HENRY

JAMES'S

LEGACY

HENRY

JAMES'S LEGACY

The Afterlife
of His Figure
and Fiction

ADELINE R. TINTNER

Louisiana State University Press   *Baton Rouge*

Copyright © 1998 by Louisiana State University Press
All rights reserved
Manufactured in the United States of America
First printing
07 06 05 04 03 02 01 00 99 98   5 4 3 2 1

Designer: Melanie O'Quinn Samaha
Typeface: Cochin, Anna
Typesetter: Wilsted & Taylor Publishing Services
Printer and binder: Thomson-Shore, Inc.

Library of Congress Cataloging-in-Publication Data

Tintner, Adeline R., 1912–
    Henry James's legacy : the afterlife of his figure and fiction /
    Adeline R. Tintner.
        p.   cm.
    Includes index.
    ISBN 0-8071-2157-6
    1. James, Henry, 1843–1916—Criticism and interpretation—
History—20th century.   2. James, Henry, 1843–1916—In fiction,
drama, poetry, etc.   3. James, Henry, 1843–1916—Parodies,
imitations, etc.   4. James, Henry, 1843–1916—Contemporaries.
5. James, Henry, 1843–1916—Influence.   6. Arts, Modern—20th
century.   I. Title.
PS2124.T55   1998
813'.4—dc21   97-32565
                                                        CIP

The paper in this book meets the guidelines for permanence and durability of the Committee
on Production Guidelines for Book Longevity of the Council on Library Resources. ♾

Frontispiece: *Portrait of Henry James.* Bronze sculpture by Michael de Lisio. Two views.

*To those legatees of James whom I have overlooked
and whose reinventions I have failed to account for,
as well as to future legatees, who no doubt stand
waiting in the wings*

ACKNOWLEDGMENTS

I wish to thank once more Mark Piel, Head Librarian of the New York Society Library in New York City, for providing me with current and out-of-print James-related novels. Donald D. Stone has read an unwieldy manuscript with his customary care and expertise and made valuable suggestions on what to keep and what to eliminate. He, as well as Charlotte Gertz, Anne Janowitz, and John Kimmey, called my attention to contemporary novels with James allusions. I wish to thank Barry Blose of LSU Press for his meticulous reading of a difficult manuscript, and John Easterly, Executive Editor of the Press, for his careful perusal of the study in the final stages of the editing. I also want to thank Michael Griffith for his attention to many details. Elizabeth Armour produced a clean manuscript. As always, I thank Daniel M. Fogel for his continuing interest in my work in spite of his heavy schedule, and, finally, this book would not have progressed at all without my husband Henry D. Janowitz's careful reading of its chapters and his sensible suggestions.

CONTENTS

PART II HENRY JAMES: HIS LEGACY

ILLUSTRATIONS

ABBREVIATIONS

AV   Donna Leon, *The Anonymous Venetian* (London, 1995)

AY   Philip Roth, *The Anatomy Lesson* (New York, 1983)

B&S   James D. Brasch and Joseph Sigman, *Hemingway's Library: A Composite Record* (New York, 1981)

BB   Edward Sklepowich, *Black Bridge* (New York, 1995)

BC   Louis Auchincloss, *The Book Class* (Boston, 1984)

BE   Louis Wilkinson [Louis Marlow], *The Better End* (London, 1969)

BF   Benjamin Franklin Fisher, "Ella D'Arcy: A Commentary with a Primary and Annotated Secondary Bibliography," *English Literature in Transition*, XXXV (1992), 179–211

BG   Edith Wharton, *A Backward Glance* (1934; rpr. New York, 1990)

BL   Elizabeth Taylor, *The Blush and Other Stories* (New York, 1959)

BO   H. G. Wells [Reginald Bliss], *Boon, the Mind of the Race, the Wild Asses of the Devil, and the Last Trump* (London, 1915)

BS   Rhoda Broughton, *Between Two Stools* (London, 1912)

BU   Edith Wharton, *The Buccaneers* (New York, 1938)

CA   W. Somerset Maugham, *Cakes and Ale* (New York, 1930)

CAL   Gertrude Atherton, *The Californians* (London, 1898)

CC   Julian Symons, *A Criminal Comedy* (New York, 1986)

CE   Graham Greene, *Collected Essays* (New York, 1969)

CF Matthew J. Bruccoli and Margaret M. Duggan, *The Correspondence of F. Scott Fitzgerald* (New York, 1980)

CH Joseph Conrad, *Chance* (New York, 1926)

CL Leon Edel, *Henry James: The Conquest of London* (Philadelphia, 1962)

CLO Anita Brookner, *A Closed Eye* (New York, 1991)

CN Hugh Walpole, *Captain Nicholas* (New York, 1934)

CO Sheilah Graham, *College of One* (New York, 1967)

COM Graham Greene, *The Comedians* (New York, 1965)

COU Philip Roth, *The Counterlife* (New York, 1986)

CP Leon Edel, ed., *The Complete Plays of Henry James* (New York, 1990)

CPA *The Collected Poetry of W. H. Auden* (New York, 1945)

CPE T. S. Eliot, *Collected Poems, 1909–1935* (New York, 1936)

CPP Sylvia Plath, *The Collected Poems*, ed. Ted Hughes (New York, 1981)

CR Daniel Mark Fogel, *Covert Relations* (Charlottesville, 1990)

CSB *The Collected Stories of Elizabeth Bowen*, intro. Angus Wilson (New York, 1981)

CSC *The Collected Stories of Noël Coward* (New York, 1983)

CSM, I, CSM, II *The Complete Short Stories of W. Somerset Maugham* (2 vols.; New York, 1953)

CSW, I, CSW, II Edith Wharton, *The Collected Short Stories*, ed. R. W. B. Lewis (2 vols.; New York, 1968)

CV Rhoda Broughton, *Concerning a Vow* (London, 1914)

DC   Edward Sklepowich, *Death in a Serene City* (New York, 1990)

DD   W. M. Spackman, *A Difference of Design* (New York, 1983)

DE   Philip Roth, *Deception* (New York, 1990)

DED   Elizabeth Taylor, *A Dedicated Man and Other Stories* (New York, 1965)

DI   Ernest Dowson, *Dilemmas* (New York, 1894)

DM   Mary Augusta [Mrs. Humphry] Ward, *The Testing of Diana Mallory* (New York, 1908)

DP   "La Dolce Prospettiva," in Jonathan Keates, *Soon to Be a Major Motion Picture* (London, 1997)

DS   Rebecca Goldstein, *The Dark Sister* (New York, 1991)

DT   Carolyn Heilbrun [Amanda Cross], *Death in a Tenured Position* (New York, 1981)

DW   Hugh Walpole, *The Duchess of Wrexe* (New York, 1914)

E   Gore Vidal, *Empire* (New York, 1987)

EB   Edward Butscher, ed., *Sylvia Plath: The Woman and the Work* (New York, 1977)

EC   Thomas Hardy, *The Excluded and Collaborative Stories*, ed. Pamela Dalziel (Oxford, 1992)

ED   Virginia W. Johnson, *An English "Daisy Miller"* (Boston, 1882)

EL   Henry James, *English Literature: Essays* (New York, 1984)

EM   Louis Auchincloss, *The Embezzler* (Boston, 1966)

ET Elizabeth Bowen, *Eva Trout* (New York, 1968)

EU Henry James, *The Europeans* (1878; rpr. New York, 1964)

F Hugh Walpole, *Fortitude* (1913; rpr. New York, 1930)

FA Philip Roth, *The Facts* (New York, 1988)

FB Frances Hodgson Burnett, *A Fair Barbarian* (Boston, 1881)

FF Edward Sklepowich, *Farewell to the Flesh* (New York, 1991)

FG Louis Auchincloss, *False Gods* (New York, 1992)

FP Louis Auchincloss, *Fellow Passengers* (New York, 1989)

FR Anita Brookner, *Fraud* (London, 1992)

FS Edmund White, *The Farewell Symphony* (London, 1997)

FW Henry James, *Literary Criticism: French Writers, Other European Writers, the Prefaces to the New York Edition*, ed. Leon Edel and Mark Wilson (New York, 1984)

GA A. R. Gurney, Jr., *The Golden Age* (New York, 1979)

GB Henry James, *The Golden Bowl* (1904; rpr. New York, 1972)

GG F. Scott Fitzgerald, *The Great Gatsby*, ed. Matthew J. Bruccoli (Cambridge, Eng., 1991)

GH David Plante, *The Ghost of Henry James* (Boston, 1970)

GL Virginia Glendinning, *Elizabeth Bowen* (New York, 1978)

GR   Constance Fenimore Woolson, "Miss Grief,"
      Lippincott's Magazine, XXV (1880)

GS   Peter Straub, *Ghost Story* (New York, 1979)

GW   Philip Roth, *The Ghost Writer* (New York, 1979)

H   Michael Hosking, *David Garnett: A Writer's Library*,
      intro. Nicolas Barker (Deal, Kent, England, 1983)

HA   Martha Gellhorn, *The Heart of Another* (New York,
      1941)

HD   Elizabeth Bowen, *The Heat of the Day* (New York,
      1944)

HE   Baroness von Hutten, *He and Hecuba* (New York,
      1906)

HF   Hugh Walpole, *Hans Frost* (New York, 1929)

HG   Hugh Walpole, *Head in Green Bronze and Other Stories*
      (New York, 1938)

HH   J. I. M. Stewart [Michael Innes], *Honeybath's Haven*
      (New York, 1978)

HL   Anita Brookner, *Hotel du Lac* (New York, 1986)

HR   Charles Poore, ed., *The Hemingway Reader* (New York,
      1953)

HS   Ruth Rendell [Barbara Vine], *House of Stairs* (New
      York, 1989)

HSL   Carlos Baker, ed., *Ernest Hemingway: Selected Letters,
      1917–1961* (New York, 1981)

HW   Alfred Bendixen, ed., *Haunted Women* (New York,
      1985)

I   Joseph Conrad and Ford Madox Hueffer, *The*

LED   Desmond Flower and Henry Maas, *The Letters of Ernest Dowson* (Teaneck, N.J., 1967)

LET   Philip Roth, *Letting Go* (New York, 1962)

LF   Andrew Turnbull, ed., *The Letters of F. Scott Fitzgerald* (New York, 1963)

LG   *The Literary Guillotine* (London, 1903)

LGC   Lev Raphael, *Let's Get Criminal* (New York, 1996)

LH   James Hilton, *Lost Horizon* (1933; rpr. New York, 1969)

LI   W. M. Spackman, *A Little Decorum, for Once* (New York, 1985)

LIB   Lionel Trilling, *The Liberal Imagination* (London, 1950)

LJ   Barbara Ware Holmes, *Letters to Julia* (New York, 1997)

LM   Richard Howard, *Like Most Revelations* (New York, 1994)

LO   Mark Longaker, *Ernest Dowson* (Philadelphia, 1944)

LS   Constance Fletcher [George Fleming], *Little Stories About Women* (London, 1897)

LT   Lucy Lane Clifford, *The Last Touches and Other Stories* (New York, 1892)

LU, I, LU, II   Percy Lubbock, ed., *The Letters of Henry James* (2 vols.; London, 1920)

M   Leon Edel, *Henry James: The Master* (Philadelphia, 1974)

MA   J. I. M. Stewart, *My Aunt Christina and Other Stories* (New York, 1983)

MB   Violet Paget [Vernon Lee], *Miss Brown* (1884; 2 vols.; rpr. New York, 1978)

MG   Thomas C. Moser, "From Olive Garnett's Diary: Impressions of Ford Madox Ford and His Friends, 1890–1906," *Texas Studies in Literature and Language,* XVI (1974)

MI   Michael Millgate, *Thomas Hardy: A Biography* (New York, 1982)

MM   Edna Kenton, *What Manner of Man* (Indianapolis, 1903)

MO   Rudyard Kipling, *Mine Own People,* with a critical introduction by Henry James (New York, 1891)

MR   W. Somerset Maugham, *The Maugham Reader* (New York, 1950)

MT   Agatha Christie, *Murder in Three Acts* (1934; rpr. New York, 1984)

MW   Graham Greene, *May We Borrow Your Husband?* (New York, 1966)

MWW   Ernest Hemingway, *Men Without Women* (1927; rpr. New York, 1970)

MY   Leon Edel, *Henry James: The Middle Years* (Philadelphia, 1962)

NCD   Graham Payn and Sheridan Morley, eds., *The Noël Coward Diaries* (Boston, 1982)

ND   Virginia Woolf, *Night and Day* (New York, 1920)

NH   Maureen Howard, *Natural History* (New York, 1992)

NN   Henry James, *Notes on Novelists* (New York, 1914)

NS   Norman Sherry, *The Life of Graham Greene, 1939–1955* (New York, 1995)

NV   James A. Michener, *The Novel* (New York, 1991)

NYE, I–
NYE, XXIV   *The Novels and Tales of Henry James* (24 vols.; New York, 1907–1909), known as the New York Edition

OD   Ursula Perrin, *Old Devotions* (1983; New York, 1988)

OG   Edith Wharton, "Ogrin the Hermit," *Atlantic Monthly,* CIV (1909), 848

OHB   W. Somerset Maugham, *Of Human Bondage* (New York, 1936)

OK   John O' Hara, *Ourselves to Know* (New York, 1960)

OM   Julius Chambers, *On a Margin* (New York, 1885)

OV   Robert Bridges, *Overheard in Arcady* (New York, 1894)

P   Veronica Geng, *Partners* (New York, 1979)

PA   Dwight Macdonald, ed., *Parodies* (London, 1960)

PC   Henry James, *The Princess Casamassima* (Harmondsworth, Middlesex, England, 1978)

PE   Henry James, *The Painter's Eye* (Cambridge, Mass., 1956)

PI   John Pilkington, ed., *Stark Young: A Life in the Arts* (Baton Rouge, 1975)

PL   Anne Douglas Sedgwick, *A Portrait in Letters,* ed. Basil de Sélincourt (Boston, 1936)

PLS, III   W. Somerset Maugham, *Plays* (Leipzig, 1934), Vol. III

PM   A. S. Byatt, *Passions of the Mind* (London, 1991)

PN   Louis Auchincloss, *The Partners* (Boston, 1974)

PO   Henry James, *The Portrait of a Lady*, ed. Leon Edel (Boston, 1963)

PP   Henry James, *Portraits of Places* (London, 1883)

PR   Hugh Walpole, *The Prelude to Adventure* (New York, 1912)

R   W. Somerset Maugham, *The Razor's Edge* (New York, 1944)

RC   Percy Lubbock, *The Region Cloud* (London, 1925)

RD   Kazuo Ishiguro, *The Remains of the Day* (New York, 1989)

RE   Hugh Walpole, *Reading: An Essay* (New York, 1926)

REJ   Louis Auchincloss, *The Rector of Justin* (Boston, 1964)

REY   Michael S. Reynolds, *Hemingway's Reading, 1910–1940* (Princeton, 1981)

RF   Jean Pavans, *Retour à Florence* (Paris, 1986)

RHJ   Louis Auchincloss, *Reading Henry James* (Minneapolis, 1975)

RJ   Louis Auchincloss, *Reflections of a Jacobite* (Boston, 1961)

RS   Robert Secor, "Henry James and Violet Hunt, the 'Improper Person of Babylon,'" *Journal of Modern Literature*, XIII (1986), 3–36

SB   O. Henry, *Strictly Business* (New York, 1914)

SC   Louis Auchincloss, *Second Chance* (Boston, 1970)

SE   Brad Leithauser, *Seaward* (New York, 1993)

SF   Henry James, *The Sacred Fount* (New York, 1901)

SH   Constance Fenimore Woolson, "The Street of
      Hyacinth," in *For the Major, and Selected Stories*, ed.
      Rayburn S. Moore (New Haven, 1967), 144–84

SHJ   Leon Edel, ed., *The Selected Letters of Henry James*
      (Cambridge, Mass., 1987)

SL   Violet Hunt, *Sooner or Later* (London, 1904)

SM   Louis Auchincloss, *The Style's the Man: Reflections on
      Proust, Fitzgerald, Wharton, Vidal, and Others* (New
      York, 1994)

SNS   Simon Nowell-Smith, *The Legend of the Master* (New
      York, 1948)

SO   Yasunari Kawabata, *The Sound of the Mountain*, trans.
      Edward M. Seidensticker (New York, 1970)

SR   Ernest Hemingway, *The Sun Also Rises* (New York,
      1926)

SSF   Matthew J. Bruccoli, ed., *The Short Stories of F. Scott
      Fitzgerald* (New York, 1989)

ST   R. W. Stallman, *Stephen Crane: A Critical Biography*
      (Ames, Iowa, 1972)

SU   A. S. Byatt, *Sugar and Other Stories* (New York, 1987)

T   W. Somerset Maugham, *Theatre* (New York, 1937)

TA   Louis Auchincloss, *Tales of Manhattan* (Boston, 1967)

TAT   Gertrude Stein, *Things As They Are: A Novel in Three
      Parts* (Pawlet, Vt., 1950)

TD   Edmund Wilson, *I Thought of Daisy* (1929; rpr. New
      York, 1967)

TH   Agatha Christie, *Thirteen at Dinner* (1933; rpr. New
      York, 1984)

TL   Louis Auchincloss, *Three Lives* (New York, 1993)

TM   Henry James, *The Tragic Muse* (1890; rpr. London, 1948)

TN   Thornton Wilder, *Theophilus North* (New York, 1973)

TR   James McCourt, *Time Remaining* (New York, 1993)

TT   Daniel Stern, *Twice Told Tales* (New York, 1989)

TY   Leon Edel, *Henry James: The Treacherous Years* (Philadelphia, 1969)

VA   Violet Paget [Vernon Lee], *Vanitas: Polite Stories* (London, 1892)

VC   O. Henry, *The Voice of the City* (New York, 1908)

VE   Louis Auchincloss, *The Vanderbilt Era* (New York, 1989)

VK   J. I. M. Stewart, *Vanderlyn's Kingdom* (New York, 1967)

VL   Edward Field and Neil Derrick [Bruce Elliot], *Village* (New York, 1982)

VU   Anne Douglas Sedgwick, *Valerie Upton* (Boston, 1907)

W   Edward Wagenknecht, *Willa Cather* (New York, 1994)

WA   Lucy Lane Clifford, *A Woman Alone* (New York, 1901)

WC   Mildred Bennett, ed., *Willa Cather's Collected Short Fiction, 1892–1912* (Lincoln, Nebr., 1965)

WD   Henry James, *The Wings of the Dove* (2 vols.; New York, 1902)

WG   Alison Lurie, *Women and Ghosts* (New York, 1994)

WH   O. Henry, *Whirligigs* (New York, 1914)

WI   Charles Eustace Merriman, *Who's "It" in America* (New York, 1906)

WL   Joyce Johnson, *What Lisa Knew: The Trials and Lies of the Steinberg Case* (New York, 1990)

WR, I, WR, II   Mary Augusta [Mrs. Humphry] Ward, *A Writer's Recollections* (2 vols.; New York, 1918)

WRW   Violet Hunt, *White Rose of Weary Leaf* (New York, 1908)

WS   Henry James, *Washington Square* (New York, 1901)

Y   Joseph Conrad, *Youth* (New York, 1926)

YB   *Yellow Book* (April, 1895)

YE   Louis Auchincloss, *Tales of Yesteryear* (New York, 1994)

ZU   Philip Roth, *Zuckerman Unbound* (New York, 1981)

HENRY

JAMES'S

LEGACY

INTRODUCTION

The very provocation offered to the artist by the universe, the provocation for him to *be* . . . an artist . . . what do I take that for but the intense desire of being to get itself personally shared? . . . I invoke and evoke, I figure and represent, I seize and fix, as many phases and aspects and conceptions of [being] as my infirm hand allows me strength for. . . . The truth is that to live, to this tune, intellectually . . . is to find one's view of one's share in it, and above all of its appeal to be shared, in an infinite variety, enormously enlarged.
                              —Henry James, "Is There a Life After Death?"

In this volume about Henry James's legacy, I invert my usual purpose of identifying traces of the art and literature of others in James's fiction. It is now the biter bit, as I turn my sights toward showing how James is present in the fiction of other writers—how as both a figure and the author of a body of work he has entered the creative writing of his contemporaries and successors. Very often his late masterpieces allow the present-day writer the opportunity to produce a pastiche of or indirect comment on the classic tales. Even the lesser-known works have been assimilated by twentieth-century authors to yield the fabric of new versions. So absorbed is Henry James eighty years after his death that it is possible to find countless instances fitting his own definition of the afterlife we are able to achieve—according to which our life after death lies not only in the art we produce but

1. Portrait of James
on Barnes & Noble plastic book bag
Courtesy Barnes & Noble.
Illustration © Mark Summers.

in the conscious memory others have of us. James's afterlife is sustained by
the recorded memories of fellow writers and fellow artists.

The fiction and plays in which I perceive a Jamesian content disclose
that content without the operation of any abstruse methodology. It is hard
to avoid falling over the evidence, so frequent is James's appearance in fictive creations and barely disguised portraits. I am sure my lists are incomplete, and as in my previous volumes, in which I explored James's worlds,
I urge readers to add to my picture by contributing their own findings.

My compilation is open-ended, and additions to it can keep being made
until writers lose interest in James. At present there is no sign of that. Nor
is there any sign that James is releasing his grip on the popular imagination. The frequency in advertising of both James's likeness and familiar
quotations from his work attests to that. When Barnes and Noble, the gigantic bookseller, wants a striking image for its plastic bags, it chooses
James's familiar face and his familiar formal clothes (Figure 1). When Banana Republic, a chain of stores selling informal clothing, seats his figure
among the modern expatriates in a café (Figure 2) and Rolls Royce quotes
from *The Ambassadors,* "Live all you can," to market the most costly of production motor cars (Figure 3), it is plain that James has penetrated com-

2. Cover for Banana Republic clothing catalog featuring
expatriate cultural figures, along with key to the persons pictured,
which appeared inside the catalog.
James is in the middle of the back row.

Illustration by H. Craig Hannah. Reproduced courtesy of The Gap, Inc.

3. Advertisement for Rolls-Royce quoting James's *The Ambassadors*
Reproduced by permission of Rolls-Royce Motor Cars Inc.

munication addressed to the general consciousness. The caricature of James as a traveler that adorned the cover page of the *New York Times Book Review* when it featured the republication of his travel books (Figure 4) continued a tradition of caricaturing James that began at the turn of the century.

In 1919, when Boni & Liveright published *Travelling Companions,* a volume consisting of reprints of James's early tale of that title along with six of his other stories from the 1870s, the book's dust jacket (Figure 5) pictured figures dressed in fashions of the Jazz Age, not of the 1870s. This book cover reflects the post–World War I mania for transatlantic tourism, bidding for a readership far removed from the tourists who inhabit the tales included in the volume. It is also an early suggestion of the tendency

4. Drawing of James in the
New York Times Book Review of December 12, 1993
Reproduced courtesy of the artist, Mark D. Summers.

of twentieth-century writers and other artists to update and reinvent James's fiction.

The legacy James has left by being incorporated as a figure in the writings of others took its first form around 1900, if not a few years before, when several women writers who were his friends—some of them reacting to his criticism of their work and taking revenge—fashioned often unprepossessing fictional characters in whom he is recognizable. These thirteen women ranged from Violet Paget, who wrote under the name of Vernon Lee, to Virginia Woolf, who as a young girl observed James as a part of the personal circle of her father, Leslie Stephen. The women also brought into their fiction elements of James's fiction.

In the work of five of James's male contemporaries—Hugh Walpole, W. Somerset Maugham, Ford Madox Ford, H. G. Wells, and Percy Lubbock—there are even harsher portraits of James. Only in Rudyard Kipling's Mr. Cleever is there a kindly and generous portrait of the senior

5. Cover of *Travelling Companions,* a collection of
James's stories published by Boni & Liveright in 1919

writer. For these men, James was a rival, a "lion in the path."[1] Hugh Walpole alone among them not only introduced into the character he portrayed
the less admirable qualities of James that later literary representations
were to emphasize and extend but paid the homage, in Henry Galleon, of
rendering James's heroic genius.

When James's figure enters fiction by the hand of writers who never
knew him personally, starting with David Plante's *The Ghost of Henry
James,* of 1970, the homoerotic findings of Leon Edel in *The Treacherous
Years,* Volume IV of his *Henry James,* bulk large. Bruce Elliot's mass market
novel *Village,* of 1982, and Louis Auchincloss' short story "They Who Have
Power to Hurt," of 1994, show James—or in the case of Auchincloss, show
Horace Scudder, who is based on him—as an avowed homoerotic, if not a
practicing homosexual. James is made to scamper with Edith Wharton,

1. Henry James, *Selected Literary Criticism,* ed. Morris Shapira (London, 1963), 109.

along with Freud and Jung, to solve a murder in Carol De Chellis Hill's farcical and playful novel *Henry James's Midnight Song*, of 1993, and in Rebecca Goldstein's *The Dark Sister*, of 1991, not only he has a part in the story but also his brother William, and several characters from his novels.

But it is where writers appropriated James's work that his legacy is most evident. Among his contemporaries, Joseph Conrad, Ernest Dowson, and Thomas Hardy all chose to rewrite tales by James, either confirming their models or differing from them.

The post–World War I generation, in both the United States and England, drew literary icons for their fiction from James. James Huneker's novel *Painted Veils*, of 1920, which I do not consider at length later, includes in its imitation of French fin-de-siècle symbolism and satanic literature a review of literary heroes, among whom Henry James serves as a model. It was in the 1930s, however, in spite of the short-lived vogue for proletarian literature, that writers from Noël Coward, the art deco representative, to F. Scott Fitzgerald and Ernest Hemingway looked to *The Ambassadors* and James's short stories for material to redo, improve on, or extend. The greatest absorption of James is apparent, though, in the large fictional output of two American writers from sharply different backgrounds and with different ends: Philip Roth and Louis Auchincloss. I develop in detail their very different relationships to the Master.

Movie adaptations of James have been numerous, but I concentrate on one that has not received the attention it deserves. It is the most reimagined and original of them all. François Truffaut's *La Chambre verte* (The green room), of 1978, relies chiefly on "The Altar of the Dead," with the hero and time changed to after World War II.

Out of the many operatic versions of James's tales, I also confine my attention to one example, that by Dominick Argento of "The Aspern Papers." Among dramatic adaptations, I pass over *The Heiress*, by Augustus Goetz and Ruth Goetz, because, except in the last scene, it hews closely to *Washington Square*. Instead, I attempt a thorough examination of A. R. Gurney's *Later Life*, a dramatic re-creation from 1984 of "The Beast in the Jungle."

The spate of detective stories from Agatha Christie to the Venetian mysteries in the 1980s and 1990s includes a continual reappearance of allusions to James. The references are particularly pronounced in the many mysteries of J. I. M. Stewart written under the name of Michael Innes.

The bountiful source that James's body of writings has proved to be for other authors comes out with utter clarity in a canvass of particular titles of his. In a list of works in descending order of appropriation by others, "Daisy Miller" is at the head. Writers have mined it from the year following its publication down to Barbara Vine's *Kissing the Gunner's Daughter,* of 1992. The most rewritten of James's novels are *The Portrait of a Lady,* rediscovered by the moderns Ezra Pound and T. S. Eliot; *The Ambassadors,* a resource both for novels as a whole and for just passages in them, as in James McCourt's satirical gay novel *Time Remaining,* of 1993; and *The Golden Bowl,* the basis for interesting postmodern variations. There are also outstanding postmodern reinventions of some of the classic short stories. A French dramatist and translator of the present day, Jean Pavans, has transformed a story into a play, and A. S. Byatt has manipulated themes of intertextuality. Even so traditionalist a popular novelist as James Michener has taken on "The Aspern Papers." Orhan Pamuk, a Turkish novelist based in Istanbul and educated in his homeland, has asserted, "The geography of my literary heritage began with Henry James." James's legacy extends to the Bosporus and a "savage country," as Pamuk calls it.[2]

In all this, the role of Edel requires acknowledgment, for he not only has served as a Baedeker to the Jamesian territory for today's writers but at times has also substituted for a reading of James.

Why do writers enfold James's fiction into their own work? Answering that question requires zeroing in on the specifics of what they have plundered and rewritten. The motive behind the appropriation varies from author to author. And what the appropriation achieves depends, too, on the reader's engagement in the transaction, for his acquaintance with James has advanced through the Library of America's recent republishing of James's novels and travel writings, and soon all of James's short stories will be in print. The Library of America's two volumes of critical essays and reviews by James have helped fuel the gigantic appropriation of his work in the 1980s and 1990s, but the stream of quotations from James's critical production is not the concern of the present study, which deals with reinventions of his creative work.

Others' readiness to batten off James is simply the counterpart to his own willingness to make adaptive use of the works of others. Appropriation was for him an act of criticism: "To criticise is to appreciate, to appro-

2. Fernanda Eberstadt, "The Best Seller of Byzantium," *New York Times Magazine,* May 4, 1997, p. 37.

priate, to take intellectual possession, to establish in fine a relation with the criticised thing and make it one's own." (*FW,* 1169). One hundred years of weaving James into the fabric of new fiction attests to a reverence for him, but it also amounts to criticism of him. Each time that it occurs there is personal revision or comment, a change in the picture that James composed, some new figure in the carpet.

HENRY JAMES THE FIGURE

THE FIGURE OF JAMES

O ther writers began to include Henry James as a figure in their novels with some frequency toward the end of the nineteenth century and the turn of the twentieth, by when the older James had indeed become a figure in English literary society, evolving his public persona with his full-blown mannerisms. A master of anecdote and the object of caricature, he offered irresistible lineaments for the novels of his contemporaries whose literary styles he had influenced.

Writers among his women friends gained but also suffered from his severe criticism of their work. Their revenge was to place him bodily in their novels under some disguise. But it is not especially difficult to recognize him, and the assumption must be that in most cases he too saw through the concealment. On the whole, the revenge these women writers took on the Master was kindhearted.

Fiction Is the Best Revenge

In particular, two women writers—Violet Paget and Mrs. Humphry Ward—were lucky enough to have had James interested in their fiction

The material in this section appeared in somewhat different form as "Fiction Is the Best Revenge," in *Turn-of-the-Century Women*, II (Winter, 1985), 42–49.

but unlucky enough to have had him so interested that he could not keep from rewriting it his way. For James there was only one way to write — *his* way — and his notions about structure, organization, and the condition of the whole, as he kept telling them in his letters, were conceptions only he could execute to his satisfaction. Consequently, he felt compelled to redo what they had done. No one escaped his strictures. H. G. Wells, Hugh Walpole, and Howard Sturgis also came in for criticism of their work, but James did not rewrite them as he did the women, nor did he rewrite Edith Wharton, despite the objections he voiced regarding her work. Violet Paget, and two other women writers, Constance Fenimore Woolson and Olive Garnett, were attracted to James as a man, and their resentments carried an amatory charge. Garnett did not write anything for publication until two years after James was dead, undoubtedly out of fear of his critical mercilessness. But all five women writers eventually avenged themselves by placing him under their control as a character in their stories.

Violet Paget

James's relation with Violet Paget (1856–1935), who published under the name of Vernon Lee, passed through three stages. The first occurred during 1884, when he met her and at the end of which year her novel *Miss Brown*, dedicated to him, was published. The second ran from 1884 until 1892, when she caricatured him in her story "Lady Tal," turning him into a figure of fun by calling attention to some of his embarrassing habits and the peculiarities of his personality. The third continued until his death; during this stage he more or less broke off relations with her because of "Lady Tal," although he was "civil" when they met at gatherings (*L,* III, 403). Nevertheless, her books continued to gain the shelves of Lamb House. Whether James purchased them or she sent them to him is unknown.

Paget's letters included comments about James from her first meeting with him. On June 24, 1884, in spite of Matthew Arnold's presence, she professed that there was "no one to amuse me except Henry James." Two days later they met again, and he was "most devotedly civil to me. . . . I talked half the time with Henry James." A week later she noticed that he wrinkled his forehead, "as usual for tight boots," and later she wrote that he took the "most paternal interest in me as a novelist" and would "do all in his power to push" *Miss Brown*, which was about to appear (*MY*, 115). Yet when he received *Miss Brown* he found it inferior to her other works, such as *Studies in the Eighteenth Century in Italy*, written when she was barely twenty-four, and *Euphorion*, a group of essays, one of which was on medieval love. He told her this months later, on May 10, 1885, when he also wrote her that her error lay in a "certain ferocity . . . you take the aesthetic business too seriously" and "with too great an implication of sexual motives. . . . You have impregnated all those people too much with the sexual, the basely erotic preoccupation." He was convinced that her interest in the moral sense was too pronounced and that she had dealt too little with the "plastic, visual, formal." She had been "too much in a moral passion!" He counseled, "Cool first—write afterwards. Morality is hot—but art is icy!" (*L*, III, 86–87).

It is not hard to imagine Paget's reaction to this after the attention James had paid her. She must have ascribed his comments to his fear of sexuality, his entrapment in form, and his worry about romans à clef. She could convince herself that the reproaches simply meant that her talent ran in the opposite direction from his. When we read *Miss Brown* today, we wonder why James thought it so bad. It is an extremely readable and amusing parody of the life and ideas of the Pre-Raphaelite group, subjecting its leaders, Dante Gabriel Rossetti and Algernon Charles Swinburne, to easy satire. Rossetti's house is carefully and recognizably described as the house of the hero-villain, Walter Hamlin, confected partly out of Walter Pater and partly out of Violet's invalid half brother, Eugene Lee-Hamilton, with whom she lived. Whatever James's dissatisfactions with the novel's form and content, he may also have been annoyed by something that had nothing to do with such deficiencies. The three-decker opens with young Hamlin, like Rossetti a rich painter and poet, paying a visit to another painter in his villa in Italy. There he encounters a ridiculously aestheticized art-worshiping environment and the painter's even more ridiculous wife, an ugly culture vulture. Telling the arrival at the house from Hamlin's point of view imitates the narrative tactics of James's "The Author of Beltraffio," which opens by describing a visit to a Pre-Raphaelite writer in his arty home from a young writer's point of view. James's entire story—in which the Pre-Raphaelite, Mark Ambient, is patterned on John Addington Symonds—is organized from the young writer's perspective, but in *Miss Brown*, Paget, after the first few chapters, switches the point of view to the heroine, Anne Brown, who looks like Jane Burden Morris, the famous model of Pre-Raphaelite beauty. Even this stems from "The Author of Beltraffio," for there Ambient's sister is also got up to resemble Jane Morris. James's story had appeared in June and July, 1884, in the *English Illustrated Magazine*. Since *Miss Brown* appeared in December, 1884, it looks as if Paget made late adjustments to the introductory chapters, because they alone are done from Hamlin's point of view. When the scene shifts to London after he has fallen in love with the maidservant Miss Brown and taken her as his fiancée into his Pre-Raphaelite house, he becomes an object of derision and the story becomes Miss Brown's. If Paget consciously adapted James's devices to open her novel, what she created was a parody of his wonderful story, but whether she acted intentionally in this or not, James must have felt the debasement of his vision in her opening sections. Furthermore, when he saw how Paget later roasted the Pre-Raphaelite set without attempting to mask the identity of the originals, he had justification for feeling apprehensive. Paget's ardent feminism was a new phenomenon, and the males she attacked were off guard. Surely James felt let down after his kindness to her. But his distaste for her exposure of what she considered follies, moral and sexual, did not keep him from devouring her nonfiction, chiefly history concerning the medieval period and the eighteenth century. Writing to Grace Norton in January, 1885, he praised Paget's "very able and interesting books on the Italian Renaissance—*Belcaro*, *Euphorion*, etc." (*L*, III, 66), both of which he owned.

Whatever James's opinion of her novel two years after its publication, *The Bostonians* incorporates the King Cophetua and the Beggar Maid themes of *Miss Brown*, and *The Princess Casamassima*, in Hyacinth, repeats the poet Chouch's fantasy that he would "dearly like to be thought a bastard, especially a duke's" (*MB*, I, 279). The theme of socialism in *Miss Brown*—Anne Brown's brother is a socialist and she herself becomes interested in working in the East End—also recurs in *The Princess Casamassima*. James adapted, converted, and introduced into his two novels of 1886 the perversity and sexuality that embarrassed him so in Paget. In *The Bostonians* he dealt covertly with lesbianism, and in *The Princess Casamassima* not only with socialism but also with bastardy. Paget went so far as to bring incest into her novel, in connection with showing how Walter will not clean up his slum holdings so as to wipe out the sin that results from poverty, but here James revealed what Paget would have deemed weak points in his character. He could not bring himself to appropriate this part of her novel, giving weight to Hugh Walpole's assertion that James was aware of every crudity in life "but did not wish that crudity to be named."[1]

In "The Aspern Papers," of 1888, James made use of material Paget's half brother, Lee-Hamilton, had related to him: the tale of Silsbee, the Boston sea captain who was a "Shelley fanatic." In Paget's *Ottilie: An Eighteenth Century Idyll*, a semi-incestuous tale of a brother and sister clearly modeled on Paget and her half brother that was published the year before *Miss Brown*, the unusual name of Aspern appears. James made that name famous, but Jeffrey Aspern may owe his name and his tale to Paget. The pair, Paget and Lee-Hamilton, excited James's mind. James wrote at the time that they were "altogether the best people for talk and indeed the only ones" (*L*, III, 159), and that "the most intelligent person in Florence is Violet Paget" (*L*, III, 166). He added, though, that she was "exceedingly ugly" and "disputatious, contradictious and perverse" (*L*, III, 165–66). Whether or not the severe way he greeted her novel and yet fed upon her and her half brother's ideas contributed to her feelings that he had given her a raw deal, she in 1892 let him have it in a short story, the famous "Lady Tal." Everyone they knew recognized that in it she was mocking James. Both his person and his attitudes are ridiculed, if in a fairly good-natured way. By this time she had had eight years to watch him in various social settings, and being very clever, she perceived his weaknesses. Perhaps she felt hurt by his reaction to her plainness and her men's attire. Her tastes seem to have been lesbian, but even so she may have expected something more from this cautious bachelor.

All Jamesians know about the stir "Lady Tal" created, since Edel recounted it in *Henry James: The Middle Years*, but few have read the story despite its availability in libraries. In *Vanitas: Polite Stories*, the volume in which it is contained, the tale is succeeded by one in which Paget satirizes *The Princess Casamassima*. Lady Tal, the heroine of the story bearing her name, lives in a house opposite the Salute, its location like that of Katherine De Kay Bronson's Casa Alvisi, where James stayed when in Venice if he was not at the Palazzo Barbaro, the much grander establishment of the Boston Curtises. Lady Tal is a rich young widow of strange and erratic habits. Six feet tall, she is aristocratic and brutish—a glorified Violet Paget, who was tall, thin, and bespectacled. Her companion, the parodied Henry James, is Jervase Marion, called Mary Ann by everyone because of his

1. Hugh Walpole, *The Apple Trees* (Waltham Saint Laurence, Eng., 1932), 53.

old-maidish personality. He wears his mother's ring on his watch chain (*VA*, 82). Three times she makes note of how Marion looks as if his boots pinch (*VA*, 75, 91, 110)—as she had also commented about James (see above, p. 14). Marion, a subtle and psychological novelist, is helping her write her novel, which has been "dissected" by him and is now being "re-written" by her (*VA*, 132). So that no reader is left in the dark about who Jervase Marion is, the novel they are writing together is called *Christina*, an allusion to Christina Light of *The Princess Casamassima*. It seems that Marion is also going to write a novel about Lady Tal, who is toying with the idea of marrying one Clarence, who would give her "complete leisure for enjoying the company of men not quite so well off as himself" (*VA*, 32). This is a reprise of Christina Light's marriage to the Prince. The story is for the most part from Marion's point of view and makes explicit his thinking: "He had long made up his mind to permit himself only such friendship as could not possibly involve any feeling, as could not distress or ruffle him by such incidents as illness, death, fickleness, ingratitude" (*VA*, 137). But "the very recognition of feeling in others presupposed a certain minimum amount of emotional experience in oneself" (*VA*, 112), which he is aware of lacking. He consequently lets himself in for trouble, but even though he has an "aversion to being ridiculous," he is equally impelled to resist his grow-ing involvement with Lady Tal. Thus Paget took James to task for not un-derstanding the feelings he had presumably aroused in her. Her tale offers her womanly interpretation of James's carefulness not to get involved with her even though he had been so enthusiastic when they met. Some men think that if a woman is ugly, she is immune from the need for love, and Paget came to understand that James was one of them. Since she fathomed this about him, she must have anticipated how riled he would be by the out-come of the relation between Marion and Lady Tal. The other book Mar-ion is writing is about an "old artist, elderly, going on fifty—who was silly enough to imagine it was all love of art which made him take a great deal of interest in a certain young lady and her paintings" (*VA*, 118). Here, only slightly cloaked, is James's interest in *Miss Brown*. Since Marion cannot ar-rive at a denouement for his novel, she suggests one. "Why shouldn't we write that novel together?" she asks, venturing also, in order to make a good ending for it, "Suppose we get married." (*VA*, 143). On that, the tale, surely meant to be a joke, ends. But the parody of James ruminating in his complicated way is marvelous and totally true to form.

James was upset by the gossip he heard about the story, although he insisted that he had not and would not read it. For his sake, it must be hoped that he remained ignorant of the details of the satire. "I don't know what it is," he wrote to W. Morton Fullerton on January 16, 1893, "and if I should know I should have to take upon myself the burden of 'caring' in some way or other established of men, or of women—and oh, I don't *care* to care" (*L*, III, 399)—in this proving one of the points of her caricature. To his brother William, he wrote that Paget had "directed a kind of satire of a flagrant and markedly 'saucy' kind at me (!!)—exactly the sort of thing she has repeatedly done to others . . . [a] particularly impudent and blackguardly sort of thing to do to a friend and one who has treated her with such particular consideration as I have. . . . I haven't read these tales and never mean to. . . . She is as dangerous and uncanny as she is intelligent. . . . She's a tiger-cat!" (*L*, III, 402). Ten days later, in a letter to his sister-in-law, he asserted that he had come to feel "genially indifferent about it," adding, "Should I meet her . . . I should myself be perfectly civil to her" (*L*, III, 403). William James wrote to Paget that the portrait of Henry "is clever enough, and I cannot call it exactly malicious." But he remonstrated that using a "friend as so much raw material . . . implies on your part such a strangely *objective* way of taking human beings." After Violet wrote a contrite letter, William cautioned, "You must never, *never*, NEVER do such a thing again in any future book! It is too serious a matter" (*MY,* 334). Henry James told William that he was "partly amused and partly disconcerted" (*L*, III, 408) by this exchange but that he "would have preferred silence" (*L*, III, 404*n*1).

Neither Henry nor William must have read the next story in *Vanitas,* or there would have been a further exchange between the brothers. The heroine is tall, aristocratic, and like Christina Light, interested in social agitation. The lowly hero, a potter, the Hyacinth counterpart, shares that interest. The heroine wonders whether "she herself is a Princess Casamassima." Her maid is even called Assunta, like Christina Light's maid.

After all the hue and cry, "Lady Tal" was a clever story, as William James conceded, and not very malicious, but it hurt Henry James's feelings, for it spoke of Marion's fear of appearing ridiculous, thereby exposing to that private public of interlocking worlds which their mutual friends made up an anxiety James suffered but would rather have kept to himself. Paget took her revenge for whatever unintended slight this sexually ambiguous male had inflicted by paying too much attention to her brains and not enough to her person, and possibly by his lifting of her and her half brother's ideas.

Mrs. Humphry Ward

They will come no more,
The old men with beautiful manners.

. . . .

Blagueur! 'Con gli occhi onesti e tardi,'

And he said:
"Oh! Abelard!" as if the topic
Were much too abstruse for his comprehension,
And he talked about "the Great Mary,"
And said: "Mr. Pound is shocked at my levity."
When it turned out he meant Mrs. Ward.

—Ezra Pound, "I Vecchii," VII,

in *Moeurs Contemporaines*

With Mrs. Humphry Ward (1851–1920), James had a relationship that was almost purely literary. Mary Augusta Ward, who of these five women was closest in age to Henry James, was the niece of Matthew Arnold and the granddaughter of Thomas Arnold, a headmaster of Rugby. She was a bluestocking in her Oxford days, when she lived near Walter Pater and was interested in problems of religion and morality. Her best seller *Robert Elsmere* is now unreadable. Edel thinks that James put her into his story "The Next Time" as Mrs. Highmore, the best-selling writer who wanted an artistic success. James had exclusively a teacher-student relationship with her, trying to get her to understand what he meant by the art of fiction done his way—though he described it to her as being the only way. Since he wrote to Edmund Gosse that when "talking art and letters" he could not "*communicate* with her worth a damn," it is puzzling that he continued to try, except that he had a thing about rewriting her novels in a way that satisfied him (*TY,* 293). He visited her in Italy and kept seeing her for the rest of his life. He continued to show her how her books should have been written until 1905.

Mrs. Ward wrote about his obsession to do that in Volume II of *A Writer's Recollections:* "As he often said to me, he could never read a novel that interested him without taking it mentally to pieces and rewriting it in his own way. Some of his letters to me are brilliant examples of this habit of his" (*WR,* II, 206). In her novel *Diana Mallory,* of 1908, she was determined to do to him what he did to her. The novel of his that she chose to rewrite her way was *The Awkward Age,* of 1899. She felt that it and James's last novels, except for *The Ambassadors,* had suffered from being dictated. From *What Maisie Knew* onward, James had, in her opinion, missed the "slight curb" that a pen imposed. "The diffuseness and over-elaboration which were the natural snares of his astonishing gifts were encouraged rather than checked by the new method" (*WR,* II, 209).

Since she read his books carefully, it was apparent to her that he not only rewrote her fiction for her improvement but also pilfered for his own fiction from the very books he was rewriting. He had without doubt imitated quite closely *Miss Bretherton,* of 1884, in the opening scenes of *The Tragic Muse,* of 1890. Both are stories of actresses who reject appropriate husbands because of their strong professional interest in their art. James's *The Sacred Fount,* of 1901, is indebted to Mrs. Ward's *Eleanor,* of 1900, which he also revised to his satisfaction for her. He was never too busy, he wrote her, to pass up "the chance to overflow into my favorite occupation of re-writing as I read, such fiction as — I can read. I took this liberty in an inordinate degree with *Eleanor* — and I always feel it the highest tribute I can pay. I recomposed and reconstructed her from head to foot — which I give you for the real measure of what I think of her" (*WR,* II, 223). He praised the book but, of course, did not suppress the mention of flaws. *Eleanor* appeared after James and Mrs. Ward had together visited the temple of Diana at Nemi, with the fountain of Egeria. The greatest resemblance between Mrs. Ward's novel and *The Sacred Fount* lies in the Egeria episode, which becomes translated into the cannibalistic conception of one person feeding off the other in a relationship. Eleanor is an emotionally depleted woman in Mrs. Ward's novel, like Mrs. Server in *The Sacred Fount.* Like her she has lost her child and her husband in a tragic double death.

After *Miss Bretherton* and *Eleanor,* James began to lose interest in reconstructing Mrs. Ward's novels and in discovering in them the germ for his own. By 1905, he was writing to Edith Wharton that "all power to read her has abandoned me."[2] He wrote of her to his brother William that "she, amiable and culture-crammed woman as she is, is strangely stupid" (*L,* IV, 375, 381). Nevertheless, there has turned up recently James's copy of *Diana*

2. Lyall H. Powers, *Henry James and Edith Wharton: Letters, 1900–1915* (New York, 1990), 54.

Mallory, which was not a presentation copy, as all the other of her novels in his library were. If he bought it, he had good reason to do so, given the part that *The Awkward Age* played in its design.

In *Eleanor*, Mrs. Ward had introduced a figure, a Mr. Bellasis, who is personally unlike James but who emits two sentences that evidently made James think himself the model. Mr. Bellasis affirms, "There's not a phrase—not a word that I don't stand by" when he asks whether Eleanor has reread his book. He also holds that "the book cannot be really appreciated except at a second or third reading."[3] James was prompted to write to Mrs. Ward, "And is Mr. Bellasis, by the way, naturally—as it were— H. J. ???!!!" (*TY*, 301). This figure in the novel is rather arrogant and self-centered. Even so, if Mrs. Ward intended to comment on James's manner, her thrust was in comparison with what James's very personal standards of composition were dealing out to her. A letter of July 26, 1899, to her shows James in extreme form. In it, he declared that he did not believe there is "but *one general* 'hard and fast rule of presentation'" (*L*, IV, 109), but he then went on to proclaim that the writer must have a "perception of the interests of his subject that grasps him as in a vise" and "must there choose and stick and be consistent" (*L*, IV, 111). He took an inflexible stand against the "promiscuous shiftings of standpoint and centre" (*L*, IV, 112).

Mrs. Ward contained herself until *Diana Mallory*, in which she placed the figure of Sir James Chide—whose not oversubtle name at once denominated one of the figure's originals and that original's offense against her in harping on her lack of method in the construction of her fiction. But Sir James Chide also embodied Mr. Longdon, of *The Awkward Age*, the novel she had resolved to rework according to her notions about how to write a book. In her revamping of James's basic plot, Sir James, like Mr. Longdon, loves and wishes to protect a young woman he cherishes—in Sir James's case, because she is the daughter of the only woman he ever loved. Diana, who corresponds to James's Nanda, is "tainted" because Juliet, the woman he loved—who parallels Julia, Nanda's grandmother—has committed a murder. Even though she acted in self-defense, as Sir James, who served as her lawyer, proved, a stigma attaches to her daughter, who only gradually finds out about the killing. As Vanderbank, in *The Awkward Age*, did with Nanda, Oliver Marsham, Diana's fiancé, rejects her. Sir James

3. Mary Augusta [Mrs. Humphry] Ward, *Eleanor* (New York, 1900), 87, 86.

can only watch with sympathy and sorrow the unhappiness she goes through.

Like Vanderbank, Marsham lacks resolution, and like him, he is a "brilliant" though "unstable, attractive fellow" (*DM*, 351).[4] When he discovers that Diana's mother was a murderess, even though exonerated, he reacts to her taint as Vanderbank did to Nanda's. But the taint in *Diana Mallory* is real, Mrs. Ward must have felt, in contrast to that borne by Nanda, whose mother's transgressions could hardly be called crimes, being merely those of the drawing room. Mrs. Ward's social set was filled with divorcées and adulteresses, guilty of tepid social infractions.

As for Sir James, he makes Diana feel that in a "hundred ways, practical and tender . . . she [is] to him as a daughter" (*DM*, 459). Diana is told that Sir James "fell in love with you!" (*DM*, 203), since he "never got over" the death of her mother (*DM*, 204). There is a natural understanding between Sir James and Diana even though he "had not said a word to her, nor she to him. They understood each other" (*DM*, 410). Of Diana, Sir James says, "And there is no one in whom I feel a deeper interest" (*DM*, 369), for Diana treats him "already like a daughter" (*DM*, 368). Like Longdon with Nanda, Chide has left his fortune to Miss Mallory. In the way Nanda is protected by Mr. Longdon, it "often seemed to Diana as if the protecting kindness of Sir James Chide was never far away" (*DM*, 104).

As was true of Henry James, Sir James is the "best of gossips" (*DM*, 525), as well as an "admirable story-teller" (*DM*, 364). Mrs. Ward had described James in her *Writer's Recollections* as having a "smooth-shaven, finely cut face, now alive with talk and laughter, now shrewdly, one might say coldly, observant; the face of a satirist—but so human!—so alive to all that underworld of destiny through which move the weaknesses of men and women" (*WR*, II, 201). Sir James is similar: "A natural majesty expressed itself in the domed forehead, and in the fine head, lightly touched with gray; the eyes too were gray, the lips prominent and sensitive, the face long, and, in line, finely regular. A face of feeling and of power; the face of a Celt, disciplined by the stress and conflict of a non-Celtic World" (*DM*, 63). James was half Irish, and Mrs. Ward undoubtedly knew that. Like James, the unmarried Sir James is usually paying country-house visits, so he is al-

---

4. For *Diana Mallory*, I am using the American edition entitled *The Testing of Diana Mallory*, but the title of the first English edition.

ways around. He is the supreme witness of all that happens, and he travels with the whole party to Assisi, as James made trips with Mrs. Ward and her group (*DM*, 328). Some of his expressions are those of James himself: An "odious young woman" he calls a character, "lifting his hands and eyebrows" (*DM*, 524).

Because Mrs. Ward sought to make money from her novels, she had to fashion an end that was satisfactory for Diana. Marsham, invalided and tamed by life, is finally happy to marry Diana, who will take care of a curable sick man for a while—all through the influence of Sir James.

Mrs. Ward, as if to atone for the liberties she took with James's novel, made the character she based on him a figure of great kindness and help. Although he had chided her, his rewriting of her novels stood among his attempts to help her become a better writer, for which she was grateful. But if he wanted to do over in his way the fiction of writers who interested him, Mrs. Ward was inclined to do his work over in her way. Her revenge is not in portraying the personality of James but in making free with the basic situation in *The Awkward Age*. It is clear that she felt she was improving on it, for his novel had suffered from being unreined by the "physical toil of writing" as a result of being dictated to a typist. Since James had written her that he never got "behind" in *The Awkward Age*, "*never at all*" (*L*, IV, 110), she was going to spell everything out so the reader knew what was going on. She chose to get behind actual events but not states of mind. In a sense, Sir James Chide's having argued his case for a murderess recapitulated Henry James's having argued his case for the art of fiction.

Edith Wharton

Edith Wharton (1862–1937) had a much different relationship with James, for he and she became very close personal friends despite the criticism he made of her fiction before he met her. Later, especially after his visit to her at The Mount, when he came back to the United States in 1904 and 1905, he sidestepped any serious discussion of her work, nor did she bother him. She was highly critical of his work, and I think he was slightly afraid of her; she was imperious and officious, and he wished to keep calm and have undisturbed relations with her.

He gave up, apparently, on Mrs. Ward after the rewriting of *Eleanor*, but he impugned all the women who wrote novels, from Violet Paget to Edith Wharton, for poor construction. He criticized the "composition and construction" of Wharton's *The Fruit of the Tree,* of 1907, and in spite of his admiration for *The Reef,* of 1912, he had strictures regarding its format.

Edith Wharton never attempted to redo James's novels, except in *The Age of Innocence,* of 1922, when he was safely dead, and he never attempted to redo hers, although he stole a few details from *The Touchstone,* of 1900, and from the tale "The Angel at the Grave," in *Crucial Instances,* of 1901, which were sent to him before he met her. In contrast to Mrs. Ward, Wharton brought only his personality, and not both his work and his personality, into her pieces. Characters resembling James appear in three of her stories and in a poem.

The tale "The Hermit and the Wild Woman," of 1906, takes place before she met Morton Fullerton and he became her lover. Yet it expresses her need for that kind of release. Her fable is presented in the semblance of a medieval legend, and the wild woman is undoubtedly Edith herself, the Hermit seeming to be Henry James.[5] Percy Lubbock called her a "wild woman" and James the "literary hermit" on the first page of his *Portrait of Edith Wharton.*[6] Wharton herself, in *A Backward Glance,* referred to James's "hermit-like asceticism." The wild woman feels the need to "wash the dust from my body in cool water" (*CSW,* I, 582).

"The Hermit and the Wild Woman" is filled with places and things that are transparently Jamesian icons. The Hermit lives in a region with two hills, like Rye and Winchelsea. He longs to live hidden from life, as James did when he was working alone at Lamb House. He fusses over his garden, but his chief pleasure is in the composition of "lauds in honor of Christ and the saints," as James's was in the writing of his fiction. The Hermit even dictates his lauds: he "feared to forget them . . . he decided to ask a friendly priest . . . to write them down" (*CSW,* I, 573).

He visits a saint who lives far away, as William James lived in Massachusetts. The saint criticizes the Hermit, in imitation of the reservations William conveyed about Henry's stories. On his way back he sees the wild woman. There is "nothing pleasing to him in the sight of this female," so he runs "no great danger in looking at her." A renegade nun, she has fled her convent because she sinfully bathed in pools of cold water, and is being

---

5. R. W. B. Lewis thinks Walter Berry, or Morton Fullerton, is the Hermit, but his argument tends to break down when it becomes clear that the Hermit was not the object of the woman's longings nor the woman the object of his.

6. Percy Lubbock, *Portrait of Edith Wharton* (New York, 1947).

hunted down. "The Hermit . . . was much perturbed by her story . . . yet, remembering the desire that drew him to his lauds, he dared not judge his sister's fault too harshly" (*CSW,* I, 582). Treating the relationship as like that of sister and brother captures Edith's relation to Henry. The Hermit advising her "to return to her cloister" is James advising her to commit herself to her marriage. He encourages her to "endure the condition of her life," as James's letters encouraged her to do in real life. When the Hermit finds her dead in the pool, he worries just as James might have: "he thought how the people would find him bending above the body of a naked woman . . . whom they might now well take for the secret instrument of his undoing" (*CSW,* I, 588). His reactions are not those of a lover but of a man worried about his reputation, and James was afraid of any kind of association with scandal. In her fantasy, Edith makes the wild woman a saint and kills off the Hermit, who collapses when he realizes he has doubted her holiness. The consolation for him is that his lauds are sung in heaven—that is, James is promised a future popularity. Perhaps the Hermit's lauds are a medieval proxy for James's New York Edition, which she knew he was readying for print. The fable was Wharton's justification of her ways to James, who wanted her to restrict her life. She had herself been dipping into forbidden waters but coming out a saint. She was prepared to acknowledge his immortality as a writer, the secret passion of his life, if he accepted her point of view. She showed that she was aware of his basically worldly interest, fame, and told him that her need for life was as important as his needs. He who a couple of years before, in *The Ambassadors,* had written, "Live all you can," should, she thought, be able to extend the principle he enunciated to her life as well.

In the narrative poem "Ogrin the Hermit," of 1909, James appears as a confidant. Wharton had now met Fullerton and since 1907 had been having an adulterous affair with him. As Iseult in the poem she accepts advice from the Hermit that expresses poetically what James had written her in the midst of the comparable situation in her real life: "Only sit tight yourself *and go through the movements of life.* That keeps up our connection with life . . . behind which . . . the deeper and darker . . . learns . . . to stay in its place. Let it get out of its place and it swamps the scene" (*L,* IV, 495). In the poem, the Hermit tells her that "after the heart amazed / Swoons of its glory," it "Craves the dim shelter of familiar sounds . . . And the slow world waking to its daily round" (*OG,* 848). In 1909, Wharton was no longer poking fun at the Hermit's—and James's—peculiarities, vanities, and fears but showing him sympathetic to the idea of physical love. James had in 1909 seen Wharton and Fullerton at the Charing Cross hotel where they were spending the night before Fullerton left for a quick trip to the United States (*M*, 415).

"Ogrin the Hermit" appeared in December, 1909, and had been written in the spring of the same year, right after James's story "The Velvet Glove" had come out. James may or may not have read "The Hermit and the Wild Woman"— it was not on a shelf at Lamb House—but "The Velvet Glove" seems to respond to Wharton's portrayal of him in that story. In "The Velvet Glove," the beautiful and rich Princess wants a literary puff for her bad novel. What the writer tells her is, "Only live. Only be. *We'll* do the rest" (XII, 263). Live, don't scribble, is his advice, and Wharton seemed to take this into account in the Hermit of 1909, for Ogrin, in "his old age," takes over the writing and allows the living to Iseult, that is, to her.

If "Ogrin the Hermit" was Wharton's way of acknowledging "The Velvet Glove," a fable through which the Hermit was allowing her her life, "The Eyes," of 1910, is her riposte to James's collection of stories, *The Finer Grain*, published in 1910 but containing stories that appeared in journals in 1909. In addition to "The Velvet Glove," these include "Mora Montravers," "Crapy Cornelia," "A Round of Visits," and "The Bench of Desolation," each of which, like "The Velvet Glove," is built around the effect that a woman of coarser grain has on a man of finer grain. Careful attention to the five tales leaves no doubt that, in a kind of a black joke, Wharton was the model for every one of these women: the Princess, Mora Montravers, Mrs. Worthingham, Florence Ash, and Kate Cookham. The last of the tales even makes use of the breach-of-promise suit filed against Fullerton by his French mistress, whom Wharton bought off for him. In that tale, Edith's country house, The Mount, is also brought in by name (XII, 422).

The portrait of James in "The Eyes" is nastier than those which either Paget or Mrs. Ward produced and much nastier than those in Wharton's earlier work. I believe the reason for this lies in Wharton's recognition of herself in *The Finer Grain*, though she concealed her awareness of James's joke. Jervase Marion in "Lady Tal" may have been a caricature of James, but he was not the object of malice. Sir James Chide was benevolent and providential. But in "The Eyes" Andrew Culwin is a cold-blooded homosexual surrounded by young acolytes off whom he feeds. Setting the description that Wharton offers in *A Backward Glance* of Howard Sturgis' Qu'Acre group of literary young men, which had James as the dominant center, against the description she offers in "The Eyes" of the group surrounding Culwin leads inescapably to the conclusion that Culwin is James. Here is the passage in *A Backward Glance:*

> This inner group I see now, gathered around [James] as the lamps are brought in at the end of a foggy autumn afternoon. In one of the arm-chairs by the fire is sunk the long-limbed frame of the young Percy Lubbock, still carrying in his mind the delightful books he has since given us, and perhaps as yet hardly aware that he was ever to put them on paper; in another sits Gaillard Lapsley, down for the week-end from his tutorial duties at Cambridge, while John Hugh-Smith faces Percy across the fireside, and Robert Norton and I share the corners of the wide chintz sofa behind the tea-table; and dominating the hearth, and all of us, Henry James stands, or heavily pads about the room, listening, muttering, groaning disapproval, or chuckling assent to the paradoxes of the other tea-drinkers. And then, when tea is over, and the tray has disappeared, he stops his prowling to lean against the mantelpiece and plunge into reminiscences of the Paris or London of his youth, or into some slowly elaborated literary disquisition. (*BG,* 231)

The group of men friends at the opening of "The Eyes"—including one member whose "slender height" conjures a memory of Lubbock—has all the marks of the Qu'Acre group. Eight men sitting and talking by the "drowsy gleam of a coal fire" are gathered around Andrew Culwin, who is "listening and blinking through the smoke circles with the cheerful tolerance of a wise old idol," (*CSW,* II, 115). He dominates the conversation, to everyone's delight: "His mind was like a forum, or some open meeting place for the exchange of ideas: somewhat cold and drafty, but light, spacious and orderly—a kind of academic grove from which all the leaves have fallen. In this privileged area a dozen of us were wont to stretch our muscles and expand our lungs; and, as if to prolong as much as possible the tradition of what we felt to be a vanishing institution, one or two neophytes were now and then added to our band" (*CSW,* II, 116). The description by Culwin of one young man he encourages—"slender and smooth and hyacinthine, he might have stepped from a ruined altar—one to Antinous, say" (*CT,* II, 123)—makes gentle but unmistakable reference to the homosexuality of Hadrian. Culwin's ghosts turn out to be his own eyes, which he twice sees haunting him, both times after he has performed acts of generosity that go against the grain of his own egotism: "They were an hallucination, then: that was plain. . . . I had gone deeply enough into the mystery of morbid pathological states to picture the conditions under which an exploring mind might lay itself open to such a midnight admonition" (*CSW*, II, 121). "Those eyes hung there and drew me. I had the *vertige de l'abîme*, and their red lids were the edge of my abyss" (*CSW*, II, 122). Here Wharton incorporated a phrase from "Crapy Cornelia" employed in connection with Monteith's deliberation about whether he could live the kind of life Mrs. Worthingham—by inference, Edith Wharton—could offer him: "He could have lived on in *his* New York . . . the sentimental . . . the more or less romantic visitation of it; but had it been positive for him that he could live on in hers?—unless indeed the possibility of this had been just (like the famous *vertige de l'abîme*, like the solicitation of danger, or otherwise of the dreadful) the very hinge of his whole dream" (XII, 354). Wharton repeats this phrase from James's story at exactly the point in her story where her hero is brooding, like Monteith, about whether to propose to a woman he does not desire. Still, the most conspicuous borrowing from James's fiction is in the theme of the man haunted by himself, as in both his "The Jolly Corner," of 1909, in which Spencer Brydon is haunted by his alter ego, a projection of his egotism, and his "The Beast in the Jungle," of 1902, in which the beast is also a "hallucination" of Marcher's egotism.

The fourth portrayal of James in a character of Wharton's is kinder to him, and she wrote the story in which it appears a few years after his death. While she was working on *The Age of Innocence* she composed "Writing a War Story," which was published in September, 1919, about Ivy, a young woman who serves tea in an Anglo-American hospital in Paris during the First World War. A famous novelist, Harold Harbard, one of her patients, reads a short story she has written for a war magazine and criticizes it in almost the same terms James had employed in commenting on Wharton's "The Custom of the Country" in a conversation with her. When Ivy asks Harbard why he is laughing, he tells her it is very hard to explain it to her.

> He shook his head. "No; but it's queer—it's puzzling. You've got hold of a wonderfully good subject; and that's the main thing, of course—"
> Ivy interrupted him eagerly. "The subject is the main thing?"
> "Why, naturally; it's only the people without invention who tell you it isn't."

"Oh," she gasped, trying to readjust her carefully acquired theory of aesthetics.

"You've got hold of an awfully good subject," Harbard continued; *"but you've rather mauled it, haven't you?"* (*CSW,* II, 369; italics mine)

In *A Backward Glance,* Edith Wharton has quoted James: "But of course you know—as how should you, with your infernal keenness of perception, *not* know?—that in doing your tale you had under your hand a magnificent subject, which ought to have been your main theme, and that you used it as a mere incident and then passed it by?" When she tried to justify herself to James, "he could merely answer, by implication if not openly, *'Then, my dear child, you chose the wrong kind of subject'*" (*BG,* 182–83; italics mine).

"Writing a War Story" is an elaboration of the idea that it is necessary for an author to have both a subject and the management of that subject well in hand—the "donnée" and its "treatment," about which James always talked and wrote. In the essay "The Art of Fiction," of 1884, James had written, "The story and the novel, the idea and the form, are the needle and thread, and I never heard of a guild of tailors who recommended the use of the thread without the needle or the needle without the thread" (*EL,* 60).

Henry James's persona is clearly discernible in the sketch of the wounded Harbard. Harbard is the author of the novel *Broken Wings,* as James was the author of the story "Broken Wings," of 1900, about an authoress who considers herself a failure.

The end of *The Age of Innocence* may also draw on an anecdote that is one of the few about James's affective life presented in Simon Nowell-Smith's collection of Jamesiana, *The Legend of the Master,* as transmitted by Edmund Gosse. James described the incident to Gosse and confided it also to Hugh Walpole, "who says that it occurred in James's youth in a foreign town." Walpole saw the story as suggesting that James may have suffered some frustration in love. It is possible that James also mentioned what had happened to Edith Wharton, as well as to other close friends. James was, in Nowell-Smith's words, "standing on the pavement of a city, in the dusk, and . . . gazing upwards . . . watching for the lighting of a lamp in a window on the third storey. . . . [He] strained to see what was behind it, the unapproachable face. And for hours he stood there . . . and never from behind the lamp was for one moment visible the face" (*SNS,* 119–20). At the end of *The Age of Innocence,* Newland Archer is in Paris sitting on a bench at evening and watching the fifth story. Archer, like James, peers through the "thickening dusk, his eyes never turning from the balcony. At length a light shone through the windows, and a moment later a man-servant came out on the balcony, drew up the awnings, and closed the shutters. . . . Newland Archer got up slowly and walked back alone to his hotel" (*AI*, 361).

In *The Buccaneers*, of 1938, Wharton's nostalgic last, unfinished novel, there is a theme that James had broached in his "The Siege of London," of 1883: the idea of the invader, the woman from America who marries into the British aristocracy. The great country house that Annabel St. George, or Nan, Wharton's heroine, lives in as the Duchess of Tintagel is named Longlands, the same as the great country house of which Mrs. Headway, James's heroine, is someday to become mistress. The governess in *The Buccaneers*, Laura Testvalley, who serves as the *dea ex machina* for the American girls who do the invading in the 1870s, seems to parallel James's little hero Hyacinth Robinson, the "most civilized little man in Europe," inasmuch as Laura Testvalley is Edith Wharton's alter ego. Like her, she is a "little, brown" woman, and she is presented as an "adventuress with morals," which seems to fit Wharton's picture of herself as a maternal figure in her last years. That corresponds to James's identification of himself with Hyacinth in his preface to *The Princess Casamassima*, where he tells the reader that he might have been Hyacinth had he not had a background of privilege. Hyacinth was "watching the same public show . . . I had watched myself . . . save indeed for one little difference," that "every door of approach" was "shut in his face. For one's self . . . there had been doors that opened" (*AN*, 61). But Laura Testvalley, unlike little Hyacinth, has power. In *The Buccaneers*, Wharton has evolved not into a mother but into a woman who has the authority of a mother without being one.

The infusion of Wharton into an important character who vies with Nan as heroine may have an antecedent in James's *The Golden Bowl*, of 1904. James has been descried in the character of the little Jewish antiques dealer who plays the key role in reintroducing the golden bowl back into the plot, thus enabling Maggie to figure out the mysterious evil lurking in her family.[7]

There are other signs that Wharton was tapping James for *The Buccaneers*. He, dead for twenty years, had by the 1930s engaged her sense of nostalgia and heritage. Miss March, the American woman in the novel who, though jilted in her youth by a British aristocrat, has remained in England,

---

7. Lawrence Holland, *The Expense of Vision* (Princeton, 1964).

harks back to Mamie Cutter, the heroine of James's "Mrs Medwin," of 1901. Especially telltale is the description of Miss March's apartment. Her room "was crowded with velvet-covered tables and quaint corner-shelves, all laden with photographs in heavy silver or morocco frames, surmounted by coronets, from the baronial to the ducal—one, even, royal— ... of young or middle-aged women, with long necks and calm imperious faces" (*BU,* 104). Mamie Cutter's "small rooms had the peculiarity that everything they contained appeared to testify with vividness to her position in society," and the effect "would have been luxurious if luxury consisted mainly in photographic portraits slashed across with signatures, in baskets of flowers beribboned with the cards of passing compatriots" (XI, 257). Like Mamie Cutter, Miss March is the "oracle of transatlantic pilgrims in quest of a social opening" (*BU,* 99).

It seems evident that the late work of James lent narrative strategies to *The Buccaneers.* For instance, the role that the Bronzino and the Veronese play in *The Wings of the Dove,* of 1902, is translated here into a role for the paintings hanging on the walls of Nan's boudoir in Longlands—Correggio's pastoral-mythological scenes of an earthly paradise—and for Rossetti's *Bocca Baciata,* hanging in the happier place, Honourslove, belonging to the Thwartes. The Correggios are holdings of museum caliber that the highest nobility had inherited, and the Rossetti is a work of rebellious art unacceptable to the property-owning classes of the 1870s, when the Pre-Raphaelites were just becoming influential. In *The Wings of the Dove,* Veronese is the accepted artist of the Renaissance, whereas Bronzino appeals to the new taste for Mannerism.[8]

Wharton handles the division between Nan's unmarried life and her married life in an abrupt transition, much as James, in *The Portrait of a Lady,* had had an abrupt transition between Isabel's courtship by Osmond and her life after four years of an unhappy marriage and the loss of her child, when everything has changed for her. In *The Buccaneers,* two years have elapsed, and Nan's acceptance of the Duke of Tintagel as a husband comes out only when she is found writing invitations to a Christmas party to be given at Longlands, a party that is the setting for the Virginia reel and the meeting between Guy Thwarte and Nan in front of Correggio's paintings of terrestrial paradise in her boudoir. When Nan wants money for her

---

8. Adeline R. Tintner, "Pre-Raphaelite Painting and Poetry in Edith Wharton's *The Buccaneers* (1938)," *Journal of Pre-Raphaelite Studies,* n.s. II (Fall, 1993), 16–21.

friend Conchita, the friend who has carried all the girls into her aristocratic milieu, she is unwilling to tell her husband why she is asking for the sum. He is agreeable to her request, however, provided that she resumes sexual relations with him. This recalls Densher's bargaining in *The Wings of the Dove* for sexual favors if he is to help execute Kate's plan of assault on Milly's money.

Although Wharton declared that James's late work held no interest for her, much from his tales after 1900 seems to have infiltrated *The Buccaneers*. Her plot, in which Nan runs off with Guy Thwarte, seems to derive from the scandal that reverberated through Europe and England when Consuelo Vanderbilt left the Duke of Marlborough, whom she had wedded under the force of her mother's ambitions, and after a divorce married Colonel Balsam for love.[9] James's tale "The Special Type," of 1900, may have been a prompt to Wharton, for it took off from the scandal that occurred when William K. Vanderbilt, Consuelo's father, obtained his divorce a year or two before the marriage into which her socially ambitious mother drove her. The talk was that her father had used a professional corespondent to engineer the proper grounds for a divorce, and James made a masterly little tale out of it.

The rescue that, in Wharton's unfinished novel, the governess brings off for Nan from the stifling traditions of the higher aristocracy correlates with the rescue, in James's *The Sense of the Past*, also an unfinished novel, that Aurora Coyne effects for her fiancé, Ralph Pendrel, from the Regency past that has trapped him in his inherited house. When Wharton wrote a novel set seventy-five years in the past, she seemed nostalgically pulled toward her first master, Henry James.[10]

Constance Fenimore Woolson

Constance Fenimore Woolson (1840–1894), a close friend of Henry James's, took mild revenge against her sometime partner on visits to art galleries by fashioning characters after him in three of her stories, but what she took the revenge for is a matter of argument. Leon Edel has detected James's figure in two of Woolson's stories: "Miss Grief," of 1880, written

9. Adeline R. Tintner, "Consuelo Vanderbilt and *The Buccaneers*," *Edith Wharton Review*, X (Fall, 1993), 15–20.

10. See *The Buccaneers* as completed by Marion Mainwaring (New York, 1993).

just before she met him, and "A Florentine Experiment," written and published that same year, a few months after she spent three weeks with him, during which he showed clear signs of enjoying her company (*CL*, 410; see also pp. 407–41 *passim*). John Dwight Kern in 1934 discerned "echoes of James in the cultivated Trafford," the hero of "A Florentine Experiment." He considered these to be "adventitious reminders of the association of the two expatriate writers under circumstances in many ways analogous to the situation of the lovers in the story."[11] In 1963, Rayburn S. Moore could not "help wondering how closely 'analogous' the 'situation' of Miss Woolson and James was to that of the lovers in the tale."[12] Just a year before, Edel had built a strong, although speculative, case for believing that Woolson and James are in both tales.

I would add a third story, "The Street of the Hyacinth," of 1882, where the same kind of male figure, there a writer of art criticism, and possessed of physical characteristics and habits that fit what we know about James, appears. It is interesting how the couple Woolson invented in each tale acts out a different fantasy concerning her relationship with James.

"Miss Grief" has in recent years received the attention of a feminist scholar, Cheryl B. Torsney, in view of its presentation of a poor, unrecognized but powerful woman writer, Aaronna Moncrief, the Miss Grief of the tale.[13] Aaronna Moncrief contrasts with a renowned male writer, based on a figure like James, who nonetheless is not as powerful as she. Like Woolson, who had not yet caught up with James though, as James put it in his correspondence, she had "been pursuing me through Europe with a letter of introduction" (*CL*, I, 288), Miss Grief has been following the narrator. Although Miss Grief dies in poverty without having her power recognized by the world, the James-like narrator comes to acknowledge, "She, with the greater power, failed—I, with the less, succeeded" (*GR*, 585).

Even the most cautious of writers on Woolson, including Moore, agree that "A Florentine Experiment," published a few months after James and Fenimore's gallery tours in Florence in the spring of 1880, reflects their time together, and the hero of the tale carries the imprint of her observation of her friend. "Miss Grief" opens with the narrator's confessing that he is

11.   John Dwight Kern, *Constance Fenimore Woolson: Literary Pioneer* (Philadelphia, 1934), 119.

12.   Rayburn S. Moore, *Constance Fenimore Woolson* (New York, 1963), 73.

13.   Cheryl B. Torsney, *Constance Fenimore Woolson: The Grief of Artistry* (Athens, Ga., 1989).

conceited, and in "A Florentine Experiment" he is both conceited and aloof. The "experiment" in Florence is conducted by Margaret Stowe, the heroine, who retails to Trafford Morgan, the character patterned on James, an invented account of having been in love and having given up her loved one. Her aim is to get Morgan interested in her, and she succeeds at her scheme.[14] He was once engaged to Beatrice Lovell, and had confected a similar story for her, but she has married another man. All the same, he falls for the marital trap Margaret has set for him.

In "Miss Grief," Woolson was content to show that the James-like figure realized she was the better artist. In "A Florentine Experiment," after she met James, she was inclined to make her fantasy more personal, ending in a marriage that her encounter with him did not rule out, at least as a fantasy.

The outcome is similar in the third tale, "The Street of the Hyacinth." There the heroine, Ettie Faith Macks, is a painter who, unlike Miss Grief as a writer, shows no talent at all. Still, her outspoken independence and forthright expression gain the interest of the Jamesian figure, who, in the way of his counterparts in the other stories, is "wonderfully smooth-spoken; but yet, somehow—awfully indifferent" (*SH*, 146). Mr. Raymond Noel is a writer of art criticism, and Ettie Faith Macks pursues him as Aaronna Moncrief does the writer in "Miss Grief," and Woolson did James in real life. Woolson has chosen an occupation for Noel by selecting from James's gainful activities. Ettie Faith Macks finally meets Noel and implores him to visit her in order to render an opinion whether her paintings show talent. But it is only after Ettie refuses a count's proposal of marriage and after she takes care of Noel when he falls from a horse that he becomes interested in her. Although she admits her love for him from the very beginning, she tells him that she does "not respect you or admire you, you have been completely spoiled and will always remain so" (*SH*, 176). Noel, however, continues his courtship of her when she is forced to leave the country for a while. Finally, his indifference completely cracked, he proclaims himself to be very much in love with her, and they marry.

Why Ettie would elect to learn how to paint from a writer on art can be explained only by Woolson's desire to make her male character true to James at this period and to rationalize an intense interest in him. The inde-

14.   Constance Fenimore Woolson, "A Florentine Experiment," *Atlantic Monthly*, XLVI (1880), 123–86.

pendence of Ettie Macks is the same that Woolson exposed in "A Florentine Experiment," though further exaggerated.

It is interesting that in the third story, the hero calls the heroine by her middle name, Faith, as James called Woolson by her middle name, Fenimore (*SH*, 159). Woolson also duplicated in this fantasy her own history of having read and memorized everything James had written by having Ettie write down everything Noel has said to her about the pictures they have seen when she has visited galleries with him. A talkative woman of great originality and strong opinions, she still wants to learn (*SH*, 163). This story may well embody the fantasy that was most satisfying to Woolson, so that it became the final one of her tales with a foundation in her relationship with James during the period when he first became friendly with her and they visited the galleries in Florence.

Woolson's revenge took three shapes. "Miss Grief" consisted of showing that, in comparison with James, she was a more powerful, although an unrenowned, writer; there is nothing personal about him in it because she had not yet met him. "A Florentine Experiment" displays how, after she met him, she was susceptible to his personal attraction though perfectly aware of his indifference to her. Yet she fantasized herself capable of capturing his fancy so that, almost reluctantly but surely, he ends up marrying her. In "The Street of the Hyacinth," she portrays an even greater indifference and reluctance, but here her personality, her independence, her originality, and her responsiveness finally, although slowly, succeed in conquering the indifferent heart. What is the revenge in this? The relationship between Woolson and James was, according to the evidence we have, a fond but impersonal one. In these three stories, written within the space of two years, she avenges herself on him in fantasy by creating herself as a more powerful writer, a sensitive and clever, passionate woman, and finally, an original and multigifted human being. Her revenge lies in fictionally commanding a declaration of love from the James-like figure, as well as in his recognition of her estimable qualities.

Olive Garnett

Olive Rayne Garnett (1871–1958) was the unmarried sister of the English author and playwright Edward Garnett. Her sister-in-law was Constance Garnett, who, involved with Russian exiles, learned their language and produced translations that introduced Russian novelists like Turgenev and

Tolstoi to the English-speaking world. Olive Garnett had a platonic love affair with one of the exiles, Sergei Stepnyak. She traveled in Russia and wrote two books, one of short stories, *Petersburg Tales*, published in 1900, and the other a novel, *In Russia's Night*, published in 1918. Her biographer, Thomas C. Moser, sees among the novel's important characters a "version of Henry James."[15] Unlike the four other women who have fictionalized the figure of James, however, Garnett simply had a crush on him, had seen him in the flesh only a few times, through his associations with the circle of Ford Madox Ford and with her brother Edward, and had no real contact with him except by way of his books. James had not given her any editorial or critical assistance. There were random encounters in the streets of Rye and one tea at Lamb House, during which she was tongue-tied by her schoolgirl passion for the portly writer. The sale catalog for her nephew David Garnett's library corroborates that she owned everything James published, as well as that part of Leon Edel's biography which appeared before her death and the books about James that appeared in the 1940s by F. O. Matthiessen. She also possessed Matthiessen's edition of the *Notebooks* and Edel's of the *Selected Letters* (H, 82; MG, 527). All this began with the gift from her grandfather, Richard Garnett, of James's *The Siege of London*, when she was twelve.

The novel tells of a young Englishwoman, Katia, who marries a spoiled young Russian painter. The first half of the book enlarges on their relationship to Arabagine, a rich middle-aged bachelor and art collector whose patronage makes it possible for Dmitri to paint and for Katia to have a beautiful friendship with an unusual man. Garnett's attitude toward the Henry James inhabiting the character of Arabagine is one of admiration, although she does not blink at some of James's peculiarities, of which the members of all the interconnecting circles in which he moved were aware.

Parts of Garnett's diary pertaining to James have been published by Edel in *Henry James: The Master*. Other parts she apparently deemed too personal, however, and she cut them out. In 1899, before she ever met James, she dreamed he looked up from his writing, smiled, and said, "You know, life isn't *only* reality, it's a small part of a great whole." In her dream she was working on a story "of what it would be like to love and be loved by Henry James" (*M*, 46). Later, in a description of coming unexpectedly

---

15. Thomas C. Moser, "An English Context for Conrad's Russian Characters: Sergey Stepniak and the Diary of Olive Garnett," *Journal of Modern Literature*, XI (1984), 43.

upon James at one of Ford's parties, she wrote, "It was Henry James!" She went on to quote him as saying to her, "I am a crushed worm, I don't even revolve now, I have ceased to turn." She recorded interjecting, "That is a happy and restful state." James countered with, "Ah, you are young— youth—youth." Apparently that cliché so affected her that three days later she wrote, "Henry James seems to obsess me, or is it the spring coming? Anyway I really *am* a crushed worm" (MG, 528). This was in 1904, when she was thirty-three years old, hardly an adolescent. Her crush endured for a lifetime.

Sergei Stepnyak, who was killed in an accident in 1895, during Garnett's friendship with him, and Henry James, with whom she may have had only this conversation and tea at Lamb House, were the two great loves and influences she memorialized in her one novel. James dominates the first part as Arabagine, though he is not as immediately recognizable in this character as he is in other writers' rendering of him, and Stepnyak dominates the second as Muromsky. James was an outsider to English society, considered by the English literary establishment to be a kind of exotic foreigner, and she said of Arabagine that he is "thought to be an Armenian Jew." He is, in any case, the epitome of civilized and cultivated tastes. Although James was dead by the time Garnett wrote her novel and his feelings would not have been wounded if she had parodied him, her inclination was not in that direction. In some ways Arabagine is closer to Mrs. Ward's Sir James Chide, in *Diana Mallory*, than to the other fictional portraits of him. Both characters comprise flattering images, Mrs. Ward's tinctured only with slight criticism and capturing James younger by ten years.

Garnett's depiction of Arabagine was influenced by James's kindly interest in young people during the last years of his life, but its substance depended on her feelings, above all, as in her dream, about "what it would be like to love and be loved by Henry James." In making Arabagine a very rich amateur of the arts, something James was not, Garnett was probably bowing to the way James professed to be a collector of impressions. Arabagine had to be very rich for the sake of his role as a fairy godfather in her fairy tale. Possessed of the "painter's eye," he spots out genuine masterpieces and is given to Jamesian locutions. "Oh, delightful, deliciously characteristic," he exclaims. His "Oh, oh, oh" sounds straight from *The Ambassadors* (*IR*, 123). As the next best thing to keeping James's nationality for him, she had him spend a lot of time in Canada, where he buys beautiful and costly furs for Katia. He is an aesthetic Santa Claus. Garnett could touch on his homoeroticism, inasmuch as James was dead; it was something that, in spite of her crush on him, she was conscious of being common knowledge. Dmitri's mother does not like it that Arabagine, who has allowed the young couple to live in some unused rooms of his vast apartment, is known to be a "man with queer morals" (*IR*, 127). He is cosmopolitan, "so much at home in London and Paris" (*IR*, 140).

In consonance with events in *The Spoils of Poynton*, of 1897, Arabagine leaves Katia a "small cross set with pearls," as well as his gallery of paintings (*IR*, 260). After tea at Lamb House, Olive may have dwelt in her imagination on being James's heiress, as Nanda was Mr. Longdon's in *The Awkward Age*. It was no doubt James's paternal interest that captivated her. "He spoke perfect English, and no man's talk til now had so subtly flattered me," Katia says of Arabagine (*IR*, 96). The feminine yearning for masculine attention was strong in Garnett, who received little of it as one of six rivals in a productive literary family, if her sister-in-law Constance is counted. Arabagine, wearing a "double gold eyeglass," also seen in late photographs of James, is described as having a good eye, noticing everything. It "is not too much to say that I was educated by his casual talk," Katia remarks. "I had never before been treated as an equal by a man of this new friend's attainments" (*IR*, 98). When Arabagine more or less adopts the young couple, he says, "The situation of young people interests me—your actions and reactions in the face of life and art" (*IR*, 99). Arabagine accords worth to the women and young he lets occupy his attention, and the measure in which he holds them is that of the Master, the James after 1900.

Theodora Bosanquet's diary of the man who dictated to her his last novels also recorded how he liked to nibble on sweets and to clown it up a bit. And Arabagine "liked a tour of the people's theatres, circuses, . . . munched gingerbread and sunflower seed, and generally played the fool in a way I should never have expected from a 'swell' like [him]," Katia observes (*IR*, 101). Garnett was aware of Theodora Bosanquet's life with James, mentioning in her diary that she saw the two pass together on the streets of Rye. When she had Dmitri and Katia live in the empty part of Arabagine's picture gallery, in rooms opposite his flat, she may have been envying Bosanquet's proximity to James in their separate quarters on the same floor in London. It is appropriate to live near but not with the ideal father-lover.

Certainly, Garnett perceived in her fantasy figure of James a good father, someone who appreciated her thoughts, admired her reactions, and educated her. Her desires were not for sexual relations with a man. Katia is shocked by the sex she has with her own husband. How much better was Arabagine than Dmitri, and in real life how appealing was the asexual figure of the sexagenarian James. After the first part of the book, Garnett could invent many letters from him in a typical Jamesian vein. Thomas Moser has written to me that "the Hueffers [the Ford Madox Fords] and the Garnett family were quite aware of her passion. Everyone knew that Olive would be excited when the Hueffers moved near James. He was in Rye and they were in Aldington, Kent and then near Winchelsea."[16]

Olive Garnett consoled and avenged herself for not having any real relation with James, either professional or personal, by creating a fairy godfather who gave her all the things Henry James did not and whom she could spurn by killing off as a literary character, making way for a real relationship with Stepnyak, incomplete though it was.

Allusions Without Malice

The five women writers who tried to square accounts with James by injecting his idiosyncratic personal figure into their work, usually with an ironic overtone, had complex personal and literary relationships with him. It was a more straightforward friendship that was important in the relationships of Constance Fletcher, Rhoda Broughton, and the Baroness von Hutten with James, and their work pays delicate tribute by alluding to him. There is no sense of revenge in the allusions.

Constance Fletcher

Constance Fletcher (1858–1938), who wrote under the pen name of George Fleming, was an old and close friend of James's. So far as is known, he never offered criticism of Fletcher's writing. Apparently she did not ask for it, and perhaps he did not wish to mar their friendship. James did read Fletcher's translation in verse of *Les Romanesques*, by Edmond Rostand, which she called *The Fantasticks*, and he seems to have lifted elements of it for "The Velvet Glove," of 1909.[17]

Fletcher with one of her tales, "The Next House," seems to have stood in

16. Thomas C. Moser to author, June 26, 1984.
17. Adeline R. Tintner, *The Cosmopolitan World of Henry James: An Intertextual Study* (Baton Rouge, 1991), 99–103.

a connection of reciprocal influence with James. The tale appeared in *Little Stories About Women,* the only volume by her to be found in James's library. Interestingly, she did not present the book to James. Rather, he seems to have purchased it and signed it. Published in 1897, it followed by one year the publication of his novel *The Other House.* The nod to James's title by Fletcher's does not appear unintended.

The action of the tale takes place at a dinner party, where Vyner Sherman, a bachelor with civilized tastes, tells a young woman seated next to him that the money of the house—money that bought the many porcelain dragon gods in the drawing room—came from China (*LS*, 113). This "quiet-looking man with the dark, oddly smiling face" (*LS*, 118) is described by his hostess as "one of the most important men in London" (*LS*, 120). The young woman and he step out onto the balcony overlooking the embankment, from where they can hear someone, whom the young woman identifies as Lady Lascelles, playing Wagner on the piano. After the young woman leaves him, Sherman stands looking at Lady Lascelles' house. He can see in the drawing room "lamps burning on a table—two yellow spots of light like two eyes in the white moonlit facade of the house. . . . Although moonlight is shining, there floated a pale, a very transparent haze, dulling it" (*LS*, 130). He is lost in reverie and living in the past, when they were engaged. But she rejected him, since he had "no family connection to boast of; no money; no prospects in particular except his profession; not even looks—! Oh, he was clever enough, of course . . . and of course he was a gentleman" (*LS*, 133–34). He thinks of what it would be like to go up to her and say, "There are other women in the world and, because of you, it has been impossible for me to love one of them" (*LS*, 138). He reckons that only if he realizes "in her own presence that she had ceased to need him, *then* he could believe in their real separation. . . . So much would be finished, but there would be peace" (*LS*, 139). With that in mind, he crosses over to her house to have it out with her, but as he approaches it, her husband alights from a cab and enters the building with his latchkey. Sherman abandons his intention and hails the cab that has brought Lord Lascelles home.

The tale appears to depend on the anecdote James told about himself to at least two of his friends, Edmund Gosse and Hugh Walpole, and probably also to Edith Wharton. This is perhaps James's only description of a love experience of his own—one he seems to have had in his youth. Although James watched with interest how human beings "plunge into experiences," Gosse commented, "he proposed to take no plunge himself, or at least to have no audience when he plunged."[18]

Sherman's reaction to knowing that the woman who rejected him lives in the house and is the one whose lamps he watches fills in the lacuna left by James's failure to explain the background of the episode he recounted to Gosse. Both Lubbock and Wharton called James a hermit, and Sherman on the first page of the tale is called a hermit by his hostess. Like James as Gosse described him, Sherman "never made confidences to anybody, or wished to make them" (*LS*, 134). But Fletcher created a story in which James's simple and unexplained anecdote became understandable despite the reticence of both its original teller and her tale's chief character.

Aside from whatever basis the plot has in the anecdote, the man at the dinner table in the story is close in appearance and general temperament to Henry James, though he is not a novelist but a gifted travel writer. He knows all about art, he gossips about the origin of the wealth of their host, pointing out a masterpiece by James's friend, Burne-Jones, in the room where they are dining, and he is in his middle fifties, as James was when Fletcher wrote the story.

The reciprocal influence that the story may have had on James involves a figure of speech in it that it is possible James lifted the next year when he wrote "The Great Good Place." The figure occurs when the young woman tells Sherman the name of the piano player, reawakening in him the memories of his suffering: "She felt the difference in his manner . . . precisely as you feel the sudden shock . . . of a line from which the fish has parted. The captured bit of life was drawing towards you at the end of that six inches of gut only a moment ago. It was there, and it is gone, and there is no more to be done about it." James refined the figure in his tale, written in 1898 and published in 1900, but the basic image is the same. The hero's "genius . . . was what he had been in danger of losing. . . . The change was that, little by little, his hold had grown firmer so that he drew in the line . . . with a pull he was delighted to find it would bear" (XI, 30). Later, "he had drawn in by this time . . . the whole of the long line, and that fact just dangled at the end. He could put his other hand on it, he could unhook it, he was once more in possession" (XI, 35).

Constance Fletcher was one of James's friends of longest standing. He had reviewed two of her novels, *Kismet* and *Mirage*, extremely favorably in

18. Edmund Gosse, *Aspects and Impressions* (New York, 1922), 42–43.

1875 and 1876, and he depended on the Palazzo Capello, where Fletcher lived with her stepfather, Eugene Benson, for the mise-en-scène of *The Aspern Papers*. It would not have been odd for him to have confided to her, in the at once revealing and concealing way of his anecdote, a sentimental attachment of his younger years. She had none of the personal or literary motives of many of the other women he knew for taking revenge on him. Her assimilation and reconstruction of his one anecdote about his romantic susceptibility would have appealed to her imagination of emotional disaster and subsequent regret. It looks as though her rapport with James was what enabled her to turn this material into the finest short story of her career. The inclusion in James's library of the volume in which the tale appeared suggests that he may have had a special reason for holding on to "The Next House." But of all this there is no proof except the uncanny resemblance of the plot of the tale to a singular moment in James's emotional life, a glimpse of which he gave his friends, after which he drew the curtain down again.

Rhoda Broughton

James had in 1876, as a sharp young critic, reviewed the novel *Joan*, by Rhoda Broughton (1840–1920). He was thirty-three, and she, at thirty-six, was already the well-known author of several novels. In the *Nation*, of December 21, 1876, he compared *Joan* disparagingly with a novel, *Mercy Philbrick's Choice*, by Helen Hunt Jackson: "*Mercy Philbrick's Choice* is a very rare and perfect work of art in comparison—so much so that it is really almost an offence to couple it, however discriminatingly, with such a farrago of puerility and nastiness, inanity and vulgarity [as *Joan*]" (*EL*, 514). He went on that, representing what fashionable fiction for young ladies concerns itself with, "horses and dogs, and the 'longevity' of first kisses," *Joan* must deal with a "beautiful young orphan who becomes a governess, and captivates the tall young men who visit the family, etc. But, as young girls have become 'fast' . . . the novel . . . must insidiously furnish them with the emotions in which 'fastness' delights. Miss Broughton's insidiousness is like the gambols of an elephant; but it is curious to see how she fulfils the conditions required of her—by what immaturity and crudity of art, what coarseness of sentiment and vacuity of thought" (*EL*, 515). If Broughton ever saw this—and one of her novels shows that she may have seen it—it must have rankled.

A year later James met Broughton and took to her immediately, as he frequently did to strong-minded spinsters. She became not only a friend for life but the person to whom he wrote his finest war letter, as the hostilities of World War I began (*L*, IV, 713–14). She comforted his last lonely years, during which he was wont to invite himself up to her flat for a cup of tea. His letters never mentioned her books, until, in 1897, writing to Francis Boott, he declared, "We are excellent friends, but I really don't know whether I like her books or not; it is so long since I read one. She is not in the least a person to whom you have to pay that tribute" (*M*, 32). He never referred to her books in the many letters he wrote to the "gallant and intrepid Rhoda" herself. And he surely never reviewed another of her books.

It was Broughton's early novels, written during the 1870s, that won her popularity among lady readers in England. Typical is *Red As a Rose Is She*, with the same plot as that of *Joan*, in which the governess marries one of the eligible young men who visit the house. What sparks her novels, however, is the lively dialogue, and this continued to become more pronounced in her later novels, which extended to 1920, the year of her death. In the sharp dialogue, she came closest to an alignment with the twentieth-century woman's point of view.

If we were to assume that Broughton, like others, sought revenge on James's critical asperity, we would be hard put to find a portrait of him in her novels, except possibly in *Concerning a Vow*. She was the only woman friend of James's to have learned of his closeness to Constance Fenimore Woolson and of his sharing a house with her in Bellosguardo. Broughton had visited them when they were there, and it is possible that the plot of *Concerning a Vow*, of 1914, involves the figure of James. Two sisters are there paid attention by the novelist Edward Bromley, and they nurse a jealousy of each other as a result. One of them, May, on her deathbed extracts a vow from the other, Sally, that she will never marry the novelist. But Sally, though true to her vow, is soon going around pretending to be Bromley's wife. Officially free, Bromley applies himself to other women, and in despair Sally commits suicide by overdosing on a drug. The shock of the death drives Bromley to a madhouse. Because the novel shows a writer of repute with two women who love him—one who dies (Woolson had committed suicide twenty years before) and one who is rejected—there can perhaps be read into it the attachment between Woolson and James, with Broughton as a somewhat envious observer. Was Broughton offering a riposte to James for having roasted her so mercilessly in his review of *Joan,* by exploiting privileged information she had concerning him and Constance Woolson?

Concerning a Vow may hold veiled evidence that Broughton remembered James's adverse criticism of many years before. One of her characters reviews Bromley's book, running in a leading American periodical: "Such a hotch-potch of morbidity, irreverence, ugliness I have seldom come across" (*CV,* 104). Bromley, in any case, shares James's quality of voice: "His voice had always been one of Edward Bromley's greatest attractions; cajoling when he had no wish to cajole; flattering when he had no intention of flattering; tender when he meant only to be courteous!" (*CV,* 269).

Broughton's novel *Between Two Stools,* of 1912, seems to hark back to a short story James published in 1884, "The Path of Duty," a tale in which Ambrose Tester loves a married woman, Lady Vandeleur, yet keeps a virtuous relation with her despite spending all his time in her presence. Knowing that sooner or later he must marry, he becomes engaged to an appropriate young woman for whom he has no feelings. When Lord Vandeleur dies unexpectedly, Tester goes through with his marriage even though his loved one has become free, since his mentor, the female narrator, convinces him that the young woman would die of heartbreak if she were jilted. Nevertheless, he continues his "virtuous relation" with Lady Vandeleur. Broughton followed James's plot fairly closely, except for eliminating the virtue and allowing her true lover to consummate the affair. In *Between Two Stools,* Mrs. Delaney, married to a disagreeable invalid, has been having a relationship with a Mr. Doughty. Finding herself under stress, she insists on a two-week moratorium with her lover prior to a final breakup. During those two weeks, Doughty meets and becomes engaged to a young woman. At that point Mr. Delaney dies, and the widow is free to marry. But here the end is somewhat ambiguous: the suggestion is that Doughty leaves his fiancée, with much sorrow and sympathy, but it seems open to the reader to choose whichever ending is judged to make for greater contentment. Arethusa, the young woman who is learning to love Doughty, hears that the woman he has loved for so long is free and asks him, "'Is it true?' His bowed head was answer enough for her" (*BS,* 366). "With an accent of divine compassion, understanding and forgiveness, she tells him, 'You will not have to suffer anymore'" (*BS,* 367). "In bitter humiliation and reverence, he answers, 'Are you so sure of that?'" This is a sharp descent from the extreme subtlety and irony of James's tale of twenty years earlier. But if Broughton borrowed from James in 1912, it was not until two years later that there was any sign of him as a character in her fiction.

Baroness Von Hutten

Bettina Riddle (1874–1957), of Erie, Pennsylvania, came from a well-to-do American family. She was the niece of the president of the Pennsylvania Railroad, and like Eugenia in *The Europeans*, she married a Bavarian nobleman. In 1897, she became the Baroness Von Hutten zum Stolzenberg, but like Eugenia, she very soon separated from her husband and moved to England, where, unlike Eugenia, she became a prolific novelist.[19] Some time after 1900, she must have met or corresponded with James. So far the only solid evidence of that is in the very explicit dedication to James of her novel *He and Hecuba*, of 1906:

> To Henry James, Esq. whose kindly criticism
> of the short story of the same name
> encouraged me to lengthen it to its present form,
> I dedicate this book
> on the
> principle that
> a cat may look at a king
>   (*HE*, flyleaf)

Von Hutten's gratitude is upheld in the novel by a fictive portrait of James that is adulatory but not effusive.

The novel concerns King Hardy, a rector in a small English town, who has anonymously written a novel, chiefly autobiographical, that becomes a best seller. The novel holds the confession of a sin and achieves a succès de scandale. The press attributes the book to many different authors, "all of them men of note and two of whom answered the accusation in a London paper." Von Hutten allots to these two men qualities from two aspects of James, as private person and as public author. The two men embody different sides of James's genius. One of them, exhibiting the private side, fits the

19. Obituary of Baroness Von Hutten, *New York Times*, January 29, 1957, p. 31.

James "whose kindly criticism" Von Hutten appreciated. That one, an "American, Anglicized by years of living in England, wrote with a sort of plaintive dignity, asking what he had ever written that laid him open to the charge of being guilty of 'He and Hecuba,' which, clever as it undoubtedly is, and pulsing with life, is so obviously a *first book?* Then, gently, with much kindness and a little mild sarcasm, he drew attention to the slight crudities of style of which he had never, even in his earliest efforts, been guilty" (*HE*, 151).

The other "great man to whom the book was attributed" was, like Thomas Hardy, a "west country man, who had suddenly, a few years before, astonished the English-speaking world with a psychological novel which in keenness, ruthlessness, and knowledge of the world, was still unrivaled." King Hardy did not know enough "of contemporary literature" to realize the "compliment paid to him . . . in attributing his work to the author of 'Puppets,'" but then "Henry Crawford himself stepped quietly into the arena, and in a short, pithy letter proved his ignorance but intense admiration of the man who had written 'He and Hecuba'" (*HE*, 152). The name of Crawford's novel, "Puppets," seems to suggest the manipulations that occur in *The Golden Bowl*, of 1904. James often used the word *puppets* to refer to his characters. This second great man suggests the public side of James, whose reputation in England was in 1906, surely among other writers, at the highest point it reached during his lifetime. The first name Henry is also a possible clue steering the reader away from Hardy and back to James. Describing his "psychological novel" as "still unrivaled" suggests the esteem in which *The Golden Bowl* was viewed at the time of its appearance. The figure that Von Hutten conjures up in the two authors who write to the London newspaper is not a physical one, but it joins together the kindly, though genuinely critical, comments that James made to writers who sought his professional advice, and the prestige of the Master, who was capable of the psychological intricacies of *The Golden Bowl*. Von Hutten's novel appeared just after James had been in the public eye during a highly publicized trip to the United States in 1904 and 1905.

In the baroness' fiction, which is chiefly of the "society novel" genre, there appear other references to James the novelist. In *Julia*, of 1924, a woman acknowledges that James was "so gentlemanly."[20] That accords

---

20. Baroness Von Hutten, *Julia* (London, 1924), 26.

with the baroness' experience when he commented on her story. In *Mice for Amusement*, of 1934, a character seems to be modeled after James's Mrs. Headway from "The Siege of London," and the baroness employs a figure of speech clearly related to Adam Verver's burning of his boats in *The Golden Bowl.*[21]

Mixed Emotions

James's relationships with another group of women excited mixed emotions in them. Gertrude Atherton and Violet Hunt wanted James to respond to them as attractive women, little realizing that a candid demonstration of their wish was probably the worst imaginable approach to gaining his attention. Cora Crane reacted violently to him and to his attitude to her by destroying the copy she had of one of his published stories.

Gertrude Atherton

Gertrude Atherton (1857–1948) took revenge on Henry James despite idolizing him as a writer, as she related in 1932 in *Adventures of a Novelist.* One motive was undoubtedly the rather ungracious reviews James wrote concerning her work in 1898. James noted in a series of papers, "American Letters," for the journal *Literature,* that Atherton's novel *American Wives and English Husbands,* of 1898, showed that the author was "looking for a situation rather than . . . finding one" (*EL,* 658). Not only did she fail "to see it" but she left "us wondering what she has supposed herself to see instead" (*EL,* 659). Nor was he any more enthusiastic a few weeks later about her novel *His Fortunate Grace,* which he said was about a "managing mother who brings to pass, in the teeth of a protesting father, that her daughter shall marry an extremely dilapidated English duke" (*EL,* 669). The reader is, James continued, "at a loss with her, too uncertain as to the degree of intelligence and intention with which she presents these wonderful persons as so uncannily terrible" (*EL,* 669).

But Atherton had a second and stronger motive for seeking revenge, in James's rejection of her lifetime infatuation with him. In her memoirs, she told how, as a girl, she and a friend were both in love with him: "It was dur-

21. Baroness Von Hutten, *Mice for Amusement* (New York, 1934), 205.

ing the following summer that I had my first introduction to Henry James. . . . The girls . . . had 'caught the Henry James craze,' and had all his books to date. I became an immediate convert. . . . I remember an irritated male calling us 'Henry James fools'" (*ADN*, 101–102). Their discussions were speculative.

> As he looked dark in his pictures I maintained that I had the best hope of winning his affections—did we ever meet!—as I was a blonde and she brunette. Then she came down one day with a copy of *Roderick Hudson* in her hand, and pointed triumphantly to a line in which the heroine was almost gloatingly described as having "a mass of dusky hair over a low forehead." I gave up. . . . Years after, when I met Henry James at a garden party in London, I told him the story of this old rivalry and my final capitulation. I wish I could remember his reply. But it was so involved, there were so many colons and semi-colons, so many commas and dashes, with never a period. (*ADN*, 110–11)

She corresponded with him, and according to Theodora Bosanquet, "When he dictated a letter to Atherton to give her some information that she requested about hotels in Paris," he prefaced the dictation by saying "I abominate the woman." Yet, although "he groaned about having to write to her," it seems he did write to her.

In 1904, she met James, and during that year Gosse had advised her about what works of the author to read. He cited "The Turn of the Screw," *What Maisie Knew*, and *The Ambassadors*, which she followed with the later novels as they appeared. Six years earlier, however, in her novel *The Californians*, Henry James had made an appearance that shows she had certainly read him diligently by then. Her heroine, Magdalèna Yorba, the plain but intelligent daughter and heiress of a California grandee with a fortune in land, yearns to be a writer, and although her father, very much modeled on Balzac's M. Grandet—perhaps through Dr. Sloper, in *Washington Square*—is against her writing, she spends much of her time at it. She is finally dissuaded from trying to become an author by the appearance of the work of Henry James in the San Francisco community. Helena, her beautiful and bright friend, discovers him, and "he immediately becomes a fad." Another friend brings two volumes of James to Magdaléna. She leaves "Magdaléna alone with Henry James" (*CAL*, 322). "She took up one of the volumes. As she did so, something stirred in the cellars of her mind. . . . She stood on the porch in the late evening: alone in a fog" (*CAL*, 322). After a week "she could not write. . . . It took a great contemporary to bring her despair" (*CAL*, 323). Atherton wrote in her memoirs,

> I met Henry James during that spring for the third and last time. It was at a luncheon at the house of Sidney Lee, the Shakespearean scholar. . . . Until this visit to London I had not read Henry James for years. I didn't like the books of his second period: his *Princess Casamassima, Spoils of Poynton, The Tragic Muse, The Sacred Fount;* I had been unable to read any of them through. They were dull; he had lost his light touch. At Mr. White's dinner I expressed this opinion to Edmund Gosse and he replied peremptorily: "Oh, but you must read his later novels. He has entered upon his period of real greatness. *The Ambassadors* is his last. Get it tomorrow and read it." I did, and then I read all the others: *What Maisie Knew, The Other House, The Two Magics* (surely "The Turn of the Screw" is the most horrifying ghost story ever written), *The Golden Bowl, The Wings of the Dove*—which still seems to me one of the greatest novels in the history of fiction. . . . A day or two after the luncheon at Sidney Lee's I wrote to Henry James asking if I might dedicate [a volume of short stories] to him. . . . His reply was rather pathetic, none too well expressed, and written in a hand that caused me hours of agony. "It would give me great pleasure that you should dedicate a book to me—if you should see your way, in your own 'interest,' to doing anything so inauspicious as to invoke my presence in respect to the popularity of the outcome. May my name, I mean, contribute to bring your work better fortune than it usually contributes to bring mine." (ADN, 373–75)

Atherton felt that in James's second period "aridity descended upon him; but in the third he surely gave the world the genius that was in him" (*ADN*, 375).

The tribute Atherton paid James in her fiction pictured him as sensitive to the possibilities of the occult by way of his sensitivity to children. She reached that conclusion about him in 1904 and 1905, after a number of years of reading his work. "The Bell in the Fog," of 1906, is her highly successful, deeply felt tale about a writer she patterned on one whose stories regarding children she had read with devouring interest. Learning about James not through frequent encounters with him but through his friend Gosse, she decided that he lacked human feelings for anyone except children, and among them only those of great beauty and mysterious personality. Recent rereadings of her tale have led some to deem it a "feminist critique," for it questions "both James's values and . . . a literary tradition dominated by men" (*HW*, 205).

The tale's hero is the great author Ralph Orth, a creative genius with personal characteristics of a superior order—specifically, the personal characteristics of Henry James. He had "left the United States soon after his first successes, and, his art being too great to be confounded with locality, he had long since ceased to be spoken of as an American author." Like James's, Orth's "following was not a large one, but it was very distinguished. The aristocracies of the earth gave to it" (*HW*, 206). Like James, too, Orth had "inherited a sufficiency of ancestral dollars" to purchase his home in England, and "the fashionable and exclusive sets of London knew and sought him." His coterie, like James's, was a group of "young literary men—and one or two women"—who "imitated him" and for whom he sooner or later wrote "'appreciations' . . . which nobody living could understand" (*HW*, 207). But behind the approval Atherton evinces for such a figure is criticism of a man who does not have feelings for others, especially for women. His emotion revolves around the English country house his legacy has permitted him to purchase. Like James's Lamb House, it is "not a castle nor a great property," but it is "quite perfect" (*HW*, 207). In spite of loving friends, he is "on the whole . . . rather a lonely man" (*HW*, 208).

Atherton's reading of "The Turn of the Screw," *What Maisie Knew*, and other fiction by James must have contributed to her impression that, impervious to her feminine charms, he had definite feelings for children and children only. So she made her hero aware of a "human stirring at the foundations of his aesthetic pleasure" (*HW*, 208) only when he sees the portraits of two beautiful children painted by the same artist that have come with his "ancestral hall."

It is that of a six-year-old girl which captivates him, for he admits he is "rather fond of children," especially, he adds, "when they are pretty enough" (*HW*, 209). To rid himself of his obsession with the two, whom he wishes "were my own" (*HW*, 211), he writes them "out of me," and produces a masterpiece of literature, so that by art they "were his now," as Miles and Flora of "The Turn of the Screw" were James's (*HW*, 212).

Although Orth's other fictional characters had been "so remote and exclusive as barely to escape being mere mentalities," he "had loved" the children in his new work, with the result that "they danced out alive" (*HW*,

211). The book is a great success, and Orth at fifty years of age is "hailed as a genius" (*HW,* 213; James was fifty-five when "The Turn of the Screw" appeared).

One day Orth meets a little girl on his property who is the image of the girl in the portrait. He feels as if he is "moving through the mazes of one of his own famous ghost stories" (*HW,* 215). He has learned that the little girl in the picture grew to be Lady Blanche Mortlake, who seduced one of the local yeomen. The man had killed himself when she discarded him, and she herself then committed suicide. The little girl, who shares the name Blanche with the lady, clearly is one of the "descendants" of the people Lady Blanche "wronged," and she has been sent back "to work out [her] final salvation" (*HW,* 220).

Orth, in his admiration for the child, wants to give her her chance in what he recognizes is becoming the "woman's age. Your opportunities will be infinite. . . . What you wish to be you shall be. . . . You shall be trained to self-control. . . . You shall become that finest flower of civilization, a woman who knows how to use her independence" (*HW,* 223). This statement makes it hard to accept the feminist interpretation of the story according to which Atherton is criticizing James's attitude toward women. Orth is clearly trying to give the girl the advantages of the modern woman in order to avert for her the kind of death her ancestor had. The child, however, "stirred no response in him. . . . The paternal was all he had to give, but that was hers forever" (*HW,* 224). Atherton must have been thinking of Longdon's adoption of the adolescent Nanda in *The Awkward Age* when she had Orth offer to adopt little Blanche. But Blanche's mother has to take the girl back to the United States, for her other children there need Blanche to keep them happy. The idea is that Lady Blanche Mortlake may be acting through the small Blanche to make up for her damage to the child's family. "I think she is Blanche Mortlake working out the last of her salvation," Orth thinks (*HW,* 228). The "bell in the fog" may be the warning afforded by the resemblance of a child in a painting to a child alive years later that the occult exists and certain spirits live on.

The view of the story as a feminist critique of James understands that for Orth artistic creation is a "coldly intellectual substitute for warm human relationships" and that his "repressed desires lead to his obsession with the children." That, "in turn, leads to a series of ironic revelations, most of which focus on Orth's failure to understand women" (*HW,* 7). But cannot Orth's desire to offer little Blanche all the advantages of modern education equally be taken as revealing his—and implicitly, James's—wish to give women independence? Orth recognizes that Lady Blanche Mortlake's misfortune lay in her circumstances. "To-day . . . she certainly would use her gifts and become famous, the while living her life too fully . . . even for the trivial business of breaking hearts" (*HW,* 223).

Either way, though, there is obvious regret on the part of Atherton that James was not stirred by the grown woman. At the same time, she pays tribute to James as a writer of superior modern ghost stories.

Violet Hunt

Two of the novels of Violet Hunt (1866–1942), a friend of James's and the recipient of fifty-two letters from him—until she was named a corespondent in Ford Madox Ford's divorce proceedings and James disconnected himself from her—contain portraits of writers with characteristics seemingly like James's and with roles apparently mirroring his in her life. From Hunt's diary and the letters James wrote to her, Robert Secor traces the picture, already sketched by Edel, of a young woman—the daughter of an influential writer and painter—who was able to bring James tidbits from the upper Bohemia of London (RS, *passim*). He also advised her in her love affairs, but he never wanted to hear what must to him have seemed the sordid details. Hunt wrote in her diary for November 2, 1907, about her weekend visit to James at Lamb House, where she wore her purple coat and matching accessories, thereby becoming his "Purple Patch" (*M,* 421–25). "He always wants my news but never more than half of it, always getting bored or delicate," she recorded (RS, 19). Two years later to the day, James canceled another visit to Lamb House set for Hunt, because he had learned of Ford's wife's divorce proceedings. In answering a letter by Ford that commented on his unchivalrous behavior, James wrote that what he "deplored and lamented was the situation in which . . . her general relations with you had landed or were going to land her—the situation of her being exposed to figure in public proceedings" (RS, 30). Passages in Hunt's diary leave little doubt that James wanted no confessions from Hunt about her affairs. He even loathed reading about a fictional sexual encounter, finding it disgusting, as he told Paul Bourget.[22] Twenty-three years older than Hunt and temperamentally averse to female flirtatiousness, he surely

22. Tintner, *The Cosmopolitan World,* 311–12.

felt no personal vulnerability in their friendship except in the eyes of the inhabitants of Rye, but he cared about what people thought, and Hunt observed how on a walk during her one weekend at Lamb House, James avoided being seen with her by Theodora Bosanquet, his secretary. How much more imperative he must have felt protecting himself from peripheral association with a scandalous divorce.

Both of Hunt's portraits of James are in books published prior to their rift. In *Sooner or Later*, of 1904, the dedication is to James. This novel is evidently a rewrite of James's *The Awkward Age*. Assheton falls in love with a girl of seventeen whose mother he had loved and whom she resembles. Longdon, in James's novel, loves Nanda for her resemblance to her beloved grandmother and because she is the victim of her mother's sophisticated set. Assheton's mistress also marries a man who has been in love with her mother and whose ward she is (*SL*, 141).

James appears in the figure of the writer Guy Quain, described as very plain—as James must have seemed to Hunt in his portly late sixties. Quain, like James, is an adviser to the heroine. He tells her, "There never was nor never will be an illicit romance without its ending in weariness" (*SL*, 325). Like Atherton, Hunt took James's failure to manifest a romantic interest as establishing that he had no feelings. When Quain remarks that he is "assisting at a woman's agony," Assheton ventures that "these authors get so subdued to the trade they work in, that they have no ordinary feeling left" (*SL*, 335).

Hunt, in her autobiography, *I Have This to Say*, called James a "Literary Flirt"(*IH*, 39), and in her novel she had Quain write a book in which she is in effect the main character. Someone says to the heroine, "He is a great pal of yours, isn't he? Odd, I never thought of him as a flirt," and the heroine replies that "his interest in me was only, oh, it's no use explaining to you." The complex relationship between Hunt and James was difficult to describe, yet it is not especially difficult to understand. For Hunt was a part of literary and artistic Bohemia by inheritance, a milieu that could furnish James with interesting gossip and discussion, fuel for his fiction. She was over forty at the time of their rupture, but he remembered her as the young girl he had met in the 1880s. Hunt described James in her autobiography as being like Daisy Miller, "flighty and deep, pure and simple in spite of appearances, and appearances are all that Mr. James's art ostensibly concerns itself with" (*IH*, 39). Quain represents the heart of James's relation to Hunt, that of an adviser and confidant, since the book parallels the affair of

Hunt with Crawfurd. At the Louvre, Quain advises Rosette to "break an odious chain, before it breaks you and him. . . . Give him up . . . before he gives *you.* . . . When romance leaves off, the grotesque begins to creep in. . . . You are like an unpaid bill in the room" (*SL*, 324–25).

The other novel in which there is a portrait recognizably of James is *White Rose of Weary Leaf,* of 1908. In it, Alec Johnson, a writer, possesses some of the nonresponsiveness Hunt regretted in James. "Books were more vital to him than persons, at least it was his pose to assume this" (*WRW,* 39). Dürer's *Melancholia* is mentioned, repeating a reference James had introduced in his revisions of his tale "The Siege of London."

It is rather hard to understand how this homoerotic man, a generation older than Hunt, could have retained such a close, friendly advisory relationship with this woman who had such a series of love affairs. Her character and the sexual overtures she made even to him distinguished her from the other women who became close friends with him and concerning whose writing his interest and counsel were understandable in a man of his temperament. But he seems not to have recoiled from Hunt's flirtatiousness the way he did from Atherton's. Perhaps it was Hunt's family associations that made him feel avuncular. Nor did she inform his creative work, unless she helped shape the conceptions he had of London society that colored *The Awkward Age.*

Lucy Lane Clifford

James had known Lucy Lane Clifford (?–1929) since the 1880s (*M*, 105). While an art student, she had married a great mathematician, but when he died at the age of thirty-four, she set to writing novels and plays to support her family. By then she had a Sunday salon, at which many distinguished writers and politicians met, and she was responsible for getting *The Other House* published for James in the *Illustrated London News.* She was very generous and did not have a sharp tongue (*M*, 106). James remembered only three of his London friends in his will, and one of them was Clifford. What he thought of her writing can only be inferred from his fairly critical letters to her. Six of her novels remained in his library, though his letters establish that he read other books of hers as well. For her play *The Likeness of the Night,* of 1901, he had sharp words: the play "halts" for a number of reasons, most of them slight (*L*, IV, 216).

James's fiction had some impact on Clifford. In her short story "The

Last Touches," of 1892, Henri Carbouche, the "greatest painter in France," was abandoned in his youth by a girl who preferred to marry into the English aristocracy. That experience has left him so disillusioned with women that he refuses to paint another until Lord Harlekston offers him a fortune to do a portrait of his wife. When the sitter turns out to be Carbouche's old love, he paints her with such a jaundiced eye, "as merciless as a looking-glass," that "every year that she had lived could be counted. She was in despair" (*LT*, 24). The brutally truthful likeness was something Clifford had encountered in James's "The Liar," of 1888, where the painter, Oliver Lyon, depicts Colonel Capadose as the flamboyant liar he is. Lady Harlekston's recourse is to return to the studio and insist that Carbouche give her painting a few "last touches." She puts on the squirrel collar she had worn when she and the painter had been in love. The addition to her attire reminds him of their happy times at the same time that it conceals the ravages of her face. Softened, he paints her face as she was twenty years before. "The last touches were perfect," and she can leave the studio with a portrait that gratifies her. (*LT*, 31–32).

After the story was converted into the play *The Long Duel* (in 1901), James read the script that appeared in a periodical. He wrote to Clifford from Lamb House on October 3, 1901,

> I read your play in the Nineteenth Century, as you invited me. . . . I don't think it a scenic subject *at all;* I think it bears all the mark of a subject selected for a tale and done as a play as an after-thought. I don't see, that is, what the scenic form does, or *can* do, for it, that the narrative couldn't do better—or what it, in turn, does for the scenic form. The inwardness is a kind of inwardness that doesn't become an outwardness—effectively—theatrically; and the part played in the whole by the painting of the portrait seems to me the kind of thing for which the play is a non-conductor. And here I am *douching* you on your doorstep with cold water. (LU, I, 390)

The amusing thing is that, begun as a story influenced by "The Liar," the play had been fleshed out to the length required by its new form by drawing upon an even older tale of James's, "The Diary of a Man of Fifty," of 1879. In that story, a man who becomes disillusioned about a woman when she jilts him tries to dissuade a young suitor from marrying her daughter. The young man is not deflected by the older man's warnings, and he marries happily. In Clifford's play, two young characters, Gaston Vignet and Gabrielle Berton, have been added to complement Carbouche and Lady

Harlekston. Carbouche offers to help Vignet, who is also a painter, if he gives up Gabrielle, since she will destroy the younger man as Lady Harlekston has destroyed the older.

A play must conform to the preferences of a popular audience, however, and this means that everybody must marry happily. Not only, as in "The Diary of a Man of Fifty," do the young people wed but in the stage version it turns out that Lord Harlekston, who commissioned Carbouche to paint Lady Harlekston, is her stepson and she is a widow, so that she and Carbouche can marry too.

In another of Clifford's novels, *A Woman Alone*, of 1901, Blanche has been brought up with great freedom in Austria and runs a salon in London with the aim of advancing her husband's political career. He has not the slightest interest in her efforts in his behalf, and soon their different views of life cause them to separate and her salon to deteriorate. By the time Blanche realizes that she loves her husband despite the divergence between their interests and outlooks, he has died. The Jamesian element enters the tale in the character of Henry Langton, who combines James's given name and a surname close to that of Mr. Longdon, his alter ego in *The Awkward Age*. Somewhat on the pattern of *The Awkward Age*, Blanche leads Henry Langton to fall in love with a girl of twenty-one, although he does not realize that he is in love with her. "He was forty-two . . . but of the world; in spite of his travels, his scholarship and occasional efforts to be cynical, he was inexperienced." He had "known men and manners . . . yet he remained a simplehearted gentleman living in an agreeable dream world created by his books." He was "well-off and a bachelor" (*WA*, 203). Is that the way Clifford saw Henry James? The name she gave the character and a number of the attributes she ascribed suggest that she was representing James.

Clifford's novel *Margaret Vincent*, of 1902, called *Woodside Farm* when it was published in the United States in the same year, is one James had in his library, though he never commented on the work. It seems to reveal the influence of some of the things James wrote during his playwriting period, from 1890 to 1895. The original title is reminiscent of one of the short stories he wrote during those years, "Nona Vincent." That tale concerns a young playwright who has a sophisticated friend, a lady on whom he has modeled the heroine of his play. She teaches the young actress who plays the heroine how to perform the part effectively. The playwright finishes by marrying the actress. It may be that the title *Margaret Vincent* was changed because of the novel's close connection with James's fiction. Clifford's heroine, Margaret, goes to London and falls in love with the theater, but un-like Miriam Rooth of *The Tragic Muse*, of 1890, who refuses her suitor, Peter Sherringham, she accepts Tom Carringford. Clifford's Mr. Dawson Farley to a degree reprises Basil Dashwood, who finally marries Miriam Rooth. *Mrs. Keith's Crime*, of 1885, by Clifford, had perhaps suggested to James some of the characteristics with which he endowed Miriam's mother, Mrs. Rooth, and Clifford in reply poked a bit of fun at *The Tragic Muse*. But Margaret is very different from Miriam Rooth, abandoning the theater as soon as Tom proposes. Clifford was casting back to both "Nona Vincent" and *The Tragic Muse*.

James wrote to Mrs. Clifford in 1912 as he criticized her latest novel, "My only way of reading . . . is to imagine myself *writing* the thing before me, treating the subject—and in thereby often differing from the author and his and/or *her* way" (*L*, IV, 617), but she had exhibited that approach to his fiction a good ten years before, in taking up some of his basic situations and giving them her own twist. A woman as worldly and as affectionate to James as Clifford assuredly knew exactly what she was doing.

Cora Crane

An inscription in a copy that has recently surfaced of Volume I of the *Anglo-Saxon Review*, a quarterly magazine edited by Lady Randolph Churchill, suggests a curious—and hitherto unknown—aspect of the relationship between Cora Crane (1865–1910) and James. "Stephen Crane/Brede Place/Sussex/England/March, 1900," read the words on the front endpaper. Above this inscription is placed the note "The book was given by Henry James to Stephen Crane." Between the note and the inscription, Cora Crane, Stephen Crane's common-law wife, has made an addition in her own hand so that what appears is, "The book was given by Henry James to Stephen Crane/and by him to/Mrs. Stephen Crane/Brede Place/Sussex/England/March, 1900" (Figure 6).[23]

James presented the volume to Stephen Crane—or to Cora Crane—just

The material in this section appeared in somewhat different form as "Cora Crane and James's 'The Great Condition': A Biographical Note," in the *Henry James Review*, XIII (1992), 192–98.

23. MacDonnell Rare Books, Supplement to Catalog 4, December, 1990, item 129. See Tintner, "Cora Crane and James's 'The Great Condition.'"

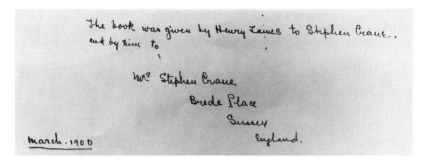

The book was given by Henry James to Stephen Crane. and by him to

Mrs Stephen Crane
Brede Place
Sussex
England.

March. 1900

6. Cora Crane's inscription
Courtesy MacDonnell Rare Books, Austin, Texas

three months before Stephen's death, according to the date recorded, because it contained James's story "The Great Condition." Stanley Wertheim, an authority on Stephen Crane and Cora Crane, has explained, "Cora had a remarkable variety of handwritings, and at this time it is sometimes very difficult to distinguish between her hand and Stephen's. Having made a careful personal examination of this inscription, however, I am convinced that it is entirely in the hand of Cora Crane."[24]

Kevin MacDonnell, a rare-book dealer, has enlarged on the situation in his catalog: "The story James contributed to the present volume is a variation on his stories about a woman with a 'past.' Cora may have sympathized with such a woman. She met Crane while operating a brothel in Jacksonville, Florida, and, at the time of their moving to Brede Place, had not obtained a divorce from her previous husband." MacDonnell, in a typed summary, has offered details absent from the catalog. The biggest surprise is that "the leaves containing ["The Great Condition"] had been excised!" MacDonnell surmised that the reason for this is that James's story is about a woman with a "past"—"about something or other in her life; some awkward passage, some beastly episode or accident . . . some unlucky page she'd like to tear out. God forgive me, some slip," he wrote, quoting from the tale (X, 392). Cora may have identified with this woman. MacDonnell also believes she may have been reacting to James's unwillingness to send her money, though he had been very generous to them both while Stephen

24. Stanley Wertheim, "Stephen Crane Letters and Inscriptions," *Stephen Crane Studies,* I (1992), 18–20.

was alive. Wertheim agrees that the excision occurred after Stephen's death.[25]

But if Cora was offended by the story, why did she not just throw away the entire copy of the volume? Perhaps it was because of the association she and Stephen had with Lady Churchill, for the couple had rented Brede Place from her brother-in-law, Morton Frewen. Also, "tipped to the front side inside cover," writes MacDonnell, is a "letter from Lady Churchill . . . to Stephen Crane regarding his manuscript of his story ('War Memories') that he contributed to Volume III (Dec., 1899) of this journal." Also laid in is a "superb portrait photograph (cabinet size) of Lady Churchill."[26] Bertram Braddle, a character in the story, thinks that the heroine, Mrs. Damerel, would have liked to tear out the unlucky page that had to do with a lapse; Cora availed herself of that very expedient to be relieved of an embarrassment from her past.

But why did she not see that the suspicions of Mrs. Damerel's suitor are at the end of the story shown, if perhaps ambiguously, to be ungrounded, with Mrs. Damerel emerging as pure as snow? No doubt Cora never finished the story or did not quite see the subtle way in which Mrs. Damerel's reputation is vindicated and her innocence attested to. What weighed on Cora were only the intimations of a compromised life that James described through seven-eighths of the story as preoccupying Braddle. Indeed, it is possible that James wrote the tale under the impetus of assimilating the particulars of Cora's past, for it was published in June, 1899, five months after the Cranes moved to their rented house a few miles from Rye.

In the story, Mrs. Damerel is an attractive American widow two Englishmen have met on a ship going to England and fallen in love with. Braddle, the more aggressive of the two suitors, proposes and learns that Mrs. Damerel attaches a condition to her acceptance. Braddle feels uneasy about the unknown past of his fiancée, but she insists that she will tell him about it only after they have been married for six months, when she feels it will not matter to him. He cannot accept the condition, and while he travels around trying to uncover something of her past in the places where she has been known to have lived, she marries Henry Chilver, the other man and Braddle's friend, who accepts her terms.

25.   Kevin MacDonnell to author, December 3, 1991; Stanley Wertheim to author, September 7, 1993.

26.   MacDonnell to author, December 3, 1991.

There is an exchange between Braddle and Mrs. Henry Chilver after he returns that, if read carefully, discloses that she has nothing in her background that is shameful: ". . . anything hidden, from so much labour, so well . . . may not have existed?" he stammered, "Then what did you mean — ?" "Ah, sir, what did *you?* You invented my past." The reader accepts as the truth that the suspicion is born of invention and that the American has made a fine gesture to her husband, to whom a dubious past means nothing because he loves her. If Cora continued reading as far as this last part of the tale, she would long have perceived herself as the woman guilty of misconduct and may not have appreciated the subtle, indirect way in which Mrs. Damerel affirms her innocence. For when Braddle asks her, "There's *nothing?*" she, instead of answering a clear-cut no, responds, "There's the upshot of your inquiry" (X, 425). To Cora, Mrs. Damerel's reply could easily sound evasive, the hedging of the guilty.

Although there is no evidence that Cora dwelled on or fretted about her situation, since she was fully accepted by the literary crowd of the Cranes, she could not have enjoyed seeing it all advertised in cold print. Cora, a fairly close friend of James's and the onetime madam of the Hotel de Dream, a whorehouse, who was twice married, once divorced, and forced to be content as the soi-disant Mrs. Crane, may have been especially sensitive to certain developments in "The Great Condition." Mrs. Damerel is, like Cora, American. Braddle "struck up . . . a friendship" with her, "of which the leaps and bounds were . . . not less remarkable than those with which the great hurrying ship took its way through the sea." Cora's courtship with Stephen had been very rapid. "With none of the ladies [on the ship] had [Mrs. Damerel] found it inevitable to exchange . . . three words" (X, 386). For obvious reasons, the madam of a brothel has no woman friends. Mrs. Damerel is, of all the women Braddle and Chilver met in the United States, the only one who is "not celebrated" (X, 388). Braddle thinks there is something "off colour" (X, 389) about her, apart from the signs that "she's so poor" (X, 391). The Cranes were penniless (ST, 462). Braddle feels she "keeps back" (X, 372) what "I'm sure she knows well enough I want to know" (X, 392). And then, when Chilver asks what it is he wants to know, he answers, "Well, about something or other in her life . . . the things that do happen, that often *have* happened, to women you might think perfectly straight . . . some chapter in the book difficult to read aloud — some unlucky page she'd like to tear out. God forgive me, some slip" (X, 392). At that point, Cora may have had enough, but if she went on, she saw that Mrs. Damerel "hasn't really *any* references." There had been many rumors in London, especially among Americans, of unspecific and unmentionable facts about Cora's past. Chilver says, "It's not as if you're engaging a housemaid." Braddle broods, "But suppose it should be something rather awful?" (X, 393). Now, what at that time could have been more awful than running a whorehouse, unless running one that was American? In England, extramarital affairs were common among some sets at the end of the century, but running a house of prostitution was something else. Braddle wonders what Mrs. Damerel's life was like when she lived in the Sandwich Islands and in California (X, 394). "She admits that . . . she has kept some queer company" (X, 395). A widow with a child, she had to. In spite of all the questions troubling Braddle, he and Mrs. Damerel become engaged and Henry Chilver wants to know, "What *was* it, the queer suppressed chapter; what was the awkward page they had agreed to tear out together?" (X, 397). This is the second mention of tearing out the page, and possibly a second prompt for Cora. Chilver himself acknowledges, "She might well strike a fellow as having had more history than she . . . owned up to" (X, 398). That possibility is enough to drive Braddle to break the engagement until he can make investigations.

Mrs. Damerel is much older than Braddle, and Cora was six years older than Crane. How would Cora have felt if she read that Mrs. Damerel had made her "great condition . . . because, after all, that left the door open to her imagination, her *dream*, her hope?" (X, 409; italics mine). To Cora's oversensitive mind, the word *dream* might well have seemed a malicious reference to her Hotel de Dream. Cora knew the gossip about herself, and an Englishman is reported to have visited James and told him that he "liked Mrs. Crane [though he] knew there were unpleasant stories in regard to her early life circulated among Americans in London. But what of it?" (ST, 467). Cora, however, like Mrs. Headway in James's earlier story "The Siege of London," craved acceptance by women and a real place in society.

Whether James was thinking strictly of Cora as he laid out the extended inquest that Mrs. Damerel's suspicious suitor conducted we do not know. But given Cora's consciousness of her past, and the details of her life that she wished to keep hidden, she could have convinced herself that fingers were pointing to her own case. James, with his ingenuity and his occasional mischievous wit, might have seen Cora's real life as a model for the supposed life of Mrs. Damerel. If Cora divined that, the ending, which in an indefinite way exonerates the heroine, probably would not have appeased her, even if she understood it.

Her excision of the story seems to be a spontaneous act of indignation and anxiety, yet it is probable that she performed it only after Stephen's death. She responded violently to personal innuendo too close to the truth for someone suffering an access of guilt feelings to tolerate, and Cora felt guilty, notwithstanding that her set cared little what her past had been, as Mrs. Damerel's new husband ends indifferent to hers. That James sent the magazine in which the tale was published to her "husband" could only have heightened her conviction that the story trespassed on her secrets.

Struggles with an Indebtedness to James

Two women writers, Anne Douglas Sedgwick and Willa Cather, found themselves labeled as Jamesian but emancipated themselves from James's influence.

Anne Douglas Sedgwick

On Monday, April 6, 1908, Theodora Bosanquet, the secretary to whom James dictated, wrote in her diary, "Worked at a new preface—to 'Lady Barberina' etc. this morning—and read 'Valerie Upton' which Mr. James says 'copies another writer rather remarkably'—of course the 'other writer' is himself!"[27] James was aware of how Anne Douglas Sedgwick (1873–1935) had absorbed his style, as well as invested her characters with the personalities of his—their ideals, their vocabulary, and their lineaments. Sedgwick's background was similar to his, too. Born a New Englander, she was brought to England as a child. She first trained as an artist in Paris, but her father encouraged her to write a novel, and her first, *The Dull Miss Archinard*, of 1898, proved very successful. From then on until her death, she wrote a novel a year.

The novel that James gave Miss Bosanquet to read was essentially Jamesian, even though Sedgwick, in her letters, avowed that she was never a follower of the Jamesian style: "I am cited, tiresomely, as a disciple; which I've never been, though doubtlessly we lesser writers of his *epoch* must have

---

27. Diary of Theodora Bosanquet, in Houghton Library, Harvard University.

caught something of his vocabulary" (*PL*, 160). Still she showed critical acumen regarding James's techniques when she commented on "his way of never abandoning a clue" and of seeing "resolutely to the end of everything." When she met him, in 1900, she remarked his "look of a clever French priest in secular dress," adding, "The thought is decisive and the search for its expression gives one an impression of fastidious choice" (*PL*, 14). Her sense of morality was more puritanical than his, though, for she bridled that in *The Awkward Age*, which she admitted is a masterpiece, "one gets a little tired . . . of the decadent *milieu* he depicts so constantly of late — and of people who have no moral sense but only exquisite consciousness of everything and perfect taste" (*PL*, 5). As a counterweight to the amorality of the fin de siècle that she reproached James for not combating, she delineated the noble sacrifice by her heroine in *Valerie Upton*, of 1907. It is not hard to see why James viewed her as an imitator.

The eponymous heroine of *Valerie Upton* has left her husband and children because of the unhappiness of her marriage and has been leading a comfortable rural life in England with a friend, Sir Basil. On the death of her husband, she returns to the United States at her daughter's request. James may have recognized here echoes from his tale "The Chaperon," of 1892, as Imogen, the daughter, takes on the role of Valerie, who becomes a "guest" and who seems to her daughter "so much younger than I" (*VU*, 46). Valerie's maiden name was Cray, suggesting Kate Croy of *The Wings of the Dove*, a novel that in one way or another seems to have influenced a great many of Sedgwick's books. But the relationship changes again when Valerie takes financial charge of the household. The shifting of relations among the characters clearly imitates the reversals of role in James's *The Golden Bowl*. The climax of Sedgwick's imitation occurred when she almost plagiarized a passage from *The American Scene*, which had been published as a book by the time Sedgwick was writing her novel. While Valerie is walking in Boston with Jack Penington, the suitor for Imogen's hand who comes to long more for Valerie, they both see the city "silhouetted in the vague grays and reds of its old houses . . . to where the dim bubble of the State House dome rounded on the sky. It almost made one think, so silhouetted, of a Dürer etching" (*VU*, 147). James had looked at Boston from the same viewpoint and seen the city "appear to make as black and minute and 'composed' a little pyramidal image, as the finished background of a Dürer print" (*AS*, 245). Sedgwick's novel was published in England under the title *A Fountain Sealed*, reminiscent of *The Sacred Fount*, but there are in it none of the hypothetical assumptions of James's novel, where one person feeds off another. Sedgwick referred to the figure of the fountain often and enlarged on it. Valerie, who gives up Penington's love because of his youth—she is old enough to be his mother—is a "fountain sealed." Preferring a noble righteousness to the decadence of James's late novels, Sedgwick had the fountain nourish without depletion, although it is sealed off at the end. She also took the image of the torch from *The Sacred Fount.* There it conveys analogy, whereas here it shines in a real cavern, illuminating Imogen so that Jack sees how her character is not what he thought. At the end, with her fountain turned off, she rejects Jack's renewed offer and has finished with life. Jack sees her as Strether sees Madame Vionnet in *The Ambassadors,* of 1903, as "mounting the steps of the guillotine" (*VU,* 142).

In *Christmas Roses,* of 1920, a collection of short stories, the tale "Carnations" repeats an image from James's "The Birthplace," of 1903, almost twelve years after its appearance in the New York Edition. Sedgwick wrote, "There came into his mind the memory of a picture seen in childhood, some sentimental print that had strongly impressed his boyish sensibilities."[28] James had written, "The three together . . . had the effect of recalling to him—it was too whimsical—some picture, some sentimental print, seen and admired in his youth" (XI, 464). Sedgwick, perhaps unconsciously, had assimilated these figures of speech in a kind of passivity before James's style.

As with the other women whose fiction James's example shaped, Sedgwick increasingly imitated James, to the degree of bordering on plagiarism, especially in the years after his death. In *The Little French Girl,* of 1924, Alix' consciousness is very Jamesian. Although sixteen years old, Alix is more like Maisie than Nanda, for she is told that she is younger than her age yet so grown up. In *Dark Hester,* of 1929, the consciousness is all that of Monica Wilmott, who calls herself a "creeping thing," as Maggie Verver had described herself in *The Golden Bowl,* and again the shifting relations among four people recall that novel.[29] Despite Sedgwick's objection to being typed as a disciple of James and her struggle to avoid indebtedness to him, the presence of the elder writer is unmistakable in her work. But her style became her own, and not James's.

28. Anne Douglas Sedgwick, *Christmas Roses* (Boston, 1920), 199.
29. Anne Douglas Sedgwick, *The Little French Girl* (Boston, 1924), 63; Anne Douglas Sedgwick, *Dark Hester* (Cambridge, Mass., 1929), 223.

Willa Cather

"I began by imitating Henry James," Willa Cather (1876–1947) said of her early stories, many of which take place in New York City. Mildred Bennett, in an introduction to a volume of Cather's early stories, quotes this remark as well as Cather's belief that "nobody seems so wonderful as Henry James" (*WC*, xxvi). In one of Cather's tales, "The Affair at Grover Station," the mark of the ghostly fingers on the throat of a victim reminds Bennett of James's "The Romance of Certain Old Clothes," a very early story that, at that time, had not been republished. In naming certain collections of stories, such as *Obscure Destinies,* Cather emulated James's style of naming. She apparently digested all James's tales, even digging out early ones in old journals. In her "A Singer's Romance," the person cuts a "figure like a malicious Beardsley poster" (*WC*, 333), recalling a similar metaphor in James's "The Real Right Thing." "In those days," she told an interviewer, "for me [James] was the perfect writer" (*WC*, xxvi). The model of "The Jolly Corner" lay behind Cather's "Consequences," of 1915. Kier Cavanaugh's future self, his alter ego, takes form alongside him, but as a real person, unlike the dream vision in James's story. Henry Eastman is Cavanaugh's mentor and adviser, and he seems to be named after Henry James, who symbolically also watches him. The alter ego is not willed, as in James's tale; he just appears. Shadows of James's "Sir Dominick Ferrand," of 1893, occur in "Coming, Aphrodite!" of 1920, which is a New York tale of a young singer that also invokes the atmosphere of *Washington Square,* of 1881. "A Death in the Desert" seems to be a transposition of James's "The Middle Years." In it Cather repeats a famous line from that tale of 1893: "the madness of art was over." She in 1925 finally did bring the name of a novel by James into a novel of her own, *The Professor's House.* "Do you happen to have read a novel of Henry James, *The American?*" asks a character. "There's a rather nice scene in it, in which a young Frenchman, hurt in a duel, apologizes for the behaviour of his family. I'd like to do something of the sort."[30]

In 1949, in *On Writing,* Cather asserted that "Henry James and Mrs. Wharton were our most interesting novelists, and most of the younger writers followed their manner, without having their qualifications." When,

---

30.   Willa Cather, *The Professor's House* (New York, 1925), 169.

in 1926, she included a description of Madison Square Garden as an "open-air drawing room" in *My Mortal Enemy*, she was borrowing James's well-known description of Venice from "The Aspern Papers." She also adopted colloquial phrases that James often repeated, such as "You give yourself away."[31] Amerigo knows that Charlotte will do just that, in *The Golden Bowl*.

Interestingly, Cather at the end of her life went again to Europe, so that her late stories, such as "The Old Beauty," concern the international set of Americans living in hotels and resort towns and thus return to the milieu of James and Wharton. Cather had to become cosmopolitanized, the way James had to, and finally, at the end of her life, she reverted to him as a model for some of her tales in European settings. But her more characteristic and important novels show her as an original writer exploring a locale, a vein, and characteristically midwestern or southern life, which James kept his hands off, since he knew nothing about such things.

It has been maintained that Cather's *Alexander's Bridge*, of 1912, is "heavily indebted to Henry James both in form and in choice of an upper-class, cosmopolitan milieu."[32] The novel has also been seen as a study of a split personality or the "lost" self. That would imply the influence on it of James's "The Jolly Corner," published four years before Cather's novel, with its depiction of the different self. In *Alexander's Bridge*, Bartley Alexander has, during a successful career as an engineer, repressed his other self, but he is undone by the tension between the two parts of his personality. In a preface to a reprinting of the novel, Cather recalled that she had felt that an author "must imitate and strive to follow the masters he most admires" but had soon learned that a writer is above all "starving for reality and cannot make this go any longer" (*AB*, 1922 reprint, viii). Her discovery was that an artist "must learn to distinguish what is his *own* from what he admires."[33]

Alexander's Bridge may thus be an attempt to redo James's *The Ambassadors* in Cather's way. Unlike Strether, who sensibly runs away from personal experiences that would confuse and muddle him, Alexander rejects his "looking on at life" (*AB*, 8), since "no creature ever wanted so much to

---

31. Willa Cather, *On Writing* (New York, 1949), 93; Willa Cather, *My Mortal Enemy* (New York, 1926), 34; Willa Cather, *A Song of the Lark* (Boston, 1915), 391.

32. Ann M. Begley, "Remembrance of America Past," *American Scholar,* LXIII (1993), 457.

33. *Ibid.,* 460.

live" as he did (*AB*, 130). His repressed self makes him feel as if "a second man had been grafted into me. . . . He is fighting for his life at the cost of mine." His conflict with two women leads to his failure as a bridge builder, and he dies when his greatest bridge falls. The outcome is hardly Jamesian, for Strether knows his limitations and forgoes the temptations of the two Marys, Maria Gostrey and Marie de Vionnet.

Edward Wagenknecht, in a recent study of Willa Cather, goes along with the prevailing idea that *Alexander's Bridge* is a "tightly knit, very Jamesian novel (or nouvelle)." But even if "its characters were sophisticated, cultivated, prosperous people of the kind readers of the best fiction of the time were accustomed to meeting in the pages of James and Edith Wharton," the hero, he has to concede, is no Jamesian character but an "authentic Cather character" (W, 64). Wagenknecht, incidentally, finds Jamesian elements in some of Cather's earlier stories, such as Isabel's vigil from *The Portrait of a Lady*, of 1881, in her "The Garden Lodge," of 1905 (W, 56), and a valet possibly from James's "Brooksmith," of 1891, in her "The Marriage of Phaedra," of 1905 (W, 57).

Cather's next to last novel, *Lucy Gayheart*, of 1935, is Jamesian in two senses. First, it seems to show the influence of James's short tale "The Story in It," of 1902, which offers the implicit argument that a one-sided love affair—in which the woman never reveals her feelings to the man she loves and with whom she has nothing physical to do—is preferable to an active love affair. In James's story, the adulterous couple are manifestly less happy than the young woman whose feelings for the man are solitary and without expression or overt reciprocation. Lucy Gayheart's love for Clément Sebastian, the distinguished singer in Cather's novel, is like Maud Blessingbourne's love in "The Story in It," and, although Clément feels great affection for Lucy and knows of her love for him, he never endangers their relationship by pursuing the love's physical ramifications.

Second, Lucy, after Sebastian's drowning, returns to her native town and visits Mrs. Ramsey, the one cultivated woman there, whose advice to her is to live all she can: "I don't like to see young people with talent take [life] too seriously. Life is short; gather roses while you may. I'm sure you gathered a few. . . . Make it as many as you can, Lucy. Nothing really matters but living. . . . Sometimes people disappoint us, and sometimes we disappoint ourselves; but the thing is, to go right on living."[34] Mrs. Ramsey

---

34.   Willa Cather, *Lucy Gayheart* (New York, 1935), 165.

acts as a stand-in for Strether of *The Ambassadors,* translating his counsel to "live all you can" into the message that Lucy has had the great love experience of her life with Sebastian but, when it comes to taking up life once more, she and Harry Gordon, who love each other in a more wonted way, do not know how to express to each other their feelings, and hence are not living all they can.

2

TH∈ PÀRODYIN(OF JÀM∈S

Parodies at the Turn of the Century

The twentieth century seized upon Henry James's idiosyncratic style, especially that of his late works, and his idiosyncratic personal appearance and social mannerisms as an ideal field for parody, especially in the United States. Some of the parodies I discuss shed light on the persona James presented to his contemporaries, and some are bits of the popular literary criticism of his time. As early as 1887 there was "Another Chapter of the Bostonians," by one Henrietta James.[1] "The Holy Pump," by H-n-y J-m-s, of 1902, condensed by Grace E. Martin, is a singularly amusing parody of *The Sacred Fount*, transferring the setting from an aristocratic English country house with weekenders in attendance to the porch of a summer boarding-house somewhere in the United States.[2] Figures of speech involving the popping of corn and teeing on the green, suitable to this different world of homespun America, instead of the references in *The Sacred Fount* to the Commedia dell'Arte and the *école gallante*, impart an air of the ridiculous to the nameless narrator and his pattern of speech.

In 1894, before James made his visit to America, Robert Bridges, in

---

1. Henrietta James, "Another Chapter of the Bostonians" (Bloomfield, N.J., 1887).
2. H-n-y J-m-s, "The Holy Pump," condensed by Grace E. Martin (Privately printed, [1902]).

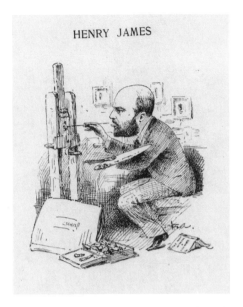

HENRY JAMES

7. James at an easel, as imagined by Robert Bridges
in *Overheard in Arcady* (1894)

Overheard in Arcady, produced a gentle parody in which he fantasized the households of a number of eminent writers. He illustrated James as a painter sitting at his easel (Figure 7), and had him enter into conversations with his own characters.[3]

In the early 1900s, cartoons and comical books burlesquing the complicated sentences of James's later style abounded (Figure 8). The majority were published in America, where plain speaking was more the vogue. But even in England, where a tolerance for the obscure language of writers like George Meredith and, to a degree, Thomas Hardy was higher than in the United States, there were parodies of James. Such compilations as *The Literary Guillotine*, anonymously published in 1903 by John Lane at the Bodley Head, were not uncommon. The book was printed in the United States but was also distributed in England. It proclaimed itself "An Authorized Report of the Proceedings before The Literary Emergency Court holden in and for the District of North America" (*LG*, 34).

Another little book, published in 1906, just after James's trip to the

3. Robert Bridges, *Overheard in Arcady* (New York, 1894), 13.

8. James in a tangle of his own words

Cartoon that appeared in the New York press in 1905,
from a scrapbook formerly in the New York Public Library,
whereabouts now unknown

United States in 1904–1905, constitutes proof of James's evolution into a personage to lampoon, a celebrity rather than a writer to read. This, written by Charles Eustace Merriman, bore the title *Who's "It" in America, Being a Sort of Biography of Certain Prominent Persons, with Some Facts About Them Hitherto Unpublished in a Work of This Nature, Edited and Compiled from the Latest Unavailable Data.* It was dedicated "to all whose 'biographies' have been omitted, with the hope that they will not feel slighted" (*WI*, 7). About James it expatiated in a parody of his late style, "Whether his environment shaped his heredity—for it is logical to say that he had both heredity and environment—or his heredity his environment, it is, beyond peradventure, certain that both heredity and environment, taken concretely or in the abstract, were fundamentally, or to state it in another way, basically, at the bottom, or beneath, his novelistic style." It appended as an editor's note that "the assistant editor delegated to prepare this particular biography, came to his task fresh from perusal of Mr. James' latest novel; further comment is

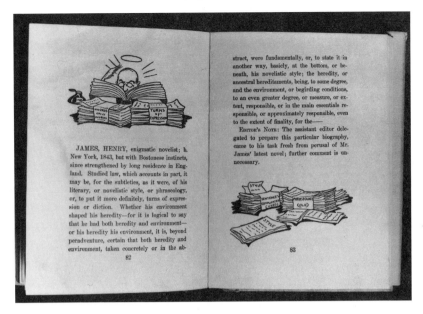

9. Entry on James from Charles Eustace Merriman's *Who's "It" in America* (1906)

unnecessary" (*WI*, 83). At the beginning of the two-page biographical sketch there is a drawing of a bespectacled James with his nose in a book and a halo above his head (Figure 9). Since Merriman's betters, such as Max Beerbohm (who wrote two parodies) and O. Henry (who parodied James in his fiction), admired James as a writer, Merriman need not be presumed to have harbored malice. He was simply obeying a natural impulse excited by the idiosyncrasies of James's late style.

The Champion of the Four Million Observing the Champion of the Four Hundred: O. Henry

One of the curiosities of James's reputation in America is the special fascination it held for William Sydney Porter (1862–1910), who wrote short stories under the name of O. Henry in a career that covered many of the same years as James's but who took care of the four million as James pre-

The material in this section appeared in somewhat different form as "O. Henry and Henry James: The Author of the Four Million Views the Four Hundred," in *Markham Review*, XIII (Spring–Summer, 1984), 27–31.

10. Urban crowd and streetcar in New York City, emblematic of O. Henry's
four million as opposed to James's four hundred

sumably attended to the four hundred (Figure 10). O. Henry, born almost
twenty years after James and dead six years before him, parodically en-
folded curious references to both James and his brother William in his
New York Stories. But he concentrated on Henry James pointedly and
specifically, mentioning him in six stories—in one of them twice. The very
first mention of James occurs, however, not in a story but in the introductory pages of *The Voice of the City*, of 1908, the third volume of stories by
O. Henry to center on New York. In this collection he mentioned a number
of the authors he had read in his unorthodox self-education, ranging from
Shakespeare to Swinburne. Fittingly for an author who was called the Ca-
liph of Broadway, he in one tale had a character refer to Stevenson's *Arabian
Nights*. But in his total corpus of 250 stories, he has reserved for Henry
James the largest number of mentions, which encompass rather elaborate
parodies and numerous metaphors. His focus was on James's complicated
late metaphoric style, so antithetical to his own, given that he is reputed to
have said that the one thing he could not do was write metaphors. The introductory pages of *The Voice of the City* attempt to define the city's voice,
and in that eventually invoke the voice of Henry James. O. Henry remarked, "We can understand the song of the poet, the ripple of the brook,

the meaning of the man who wants $5 until next Monday, the inscriptions on the tombs of the Pharaohs, the language of flowers, the 'step lively' of the conductor, and the prelude of the milk cans at 4 A.M." He added, "Certain large-eared ones even assert that they are wise to the vibrations of the tympanum produced by concussion of the air emanating from Mr. H. James. But who can comprehend the meaning of the voice of the city?" (*VC*, 4). The author of this proceeded "scholastically," with a pretty good parody of how the late James might analyze the investigation: "It is, as you might say, a consensus of translation, concentrating in a crystallized, general idea which reveals itself in what may be termed the Voice of the City" (*VC*, 5).

Inasmuch as the late New York stories of James did not appear until 1909 and 1910, a possible conjecture is that the publication of Henry James's "Julia Bride," a New York story, in *Harper's* magazine for March–April, 1908, made O. Henry sensitive to James's voice on New York life, and the life of Julia may be the model for that of O. Henry's heroine, Masie, in "A Lickpenny Lover." As James's Julia lives in a back bedroom and can meet her friends only in Central Park or at the Metropolitan Museum, so Masie's "park is her drawing-room; the avenue is her garden walk" (*VC*, 26). The New York Edition of James's fiction began appearing in 1907, and by 1908 Volume XIV had been published. The stories in that volume, which include "Lady Barberina" (half of which is a New York story), "A Bundle of Letters," and "A Point of View," often refer to New York and New Yorkers. But James's New Yorkers are the four hundred.

The Voice of the City also mentions James in a story, "Extradited from Bohemia," about a young lady artist and her Bohemian circle. The young people go to the Café Terence, a hangout of artists and models where they meet "Miss Elise and Miss 'Toinette. Perhaps they were models, for they chattered of the St. Regis decorations and Henry James—and they did it not badly" (*VC*, 204). O. Henry here latches on to James's popularity among artistic, Bohemian circles. Perhaps O. Henry was aware of James's *The American Scene*, published on January 30, 1907, and its chapters on New York that suggested its author was in terror of skyscrapers. In any case, the general criticisms James leveled against the New York he encountered must have come to O. Henry's attention.

When James came to the United States in 1904, he was greeted as an important figure, and when he returned to England, he left in his wake caricatures and journalistic editorials transfixed by his elaborate speech. By this time, William James had become reconciled to his brother's late style, but what he wrote in a well-known letter leaves no doubt that he understood the difference between his own literary "execution" and his brother's to reflect their different purposes, "mine being to say a thing in one sentence as straight and explicit as it can be made, and then to drop it forever; yours being to avoid naming it straight."[4] O. Henry could be sure that his four million readers would understand his sly references to James's style. *The American Scene*; the eight papers James wrote for Elizabeth Jordan, of *Harper's Bazaar*, on the speech and manners of American women; and the tales he published in 1908 and 1909 that went into the New York Edition and into *The Finer Grain*, of 1910, kept him in the public eye, or at least in the cultivated public's eye. But the chapters of *The American Scene* on New York had first appeared in 1906 in a couple of periodicals —*Harper's* magazine and the *North American Review*—and O. Henry may have seen them there rather than in the book.

Strictly Business, a collection of stories O. Henry published in 1910, included "The Girl and the Habit," which his biographers seem to think was based on a famous chapter by William James on habit. The opening sentences of the story acknowledge that the critics have accused O. Henry of getting "sources[s] of inspiration" from other writers: "When we strove to set forth real life they reproached us for trying to imitate Henry George, George Washington, Washington Irving and Irving Bacheller." The interlacing in this list is the playful operation of O. Henry's interest in names, especially in the name Henry at its head. He then continues, "We wrote of the West and the East, and they accused us of both Jesse and Henry James" (*SB*, 231).

By the time *Strictly Business* was out, *The Finer Grain*, as well as the later volumes of the New York Edition, had also been published. In those volumes a number of stories, like "The Jolly Corner," "Julia Bride," "Crapy Cornelia," and "A Round of Visits," dealing with the New York James had visited during his American trip, sharpened O. Henry's awareness of himself as the very opposite of James —as the chronicler of the "Bagdad of the Subway," not of the Upper East Side, Washington Square, and points east. O. Henry's New York was the West Side of Wall Street, the Bowery, up through Union Square and Madison Square. Hell's Kitchen was, as he wrote, just seven blocks away from the "private clubs" where James's characters, such as Spencer Brydon, stayed. The Waldorf-Astoria, which

---

4.   *The Letters of William James* (2 vols.; Boston, 1920), II, 277.

O. Henry called the "hyphenated hostelry" and, at other times, the "W——f A——a," became the center of James's "A Round of Visits," of 1909. Thus, 1910 was a collision year for their two stars above the New York skyline. O. Henry's "The Girl and the Graft," in *Strictly Business*, presents its hero, Ferguson Pogue, as a kind of Jamesian character gone haywire. He is a "conscientious grafter of the highest type." His "line of business" is expressed in the hyperbolic juxtaposition of opposites out of which so much of the bounce and vigor of O. Henry's style is compounded (*SB*, 90).

The narrator sits "on the trunk while Pogue talks" and finds that "no one could be franker or more candid in his conversation. Besides his expression the cry of Henry James for lacteal nourishment at the age of one month would have seemed like a Chaldean cryptogram. He told me stories of his profession with pride, for he considered it an art" (*SB*, 91). The comparison of the grafter—who sits in "stocking feet" playing on a "small zither" a song called "The Banks of the Wabash"—with the genteel James draws comic value from the image of the dignified and rather stout novelist, always formally dressed, crying for milk at the age of a month.

O. Henry had commented before that something was a "cross between Tolstoy and a June lobster." In his collection of stories *Whirligigs*, also published in 1910, he continued to exploit James as a model of the genteel life in order to heighten his own emphasis on the rough and very ungenteel side of New York. In *Whirligigs*, O. Henry mentioned James once more, along with other masters of literature, James's company indicating that O. Henry placed him high in the pantheon. He also signaled his consciousness of James's dedication to his art, the sort of dedication O. Henry disclaimed in reference to himself but to which his writing habits testified. "A Sacrifice Hit" is a story about the office of a newspaper that publishes books on the recommendations of an "army of volunteer readers" consisting of the elevator man and the "office boys, the former of whom (gossips say) passed up *The Rise and Fall of Silas Lapham*" (*WH*, 153). Slayton, who wrote a story called "Love Is All," marries an old-maid stenographer in order to get his manuscript accepted. O. Henry commiserated, "Brave Slayton! Châteaubriand died in a garret, Byron courted a widow, Keats starved to death, Poe mixed his drinks, De Quincey hit the pipe, Ade lived in Chicago, James kept on doing it, Dickens wore white socks, De Maupassant wore a strait-jacket" (*WH*, 157). That Slayton does not get his manuscript accepted is irrelevant to the pointed mention of Henry James, who appears cheek by jowl with figures of literary renown from several periods. O. Henry is fairly accurate in the selection of the authors' distinguishing characteristics, but of them only James's constant application and commitment to literature are pertinent to a writer's intentions in regard to his art, and admired by O. Henry.

Perhaps the most amusing mention of James also came in 1910. It is in the autobiographical story "Let Me Feel Your Pulse," about a visit O. Henry made to a doctor after excessive drinking. The narrator is told he is in trouble but that some time in a sanitarium would help: "So [the doctor] took me to a mad-house in the Catskills." That is followed by a stint in a hotel on Long Island's main shore. When nothing works, he is taken to a consulting physician who, after putting him through some ridiculous tests, "held his forefinger within three inches of my nose. . . . 'Look at my finger,' he commanded. . . . 'Now look across the bay. At my finger. Across the bay. At my finger. At my finger. Across the bay. Across the bay. At my finger. Across the bay.' This for about three minutes." Explaining that this was a "test of the action of the brain," O. Henry concludes that it "seemed easy to me. I never once mistook his finger for the bay. I'll bet that if he had used the phrases: 'Gaze, as it were, unpreoccupied, outward—or rather laterally—in the direction of the horizon, underlaid, so to speak, with the adjacent fluid inlet,' and 'Now returning—or rather, in a manner, withdrawing your attention, bestow it upon my upraised digit!'—I'll bet, I say, that Henry James himself could have passed the examination."[5]

Waifs and Strays, posthumously published in 1917, makes a sixth mention of James. This occurs in a story written during the last year of O. Henry's life. The narration is by a rubber plant up for sale as a result of the divorce of a musical-comedy actress, "along with the jobbiest lot you ever heard of being lumped into one bargain. Think of this little cornucopia of wonders, all for $1.89: Henry James's works, six talking machine records, one pair of tennis shoes, two bottles of horse radish, and a rubber plant—that was me!" A young girl comes along and "proceeds to turn down Mr. James and the other commodities," and for thirty-nine cents she gets the rubber plant.[6]

Besides these six mentions of James, there overflow allusions to both Henry James and William James connected with O. Henry's peculiar and

5.   C. Alphonso Smith, ed., *Selected Stories from O. Henry* (New York, 1928), 248.

6.   O. Henry, *Waifs and Strays* (New York, 1919), 27.

inexplicable attraction to both their first names, especially when conjoined. William was O. Henry's real given name, and he was called Will by his family and friends. One of his biographers, coincidentally blessed with the name William W. Williams, or perhaps inventing it for reasons related to O. Henry's predilection, tells of the origin of the pen name O. Henry. Deeply humiliated by an imprisonment of three and a half years for embezzlement, William Porter decided he needed a new name, and the name he liked was Henry. He later recalled that he had insisted that "the only name I had in mind was Henry: that I like the name of Henry."[7]

His own name, William, and his liking for the name Henry may not have issued in a conscious decision to dog the two James brothers, by this time famous as a psychologist and a novelist. But in view of his preoccupation with them, it is apt that William James liked O. Henry's fiction. John Reed is quoted as writing that when he was looking in the window of a bookstore in Harvard Square at a new volume by O. Henry, "a quietly dressed, unimpressive man with a sparse, dark beard came up and stood beside me. Said he, suddenly: 'Have you read the new one?' 'No,' I said. 'Neither have I. I've read all the others, though.' 'He's great, don't you think?' 'Bully,' replied the quietly dressed man; 'let's go in and buy this one.' The quietly dressed man was William James."[8]

"Sisters of the Golden Circle," in *The Four Million*, of 1906, tells of a just-married young couple, Mr. and Mrs. James Williams, who, because of Mrs. Williams' sympathy for a young criminal's new bride, help the man escape. *The Gentle Grafter*, of 1908, includes "The Hand That Riles the World," in which William Henry Humble, who wants an ambassadorial appointment, is named instead postmaster of Dade City, Florida. William James may have been a source of inspiration not only for "The Girl and the Habit" but also, in *The Gentle Grafter*, "The Higher Pragmatism." In another tale in the same collection, there appears a Mr. Henry who writes a story about the sparrows in Madison Square. The bum in the story who asks for a dime is called Mr. Henry Willie. "Out of Nazareth," also in the collection, describes a Henry Williams who owns a bookstore.

O. Henry's chief complaint about James's fiction comes out in something Anne Partlan, one of O. Henry's friends, wrote about an evening

---

7. William W. Williams, *The Great Lodger of Irving Place* (New York, 1936), 209.

8. Richard O'Connor, in *O. Henry* (New York, 1970), 235, requotes this from C. Alphonso Smith's *O. Henry Biography* (New York, 1916).

when a few department store employees were having dinner with her: "I asked O. Henry to join us so that he might catch the spirit of their daily life. . . . On leaving, he remarked to me: 'If Henry James had gone to work in one of those places, he would have turned out the great American novel.'"[9]

"In Full Possession of My Innermost Thoughts": Max Beerbohm

> I had always regarded the fact of being parodied as one of the surest evidences of fame.
>
> —Edith Wharton, *A Backward Glance*

The two most famous parodies of James are by Max Beerbohm (1872–1956): "The Mote in the Middle Distance," in *A Christmas Garland*, of 1912, and "The Guerdon," written in 1916, when James, on his deathbed, was to receive the Order of Merit.

James constituted a dilemma for his contemporaries. His kindness, gentleness, and almost formal personal courtesy evoked solicitude for his feelings, while his prose demanded parody. Max Beerbohm was especially sensible of the problem. He told S. N. Behrman how well James had accepted his first parody, answering a question at a dinner party about his opinion by pointing to Beerbohm. "'Ask that young man,' he said. 'He is in full possession of my innermost thoughts.' But James was always gentle to me; he was very nice about that parody."[10] And in "The Mote in the Middle Distance," Max had been gentle with James. The parody is funny and clever but not punishing. It is an amusing portrait of James as a young boy, Keith Tantalus, close to the age of Miles in "The Turn of the Screw," who contemplates his and his sister Eva's stockings on Christmas Eve. The small boy thinks and talks like the mature James, and it is the incongruity between age and style on which the humor depends. James accepted the portrait's appositeness. By the end of the little piece, Beerbohm has convinced the reader that the children will not peer into their stockings before Christmas Day.

9. O'Connor, *O. Henry*, 124.
10. S. N. Behrman, *Portrait of Max* (New York, 1960), 231.

Beerbohm reserved his more satirical wit for "The Guerdon." Halfway through the parody, the Lord Chamberlain, "poor decent Stamfordham," who bears Henry James's name to Buckingham Palace for the Order of Merit, inquires of one of the sentries there, "To whom do you beautifully belong?" (*PA*, 148). The question is from James's play *The High Bid*, in which Captain Yule asks the butler Chivers, "I mean to whom do you beautifully belong?" (*CP*, 567). The adverb *beautifully* seems to have stuck in everyone's craw, and it recurs in other parodies of James. *Beautifully* seems to capture economically the essence of the late James, and Beerbohm's instincts steered him to it.

Dwight Macdonald thought that the parodying in "The Guerdon" went "about as far as it can go" (*PA*, 149), and Beerbohm probably realized that it went a bit farther, for he did not publish the story until after James's death. In this he exercised greater compassion than H. G. Wells, who in 1915 under the pseudonym of Reginald Bliss had in *Boon* caused James much private pain. Beerbohm practiced the same discretion in displaying his caricatures of James. Those Max published while the older man was alive are very easy on him and did not elicit comments from him that were recorded. *Mr. Henry James Revisiting America* (Figure 11) is one of the kindest. The one thoroughly cruel caricature, of James kneeling, with his ear to the keyhole of a hotel bedroom, was not exhibited until long after James's death.

James had suffered understandable "misery," as Edith Wharton called it (*BG*, 925), when she brought him the essay "In Darkest James," which was included in Frank Moore Colby's *Imaginary Obligations*, of 1905. This is a witty and sharp deflation of James's *The Awkward Age* and *The Sacred Fount*, the two novels with the "deepening shadows of his later language" (*IO*, 321). Colby was prepared to grant that "in *The Wings of the Dove* there were signs of a partial recovery" (*IO*, 327), but of the two novels he pilloried he wrote, "Neither of those books was the work of a mind entirely free. In one aspect it was ridiculous; but if one laughed, it was with compunctions, for in another aspect it was exceedingly painful. This only from the point of view of his admirers. It is not forgotten that there is the larger class (for whom this world in the main was made) to whom he is merely ridiculous" (*IO*, 327–28).

What is difficult to understand is why Wharton, well aware of James's "morbidly delicate sensibility" (*BG*, 926), pressed this parodic essay on him. Her own comments had provoked reactions much the same in the

11. *Mr. Henry James Revisiting America,* by Max Beerbohm

Courtesy National Gallery of Victoria, Melbourne, Australia. Purchased 1953.

past: "Once again—and again unintentionally I was guilty of a similar blunder" (*BG*, 925). The effect on James "was disastrous. I shall never forget the misery, the mortification even, which tried to conceal itself behind an air of offended dignity" (*BG*, 925).

Graham Greene

Graham Greene (1904–1991), who was by nature a double agent, could not resist the temptation to parody the author he respected so deeply. In 1939, Greene won a prize for the "best letter to the Divisional Petroleum Controller claiming a supplementary petrol ration in the style of a famous writer. Greene chose Henry James." Here is a sample of Greene's parody of James's later style:

> I simply beg you as one bred in the bureaucratic corridors, acquainted as my poor friends are not with the *moeurs*, conditions and relations responsible for the inconceivably portentous questions handed to me yesterday, to tell me *tout doucement* whether I, aged, infirm, out of the vast crowded political canvas as I am, may yet retain—practically and not as a mere fond memento of the kindest, the most amiable of ladies—a small gay gorgeous object that goes, so I am told, in the huge hideous undiscriminating world by the abrupt name of a "lighter." Believe me, very truly yours (NS, 32)

For this, Greene, as he wrote to his wife, "won a guinea's-worth of books" (NS, 32). Many years later, he in a letter entertained Katherine Walston, the great love of his life, "with a fictional sexual encounter in the style of Henry James rewriting *Fanny Hill*" (NS, 252).

The Sacred Fount Transformed into "The Sacred Front" During a Revolutionary Weekend at Newmarch: Veronica Geng

Unlike other parodists of *The Sacred Fount*, Veronica Geng (1941–1997) kept the cast of characters, the general disposition of scenes, and the plot of cannibalistic interchange of sexual energies from her original. The narrator of James's novel has been seeking a law that fits what he has observed, and in Geng's "The Sacred Front," of 1984, that law has the "tell-tale signs of the new cold war culture" (*P*, 117). Her story's comedy hangs on converting James's aristocratic country-house weekend into a convention of anarchists or self-styled revolutionaries at Newmarch. Grace Brissenden, in newfound vigor, brandishes Emma Goldman's horsewhip. Her rejuvenation is explained in Marxist terms as the "redistribution of wealth": Briss "has given *her* his youth." Gilbert Long has also been charged and invigorated, out of his lethargy as a "former mental proletarian" (*P,* 121).

The black-dressed figure of the portrait in the gallery now wears a "black mask" instead of holding a mask in his hand, and the narrator interprets the figure as a "symbol of the black man's struggle" (*P,* 126). It is no longer a question of the mask's resembling a woman or May Server. Now May sees that the "horror" of it lies in the fact that it "hasn't got any meaning. . . . It's the enigma that *is* the horror" (*P,* 127).

In contrast to the concealment in *The Sacred Fount,* Grace Brissenden in "The Sacred Front" confesses with alacrity to her affair with Gilbert Long. "Poor Briss" sees her "marital infidelity" as a "by-product of her dread of nuclear extinction," but he and May Server huddle together in their depletion and are happy. At Newmarch, the theory of living on someone else's energy is demolished. The two healthy ones are lovers, as are the two who are spent.

Geng's timing throughout the piece is masterly, striking the note of the 1980s even in her opening lines: "As Gilbert Long strode vigorously toward me on the station platform, I concluded he must be having a liberating sex experience with someone" (*P,* 117). The adaptation of the milieu of James's novel to the late twentieth century seems to accommodate all the important episodes in *The Sacred Fount,* leaving the story line not only undamaged but enhanced.

An Obscene Parody Privately Printed

In 1969, a pamphlet of seven pages by Louis Wilkinson, writing under the name of Louis Marlow, purported to be the "Conclusion of a chapter from the unpublished novel, What Percy Knew, by H*NR* J*M*S." Called *The Better End,* this was printed privately in a numbered edition of two hundred copies. The title page asserted it to have been "written about the year 1912 and now first printed LONDON MCMLXIX," and the copyright was given under the name of Kenneth Hopkins and the Estate of Louis Wilkinson. The complex later style of Henry James is parodied so elaborately that the obscenity of the scene the pamphlet describes is concealed from all but the most determined reader. In that scene an elderly gentleman is seen being sexually serviced by a younger man in front of the fire of a "gentlemen's library," while a "small company, select," watches. After the sexual climax, all the stages leading up to which have been blanketed in an almost impenetrable exaggeration of James's most convoluted style, the elder of the two men, clearly meant to be Henry James, says, "Ah well, my dear, so there, you see, we are" (*BE*, 7).

If it is credible that Louis Wilkinson composed this parody in 1912, the year in which Beerbohm's "The Mote in the Middle Distance" was published, it is also credible that 1969 was the year in which a posthumous printing for a small circle of readers became achievable. For in that year Leon Edel offered his account of James's passionate love for Hendrik Andersen in *Henry James: The Treacherous Years*. This was the first extended and factual account of James's correspondence with the handsome young sculptor. James's biographer made the "homoeroticism" of his subject public, although he found no evidence that James had "acted out" his erotic feelings (*TY*, 309–14). But James would have found scant solace in knowing that the printing of *The Better End* was mercifully small and its circulation restricted to a few.

3

PORTRAITS OF JAMES BY
HIS MALE CONTEMPORARIES

Hugh Walpole

Of all James's acolytes, Hugh Walpole (1884–1941) was perhaps closest to him. James was excessively fond of Walpole, and Walpole's feelings for James were apparent from his small book of memoirs, *The Apple Trees*, of 1932, dedicated to James sixteen years after his death, "as he knows with love." In Walpole's many novels and short stories not only the figure of James is conspicuous but also almost countless allusions by Walpole to James's fiction. Walpole suffered particularly from James's criticism of his fiction, which personal fondness did little to temper. All Jamesians know that Walpole was loved by the Master, as the younger writer called him, and thrilled by the warmth of the first great man he knew. What is less well known is that the letters from Arnold Bennett to Walpole begin in very much the same affectionate way as James's, with greetings like "Darling Hugh," and that Bennett was just as critical of Walpole's fiction as James had been. Walpole wrote in his preface to the Modern Library edition of *Fortitude* that he never learned anything from the famous writers who took him up as a young man. "I had, when I was young, an immense amount of advice from older novelists and none of it has done me any good at all" (*F*, xi). Walpole was a childish man and a hero worshiper as far as men of letters were concerned. But his enthusiasm was sincere, as is brought out even in the critical portrait of him implicit in W. Somerset Maugham's character Alroy Kear in *Cakes and Ale*. It was by his sincerity that he was known, by his honest yet gushing admiration for the great men of his time, whom he cultivated assiduously, and by his apparently genuine self-deprecation. Given the damaging gossip and the growing worldwide popularity of Walpole's novels, it is not surprising that the younger novelist concealed at the same time that he displayed his interest in James, in an invented character, Henry Galleon, a novelist who appeared first in *Fortitude*, of 1913, and then again in many of the more than fifty books Walpole published in his lifetime. The two he dedicated to James came out only in the 1930s and 1940s, after James's death, and one of these, his last novel and last book, *The Killer and the Slain*, of 1942, he dedicated not to Henry James by name but to the "great author of *The Turning of the Screw*." The favorite books of the characters who stand for Walpole himself in his fiction rarely include works by James, even in such an autobiographical volume as *Roman Fountain*. Was Walpole here concealing his attachment to Henry James, or, as he wrote in his journal, was it impossible for him to love someone who loved him a lot?

In *The Apple Trees*, Walpole was frank in his analysis of James's personality and his affection for him. Leon Edel, in a psychocritical analysis of the relation of the two main characters in *The Killer and the Slain*, thinks that the novel reenacts Walpole's love-hate relation with the older novelist. The main character kills the man who resembles James, and finally he becomes the man he has killed. But a review of the other novels by Walpole pivoting on hatreds that issue in murders may modify that view. According to Rupert Hart-Davis, Walpole's fits of temper and spells of hatred were part of his personality, not just of his attitude toward James, and it is clear that he scrutinized his own temperament in constructing not only his macabres, a genre to which *The Killer and the Slain* belongs, but also his London social novels. Hatred was one of the catalysts of his plots, and I will deal later with his macabres and their Jamesian elements.

Walpole was twenty-six when he met James, in 1909. In *The Prelude to Adventure*, of 1912, Galleon is the author of a book called *The Routes* that is placed side by side with James's *The Ambassadors* and *The Awkward Age* in the library of the hero. This is Walpole's first novel about the hatred of one man for another. Set in Cambridge, it ends in the murder of the hated man. There is a faint whiff of "A Round of Visits" in it. In James's tale, Newton Winch confesses his crime to Mark Monteith, as Olva Dune does to his friend Craven in Walpole's novel. Craven repeats what Monteith says to the embezzler Winch: "You're wonderful!" (*PR*, 279). Both auditors utter this at the same point in the criminal's confession of his crime (XII, 458).

Walpole's first book to transform James into Henry Galleon, instead of standing the two novelists beside each other on a shelf, was *Fortitude*, a year later. As Peter Wescott, the hero, describes Galleon, he is a "little, round, fat man with a face like a map, the body of Napoleon . . . eyes that saw everything, understood everything and forgave everything, a brown buff waistcoat with gilt buttons, white spats and a voice that rolled and roared." What is more, he is the "tenderest, most alarming person in any kind of a world." He is "so gentle that any sparrow would trust him implicitly and so terrific that an army would most certainly fly from before him" (*F,* 278). Almost twenty years later, in *The Apple Trees*, Walpole described James in similar antithetical terms: "I loved him, was frightened by him, was bored by him" (*AT,* 54). Galleon's Edition Deluxe has the earmarks of James's New York Edition. Walpole's Galleon has a habit of putting his arm in Peter's so that Peter feels the "weight of the great man's body" (*F,* 290). This duplicates a habit James had. He criticizes Peter's fiction as James criticized Hugh's. Galleon's book, *Reuben Hallard*, bears a title that bows to Henry James's first novel, *Roderick Hudson*, and it is criticized by Galleon in words used by James to criticize the youthful efforts he examined: "It is not written at all—it is loose and lacking in all construction . . . but the Spirit is there" (*F,* 291). James's letters to Walpole and his "The New Novel," an essay of 1914, articulate such judgments.

In *The Duchess of Wrexe*, of 1914, Walpole's society novel, there is the specific importation of James's theme in "The Beast in the Jungle." The metaphor of a tiger, introduced in Walpole's novel by the writer Brun, crops up frequently like a children's version of James's "beast in the jungle." Brun's tiger is what is addressed by "the force in people, the way they either grappled with the creature, and at last trained it to help them out with their work in the world, or ignored it, silenced it, allowed it at last to die, and so cozy and lazily comfortable, passed to their day's end, but had, nevertheless, missed the whole purpose of life" (*DW,* 279). The tiger confronts the old Duchess of Wrexe, for "even as she sat there, her darkest hour was suddenly upon her. It leapt upon her, as it were a beast out of some sudden darkness—leapt upon her, seized her, tore her, crushed her little dire, withered soul in its claws and tossed it to the fire" (*DW,* 278). The tiger also talks to her: "'Reality has never touched you. . . . You have enjoyed their terror—now your own terror has come.' . . . The beast crouched nearer. The room darkened. She could feel the hot breath, could be dazed by the shining of those eyes" (*DW,* 279). This tiger must be faced by all the characters. Brun explains it as being "an Ambition, or a Passion, or a Temptation, or a Virtue. . . . If he faces the Beast, it can be used, magnificently used. If he's afraid . . . the Tiger will make his spring" (*DW,* 100). Rachel's tiger is "the pursuit of Truth . . . the restive Tiger" (*DW,* 191). Roddy's tiger, after his accident, wants him to commit suicide, but Dr. Christopher tells Brun that, in the end, the only curb for the tiger is "self-denial" (*DW,* 499).

In the critical piece entitled "The Younger Generation" in the *Times Literary Supplement* and reprinted as "The New Novel," James put in an equivocal good word for *The Duchess of Wrexe,* which had just been published. No doubt recognizing Walpole's childish tribute to his work, he punningly remarked, " 'The Duchess of Wrexe' reeks with youth" (*EL,* 143). He saw it as a "juvenility reacting, in the presence of everything," but he concluded that the "happy-go-lucky" taken as "refreshment" is not "trustable to the end" (*EL,* 144). So, as to Walpole's "interest in life, in London, in society, in character, in Portland Place"—James had made it a literary locale in *The Golden Bowl*—he was advised to work himself free of the "crude fact of the convulsion itself" (*EL,* 143) and to learn how to make method, "learn how to bite."

Walpole finished his novel *The Green Mirror* in 1916, while James lay dying, and Hart-Davis thinks it may have been influenced by James's *A Small Boy and Others,* of 1913, which the young man read when it came out, but the atmosphere of relations is suffocating. In 1926, ten years after James's death, Walpole indicated how much his interest in James's fiction had waned, for in his small book *Reading: An Essay* he never singled out even one book by James among the dozens of novels he enjoyed throughout his life as a reader.[1]

The Silver Thorn, of 1928, a collection of short stories, contains "The Tarn," which anticipates *The Killer and the Slain.* Also in *The Silver Thorn,* "Chinese Horses" reveals itself to be a redoing of James's short tale "Crapy Cornelia," of 1909, in which an older gentleman prefers a woman of his own generation to a young beauty. But unlike Mrs. Worthingham in James's tale, the preferred woman in Walpole's story rejects the man. "The Enemy," of 1928, is about a bookseller whom a man called Tonks bothers

---

1. Hugh Walpole, *The Green Mirror* (London, 1918); Rupert Hart-Davis, *Hugh Walpole* (New York, 1952), 102, 108; Hugh Walpole, *Reading: An Essay* (New York, 1926), *passim.*

and antagonizes but who, when Tonks is killed, proves to have been the man's only friend. The intermixture of hatred and love is a theme running through Walpole's work, responsive perhaps to his feelings toward James, as well as toward everyone else.

In the novel *Hans Frost*, of 1929, Walpole combined his memories of James with plot features from James's novel *The Awkward Age*. Henry Galleon is mentioned eleven times in the novel, but Hans Frost is a James-like figure as well (he is called "a Figure"). The novelist Frost's friends give him for his seventieth birthday a special presentation that has the lineaments of James's seventieth-birthday celebration. The young Hugh Walpole, asked to join with 250 other friends of James, had played a role more prominent than the others did in that observance. James received a portrait of himself by John Singer Sargent and a golden bowl. Hans Frost is given a small painting by Manet rather than a self-portrait, for that was what Walpole, by then an avid collector of modern paintings, would have liked to get at such a celebration. The signers of the tribute to Frost are listed alphabetically, just as those of the one to James had been. Frost's wife, Ruth, jealous of a girl, Nathalie, for her attachment to the novelist, induces her to leave the house by lying that Frost wants her out too. But he trails her from town to town, finally catching up with her at a small seaside place. There he decides to stay. He will leave his wife and again set to writing his great book. The plot may capture, with an adjustment of sex, the relation between James and Walpole, as well as Walpole's decision to live with another man.

Hans Frost is accoutred with James's characteristics. He has "deep penetrating eyes . . . the shoulders broad, the body rather squat, the short sturdy legs. Rather priest plus prize-fighter" (*HF,* 4). His accustomed gestures are similar: "He put his hand on Sir Giles's massive shoulder" (*HF,* 20). He even has a dachshund, as James did. And the time he spends with Nathalie bears a likeness to the time James spent with his niece Peggy: "Does he take you to theaters when you are in London?" (*HF,* 4). Then, on the same page where he rests his hand on Sir Giles's shoulder, it is mentioned that he has written an article on Henry Galleon—a "great man," he calls him. "There is not a day I don't miss him." On Frost's desk there is a photograph he keeps looking at of this invented writer whom we feel we know (*HF,* 39). James's New York Edition is replicated in the grand edition de luxe put out of Frost's work. The volumes in the grand edition de luxe number twenty-three, the total James had wanted for his New York

Edition but didn't quite make. Frost's trilogy of novels between 1905 and 1907 corresponds to James's trilogy of *The Ambassadors, The Wings of the Dove,* and *The Golden Bowl. King Richard the Fourth,* on which Frost is at work, correlates with *The Outcry,* the last of James's completed novels and based on *King Lear.*

Frost is James and is called the Master (*HF,* 38), yet he is a friend of Henry Galleon, Walpole's fictive James. Frost also has a lot of Walpole in him. He employs a favorite image of James's, of a gilt nail. He is reminded of Galleon with "his great tie with the red spots" (*HF,* 94), "his hand pressing one's shoulder" (*HF,* 95). "Bay" Emmett's portrait of James shows him in such a spotted tie. Like James, Frost has had tea with Turgenev in Paris (*HF,* 126). Frost wears a "buff waistcoat with brass buttons" (*HF,* 228), a vest familiar from Jacques Emile Blanche's portrait of James. When Frost leaves to follow Nathalie, he says, "I've been an artist long enough. . . . I should like before I die to see life at first hand a little" (*HF,* 299). James felt the pull of a more thoroughgoing engagement with life when the war broke out, and Walpole must have known how the elder novelist envied the young man for his chance to serve as a journalist at the Russian front.

The plot of *Hans Frost* resembles that of *The Awkward Age* in the relationship of an older man to a young woman. Frost is perhaps more passionate toward Nathalie than Longdon is toward Nanda, but in both novels the associations are without sexual relations. Nathalie is what Hugh was to James: "His love for Nathalie—protective, paternal, maternal, *passionately* protective" (*HF,* 172). But there is also a plot element of *The Golden Bowl* in the episode in which Ruth Frost, who wants the golden crystal box from Zanti's antique shop, feels that Zanti is overcharging her and storms out, harking back to Charlotte Stant's objection to the price of the golden bowl.

Certain of Walpole's titles recall James's. For instance, *The Duchess of Wrexe* suggests *The Princess Casamassima. The Crystal Box* adverts to *The Golden Bowl.* A book mentioned in *Hans Frost* is called *The Blissful Place,* close enough to *The Great Good Place* by James.

A section of *The Apple Trees* is devoted to James. "I have refrained through these years from writing about him," Walpole affirmed, apparently discounting his representations of Galleon and Frost (*AT,* 51). Certain statements in his memoirs embodied insights into James that had not previously been enunciated. "There was no crudity of which he was unaware, but he did not wish that crudity to be named," Walpole wrote (*AT,*

53). "In his novels, he showed that he knew *all* the passions, feared them, and allowed himself to reveal them only by innuendo" (*AT,* 58).

Walpole had written "Mr. Oddy" in 1925, at the age of forty-one, a story he considered his best, but it did not appear in a collection of short stories until *All Souls' Night,* of 1933. It is his closest portrait of the Master, exhibiting James pretty much as he had been in his relation to Hugh, although still concealed in the figure of the writer Henry Galleon. In the tale, Walpole told of the romance of London when he came to the city before the First World War. He wrote about a young man, Tommy Brown—in all essentials himself—who after Cambridge has settled in Chelsea. One April day, he goes into an old bookstore and discovers a variety of thin books from the nineties, among them *The Happy Hypocrite,* by Max Beerbohm. Holding it in his hand, he is aware of someone looking over his shoulder (*ASN,* 135). He notices that the man has a fine forehead, his "eyes being large and fine and the chin strong and determined. The figure . . . was short and thick-set and inclined to stoutness; he had the body of a prize-fighter now living on his laurels" (*ASN,* 136). The man, Mr. Oddy, wants to make friends with someone of Tommy's generation (*ASN,* 138). That night Tommy goes to a party, and a critic by the name of Spencer Russell makes him so unhappy that he and his girlfriend, Alice, have a fight. The following day he sees Mr. Oddy for tea and relates his cares to him. Mr. Oddy explains that he now gets his own romance in different ways: "There was a lady once beneath whose windows I stood night after night merely for the pleasure of seeing her candle outlined behind the blind" (*ASN,* 141).

At the third meeting, Tommy asks whether Mr. Oddy has ever heard of Henry Galleon, adding, "Of course he's a back number now" (*ASN,* 143). Mr. Oddy prevails on Tommy and attends one of the young man's evening literary gatherings, and while he is there, Spencer Russell holds a book by Galleon up to ridicule. Tommy, however, publicly rises to Galleon's defense. Then Mr. Oddy takes tea in Tommy's room, and Tommy admits he thinks Galleon is "the greatest novelist we've got." He exclaims that he would like to see Spencer Russell write anything as fine as *The Roads* or *The Pattern in the Carpet* (*ASN,* 147–48).

Mr. Oddy invites Tommy to dinner at his home in Eaton Square to console him for Alice's betrayal. There an elegant young man appears, probably Mr. Oddy's secretary, announcing that Mr. Galleon "will be with you in a moment" (*ASN,* 152). The man who appears is Mr. Oddy. This story clinches the portrait of Henry James: Henry James and Mr. Galleon are one and the same in Walpole's novels and tales, as Mr. Oddy and Mr. Galleon are one and the same.

After 1916, the farther from James's lifetime, the more Walpole's novels recall James's fiction. In *Captain Nicholas*, of 1934, the tale of a demonic hero, one of the characters talks of reading *The Wings of the Dove* by Henry James, which he declares is "most awfully old-fashioned" (*CN*, 234), although "only thirty years ago it was considered the last word in modern brilliance" (*CN*, 235). The last lines of *The Wings of the Dove* get applied to a situation succeeding an incriminating letter, for it makes it impossible for anything to "be as it has been before" (*CN*, 361). Nell cannot put *The Wings of the Dove* down, for it has brought to mind Hector and her love. She reflects, "Perhaps if we're shabby and secret . . . we'll destroy our love for one another. It won't ever be the same after. *We* won't be the same," adding, "Henry James makes you feel that acting nobly is the *only* thing to try for" (*CN*, 235).

The Joyful Delaneys, of 1938, is about an unusually cheerful family, even if they are forced to live shabbily in an ancestral London town house they must partly let out in order to survive. *The Wings of the Dove* casts its shadow over this novel too, since Captain Nicholas Coventry reappears and his relation to Lionel Croy is again a focus. When the Delaneys lose all their boarders and walk through their house with their Georgian candlesticks, the atmosphere is that first created by James in "The Jolly Corner" and *The Sense of the Past*. But this is a fairy tale, and Lord Ragadoon, an eccentric art collector, gets the family out of its plight by renting the entire house and allowing the poor to live there rent-free. There is much here iconic of James's tales. The characters, bent on adultery, meet in the Tower of London, as Selina Berrington and her lover in "A London Life," of 1888, meet in Sir John Soane's museum. The rose-colored bowl in an antique shop has its origin in *The Golden Bowl*.

Perhaps Walpole's greatest tribute to James is in *Head in Green Bronze and Other Stories*, also of 1938. In "The Adventure of the Beautiful Things" of that collection, Walpole clearly stated that he was "redoing" James's *The Spoils of Poynton* his way. The question is "of the living and breathing vitality of concrete objects. . . . You either feel it or you don't. It is one of the really great divisions between people, and the exact essence of this division has never been better put, I imagine, than by Henry James in his exquisite *Spoils of Poynton*. I must ever apologise to that great man for this little ghost of his magnificent art" (*HG*, 178).

The divergences from James's novel are arrestingly original. Instead of having the collector's knack, like James's Mrs. Gereth, the widow who is here in possession of valuable things has no feeling for or interest in the objects of beauty, which her husband, not she, collected. Being the sole heir, however, she is indisputably their owner. Her son, David, on the other hand, so unlike Owen Gereth, Mrs. Gereth's son, who is totally insensible to beauty, loves "his father's things passionately" and he loves them "simply for themselves" (*HG*, 179).

His mother plans to sell "the things"—to employ the term Walpole takes from James's novel. The narrator is delighted by the son's attempt to try to deflect his mother from the act. The narrator says that "if you care very much you will be for ever wanting more than you can get, not possessively wanting, of course, but imaginatively" (*HG*, 182). Here the narrator is at one with Fleda Vetch, who possesses only imaginatively the beautiful "spoils" of Poynton. Unlike James, Walpole specified the objects: a Tang horse with a blue saddle, a Constable study of a landscape, an "exquisite, jewelled crucifix," which recalls the Maltese cross, the one object Fleda wants from Poynton but never gets, and "two Rembrandt etchings," each identified by title. The difference between James and Walpole is that Walpole was an insatiable collector and James was not, for Walpole had made a fortune from his novels and James had not. The paintings Walpole mentioned include Corots, a Daubigny, and a Sisley, which show a modern taste beyond James's. Like Mrs. Gereth, David decides to steal the things. He is certain that his mother will never miss them: "If someone has a beautiful thing, and doesn't even know he has it, then he's got no right to it whatever" (*HG*, 185). Deciding that "of course we won't take everything . . . only a few of the most beautiful things," he joins Mrs. Gereth in carrying off more than trifles. David walks away with the Tang horse, two Rembrandts, two plates, the Daubigny, the Constable, and the jeweled crucifix. He and the narrator execute the theft after his mother leaves to go on a trip, but because of the fog that shrouds London, she returns from the railway station. She fails to notice that anything has been removed, and when she comes to lunch at David's house and is oblivious to the paintings, which have been rehung on her son's walls, David is vindicated.

This variation on *The Spoils of Poynton* is one of Walpole's best short stories, and it depends on its model for its superiority. It may be the only case where his redoing of a tale by James truly succeeds.

When Edel says that *The Killer and the Slain*, Walpole's last novel and the best of his macabres, replays the author's reaction of love and hate toward James, he is attempting to explain two peculiarities of the book's dedication to James. Phrased, "To the great author of *The Turning of the Screw*," the dedication omits James's name and misstates the title of James's tale. Hart-Davis, Walpole's biographer, had asked Edel to make a psychocritical "diagnosis" of the two oddities,[2] and Edel ventured his interpretation in an article in *American Imago* that brought under consideration the story line of the novel Walpole had finished in the midst of World War II, during the terrors he experienced in the bombings and disasters of beleaguered London, but which was not published until after his death.[3]

The novel's ineffectual protagonist and narrator, John Ozias Talbot, kills James Oliphant Tunstall, his opposite — or deuterogonist, as Elizabeth Steele, the Walpole scholar, designates the oft-occurring type in Walpole's novels — only to become the slain man. Driven by his transformation into a brutal personality, he ends by killing himself. On Edel's account, Walpole, the ineffectual novelist, is here killing Henry James, the great novelist, in effigy. After becoming James and possessing James's genius, Walpole the novelist dies.

In substantiation, Edel finds certain emblematic pointers to James in the naming of the novel's characters. Oliphant is a distortion of *Elephant,* a self-description James offered of himself in some letters to Walpole. Tunstall contains the word *tun,* which according to Edel is another reference to James's shape, and *stall* "would be where an elephant might be tethered."[4] But Steele has argued that "shortly after the novel-planning entry in Walpole's journal," a John Tunstall was tried for "assault and battery against his wife's lover."[5] In a published history of Walpole's family in the Walpole files at the University of Texas, she has also found it mentioned that a Tun-

---

2.   Leon Edel, *Stuff of Sleep and Dreams* (New York, 1982), 310.

3.   Leon Edel, "Hugh Walpole and Henry James: The Fantasy of the 'Killer and the Slain,'" *American Imago,* VIII (1951), 351–69.

4.   *Ibid.*

5.   Elizabeth Steele, "A Change of Villains: Hugh Walpole, Henry James, and Arnold Bennett," *Colby Library Quarterly,* XVII (1981), 188.

stall married a Walpole in the eighteenth century. Farther along in the same history the name Talbot appears, as belonging to a family in the same town. That casts doubt on Edel's supposition that Walpole named his protagonist by playing with the letters in his own name.[6]

In *Harmer John*, of 1926, Walpole wrote,

> When I was a child I read a book that had a very odd effect upon me—Mrs. Oliphant's *A Beleaguered City*. It is, I think, as forgotten to-day as all the other books by that fine and plucky lady. I cannot myself very clearly recall it, but as I recollect it had for its theme the invasion of a certain town by the spirits of the departed. These returning citizens crowded the streets, pressed in upon the doors, peered from the windows and invaded the churches, with what dramatic effect or to fulfil what purpose I cannot remember.[7]

Paul Lecamus, the narrator of *A Beleaguered City*, is the only man living in Semur, a town that has been taken over by its own dead, who are rebelling against the suspension of the masses that were said for them in the cathedral. The narrator of *The Killer and the Slain* is possessed by the man he murders, as Semur is possessed by its former inhabitants. "The Turn of the Screw," too, is a tale of possession, and therein lies a possible basis for Walpole's choosing to dedicate his book to the tale's author.

Walpole's adoption of James's metaphor of a "beast in the jungle" is evidence that he took seriously the opposition between antagonistic forces, but this just shows an intentness on the reality behind James's metaphor and does not implicate him in a hatred of and wish to annihilate James, conscious or unconscious. Nor is there evidence that Walpole envied James for being a better writer than himself, whom he therefore had to destroy. To all appearances, Walpole was willing to believe that his great popularity was a sign of his aptitude. He wrote in his preface to *Fortitude*, "The last twenty years have been attempting, I think, to make the novel too deliberately and self-conscious an art. Its great glory lies in its quality of creative and almost amateur spontaneity" (*F*, xi). Walpole plainly separated himself from James's reverence for self-conscious art. The tastes Walpole displayed in *Reading: An Essay* did not seem to include James. He referred to James only once, saying that "every reader who is the real thing has an

---

6. *Ibid.*, 187.
7. Hugh Walpole, *Harmer John* (New York, 1926), 363.

appreciation for all sorts, Beaudelaire [*sic*] as well as Hugo . . . Smollett as well as Henry James."[8] The misspelling of Baudelaire, which occurs in all editions of the book, is not just the result of bad proofreading but is symptomatic of Walpole's insouciance concerning detail, which was well known and documented by Hart-Davis. "The Turning of the Screw" can also be seen as springing from Walpole's carelessness, a fault he acknowledged himself.

I see the dedication to the author of "The Turn of the Screw" as revealing Walpole's desire to present the older writer of a classic tale of possession with an equally masterly tale in the same genre. But that is not to deny that Walpole may have smarted under the criticism he received from James in "The New Novel" and that other unconscious drives, as Edel suggests, may have made Walpole's relationship with James as complicated as his relationships seem to have been with everyone else.

In the preface Walpole wrote to *The Duchess of Wrexe* for the Cumberland Edition of his works, in 1934, he remarked, "I think of it now with affection, . . . because it was one of the half dozen novels chosen by Henry James in the *Times* article on 'The New Novel in England.' . . . I do not think that James's judgments were very perspicacious. He talked, I remember, of D. H. Lawrence today in the dusty rear — Lawrence, the one genius among the younger novelists! But I do remember that he gave a column to *The Duchess* and that, at the end, I was bewildered, unable to decide whether he praised or blamed" (p. viii).

In the preface he wrote to *Hans Frost* for the Cumberland Edition, he proclaimed that "no Portrait of any living person is intended in the pages of this Novel" (p. viii). Since James had been dead for thirteen years, the assertion did not rule out the likeliest model. Walpole went on,

> People in general are not interested in the queer things that happen to a novelist when he writes his novels. . . . This is something of a pity, because the subject of an artist struggling to make something of his art is a fine subject, not because the artist is interesting, but because creation is. . . .
>
> Henry James, of course, did this kind of thing better than anyone living or dead. It is a fashion at the moment to disregard Henry James because, it is said, he cared so much more for art than life and, to-day, life is all that matters. But did he? No one felt the actual horror and brutality of the War more

8.   Walpole, *Reading: An Essay*, 22.

than he did, no one cared more directly and passionately for his friends than he did. And where can light be found more sharply and movingly depicted than in "The Turn of the Screw," the death of the heroine of *The Wings of the Dove* or the sufferings of a child in "What Maisie Knew"? There will be a time when all this will be apparent again. (p. x)

W. Somerset Maugham

The literary criticism that W. Somerset Maugham throughout his long life (1874–1965) marshaled against Henry James provocatively attests to the influence the older man exerted on the younger British writer, and to the complex love-hate response the American evoked in him. If Guy de Maupassant, who commanded the deep admiration of both and pointed the way to both as short-story writers, was a "lion in the path" of James—as James himself put it—the American, it seems, was a lion in Maugham's path, an obstacle to be overcome or at least outflanked.

By juxtaposing the curiously ambivalent criticism that Maugham made of James's work and character, the figure of James as he appears in Maugham's fiction, and the resources Maugham found in James's stories for his own creations, it will be possible to discern the contradictions inherent in Maugham's posture toward James, as well as the presence, both vexatious and technically fruitful, in his writing, of the great oeuvre left by the American writer who reappears more consistently in Maugham's pages than any other of the many authors he passed judgment upon.

In 1940, in *Books and You,* Maugham at sixty-six introduced James by calling him an author "who turned his back deliberately on the American scene." Yet, he acknowledged, "His gifts were conspicuous; but there was some defect in his character . . . that prevented him from making the most of them. He had humour, insight, subtlety, a sense of drama; but a triviality of soul that made the elemental emotions of mankind, love and hatred, the fear of death and the sense of life's mystery, incomprehensible to him. No one ever plumbed the surface of things with a keener scrutiny, but there is no indication that he was ever aware of the depths beneath it."[9] In the same book, Maugham's opinion of *The Ambassadors* was unfavorable: "He looked upon The Ambassadors as his best novel. I read it again the other day and

The material in this section appeared in somewhat different form as "Henry James and Maugham," in *A. B. Bookman's Weekly,* November 7, 1983, pp. 3092–3120.

9.   W. Somerset Maugham, *Books and You* (New York, 1940), 93–94.

I was appalled by its emptiness. It is tedious to read on account of its convoluted style; no attempt is made to render character by manner of speech, and everyone speaks like everyone else, in pure Henry James."[10] But three years later he had revised his judgment: "To my mind his best novel is *The Ambassadors*. In this he perfected his device of telling his story through the observations and reactions of a single character who is not directly concerned in the action. . . . But besides this *The Ambassadors* is an entertaining and amusing book and the delicacy of its descriptions of Paris has never to my knowledge been equaled" (*IM*, 525). Maugham's pervasively ambivalent attitude to James makes the sharpest impression when in a single passage he both gives and takes away his praise:

> But in such a book as this it would have been shocking to leave out a story by Henry James; for, though not the most gifted writer that America has produced (I should place far above him for power and originality Herman Melville, Edgar Allan Poe, Walt Whitman, and Mark Twain), he is its most distinguished man of letters. His influence on fiction, especially in England, has been great, and though I happen to think it has been a bad influence, its enduring power makes him an important figure. Nor should it be forgotten that the passionate seriousness with which he took his art has been, if not an incentive, at least an encouragement to those who came after him to look upon their craft as something that demanded the best of their powers. (*IM*, 524)

By 1948, Maugham must have been conscious of what he had derived from James's technique, for in spite of his earlier dismissal of *The Ambassadors*, he analyzed with care James's investigations into a "sub-variety of the method of omniscience," a method Maugham was to develop a stage further and use as the only technique of story delivery. The placement of the total consciousness in Strether, Maugham asserted, accounts for the compactness of *The Ambassadors*. Seeing from Strether's point of view, "the reader enjoys the pleasure of the elucidation, step by step, of what was puzzling, obscure and uncertain." Still, Maugham picked holes in the approach: "I don't suppose anyone can read *The Ambassadors* without growing impatient with Strether's obtuseness. He does not see what is staring him in the face, and what everyone he comes in contact with is fully aware of."[11]

10. *Ibid.*, 94.

11. W. Somerset Maugham, *The Art of Fiction* (New York, 1955), 21. This had been published as *Great Novelists and Their Novels* in 1948.

The following year, in 1949, he included a paragraph about James in *A Writer's Notebook* that implicitly contrasted the solitary life of the American-born writer to the life full of experiences that he himself led: "He did not live, he observed life from a window, and too often was inclined to content himself with no more than what his friends told him they saw when *they* looked out of a window."[12]

Ten years later, at the beginning of the chapter "The Short Story" in *Points of View*, Maugham displayed his nagging contradictory feelings: "It is impossible, I imagine, for anyone who knew Henry James in the flesh to read his stories dispassionately. He got the sound of his voice into every line he wrote, and you accept the convoluted style of so much of his work, his long-windedness and his mannerisms, because they are part and parcel of the charm, benignity and amusing pomposity of the man you remember."[13]

Garson Kanin, in *Remembering Mr. Maugham*, which was published in 1966, recalled an entry from his diary for September, 1953, when Maugham was seventy-nine, about how he told Maugham of his own interest in James's *Notebooks*, published in 1947. He had recorded, "WSM says, 'I am not interested in Henry James. I never . . . liked him, nor what he wrote.' This seems to end that part of the discussion" (K, 143). Kanin wrote of "the case of Maugham vs. James" that it "became one of the few mysteries I have ever attempted to unravel. I wondered what could have caused this bitterness. On the face of it, it would seem that Henry James and Somerset Maugham were two men of a piece: both gentlemen; fastidious writers, travelers, social lions, and extremely industrious. I should have thought they would have liked each other and admired each other's work. With James long gone it is almost impossible to find out what, if anything, happened between them" (K, 143). He hypothesized, however, that the omission of any mention of Maugham in James's essay "The New Novel" may have had something to do with the antagonism. The omission, Kanin speculated, owed to James's sensitivity to Maugham's success as a dramatist. Maugham had reported to Kanin an unflattering and scornful opinion of James's play *Guy Domville*, and Kanin speculated, "What I am thinking is this: Could it be that he had somehow made this fact known to Henry James, and if so, would this not have upset James? In any case, twenty

---

12.   W. Somerset Maugham, *A Writer's Notebook* (New York, 1949), 273.

13.   W. Somerset Maugham, *Points of View* (New York, 1959), 163–64.

years passed, and when James wrote his article for *The Times Literary Supplement,* he deliberately snubbed Maugham. And so began, as far as I can make out, a feud which lasted for two lifetimes" (K, 149).

If there was a continuing feud, it seems to have been waged only by Maugham. And it is worth keeping in mind that during the very period when Maugham was showing so much animus toward James in his conversations with Kanin, he was writing in the preface to Volume II of the *Complete Short Stories of W. Somerset Maugham,* "All the greatest short-story writers have published their stories in magazines, Balzac, Flaubert and Maupassant; Chekhov, Henry James, Rudyard Kipling" (*CSM,* II, viii). In addition, only the year before, in 1952, he had written in *The Vagrant Mood,* "The fact remains that those last novels of his, notwithstanding their unreality, make all other novels, except the very best, unreadable."[14]

Yet, in Nice, five years after the original diary reference to Maugham's admission of a dislike for James, Kanin found that when the question of *The Wings of the Dove* was brought up, Maugham was still ready to go off on "one of his devastating screeds on the subject of James" (K, 230).

Perhaps the most important personal encounter between Maugham and James occurred in 1910, when the younger writer was in Boston visiting Charles Eliot Norton and his sister. James was there at the time, and Maugham was invited to dinner with James and his widowed sister-in-law, William's wife, Alice. Maugham remembered in *The Vagrant Mood* that James said "America seemed to him a strange and terrifying labyrinth." He recalled that in Cambridge, James "felt himself forlorn. . . . 'I wander about these great empty streets of Boston,' he said, 'and I never see a living soul. I could not be more alone in the Sahara.'" *The Razor's Edge,* of 1944, which, as I will show, is Maugham's James novel, adapts this anecdote. When Elliott takes the narrator, Maugham, to the museum in Chicago, he says, as James did in Boston, "I'm like a lost soul in this great city. . . . I'm counting the days till I can get back to Paris" (*R,* 23).[15]

There are also many references to James in Maugham's autobiographical writing. In criticizing his own early novel *The Merry-Go-Round,* of 1904, he conceded, "I failed from my ignorance of the very simple device of seeing the diverse events and the characters that took part in them through the eyes of a single person. It is a device which of course the autobiographi-

14. W. Somerset Maugham, *The Vagrant Mood* (London, 1952), 209.
15. *Ibid.,* 202.

cal novel has used for centuries, but which Henry James has very usefully developed. By the simple process of writing *he* for *I* and stepping down from the omniscience of an all-knowing narrator to the imperfect acquaintance of a participator he showed how to give unity and verisimilitude to a story" (*MR*, 590). He elaborated, "The method that Henry James devised and brought to a high degree of perfection of telling his story through the sensibilities of an observer who had some part in its action was an ingenious dodge that gave the dramatic effect he sought in fiction" (*MP*, 620–21). Nevertheless, five years later, in *Introduction to Modern English and American Literature,* he rescinded his thanks for the technical device he had adopted from James and to which his popularity as a storyteller was almost entirely due. When he mentioned Joyce's "stream of consciousness," he called it a "technical device just as is Henry James's method of telling his story from the standpoint of a more or less disinterested observer; and like that, it can be of service when ingeniously applied; but it remains a technical device and is of no intrinsic importance" (*IM*, 527).

As Maugham's preoccupation with James grew over the years, it became an argument with a ghost, the American-born author having been safely dead since 1916. It spurred him to make reference to the historical James in one short story, "Mirage," of 1929, and in two novels, *Cakes and Ale,* of 1930—according to some critics his masterpiece—and *The Razor's Edge.*

"Mirage" mentions James parenthetically but directly. When the narrator asks the main character about the luggage he transported from the East to London, he explains his interest to the reader in an aside: "I have often asked myself how the characters of Henry James in the intervals of subtly examining their situation coped with the physiological necessities of their bodies" (*CSM*, II, 203).

Cakes and Ale is a novel about writers and their interrelations, and although many are referred to, only James crops up in three different passages. The first is about halfway through the novel. Alroy Kear, based on Hugh Walpole, and Willie Ashenden, based on Maugham, are discussing the opinions Driffield, based on Thomas Hardy, has voiced concerning certain writers, and Willie conveys the critical estimates Driffield expressed regarding the plays of Shakespeare. Kear asks, "Didn't he say anything about anyone more modern than Shakespeare?" Ashenden answers pointedly that he "overheard him saying that Henry James had turned his back on one of the great events of the world's history, the rise of the United

States, in order to report tittle-tattle at tea-parties in English country houses." He proceeds, "Driffield called it *il gran rifiuto*. . . . He said: 'Poor Henry, he's spending eternity wandering round and round a stately park and the fence is just too high for him to peep over and they're having tea just too far for him to hear what the countess is saying.'" Then Kear "shook his head reflectively. 'I don't think I could use that. I'd have the Henry James gang down on me like a thousand of bricks'" (*CA*, 152). Since Walpole was publicly known to be a votary of the Master, his grounds for not embracing Driffield's appraisal seem astonishingly peripheral. It is interesting that *il gran rifiuto* is the very phrase James put into the mouth of Christina in *The Princess Casamassima*, which Maugham's fiction gives signs of his having read. She tells the little nucleus of friends that Madame Grandoni is still with her: "Oh yes, still, still. The great refusal, as Dante calls it, has not yet come off" (*PC*, 347). What Driffield is alluding to is *Purgatorio*, Canto III, in which the Trimmers are introduced: "After I had recognized some amongst them, I saw and knew the shadow of him who from cowardice made the great refusal." The implication is thus that Henry James made *il gran rifiuto* from cowardice.

Since Maugham admitted that Alroy Kear reflected Hugh Walpole, it is not surprising that Kear urges Willie Ashenden, the narrator as a young man, to read words on the craft of fiction: "I read *The Craft of Fiction* by Mr. Percy Lubbock, from which I learned that the only way to write novels was like Henry James" (*CA*, 216). The irony is obvious.

In Maugham's penultimate novel, *The Razor's Edge*, the first chapter begins with a passage that compares his situation to James's. That is appropriate since *The Razor's Edge* is Maugham's only novel about Americans, with a Euro-American theme he came to grips with only twice in his career, the second time in the play *Our Betters* after an interval of almost thirty years. Maugham asserted that in his novel *The Moon and Sixpence*, of 1919, he had to invent even though his main character was drawn from the painter Paul Gauguin. Now, he contended, he invented nothing, his story was all true. Still, he was conscious that since his characters were Americans, he could not know them thoroughly. "Even so subtle and careful an observer as Henry James, though he lived in England for forty years, never managed to create an Englishman who was through and through English." But in keeping with his contradictory attitude to James, he went on at once to bring out a way in which James's observation was less subtle and careful than it might have been. Unlike James he planned to show the

American through English eyes, because if he attempted American slang, the "great pitfall"—he can see, as James, who "made constant use of" British slang, apparently could not—he would "too often" give the reader an "uncomfortable jolt" (*R*, 3–4).

It is even more interesting to look at the evidence of James's influence as a storyteller and fictional technician in the novels and stories of Maugham, given Maugham's zeal concerning the craft of fiction and his fixation on James. One story by James and two by Maugham reveal their debt to Maupassant's "La Parure."

James in a long essay on Maupassant in 1888 praised him for "his stand on simplicity, on a studied sobriety. . . . Nothing can exceed the masculine firmness, the quiet force of his own style, in which every phrase is a close sequence, every epithet a paying piece, and the ground is completely cleared of the vague, the ready-made and the second-best."[16] Maugham, in achieving the concision and brevity James praised but could not imitate in Maupassant, often freighted those virtues with "the ready-made and the second best." For Maugham, Maupassant was "that master of the short story."[17] In the preface to the first volume of *The Complete Short Stories of W. Somerset Maugham,* he at seventy-nine nodded to the writer who had meant the most to him, observing that "an intelligent critic . . . has found in my stories the influence of Guy de Maupassant. That is not strange. When I was a boy he was considered the best short story writer in France and I read his works with avidity. . . . It is natural enough that when at that age [of eighteen] I began writing stories myself I should unconsciously have chosen those little masterpieces as a model" (*CSM*, I, vi–vii).

James published his Maupassant story, "Paste," in Frank Leslie's *Popular Monthly* in December, 1899. Maugham published the first of his two, "Mr. Know-All," after the end of World War I. James told the reader in his preface to the volume of the New York Edition containing "Paste" that his story was based on a Maupassant tale; Maugham never declared the source for his two reworkings of Maupassant's theme. But both James and Maugham produced variants on Maupassant's "La Parure" in which the diamond necklace (*la rivière de diamants*) is changed to a pearl necklace. James in his preface seemed to think that Maupassant's tale also involved

16.   Henry James, *Partial Portraits,* ed. Leon Edel (Ann Arbor, Mich., 1970), 262–63.

17.   W. Somerset Maugham, *Ashenden: The British Agent* (Harmondsworth, Eng., 1941), 7.

a pearl necklace. At any rate, the two stories had a common source. Maugham's second version, "A String of Beads," written two years later, shows acquaintance with James's story. Both authors, in James's words, found that it "seemed harmless sport simply to turn [Maupassant's] situation round . . . making this a matter not of a false treasure supposed to be true and precious, but of a real treasure supposed to be false and hollow" (*AN*, 238).

Maupassant's story tells of the wife of a petty clerk who borrows a diamond necklace from a rich friend to wear to a ball, where her success is so complete that, distracted, she loses the borrowed jewelry. The couple are reduced to poverty for ten years as they struggle to pay for their replacement of the ornament they suppose to have had a value of forty thousand francs. Only then does the wife learn from her friend that the necklace was an imitation worth barely five hundred francs.

In James's "Paste," a necklace of pearls, thought false but actually genuine, is found among the discarded stage effects of the heroine's deceased aunt, a retired actress. Mrs. Guy—James was not trying to hide his source—is a brilliant *femme du monde* who requires stage jewels to put on tableaux vivants at a country house. She detects the authenticity of the pearls, wears them to dinner, and is a sensation. "They're things of love!" she says. The result is that "the pearls had quite taken their place as a revelation" (X, 466). James makes the connections between pearls and life, pearls and love, pearls and passion—a theme Maupassant never suggested but Maugham assumed in both his tales.

In "A String of Beads," Maugham seems to refer to James's "Paste" rather than to the French original. He begins this story in a typical Jamesian way, with the narrator sitting next to him and telling him the "germ" of a story he might develop. It is about a Miss Robinson, who, like Charlotte Prime in James's tale, is a clergyman's daughter and a governess. Maugham repeats the situation of his first story, "Mr. Know-All," in having a man who knows jewels detect the true value of the pearls at a dinner party, only here he is a count, not a businessman. He puts the worth of the necklace at fifty thousand pounds although the governess has insisted she "paid fifteen shillings for it." The narrator tells Maugham, "'We've all heard of wives palming off on their husbands as false a string of pearls that was real and expensive. That story is as old as the hills.' 'Thank you,' I said, thinking of a little narrative of my own" (*CSM*, II, 797). That little narrative is, of course, "Mr. Know-All." Such an allusion to his own work follows a Jamesian precedent in "Pandora" and "The Point of View."

When two men come at the dinner hour and ask to speak to Miss Robinson, everyone assumes the police are there to arrest her for theft. But returning to the table, she throws down a string of beads that the count recognizes as different from the pearls she was wearing. The cheap beads she had taken to be fixed had been switched with a necklace of real pearls.

She completely squanders at Deauville the large reward she receives for surrendering the pearls she has been handed by mistake, and she ends a professional cocotte, with many ropes of genuine pearls around her neck. The pearls she has worn for a time by accident have done this to her, for, as James wrote in his story, "they're things of love" and "they're things of passion." They always find their way to women capable of both love and passion, like Mrs. Guy. Having worn the pearls, the governess sees them as a "revelation," to adopt James's word, but the revelation for her becomes a way of life.

During the nineties, Maugham, because of his critical obsession with James, seems to have read every story the American-born author wrote. The image of the figure in the carpet, from James's tale "The Figure in the Carpet," of 1895, ran through Maugham's *Of Human Bondage* twenty years later as a leitmotiv. In the novel, Cronshaw gives Philip Carey some advice: "You were asking just now what was the meaning of life. Go and look at those Persian carpets, and one of these days the answer will come to you" (*OHB*, 193). In his will he leaves Philip a piece of carpet: "It appears to be a Persian rug. He said you'd asked him the meaning of life and that was the answer" (*OHB*, 289). The lesson is spelled out: "As the weaver elaborated his pattern for no end but the pleasure of his aesthetic sense . . . so might a man look at his life, that it made a pattern" (*OHB*, 487). The carpet teaches the power of "forming . . . a pattern out of the manifold chaos of life" (*OHB*, 533). This is true to "The Figure in the Carpet," where the pattern is Vereker's own invention, which is his special handling of life.

The material from James in Maugham's *Theatre*, of 1937, his novel of the theater, stems mainly from James's novel of the theater, *The Tragic Muse*, and from the better of his two stories on the theater, "The Private Life," of 1892. Echoes of *The Tragic Muse* reverberate first in Julia Lambert, the actress who is the heroine of *Theatre* and who plays a role similiar to that of Miriam Rooth in James's novel, which also has a character named Julia. She, like Miriam, marries a manager-actor. As in the case of Miriam, her acting is superior to that of her husband—something they both recognize.

Mrs. Siddons, who had been painted as *The Tragic Muse* by Sir Joshua

Reynolds, is alluded to by the name of the Siddons Theatre, the theater Julia Lambert and her husband run. If Mrs. Siddons underlies the whole of James's novel insofar as Miriam is compared all through the novel to the woman in Reynolds' painting, Julia Lambert presses a like comparison for herself: "Mrs Siddons was a rare one for chops; . . . I'm a rare one for steaks" (*I*, 292). Maugham also invoked George Romney's portraits of Lady Hamilton (*I*, 230), as James had done. In Maugham's novel, Roger says to Julia, his mother, "When I've seen you go into an empty room I've sometimes wanted to open the door suddenly, but I've been afraid to in case I found nobody there" (*T*, 261). This refers to Lord Mellifont in James's "The Private Life," who is theatrical and picturesque but does not exist if nobody is with him. Maugham repeated James's conceit a few pages later: "There was one point in particular that unaccountably worried her; this was his suggestion that if she went into an empty room and someone suddenly opened the door there would be nobody there" (*T*, 267).

Maugham's "The Social Sense" is a redoing of James's "The Path of Duty," of 1884, which concerns two people who over the years maintain an emotional attachment that everyone knows about. In "The Human Element," of 1931, Maugham wondered whether the main characters should write a story about such a situation, but he decided against that, adding, "Besides, there's no story there" (*CSM*, I, 704). That parallels the trick ending of "The Story in It," where James asked, "Who but a duffer . . . would see the shadow of a 'story' in it?" (XI, 326). The story in each is the story we have read.

In Maugham's *Christmas Holiday*, a novel of 1939, young Charley evokes Lance, the artist's son in James's "The Tree of Knowledge," of 1900, for when Charley, having gone to Paris and realized he lacks talent as a painter, becomes a businessman, his father sends him back to Paris for Christmas as a reward. Here Maugham repeats James's phrase "the beast in the jungle" without saying so (*MR*, 1114). Charley and Lydia, a communist prostitute, go to the Louvre and look at the *Mona Lisa*. His parents considered *L'Homme au gant* "one of the finest portraits that's ever been painted. Of course one can't compare it with a portrait by Cézanne or even by Manet. . . . Personally I think it's a finer portrait than Velasquez's Pope, the one in Rome" (*MR*, 1129). The pictures Charley mentions are two James focused on, Velázquez' pope in "Daisy Miller," *L'Homme au gant* in *The Ambassadors*. After this, Charley enters the Salon Carré, since for Maugham's Lambert Strether the trip has left no room to doubt that "the bottom had fallen out of his world" (*MR*, 1187). Charley's trip to Paris has kindled the same sort of revolution in values that Strether's in *The Ambassadors* did.

In *The Razor's Edge*, James's impact is apparent not only in the first pages, where Maugham commiserates with James on his failure to create an authentic Englishman, and reproves him for his unconvincing use of British slang. Maugham's criticism may mean that he knew James's "An International Episode," of 1878, which was severely taken to task by the British for an incorrect use of their slang. Maugham had in any case read Andrew Lang's articles on the art of fiction, probably including Lang's piece in the *Pall Mall Gazette* on Walter Besant's lecture "The Art of Fiction," in which "An International Episode" is discussed.[18] This piece stimulated James to write "The Art of Fiction" as his reply. It is significant that Maugham called his collection of essays on ten novelists *The Art of Fiction*.

In *The Razor's Edge*, of 1944, Elliott Templeton is an American midwesterner who lives in Europe. Some readers have discerned James in Templeton, and at the least, Templeton's terror at America resembles James's as Maugham described it in *The Vagrant Mood* (see above, p. 101). Elliott has the "feeling I have noticed in some Americans who have lived many years abroad that America is a difficult and even dangerous place in which the European cannot safely be left to find his way about by himself." Certain names from James's last novels also appear in this novel. That of Gregory Brabazon echoes James's mention of the painter Brabazon-Brabazon, a friend he put in the list of great native painters in his novel *The Outcry*, of 1911.

In *The Razor's Edge*, as in *The Explorer*, a novel Maugham had written thirty-seven years before, a character reads William James. Larry, the saintlike hero, spends ten hours straight with *The Principles of Psychology* (*R*, 32). Twelve pages later, the work is referred to again. Larry reminds Elliott of a "portrait by Botticelli," evincing a habit of comparison Maugham could have picked up from Proust later, but from James earlier. When Sophie MacDonald becomes engaged to Larry, the jealous Isabel takes her shopping. Isabel will do something to ruin her rival, but not by dressing her in bad clothes, as in James's "The Two Faces," of 1900. James's tale is alluded to when Isabel helps Sophie buy her Parisian attire, but she hits on a

---

18. See Adeline R. Tintner, "'An International Episode': A Centennial Review of a Centennial Story," *Henry James Review*, I (1979), 24–60. There the author of the piece in the *Pall Mall Gazette* is identified as Andrew Lang, a close friend of Henry James.

much better way of destroying her. She sees that Sophie is alone with a bottle of vodka so that she reverts to her alcoholism.

In the last page the narrator says, "Without in the least intending to I had written nothing more nor less than a success story. For all the persons with whom I have been concerned got what they wanted: Elliott social eminence; Isabel an assured position . . . ; Gray a steady and lucrative job . . . ; Sophie death; and Larry happiness" (*R,* 343). This idea of "success in life" stems from Walter Pater, a strong influence on Maugham's early thinking. But it also plays an important role in James's *The Portrait of a Lady,* where both Isabel Archer and Henrietta Stackpole find that their notions have to be radically altered.

In Maugham's works, James's influence is strongest in the play *Our Betters,* written in 1915, the same year that *Of Human Bondage* was published. Since this is his only play about Americans, as *The Razor's Edge* is his only novel about Americans, it is not surprising that there is a lot of James in both. Maugham's play has affinities with two of James's stories. One of those, "An International Episode," achieved notoriety both because it was perceived to project an anti-British attitude and because the American heroine dared reject an English nobleman. The second, "A London Life," of 1888, was noteworthy for its candid exposure of corruption among the British upper classes and of the effects of it on the transatlantic girl. *Our Betters* was Maugham's first attempt at the Anglo-American theme, James's subject, and a trial run for the East-West stories that were to make him famous. It takes place at the city and country houses of Lady Pearl Grayston, a young American woman married to a British aristocrat. She is flagrantly unfaithful, offstage, with the younger lover of another American woman married to a titled European. An English nobleman, Lord Bleane, courts her younger sister, Bessie Saunders, but she refuses him for fear that she will become corrupt like her sister. The relation of the two women suggests the one between the heroines of "An International Episode," Mrs. Westgate and her younger sister, also named Bessie. Like Maugham's Bessie Saunders, James's Bessie Alden rejects her suitor, Lord Lambeth. In James's tale, the Yankee women, after entertaining two aristocratic Britishers in Newport, pay a return visit to London, where Bessie, objecting to Lord Lambeth's lack of responsibility to his hereditary privileges, rejects his proposal of marriage.

In the relation of Bessie Saunders and Lady Pearl Grayston, there is a marked resemblance also to that between Laura Wing and her older sister,

Selina Berrington, in "A London Life." The young United States–bred Laura is scandalized by the behavior of Selina, the wife of a British aristocrat and the participant in an adulterous affair much like the offstage adultery of Pearl and Tony Paxton in *Our Betters*. In both play and tale, a young American male of probity equaling the younger sister's appears as a suitor for her hand. Fleming in Maugham's play is the counterpart to Wendover in James's story. Fleming "wants to see life in London" (*PLS*, III, 27), just as Wendover "had come over really to see London" (VII, 141). His clothes, like Wendover's, are made in America and look it.

James's trio of the older sister, Selina Berrington, her naïve younger sister, Laura, and the young American, Mr. Wendover, is repeated in Pearl, Bessie, and Fleming in *Our Betters*, but Maugham has given Fleming the moral indignation of Laura. He sounds significantly like her in some exchanges with her protectress, Lady Davenant. "There's something," Fleming says, "in these surroundings that makes me feel terribly uncomfortable. Under the brilliant surface I suspect all kinds of ugly and shameful secrets that everyone knows and pretends not to. . . . Surely there are women who don't have lovers, there are such things as honour and decency and self-restraint" (*PLS*, III, 65).

The revelation of the adultery of Bessie Saunders' sister has changed Bessie Saunders from an echo of Bessie Alden of "An International Episode" to an echo of Laura Wing, but Fleming echoes even more distinctly the kind of thought that James put into Laura Wing's mind. "It's come," he says, "as well, as a shock to discover exactly what the relations are between all these people. And what I can't very easily get over is to realise that I'm the only member of the party who doesn't take it as a matter of course" (*PLS*, III, 93).

Bessie Saunders tells her sister she is leaving her house: "You fill me with shame and disgust" (*PLS*, III, 120). Revolted at the placid corruption of her sister and her sister's set, she exclaims, "They're not worth making a fuss about. I'm sailing for America next Saturday!" (*PLS*, III, 130). That is the curtain line of the final act, and it chimes with Bessie Alden's line after her refusal of Lord Lambeth: "I should have liked to see the Castle. . . . But now we must leave England" (IV, 327).

A number of the specific details of Maugham's play indicate that the two stories by James that presented him with a theme also guided him in building on it. Pearl's monologues about the English resemble Mrs. Westgate's monologues in "An International Episode" (IV, 264–66). When Bessie refuses Lord Bleane's hand and tells him that his is a "life of dignity, of responsibilities, of public duty," as Bessie Alden more or less also says to her aristocratic suitor (*PLS*, III, 124), he responds, "You make it very strenuous" (*PLS*, III, 124), in the same vein as Lord Lambeth. Since she does not love him, she will not make a sacrifice of her own identity and freedom. "If I marry ever," Bessie Saunders says, rephrasing Bessie Alden's decision, "I want to marry in my own country." In England, she tells him, "we fall to pieces. But in America we're safe" (*PLS*, III, 125).

Maugham correctly interpreted the symbolism of the name Laura Wing. Pearl says to Thornton, the rich American bachelor, that since Fleming wants to see life in London, he should put himself under the other man's wing. Mr. Wendover in "A London Life" is put under Laura's wing, as it were, and sees London—its sights, its adulteries, and its scandals. What Laura Wing shows him are both the good and the bad, but what she wants is protection under his wing through matrimony. So too Bessie Saunders plans to be under the protection of the Princess when she leaves in disgust for Paris.

Maugham appears to have quarried other fiction by James, as well, in writing his Anglo-American play, and *Our Betters* is a compendium of allusions to James's works. Thornton Clay, the most Anglicized American, discourses on the virtues of the afternoon tea ceremony: "You Americans . . . despise the delectable habit of drinking tea because you are still partly barbarous. The hour that we spend over it is the most delightful of the day. . . . We drink tea because we are a highly civilised nation" (*PLS*, III, 30). The opening lines of *The Portrait of a Lady* read, "Under certain circumstances there are few hours in life more agreeable than the hour dedicated to the ceremony known as afternoon tea. There are circumstances in which, whether you partake of the tea or not, . . . the situation is in itself delightful" (*PO*, 5).

The Duchess de Surennes, in love with the young wastrel Tony Paxton, says that she will not be "such a fool" as to marry him. "If I married him I'd have no hold over him at all" (*PLS*, III, 34). This may be a universal joke about modern marriage, but the line is also straight from James's late tale "Mora Montravers," of 1910, in which Walter Puddick, the young artist with whom Mora is living, tells her uncle, "Certainly, sir, I'll marry her if you and Mrs. Traffle absolutely insist. . . . But I warn you that if I do, and that if she makes that concession, I shall probably lose my hold of her" (XII, 270).

The Princess in *Our Betters*, like the Princess in *The Golden Bowl*, is married to an Italian nobleman who had a "pope in his family." In this case there are also a "dozen cardinals [and] one of his ancestors had been painted by Titian. . . . I thought it was splendid to take my place after all those great ladies. . . . I loved him." She adds, as if she is indeed Princess Maggie, that "he was obliged to sell himself. He sold himself for five million dollars. And I loved him" (*PLS*, III, 67).

Maugham's Prince takes a mistress, as Amerigo does. When the Princess explains to Fleming that "English society is a little pompous; they welcome a man who can make them laugh. Thornton is very useful. He has high spirits, he's amusing, he makes a party go" (*PLS*, III, 63), there is the whiff of James's "Mrs. Medwin," of 1901. In that tale, an invitation to a country weekend of a down-and-out American who amuses the English aristocracy is the price his sister must pay Lady Wantridge for getting her client, a rich American woman, into English society. Traces of James's *The Better Sort*, of 1903, a collection of eleven stories, appear so frequently that Maugham's ironical title *Our Betters* begins to seem a broad hint about his debt to James's volume.

But Maugham more often bit the hand that fed him. James had provided him with the very form of, and even some of the names in, his two attempts, *Our Betters* and *The Razor's Edge*. More fundamentally, Maugham made his reputation and fortune by extending, from Euro-American transactions to East-West relationships, the attention James paid intercultural dynamics, and he set everything in motion by accepting James's innovations in narration from a point of view and in the first person. The first-person narrator, which in James's hand had been an extremely flexible and elastic device, became with Maugham never anyone but Willie Maugham himself, whom others might accuse of being the unreliable narrator. In this way he made himself accessible to the millions of readers for whom the subtlety of James was daunting.

Rudyard Kipling

Henry James repeatedly said what he thought of Rudyard Kipling (1865–1936). There are the famous letters to Robert Louis Stevenson in which he expressed disbelief that so young a writer, merely twenty-four, should have produced those wonderful blue-wrapped tales of 1888, prior to his settlement in England. James's, and surely Stevenson's, comments were tinged by a natural jealousy: "Kipling is too clever to live." There is also the fore-word by James to Kipling's *Mine Own People*, of 1891, in which he made plain his admiration for the young man's extraordinary talent but worried that Kipling would not be able to keep it up.

But what of Kipling's opinion of James? They had met in 1890, and a month after Wolcott Balestier, the young literary agent, died in Dresden, James gave his sister, Caroline Balestier, in marriage to Kipling. Kipling must have in those early years, if not in his preschool years, read James. Surely Kipling had heard of him and knew him to be a writer of extraordi-nary short stories and novels, since the colonial came from a literary and artistic family. His aunt and uncle were the Edward Burne-Joneses, close friends of James's, and Kipling spent 1890, his "first full year" in London, meeting Balestier, Gosse, James, and their literary circle.[19]

Kipling's "A Conference of the Powers," in *Mine Own People*, portrays a novelist whose work brings in nature in a way that suggests Hardy, but Kipling did not know Hardy in 1890, when the story was written. Given that the story's novelist, Eustace Cleever, is called a "great man" (*MO*, 198) and his personality and peculiarities resemble Henry James's, it is unlikely that he is anyone but James. At this time, as J. I. M. Stewart has remarked, "With the exception of the equivocal James, indeed, the great are absent" from Kipling's life.[20] In "A Conference of the Powers," what Kipling thought of James emerges. In the tale, three young men of the 45th Bengal Cavalry encounter Eustace Cleever in London during their leave from mil-itary service in India. Cleever begins speaking to them with an apologetic stutter, a disability James had. Since Cleever "was a great man," they wel-come him, thanking him for his books, the content of which Kipling pre-sents as un-Jamesian, probably in order to disguise the identity of his model. About a book they all admire, his *As it Was in the Beginning*, the nov-elist does not mind speaking, "for he was a golden talker" (*MO*, 199). "His big eyes twinkle"—those eyes everyone who knew and wrote about James commented on. He has a "gray beard," as James did at the time, and his speech seems idiosyncratic to the young men; they notice the "indefinable 'euh' that runs through the speech of the pundit caste—and the elaborate choice of words" (*MO*, 200).

He is puzzled by the boys. He "could create men and women, and send

19.   John Gross, ed., *The Age of Kipling* (New York, 1972), 155–56.
20.   *Ibid.*, 156.

them to the uttermost ends of the earth to help, delight, and comfort . . . and he knew the hearts of many in the city and country, but he had hardly in forty years come into contact with the thing which is called a Subaltern of the Line" (*MO*, 200). The boys say that this is natural, and he admits, "I live chiefly among men who write and paint and sculp and so forth. We have our own talk and our own interests, and the outer world doesn't trouble us much." Then these young men, children in comparison with the novelist, begin talking about the bloody warfare they have seen. "To me," says Cleever softly, "the whole idea of warfare seems so foreign and unnatural — so essentially vulgar, if I may say so — that I can hardly appreciate your sensations" (*MO*, 201). When he realizes that they have all been under fire, he asks, "as a child might ask, 'Tell me — tell me everything about everything'" (*MO*, 201).

He inquires of the young soldier called the Infant, "Has the Army a language of its own?" The Infant describes the carnage and destruction he has seen, to the amazement of Cleever, and emphasizes the violence of the things he tells, the pleasure the natives take in "filling women up with kerosene and setting 'em alight, and burning villages, and crucifying people" (*MO*, 202). Kipling proved himself aware of James's civilized manner of living alone but among his kind: "Solitude of the soul [Cleever] knew — none better; but he had never been ten miles away from his fellow-men in his life" (*MO*, 203).

The novelist shows interest in the slang of the army. When the Infant sings barracks verses, he responds, "Oh, gorgeous! . . . And how magnificently direct! The notion of a regimental bard is new to me. It's epic" (*MO*, 204). He is shocked to hear that each of the young men has killed others. He exclaims "Good heavens!" — exactly the kind of oath it would have been in character for James to make at hearing of carnage by charming young Englishmen. Kipling knew that James was squeamish about violence from early in their association.

After hearing of the violence among fighting men, Cleever says, "I think I am beginning to understand a little. . . . It was a pleasure to you to administer and fight?" (*MO*, 207). The Infant goes on to describe how Dennis thought he had killed a *∂aku* though he had not, and when he could not eat the sandwiches meant for him, they were given to the *∂aku*. Cleever exclaims, "That's art! . . . Flat, flagrant mechanism. Don't tell me what happened on the spot!" The Infant answers stiffly, "I beg your pardon . . . but

I am telling this thing as it happened." Cleever apologizes: "My fault entirely. . . . I should have known" (*MO*, 210).

After these graphic accounts, Cleever says, "I can't understand it. Why should *you* have seen and done all these things before you have cut your wisdom-teeth?" The young men have seen "dead men and war and power and responsibility. . . . You won't have any sensations left at thirty if you go on as you have done. But I want to hear more tales — more tales" (*MO*, 212).

They invite him to eat and then to go with them to the Empire Theatre. He keeps ejaculating "Good heavens!" regularly, "in a manner that the boys could not understand." He confesses, "I don't think I've been to the Empire in my life. . . . But, good heavens! what *is* my life, after all? Let us go back." The narrator of the tale, who is left at home when the boys go "over to the better man," knows they are with a "person in whose company it [is] an honor to go abroad." He learns later that Cleever "had taken no less interest in the performance before him than in the boys' conversation, and they protested with emphasis that he was 'as good a man as they make, knew what a man was driving at almost before he said it, and yet he's so dashed simple about things any man knows'" (*MO*, 212). They return at midnight with the "eminent novelist." The narrator writes, probably punningly, "I am certain that he said he had been moving in worlds not realized, and that they had shown him the Empire in a new light" (*MO*, 212).

James's foreword to *Mine Own People* shortly followed his own first acquaintance with Kipling's tales, for on March 21, 1890, he professed astonishment to the Stevensons at the talent of the young novelist and on January 19, 1891, he sent Stevenson a copy of his introductory text to the American collection by the "infant monster" (*L*, III, 327). Of the dozen tales in the volume, James mentioned only three in the foreword. He did, however, refer to four from other collections. He saw the tales of the soldiers, especially those of Mulvaney, as the beneficence of "Mr. Kipling's tutelary deity — a landmark in the direction in which it is open to him to look furthest" (*MO*, xvi).

That James refrained from commenting critically on the tale with Cleever in it may be a sign of discretion arising from recognizing himself, or it may be a sign that he did not catch on. Either way it is a mark of Kipling's insight that James, who judged the soldiers' tales the most fascinating of Kipling's contributions to the genre of the short story, turned out to have the same tastes as Cleever, who was smitten by the tales. Even though the young men who regale Cleever with their tales of warfare in "A Conference of the Powers" are not common soldiers, it is the adventures they have shared with the common soldier that enthrall the novelist. His critical comment certainly squares with the present-day idea that James suffered guilt for not having participated in the American Civil War because of his "obscure hurt." When World War I broke out in Europe, it would be an opportunity for him to throw himself into the atmosphere of hostilities and the comradeship of soldiers, permitting him a taste of the kind of wartime experiences he had missed in life but had heard about in his realization as Eustace Cleever in "A Conference of the Powers."

Compared with Hugh Walpole's Mr. Oddy and, as will come out later (see below, pp. 121–23), with Percy Lubbock's Channon in *The Region Cloud*—which, although recognizable as renderings of James, are above all caricatures—Kipling's Cleever is true to the James who was drawn to young men with a connection to life more direct than his own. This trait became more insistent as James grew older and fell under the spell of the twentieth century. Kipling's perception of James's nature seems to be absolutely sure and accurate, and the acute observations behind the figure of Eustace Cleever amount to one more piece of evidence pointing to the great genius of the "infant monster."

Ford Madox Ford

The relationship of Ford Madox Ford (1873–1939) with James has been thoroughly investigated recently, and it is generally conceded that the representation of Callan in *The Inheritors*, the novel that Ford wrote as Ford Madox Hueffer and published as a collaborator with Joseph Conrad in 1901, is a physical portrait of James, as well as a sketch of his personal and professional peculiarities.[21] Callan is without doubt first of all a portrait of

---

21. See Joseph Wiesenfarth, "Henry James and Ford Madox Ford: A Troubled Relationship," *Henry James Review*, XIII (1992), 172–91; Brita Lindberg-Seyersted, *Ford Madox Ford and His Relationship to Stephen Crane and Henry James* (Atlantic Highlands, N.J., 1987); Miranda Seymour, *A Ring of Conspirators: Henry James and His Literary Circle, 1895–1915* (Boston, 1989); John Tytell, "The Jamesian Legacy in *The Good Soldier*," *Studies in the Novel, III* (1971), 365–73; Lydia Rivlin Gabbay, "The Four-Square Cotery: A Comparison of Ford Madox Ford and Henry James," *Studies in the Novel*, VI (1974), 439–53; Paul B. Armstrong, *The Challenge of Bewilderment: Understanding and Representation in James, Conrad, and Ford* (Ithaca, N.Y., 1987); and Nicholas Delbanco, *Group Portrait: Joseph Conrad, Stephen Crane, Ford Madox Ford, Henry James, and H. G. Wells* (New York, 1982).

R. S. Crockett, the Scottish kailyard novelist, but there is really more than the "touch or two of Henry James about him" that Arthur Mizener descried.[22] Ford, who had the eye of a painter and was the grandson of the great painter Ford Madox Brown, saw James remarkably clearly.

Ford's narrator, Arthur Etchinham Granger, describes Callan as someone who "spoke—very—slowly—and—very—authoritatively, like a great actor whose aim is to hold the stage as long as possible. The raising of his heavy eyelids . . . conveyed the impression of a dark, mental weariness; and seemed somehow to give additional length to his white nose. His short, brown beard was getting very gray, I thought. With his lofty forehead and with his superior, yet propitiatory smile, I was of course familiar. . . . One hand supported his head, the other toyed with his watch-chain. His face was uniformly solemn, but his eyes were disconcertingly furtive" (*I*, 18). Callan speaks to the young journalist who is the narrator about the originals of certain characters in his novels. Granger also meets an actress, Mrs. Hartly, who tells him "what a dear, nice man [Callan] is! You should see him at rehearsals. You know I am doing his 'Boldero.' . . . And the trouble he takes. He tries every chair on the stage" (*I*, 35). James, during his playwriting period, was renowned for his generosity and the help he showered on the casts of his plays (*TY*, 338).

Callan is sent to Greenland to write an article, and Granger's description of encountering him at the railway station captures James as a traveler: "He was rather unhappy—found it impossible to make an already distracted porter listen to the end of one of his sentences with two-second waits between each word. For that reason he brightened to see me." Callan talks to Granger "in his most deliberate, most Olympian tone" (*I*, 90–91). Later it becomes plain that on his assignment "Callan *had* been shown things he had not been meant to see, and had written the truth as he had seen it." He is "*the* man who could be believed" (*I*, 184), comparable to Henry James in his strong principles. At the beginning, Callan objected to taking on the task, because, regarding autobiographical writing, "it would verge upon self-advertisement to do more. You know how much I dislike *that*" (*I*, 20). James no less abhorred publicity.

Callan keeps all the things necessary for his writing ready at hand: "He had an appropriate attitude for every vicissitude of his life. . . . Beside him

22. Arthur Mizener, *The Saddest Story: A Biography of Ford Madox Ford* (New York, 1971), 53.

he had every form of labour-saver; every kind of literary knick-knack. . . . There were piles of little green boxes with red capital letters of the alphabet upon them" (*I*, 22). This gear fills the same need as James's multitude of desks, letting the writer continue regardless of the conditions he preferred at the moment.

Joseph Wiesenfarth has explored the infusion of James into Ford's characters, as in *A Call*, of 1910, and especially in *The Good Soldier*, of 1915, and *An English Girl*, of 1907.[23] *Parade's End* was inspired, Ford owned, by "What Maisie Knew," and references to Maisie occur in more than one novel. But despite the respect, even reverence, for James's style that Ford demonstrated in 1913, in the earliest major, and extremely laudatory, study of James the novelist, he in *The Inheritors* allowed himself a slur against Callan, who, he said, could write "seven goodly pages" and "seven unreadable packed pages of a serial," as well as a "dully readable novel" (*I*, 20).

H. G. Wells

The unfortunate end of the friendship of H. G. Wells (1866–1946) and Henry James is open to public view in the correspondence between them that Leon Edel and Gordon Ray have published. *Boon*, a literary lampoon by Wells that appeared under his pseudonym of Reginald Bliss in 1915, was a work in the manner of William Mallock's *The New Republic*, of 1877, but one chapter spoofed James cruelly as a figure and a novelist and brought the contention between them to a head. Wells wrote in his preface, "Bliss can write all sorts of things that Wells could not do" (*BO*, 6). Edel, in the final volume of his biography of James, enlarged only slightly on Wells's characterization of James in the novelist Mr. Blandish of *Boon*. The scant paragraphs he gave in illustration of Wells's parody, however, bore upon James's figure, personality, and writing style, the aspects of James that most other writers who based a fictional character on him selected from rather than combined. The parody in *Boon* deserves a more detailed discussion, because the harsh criticism implicit in it touched James to the quick and elicited a grave and touching letter of response.

Wells felt that James had dealt him an injustice in "The New Novel." Although James praised his "saturation" (*EL*, 128) in his material, he wrote that this is only one part of a novelist's job. Some of his novels, James

23.   Wiesenfarth, "Henry James and Ford Madox Ford," 183.

Mr. James converses with Mr. George Moore upon matters of vital importance to both of them.

12. James converses with George Moore
in H. G. Wells's *Boon.*

wrote, "are so very much more attestations of the presence of material than attestations of an interest in the use of it" (*EL,* 138). In other words, Wells's method and material are at odds with each other. Wells inserted the chapter of *Boon* critical of James's method of writing only in a later draft, after "The New Novel" had made its initial appearance, in 1914, as "The Younger Generation" in the *Times Literary Supplement.*

Chapter 4 of *Boon* discusses James by name, and in a cartoon in the second section of the chapter Wells has James and George Moore conversing not with each other but alongside each other independently (Figure 12). In the third section of the chapter, Boon says to a group of men, which includes Ford Madox Ford, "James is to criticism what Immanuel Kant is to philosophy." Still, he adds, James "has no penetration. . . . But here he is, spinning about like the most tremendous of water-boatmen—you know those insects?—kept up by surface tension" though he is "as big as an elephant." Boon is equally disapproving of James's fiction: "Then with his eviscerated people he has invented he begins to make up stories. . . . These people cleared for artistic treatment never make lusty love, never go to angry war, never shout at an election or perspire at poker" (*BO,* 106). A novel of his "is like a church lit but without a congregation to distract you, with every light and line focused on the high altar. And on the altar, very reverently placed . . . is a dead kitten, an egg-shell, a bit of string. . . . Upon the desert his selection has made Henry James erect palatial metaphors. . . . The chief fun, the only exercise, in reading Henry James is this clambering over vast metaphors" (*BO,* 106–107). "His vast paragraphs sweat and struggle. . . . And all for tales of nothingness. . . . It is leviathan retrieving pebbles." James is a "hippopotamus . . . picking up a pea" (*BO,* 108).

In the fourth section of Chapter 4, Boon tells about a novel of his own, "rather in the manner of Henry James. . . . It is to be called 'The Spoils of Mr. Blandish,' and it is all about this particular business of the selective life. Mr. Blandish . . . was pretty completely taken from the James ideal. . . . He was a man with an exquisite apprehension of particulars. . . . He believed that in speech and still more that in writing there was an inevitable right word. . . . He was, in fact, the very soul of Henry James—as I understand it." Mr. Blandish "didn't marry. . . . Lust, avarice, ambition . . . were not for him. . . . He went about elaborately, avoiding ugliness, death, suffering, industrialism, politics, sport, the thought of war, the red blaze of passion" (*BO,* 109–11).

Boon explains how the story will develop, offering as its beginning a long, complicated sentence in imitation of James's late style. He says the chapter "expands and expands" until you realize that Mr. Blandish has come upon a house he is looking for to live in himself: "*This is it.*" In the details of Mr. Blandish's possession of the house, Wells is clearly making fun of James's acquisition of Lamb House. Wells calls it Samphire House, probably after the reference to *King Lear* and the Samphire collectors in James's story "Mora Montravers," which he apparently had read. Boon goes on, "And to crown it all I am going to write one of those long crescendo passages that James loves," until at last the perfect butler and his wife, the cook, arrive, with to "crown all, the perfect name—Mutimer!" (*BO,* 116). "But," promises Boon, "there is an effect piled up very wonderfully, of Mr. Blandish, obsessed, uneasy, watching . . . his guests, . . . continually asking himself 'Do they note it? Are they feeling it?'" (*BO,* 118–19).

There is a treasure, an 1813 brandy, bricked up in a disused cellar of Samphire House. "Samphire House, instead of being the fine claret of a refuge Mr. Blandish supposed, is a loaded port. . . . For a long time you will be by no means clear what the 'spirit' is that Mr. Blandish is now resolved to exorcise. He is, in fact, engaged in trying . . . to sell the stuff" (*BO,* 125–26). In the novels, Henry James just cannot sell it, Wells intimates. The reader will learn "by circumlocution the most delicate that . . . the last drop of the last barrel has gone and that Mutimer, the butler, lies dead or at least helpless—in the inner cellar. And a beautiful flavour, ripe and yet rare, rich without opulence, hangs—*diminuendo morendo*—in the air" (*BO*, 127–28).

The plot relates to the episode at Lamb House in which James's butler and the butler's wife, appearing dead-drunk one day, were belatedly discovered to have been drinking his liquor all through the years and were summarily dismissed.

Wells devoted thirty pages to roasting James and his works, without any masking of his identity and without the relief of any good humor. James's considerate and noble response impelled Wells to soften the sting in a letter (*M*, 537), but their relationship was ended. Whatever caused him to be so blunt in his presentation, there were certainly others who agreed with his disparaging estimate of James's idiosyncrasies as a person and a writer.

Percy Lubbock

Percy Lubbock (1879–1965) wrote a novel that, although not superficially biographical, has struck some readers as in part a greatly disguised portrait of Henry James. Leon Edel sees Lubbock's *The Region Cloud*, of 1925, as a "portrait-caricature of James of considerable power and a certain amount of truth" (*M*, 189). He detects James in Lubbock's character Channon, a great painter, though Lubbock gave him what James never had, a decorative wife and a lavish country estate. But Channon's genius needs to feed off young men who are his acolytes and, moreover, needs a constantly renewed company of them, something that seems to have been noticeable about the older James's intellectual temperament as well during the time that the group at Howard Sturgis' country house, Qu'Acre, was at its height, with James at its center. In "The Eyes," Edith Wharton showed the domination of a group by such a figure (see above, p. 28).

Five years before Lubbock wrote *The Region Cloud*, he had tried to put down his definition of James's personality as an artist in an introduction he prepared to two volumes of James's letters (LU, I, xiii–xiv). He remarked how even James's friends, of whom he had many, must have felt that at heart he lived in solitude: "He disliked that the service of art should be questioned and debated in the open. . . . Sometimes . . . to one in whom he felt an understanding, he would speak out with impressive authority. . . . He was insatiable for anything that others could help him from their personal lives" (LU, I, xvi). The assumption can be that Lubbock attempted to transmit these traits to Channon as he relates to a young admirer, whom the artist sees as his doppelgänger or the mirror of his thoughts. But Lubbock also endowed Channon with some of the qualities James had that it would not have been tactful to mention in an introduction to the volumes of letters. No one can know whether Lubbock had only James as a model for his egocentric painter, but James is patent at least in Channon's emotional attachments to the members of his circle.

Eye contact occurs between Austin, the first-person narrator and admirer of the painter, and Channon in the dining room of a grand hotel while the two men are still unacquainted. James had famously arresting eyes. Later, Channon keeps putting his arm on Austin's shoulder, which was also James's wont. The young man to whom the great man is drawn carries the name of the young secretary to an elderly character in an early story by James, "A Light Man," of 1869. In that tale, Max Austin displaces the secretary who precedes him, just as in Lubbock's novel, Austin displaces Blake, the secretary to Channon. The attraction Channon feels to Austin rests on the young man's intelligence and understanding of himself, which do not issue in the vulgar and blind admiration Channon receives from everybody else. Although Austin has been "smothered in his presence" (*RC*, 120) — as Lubbock may have been in James's — Channon likes Austin because he senses that the young man lives his "own life in [his] brain and it's a real life" (*RC*, 122). He is persuaded that the "brain ticking away there in silence . . . gives me the measure of myself," although one of his circle says, "His genius uses him, as he the rest of us" (*RC*, 155).

Channon transports Austin to his big estate, Bintworth, where the young man inhabits a lavish world among the admirers whom Channon considers vulgar. The painter appreciates Austin's wordless presence for allowing him to think his own thoughts without the solitude they usually entail — solitude of the sort Lubbock mentions in his introduction to James's letters. But Austin loses his hold on Channon's imagination when he answers the painter's question about what he has brought Austin of value. "What becomes of all that rubbish if across it and over it I can catch your eye?" asks the young man in response (*RC*, 196). Channon promptly drops him, remonstrating, "You don't seem to be able to understand me after all" (*RC*, 197). The outcome is similar to that in James's "The Jolly Corner," only here talk rather than physical aggression breaks the spell between the alter ego and the chief character. So it is that the sun, for

Lubbock and Austin, is "but one hour mine," to quote the sonnet of Shakespeare's from which Lubbock takes the title of the book and its epigraph, "The region cloud hath masked him from me now."

Since nobody can give Channon what he needs, Austin is allowed to stay at Bintworth only if he does not break his silence. At the same time that Lubbock set in relief James's cannibalistic habits toward his admirers, he did not lose the deep respect and admiration for James the artist that he had demonstrated in his *The Craft of Fiction,* of 1921, and in his introduction to James's letters. He was willing to have such a novel appear only long after James was dead, and after his letters had come out. He also practiced a decorous concealment by ascribing the human failings at the center of his attention to a character with a different occupation from James's who was a married man and a wealthy landowner. It is not surprising that James's presence in the novel eluded critics for so long, for even in Wharton's story "The Eyes," written during James's lifetime in his own milieu, critics on the whole did not recognize his figure.[24]

Had James administered some slight to Lubbock that sharpened his sensitivity to James's control over his young admirers and made him see the older man as a vampire feeding off young men? Perhaps the other young men the Master favored excited his jealousy (*M,* 99). When Lubbock visited Lamb House for the first time, in 1901, Hendrik Andersen was about to arrive and James's relationship with Morton Fullerton was in full flower. In 1903, James was to meet Jocelyn Persse, with whom he formed an immediate attachment, and in 1909 his emotional involvement with Hugh Walpole began. But the cannibalistic effect troubling Lubbock may have been restricted to Sturgis' Qu'acre circle, where James shifted his affections from one young man to the next. Hugh Walpole never referred to this aspect of James's personality in *The Apple Trees.* The long and deep, yet simultaneous, emotional attachments to Fullerton, Andersen, Persse, and Walpole do not, on the evidence available, appear to have been blighted by James's cannibalistic tendencies. The four young men remained strong love objects and did not endure the kind of shifting favoritism on which Lubbock's eye fastened.

24. Adeline R. Tintner, "The Metamorphoses of Edith Wharton in Henry James's *The Finer Grain," Twentieth-Century Literature,* XXI (1975), 355–79.

4

THE RETURN OF JAMES THE FIGURE

The stock figure of James in the fiction of more than fifty years ago usually built on the memories of those who had known him in the flesh. A strong impression remained with them of James's idiosyncratic appearance, his formal dress and mannered speech with its endless parentheses, and his timidities and reticences. Even the most exaggerated caricatures of him in the fiction of this period bore a large degree of fidelity to the historical Henry James. In the past fifty years, however, portraits of him have taken on a freer shape in works of fiction as the authors re-creating him have highlighted particular aspects of his personality to serve their purposes. Whereas Gore Vidal in 1987 followed the historical James and his friendship with Henry Adams for his novel *Empire*, David Plante had in 1970 already brought James out of the closet despite fabricating another last name for the James family. The giveaway is in the title, *The Ghost of Henry James*. The two men writing together under the pseudonym Bruce Elliot had no compunctions about attaching James's name in their mass-market novel *Village* to a character whose homosexual orientation conflicts with a romantic young woman's expectations. In the more recent evocations of James by Rebecca Goldstein, Susan Sontag, and Carol Hill, the stress is not on his homoeroticism but on his position vis-à-vis his siblings, his relations with Edith Wharton, and his delight in the criminous.

"I Have a Feeling Henry Will Come Back": David Plante's *The Ghost of Henry James*

"I have a feeling Henry will come back" is a statement made by Charlotte, a stand-in for Alice James, in one of the earliest novelistic attempts to tinker with the facts about the James family in confecting a fantasy. The title, *The Ghost of Henry James*, of the first novel by David Plante (1940–) offers assurance that Charlotte's expectation will not be disappointed. The first chapter of the novel, published in 1970, exposes Plante's intentions regarding the James siblings: he will show that no matter where they might live today or what they might do, they would still enact their essential family drama. It is significant that the only member of the family in the novel to keep a name from the James family is Henry. At the start of the novel, the brothers and sister meet at Henry's grave in the Cambridge cemetery where in real life the ashes of the Jameses are buried. The rest of the book is a flashback to Henry's life—to the life that, Plante intimates, Henry James would have led in these loose and open times. The Jameses would have the same facility of intellect they had before, but now they would not be afflicted by repression. Charles wants "to hear Henry talk about his sexual adventure as he had always done whenever they came together" (*GH*, 181), and Henry attends "a whore house in Beirut, steam baths in New York, a party in the banlieu of Paris." He lives amid a "wealth of sensual suggestions" and visits the Far East. Henry tries "to think of all the cities he had made love in. He tried to think of all the people whom he had had in bed. He tried to recall the names of young men and women whom he could recall only as smooth accommodating bodies"(*GH*, 147). Henry is voraciously bisexual, clearly living all he can.

This is not the historical Henry and, just as surely, not a Henry with the repose to conceive and fashion James's 20 novels and 112 stories. Plante would probably argue that his fulfillment would not have required him to write them. When Henry dies in Italy, in Charles's villa, his body is taken back to Cambridge. Although Henry James was predeceased by at least three of his siblings, in this fantasy Henry is the first to go and the first to come back as a ghost—for, on the last page, in the old family house surrounded by ice and snow, "the door, with a sudden horrible bang, flew open to them" (*GH*, 247). Thus the reader returns to Chapter 1, as in *Finnegans Wake*.

A volley of reminders of the historical James punctuates the text. Someone reads *Italian Hours*, they all visit Rye and Lamb House, they remember Tremont Street, the location of the Boston art gallery in *The Ambassadors*, and Julian reads about the life of William Wetmore Story and his friends. Yet this may be the first fictional representation of James that detaches him from his authorial distinction. It may also be the first to position him as the most influential member of his family of four brothers and a sister. A few years later, Plante wrote a memoir about three "difficult women" writers, in which he quoted Jean Rhys as telling him, "You've got to forget about all past American writers. You've got to forget about Henry James."[1] At the time of his first novel he was not only writing about James's ghost but was haunted by it.

The Homosexual Artist:
Bruce Elliot's *Village*, a Mass-Market Paperback

A mass-market novel written a decade later by a team of two men — Edward Field, a distinguished poet, and Neil Derrick, a novelist — under the name of Bruce Elliot, makes James the hero of one of its chapters. *Village*, of 1982, is the saga of five generations of a family living in an old house on Perry Street, in Greenwich Village, that enduring section of downtown New York City from which the book, in currently stylish, truncated form, takes its name. The novel deals with the young James.

The sections of the volume are associated with dates, beginning with 1845 and ending with 1975. Henry James appears in the section for 1870. There Thomas Endicott, a member of the family occupying the house, has been printing in pamphlet form a tale by James identified as "The Passionate Pilgrim." In reality, "A Passionate Pilgrim" first appeared in the *Atlantic Monthly* of 1871 and was in 1875 reprinted in James's first book of collected tales, published not in New York but in Boston.[2] Veronica, Tom's poetry-writing daughter, hears from her father "about his well-dressed customer

---

The material in this section appeared in somewhat different form as "The Figure of the Homosexual Artist in Bruce Elliot's *Village*: A Mass Market Paperback," in *Markham Review*, XI (Summer, 1982), 71–72. Dr. Anne F. Janowitz, of Warwick University, brought the chapter about James to my attention.

    1. David Plante, *Difficult Women: A Memoir of Three* (New York, 1983), 20.

    2. Henry James, *A Passionate Pilgrim* (Boston, 1875). In addition to "A Passionate Pilgrim," the tales in the collection are "The Last of the Valerii," "Eugene Pickering," "The Madonna of the Future," "The Romance of Certain Old Clothes," and "Madame de Mauves."

from Washington Square" whose story "was so fancily written he was having a devil of a time proofreading it." Veronica is thrilled, for "she already knew several of his stories from magazines—she considered him the most talented young writer in America." She sends James a sample of her poetry, which delights him, so that "he went on about it in such a complicated fashion that Tom could hardly follow," but even so he invites James to dinner, for "this was the first man who had ever expressed the slightest interest in his daughter." James is "already a sacred figure" to Veronica, and she is made shy by the great admiration James has for her poetry (*VL*, 169).

Certain liberties have been taken with some facts. The "high-toned world of Washington Square" (*VL*, 169) that the novel presents as James's milieu was no longer his home at this time. He had lived there only as an infant and after that his family resided on Fourteenth Street, until his eleventh year, when they moved to Europe. During the one year that he as an adult was in New York, he lived on Twenty-Fifth Street, not in the Washington Square area at all, nor with his family, by then settled in Boston, but alone. The special booklet that Tom makes for James out of "A Passionate Pilgrim" is completely fanciful, as are the five copies that James says the New York Society Library requested (*VL*, 172). It is hard to imagine James waxing eloquent about a young woman's poems, since James never liked poetry particularly, except that by the great traditional poets. The authors are fully familiar with the facts of James's life, but they modify them in order to quicken the narrative flow and relate the characters to James in the service of their plot.

The general impression James makes on Tom Endicott's family is not very favorable. He is "conceited as well as pretentious," Elizabeth, Veronica's sister-in-law, thinks, but she is "pleased that Veronica seemed to be drinking in every syllable." When his "meticulous way of speaking" prompts the question whether he is English, he explains, "I was born right here in New York" (which was a fact) "in the same house I still live in with my family" (which was not a fact). He tells them he is going to London very shortly "for an indefinite stay" (*VL*, 172). He complains that very "few Americans give a hoot about the Middle Ages"—one of the few periods of history that did not interest the real James very much either. As for James's comment that "the only thing I disapprove of is that ghastly means of public locomotion they have installed underground" (*VL*, 174), this does not square with his remarking in 1869 in a letter that he enjoyed the underground, thinking it a "marvellous phenomenon" (*L*, I, 91). Moreover, his brother William, who was in Cambridge at the time, could not have taken him there. But in the novel, James's objection to the innovation is meant only to attract Patrick's attention—since he is going to start building the first subway in New York—and hence to establish the writer's homoeroticism. As soon as Patrick begins on his favorite topic of how he will conquer the obstacle of granite in building the subway, James appears deeply engrossed in what he is saying. It dawns on Elizabeth that Patrick, not his subject matter, has captured James's interest and that Tom's hope of finding a suitor for Veronica will not be realized. "To think that all that stuffy pretension hid a shocking secret" (*VL*, 176). Would her husband, Patrick, be up to "such subtleties and complexities?" Veronica is distressed when her sister-in-law cautions her that James is a "more complicated man than we knew," and the young poetess exclaims, "I just can't believe he's the same man who writes those beautiful stories . . . that one about the old maid . . . with her widowed father." Elizabeth replies that "great art has nothing to do with being kind" (*VL*, 177).

This dinner scene is James's major appearance in *Village*, but his influence is felt among members of the next generation. Eugene Endicott, an aspiring writer, who knows that his late aunt Veronica had enjoyed this "relation" with Henry James, decides to write up the episode: "Why not try a piece on Henry James?" His aunt—who also went to England and continued to write poetry—"practically had a love affair with him once" (*VL*, 330). Meeting Mabel Dodge and her circle of literary and artistic friends, Eugene is at first avid to write his piece, but he is later daunted by Theodore Dreiser's advice "not to worry about a highfalutin prose style like Henry James but just to tell his story straight out" (*VL*, 332). Every ten pages or so the unfinished piece is mentioned. Later, a character with a Jewish name takes the pseudonym of Henry Lambert when job hunting. Both names have Jamesian associations, the first name with the author and the surname with the hero of *The Ambassadors*, Lewis Lambert Strether.

None of this is accidental, and the authors, in the manner of James regarding other incidents, plant clues to keep alive the expectation that something is to come of the Jamesian episode and its fitful reminders. What emerges is the strongly resisted tendency to homosexuality Eugene exhibits. This powerful force finally takes over and thus identifies him, the writer of the family, with Henry James. The great writer born in the Village is the model and antecedent for another writer, also born and bred in the Village, except that the later writer is a failure, even if his mother had encouraged him to believe that his art would be his salvation. One of Eugene's plays, however, succeeds, and its fame continues long after his tragic, accidental death. The "obscure hurt," often interpreted as James's sexual impotence, is here construed as a basic homosexual predisposition, and Eugene's exhibited impotence is a correlate of the supposed Jamesian problem—a problem that Hemingway took up in *The Sun Also Rises*, where "Henry's bicycle" and his wound are referred to in connection with Jake Barnes's impotence, the result of a war wound.

By one of the ironic twists so characteristic of contemporary idol making, the man who had been caricatured in the popular press of 1905 because of his aestheticism, expatriatism, and complex language, was in 1982 regarded as a cultural hero, the modern artist who atones for his hidden homosexuality by his talent. The last volume of Edel's biography has James revealing his homoeroticism only late in life, in his passionate friendships with a number of young men. The chapter in *Village* devoted to the thirty-two-year-old James, who was about to leave for Paris and for Europe for good, reads more like biography than like fiction. This mass-market paperback anticipated the assertion that James's homoeroticism surfaced much earlier than Edel's biography conceded. Such a picture of James was admissible as part of a novel in 1982. Today, when an interest in James's sexual orientation usurps the attention given by scholars in the past to his work rather than to his life, the picture of the young Henry James in *Village* seems closer to the reality of the man, in spite of the liberties taken for the sake of narrative values, than do the putatively true accounts by some of the biographers who have come after Edel (see below, pp. 442–44).

John Hay, Henry Adams, and Henry James: Gore Vidal's *Empire*

The novel *Empire*, of 1987, by Gore Vidal (1925–), again introduced the figure of James by name—now in his relation to John Hay and Henry Adams, as well as to Clarence King and the Don Camerons. In the novel, James is an imagined figure with a foundation in biographical material the historian Vidal knew well. It is August, 1898, and there is a country-house party at Surrenden Dering, the place rented by the Don Camerons. The factual trappings of this chapter come largely from the Adams letters and from Edel's biography. Edel wrote that James "did go [there] for a short stay on a couple of occasions" (*TY,* 233). Henry James enters, bearded and correctly dressed. He has met Caroline Sanford, the heroine of the novel and French-bred, at Saint-Cloud, to which the Bourgets took him. James possesses a "huge barrel of a chest that contained a singer's lungs," and his "breath never gave out, no matter how long and intricate the sentence" (*E,* 17). Adams calls James's language "Remingtonese"—employing a word from one of James's letters to Charles Eliot Norton (*L,* IV, 95). "James's beautiful measured voice [is] far less British in its accent than that of Henry Adams" (*E,* 428). James mentions his review of Charles Schermerhorn Schuyler's *Paris Under the Communards.* Vidal had in 1986 reviewed the two volumes of James's complete criticism, which unearthed reviews from forgotten journals. When the Smiths, James's domestic couple, in a drunken state produce tea for the crowd, Vidal's knowledge of James is detailed enough to show him as liking sweets— he "put three teaspoons of sugar in his tea"—and as critical of "those who find [Theodore Roosevelt's] crude mindless energy attractive" (*E,* 42).

After that, James disappears from the 486-page novel as a character except for a visit to Washington and a celebration in the White House for Theodore Roosevelt. Along the way, however, this good friend of the main characters, Hay and Adams, influences the fabric of the novel. When Caroline visits the Waldorf-Astoria in New York, Vidal draws on Henry James's tale "A Round of Visits" for a figure of speech to describe the Palm Garden: it is a "wonderful jungle of palm trees set in green Chinese cachepots. . . . Noon on a tropical island, thought Caroline, half expecting to hear a parrot shriek; then heard what sounded like a parrot shrieking but was merely the laughter of Harry Lehr" (*E,* 79). James had described the same setting at the Waldorf, which he concealed under the name of The Pocahontas: "The heavy heat, the luxuriance, the extravagance . . . gave the impression of some wondrous tropical forest" (XII, 431).

Vidal certainly looked into James's Washington story of 1884, "Pandora," in which the Adamses, Henry and Clover, become the Bonnycastles, who entertain the president. James's story also includes the self-made girl Pandora Day, who imparts something to Vidal's self-made woman journalist Caroline Sanford, although Caroline's life is at first more like Isabel Archer's, since she finds herself trapped in a marriage—in her case necessary because she has become pregnant by the man who attracts her, James Burden Day. One of James's inventions, American City, the city to which Adam Verver and Charlotte return at the end of *The Golden Bowl,* is mentioned (*E,* 317). Cissy Patterson "had literary dreams; she would write novels, she said; and promptly picked up Mr. James's latest effort, *The Ambassadors,* inscribed to Henry Adams" (*E,* 379).

When, in the last part of the book, James visits the joint Washington home of the Hays and the Adamses, his entering line reads like something combining aspects of "A Round of Visits": "I have hurried home from my morning round of calls, filling the city with a veritable blizzard of pasteboard" (*E,* 426). In "A Round of Visits," a midwinter blizzard takes place as the hero makes his social rounds. Hay calls James a "fellow celebrity" to Admiral Dewey, but James says he cannot stay because "the ladies of America are waiting for me to tell them about Balzac" — for in 1905 James gave his memorable lecture. When James says they are "re-creating the house-party at Surrenden Dering," Hay thinks that a "young American woman who chose to publish a newspaper was not quite within his grasp" but that eventually "Caroline would be defined in Jamesian terms" (*E,* 427). Vidal is evidently fulfilling that expectation.

James, Augustus Saint-Gaudens, and John La Farge all attend a diplomatic reception in the East Room of the White House. The reactions Vidal ascribes to James stem from James's correspondence: "The local ladies here are plainer" than in London (*E,* 431). Jean Jules Jusserand, a diplomat, historian, and friend of James, joins the men; they all speak French, a "language James spoke quite as melodiously as his own" (*E,* 431).

However James might have felt if he had read *Empire,* he is in it as a deeply researched historical figure whose every comment is worth paying attention to. A distinguished creative artist, James has been restored to his standing as a celebrated personage on the American scene. Would he not have "modestly blushed" while accepting Vidal's generous tribute, as he reportedly did when the Order of Merit was pinned on his chest as he lay dying? The color he would turn if he learned of his place in the work of David Plante or Bruce Elliot is not pleasant to imagine.

Rebecca Goldstein's *The Dark Sister*

The novelist Rebecca Goldstein (1950–) acknowledged the impact of three members of the James family — Alice, Henry, and William — on *The Dark Sister,* her novel of 1991. In her prologue, after describing the two younger boys, Goldstein came to Alice, whom she said had the "Jamesian heightened consciousness, its gift for making itself known to itself" but not to "that outside world, which her two eldest brothers transform into their own" (*DS,* 4). She quoted Henry James's comment to William that Alice's "tragic health was in a manner the only solution for her of the practical problem of life" (*DS,* 5).

The main character of the novel is Hedda, a writer aware of her ugliness, in the way of Rosanna Gaw of *The Ivory Tower.* Much repeated is the basic thematic mode of the double, the divided self, especially its dark side. William, with his *Will to Believe,* is at the center, and there appear several members of the James family, especially William and Alice, both in double guise, in addition to figures from Henry James's fiction. All these—including Dr. Austin Sloper, the physician in *Washington Square,* and a Roderick who, now with the surname Bonnet, has exchanged his original role in *Roderick Hudson* for the acquisition of two daughters, Alice and Vivianna—are in the novel Hedda is writing.

Once again fiction has not shrunk from using the James name, but here William is the focus. In earlier fiction, whether the name was changed or not, it had been Henry who exercised the hold on the writer's imagination, even though William was personally the charmer. Goldstein's fictional world not only supersedes the world of realistic fiction but also conspires with it. Dr. Sloper, the father of Catherine Sloper, coexists in *The Dark Sister* with William James, the physician from real life on whom Henry James is believed to have based Sloper, and both play important parts. Reality and fantasy interpenetrate, usually with the effect of duality of self. Hedda herself has a beautiful sister, Stella, who is her opposite, with no sense of selfhood. The author of two novels concerned with the so-called mind-body problem, Goldstein fragments her narrative and imposes on it the notion of the double, with their opposed identities. Alice James inhabits two personalities in the subplot. In one of these, she is Alice Bonnet, Roderick Bonnet's daughter, and, considered a hysteric, has consulted Dr. Sloper about Vivianna, her sister and opposite. Dr. Sloper then consults William James, his real-life counterpart.

Goldstein weaves into her novel whole passages from James's fiction, including the description of Washington Square, which is the location of Dr. Sloper's house (*DS,* 30; *WS,* 14). Roderick Bonnet, as a sculptor, is Roderick Hudson completely transformed. Vivianna picks a rose from the Colosseum to give to her father, Roderick, paralleling what Roderick Hudson risks in James's novel for Christina Light (*DS,* 40). Hedda, however, always identifies with Henry James, and in the name Bonnet there is subordination to her "bon," Henry James, as James called his muse "mon bon."

Goldstein constitutes the figure of Henry James by means of a collage of his family letters and of quotations from his work. He becomes her muse. His personal problems, his nightmares, his relations with William and Alice—open to late-twentieth-century novels because of Edel's biographical studies—all combine in this rather intellectual portrait of the man Goldstein familiarly calls Henry.

Standing Before Sargent's Portrait of Henry James: Penelope Lively's *A City of the Mind*

Penelope Lively (1933–), in *A City of the Mind*, of 1991, has a divorced architect wooing a new girlfriend, Sarah Bridges, in the National Portrait Gallery, in London. Arriving before John Singer Sargent's likeness of Henry James, they decide that "it is easier to meet" his "benign but judgmental gaze." Sarah says, "He looks like a person you'd love to have as an uncle." They look at each other, and she says, "So there it is," echoing James's famous sentence.[3]

The intimacy between the hero and heroine is intensified in the gaze of James, who was indeed a good uncle.

Carol De Chellis Hill's *Henry James's Midnight Song*

Henry James's Midnight Song, of 1993, by Carol De Chellis Hill (1942–), can be seen as the riposte of a novelist to the tremendous amount of information available about today's literary and philosophical idols. Instead of writing a serious history of fin-de-siècle thought, tracking the paths taken of late by philosophy, psychoanalysis, the leading literary movements of America and the Continent, and scientific investigation, Hill opted to toss everything into a grab bag from which she could pluck them without regard to their traditional moorings, to rearrange in the order her creative imagination preferred.

Hill's reinvention, unlike Goldstein's, is restricted to the lives of the authors and does not place the characters they created on their own level. When she referred to their characters—as she did to Isabel Archer of *The*

---

3. Penelope Lively, *A City of the Mind* (New York, 1991), 211–12.

Portrait of a Lady—she kept them within their fictional world. Instead, she made historical personages her puppets, putting them, with their recognizable personalities, into a murder mystery. Wrapped in their cocoons of biographical data, the personae of Henry James, Edith Wharton, Sigmund Freud, and Carl Jung, along with their relatives and love objects, connect in a search for a criminal, in which they endear themselves to the reader who knows a little about them to begin with and enjoys seeing them step out of their actual lives into the camaraderie, rivalry, and detection that Hill has invented for them. Henry James and Edith Wharton come to life in ways that fit what Leon Edel and R. W. B. Lewis say in their biographies and what Lyall Powers' publication of their correspondence reveals about them. They are not mutilated but delightfully recognizable.

In the novel, James wishes to consult Sigmund Freud about his sister Alice, and Edith Wharton wishes to consult him about James and his anxieties. Unfortunately a body turns up in Freud's study, and James, as well as a troop of others, comes under suspicion. In order to deflect the inquiry from sensitive areas, each of the illustrious suspects tends to conceal secrets. What James hides is chiefly his personal guilt at the suicide of Constance Fenimore Woolson. Inspector LeBlanc, who has been brought in on the case, is equally confronted by the personal mysteries that Jung, Freud, and everyone else try to protect.

As in a story by James, a nameless narrator holds forth. James is seen reading a Gothic tale of criminality, in keeping with his interest in the criminous. Also in the novel is James's discreditable act of killing his cat in fury at its wailing. That, together with his possible culpability in the suicide of Miss Woolson, leads Edith Wharton to think he might benefit from Freud's offices.

Hill's novel is a romp in a genre that has become popular in recent years—that of fictionalized biography. Almost a dozen such treatments have appeared, assuming the standpoint of Byron's doctor, Chekhov's sister, Wittgenstein's nephew, or Rameau's niece, for instance. The authors recreated historical lives but allowed themselves the latitude of a novelist rather than a biographer.[4] Hill made an entertaining excursion in this genre, and by multiplying her biographical subjects and playing God with their temporal relationships she developed its comedic subgenre.

---

4. Michiko Kakutani, "Freedom of Fiction, Applied to Biography," *New York Times*, September 10, 1990, Sec. C, p. 15.

The mass of biographical data lets the reader picture James easily, but Hill has concentrated on aspects of his personality that the present generation is especially concerned with: personal peculiarities of his that might profit by a visit to Freud; his great friendship with Edith Wharton; his love of jokes and comical situations, along with his gregariousness. The reader who takes a jaunt with James and Wharton through the fin-de-siècle cosmopolitan world they both loved so well, and felt so at home in, is riveted by a side of them that people of the new fin de siècle find absorbing.

Susan Sontag's *Alice in Bed*

Alice James is at the center not only of Goldstein's *The Dark Sister* but also of *Alice in Bed*, of 1993, by Susan Sontag (1933–). Jean Strouse's *Alice James: A Biography*, of 1980, and Ruth Bernard Yeazell's *The Death and Letters of Alice James*, of 1981, along with R. W. B. Lewis' *The Jameses*, of 1991, have fostered the present lively interest in Alice.

The 1990s have seen contemporary fiction writers usurp, re-create, and manipulate, besides the Jameses, writing personalities like Gustave Flaubert, Anton Chekhov, and Ernest Hemingway. The widespread entrance of such figures into the fantasies of other writers springs from a context. For one thing, there has been a proliferation of biographies of the master writers which go into their activities and relations with others in exhaustive detail. The material is there begging to be usurped and reassembled by a postmodern point of view and fictional drive. For another, the example of James, actuated by his "germ" theory of fictional creation, has been a lure. James's idea was, Take what you want from others and go on from there. Writers, their habits and foibles, their friends—all this is accessible matter, permitting the search for characters to be set aside in favor of the ingenious creation of humorous or outrageous transactions between historical personages and between them and the reader. The resulting collage of serious historical and aesthetic material aligns itself with jocularity for a change.

Sontag's *Alice in Bed*, a play conceived in 1990 and performed in Europe in 1993, is, however, far from jocular. The feminists' interest in Alice James has no doubt also helped shape this work. Alice is in bed lying under the stack of many thin mattresses that serves as a suppressor during her agitated states. Her brother Henry visits her, and though he attempts to console her, the effect of his attention is to oppress her with his concern. In her agitation she thinks of a scene with her father in which, as a young girl, she asked him whether she could commit suicide and he told her that if she wished to, she could.

Henry is the only member of the family to exist in the same time frame with Alice in this play. Despite his frequent visits and concern, he somehow does not understand her problem, although he is affected so strongly that he bursts into tears in her presence. Sontag draws parallels between Alice James and the most famous Alice in Victorian literature, Lewis Carroll's Alice, having Alice James say, "Is there a hole I can fall into?" Carroll's Alice dreams of falling into a world that is not arranged to accommodate her sense of freedom, and Sontag's Alice James experiences a change in size relative to her environment and its pressures.

For Henry, here called Harry, Scene 4 is the big one. He appears "obese, and wears a caftan," the attire puzzling, since he never traveled farther east than Italy, unless it is to underline his monkish character or his resemblance to Balzac. He does not allow Alice her peculiar patterns of expression but says, "You'll stop being hysterical. You'll stop making me feel wretched" (*AL*, 27). His concern is chiefly with the unhappiness that her illness is causing him, not with its basis. He tries to console her with his affectionate diminutives: he calls her "dear rabbit" and a "mouse," and she bridles that he is patronizing her (*AL*, 28, 29). He tells her, "The extraordinary intensity of your will and your personality . . . would create enormous practical problems of life . . . in . . . the real world" (*AL*, 29). Sontag quotes a statement he made about her after her death: "Her tragic health was . . . the only solution for her of the problem of life—as it suppressed the lament of equality, reciprocity, etc." (*AL*, 30). The sister and brother surely have love for each other, but Harry too is a mattress on her and a weight. She again assimilates to Lewis Carroll's Alice when she shows up at a tea party. Excited by Margaret Fuller's account of her Roman adventures, Alice mentally travels to Rome, demonstrating how successfully the mind can take a human being on a journey regardless of the inaction of the body.

On Sontag's interpretation, Henry James's feelings for his sister, although expressed in frequent visits, only reinforced the repression she had experienced in her family. He meant well, but he did not have the key to release her into reality on her own. He was part of the family conspiracy, and although his love and kindness helped keep her occupied, they were unable to cure her. Emotional, with a deep sense of responsibility and guilt toward his sister, he was nonetheless insistent on leading his own life.

Probably the James family members have been seized upon for biographies and novels because of their creativity and intelligence, and because the institution of the family is back in style. For the James family is the American family at its most united and productive. At the same time, however, it is the dysfunctional family at its most destructive. The father's odd enthusiasms and his unique ways of educating his children seem to have produced "broken fortunes" for the two younger brothers. The uncomfortable youth of William James is attributed to his father's attitude to him. The pressures of the extraordinary family are seen as lying behind Henry's suppressed homoeroticism and his neurotic dependence on a youthful accident, as well as behind the neurotic problem of the lifelong invalidism of Alice.

Postmodernist tenets sharply distinguish between the author and the text, thereby licensing appropriation of the text's pieces by anyone so inclined. There is no question of plagiarism when the deconstructed text belongs to no one and to everyone. Pieces of it become matter to be absorbed and pieced together again in a new text. The authority of the postmodern author supervenes in manipulating the appropriated text, but all text has been removed from its creative hegemony.

Hiram Scudder as Henry James: Louis Auchincloss' "They That Have Power to Hurt"

Louis Auchincloss (1917–) has amused himself and his readers in three fictional renderings of Edith Wharton's relationship with her innermost circle of men—which included Teddy, her husband; Walter Berry; and Morton Fullerton. In each of the three tales, although there are abundant clues for the reader who knows something about Wharton and her men that they are the original models, Auchincloss' cast has been so totally transformed that its members are narrative inventions much in the manner of postmodern adaptations of historical figures. It is only in the most recent of the three tales, "They That Have Power to Hurt," of 1994, that Henry James joins the cast. In Hiram Scudder, "that grand old ham of Yankee fiction" (*YE*, 38), James undergoes a transformation, however, that places Scudder's role at some distance from James's known character.[5]

The tale is told by a first-person narrator, Martin Babcock, based on

---

5. Louis Auchincloss has acknowledged that he used a lot relating to Henry James for the portrait of Hiram Scudder (Louis Auchincloss to author, February, 1994).

Morton Fullerton. Like Fullerton, Martin is a journalist of meager accomplishments, physically small and dapper, and now in his old age a resident of Paris. He is the inheritor of an "indistinguished but amusing past" (*YE*, 55) who recounts his affair with Arlina Randolph—a successful and great novelist, and the figure drawn from Wharton. Babcock is introduced to Arlina at one of her Wednesday salons when she, married to a now impotent but complaisant invalid, is at the height of her fame. She takes a fancy to Martin, quoting to him from James's prefaces, and at one of her parties Martin meets Hiram Scudder. From one of Scudder's letters, now in the archives of a university, comes an initial description of Martin:

> Few of Arlina's friends felt that he was worthy of the affection she lavished on him. It is always sad to see a person of the first order chained to one of a baser tier. Martin undeniably had charm and a kind of elfin beauty. He seemed to be trying, by a sort of osmosis, to imbibe from more gifted souls some of the talent with which he had not been endowed. But *his* soul, like his personal stature, was small; he was a busy little animal who played below the belt with both sexes and had no real concept of what went on in their minds or hearts. (*YE*, 58)

After quoting this passage, Martin comments, "Not below *your* belt, horrid old man, embracing young men in homoerotic hugs and extolling their youth and vigor with your stale breath!" These words surely capture James as he behaved in his latter years toward the young men he was interested in, of whom Fullerton was one. A letter from James to Fullerton in 1900 is an effusion in no uncertain terms: "You are dazzling, my dear Fullerton; you are beautiful; you are more than tactful, you are tenderly, magically *tactile*" (*SHJ*, 325). Yet the role that Scudder plays in the story is one that James would have found abhorrent, although in certain aspects the tale extends and embroiders facts about James. James accompanied Wharton and Fullerton when they met clandestinely in a hotel in London, and he had tea with them. But that is a far cry from acting as a pander, which is exactly what Scudder does. He encourages Fullerton to have an affair with Edith Wharton:

> It was Hiram Scudder who first hinted to me that my project was not entirely unfeasible. I had become a great favorite of the paunchy, bald old boy, who was always asking me to lunch, ostensibly to discuss my writing but really to hold forth about his own, and we would walk slowly down the avenue after-

wards, his arm entwined with mine while he chanted about what he would do if he had again, like me, "a manly vigor and youth." In parting he would seize my head with both his hands and plant a wet kiss, presumably of benediction, upon my forehead. Perhaps he thought of the emotion I aroused in him as paternal. . . . Hiram was a bachelor and very possibly a virgin to both sexes. Such things were not uncommon to his generation. (*YE*, 73)

The affair blossoms. It collapses only when Scudder pays a visit to an old, openly homosexual sculptor, Dan Carmichael, who has persuaded Martin to pose in the nude for him, as well as to allow him to make love to him. Scudder breaks into the studio during a posing session, and the "jealous Hiram's lecherous eyes" at once take in the situation. He writes to Arlina, telling her about her lover's infidelity.

It is difficult to believe that Auchincloss would want the pimping side of his fictitious character to be seen as springing from the real-life James. But the unfulfilled homoeroticism of the older James is surely made the most of in a tale that does reproduce with considerable precision the triadic relationship between James, Wharton, and Fullerton. Auchincloss' adroit but somewhat disillusioned portrait of James suggests that he has come out from under the Master's influence and is ready to parody the writer as a more or less grotesque and pitiful character.

Virginia Woolf's Mr. Fortescue in *Night and Day*

The reason we are taking out of its normal chronology the portrait of Mr. Fortescue as Henry James in Virginia Woolf's early novel *Night and Day* (1920) is to put it beside Auchincloss' Hiram Scudder, a portrait of James that is truly postmodern in its view of the Master as an invert, a gossip, and one who lived off others' experiences. For Woolf, who joined the nineteenth century to the twentieth, James was the elder statesman who was part of her father Leslie Stephen's circle. Mr. Fortescue opens *Night and Day* during a tea party, and he is a figure who contrasts better than any other portrait with the figure recreated by our contemporaries. On the novel's second page, a character enters just "as Mr. Fortescue, the eminent novelist, reached the middle of a very long sentence," which he kept "suspended while the newcomer sat down" (*ND*, 10). This sentence puts the knowledgeable reader into the very heart of Woolf's portrait of Henry James. Mr. Fortescue's vivid appearance begins the book's action, but he disappears after he has made an impression on Mrs. Hilberg, who appears at the gathering with an expression on her face "as if a scene from the drama of the younger generation were being played for her benefit" (*ND*, 20–21). The first word she speaks involves Mr. Fortescue: "The truth is, dear Mr. Fortescue has almost tired me out. He is so eloquent and so witty, so searching and so profound that . . . I feel inclined to turn out all the lights" (*ND*, 21). I see the words "the younger generation" as a conscious reminder of James's epoch-making essay of that name. Woolf had been writing for the *Times Literary Supplement* since 1905, and the essay most surely was known to her. As for her view of James as a figure, we learn from a letter she wrote to Stephen Spender in 1935 that James "loomed up in my young days almost to the obstruction of his works."[6] James's benign figure "obstructed" his works, and no matter how hard critics have tried to find James's influence in Woolf's fiction, the evidence is, as Daniel Mark Fogel proves in *Covert Relations*, his book on James Joyce and Virginia Woolf, covert: "James stirs beneath the arras, as it were, throughout Woolf's novel" (*CR*, 137). Yet Fogel sees that her portrait "embodies a strategy of emptying Henry James of his divinity" (*CR*, 137). Thus, in her own way, Virginia Woolf prepares us for Hiram Scudder of 1994.

6.   See Nigel Nicolson and Joanne Trautman, eds., *The Letters of Virginia Woolf: Volume Five, 1932–35* (New York, 1979). See Fogel's *Covert Relations*, 130–37, for further details of Mr. Fortescue as Henry James.

HENRY JAMES: HIS LEGACY

5

JAMES AND HIS CONTEMPORARIES

There are many twentieth-century descendants of Henry James, but it is
not the legacy James left to twentieth-century criticism that is the topic
here. Rather, my concern is with how creative writers of this century
have handled their inheritance of the 20 novels and 112 short stories by
James. The vast critical apparatus that surrounds his fiction has meant that
different people read him in different ways, but what I address is the reading by the writers and short-story tellers of our time. It is now a question
not of the figure of the master of the art of fiction but of the appropriation
of his work.

Joseph Conrad Meets James

In 1898, when James moved to Rye, he came to an area where Joseph Conrad (1857–1924) had also settled and where their first meeting, which had
occurred in February, 1897, could lead to others (Figure 13). Conrad, who
was a long-standing admirer of James's work, had sent him an inscribed
copy of *An Outcast of the Islands* in October, 1896, shortly after its publication. James probably read this, the first sample Conrad tendered him of his
fiction, because he was then writing *What Maisie Knew* and would have
been interested in the little girl in Conrad's book, Nina, Almayer's daugh-

13. *A Memory of Henry James and*
Joseph Conrad Conversing, by Max Beerbohm

Reprinted by kind permission of the Max Beerbohm Estate, London Management

ter, who is clever and quick and, like Maisie, has the childish inability to put adult behavior into words. Conrad wrote, "Small children have many more perceptions than they have terms to translate them; their vision is at any moment much richer, their comprehension . . . stronger than . . . their reproducible vocabulary."[1] Yet Nina is the opposite of Maisie in that her father has pampered her and has transferred his worship of idols to the worship of his little girl. Maisie has not been similarly coddled. James expressed his pleasure in Conrad's novel by sending him "The Spoils of Poynton." In 1898, "The Turn of the Screw" appeared in *The Two Magics*, and it impressed Conrad immensely.

In the table of contents of a copy of Conrad's *Youth*, of 1902, which also contains "Heart of Darkness" and "The End of the Tether," Olive Garnett wrote, "Henry James liked this best," under the latter title. It probably interested James that the blindness of the central character, Captain Whalley, is not revealed until the last part of the story, though there are clues throughout (*Y*, 235). The mate Massy, wishing to get rid of Captain Whalley, carries soft iron in his pockets to deflect the magnetic needle of the ship. But Whalley feels Massy's coat, and "the game was up" (*Y*, 335). Before the captain goes down with his ship, he writes a letter to his daughter and leaves her five hundred pounds: "My dear, I am at the end of my tether" (*Y*, 338). In preferring this story to the other two in the collection, "Youth" and especially "Heart of Darkness," which has come to be considered Conrad's best, James was no doubt responding to the pathos of this courageous old man and Conrad's strategy of concealing the reasons for his behavior. Jack London reacted comparably and repeated the situation in *The Sea-Wolf*.[2]

Joseph Conrad, for his part, also liked some of James's stories more than others. In a copy of James's *The Lesson of the Master* that he gave to Edward Garnett, Garnett wrote in ink on the upper half of the inner title page, "This copy was given me by Joseph Conrad on a visit to Ivy Wells. Stanford-le-Hope." J. C. had a particular admiration for the story "Brooksmith," and in the same book he also liked the story "The Pupil."

When, in 1902, James read "The End of the Tether," he also read the accompanying "Heart of Darkness," which seems to have affected a passage

---

1. Joseph Conrad, *An Outcast of the Islands* (New York, 1926), 249.
2. Adeline R. Tintner, "Jack London's Use of Conrad's 'The End of the Tether' in *The Sea-Wolf*," *Jack London Newsletter*, XVII (1984), 61–66.

in the chapter he wrote for *The Whole Family,* a collaborative novel of 1908 with a dozen authors: "For, like all of us, she lives surrounded by the black forest of the 'facts of life' very much as the people in the heart of Africa live in their dense wilderness of nocturnal terrors, the mysteries and monstrosities that make them seal themselves up in the huts as soon as it gets dark."[3] James wrote this chapter during 1906, the year he was most intimate with Conrad.

Conrad's *The Secret Agent,* of 1907, employs a phrase out of James. Mr. Vladimir says to Mr. Verloc, "Couldn't you have managed without [marriage]? This is your virtuous attachment—eh?"[4] The phrase *virtuous attachment* is well known from *The Ambassadors,* referring there to Chad and Marie de Vionnet's relationship. The "red tip of the cigar seen for a few seconds in the dark" that James introduced into the 1907 revision of *Roderick Hudson* (*NYE,* 389) likely came from *Lord Jim,* of 1900, a novel he liked: "Perhaps it was the after dinner . . . in the deep dusk speckled by fiery cigar ends. . . . Now and then a small red glow would loom abruptly."[5]

When Conrad wrote to Garnett that James had sent him *The Spoils of Poynton* in return for the gift of *An Outcast of the Islands,* he remarked, admiringly, that James's mind seemed "like a great sheet of plate glass—you don't know it's there till you run against it."[6] But on reading *The Two Magics,* he had mixed feelings. "The Turn of the Screw" was published in 1898 in the Christmas number of *Collier's Weekly,* but when Conrad read it in *The Two Magics,* where it was followed by "Covering End," he wrote, "The first story is all there. He extracts an intellectual thrill out of the subject. The second is unutterable rubbish. Quite a shock to one of the faithful."[7] "The Turn of the Screw" left its impression on Conrad's mind, and he kept copying and getting ideas from it.

In "The New Novel," James wrote what amounted to a critical appreciation of Conrad, though at fifty-seven years Conrad was scarcely a new novelist. With regard to his latest novel, *Chance,* of 1912, James declared that his method was "without a precedent in any like work." He described Con-

---

3. William Dean Howells *et al., The Whole Family: A Novel by Twelve Authors* (New York, 1908), Chap. 7, pp. 144–45.

4. Joseph Conrad, *The Secret Agent* (New York, 1926), 36.

5. Joseph Conrad, *Lord Jim* (1900; rpr. New York, 1920), 24.

6. Frederick R. Karl and Laurence Davies, eds., *The Collected Letters of Joseph Conrad* (5 vols.; Cambridge, Eng., 1983), I, 339.

7. *Ibid.,* II, 111.

rad "as absolutely alone as a votary of the way to do a thing that shall make it undergo most doing. . . . To be 'art' exclusively or to be nothing" (*EL*, 147). James did, nevertheless, criticize a foible apparent in this novel that seems engendered by the author's infatuation with "The Turn of the Screw." James complained that Conrad was guilty of "so multiplying his creators or . . . producers as to make them almost more numerous . . . than the creatures and the production itself. . . . Mr. Conrad's first care is . . . to set up a reciter . . . who immediately proceeds to set up another, to the end that this other may conform again to the practice" (*EL*, 148). When James resorted to the device of the narrator within the narrator in the prologue to "The Turn of the Screw," he quickly moved on to the governess' version of the story. But James believed that in *Chance*, shifting the narrative from one reporter to another resulted in a "general and diffused lapse of authenticity" (*EL*, 150).

Among other ostensible carry-overs from "The Turn of the Screw" in *Chance*, the young heroine's given name, Flora, is that of James's little girl; and Flora's governess, unnamed by Conrad as by James, is the evil influence that many in the end have come to the conclusion James's governess is. But Conrad's governess is an obvious villainess. Her behavior is not something that needs interpretation; it is obvious and is accorded authorial comment. Like James's governess, she is "very jealous of any outside influence" (*CH*, 89). She is "apparently shy, but . . . probably nursing under a diffident manner a considerable amount of secret arrogance," and she is "hatching a most sinister plot under her air of distant, fashionable exclusiveness" (*CH*, 90). Her scheme involves marrying off someone she calls her nephew, who is really her impoverished lover, to Flora the heiress. But when Flora's father loses his money, the forty-year-old governess decamps with her lover, leaving Flora alone in the household. Conrad presented Flora, who is sixteen, as if she were a child as small as James's Flora. As the governess goes from the house, she berates the girl, who has the "feeling of being personally attacked" (*CH*, 116). "The wretch put her face close to mine and I could not move" (*CH*, 118). This is resonant of the final scene the governess has in "The Turn of the Screw," when she holds Flora's brother, Miles, closely and terrifies him, it has to be believed, to death. After the governess abandons Flora, she flees to her friends, the Fynes, "To resist what? Force or corruption?" (*CH*, 126)—evincing another kinship with "The Turn of the Screw."

Conrad's preference for "Brooksmith," the tale of a butler, may bespeak a sympathy for the oversensitive character who cannot accept the downhill course of his life, a type he wrote about throughout his career. Conrad, who felt that James was an impersonal artist and craftsman, must have approved of the compassion that James showed for his butler hero. The subject of this story is straightforward and does not touch on anything as elaborate as the conundrum at the center of "The Lesson of the Master," of 1892, or the unresolved reasons for the death of Morgan Moreen in "The Pupil," of 1891. Comparably with Conrad's heroes, Brooksmith cannot endure the loss of his utopian garden, and although his ultimate "doom" is obscure (VIII, 31), there is no ambiguity about his loss of the desire to live after the exigencies of life expel him from his eden. The plot is simple, unusually so for James but in consonance with Conrad's. The legacy Conrad gained from James occurred through mutual influences by two strong writers rather than through one-way transmission.

Ernest Dowson and James

Ernest Dowson (1867–1900), that peculiar genius of the fin de siècle, was smitten with James's earlier works from his youth. His collaborative novel *A Comedy of Masks*, of 1893, is strongly imitative of certain basic structures in *Roderick Hudson*, of 1876. A book of his short stories, *Dilemmas*, published in 1894, is dependent on such stories by James as "The Diary of a Man of Fifty," of 1879, and "Madame de Mauves," of 1874, as well as on two of James's early novels, *Watch and Ward*, of 1878, and *The American*, of 1877.

Dowson's life was somewhat irregular. The son of a literate and intelligent man who met Robert Louis Stevenson on his journeys, he was the inheritor of a London dry dock property that had been extremely productive and lucrative for his family. But as Ernest grew up, the dry dock company became unprofitable, and he was eventually reduced to living in a derelict house that had been the company's office. Without any education except home instruction, Dowson managed to matriculate at Queen's College, Oxford, but he left after the family fortune failed.

His letters to Arthur Moore, a friend from Oxford, made plain the works of literature he admired. In addition to Ivan Turgenev, Gustave Flaubert, and George Meredith, there was Henry James, whom he preferred to them all (*LED*, 10). He seems to have been involved in love affairs with very young girls, and he tried to educate one of them "to the point of view of James" (*LED*, 49). In April, 1889, he wrote, "I haven't seen the new edition of the Master"—which the editors say may have been the "'yellowback' reprint of *Washington Square*" (*LED*, 60). Five days later he reflected, in connection with a young girl, "I am in the condition of the perplexed lover in 'Daisy Miller.' Is she amazingly innocent or impudence personified?" (*LED*, 62). No matter the level of education of Lena, his young girl friend, he decided that he was "going to send her a James—'The Madonna of the Future' vol. 1 tomorrow. *Will* she appreciate it???" (*LED*, 63). When Lena at last fled, he was reminded of James: "Do you remember the episode of Mdlle Niniche [*sic*] in 'The American'?" (*LED*, 87). In comparing writers, he ventured, "But when you come to delicacy—subtlety— there is only H. James & his master, Tourguénef of novelists" (*LED*, 93). That same year he postured, "There is nothing in the universe supportable save the novels of Hy. James, & the society of little girls" (*LED*, 108). When, a little later, he was reading "Stendhal . . . Turgénef . . . —Balzac," he concluded that "the three above-named masters are responsible for the evolution of Hy. James" (*LED*, 112). He bade Moore, who was collaborating with him on the novel *A Comedy of Masks*, to "go on writing Chapters like . . . that [of] Elsie [reflecting more of] Pansy [from the] 'Portrait of a Lady,'" with the consequence that the novel would draw on James's characters for their own (*LED*, 118). He said that *Partial Portraits* "fill[s] me with wonder & amazement" (*LED*, 132). He commended Browning's work for some resemblance to James's: "'My Last Duchess,' *par example*, is pure Henry James" (*LED*, 146). Here it is interesting to note that James in a tale of 1868, "The Story of a Masterpiece," had assigned the title *My Last Duchess* to a painting of the young man's fiancée that the jealous suitor hacks and destroys.

Dowson did not think much of William Dean Howells' *The Rise of Silas Lapham*, considering it "banal" and mere reportage. "Thank god for James!" he countered (*LED*, 184). In 1891, he looked forward to April, because it would "bring with it the rest of 'The Pupil'" (*LED*, 189). He did not care for Nathaniel Hawthorne, although "Henry James, as you know, rates Hawthorne high" (*LED*, 199). He adverted to "James['s] study of Hawthorne, which, I admit, with shame, I prefer to anything Hawthorne has done himself" (*LED*, 201). When he traveled on the Continent, he contemplated sending a letter from Saint-Germain-en-Laye, "which you will remember, like a good student of James, was the place where the young American met Madame de Mauve[s]" (*LED*, 336).

But it was Roderick Hudson with whom he identified: "If you could realize the immense temptation I have to retire like Roderick Hudson to my sofa, and lie with my eyes shut smelling a rose" (*LED*, 221). *A Comedy of Masks* is really modeled less on *The Portrait of a Lady* than on *Roderick Hudson*.[8] In the collaborative novel, there are two friends, as in *Roderick Hudson:* Philip Rainham, a tubercular and pessimistic man, and his friend and protégé, Richard Lightmark, who as a painter is an artist like the sculptor Roderick. Philip, who stands to Richard as Rowland Mallet does to his protégé, Roderick, lives in a London dry dock like the one in which Dowson grew up. Philip allows Richard to use a set of rooms there for painting. His effect is to restrain Dick's behavior. He too loves the girl Dick is to marry, as Rowland and Roderick both love Mary Garnett. Philip exceeds Dick's age by about ten years, roughly the same margin by which Rowland exceeds Roderick's. Dick is on a downhill course like Roderick, but Dick has fallen farther than Roderick. He is a cheat, a liar, and a seducer, which James's hero is not.

A circle of artists and writers meets in Dick's studio in the dry dock — corresponding to the circle in Rome of which Rowland and Roderick are part. Dick is engaged to Eve, the young woman who as a child Philip has loved. Into this basic situation paralleling *Roderick Hudson* certain elements from *The Portrait of a Lady* wedge. Philip is dying from tuberculosis, as Ralph Touchett is. Philip is in love with Eve, and in order to keep her from being hurt, he asserts responsibility for the child Dick has fathered by another woman. Philip dies, but he allows Eve to know that "she has been fervently loved."[9] In this he behaves much like the dying Ralph Touchett, who reveals his love to Isabel.

After Dowson's death, Arthur Moore wrote to Mark Longaker, the biographer of Dowson, "I believe that we discussed little else but Henry James . . . and I recall that it was not long after that I read a paper on the subject of this author to a College Literary society (the 'Addison') of which we were both members" (LO, 30). Moore continued, "It was, in fact, the discovery that we were both enthusiastic about the earlier work of Henry James which first brought us together in our Oxford days" (LO, 125).

In *Dilemmas*, the collection of stories Dowson brought out during the year following *A Comedy of Masks*, almost every story ends with a series of

---

8. A two-volume set of the 1883 Macmillan edition with Dowson's signature is in my possession.

9. Ernest Dowson in Collaboration with Arthur Moore, *A Comedy of Masks* (London, 1893), 30.

unanswered questions, in the way of James's "The Diary of a Man of Fifty." But James's tale is reflected most clearly in Dowson's story of almost the same name, "The Diary of a Successful Man." Here the narrator, Lorimer, is fifty years old, like James's nameless narrator, and like him, he revisits the old house where, twenty years before, lived the countess he loved. Dowson's Countess Savaresse, whose name has at least a passing resemblance to that of James's Countess Salvi-Scarabelli, is also a widow. The section of James's "Madame de Mauves" in which the narrator sees the painter and his girl friend together on a picnic, with the girl reading Chenier's poems to him, makes it into Dowson's tale, but Dowson's girl sings little French songs. As in "The Diary of a Man of Fifty," an older man in "The Diary of a Successful Man" advised the young man not to marry the woman he loved, and the young man took the advice. In James's tale, the disappointed man asks himself, in the last words of the story, "*Was* I wrong—*was* it a mistake? Was I too cautious—too logical?" (IV, 425).

The mistake in Dowson's tale, "The Diary of a Successful Man," is that of the woman, who marred her happiness by sending the letter of rejection to the wrong suitor, the narrator, whom she loved. When she asked Lorimer to tell the narrator that he was the one she chose, Lorimer never gave him the message (*DI*, 18). She became a nun, and they go hear her voice dominate the choral singing. This episode springs from *The American*, in which Newman goes to the Convent of the Carmelites and thinks he hears the voice of Madame de Cintré.

It is striking that *Dilemmas* anticipated, in indicating the form of its content, James's first named collection, *Terminations*, which did not appear until the next year, 1895. In "An Orchestral Violin," another of the stories in *Dilemmas*, the influence of James's *Watch and Ward* is evident, in keeping with the intense interest Moore testified to on the part of him and Dowson in James's earlier fiction. The narrator of "An Orchestral Violin" is taken to *Fidelio* to hear a famous opera singer whom his friend says he found and developed. When the opera singer was a small child, the friend adopted her after her father's death, but he then fell in love with her. That is the basic plot of *Watch and Ward*, as well. When the friend in Dowson's tale dies, he leaves the narrator his violin. The narrator meets the opera singer, and she asks him to bring the violin to her house, but he shrinks from that, because she is a dangerous woman. He asks himself, "Pusillanimous or simply prudent? . . . It is a point I have never been able to decide. . . . Have I been pusillanimous, prudent or merely cruel? For the life of me I cannot say!" (*DI*,

84–85). The question has the flavor of James's last lines in "The Diary of a Man of Fifty."

These stories, now out of print, had a certain vogue in their day. Dowson, who died in 1900, never knew James's later novels and stories. It is an open question whether James, who touched on the "larger latitude" in his *Yellow Book* story "The Death of the Lion," was aware of how he held a notorious decadent of the fin de siècle in thrall.

"Our Hichens": James's "In the Cage" and Robert Hichens' *The Londoners*

Although James insisted he was amused by Max Beerbohm's parody of his prose in "The Mote in the Middle Distance," it is not certain he found it droll when Robert Hichens (1864–1950), in *The Green Carnation*, of 1894, asserted that it was James's habit to leave a party as soon as "he has thought of a clever thing. . . . He rushes home to write his thoughts down."[10] The next year Hichens again required James's indulgence when he mentioned him in a witty playlet, *The New Lover*, written à la Gyp, the French writer. Mrs. Delane, a young widow in the play, explains that the "modern art of lovemaking" is very subtle. The new lover "will do and say nothing that is not restrained, light, cultured and artistic. You will assist at a scene from Henry James, not at one, from, shall we say, Rhoda Broughton. He will imply his proposal. I shall infer my acceptance."[11]

Hichens recorded in his autobiography, *Yesterday*, that as a young man he often had tea with other young literary people and Henry James at Lamb House and that he knew well James's friends Antonio and Mary Anderson Navarro.[12] Their relationship seems to have been friendly, and on James's part benevolent. Hichens had great respect for him and not only brought him into his work twice by name but apparently also felt he was sufficiently a classical source that it was permissible to grab one of his famous lines.

There is a curious resemblance between Hichens's *The Londoners*, of 1898, and James's "In the Cage," of the same year. Both works were published by the same publisher in Chicago. It is as if James was demonstrat-

10.   [Robert Hichens], *The Green Carnation* (London, 1894), 127–28.
11.   Robert Hichens, *After Tomorrow* (New York, 1895), 55.
12.   Robert Hichens, *Yesterday* (London, 1947), *passim*.

ing in his long tale what Hichens kept saying over and over again metaphorically, that is, that society is a prison. Mrs. Verulam in Hichens' novel
wishes to leave London society, because it has for her become confining,
"like the cage of my squirrel," with the women the "wretched captives."[13]
There are at least six drawn-out figures of speech in which the cage is a referent. Finally, when the heroine's friend, Chloe, who dresses like a man and
passes for one, compromises Mrs. Verulam, she has "opened the cage-door
to the squirrel."[14]

In James's tale, a telegraph operator occupies a cage in a grocery store.
The members of London society whom she serves are freer of physical
curbs than she, but rescue from the disastrous mistakes in which their in-
trigues enmesh them comes only by virtue of a free mind like hers. Who anticipated whom in these two stories is a teasing question, just as it is provoc-
ative to ask whether Hichens's popular *The Garden of Allah*, published in
1904, contributed something to the vivid figures involving the African desert in especially the last part of James's *The Golden Bowl*, which was not
published until November of that year. In at least one instance, however,
the direction of dependence is patent. In *Barbary Sheep*, of 1907, Hichens
wrote, "She did not love him, yet she felt a strong inclination to follow him
and to obey him. It was as if he held in his hands a thin cord to which she
was attached, and whenever he pulled, however gently, at this cord she felt
that she must move in the direction he desired. . . . She was conscious of the
subtle tugging."[15] Compare this figure of speech with James's in *The Golden
Bowl:* "[It is as] if he had been thought of as holding in one of his pocketed
hands the end of a long silken halter looped round her beautiful neck. He
didn't twitch it, yet it was there; he didn't drag her, but she came" (*GB*, 491–
92). James's metaphor appeared almost four years before Hichens'.

Hichens redid "The Jolly Corner" in a story of a double involving a clergyman and his weaker subordinate: "Chichester seemed to suck my will
away from me."[16] The connection with "The Jolly Corner" is just as obvious in another passage of the story: "But if, by a miracle, the average self-
contented man could look at himself with the eyes of his soul full of sublim-
inal self-knowledge . . . he would be stricken down by a great horror."[17] In

13.   Robert Hichens, *The Londoners* (Chicago, 1898), 13.

14.   *Ibid.*, 273.

15.   Robert Hichens, *Barbary Sheep* (New York, 1907), 221.

16.   Robert Hichens, *The Dweller on the Threshold* (New York, 1911), 161.

17.   *Ibid.*, 115.

Bella Donna, of 1909, Hichens seizes a well-known line from James's "The Two Faces," of 1900: "But the face—the face!"[18] The phrase is a copy of the one in James's tale even to the punctuation (XI, 254).

In 1911, James wrote a letter to Edith Wharton referring to a play based on *Bella Donna* as a "dramatization of our Hichens—yours and mine, the one we back so against Lady True Benson."[19] This private response to *Bella Donna* suggests that both James and Wharton were rather fond of Hichens. Although the letter does not go into any detail, it is common knowledge that this charming, cultivated extra man who had traveled so much in the East was a familiar of many of London's drawing rooms, where he was accustomed to see James and Wharton.

A Tribute to James's "The Abasement of the Northmores" and "Sir Dominick Ferrand": Thomas Hardy's "The Unconquerable"

Michael Millgate, Thomas Hardy's biographer, has researched the sticky relationship between James and Hardy (1840–1928). He holds that Hardy learned to "dislike James as a man, much as he always admired him as an artist" (MI, 208). The unfavorable review James gave *Tess of the d'Urbervilles,* of 1891, could not have pleased Hardy at the time, and "when he learned, years after the event, that Henry James and Robert Louis Stevenson had exchanged views on what they considered the abominable style and factitious sexuality of *Tess of the d'Urbervilles,*" he exclaimed, "How indecent of those two virtuous females to expose their mental nakedness in such a manner" (MI, 373). Yet, in spite of his personal dislike of James, he praised him "for being a dedicated artist, a real man of letters" (MI, 374).

Millgate asserts that "at one time [Hardy] thought of rewriting some of his early hurried and immature novels, nobody knowing their faults better than he did. But, being convinced that no really live and creative minds ever condescended to such tinkering, it being the mark rather of uninventive and plodding temperaments, he left the faulty novels alone, taking the tack of showing his enlarged perceptions by creating entirely new work" (MI, 352). That Hardy may have had Henry James especially in mind is

18.   Robert Hichens, *Bella Donna* (New York, 1911), 117.

19.   Lyall H. Powers, ed., *Henry James and Edith Wharton: Letters, 1900–1915* (New York, 1990), 198.

plausible in light of some recollections a visitor to his home, Max Gate, heard from him in 1920: "Hardy noticed the fastidious retouching in which Meredith and Henry James habitually indulged. He became particularly entertaining when speaking of James's fondness for emendation. Hardy had asked him if he ever saw his work finished, completed. No, James had replied, it was never finished because he was never satisfied with it and he believed in constant revision. Hardy looked upon that as a sort of 'eternal proofreading'" (MI, 354). James's notorious review of *Far from the Madding Crowd*, of 1874, in the *Nation*, with his call for novelists to observe the three unities, may conceivably have prompted Hardy to attend to the unities more scrupulously four years later in *The Return of the Native*. But his description of James as the "Polonius of novelists" encapsulates his attitude to James's acknowledgment of a fondness for form.

According to *The Early Life of Thomas Hardy*, of 1928—which Hardy wrote but which listed his wife, Florence Emily Hardy, as author—when he read James's *Reverberator*, of 1888, his reaction was to think that "after this kind of work one feels inclined to be purposefully careless in detail. The great novels of the future will certainly not concern themselves with minutiae of manners. James's subjects are those one could be interested in at moments when there is nothing larger to think of" (MI, 227). Yet it is of significance that Hardy should have been reading James at all and that, though he rarely permitted himself a comment on a contemporary author, he should have recorded his opinions. Surviving notebooks show that he also read other books of James's, including *Roderick Hudson*, and *Hawthorne*, of 1879. In 1919, he was recorded as saying that, although he could read only a page or two of Meredith, "Henry James he could always read to the end." He had thought independently of many of the subjects James chose, such as that of *The Wings of the Dove*, about a man marrying a woman and knowing that she was going to die (MI, 358). But when he first read that novel, he and his wife entirely failed to agree on what actually happens in the novel.

It is only with the appearance in 1992 of a volume of hitherto unpublished short stories, some by Hardy alone and some written in collaboration with others, that an instance—an unusual and unexpected one—of Hardy's indebtedness to James for several fictional ideas has come to light. The story is "The Unconquerable," written with Florence Dugdale, probably in 1912, before she became his wife, and it amounts to an amazing reworking of two stories by James, "Sir Dominick Ferrand," of 1893, and

"The Abasement of the Northmores," of 1900. It is the best tale in the volume.

"The Unconquerable" focuses on the dominant will of Roger Wingate and the submission of the narrator of the tale, Philip Fadelle, to it. The story is also about the finding and burning of a set of compromising letters. These are themes conspicuous in "The Abasement of the Northmores." In addition, there is the high-minded destruction of letters in "Sir Dominick Ferrand."

"The Abasement of the Northmores" revolves around two men—Lord Northmore, who became successful in life by exploiting the talent of his best friend, and Warren Hope, that friend, whose wife, after his death, is the virtual narrator of the tale. Lady Northmore writes to all her husband's friends to collect her late husband's letters for a memorial volume. Mrs. Hope returns his letters to her husband in good faith, but Lady North-more's volume is monotonous and receives bad reviews. When Mrs. Hope decides to collect her husband's letters for a similar volume, she discovers that no one has kept them, since he did not seem important enough for that. Mrs. Hope's reprisal is to do an edition of her husband's letters to her, nota-ble for their literary excellence, which she reduces to one volume. She plans for this edition to be published after her death, when it will expose the superiority of her husband's talent to Northmore's. Although Mrs. Hope also had a packet of love letters in Lord Northmore's hand to her, she destroys them once her feelings of injury are assuaged.

In this tale, a cache of letters sets in stark relief a relationship between a dominant character and a submissive one, between a successful scoundrel, a nonentity on his merits, and a man of integrity but of timid and weak resolution. Mrs. Hope tells her husband, after they have been to Lord Northmore's funeral and just before he dies, "He never recognised you, but he never let you go. You kept him up, and he kept you down. He used you, to the last drop he could squeeze. . . . He made his way on your back. . . . *You* were his gift!" (XI, 113). Hardy's point about the two men in "The Un-conquerable" is essentially the same.

That tale, from the very first paragraph, is more in the vein of James than in that of Hardy: "There were times when Philip Fadelle acknowl-edged to himself with a sense of amusement not untinged with bitterness that even death had scarce succeeded in tempering the force of that inflex-ible will which he had ever recognized as an essential part of the being of his friend Roger Wingate" (*EC*, 357). The style announces the entrance into James's territory. The central consciousness here is Philip Fadelle's, in a shift to the vanquished but surviving rival for the beloved woman from the woman herself in "The Abasement of the Northmores." In Hardy's tale, Fadelle's courtship of Gertrude Wingate is doomed even when he has every advantage after Wingate's death. That enables a heightening of amatory pathos, imparting great unity to the plot.

The opposition between the two men's characters—one an "astute and rising young politician," the other a "struggling man of letters" (*EC*, 357)—is directly from "The Abasement of the Northmores." But Fadelle is less effective as a defender of his own interests than even Warren Hope, because Hope gets the girl both favor but Fadelle loses out on her all the way. When, earlier in life, he could have proposed, he "linger[ed] irresolutely a day or two in an old Cathedral town" (*EC*, 358) while Wingate proposed and was accepted. Wingate has guaranteed his subservience by appointing him his biographer.

A statement by Gertrude Wingate supports the inference that Hardy had beside him "The Abasement of the Northmores," which was first published in the collection *The Soft Side*, of 1900, and then republished in the New York Edition, of 1909. In Hardy's tale, Gertrude tells Fadelle, "Sometimes I am afraid that [the biography] is going to be something of an obsession" (*EC*, 361), echoing Mrs. Hope's situation of being "perfectly aware that her obsession had run away with her" (XI, 122)—the obsession, that is, of her husband's worth and Northmore's mediocrity.

Gertrude returns to a large packet of letters she had ignored before in the drawer of a bureau and tells Phillip Fadelle to go over them. The letters leave no doubt that Wingate betrayed both his country and his wife. In typical Jamesian fashion, Fadelle, whom Gertrude has told that loyalty to her husband makes it impossible she should remarry, burns the evidence, as Mrs. Hope burns Northmore's love letters to her.

Peter Baron in James's "Sir Dominick Ferrand" also destroys letters. When he finds communications in his davenport involving the paternity of the woman he loves, he has no hesitation about protecting her from scandal. In Hardy's tale, a man who has been exploited by a glamorous yet unscrupulous friend destroys the evidence that would incriminate the exploiter, but there is a difference between Fadelle and James's doers of the noble thing. In "The Abasement of the Northmores," Mrs. Warren Hope has grounds for hoping that the privately printed volume of her husband's letters will eventually redeem his reputation, but in Hardy there is no comparable hope for the victim of another's selfish control. Fadelle has from beginning to end been Wingate's tool. It is enough for Gertrude to show him a letter from Wingate telling her that he trusts the loyalty of Fadelle as the only friend in his life for Fadelle's self-assertiveness to be snuffed out so that he leaves without making use of the material that could have won him the hand of the widow. Hardy's undeviating determinism rules in this and all his tales. Fadelle, even in his moment of moral triumph, acknowledges his "weakness" (*EC,* 368), for "the opportunity had presented itself so aptly, and yet he had omitted to make use of it" (*EC,* 367). Wingate "from the other side of the grave . . . had played his last cards and won" (*EC,* 370). A rogue who has "lied and cheated in a calm deliberate manner, using . . . that unconquerable will," wins in life and death (*EC,* 366). Hardy's tale in James's mode is a clear literary tribute, but he has given his reinvention his own theme.

A Minor Offstage Character in James's Life: Stark Young

The measure of James's reputation in the first decades of the century is the way the publication of a letter of his to Stark Young (1881–1963), an unknown young man, made Young's career as a writer. The transaction between James and Young began in a comedy of errors. Somehow, Fanny Prothero, a friend of Henry James's who had invited the young Stark to tea while he was visiting London in 1913, got the impression from his perfunctory politeness that he was interested in advice on how to read James's novels. She interceded with James, who enclosed in an envelope marked "For the Young Man from Texas" a response that enthusiastically directed someone he did not know and whom he would never meet in a course of reading his work. What James wrote may not constitute the most important letter in his vast correspondence. But to the nonspecialist world it is surely his most famous, the most charming, and in a way the saddest. Believed lost in a fire and known only through an incorrect copy and Stark Young's comments, it has recently turned up intact and is accompanied by the letter from Young making a gift of it to Mrs. Isaacs, his patroness.[20] For

---

The material in this section appeared in somewhat different form as "Henry James and Stark Young: The Correct Version of the Legendary Letter," in *American Literature,* LVII (1985), 318–21.

20.   Adeline R. Tintner, "Henry James and Stark Young: The Correct Version of the Legendary Letter," *American Literature,* LVII (1985), 318.

James it was enough that a young man wanted to read him. Not many people did. To one who "shows such excellent dispositions," James suggests

as alternatives these 2 slightly differing lists.

1/ Roderick Hudson
2/ The Portrait of a Lady
3/ The Princess Casamassima
4/ The Wings of a Dove
5/ The Golden Bowl.

1 The American
2 The Tragic Muse
3 The Wings of a Dove
4 The Ambassadors
5 The Golden Bowl.

The second list is, as it were, the more "advanced." And when it comes to the Shorter Tales the question is more difficult (for characteristic selection) & demands separate treatment. Come to me about that, dear Young Man from Texas, later on—you shall have your little tarts when you have eaten your beef & potatoes. Meanwhile receive this from our admirable friend Mrs. Prothero. Henry James.[21]

Young related the circumstances of the letter with humor and candor in *The Pavilion*, of 1948. "Considering my earlier connections with the novel

21. *Ibid.*, 318–19. The text of the letter has been recently corrected by Leon Edel in *Selected Letters of Henry James* (Cambridge, Eng., 1987) after the publication in *American Literature* of an accurate version. All three previously published copies of the letter—Lubbock's, Young's in *The Pavilion*, and Edel's of 1984—show errors when compared with the original. The most significant occurs in the last sentence, where the original letter reads, "Meanwhile receive this from our admirable friend Mrs. Prothero," followed by the writer's signature, "Henry James." In Lubbock we read, "Meanwhile receive this from your admirable friend, Mrs. Prothero, HENRY JAMES" (LU, II, 333), showing a substitution of "your" for "our," an understandable error by the original copyist, since James contracted the handwriting in order to get the last line on the page. Edel's 1984 version reads, "Meanwhile receive this from your admirable friend Henry James" (L, IV, 683). Here the omission of "Mrs. Prothero" makes Henry James Stark Young's "admirable friend," very unlikely wording, since the two had never met. Other errors in earlier copies show the substitution of "different" for "differing" and a correction of what James wrote, "The Wings of a Dove," to "The Wings of the Dove," the real title of the novel.

as a literary form there is a certain irony in the fact that I should some day become the innocent object of a small degree of interest among students of Henry James and the recipient of one of his most famous letters," he wrote. Recalling how Mrs. Prothero, at tea, had taken "advantage of the moment to ask me what I had done about Mr. James' books," he recounted that he did not answer the "simple truth that I had never read anything of his except some scenes from *Daisy Miller* and the two volumes in purple moiré silk of *The Golden Bowl*." Here, however, his memory was fanciful, since there was never such an edition. He was thinking of the plum-colored cloth volumes of the New York Edition that he read "with limited enthusiasm" on shipboard, for he was "deep in *Wuthering Heights*." So indifferent was he to James that when he landed he gave the volumes to the customs inspector. He recognized, though, as a "painful truth" that it would have been "ungallant indeed" to tell Mrs. Prothero all this. "And so it came about that I said that Mr. James had written a great many books and I wondered where I should begin." Any one of Young's "Southern cousins would have understood that I meant I did not at the moment plan to begin at all," but the message was too nuanced for Mrs. Prothero. Instead, he was "greatly surprised soon after that to receive a letter from Mr. James, on blue stationery, in his own handwriting, with an envelope 'To a Charming Young Man From Texas,' in reply to my reported cry for guidance through a course in his works." After thirty years, Young got some of the details wrong. The envelope does not read, "To a Charming Young Man From Texas," but, "For the Young Man from Texas." The letter paper is off-white, not blue, with "Lamb House, Rye, Sussex" in centered red letters. This is James's regular writing paper of the period. But since Young did not keep the letter long, it is understandable that he forgot some particulars. In 1921, the year after Lubbock's collection of James's letters appeared, Young sent his letter, an inexact copy of which was included in the collection, to Mrs. Isaacs. An ardent fan of James, in contrast to her protégé, Mrs. Isaacs seems to have sensed the letter's historical importance, even beyond its importance to Young. For Young, the holograph was a watershed, since as soon as Lubbock's edition appeared, the young man was in possession of a literary reputation, with its basis only in the fact that he was James's "young man from Texas," irrespective of his Mississippi origins. The gift of the letter to Mrs. Isaacs was in gratitude for her generosity to him. He explained, "I brought it home and gave it to the Isaacs, who soon after lost it in a fire," adding, "None of that is of any great importance, but it is interesting to see how differently it adds up from the little myth that has accumulated around the actual circumstance."[22]

Young's letter to Mrs. Isaacs from 1921 is dated only "Amherst, Friday," but the contents disclose that it was written just after he returned from a trip to Europe eight years subsequent to the one in 1913. It has been reported how, "while abroad in the winter and spring of 1919–1920, . . . Young, perhaps rashly, resolved to sever his ties with Amherst; and in the fall he began his final year of teaching. . . . During the summer [of 1921], while once again in Europe, Young received an invitation to join the editorial staff of *Theatre Arts Magazine.* . . . In the fall of 1921, he moved to New York" (PI, 70). He probably wrote the letter to Mrs. Isaacs at the end of September or during the first few days in October. In it he touched on how the letter from James that he had promised her had turned up "in a mass of old papers." He went on, "You probably thought I had changed my mind since I promised it. As a matter of fact it gives me no end of satisfaction to give it to you, however much I hate to part with it."[23]

On October 18, 1920, some time after the publication of Lubbock's collection of James's letters, which had taken place in April, Young wrote to Julian Huxley, apparently responding to an inquiry about James's letter,

> The Henry James letter has an odd angle. It was ages ago, but I remember the occasion. Mrs. Prothero his good friend and daily visitor asked why I didn't read Mr. James. Instead of telling the truth I tried to be polite and said that I couldn't read them all, what should I begin on? She told Mr. James. If I had said the truth, which was that I admire him, think him very sure and true and delicate etc. I find his books not what I want to feed on when I read, since I don't like to read for mere diversion and gentle brooding as a rule — If I had said all that the result might have been different. *The Golden Bowl*, I'm damned if I'll read all that, though I could see how very good it was. But I prefer to watch people for myself often instead. (PI, 143)

When Bernard Bandler II asked him to write up the episode for the Henry James number of *Hound and Horn*, in 1932, Young replied that "it all comes out as a joke about that Henry James note to the 'dear young man from Texas.' I have never had much feeling for Henry James and the letter came about through some friends with whom I had been talking. I never took his

22. Stark Young, *The Pavilion* (New York, 1948), 131–32, 134.
23. Tintner, "Henry James and Stark Young," 321.

advice and read the book. If you would like a short account of how the letter came to be written, I should be delighted to write it out for you. It will have very little to do with Henry James" (PI, 392). Forewarned by that last sentence, Bandler published nothing about the letter.

It is obvious that Young wished to avert the natural inference by readers of the letter in Lubbock's edition that he liked James's work. When, in 1936, Allen Tate wrote Young that he felt James had refused to deal with nature directly, Young concurred: "You expressed exactly what I have felt—and more or less thought—about him for years." But that did not keep him from adding, "I suppose you have seen the celebrated letter to me in his published correspondence" (PI, 698). For despite criticizing James, Young continued proud of the letter. And regardless of his professed indifference, James appeared in his work. In his novel *The Torches Flare*, of 1928, Lena, the heroine, meets Mrs. Courtlandt, who lives close to Washington Square: "She had known every one to be known for two decades, Presidents of the United States, Chief Justices, and the writers and artists who flourished in the heyday of *The Century Magazine* and the epoch of Henry James and William Dean Howells."[24] Her house is open to Lena, the young actress. The air of her drawing room "seemed to say that history was long and human nature constant . . . and it was delicious to remember Henry James when they drove him up to see Broadway in its theatrical district of lights and blazing signs. 'Why,' he said, 'It's the effort of a mining town.' " [25] Fifteen years after the event, Henry James entered into Stark Young's imagination, but as a personality rather than the author of books he was never inclined to read.

Young's mixed feelings about the whole episode were not hard to understand. The irony of it was grist for his mill creatively. Young may have relished the contrast between his own lack of reverence for the Master and the Master's late works, on the one hand, and James's generosity to a young man unknown even by name to him, on the other. Certainly, he lived off his anecdote for many years. But in appreciating the irony of the situation, he in all likelihood also worried about how in the long run he would be remembered.

At least at one place in his work he gives evidence of having read James. In his first volume of theater criticism, *The Flower in Drama*, which he wrote

24. Stark Young, *The Torches Flare* (New York, 1928), 126.
25. *Ibid.*, 127.

in 1923, after only two years of doing reviews for *Theatre Arts Magazine* and a mere three years after he had been an offstage character in Lubbock's compilation, the opening chapter, "Acting," not only reflects James's enthusiasm for the French theater but also quotes from an essay by James. James's writing on the theater seems to have had a stronger effect on Young than the rest of his writing did, and the effect was in greatest evidence in Young's writing on the theater, published in four small books from 1923 to 1948, which many critics consider his most lasting contribution. Here is Young: "There is, of course, a vast amount of bad acting in France; but at its best French acting may easily be called the most discreet, the best regulated, the best placed of all. It exhibits not seldom a brilliantly *observed propriety* that might be said to affect one, as Henry James declared it affected him, as an almost celestial order."[26] Young was quoting verbatim from an essay by James on the French actor Constant Coquelin that had originally appeared in *Century* magazine in January, 1887, but that James thoroughly revised in 1915, when Brander Matthews, the theatrical historian and professor of drama at Columbia University, asked him to contribute it as an introduction to a translation of Coquelin's lecture *Art and the Actor*, in a series of books the Dramatic Museum at Columbia was publishing. In *Century* magazine, James had commented on the Théâtre Français: "I was dazzled by the unusual finish, by an element of control which at that time seemed to me supreme."[27] This he expanded in the introduction to *Art and the Actor*: "I remember that the first evenings I spent in the Rue de Richelieu I thought everyone equally good. I was dazzled by the general finish, by the harmony unbroken, a regulated tone and *observed propriety* which at that time affected me as an almost celestial order."[28] It was the revised essay that Young quoted, though he did not bother to put quotation marks around the phrases he repeated. He undoubtedly also looked into Coquelin's text for hints about how to proceed in his own disquisition on the art of acting.

In the "more 'advanced'" list that James put together for Young (see above, p. 159), *The Tragic Muse* appears, a novel about the theater, actors,

---

26. Stark Young, *The Flower in the Drama* (New York, 1923), 31 (italics mine).

27. Henry James, "Coquelin," *Century*, XXXIII (1887), 408.

28. Constant Coquelin, *Art and the Actor*, trans. Abby Langdon Alger, intro. Henry James, Dramatic Museum of Columbia University Papers on Acting, II (New York, 1915), italics mine. James's introduction is reprinted in a collection of his authorship, *The Scenic Art*, ed. Allan Wade (New Brunswick, N.J., 1948), 119–218; the passage in quotation marks is from pp. 201–202.

and actresses. Published in 1890 and ending James's early period, this would have struck someone who could not finish *The Golden Bowl* as much more readable. It would be a shame if Young did not delve into the book, for it concerns a passion like his for the theater. Peter Sherringham, a young diplomat, explains this passion as an art that is possible for him, who is neither a playwright nor an actor, by saying, "I am fond of representation—the representation of life: I like it better, I think, than the real thing. . . . One can lose oneself in it, and it has this recommendation (in common, I suppose, with the other arts) that the further you go in it the more you find" (*TM*, 78–91). Stark Young was in a sense Peter Sherringham come to life, if a novelist rather than a diplomat. To the degree that Peter was also part of James, the passionate theatergoer, and that the diversity of Young's writing emulates James's, Young and James turn out to intersect in their interests and accomplishments.

From Henry James there was never any follow-up on the letter to Young either in his letters to others or in anything conversational his friends have recorded. Leon Edel's biography (as well as Fred Kaplan's, of 1992, entitled *Henry James: The Imagination of Genius*) establishes that by 1913 James's homoerotic tastes were well established and his emotional dependence on the attractive young men writers he knew great. That a young man such as Stark Young, even if unseen, wanted very much—so James was told—to read his fiction, which at that moment was not doing particularly well, must have appealed to him. He rose to the bait with great enthusiasm.

The notion that the young man hailed from Texas was doubtless exciting to James, who in his lecture tour through the United States, in 1904–1905, had visited almost every part of the country except the Southwest. Texas was for him the unknown, the romantic spot beyond his acquaintance. In "The Siege of London," the Territories—from which Mrs. Headway, the beautiful and aggressive widow comes—were so vague in his mind that he put San Diego in the wrong place and made other geographical mistakes.[29] In the short story as it first appeared, in 1883, Texas was never mentioned, but in 1908, after the lecture tour, when James revised the tale for the New York Edition, he called Mrs. Headway the "well-known Texas belle" at least five times (*NYE*, XIV, 159, 181, 192, 195, 223)

---

29. George Monteiro, "Geography in 'The Siege of London,'" *Henry James Review*, IV (1983), 144–45.

and the "Texan belle" once (*NYE*, XIV, 242), and he applied *Texan* as an adjective to her twice (*NYE*, XIV, 176, 254).

The invitation James extended in his letter, to "come to me . . . , dear Young Man from Texas, later on" for advice about the shorter tales, intimates that he fully expected an answer from Young and that he probably thought it was the beginning of a lovely friendship. The short stories demanded "separate treatment," and Young would have his "little tarts" only after his "beef & potatoes."

JAMES AMONG THE MODERNS

I n the atmosphere of the 1920s and 1930s, the use authors made of Henry James altered.

Art Deco and the Turn of the Century Face-to-Face: Noël Coward and James

Noël Coward (1899–1973) often created titles out of quotations from literary masters. In *Remembered Laughter,* of 1976, he took his phrase from *Twelfth Night,* and in *Private Lives,* of 1930, he transformed James's "The Private Life" into a plural. One of the "pair of conceits" (*AN,* 252) on which James rested his tale "The Private Life," of 1893, was that of the double, with one man in society and his alter ego in private, the first a frivolous figure, the second a serious and great playwright. The other conceit behind the "piece of ingenuity" (*AN,* 249) was that of an artist who is there only when he is seen. James excused "this pair of conceits . . . under the plea of my amusement in them" and his wish that "others might succeed in sharing" the amusement (*FW,* 1253). The tale relates to the theater, in that the heroine is an actress and the men are playwrights, at least two of them, and a musician, besides the artist. But it is also theatrical insofar as its accumulation of paradoxical incidents and paradoxical language are adapted to a dramatic situation in a single setting. Between 1890 and 1895, James was writing mainly for the theater, and this was one of the few short stories he allowed himself as relief from his struggle for success on the stage. Confoundingly, James's most successful play, however, may have been this short tale. Blanche Adney, who has an adoring husband but who nonetheless exercises a seductive way with other males, is a thematic ancestor of Gilda in Coward's *Design for Living,* Judith Bliss in *Hay Fever,* and Amanda Prynne in *Private Lives.* *Private Lives* has been compared to Congreve's and Wilde's dramatic works, for paradox animates his play as much as it does James's tale. Doubling also takes place in *Private Lives,* and Coward also claimed that he had only a "talent to amuse." The doubling animates the whole of Act I. Elyot Chase and his new wife, Sibyl Chase, and Amanda, Elyot's former wife, and her new husband, Victor, occupy two adjacent suites in a Deauville hotel, as James's double Clare Vawdrey and the half-person Lord Mellifont occupy adjacent quarters in a Swiss resort hotel, an equally cosmopolitan setting. In rooms overlooking the harbor, as the rooms in James's Swiss hotel look out on an alp, Amanda and Elyot, who have married on the rebound, are for a while unaware that they have landed in such close proximity, but after they recognize each other, they regret their new marriages, realize they are still in love, and run away together. The second act is, as Coward says in the preface to an anthology that includes the play, essentially a "dualogue" for two experienced performers. For the author its greatest interest was, according to the preface, "from the point of view of technical acting." Since everything depended on the interactions of the two stars—in the play's opening run Coward himself and Gertrude Lawrence—"every night, according to the degree of responsiveness from the audience, the attack and tempo of the performance must inevitably vary."[1]

The outcome in *Private Lives* ties the play to the modern theater of the absurd, for Amanda and Elyot are destined to live out their relentlessly recurring hatreds and hellish confrontations in a renewed life together in Paris, as are the now equally united and bitterly quarreling Sibyl and Victor.[2] The doubleness is thoroughly invasive and as frustrating as it is at the end of James's "The Private Life." In that story, the actress will never get the part she wants from the real dramatist, Vawdrey, nor does she want what she

---

1. Noël Coward, *Play Parade* (New York, 1933), xiii.
2. Archie K. Loss, "Noël Coward as Comedian of the Absurd," *Journal of Modern Literature,* XI (1984), 299–306.

can get, the play the narrator-playwright can give her. The reader realizes at the end that her best performance will be in the tale that is being read and that the ideal part will never come.

The characters in "The Private Life" were patterned on real people. In James's preface to the New York Edition he admitted that Robert Browning was the inspiration behind Clare Vawdrey, and although he did not name the person behind Lord Mellifont, there are in the original preface broad hints that the F. L. he refers to is the painter Frederick Leighton. But as Coward put himself into the play as an actor, so James put himself into the tale as the playwriting narrator, with his female lead also an actress. Coward in his preface referred to his "puppets," as James did in his prefaces. Coward also listed the places where the play was conceived and written: "*Private Lives* was conceived in Tokyo, written in Shanghai, and produced in London."

When Coward in his mature years was called the Master, the title may have parodied James's or it may have been a sincere homage by comparison. J. B. Priestley asked Coward in 1964, "What is all this nonsense about you being called the master?" and Coward allowed, "It started as a joke and became true" (LE, xx). Certainly from an early age he was finding nourishment in sophisticated forms of the written word. According to his autobiography, he had read Oscar Wilde when he was fourteen, and when he was eighteen and nineteen, he met Charles Scott-Moncrieff, Rebecca West, Hugh Walpole, H. G. Wells, and Compton Mackenzie, all friends of James.[3] Later, Coward's wide and voracious reading, which took place in any free hours from his acting and social life, was implicit in his naming of four puppies after the Brontës, in his imitation of Wilde's *Lady Windermere's Fan* in *After the Ball*, and in his confidence in pronouncing that "no new writers of the stature of Henry James, Edith Wharton and Scott Fitzgerald had emerged . . . in America" (*NCD*, 307). Although he did not set his hand to writing short stories — or his one novel — until his reputation declined after the Second World War, especially during the 1950s, and he was no longer active as a playwright, he then began to cart "many volumes of Balzac, Thomas Hardy, Henry James, all of Jane Austen, and *Wuthering Heights*" around with him (LE, 375). In 1958, he mentioned, "I have also waded through a long biographical analysis of Henry James and his oeuvres and oh dear my heart is in my espadrilles. I shall press on, for from

---

3. Noël Coward, *Present Indicative* (Garden City, N.Y., 1937).

time to time he has interested me, but I have a feeling that I shall be mad-
dened" (LE, 376). Other comments from his diary of the period confirm his
interest in James. He compared Maugham with James, observing that the
elder writer "trudges and writhes and wriggles through jungles of verbiage
to describe a cucumber sandwich. And yet, with all this undue emphasis on
meticulousness, with all his interminable parentheses and attenuated sentences, he manages to convey a true and perfectly moving sense of the facts
and also an indefinable gilding of literary elegance" (*NCD*, 352). In the
next entry, dated some two months later, he wrote, "I have just finished the
first volume of *The Portrait of a Lady* and have been entirely charmed by it.
Mr. James's urbanity, taste and sense of behaviour are so consoling in
these jagged *Look Back in Anger* years. It is pleasant to feel there is so much
of his I have not read. Some, I know, of the later, involved novels and stories
I shall find tedious but this one, written in his middle years, is lucid and delightful" (*NCD*, 353).

   Yet, on October 25, 1966, when he criticized Rebecca West in his diary
for the verbosity of *The Birds Fall Down* (*NCD*, 637), he appended, "Henry
James, of course, was one of the double-dyed, double-Dutch deans of this
particular school and, now I come to think of it, Rebecca was a great James
girl; in fact, her first book was a monograph on him. I do wish she hadn't
been" (*NCD*, 637–38). If he had read her book, he would have known she
was not.

   In deciding that it was pleasant knowing there was so much of James
still to read, Coward was not conceding that he had read very little of
James. In addition to putting the line "Then there we are!" from *The Ambassadors* in both *The Vortex* and *Private Lives*, he introduced a Sholto as a
namesake of Captain Sholto in *The Princess Casamassima*.

   As a boy of fourteen, Coward had been put in the charge of Hugh Walpole, who may have talked of James, since at that time he was deep within
his spell (LE, 47). Coward in any case viewed Oscar Wilde with the same
deprecation James did, however he came by his opinion: "What a tiresome,
affected sod" (*NCD*, 60), "What a silly conceited inadequate creature" (LE,
306). With reference to his own *After the Ball*, he wrote, "The more Coward
we can get into the script and the more Wilde we can eliminate, the happier
we shall be" (*NCD*, 235). In 1962, reading Wilde's letters reinforced his
conviction that Wilde "was one of the silliest, most conceited and unattractive characters that ever existed" (*NCD*, 508).

   Still, in Coward's *Design for Living*, first presented in 1933 and recently revived, Wilde's influence is foremost. The play could have been entitled "The Unimportance of Being Ernest," for Ernest, an art dealer, is a mere spectator, whom Gilda marries to escape between the horns of the dilemma of loving both Otto and Leo. She flees them both—after each has spent the night with her—by marrying Ernest and moving into his penthouse apartment in New York City. Leo and Otto go on a drinking spree that is an improvement on the drunken scenes in Henry James's play *Guy Domville,* of 1894, and Oscar Wilde's *An Ideal Husband,* of 1895, both of which Coward may have read. The men drink so much that they end making love to each other, after bemoaning Gilda's fickleness in freeing herself from them.

In 1929, Coward took a break and traveled around the world by himself. He probably read a lot while on his own, and in Tokyo he got the idea for *Private Lives.* In bed with the flu by the time he got to Shanghai, he wrote it very rapidly. St. John Ervine unfairly remarked that "Coward's entire existence had been spent in a corner of the theatre" and that he was "amazed and disturbed at the slenderness of this intellectual resource. . . . We might well wonder whether he has ever read a great book." And although he adds that it seemed unlikely "that the journey around the world gave Noel a chance to catch up on all that . . . it was at least a beginning."[4] But *Present Indicative* and Coward's diaries, published only recently, prove how much he read. When Laurence Olivier was offered the part of Victor in *Private Lives,* Coward told him to read Emily Brontë's *Wuthering Heights,* Maugham's *Of Human Bondage,* and Arnold Bennett's *The Old Wives Tale* to prepare himself for his role.

Two other plays by Coward suggest a connection with James. One is *Easy Virtue,* of 1924, which relates to James's "The Great Condition" (1899). The other is *Point Valaine,* mounted with the Lunts in 1935 and a theatrical failure. This was supposed to be heavily influenced by Maugham, but in it, Quinn, the writer who is a steady guest at Mrs. Valaine's hotel, could be either Maugham or Henry James—"an ironic observer and recorder of other people's passions."[5]

In 1939 in Honolulu, Coward wrote some short stories, seven of which are in his volume *To Step Aside.*[6] While writing them, as when he wrote *Pri-*

---

4. Sheridan Morley, *A Talent to Amuse* (New York, 1969), 182–83.
5. Noël Coward, *Curtain Calls* (New York, 1940), 558.
6. Noël Coward, *To Step Aside* (Garden City, N.Y., 1939).

vate Lives, he was removed from the theatrical world and dependent on books. Again Henry James appeared in his work, if indirectly.

In the tale "What Mad Pursuit?" of 1939, and in the novel *Pomp and Circumstance*, which he kept at between 1951 and 1960, Henry James seems to have stimulated some part of Coward's imagination, as he did in *Private Lives*. Although *Pomp and Circumstance* is dedicated to Nancy Mitford, it is more like Henry James, who wrote six short stories in the first person as a woman (as a man was Maugham's technique). When Coward's hero, Bunny, tries to enlist the narrating woman's aid in covering up his love affair with the duchess, the device in use is James's of the female narrator as confidante. In addition, *Pomp and Circumstance* has a beginning like *The Spoils of Poynton*, with its description of ugly houses.

Coward recorded in his diary on November 20, 1955, that he had decided "to begin an entirely new novel . . . writing it freely in the first person as a cheerful married woman with two children and a nice husband" (*NCD*, 293). In September, 1959, he saw a theatrical version of "The Aspern Papers," which he called "well done but a little dull" (*NCD*, 416).

In "What Mad Pursuit?" Evan Lorrimer, an Englishman who has written eleven novels, one play, and criticism, is in the United States on a lecture tour when he meets a woman at a noisy New York cocktail party on the eve of having to give a lecture. She insists that, since he needs peace and quiet, he must be a guest at her country house on Long Island, where nothing will disturb his work (*CSC*, 77). Coward mentioned Henry James twice in the course of the tale, along with *The Wings of a Dove* (*CSC*, 79).

In the story "Nature Study," of 1951, Coward mentioned *The Portrait of a Lady* (*CSC*, 168–69). And in another short story, "Pretty Polly," of 1965, there is a faint resemblance to James's "Glasses," of 1896. Polly is the poor companion of a disagreeable, rich aunt, traveling with her to Singapore. The aunt dies suddenly from overeating, and Polly is left to bury her but now owns her jewels and is accompanied by a charming, half-Indian lover who gets her contact lenses and pretty clothes.

In an interview by Ed Murrow on television in 1957, Coward said that his notion of comfort was "good books, agreeable people, and first-rate plumbing." It is no accident that reading came first. Coward's serious reading in later life, which acquainted him with some of James's masterpieces and left him well aware of the contemporary estimates of the author he was reading—the verbosity, prolixity, and touch of absurdity—enabled him to recognize also the value of the detailed descriptions of people and places that James's work presented so fully. Coward did his own reading and made his own judgments and he handled James tenderly if ironically, even as late as the role he played in the film *Our Man in Havana*, of 1959, under Carol Reed's direction, in which, sixty years old, he created a figure like the older James, with "furled umbrella and Eden's hat, a figure at once correct, commanding and deeply absurd" (LE, 384).

F. Scott Fitzgerald and James

> We have all stolen . . . from Shakespeare on down. It's how the story is written that makes the difference.
>
> —F. Scott Fitzgerald

T. S. Eliot congratulated F. Scott Fitzgerald (1896–1940) on *The Great Gatsby* by calling the novel the *"first step forward American fiction had taken since Henry James."*[7] But what did Fitzgerald get from James? At Princeton, under the tutelage of Edmund Wilson and John Peale Bishop, he had read James's fiction, and there were spotty effects of that in his earlier work. James's name crops up in *Flappers and Philosophers*, of 1920, in which professors carry "thick volumes of Thomas Aquinas and Henry James and Cardinal Mercier and Immanuel Kant."[8] In *The Beautiful and Damned*, of 1922, Anthony Patch's grandfather encourages him to write about "your own country."[9] That was the advice James had given Edith Wharton, as Fitzgerald may have read in the letters of Henry James published in 1920. Anthony, in his affair with Dorothy Raycroft, does not "fall before a personality more vital, more compelling than his own, as he had done with Gloria four years before."[10] The gist of the thought seems to come from a phrase in James's "The Jolly Corner": "falling back as under the hot breath and the roused passion of a life larger than his own, a rage of personality before which his own collapsed" (XII, 226). Although the tale "The Diamond as Big as the Ritz," of 1922, may show the effect of James's "The Great Good Place," there are other utopian novels and tales that may have set the framework for the story.

Fitzgerald's *Tender Is the Night*, of 1934, harks back to James's canni-

7.   Andrew Turnbull, ed., *The Letters of F. Scott Fitzgerald* (New York, 1963), 199.

8.   F. Scott Fitzgerald, *Flappers and Philosophers* (New York, 1920), 197.

9.   F. Scott Fitzgerald, *The Beautiful and the Damned* (New York, 1922), 15.

10.   *Ibid.*, 324.

balizing theory of love, often on display in James's tales but especially developed in *The Sacred Fount*. Nicole, the mentally sick woman in *Tender Is the Night*, feeds off Dr. Dick Diver, who falls apart as she becomes healed. That same year, Maxwell Perkins, Fitzgerald's editor, had introduced the writer to *The Art of the Novel*, a collection of James's prefaces to his New York Edition, which Fitzgerald "thought was wonderful and which is difficult reading as it must have been to write."[11] *The Golden Bowl* is also evident in *Tender Is the Night:* "The silver cord is cut and the golden bowl is broken."[12] In the proliferation of metaphors, there is evidence of the late James, as well as in the format of the book. Dick Diver has his volume as he saves Nicole and then goes to pieces; Nicole has her volume as she heals and climbs out of her psychosis. Rosemary is Dick's Charlotte Stant.

If the effect of James is more apparent in the novels and tales of the 1930s, that may be because T. S. Eliot's letter probably made not only Fitzgerald's critics and friends but even Fitzgerald himself more aware of his predecessor than before. When, in *The Crack-Up*, of 1945, Fitzgerald used the expression "finer in the grain,"[13] he knew, it is tempting to think, James's series of stories *The Finer Grain*, about a man whose grain is finer than that of the women involved with him, to paraphrase James's own dust-jacket summary.

Even in *The Great Gatsby*, of 1925, there are echoes from *The Golden Bowl*. Gatsby says that Daisy's voice is "full of money" (*GG*, 91). Nick Carraway extends the figure: "That was it. . . . It was full of money—that was the inexhaustible charm that rose and fell in it, the jingle of it" (*GG*, 94). Fitzgerald may here have been remembering the Prince's reaction to Charlotte Stant, whose voice has the "chink of the metal." Her appearance is of a "long loose silk purse, well filled with gold-pieces" (NYE, XXIII, 47). James's late metaphoric style may well have influenced Fitzgerald's way with metaphors in spite of his declaration that it was the earlier James he preferred.

Fitzgerald wrote *The Last Tycoon*, of 1941, during the time that he was seriously, although with a sense of humor, conducting a "College of One" for his friend Sheilah Graham. Because he prepared a curriculum covering Western art and literature in depth—which entailed reviewing the tales and

11. Turnbull, ed., *The Letters of F. Scott Fitzgerald*, 254–55.

12. F. Scott Fitzgerald, *Tender Is the Night* (New York, 1934), 58.

13. F. Scott Fitzgerald, *The Crack-Up* (New York, 1945), 84.

novels of James's that he wanted Graham to read—*The Last Tycoon* is, of his novels, the most saturated with James. There is every inclination to think that Cecilia, Fitzgerald's young heroine, has been shaped by his familiarity with James's novels of the late 1890s. *What Maisie Knew* and *The Awkward Age* involve the points of view of girls eight and eighteen years old, respectively. Cecilia's name recalls one of the most neglected characters in *Roderick Hudson*, the young widow Cecilia, who lives in Northampton and seems to love her cousin, Rowland Mallet, who is in love with Mary Garland.

From Graham's account, some of Fitzgerald's opinions about James's works emerge, even though he tailored her reading to her deficient general education. On his recommendation, she "read six of James's earlier novels during our College of One." Fitzgerald told her, "The others would bore you. . . . James [is] too complex and intricate." He did not say that they bored him, and there is ample evidence in his work that he read and absorbed the late James as well as the early. He commented that "his critics believed he had been influenced by Henry James, especially in *The Great Gatsby*" (*CO*, 86). "It's surprising," he continued, "to read of an influence you are not aware of when writing" (*CO*, 86–87).

Fitzgerald's pedagogic technique was to mix art with literature and to combine different generations of writers. In his third list, which included James's *The Portrait of a Lady*, Leo Tolstoi's *Anna Karenina*, and William Faulkner's *Sanctuary* (*CO*, 113), there was also assigned Karl Marx's *Das Kapital*, as well as James's "Aspern Papers" and Beerbohm's "The Burlesque of Henry James." In the revised first list, *Roderick Hudson* appeared (*CO*, 81). Graham wrote that at that time she had read "Proust, Henry James's *Daisy Miller* and *The Reverberator*" (*CO*, 80). In the "Substitute List of Good Novels" that Fitzgerald compiled for her, *The Ambassadors*, *The Spoils of Poynton*, *The American*, and *The Princess Casamassima* all had a place (*CO*, 206). By this time, he must have felt that she could take *The Ambassadors*. In his "Third List: *Religion* and *Fiction*," he named Ecclesiastes, *The Portrait of a Lady*, and Dutch pictures (*CO*, 211). He included *The Europeans* on another list (*CO*, 214).

Fitzgerald found much for Graham to read in the secondhand novels by James that he had had re-bound in red (*CO*, 146). Though he never recommended *The Wings of the Dove* to her, its effect on *The Last Tycoon* is manifest in the image Cecilia conjures up of Monroe Stahr's imagination: "He had flown up very high to see, on strong wings, when he was young. And while he was up there he had looked on all the kingdoms, with the kind of eyes that can stare straight into the sun. Beating his wings tenaciously . . . and keeping on beating them . . . remembering all he had seen from his great height of how things were, he had settled gradually to earth."[14] The image corresponds to the scene in *The Wings of the Dove* where Milly Theale sits on a projection of an alp and feels she sees the kingdoms of the earth.

The Ambassadors and "Babylon Revisited"

Graham, in her second book about Fitzgerald, *The Real F. Scott Fitzgerald: Thirty-Five Years Later,* recalled that he said, "We have all stolen . . . from Shakespeare on down. It's how the story is written that makes the difference."[15] Revelation and disillusionment he got from *The Ambassadors,* but in "Babylon Revisited," of 1931, he wrote it in his own way, for he made it about a modern antihero of the sort he knew in himself, just as on James's word, *The Ambassadors* is about a man, Lambert Strether, with a lot of James in his character. In Fitzgerald's tale, a first visit to Paris was wonderful, but a second, in which Charlie Wales wants to reclaim his child, cannot undo the disaster that overtook his life during and after the earlier trip. His return is a nostalgic voyage, and bad luck hampers his transformation from an alcoholic. This inverts the sequence in *The Ambassadors.* Strether's first visit, with his now-dead wife, had no life in it, whereas his second is full of life. But both men leave the city without getting anything for themselves. Strether rejects a sensuous relationship with Maria Gostrey; Charlie is not able to take his child with him.

In Book Second, Chapter II, of *The Ambassadors,* Strether finds Paris a "vast bright Babylon . . . like some huge iridescent object, a jewel brilliant and hard" (*AM,* 84). Fitzgerald's title, taken from James's passage, shows how familiar the younger writer was with this pivotal chapter, which unrolls the beginning of Strether's mission to bring home Chad, the son of his boss lady and fiancée, Mrs. Newsome. The failure of this mission will mean for him the loss of the security that Mrs. Newsome's patronage and personal devotion guaranteed him. The passage comes after Strether has sat on a chair in the Luxembourg Gardens thinking about his dead wife and about his dead son, whom "he had stupidly sacrificed" (*AM,* 79). Strether is

14. F. Scott Fitzgerald, *The Last Tycoon* (New York, 1941), 20.
15. Sheilah Graham, *The Real F. Scott Fitzgerald: Thirty-Five Years Later* (New York, 1976), 178.

conscious that he has so far not lived, and he thinks it is too late for him. Charlie Wales, on the other hand, has liked the city "too much," for he has experienced the Paris of the wild 1920s, just before the Wall Street crash, when rich Americans set the pace. He reflects, "I spoiled the city for myself."[16] Charlie mourns his responsibility for his wife's death much as Strether has felt grief in regard to his son.

Strether says at the end of the novel, "Not, out of the whole affair, to have got anything for myself" (*AM*, 454). The pasts of both men prevent their success: Chad returns to America, but not as a result of Strether's action, and Charlie is unable to get custody of his little girl, Honoria—not because he has gone on another alcoholic binge but because his disreputable friends have ruined his sister-in-law's confidence in him. Strether's puritan repressed sexuality and Charlie's drunken and irresponsible behavior of ten years back—one man's excessive innocence and the other man's excessive corruption—are the pasts that obstruct them. Charlie, however, "would come back some day," he hoped, to take his child home with him.[17]

James, in the passage about Paris as a bright Babylon, had gone on to describe the city as a "jewel brilliant and hard, in which parts were not to be discriminated nor differences comfortably marked. It twinkled and trembled and melted together, and what seemed all surface one moment seemed all depth the next" (*AM*, 84). It is possible that this influenced the conceit of Fitzgerald's "The Diamond As Big As the Ritz," written nine years before "Babylon Revisited." In fantasy, Fitzgerald perhaps transmuted Paris, as the great good place, into an American mountain residence constituted by a solid diamond, for the key to pleasure in Paris was the American dollar. In being "as large as the Ritz," Fitzgerald's mountain is linked to James's Paris by way of "Babylon Revisited," for which the Ritz is a critical location. (The relation of *The Great Gatsby* to "Daisy Miller" is treated in Chapter 10.)

Ernest's Lover's Quarrel with Henry: Ernest Hemingway and James

That Henry James figures in Ernest Hemingway's works is apparent to anyone who reads either the novels or the nonfiction of Hemingway (1899–

---

16. Matthew J. Bruccoli, ed., *The Short Stories of F. Scott Fitzgerald* (New York, 1989), 618.

17. *Ibid.*, 633.

1961). With the publication of his letters and the lists of holdings of the libraries at Key West and Finca, in Cuba, his changing attitudes toward the older writer are part of the open record. James's name occurs in his first two novels. *The Torrents of Spring,* of 1926, includes an anecdote about James. Scripps speaks of his interest in James to Mandy, an unlikely waitress who has an anecdote to tell: "'Let's hear it,' Scripps said. 'I'm very interested in Henry James.' Henry James, Henry James. That chap who had gone away from his own land to live in England among Englishmen. Why had he done it? For what had he left America? Weren't his roots here? His brother William. Boston. Pragmatism. Harvard University" (*HR*, 50). Mandy then relates how Professors Gosse and Saintsbury came with the man who brought the Order of Merit to James's deathbed. After they left, James "never opened his eyes" but spoke to the nurse. "'Nurse,' Henry James said, 'put out the candle, nurse, and spare my blushes.' Those were the last words he ever spoke." Scripps, "strangely moved by the story," answered, "James was quite a writer" (*HR*, 51).

Where did Hemingway hear such a thing? He tells us. "Would it be any violation of confidence if we told the reader that we get the best of these anecdotes from Mr. Ford Madox Ford?" (*HR*, 57). It was indeed a yarn from Ford Madox Ford, who had known both James and Hemingway and had published four stories by James in the *English Review*, "The Jolly Corner" and "The Velvet Glove" among them. It may be that Ford introduced Hemingway to James's stories even as he was publishing Hemingway in his new *Transatlantic Review*.[18] The Key West library list indicates that Hemingway owned seven of Ford's published volumes by 1940 (on the Finca list there are only five), including *Portraits from Life,* of 1937. Ford's *Henry James,* of 1913, does not, however, appear in the earlier list (REY, 125–26; B&S, 129).

In *The Sun Also Rises,* of the same year as *The Torrents of Spring,* Bill Gorton refers ironically to an argument then current that expatriation impoverishes a writer's art and leads to creative impotence. Answering Jake Barnes's response that "I just had an accident," Gorton says. "That's the sort of thing that can't be spoken of. That's what you ought to work up into a mystery. Like Henry's bicycle" (*SR*, 118). Henry in this remark is Henry James. Fred D. Crawford and Bruce Morton have identified as the source of the comments against expatriation Van Wyck Brooks's *The Pilgrimage of*

18. Carlos Baker, *Hemingway: The Writer as Artist* (Princeton, 1973), 418.

Henry James and Hemingway's response to that volume.[19] Barnes pursues Gorton's notion about the cause of James's injury: "'It wasn't a bicycle,' I said. 'He was riding horseback.' 'I heard it was a tricycle.' 'Well,' I said. 'A plane is sort of like a tricycle. The joystick works the same way'" (*SR*, 118–19). That passage is suggesting that Jake became impotent as a result of an accident, his plane shot down in a battle during World War I, "on a joke front like the Italian" (*SR*, 31).

James, as he recounted in *Notes of a Son and Brother*, of 1914, had received his "obscure hurt" when he was about eighteen years old, at the "breaking out of the War," while helping to extinguish a fire. "Jammed into the acute angle between two high fences . . . I had done myself . . . a horrid even if an obscure hurt." It was significant to him that the hurt was associated with Civil War battles. There was the "queer fusion . . . established in my consciousness . . . by the firing on Fort Sumter" and the "physical mishap." Affecting him was the "undivided way in which what had happened to me . . . kept company . . . with my view of what was happening . . . to everyone about me, to the country at large: it so made of these marked disparities a single vast visitation." He had the sense of an "ache," and he could not tell at times "whether it came most from one's own poor organism . . . which had suffered particular wrong, or from the enclosing social body, a body rent with a thousand wounds and that thus treated one to the honour of a sort of tragic fellowship. The twenty minutes had sufficed . . . to establish a relation—a relation to everything occurring round me not only for the next four years but for long afterward" (*AU*, 414–15).

It seems clear that James felt that his accidental wound made him one with the young men suffering battle wounds; he had the feeling that he, like them, had been wounded in the very thick of battle. Thus the parallel between James's "obscure hurt" and Jake's unmentionable wartime injury was even greater than Hemingway may have supposed, if his assumption was merely the general one that James's "obscure hurt" was impotence, given his celibacy and his vague reference to what had taken place.

As Crawford and Morton nicely put it, "In the process of refuting Brooks, Hemingway combined Henry James', Jake Barnes', and the critic's 'impotence' into one central image, using the bicycle allusion as a fo-

19. Fred D. Crawford and Bruce Morton, "Hemingway and Brooks: The Mystery of 'Henry's Bicycle,'" *Studies in American Fiction*, VI (1978), 108.

cus."[20] Nevertheless, they are wrong in conjecturing that Hemingway found the bicycle incident—which occurred late in James's life—in Lubbock's edition of James's letters, for Hemingway's now-published letters show that at the time of employing the bicycle image he knew that James had suffered a more serious accident in his youth. When Maxwell Perkins cautioned Hemingway not to mention complete names in *The Sun Also Rises*, since he might be sued, he replied, "But I believe that it is a reference to some accident that is generally known to have happened to Henry James in his youth." He continued (Figure 14), "To me Henry James is as historical a name as Byron, Keats, or any other great writer about whose life, personal and literary, books have been written. . . . As I recall Gorton and Barnes are talking humourously around the subject of Barnes' mutilation and to them Henry James is not a man to be insulted or protected from insult but simply an historical example" (*HSL*, 209). Several months later, they decided that James would be referred to simply as Henry (*HSL*, 215).

It is more revealing of Hemingway's attitude toward James when Bill Gorton says, "I think he's a good writer, too." He continues, "And you're a hell of a good guy" (*SR*, 119). Bill thereby relates Jake to James.

In *Death in the Afternoon*, of 1932, James is the "favorite author" of a Mrs. E. R., a discriminating lady who develops "unerring judgment for a matador's class." Her preference for James proves she is a superior woman.[21] Early in *Green Hills of Africa*, of 1935, James, Stephen Crane, and Mark Twain are cited as the "good writers" of America.[22] In *A Moveable Feast*, of 1964, a preference for James attests the impeccable literary taste of his wife, Hadley, and it is said that Ford Madox Ford considered him "very nearly" a gentleman.[23] James's appearance at intervals in Hemingway's oeuvre is as a historical literary figure with a benign, almost mythological presence.

As for Hemingway's reading in James, he had a lifelong enthusiasm for *The American*, which he owned in the 1877 edition (REY, 1169), and he had two copies of *The Portrait of a Lady*, as well as a copy Perkins had given him of Blackmur's edition of James's prefaces. Hemingway took both novels along when he moved from Key West to Cuba (B&S, 3337, 3342, 3343).

20. *Ibid.*, 109.
21. Ernest Hemingway, *Death in the Afternoon* (New York, 1932), 467.
22. Ernest Hemingway, *Green Hills of Africa* (New York, 1935), 22.
23. Ernest Hemingway, *A Moveable Feast* (New York, 1964), 38, 87.

14. James and his bicycle in Rye, England

Leon Edel Collection

The final item on a list of fifteen titles that Hemingway drew up for his young protégé Arnold Samuelson is *The American* (Figure 15). "If you haven't read these you aren't educated," he wrote.[24] The five volumes by James on the Key West list grew to thirteen on the Cuba list (B&S, 3337–48).

Establishing the influence of James's work on Hemingway's is another matter. Sheldon Norman Grebstein found between the manuscript pages of *A Farewell to Arms*, of 1929, in the John F. Kennedy Library a clipping of the purported interview with James that Preston Lockwood published in the *New York Times Book Review* of March 21, 1915. Both sides of the interview were written by James (*M*, 527). The passage that may have informed *A Farewell to Arms* reads, "The war has used up words; they have weakened, they have deteriorated like motor car tires; . . . and we are now confronted with a depreciation of all our terms, or, otherwise speaking, with a loss of expression through increase of limpness, that may well make us wonder what ghosts will be left to walk."[25] Grebstein hears an echo of these lines in Hemingway's: "I was always embarrassed by the words sacred, glorious, and sacrifice and the expression in vain. . . . There were many words that you could not stand to hear and finally only the names of places had dignity. . . . Abstract words such as glory, honor, courage, or hallow were obscene beside the concrete names of villages, the numbers of roads, the names of rivers, the numbers of regiments and the dates."[26]

A correlation may also be possible between an early tale by Hemingway and a late one by James. There is a striking similarity of basic theme between James's "The Great Good Place" and Hemingway's "Big Two-Hearted River," of 1925, and some of Hemingway's key phrases are the same as James's. James's lead story in *The Soft Side*, the collection of his that Ezra Pound praised, was reprinted in the New York Edition, and in 1925 Hemingway could have had easy access to Gertrude Stein's set.

"The Great Good Place" concerns an overburdened writer who, to escape, in a dream retreats to a haven where tired writers and artists can rest and recharge their creative batteries. Nick, in Hemingway's tale, has also found his "good place" (the story resorts to James's phrase, or parts of it,

---

24. *Books and Papers Belonging to Ernest Hemingway, 1898–1961* (Catalog of Sale by Glenn Horowitz, n.d.), p. 19, item 29.

25. Sheldon Norman Grebstein, *Hemingway's Craft* (Carbondale, Ill., 1973), 206.

26. Ernest Hemingway, *A Farewell to Arms* (New York, 1929), 196.

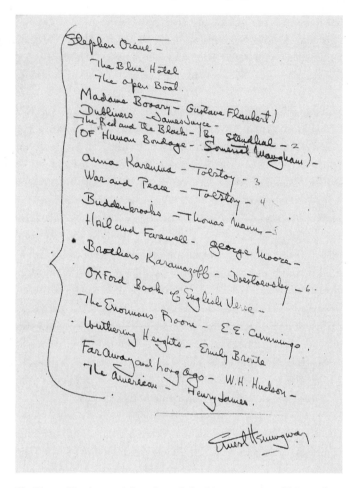

15. Ernest Hemingway's list of novels for his protégé Arnold Samuelson

Courtesy Glenn Horowitz Bookseller, Inc.

four times) after his wartime experience with death and destruction: "He had made his camp. He was settled. Nothing could touch him. It was a good place to camp. He was there, in the good place" (*HR,* 9). After eating, Nick thinks, "There were plenty of good places to camp on the river. But this was good" (*HR,* 10).

For George Dane, James's hero, the Great Good Place is the "scene of his new consciousness" (XI, 19); for Nick, it is the scene of the perfect fishing expedition. Hemingway seems to realize and actualize James's metaphors.

The feeding that James expresses in similes and metaphors becomes in Hemingway the dinners and breakfasts that Nick makes for himself (*HR*, 10).

Before George Dane came to his Great Good Place, he had "been in danger of losing" his "genius," as he called it, which was "held by a thread that might at any moment have broken. The change was that, little by little, his hold had grown firmer, so that he drew in the line—more and more each day—with a pull that he was delighted to find it would bear" (XI, 30). He found "he had got his soul again. He had drawn in by this time, with his lightened hand, the whole of the long line, and that fact just dangled at the end. He could put his other hand on it, he could unhook it, he was once more in possession" (XI, 35). Through the long fishing image, James metaphorically conveys the worth of the peace that came to his hero. Hemingway has Nick actually fish and find a peace he never had before. Nick, having felt the "tug on his line," allows a couple of trout to slip away. But after that loss, he gets over his disappointment, saying, "It was all right now" (*HR*, 18). His words are more or less those of the Brother when Dane is about to go back to his regular life: "Oh, it's all right!" (XI, 40). After settling into an existence that is now uncluttered, Dane, in the last sentence of the story, agrees with the Brother, "It *was* all right" (XI, 42). The similarity of idiom seems conscious as Dane hooks his soul and Nick hooks his trout. The part of the river that Nick decides to leave alone can be read as epitomizing the hectic contemporary world George Dane inhabits. Both Nick and Dane are withdrawing from danger. Is the relationship between these stories the sort of thing Hemingway had in mind when he wrote to Hadley on November 25, 1943, "Maybe I'll turn out to be the Henry James of the People or the comic strips" (*HSL*, 556)?

There are also striking correspondences between James's *The Ambassadors* and *The Sun Also Rises*. Alice B. Toklas' letters make clear that Gertrude Stein admired the last novels of James, of which *The Ambassadors* is the first. Hemingway must have heard those novels praised by her, by Ford Madox Ford, and by Hadley.

Not only is Hemingway's the only novel about Americans in Paris after James's to be considered a masterpiece, but the opening of his book is so close to the opening of *The Ambassadors* that it is hard to believe he had not read it. Robert Cohn's life, summarized in the early pages of *The Sun Also Rises*, bears likenesses to Strether's. Both men have been taken up by forceful women who own journals that the men edit. At the beginning of each novel the arrangement is approaching its end as the man starts thinking about really living. Robert's speech to Jake about wanting to live is a re-markable compression of Strether's speech to Little Bilham at Gloriani's party in *The Ambassadors:* "'Listen, Jake,' he leaned forward on the bar. 'Don't you ever get the feeling that all your life is going by and you're not taking advantage of it? Do you realize you've lived nearly half the time you have to live already?'" (*SR*, 11). Strether says, "Live all you can; it's a mis-take not to. It doesn't so much matter what you do in particular, so long as you have your life. If you haven't had that what *have* you had?" (*AM*, 173–74). Yet Strether himself refuses life and love in Paris because of a kind of emotional impotence. It is possible that Hemingway entertained the notion that Strether cannot respond to the advances of Maria Gostrey or Marie de Vionnet because of a "horrid" hurt, a real and not only a spiritual impo-tence. If so, Robert is not the only character of the novel mirroring Strether, for Jake's incapacity will also be Strether's.

All the characters in both novels are expatriates. The only important non-American in either is the femme fatale, in one the Countess de Vionnet, and in the other Lady Brett. Desperation is a characteristic of both women. Marie de Vionnet says, "The only certainty is that I shall be the loser in the end" (*AM*, 427). Nor is she the only loser in *The Ambassadors*. Maria Gostrey, who loves Strether, also loses, but it is Strether who is the prime avatar of the "winner take nothing" motif of all Hemingway's work. At the end of James's novel, Strether rejects Miss Gostrey's proffered love: "But all the same I must go. . . . To be right. . . . That, you see, is my only logic. Not, out of the whole affair, to have got anything for myself" (*AM*, 454).

When Brett goes off with the "bullfighter chap," Jake's reaction is like Strether's to discovering that Marie and Chad are lovers. Brett summons Jake, just as Marie, after her exposure as the mistress of Chad, summons Strether. Each woman wants to be seen through the separation from her lover by the hero. Although the women's methods of enslavement vary, they tangle erotically with all the characters and have a blocked sexual relation with the impotent heroes, Lambert Strether and Jake Barnes.

Hemingway's letters bespeak a love-hate relationship with both the figure of James and his work. Besides envisioning himself as the "Henry James of the People," he wondered "what Henry James would have done with the materials of our time."[27] As early as 1926, Pound could accuse him of following too much "in the wake of H. J." (RE, 22).

---

27. Baker, *Hemingway: The Writer as Artist*, 193.

In a letter to Waldo Peirce written around mid-December, 1927, Hemingway mentioned that his new wife liked James. In this she was like his first wife, Hadley: "Pauline has been fine and has read Henry James (The Awkward Age) out loud—and knowing nothing about James it seems to me to be the shit. . . . The men all without any exception talk and think like fairies except a couple of caricatures of brutal 'outsiders.' You have read more and better ones than this doubtless but he seems an enormous fake in this. What ho? Was he a fake? He had obviously developed a fine very easy way for himself to write and great knowledge of drawing rooms but did he have anything else?" (*HSL,* 266). Although Hemingway maintained that he knew "nothing about James," the continuing references to James in his work earn the assertion a certain amount of skepticism.

Hemingway wrote to Charles Scribner, in a letter dated September 6–7, 1949, that he had "tried for Mr. Turgenieff first and it wasn't too hard. Tried for Mr. Maupassant . . . and it took four of the best stories to beat him. . . . Mr. Henry James I would just thumb him once the first time he grabbed and then hit him once where he had no balls and ask the referee to stop it" (*HSL,* 673). He made a similar remark about Shakespeare, evidently taking on only the toughest competition. James was during this time very much on Hemingway's mind, for he wrote again to Scribner on October 4, 1949, "Of Henry James you would like, I think, Madame de Mauves. It's quite short. There are a couple of other good ones too. But the greater part of it is rather snobbish, difficultly written shit" (*HSL,* 678). The story was reprinted in *The Great Short Novels of Henry James,* of 1945, edited by Philip Rahv, which is on the Finca list.

Hemingway advised lots of drinking and a motorbike for a son traveling in Italy, which "is sort of different from Henry James in a way" (*HSL,* 679). The next year he wrote to Scribner, "Henry James was not faced with these same problems"—such as having to "clip" people who "start to paw your wife" in night clubs (*HSL,* 709). He jibed at James again in a letter to Scribner dated July 9–10, 1950: "I do not imagine this is the type of life which would have agreed with Henry James but fuck all male old women anyway. He wrote nice but he lived pretty dull I think. Too dull maybe and wrote too nice about too dull." Then he turned his attention to what James must have been like as a boy without athletic skills, against whom he contrasted his own sons (*HSL,* 703).

James's personality seemed both to fascinate and to annoy him, especially in relationship to his "obscure hurt." On June 21, 1952, he sent Har-

vey Breit a humorous reconstruction of an extract from an imaginary journal of earlier years: "Thursday.—Commenced writing a new novel. It is to
be called A Farewell to Arms and treats of war on the Italian front which I
visited briefly as a boy after the death of Henry James. A strange coincidence" (*HSL*, 768). He continued to connect his war wound with James's
wound, even in 1952. The association adds to the significance of finding the
clipping with the James interview among the manuscript pages of *A Farewell to Arms*.

From 1952 to 1954 four more references to James occur in the *Selected
Letters*, and by then Hemingway's desire to write like James was becoming
patent. In 1954, he sent an affectionate letter to Adriana Ivancich, the
young girl behind the heroine of *Across the River and into the Trees*, of 1950,
who as the object of the Colonel's love sometimes fuses with Venice itself:
"Pretty soon I will have to throw this away so I better try to be a calm like
Henry James the writer. Did you ever read Henry James? He was a great
American writer who came to Venice and looked out of the window and
smoked his cigar and thought. He was born too early and never saw you"
(*HSL*, 830). In this image he seems to be remembering a passage regarding
Venice in James's *Portraits of Places*, of 1883, the 1948 edition of which is on
the Finca list: "If you are happy, you will find yourself, after a June day in
Venice (about ten o'clock), on a balcony that overhangs the Grand Canal,
with your elbows on the broad ledge, a cigarette in your teeth, and a little
good company beside you" (*PP*, 38). And more than *Portraits of Places* may
have prompted Hemingway to think of James in connection with Venice
and the heroine of *Across the River and into the Trees*. In James's *The Wings of
the Dove*, the major theme is love and death in Venice. Just before Hemingway wrote his novel, a spate of books on James had attended and followed
his centenary, in 1943. Many appear on the Finca list, among them F. O.
Matthiessen's *Henry James: The Major Phase*, of 1944, one of the first and
best endeavors to reinstate the late James novels in the canon.

Renata, the name of Hemingway's heroine, alludes through its Latin
meaning to the rebirth of the Colonel's feeling of love and may also echo
Adriana, and thus the Adriatic, the sea wedded to Venice in the age-old ritual ceremony. The Colonel loves Venice: "Christ I love it, he said," and the
novel is the story of his love affair with it as much with Renata.[28] James, in

28.   Ernest Hemingway, *Across the River and into the Trees* (New York, 1950), 45. Renata's
name probably comes from Gabriele D'Annunzio's daughter.

writing of Venice in the first chapter of *Portraits of Places*, remarked, "The place is as changeable as a nervous woman, and you know it only when you know all the aspects of its beauty. . . . You become extraordinarily fond of these things. . . . The place seems to personify itself, to become human and sentient, and conscious of your affection. You desire to embrace it, to caress it, to possess it; and finally, a soft sense of possession grows up, and your visit becomes a perpetual love-affair" (*PP,* 8).

On February 17, 1953, Hemingway wrote to Dorothy Connable about a piece on Toronto, "We ought to get Henry James to write it" (*HSL,* 806). On March 20–22 of the same year he wrote to Bernard Berenson, "We would have to check the dates but I think I was wounded badly before Henry James received the O.M. for his patriotic sentiments" (*HSL,* 810–11). On January 3, 1954, in a letter from Kenya, he remarked, "It's like this. You sit down to write like Flaubert, H. James (not Jesse) etc. and two characters with spears come and stand easy outside the tent" (*HSL,* 826). Hemingway was at last making no secret of his wish to write like James.

Hemingway's appreciation of James, the figure and the artist, appears to have become more intense as his work progressed, and his last novels exhibited a general kinship with James's themes. *The Old Man and the Sea,* of 1952, has to do with the pursuit of an alter ego ("the fish my brother"). For Hemingway, the type for that in modern literature might well have been James's "The Jolly Corner," a story that Pound praised and Rahv's collection included. *Islands in the Stream,* of 1970, with its set of doubles, is reminiscent of James's *Roderick Hudson.* The main character, Thomas Hudson, has Roderick's last name, and Roger Davis, who Carlos Baker thinks can be viewed as Thomas' alter ego, has a correspondence to Roderick himself. Thomas himself has the character of Rowland Mallet, the sober, steady alter ego in James's novel, for he is the adviser and counselor to Roger, the romantic writer and the equivalent of James's sculptor, Roderick. Thomas is a hardworking and successful painter, and the way Hemingway handles Thomas' character indicates a habit of conversion typical not only of his craft but also of James's.

When Hemingway accepted the Nobel Prize, he paid homage to the two great sources of his literary heritage. As a Nobel winner he regretted "that it was never given to Mark Twain, nor to Henry James."[29] In linking the

29.   Carlos Baker, *Ernest Hemingway: A Life Story* (New York, 1980), 668.

two figures of late-nineteenth-century American literature who, although poles apart, most richly nourished his imagination, he intermitted for the moment his long lover's quarrel with James.

Graham Greene and James

"This, then, is the destiny that not only the young women affront—you must betray or, more fortunately perhaps, you must be betrayed," Graham Greene wrote in his introduction to a 1947 edition of James's *The Portrait of a Lady,* expressing the message he received not only from that volume but from all of James's novels. He pictured James sitting in Lamb House, listening to the "footsteps of the traitors and their victims going endlessly by on the pavement."[30] Whether we agree or not with his definition of the figure in James's carpet, it is clear that betrayal is the theme of all of Greene's fiction. He believed that "the final beauty of James's stories lies in their pity" of wrongdoers (*CE,* 38). "It is in the final justice of his pity . . . that he ranks with the greatest of creative writers" (*CE,* 40). Greene saw that the evil James delineated in his late novels and in the unfinished *The Ivory Tower*—involving the "wealth . . . connected with the treacheries he described"—did not belong more as a "part of a capitalist than of a socialist system: they belonged to human nature." Prevailing was an "egotism so complete that you could believe that something inhuman, supernatural, was working there through the poor devils it had chosen" (*CE,* 37).

Greene as an adolescent precociously read James, who was then still alive.[31] Whether he found what he did in James early enough to form his world picture or whether his own established feelings about life elicited what he detected is immaterial. Later on, he called himself an agnostic Catholic. James drew no morals regarding religion from his depiction of human betrayal, but Greene took him to be a naturally religious man, writing that James had a "sense of evil religious in its intensity" (*CE,* 23).

Greene acknowledged that his corpus, like any other, might be approached through the metaphor of James's story "The Figure in the Carpet," although like Walpole and Maugham, he substituted the word *pattern*

---

30. Graham Greene, Introduction to *The Portrait of a Lady,* by Henry James (London, 1947), x.

31. Paul Theroux, "An Edwardian on the Concorde: Graham Greene as I Knew Him," *New York Times Book Review,* April 21, 1991, p. 3.

for *figure*. Asked in old age whether a true image of him existed, he answered his interviewer, "I expect you're familiar with Henry James's
words about 'the pattern in the carpet.' In any body of work there's always
a pattern to be found. Well, *I* don't want to see it."[32]

In a number of Greene's stories, James appears as a figure. In the early
novel *It's a Battlefield*, of 1934, which was based on Lady Ottoline Morrell's
circle, the drawing room of Lady Caroline, the fictive Lady Ottoline, has
among its visitors Henry James, whose sentences are "like Chinese boxes
which held at the center a tiny colloquialism." In the room is a "signed photograph of James, a great swollen brow floating over gloved hands."[33]

As Greene's fiction developed, it became more and more imitative of
James's last tales. The stories he wrote between 1957 and 1966 and collected in *May We Borrow Your Husband?* show a distinct similarity to James's
tales in *The Finer Grain*. They too take place in resorts of Europe and other
parts of the world, and the element of pity is stressed. There are also pseu-
dosymbolic names comparable to those James used. In the title story, the
narrator, an observer of Jamesian cast, recounts the campaign of a couple
of gay men to seduce the innocent young husband of Poopy, a rich young
newly married woman. After they seduce him, he is able to satisfy his bride
sexually for the first time, and the tale ends with the prospect of all four
characters having a fine time in the young couple's home. "Cheap in August," which takes place in Jamaica, mentions James as a writer. A young
woman on leave from her husband wants a sexual adventure, but the only
one to have it with is an ugly fat old man: "Henry James had described the
type, and at that moment in her history she had been reading a great deal
of Henry James: a man of intellect whose body was not much to him and its
senses and appetites not importunate" (*MW*, 96). "The Over-Night Bag," in
which "it was as hot in the car as in a New York hotel during a blizzard"
(*MW*, 67), evokes the scene in "A Round of Visits" of Mark Monteith in bed
with the flu for a few days in the overheated Hotel Pocahontas during a
New York blizzard. "Two Gentle People" takes place in Paris, in the Parc
Monceau, and its older couple in an unconsummated relationship pertain
to the world of James. When the gentleman sees young boys kicking

32. Marie Françoise Allain, *The Other Man: Conversations with Graham Greene* (New York,
1983), 23.
33. Graham Greene, *It's a Battlefield* (New York, 1934), 89–198.

pigeons in the park, he exclaims, "Infernal young scoundrels," and the phrase sounds "more Edwardian because of the faint American intonation—Henry James might surely have employed it" (*MW,* 174).

In three critical essays on James, Greene elaborated on the conviction that James was actuated by the same concerns as he and that "his ruling passion . . . was the idea of treachery." He sees this in Milly's betrayal and in Isabel's betrayal, as well as in the "complicated culminations of treacheries in *The Golden Bowl.*" Greene surmises that James was led to his focus on treachery "by the portrait of one young woman who died," Minny Temple, which revealed to him the "inherent disappointment of existence" (*CE,* 60). Greene is particularly sharp in gauging what James intended in *The Portrait of a Lady.* As revised, the novel suggests to him that James meant by his ending that "there is no possibility of a happy ending." It is "with a kind of bitter precision" that James "presents us with a theorem, but it is we who have to work out the meaning of x and discover that x equals no way out."[34] Readers of James uncoached by Greene are not likely, however, to see unremitting pessimism in every part of his fiction. Greene's own views blinker him against seeing that there are ways out in James's novels. Morton Densher refuses Milly's fortune, and Maggie reclaims her husband. In *The Ivory Tower* there may be no way out chiefly because James did not live to invent one.

It is odd that the self-victimizing Greene was so drawn to the late work of James, since the sense of pity there is never self-pity but a strong sensitivity to the human plight. Perhaps he saw in James the "real thing" and was sensible of his own literary facade or disguise. The recent biographies of Greene, authorized and unauthorized, expose the double lives Greene lived and the "covers" he enjoyed as an intelligence officer and spy.[35]

Reading and Writing over James's Shoulder: Louis Auchincloss

Louis Auchincloss wrote that his "lifetime's reading has been over the shoulder of Henry James" (*RJ,* vii). In his novel *The Book Class,* of 1984, it

34. Greene, Introduction to *The Portrait of a Lady,* ix.
35. For Greene's "great good place," see below, Chapter 14.
The material in this section appeared in somewhat different form as "Louis Auchincloss and Henry James," in Amritjit Singh and K. Ayyappa Paniker, eds., *The Magic Circle: Essays in Honor of Darshan Singh Maini* (New York: Envoy Press, 1989), 326–42.

was more as if he had settled in his bosom. No other writer of contemporary times has been so saturated in James. Auchincloss' characters talk to each other about Henry James; they read his novels and tales, especially *The Golden Bowl, The Ambassadors,* and *The Tragic Muse.* They die with the dying James's renowned comment, "Here it is at last—the distinguished thing," and they employ Jamesian locutions like "the real thing," "the real right thing," "so there we are," and "so there we were." Those who acquaint themselves with his works read of "dear old Mr. James" more than once, as well as "dear Edith." Auchincloss' family connections included Edith Wharton, and she is the second constituent of the brew in which he has been steeped. The genealogy he has established for himself including James and Wharton makes him the heir to the American literature of manners.

In *The Embezzler,* of 1966, the tasteful Percy has a "preference for Henry James" rather than for Galsworthy, whom a less sensitive character prefers, and James occupies a good part of the consciousness of the characters. Angelica Hyde calls herself a Daisy Miller, adding, "We don't die of fevers, as poor old doddering Mr. James thinks" (*EM,* 92) — Angelica is speaking in 1910, while James was alive—and another character looks as if "he might have stepped out of *The Golden Bowl*" (*EM,* 97). In the Europe of 1914 one drives "down to Rye to see poor old Henry James" (*EM,* 234) or speeds to Paris to see "dear Edith" (*EM,* 235). In James's story "The Beldonald Holbein," of 1901, a particular social set in London is defined as being "bounded on the north by Ibsen and on the south by Sargent!" (XI, 302). The set in Auchincloss' novel is bounded by two American literary friends. A conspiracy to marry off two people is likened to a "sordid parody of a Henry James tale" (*EM,* 240)—perhaps "Lord Beaupré," of 1893, where a mother plots to have her daughter marry an aristocrat by playing a game of engagement to protect him from other marrying mothers, or *The Portrait of a Lady,* where Madame Merle conspires to have Osmond marry Isabel.

Although in *Tales of Manhattan,* of 1967, Auchincloss seems to be looking almost exclusively over Wharton's shoulder, he employs the phrase "the final turn of the screw" in a piece of figurative language (*TM,* 220). In the last tale of the collection, "The Wagnerians," a man of finer grain who is staging Wagner for the first time in New York halts the opera to wait for the matrons in their boxes to stop talking. Of course they continue. As in every one of the five stories in James's *The Finer Grain,* women of coarser grain make men of finer grain suffer.

With regularity James appears as a tutelary genius. In *Second Chance*, of 1970, "Frank did a monologue depicting Henry James lost in the London Underground" (*SC,* 103). The famous figure of speech in *The Golden Bowl* involving the "long silken halter" that seems to have been put around Charlotte's neck by Adam—"He didn't twitch it, yet it was there; he didn't drag her, but she came" (*GB,* II, 295)—mutates only slightly: "Gilbert had her as surely under control as if he had a cord around her thin white neck which he could twitch whenever he wanted her to do his bidding" (*SC,* 216). A writer in *The Partners,* of 1974, wants to write a novel as perfect as *Madame Bovary* or *The Ambassadors* (*PN,* 149).

The Book Class, however, is a fuller demonstration of what Auchincloss learned from James as a writer of fiction and as a critic of literature, and it has the densest collection of Jamesian references. Since from college on, Auchincloss had been "conducted through the literature of his time" with James as his "starting point" and "common denominator" (*RJ,* vii, viii), he constructed his novel of cross-linked short chapters with reference to the works that nine of his characters read, or at least desire to read. The actual and envisioned reading ranges from Nathaniel Hawthorne to a new life of Henry James. The one meeting of the class that takes place, in the first chapter, is devoted to *The Scarlet Letter.* That meeting is the device attaching the lives of the members to their reading. It gives clues to the future in thumbnail biographies of each member of the class, which must be read again later to be fully fathomed. The device itself is something Auchincloss most probably learned from reading James. In the first chapter of Auchincloss' novel the important fact comes out that the narrator, Chris Gates, was undersized as a young boy. His "diminutive stature" (*BC,* 15) will later identify him with the "I" of James's late first autobiographical account, *A Small Boy and Others.* Auchincloss, in *Reading Henry James,* of 1975, had called the work the "ultimate experience for the Jamesphile," and James's finest because "the artificialities of fiction are absent" (*RHJ,* 152). This autobiographical volume provided Auchincloss with the sense of the *vrai verité* that Chris Gates's nosegay of biographies of his mother's friends constitutes. For Auchincloss, "the most delightful parts of *A Small Boy* are the stories he tells of his relatives and friends" (*RHJ,* 153). Auchincloss deems *A Small Boy* superior to the autobiographical volume that succeeded it, *Notes of a Son and Brother,* because it is "more of a family memoir than a work of art" (*RHJ,* 155).

Chris Gates listens "covertly from behind the screen before the pantry door" (*BC*, 9) to the proceedings of the meeting in the dining room of his parents' house at which the women discuss *The Scarlet Letter.* The comments by the women on the adultery in Hawthorne's novel will bear on the later revelations about their sexual histories and politics. Later on in the novel, too, there will be a discussion of Marcel Proust's similar eavesdropping on Charlus and Jupien's coupling. Ending the chapter, Chris judges that the class "used books as a door. To what?" His job is "to find out" (*BC*, 12).

The books the members of the class use as a door to their lives in the outside world happen to be the books Auchincloss also uses. Like James's small self, Chris will observe and clarify the histories of those about him — in his case, of nine of the dozen former debutantes who in 1908 come together as the book class in which his mother, Cornelia, participates. The result will be to explain the members of a whole social class. Chris's story is in step with the memoir Auchincloss admired inasmuch as "the memoir is purely and simply the story of a small boy, a small James, who dedicated himself early and passionately to the role of an observer of life" (*RHJ*, 153). What James did in connection with the stories about the members of his family and their friends — "allow . . . his imagination, quite consciously, to play, to speculate, to embroider" (*RHJ*, 153) — is what Chris is doing with the members of his mother's class. Chris refers to "my young observing eyes" (*BC*, 5), which wanted to know about people: "What did they look like?" (*BC*, 7). Auchincloss was conscious of the close attention in James's autobiography to the "question of how people looked, and of how their look counted for a thousand relations" (*RHJ*, 156).

Beginning in Chapter Five, Auchincloss elucidates certain events in his portraits of ladies through artfully varied allusions to James's fiction, and in the later parts of the novel by reference to James's critical attitudes. After limiting the first four chapters to Cornelia and the Gateses' financial downfall, Auchincloss concludes his first portrait, which has depicted a lady who commits perjury to save her husband from jail. Then he eases into the tale of Justine Bannard by way of the prep school where Chris and her son Chuck are classmates. Justine is not only the one member of the book class who reads a book by James — *The Golden Bowl,* for the class is going to discuss a "new life of James" — but she is also the one who is learning Maggie's strategy of winning back a "straying husband without blowing the whistle on her stepmother." "Just as Maggie had to preserve her father's immunity from scandal," Justine has to "fight her battle" of keeping Chester in the running for headmaster of the school, "by being more aware of everything than anyone else." In other words, she has to be a Jamesian character, especially since Chester is "not reading Henry James" (*BC*, 45). Justine, "placing *The Golden Bowl* in her reticule," reflects that she is "indeed going to need a Jamesian subtlety to keep Chester from scotching their grand opportunity" (*BC*, 47).

At the end of the chapter, Justine consults Adeline Bloodgood, a Catholic like Maggie, in an attempt to comprehend what her motives have been, and whether they have been bad or good. Performing a role like James's Mrs. Assingham, Adeline decides all is well as long as Chester returns to the "path of virtue." Justine, capable of a "detached" view of herself, admits that there was "no love in my heart" when she kept her spouse from wandering (*BC*, 63). But Adeline absolves her, and Justine, as smart as ever and in the spirit of having been in a confessional, lets it be understood that condonations such as the one Adeline has just favored her with are the reason "why we all come to you for judgment" (*BC*, 64). She has surely out-Maggied Maggie.

If Justine is the paramount example of how Auchincloss does over James's characters in this book, she also demonstrates that Maggie pales in comparison with a woman of this group. James may have turned to others' fiction "to write it over my way," taking "liberties with the greatest" (*L*, IV, 238), but Auchincloss proved himself adept at the same thing by rewriting the novels of James.

Adeline Bloodgood, the "oldest member of the Book Class . . . and its sole virgin" (*BC*, 90), harks back to James's Crapy Cornelia, also an older virgin. In the manner of Cornelia, she "offers" the young man Chris has become a "sense of life." Adeline's story hangs on the supposition by most people that her devotion to Judge Melrose has kept her from marrying. A Jamesian locution creeps into the chapter about her when Judge Melrose, referring to Chris, says, "Invite the delightful young man here again" (*BC*, 105). Auchincloss knew there was only one "delightful young man" in James's letters, Stark Young (see above, pp. 158–59), and indeed he had earlier made a stab at revising James's list for Young (*RJ*, 218–19). The truth that emerges is that Melrose never gobbled Adeline up at all. The judge left her a trust whether she married or not, permitting her to live the way she wanted to.

Mylo Jessup's story is of a love for Rick Wise, the aesthetic, ailing son of a wealthy Jewish financier, and of her acquiring from him a Pateresque aestheticism. After he dies, she marries Halsted Jessup simply because he admires her for having brought joy to the dying boy. Her sense of mission shifts at that juncture to Halsted the athlete. His stroke leaves her living ostensibly for his sake but really for her own. She builds an "altar of the dead" with his money. One of her tutors in the religion of beauty was Henry James, and *The Wings of the Dove* shadows her story, for she, like Merton Densher, was converted by the spirit of a dying young person whose wings covered her. James's name and Halsted's comparison of her to Catherine of Russia also link her to Milly Theale (*BC,* 138). She asks Chris to fix up her Greek Revival temple, so as to enable "this unprecedented escape into the world of beautiful things" for Halsted after his stroke (*BC,* 139). Halsted banters, however, "The good burghers of Bracton won't recognize the old place when she's through with it. She'll be like that czarina—who was it?—that had pretty villages erected at the stages of her proposed progresses!" (*BC,* 138). In *The Wings of the Dove,* Susan Shepherd compares Milly's arrangements at the rococo palazzo she rents in Venice "to the Empress Catherine's famous progress across the steppes of Russia; improvised settlements appeared at each turn of the road" (NYE, XX, 136).

Genevieve, Marquise de Terrasson, another member of the club, has forgotten her origins and thinks she is French. When her son says, "The story of the Terrassons will have waited all these years for an American viewpoint" (*BC,* 187), he strikes a chord not only with James's *The American* but also with his *The Reverberator,* in which the members of the family into which Francie Dosson is marrying are overwhelmingly Gallicized. When Genevieve wishes to publish her memoirs, the family rises up in arms, just as in James's novel the Proberts break with the Dossons over a bit of vulgar journalism. The ability to forget one's origins and to make up a fantasy world may well have been suggested to Auchincloss by James's short and amusing novel.

Maud Erskine, who brings the date up to 1980 in reflecting on her fellow members of the class, now all dead, carries vestiges of *The Ambassadors,* for she has long been involved in a "virtuous attachment" (NYE, XX, 136), something that is today considered shameful. An ugly duckling, she enjoys a sexless marriage with an important ambassador. The last chapter of the book tries to go beyond Henry James with a summation of what Auchincloss has accomplished and failed to accomplish through the artistry he learned from James. Maud, as the chief justice of the nine old women of an earlier generation, passes down her judgment upon their judgment and lays out what readers *should* find in Chris's book. In the ninth mention in the novel of James's name, she criticizes Chris's "Jamesian" handling of the narrative. "Why not say it outright?" she asks (*BC*, 209). She concludes that the women were at least "serious . . . about their mission in life. Whatever it was" (*BC*, 210). She admits their power over their men, but holds that "they didn't waste their lives." They felt under "some kind of duty . . . to be good" (*BC*, 211).

By a witty stroke, Chris inquires what the women would say "if *this* book came up for discussion at lunch on a fleecy cloud above." The novel's last scene thus shares the form of the first scene, as he eavesdrops on the heavenly meeting. Although the members may feel betrayed by his memoir, he insists that everything "has been said with love" (*BC*, 211). On Maud Erskine's advice he stops being Jamesian and aligns himself with her unvarnished summation of what the reader should take from the "partial portraits" (*BC*, 210). In the last chapter, Auchincloss' "own way" of doing it gains its greatest ascendance as he makes the most of his own gifts and his background in the law. The Day of Judgment is truly a court proceeding, and Auchincloss puts in his bid to be a partner in the firm of James and Wharton. Auchincloss took even more seriously than Wharton did the advice James bestowed on her to stay "in native pastures" (LU, I, 396).

In 1983, the year before *The Book Class* came out, Auchincloss published *Narcissa and Other Fables*, a book of stories. In "Marley's Chain," one of the stories, there is a rewriting of James's late tale "Crapy Cornelia." James had a middle-aged gentleman who is on the verge of marrying a dazzling youngish and modern widow choose instead to spend the rest of his days with a frumpish older spinster, who can share his memories of their youth together. Auchincloss reverses this, having his hero reject the plain spinster in favor of the dashing widow with good taste. In *Diary of a Yuppie*, of 1986, there is a declaration on the first page that, although Henry James disapproved of first-person narrators on the grounds that they limit stories to what the "I" experiences, a first-person narrator will do here since "people know more about themselves today than they did in Mr. James's time—or at least they should."[36] The yuppie, Robert Service, though a crude takeover operator, seems to have read James and has had some courses in literature at Columbia University. The plot of Auchincloss' novel derives from "A Light Man," of 1869, by Henry James, in which Maximus Austin, also

36. Louis Auchincloss, *The Diary of a Yuppie* (New York, 1986), 1–2.

a first-person narrator, is playing for money. Auchincloss refers to the Roman Empire throughout, bringing to mind Gibbon's *Decline and Fall* and James's "The Siege of London," in which the Romans of the decadence are featured. "I have an imagination easily inflamed by horrors" relates to James's phrase "imagination of disaster." The yuppie has an affair with Sylvia Sands, who works for a woman in a position of responsibility with a large foundation. Sylvia shows not the slightest jealousy of the yuppie's intimacy with a rich woman who is about to die, as Kate Croy in *The Wings of the Dove* nurtures Merton Densher's romantic friendship with a dying heiress, Milly Theale, in order that he may inherit and share with her the heiress' fortune.

Auchincloss from time to time published other collections of tales joined by a common theme in the manner of the novel *The Book Class*. After 1983, six out of his eleven volumes of fiction are collections of tales, sometimes integrated, sometimes not. *Skinny Island*, of 1987, is a second volume of stories based on Manhattan situations, in form following *The Winthrop Covenant*, of 1976, though not thematically joined like it. Each tale of the newer book focuses on another step in the evolution or devolution of New York types. In the tales of the 1980s Auchincloss was no longer reading over Henry James's shoulder to the same extent as earlier. The presence of Jamesian icons does not go much beyond the naming of characters or personages connected with James. Theodore Childe, the hero of one tale, is named after one of James's close friends for no clear reason, with a final *e* added to his last name. The "painter's eye," which John La Farge had ascribed to James, becomes an attribute of Auchincloss' Eric Stair.

Anita Vogel, the heroine of *The Golden Calves*, of 1988, a novel Auchincloss set in a museum, is close to Fleda Vetch in James's *The Spoils of Poynton:* financial reasons attach her, like Fleda, to an older woman who owns a valuable collection of art. Mark Adams, the hero, in his desire to get the art collection through Anita for the museum, is compared by a friend to the hero of "*The Aspern Papers*, isn't it? You get the treasure if you marry the old girl's niece. Except it's not the niece but the . . . dim, rather faded companion."[37]

In *Fellow Passengers*, of 1989, each portrait in a gallery of ten is an independent tale from the point of view of the passenger Dan Ruggles. Auchincloss quotes the anecdote about James's having said to Ruth Draper, the

37. Louis Auchincloss, *The Golden Calves* (Boston, 1988), 65.

monologuist, "You have woven your own little magic carpet. Stand on it!" The remark is dated 1912, when James wrote his monologue for Draper (*FP*, 118). One character is named Jonathan Sturges, after the young crippled friend of James's late years to whom Howells had given the famous advice "Live all you can." In the tale "Abel Donner," the hero is not only compared to Lawyer Crick in *Ivory Tower*, the novel James worked on from 1910 to 1917 but did not complete, but James's description of Crick is offered as being equally descriptive of Donner and some of James's words are quoted without quotation marks (*IT*, 245). Ellen Emmet Rand, a member of a branch of James's family he called the Emmetry, is mentioned by name as the "poor man's Sargent" (*FP*, 36).

In *The Vanderbilt Era*, of 1989, James's name fails to appear in only five of the twenty-two chapters. James shed light on the era under consideration in *The American Scene*, touching on the persons Auchincloss is dealing with, and their possessions. He brilliantly captured Biltmore, the castle of George Vanderbilt. Auchincloss sees the Duke of Marlborough, Consuelo Vanderbilt's first husband, as a "twin of Gilbert Osmond, Henry James's frigid dilettante" (*VE*, 108), and the Grace who became a Vanderbilt as the source for "Julia Bride" by virtue of enduring in life the attitude James has society adopt toward his unfortunate girl (*VE*, 11). Auchincloss' piece on John Singer Sargent is lighted up by James's essay on the artist, and James contributes color to this chapter when he appears lunching with Saint-Gaudens at the Century Club (*VE*, 139).

In *False Gods*, a collection from 1992 in which each tale has a parallel in one of the gods or muses of classic mythology, two sorts of references to James occur, both integrated into the tales even more adroitly than previously. One consists of plot resemblances to James's novels. In "Ares, God of War," Roger Carstairs, the southern lawyer, goes to New York after the Civil War, trailing associations with James's *The Bostonians*, which has to do with the same period. The name of Basil Tremont, who is his mother's cousin and runs the law firm he joins, is close to that of Basil Ransom, the southern cousin of Olive Chancellor in *The Bostonians*. The central point of interest lies in the fact that Roger is like Basil Ransom in being a conservative who wants to establish a career in the North but unlike Basil Ransom in returning to the South with his northern bride. Kitty Carstairs was brought up in Paris and is one of those children affected by the "semiludicrous efforts of their Francophile parents to be included in the *gratin* of the old faubourg" (*FG*, 14). This is a distinct allusion to Gaston Probert's family in *The Reverberator.* In "Hephaestus: God of Newfangled Things," the architect Gilbert Kane's mother had ambitions as a young girl to be a famous actress, much like Miriam Rooth in *The Tragic Muse.* But after reciting a *"tirade* from Phèdre" before the famous French actress Réjane, as Miriam also does before a leading actress, she was forced to marry her parents' choice and had to give up a theatrical career. Auchincloss' character reversed the course of Miriam Rooth, however, who turns down a diplomat suitor to marry her stage manager. In the same tale, Gilbert's affair with his uncle's wife makes him feel "enmeshed in something a bit sickly sweet, something like a nineteenth-century French academic painting of a Roman banquet, with white robes slipping off the alabaster limbs of languidly reclining ladies" (*FG,* 119). This is an accurate transcription of Thomas Couture's *The Romans of the Decadence,* of 1847, which Auchincloss would have remembered lends itself to a striking metaphor in James's "The Siege of London."

The second sort of reference to James in *False Gods* involves naming him or introducing a quotation from his work. In "Hermes: God of the Self-Made Man," Dorothy Stonor is auditing a course on W. D. Howells, Edith Wharton, and Henry James (*FG,* 53). Two characters "exclaim, like the dying Henry James, 'At last, the distinguished thing!'" (*FG,* 93). This is the second time Auchincloss has invoked the exclamation imputed to James during his first stroke. In the tale paralleling Hephaestus, Gilbert Kane wants architecturally to carry the "spirit of the European country manor to the West in such a way as to enhance and even to enrich what Henry James had called 'the thin American air'" (*FG,* 102).

Auchincloss weaves in his quotations from James by making them spring from the minds of his characters. They, like the author, have been exposed to James's fiction, whether by taking a course or coming in touch with the European tradition surrounding him.

Three Lives, of 1993, a collection of longish tales, really novellas, seems to have been written to exhibit Auchincloss' effectiveness with first-person narrative in spite of James's caution against it. In the preface to *The Ambassadors,* James had written that the first-person novel incurs a loss in unity and composition. "The double privilege of treating the narrative in the first person," wrote James, "of being at once the subject and the object, sweeps away difficulties at the expense of discrimination. It prevents the possibility of a center and prevents real directness of contact" (*AM,* xxx). Although Auchincloss adverts to James's reservations about first-person narratives only on the last page of "The Epicurean," the first of his three tales, all the

16. Anthony Van Dyck's portrait of
James Stuart, Duke of Richmond and Lennox

The Metropolitan Museum of Art, Marquand Collection,
Gift of Henry G. Marquand, 1889 (89.15.16)

tales are told by the main character in the first person. In the first tale, the
"I," Nat Chisolm, tells his stepfather, the English diplomat Percy, that he
has been writing a memoir, maybe to assume the form of a novel. This "I"
reconstructs dialogue he could never have remembered so exactly, and he
illustrates the "self-knowing narrator Henry James so much disapproved
of. For who would have written his own life in that way? Well, sir, Nat Chisolm would have!" (*TL*, 85). Auchincloss, through his character, rebuts
James on this particular point.

In "The Stoic," when there is a "discussion of a railroad receivership"
(*TL*, 149), Henry G. Marquand (1818–1902) is involved in the character
of the collector Lees Dunbar. Dunbar asks the hero what he thinks of "that
Van Dyck" in his library. Marquand gave Van Dyck's *James Stuart, Duke of
Richmond and Lennox* to the Metropolitan Museum (Figure 16). He also

comes to mind in connection with the railroad receivership because he purchased the Iron Mountain Railroad and became the director of the Missouri Pacific system.

Although Auchincloss in these stories still relied on certain technical devices he learned from James, he modified them and claimed them as his own. Learning from James how to use, symbolically and visually, certain masterpieces in order to iconify his donnée, he went on to make those masterpieces easily identifiable ones, such as the portrait by Van Dyck of *A Young Cavalier with a Wolfhound*, recognized at once as the Duke of Richmond. He devoted a long paragraph to the painting and to the narrator's links to the young duke. But the choice of the picture has been dictated by a passage in Henry James's review "The Old Masters at Burlington House," originally published in the *Nation* of February 1, 1877, and republished in 1956 in *The Painter's Eye*. James's appreciative description reads,

> Then there is one of the fine Van Dycks I spoke of—a certain Duke of Richmond of Charles I's time. He is dressed in black satin, with wrinkled stockings of pale, faded blue, and he rests his right hand upon the head of a great deerhound which is seated on his haunches beside him, and which leans his long nose against his thigh and looks up with a canine softness that is admirably indicated. The gentleman's yellow hair falls upon his satin mantle, and his face, which is not handsome, is touchingly grave. Such a give-and-take of gentlemanliness between painter and model is surely nowhere else to be seen. (*PE*, 128)

Auchincloss offered a description of the painting when Lees Dunbar shows it to the narrator as a picture he is contemplating buying:

> The canvas before me depicted a young Cavalier with a wolfhound. The youth, lace-collared, long-legged, high-heeled, one hand casually on a hip, the other muzzling the affectionate canine, had high cheekbones, long blond hair and blue eyes serenely reflecting the security of his rank and station. . . .
>
> "He was killed by the Roundheads in the Civil War." Dunbar slowly lit his cigar. "You can see that, can't you? He has that look of doom." . . .
>
> I studied the canvas for another silent period. What did he want me to say? Could he have supposed that I might derive some instruction from a contrast between the young peer and myself? I too was long and skinny and of a pale complexion, but my eyes were closer together and my brown hair rose in a billow over my high brow. . . . Was the Cavalier laughing at me? Or

was he sneeringly suggesting that I was a kind of renegade Cavalier who had perversely turned myself into a quill-behind-the-ear Roundhead? But I didn't want to cut off anyone's head, least of all a king's. (*TL*, 149, 150)

Auchincloss, stimulated by James's charming passage, decided to do his own pastiche on the impressions this painting made on the narrator. He also used the picture and the sitter for the picture as a symbol for the financial dealings in which the narrator and the owner of the picture are involved.

The degree to which James's novels, letters, and criticism have penetrated Auchincloss' consciousness is not dissimilar from the degree to which Balzac penetrated James's consciousness, as he recorded in an essay about Balzac in 1902. Certain influential books we read when young, he held, "exist for us, with the lapse of time, as the substance itself of knowledge: they have been intellectually so swallowed, digested and assimilated that we take their general use and suggestion for granted, cease to be aware of them because they have passed out of sight. But they have passed out of sight simply by having passed into our lives. They have become a part of our personal history, a part of ourselves ... so far as we may have succeeded in best expressing ourselves" (*NN*, 109–10). Thus it is with Auchincloss after a lifetime of reading James, of writing two books of criticism devoted chiefly to his writings, and of working within and out of the Jamesian tradition. He shows a Jamesian sympathy for his women, even when he is revealing their weaknesses. In essence, as James said of himself with regard to Balzac, Auchincloss has "largely been living on [his] benefactor—which is the highest acknowledgment one can make" (*NN*, 110).

Philip Roth in Jamesian Disguise

Standing on James: James as Roth's Ghostwriter

If Auchincloss received his legacy from Henry James as a rightful heir and family member, Philip Roth, as an outsider to the Jamesian tradition, has engaged in a long struggle with James. He has needed James's blessing, but he has also needed the freedom to break away from his indebtedness to

The material in this section appeared in somewhat different form as "Henry James as Roth's Ghostwriter," in *Midstream*, XXVII (March, 1981), 48–51.

his benefactor. Out of this struggle has emerged a polarized and energized fiction.

Who is the ghostwriter in Philip Roth's *The Ghost Writer,* of 1979? In this novella of guilt about anti-Semitism, the ghost seems to be that of Anne Frank. But the delusion of Amy Bellette, his student heroine, that she is Anne Frank's ghost cannot sustain the imaginative load the ghostwriter carries. The "madness of art," not the madness of Amy, is required. The effectuating ghost reveals itself to be Henry James himself, a ghost that does the writing of the book, just as a ghostwriter should. Philip Roth (1933–) lets James's presence be seen through both quotations and references to his tale "The Middle Years," of 1893. But by a literary sleight of hand he conceals another of James's stories, "The Author of Beltraffio," of 1884, and the main line of this tale's plot is the main line of the plot of *The Ghost Writer.*

Roth elaborated his novella in just the form Henry James had developed. James's approach was to place one literary classic within his story by conspicuously taking a character or situation from it and then covertly to re-create the form of another classic by the same author through an original variation on it. James named Lewis Lambert Strether after the hero of Balzac's not very good novel *Louis Lambert,* and then he made the plot hang on a very good Balzac story, "Madame Firmiani." He has mined two literary models by the same author, one declared and one undeclared.[38] In *The Ghost Writer,* Roth followed James's approach, but he also turned to James as the author of the two literary works from which he drew. In bringing James's "The Middle Years" physically and textually into the plot by naming the story and having his writer read and mark the famous passage in it about the "madness of art," Roth introduced his fantasy about Amy and Lonoff, the established writer whom the narrator seeks out, and he created Amy's identification with Anne Frank. The invention serves to compensate for the pain Nathan Zuckerman, his hero, has caused his family by exposing in an early published story certain aspects of Jews that will make them vulnerable to anti-Semitism. But Roth covertly shaped his story through structural parallels with James's "The Author of Beltraffio," which deals with the visit an enthusiastic young writer pays to a literary master living in the country. His visit, which ends in disaster, with the death of the child of the people he is visiting, disturbs the balance between

---

38. Adeline R. Tintner, *The Book World of Henry James* (Ann Arbor, Mich., 1987), 301–308.

the great man and his wife. Although the disaster in Roth's tale does not involve involuntary murder, the dependence of *The Ghost Writer* on "The Author of Beltraffio" is evident from the first page: "It was the last daylight
hour of a December afternoon more than twenty years ago. I was twenty-
three, writing and publishing my first short stories . . . when I arrived at his
hideaway to meet the great man" (*GW*, 3). James's novella begins similarly.
A young author of twenty-five is met at the station by his great master, to
whom he has a letter of introduction. Both trips are recollected more than
twenty years later. Both young men describe the houses they are visiting
with a good deal of envy. Roth's "old farmhouse" in New England was just
what it was chic to be living in a generation ago if you were a famous writer,
and James's pre-Raphaelite cottage, "glorified and translated," an "old English demesne," seemed a wonderful place to live to a visiting American
writer in the 1850s or 1860s. Roth's character Lonoff is as fashionable in his
ethnic tastes as James's Italy-enamored Mark Ambient in his art-for-art's-
sake attitude.

The young man's impressions of the two women in Lonoff's establishment are similar to those of the young narrator concerning the two women
in "The Author of Beltraffio." As James's Mrs. Ambient, the master's wife,
reminds James's narrator of a Sir Joshua Reynolds (and his sister, Miss
Ambient, of a Rossetti), young Amy Bellette reminds Zuckerman of a Velázquez. James's hero's penchant is for the aesthetic side of life, and the resemblance of Ambient's wife to a work of art blinds him to her narrow,
rigid character and her fundamental hatred of her husband's point of view.
As an American, he fails to understand her. In his unfamiliarity with her
type, he encourages her to read the proofs of her husband's latest book,
which convince her that it would be better for their sick child to die than to
know his father's decadent works. If the young writer had not interfered
with the life of the family nor pressed Mrs. Ambient to read the book, the
tragedy might have been averted. The reader is told that the episode cured
the young man of his confusion of life with art. In Roth's story, the presence
of the young writer, who represents the outside world to the imprisoned
Mrs. Lonoff, releases her bottled-up feelings of self-disgust at being old
and of helplessness before her husband's lack of interest in her, and that
leads to her making a scene in which she offers to leave the house so that her
husband may make the beautiful young Amy his mistress. Nathan, like
James's nameless hero, is treated to a vision of domestic turmoil triggered
by his own worshipful visit to the house.

Both Mrs. Ambient and Hope Lonoff suffer from the seclusion their husband's profession means for them. There is a conversion of Mark Ambient's speculation — "As for my little boy . . . we shall probably kill him between us, before we have done with him!" (V, 317) — into Hope's exhortation to Lonoff, "Chuck me out! Please, now, before your goodness and your wisdom kill us both!" (*GW,* 44).

One passage from James's story, in which Ambient tells the young narrator, "You are very young after all," and the young man answers, "But you may treat me as if I could understand you!" (V, 318), particularly contrasts with Roth's. For Nathan is not really interested in understanding Lonoff's stories but in having Lonoff praise his.

Lonoff, moreover, never comes off as a great master of anything; unlike Dencombe of James's "The Middle Years," he is a bore. He describes his artistic activity:

> I turn sentences around. That's my life. I write a sentence and then I turn it around. Then I look at it and I turn it around again. Then I have lunch. Then I come back in and write another sentence. Then I have tea and turn the new sentence around. Then I read the two sentences over and turn them both around. Then I lie down on my sofa and think. Then I get up and throw them out and start from the beginning. And if I knock off from this routine for as long as a day, I'm frantic with boredom and a sense of waste. (*GW,* 17–18)

The sterility of the dedicated artist's life for those living with him comes across in each wife's reaction to her marriage, for in each story the wife is alien to the writer in background and temperament. Hope is a New England Gentile married to a Jew; Beatrice Ambient is a stern Calvinist married to an aesthete and devotee of sensuous experiences, the paradigm for which at that period in English cultural history lay in Italian art. After sexual fantasizing and gratification, Roth's hero reads James's "The Middle Years" twice and tells the reader its plot, annotated by Lonoff, who has marked the passage "the rest is the madness of art" (*GW,* 163). Then he does his eavesdropping, and there is a shift out of "The Author of Beltraffio" into "The Middle Years," in Amy's reading her (Anne Frank's) diary, congruently with Dencombe's reading his book, *The Middle Years.*

Dencombe, the middle-aged writer of James's tale, has forgotten what his just published book was about, and he is elated by what he finds: "Never, probably, had that talent, such as it was, been so fine. . . . The result produced in his little book was somehow a result beyond his conscious intention: it was as if he had planted his genius, had trusted his method, and they had grown up and flowered with this sweetness" (IX, 56). As Amy looks over Anne Frank's diary after ten years, she reacts like Dencombe: "But mostly she marked passages she couldn't believe that she had written as little more than a child. Why, what eloquence, Anne . . . what deftness, what wit! . . . She'd had a great subject" (*GW*, 136). James and Anne Frank combine their power in *The Ghost Writer*, one to direct the narrative curve of the story, the other to direct the fantasizing tendency in Nathan Zuckerman.

Nathan stands on a fat volume of James's stories he has just read to eavesdrop on the upstairs conversation between Amy and Lonoff, symbolically true both to his reliance on the stories for understanding what he hears and to Roth's reliance on James in writing his story. Lonoff rationalizes his rejection of Amy's offer of herself by admitting his "singularity" as far as sex is concerned — an echo of James's "obscure hurt." Lonoff's rejection of the beautiful young woman may be a version of James's rejection of his women. Next Lonoff comes "heavily to his feet; slowly and heavily, like an elephant" (*GW*, 71). Edel's biography, which Roth undoubtedly read, includes many letters in which James refers to himself as an elephant. Lonoff complains about the "pain in his back," which was a symptom of James's disorders. Close to the end of the story, Lonoff explains his wife's erratic behavior as having a cause similar to the one that emerges in "The Author of Beltraffio": "This is all because we've had visitors. This is all because somebody new stayed the night" (*GW*, 176). Lonoff with this sheds his disguise as James the master to resume his part as Ambient the master.

Hiding Behind James

In Roth's succeeding novella, *Zuckerman Unbound*, of 1981, the hero, still Nathan Zuckerman, shows a line from a letter of Henry James to his agent exactly halfway through the book: *"All this is far from being life as I feel it, as I see it, as I know it, as I wish to know it."* But the agent is neither edified nor amused: "The world is yours, Nathan, don't hide from it behind Henry James. It's bad enough that that's what he hid behind" (*ZU*, 100).

The material in this section appeared in somewhat different form as "Hiding Behind James," *Midstream*, XXVIII (April, 1982), 49–53.

Even though the title *Zuckerman Unbound* is Shelleyan and the whole gamut of Roth's reading appears between the novella's covers, once again James enters by way of two stories. This time it was his own past as well as James's that Roth was trying to free himself from. The uncrating of books in the pages of this novel marks Nathan's move from his Village flat to new bachelor quarters on the Upper East Side. "Uncarton all the boxed-in brains! Then uncarton your own!" (*ZU,* 99): the unburdening of Zuckerman's overbookishness means that Proust, Joyce, Wolfe, Tolstoi, Chekhov, Kafka, Hemingway, Dylan Thomas, either named or recognizable by a well-known tag, get flung into the text like ballast cast out of Nathan's life. Yet they do not contribute to the art of writing the book. They represent *idées reçues* ingested in the youthful devouring of literary pablum, now up-chucked by Nathan in his adulthood. They may be viewed also as the literary bricks with which he builds the story, but they are neither foundation nor support, which come from the two stories by James. If he once hid behind James, as his agent fears, he hides behind him now even more. In *The Ghost Writer,* one of James's stories is overtly present and another hidden, but here both are hidden. Yet, emulating James in pointing to his novella's hidden form, he gives the reader clues; he plays the game fairly. James is still necessary to unbind Zuckerman culturally, as he struggles to free himself from his library, his family, and his alter ego.

Roth has said he is part Henny Youngman, the master of the comic one-liner, and part Henry James. He has thought of himself as a divided self, and it is as a divided self that Nathan Zuckerman appears at the period the novella addresses, around 1969. The main plot development clearly springs from the most famous tale of the divided self written in the twentieth century, James's "The Jolly Corner," which concerns a returned expatriate's pursuit of his alter ego. In it a man plans the demolition of his past and home, just as Zuckerman plans his own liberation. But Roth reverses the situation of James's Spencer Brydon, who conjures up a ghost, the man he might have been had he stayed in his own country. In Roth's version, the aggressive alter ego, Alvin Pepler, is the one who stayed behind and failed to become a celebrity like Nathan. Yet, just like the alter ego at the end of "The Jolly Corner," Pepler attacks and threatens his counterpart.

The title "The Jolly Corner" is ironic, contrasting the once jolly and lively corner of Brydon's youth to the corner of ghostly terror it has become. The atmosphere of Madison Avenue, to which Nathan has moved, could not be jollier, yet at Eighty-First Street, opposite his new apartment, stands Campbell's funeral parlor. In front of the mortuary, Pepler's aggression against Nathan takes place. Faced with the oppressive Pepler and his accusations, Nathan escapes through the corridors of the building: "He would take the rear exit, no matter how dark or dank the subterranean corridors he had to escape through" (*ZU*, 159). His experience replays Spencer Brydon's ordeal through the many-corridored house, filled with the "dusk of distances and the darkness of corners" (XII, 211). But Roth converts and reverses the Jamesian forms. Nathan, who from his window has seen the "stiffs" unloaded at night, now goes through a "bright carpeted hallway. . . . No ghoul emerged to take his measurements." His alter ego, the fact-filled Pepler, is now "dans le vrai," in broad daylight, outside and in front of Campbell's underworld emporium.

Pepler resembles James's alter ego in certain details of his physical appearance. He wears a "black raincoat and hat" and not evening clothes, but in the final scene of aggression he wears "dark glasses," which make Nathan think he is perhaps "unfortunately blind," like the alter ego in "The Jolly Corner" with "his poor ruined sight" accompanying his dearth of insight, a deficiency Pepler shares with him. Nathan cries, *"Who is he behind those dark glasses? Me! He thinks he's me!"* (*ZU*, 149). He resists this idea less than James's Brydon, who insists, "He's none of *me*, even as I *might* have been," despite his friend Alice's insisting that the "black stranger" is Brydon as he *"might* have been" (XII, 231).

James's hero plans to tear down his house because his childhood is over and the house is merely the ruin of his youth. In a different way, Nathan's childhood home in Newark is also a ruin: his family has moved to healthier and safer places, and society has abandoned the house to decay. As Brydon in his midnight roaming through his abandoned house invites "the builders, the destroyers" to "come as soon as they would" (XII, 223), so Nathan in riding through the ruined landmarks of his youth has no further use for them. "All his lyrical feeling for the neighborhood had gone into *Carnovsky*," his new book. That part of his life is over. "Over. Over. Over. Over. Over. I've served my time." The five *over*s recall the five *never*s in King Lear. But James is not over for Roth. The James occupying Roth's mind, behind whom he is still hiding, resurges in the traces left on his book by "The Figure in the Carpet," on the surface a tale about attempts to uncover a writer's "secret" intention in his oeuvre. Roth never names the story, but those steeped in James can recognize details from it, justifying Alvin Pepler's conviction that "art is *controlled*, art is *managed*, art is *always* rigged" (*ZU,* 38).

Three clues stand out. The first is the thrice-mentioned oriental rug, which Nathan has purchased as the only piece of decor for his Madison Avenue apartment. The last mention has Nathan sitting on it in his empty room, listening to television personalities distort the meaning of his work — such distortion being the theme of James's tale.

The second clue resides in the proliferation of words beginning with the letter *p* in the first half of the novel, where they occur with a frequency far in excess of what the laws of chance would predict. At least fourteen names of people and places begin with *p* in the first half, to say nothing of the hundreds of other *p*-words, such as *paranoia* and *peritonitis,* along with phrases like "Pig Threatens Porn," "price of a pound of flesh," "police protection," and "penthouse at the Pierre," all jammed together within about fifty or sixty pages. Pepler, the alter ego, is a walking icon of the letter. There is also an epidemic of words starting with *p* in "The Figure in the Carpet," from the first page to the climax where the "preference for the letter P" gives the repetition its rationale. The writer Hugh Vereker tells the narrator that what "nobody has ever mentioned in my work is the organ of life." The young critic answers, "It's some kind of game you're up to with your style, something you're after in the language. Perhaps it's a preference for the letter P! . . . Papa, potatoes, prunes — that sort of thing?" (IX, 284). Vereker says he has the wrong letter, but the reader must discount that. The system operates on a level below the narrative. The contiguity of the organ of life with the letter *p* suggests to the modern reader the male organ, the penis. But the modern reader is also stopped by an awareness of the hold of the genteel tradition on James's writings. Hence, there are grounds for exploring whether the treasure hunt and its clues might not square with some other interpretation.

The third clue appears early in the book and seems an anachronism in a contemporary novel until it is connected to the other two clues to complete the anagram for "The Figure in the Carpet." When the young girl students stare at Nathan in the bus, he concludes that "it must be phrenology they were studying at St. Mary's" (*ZU,* 6). The narrator and his friend Corvick in James's tale become obsessed with trying to figure out the general intent of Vereker's literary works, and Corvick, in India, succeeds in figuring out the "figure in the carpet." He gets married to a girl he has been more or less engaged to, but dies in an accident on his honeymoon. Although his bride knows the secret, she refuses to tell either the narrator or her second husband, by whom she has two children. After her death the narrator and the second husband, Drayton Deane, continue to search, but never discover the secret. Phrenology crops up in connection with the very intellectual Deane, who looks "like a dim phrenological bust." The "numbers on his bumps" began "to come out" (IX, 313). Purchase is thus given for translating the organ of life into phrenological terms, as relating to the various "organs" mappable on a plaster replica of the human head.

Why has Roth chosen "The Figure in the Carpet" as one of the stories he and his hero will hide behind? The agent's advice to Nathan Zuckerman includes the complaint "It's bad enough that that's what [James] hid behind" (see above, p. 206). Close attention to "The Figure in the Carpet" confirms Roth's observation that in this tale James hides behind himself, in an apt precedent for Roth's and Zuckerman's comportment. For a character like Zuckerman "wrote *Carnovsky*" (*ZU*, 5). That novel was about a "budding soul no less bedeviled by onanism in Jewish New Jersey than [the young Jesuit priest] Douglas growing up in Catholic Wisconsin" (*ZU*, 164). There is relevance in the possible concern of James's story with masturbation, in spite of modern criticism's resistance to coming to terms with it.[39]

The series of cryptic though finally fathomable hints apparently succeeding one another as red herrings leads to the conclusion that Vereker's secret consists in the joy of having a penis whose pleasurable sensations exist outside heterosexual or even homosexual experience and are unconnected with either amativeness or progeniture, organs number one and two on the phrenological bust suggested to the narrator by Deane's appearance.

In fact, the junction of Deane and phrenology should exempt him for good from the suspicion of autoerotism that the final paragraph of the story may spark, for Orson Fowler, the leading phrenologist of the time, had written a large sex manual in which he severely reproved self-abuse and Deane never learns the secret. The language of this paragraph, metaphoric in nature, may equally be representing Deane as in the preparatory stages of an erection that achieves tumescence but not climax. At the start is the word *ejaculations*, presumably employed in its linguistic rather than sexual

39. Adeline R. Tintner, "Hiding Behind James: Roth's *Zuckerman Unbound*," *Midstream*, XXVIII (1982), 49–53.

sense. The mounting spasm is disguised as Deane's reaction to his wife's want of trust in him: "But I saw that immediate shock throb away little by little and then gather again into waves of wonder and curiosity—waves that promised . . . to break in the end with the fury of my own highest tides. I may say that today as victims of unappeased desire there isn't a pin to choose between us" (IX, 315). Vereker has told the narrator that had he had a glimpse of his secret, "the element in question would soon have become practically all you'd see" (IX, 282). That is finally all the reader sees who follows this far, realizing why the secret had to be kept. It took the author of *Portnoy's Complaint* to spot this obsession. The secret in human sexual experience that is most likely to be kept is masturbation, for with no partner and no witness there is little risk of being found out.

It would be absurd to believe that James meant us to think that Hugh Vereker wrote twenty volumes devoted to autoerotism. What he did mean us to see, if we would, in a vein of low, not high, comedy, was that the intent of a writer could be as private as the most private sexual act. Not sex, but secret sex, parallels the secret of a man's literary style. Thus a covert analogy becomes the heart of a theme seemingly remote from it. Roth, in spite of his hero's unboxing of his books and brains, continues to hide formally behind James. But more important, in selecting this story for half of his Jamesian shield, he forces us to see what "The Figure in the Carpet" is all about. Roth's novel acts as a "torch of . . . analogy" (*SF*, 66). James creates, through a systematic series of figures of speech, a private joke hidden from the average reader. It has taken Roth, sensitive to James and sensitive to masturbation, to open our eyes to it. In "The Figure in the Carpet," James not only does not name Vereker's secret, he weaves it into the carpet, or rather pushes it under the rug, which eventually Roth helps us, almost a century later, roll back.

James on Roth's Back: Roth's Anatomy of "Pain" and James's "Obscure Hurt"

At first it seems as if Henry James makes no entrance into *The Anatomy Lesson*, of 1983, the third volume of the Zuckerman trilogy. He is not conspicuously present as in *The Ghost Writer* and *Zuckerman Unbound*, and the hero

---

The material in this section appeared in somewhat different form as "Roth's Pain and James's Obscure Hurt," in *Midstream*, XXXI (March, 1985), 58–60.

appears to be heeding the agent's plea "Stop hiding behind Henry James." The novel never mentions James, nor have any of his tales slipped into the narrative. But the "restless analyst," the reader steeped in James, sees fairly soon that James is not gone, after all. The great, mostly unread trilogy of James's *Autobiography*—consisting of *A Small Boy and Others*, of 1913, *Notes of a Son and Brother*, of 1914, and *The Middle Years*, of 1917, which was unfinished at James's death—glimmers through the master plan for Zuckerman's autobiography, that is, the novel. From James's second volume, *Notes of a Son and Brother*, comes the substance of the plan.

At the core of *The Anatomy Lesson* is Zuckerman's intolerable and undiagnosable pain, a "pain that made it difficult to walk for more than a few city blocks or even to stand in one place" (*AY*, 3). The novel revolves around the account of that pain, its effect on Zuckerman's life, and his efforts to overcome it. A malady with the same features of physical location and resistance to treatment that James refers to in *Notes of a Son and Brother* as his own "horrid even if obscure hurt" has given rise to a whole literature of theories about James's sexual and psychological difficulties unequaled by that dealing with any other factor in his life. The prose describing it is as dense a thicket of language as any to be found in James, emphasizing the obscurity of the "hurt." Even James's painstaking biographer Leon Edel finds that the lines "bristle with strange ambiguities."[40]

As with Zuckerman's pain, when the eighteen-year-old James had found himself "jammed into the acute angle between two high fences" while helping to extinguish a fire—with the result that "I had done myself, in the face of a shabby conflagration, a horrid even if an obscure hurt"—the medical verdict was that there was "nothing to speak of the matter with me" (*AU*, 415). James wrote that "for a long time after" it continued as a "painful" experience and that his main therapy was "lying down book in hand" (*AU*, 419). Although the hurt was caused by a physical mishap and Zuckerman's was not, it lasted longer than it should have and became a locus of anxiety for him. James's friends related that even at forty James had to spend a good part of the day supine in order to face the ordeal of evening dinner parties. Zuckerman spends his day flat on a playmat from F. A. O. Schwarz, the toy store in New York City.

James's language shows how attached he was to his pain, or it to him. It "consistently declined, as an influence at play, to drop for a single instant.

40.   Leon Edel, *Henry James: The Untried Years* (Philadelphia, 1953), 175.

Circumstances, by a wonderful chance, overwhelmingly favoured it—*as* an interest, an inexhaustible, I mean" (*AU*, 415). Those circumstances involved the outbreak of the Civil War, so that his hurt became bound up in his mind with the battle wounds of countless young Americans. He wrote of "seeking to strike some sort of bargain" with this "less and less bearable affliction" (*AU*, 416). Perhaps the most striking affinity between Zuckerman's and James's pains rests in James's certainty that his suffering would last: "What was interesting from the first was my not doubting in the least its duration" (*AU*, 415). From James's "obscure hurt," Roth has made a characteristic leap. Zuckerman's pain, unlike James's, was not the result of an injury. Roth has eliminated the physical accident and has made the hurt into a metaphor for the burden of the writer's consciousness, the unbearable fate of the "man apart" who cannot "unchain himself" from his duties as a writer and must resist the claims of wives, family, and race.

On the first page, Zuckerman says, "Just having a neck, arms and shoulders was like carrying another person around" (*AY*, 31). No longer "hiding behind James," he is now figuratively carrying James on his back, as well as in that part of him which is fundamental for a writer, the obsessive concern with his own consciousness. James's *Autobiography* is the history of such a consciousness. The first volume begins with the "wonder of consciousness" and ends with a "lapse of consciousness" when the small Henry becomes seriously ill (*AU*, 236). The second is the record of the consciousness' fullest development, and it ends on the dying effort of James's cousin Minny Temple to "cling to consciousness" (AU, 544). Consciousness had become what a few years earlier James, in one of his New York Edition prefaces, called a "*usurping* consciousness" (*AN*, 90). Roth now has it usurp not only the mind of his character but also his entire body, creating a woe that unites it to the Jamesian notion of the obscure hurt. It is unbearable: "Then the hell with consciousness," Zuckerman cries out. "To make so much of consciousness may have been my first mistake" (*AY*, 248). That is another way of saying, To make so much of Henry James may have been my first mistake. Roth tries to extricate his hero from the intolerable situation by having him take on the profession of Henry's older, admired brother William—by becoming, in short, a doctor.

From *Notes of a Son and Brother*, Roth has taken Henry and William's father's admonition to "convert, convert"—not to discard or deny experience but to transform it into something else valuable. To get rid of his hero's burden, he converts Henry's painful vocation as a writer into one that deals with everyday pain in its ordinary appearance. "I want the real thing, the thing *in the raw*," Zuckerman cries, "and not for the writing but for itself" (*AY*, 204). When he opts for William's career, he gets moving, his pain notwithstanding, and lands in Chicago, the landscape of his education, at Billings, the great teaching hospital. By the end of the novel, however, it is plain that switching between the James brothers' careers is no solution to Zuckerman's problems. He will have to remain Henry, which is to say, Zuckerman the writer, attached to the art he has already successfully created, for to ask the question with a pun, how can he "unchain himself from a future as a man apart and escape from the corpus that was his?" (*AY*, 291).

In addition to providing Roth with the tyranny of the developed consciousness that is his hero's burden, James in his analysis of his relations with his parents and brother gives Roth a loose but recognizable model for Zuckerman's relations with his parents and his brother, incidentally also named Henry. Zuckerman and James are both essentially sons and brothers, and *The Anatomy Lesson* and James's *Autobiography* recount their histories in relation to parents and siblings. Both responded tenderly to their mothers; both entertained feelings of dissatisfaction with regard to their fathers. James felt his father was too permissive and too vacillating in planning his children's education. Zuckerman felt his father, because of his semiprofessional status, was more of an obstacle to his freedom as an intellectual than his archcritic Milton Appel's totally illiterate father was for Appel's: by not being able to enter at all into his son's educated consciousness, the elder Appel allowed his son perfect freedom in the life of the mind.

The scene in which Zuckerman accompanies his surgeon friend's father to the grave of his wife in snowbound Chicago has a kinship with James's two trips to snowbound Cambridge, one to bury his mother and the other, a year later, to visit the graves of both parents. The similarity in the episodes points to Roth's having read Edel's life of James, where the incidents in Cambridge are recorded. The line from James that Zuckerman shows his agent halfway through *Zuckerman Unbound* is from an unpublished letter as given by Edel in *Henry James*.

In contrast to Roth's earlier pilferings in the Jamesian oeuvre, *The Anatomy Lesson* shows that the James he has become interested in is the twentieth-century writer who took a retrospective view of his fiction for his New York Edition and revised it to suit the standards of a man who was writing in a different manner from earlier and seeing the world with a different vision.

The naming of *The Anatomy Lesson* after two world-famous paintings by Rembrandt may hark back to a novel by James, *The Tragic Muse,* which invoked two famous paintings, one by Sir Joshua Reynolds and one by Jean-Léon Gérôme. Calling Zuckerman's discovery that he cannot disengage himself from his body a "lesson in anatomy" is consistent with James's predilection for punning, both in his titles and in the material of his tales. That some judge Nathan Zuckerman's brother, Henry the dentist, to write "better than the writer" carries faint traces of the witticism current around the turn of the century that William was the philosopher who wrote like a novelist and Henry the novelist who wrote like a philosopher.

The principle of conversion helped James put to advantage his overcompensation for his guilt feelings by hitching his consciousness to his craftsmanship. In the last pages of *Notes of a Son and Brother,* he told how the "image" of Minny Temple's conscious dread of death—"she would have given anything to live"—led him to "lay the ghost by wrapping it, a particular occasion aiding, in the beauty and dignity of art" (*AU,* 544). He meant that in *The Wings of the Dove* he perpetuated her consciousness and personality.

In the last line of Roth's novel, Zuckerman is made to see himself "as a man apart," as James saw himself as "that queer monster, the artist." Roth seems to imply that Zuckerman has to go on writing because he is an artist. James wrote to his friend Henry Adams that the artist, "an obstinate finality, an inexhaustible sensibility," as he himself was, still at the age of seventy could find his consciousness interesting "under *cultivation* of the interest. Cultivate it *with* me" (*L,* IV, 706). Zuckerman will presumably continue to cultivate the interest of his consciousness, pain or no pain.

Still Bound to James: *The Prague Orgy*

Was Roth reacting to James as James did to the tales he had read as a young person, tales that had been, as he wrote, "so swallowed, digested and assimilated . . . that they have become a part of our personal history?" (*NN,* 109–10). Not quite, for James's influence on the Zuckerman trilogy and its epilogue, *The Prague Orgy,* of 1985, seems to have operated through a more conscious process. Still, in it, Roth as Zuckerman becomes James, as

The material in this section appeared in somewhat different form as *"The Prague Orgy,"* in *Midstream,* XXXI (December, 1985), 58–60.

James tells us he became Balzac. If we read it separated from the preceding three works, *The Prague Orgy* comes across as making a case for both unconscious and conscious modalities of literary influence. But as another segment of the whole, it discloses the appropriation of James's writings as a conscious aim. Here also two works by James underlie Roth's creation.

The Prague Orgy has for its basic model *The Middle Years*, the third, unfinished volume of James's autobiographical writings. In it, James moved away from his family and home and on "that momentous March day" of 1869 landed in Liverpool, beginning his experience of the Old World—for James, always fundamentally that of England and especially London. Because of his preparation through literature, nothing was "impenetrable . . . and still more wherever I pressed, I sank in and in up to my nose."[41]

Roth's epilogue begins in strikingly Jamesian language, the personality of Zuckerman receding from the center of the stage and Roth's other characters taking over, in a refocusing similar to that of *The Middle Years*, which, when it gets going, is primarily about English writers so far as they made an impression on the young James. *The Prague Orgy* on its first page also summons up *The Ivory Tower*, the other unfinished masterpiece by James. Roth has Eva Kalinova, the actress, appear in "black like Prince Hamlet," but her "funeral suit" shows signs of wear. Gray Fielder, the hero of *The Ivory Tower*, was also a "young black-clad figure"—black for the funeral of his uncle—but he, unlike Eva, was a "happy Hamlet" (*IT*, 191). Although Zuckerman's Europe has no happy spots, *The Prague Orgy* is always within the framework of the late James—in style, in outlook, and in tone—for *The Ivory Tower* is also concerned with the "black things" behind the fortunes of the very rich, the evil forces of society that were visible then to James if not to other writers.

For the plot, Roth went to another of James's works, and it may not be totally a coincidence that the work is considered the masterpiece of James's middle years. In "The Aspern Papers," the hero is a "publishing scoundrel," a nameless journalist who wants to obtain possession of the papers of a great deceased American romantic poet, Jeffrey Aspern. The price he must pay to get what he wants, however, is to marry Tina,[42] the unattractive,

---

41.   Henry James, *The Middle Years* (London, 1917), 8.

42.   James named this character "Tita" in the first version of the story, published in the *Atlantic Monthly* of March–May, 1888, a version that is still sometimes reprinted. But in Volume 12 of the New York Edition, he renamed her "Tina," which is the name I use throughout this book.

middle-aged spinster who is Miss Bordereau's niece. That is a price he is unwilling to pay.

The Prague Orgy has essentially the same plot. Roth has transmuted "The Aspern Papers" into a modern analogue. Zuckerman's mission is to obtain possession of some remarkable stories by Sisovsky's father, who like Aspern is now dead. The expectation is that their publication in the United States will garner a respected place for them as unique testimony to vanished Yiddish life. Eva now owns these stories, and her price is, like Tita's, marriage. Unlike her Jamesian predecessor—for she is a worldly woman, exhibiting the corrupt values and habits of the Central European middle class, distorted by Communist repression—she demands in harshly repeated four-letter words that Zuckerman sleep with her as a preliminary to marriage. Zuckerman who, like James in *The Middle Years*, has become a receptor of new experiences rather than an aggressive sexual personality, has lost his appetency for bedding down every available woman. He feels the disgust of the Aspern journalist, and verges on James's sexual ambiguity and his revulsion against women. The ending also follows the pattern of James's tale. Eva seems to be responsible for the confiscation of the Yiddish manuscripts, for although in a seemingly renunciatory gesture she allows Nathan to take them from her, the police confiscate them at his hotel. The linkage of *The Middle Years* and "The Aspern Papers" as sources for *The Prague Orgy* parallels the bimodal structure of the other parts of the Roth trilogy. The eight works by James that Roth has fundamentally relied on, two to a novel, constitute, as it were, an appreciative anthology of the writings by James most meaningful to him as a modern writer and sensibility.

Although the hero is urged to free himself from books, the trilogy is called, after all, *Zuckerman Bound*, and bound he still is. He is forced to learn that he can never "unchain himself from a future as a man apart and escape the corpus that was his" (*AY*, 697). He is an artist bound to the masterpieces of his tradition.

Turning James's "Madness of Art" to Artistic Profit: *The Counterlife*

In *The Counterlife*, of 1987, which is the fifth installment in the lives and deaths of Nathan Zuckerman, Henry James has not petered out as an in-

The material in this section appeared in somewhat different form as "Adventures in Literature and Life," in *Midstream*, XXXIII (June–July, 1987), 55–56.

fluence upon Roth's fiction. Once again two uncited works by James figure in the book's construction. There is also a continuing dependence on the works on which Roth drew earlier. The great innovation resides in the role allotted James's critical writings, which lie behind the entire work. *The Counterlife* can be considered Roth's own writing on the art of fiction, in the vein of James's. His writer-hero creates his fantasy and changes it before the eyes of the reader, so that the ideas about the art of fiction are in process, the result of invention in action. "The Jolly Corner," brought into *Zuckerman Unbound*, reappears even more identifiably, although again it is not named. The name of Henry James crops up only as exhibiting the taste in literature of the least admirable character in the novel, Maria's anti-Semitic English mother. "The Aspern Papers," conspicuous in *The Prague Orgy* for its contribution to the plot, also makes a reappearance here, but only through phrasing reminiscent of a famous descriptive passage by James on the Piazza San Marco, in Venice. Roth's eye for detail and for the relevant metaphor has been trained on James's extraordinary perspicacity in these matters.

The two uncited works by James that are formative for *The Counterlife* are two novels, *The Portrait of a Lady* and *The Ambassadors*. The mass of critical material by James on the art of fiction that Roth availed himself of had been published in book form as *English Literature: Essays* in 1984. That included his essay "The Art of Fiction," written in 1884 in response to an article by Walter Besant that stirred up a critical debate about what an "adventure" is, in which Andrew Lang and Robert Louis Stevenson also took part. In combination with the prefaces of the New York Edition, written between 1905 and 1909, and all the other criticism James produced from the age of twenty-one to seventy-one, this constitutes the greatest corpus of writing on the art of fiction by any author in any language at any time. The collective impact of it seems to have influenced Roth in arranging the elements of his plot and in developing the relationships between the author who is a character in the novel and the characters he invents in it.

The Counterlife adapts James's material in more complex ways than Roth's earlier fiction. But there are also continuations of the earlier approach. The short story "The Middle Years," of 1893, yields up its famous theme of the "madness of art," which Roth relates to the madness of Zuckerman with respect to his Jewishness, his mistress Maria, and his profession, all indistinguishable from his art since all, even his mistress, are constructs of it. As his brother's abandoned wife accuses Nathan, "You turned the madness to profit, but it's still all part of the family insanity" (*COU,* 151). The profit, in any case, is artistic as well as financial.

The recognizable elements from James's first great novel, *The Portrait of a Lady,* devolve from its heroine, who is to "affront her destiny" and who becomes entrapped in it. When, in the section "Judea," Zuckerman goes to Israel to bring back his brother Henry, who has fled his responsibilities in America, there is a reworking of *The Ambassadors,* in which Strether goes to rescue a young man who has been dallying with Parisian culture by forming a liaison with a French aristocrat. The two Marias in Roth's novel duplicate a name the way Maria Gostrey and Marie de Vionnet do in *The Ambassadors.* But Roth has reversed James's moral priority. In James's novel, the Parisians are effete and the Americans strong; in Roth's, the Americans are effete and the Israelis strong.

The very title *The Counterlife* points to "The Jolly Corner," since it captures the *donnée* of that tale by James. The counterlives of both Nathan and Henry, his dentist brother, are variations on and original interpretations of the story's theme. In "The Jolly Corner," when Spencer Brydon confronts his alter ego, who has really lived, he feels the "hot breath and the roused passion of a life larger than his own, a rage of personality before which his own collapsed" (XII, 226). Nathan's language about his visit to Henry's room in Israel preserves much of this: "The last thing he needs, I thought, is to be dwarfed by yet another personality bigger than his own" (*COU,* 136). But the chief element that Roth derives from James's tale is the ghost. The ghost of Zuckerman carries us through the last chapter and ends the book. It is a ghost of a very special kind, one capable of the erection on which the novel closes. Zuckerman gambled on an operation and lost his life in pursuit of such an erection, but attains it in his afterlife. From having to do with a "ghost writer," in the first novella, Zuckerman has passed, by his fifth appearance in Roth's fiction, to being a ghost himself, but a virile one.

But the main hold that James has on Roth's imagination in this installment in the Zuckerman suite arises from the great archive of James's statements about the art of fiction. The entire system of decoupage that determines the plot and the innovations in *The Counterlife* seems to be Roth's reaction to this. Roth has not managed to give up icons of the sort he has been accustomed to extracting from James's fiction, but it is what James said on the "art of fiction" that seems to have allowed him the freedom to revolutionize the shape of his novel, counterpointing and annihilating the various scenarios he has fantasized. Above all, there is a reaction to what James in the "The Art of Fiction" held an adventure to be. For Stevenson an adventure was something like a shipwreck; for James that was not necessarily so. "The moral consciousness of a child is as much a part of life," he wrote, "as the islands of the Spanish Main." Then he asked, "And what *is* adventure . . . and by what sign is the listening pupil to recognise it? It is an adventure—an immense one—for me to write this little article" (*EL*, 61). That offered a direction to Roth, who decided, "Life is the adventure of losing your way—and it's about time I found out!" (*COU*, 131).

James's reflections on fiction gave Roth nothing more specific than an attitude of seriousness. The prefaces of the New York Edition render no practical hints as to invention, but they take a stance toward invention and composition that places the making of fiction in a category in which impersonality is the chief characteristic. It is as if James's prefaces were cut up and collaged within the fabric of Roth's fable—a revolutionary step in that James himself had never let his theoretical statements about fiction leak from the prefaces into the fiction. It is the light of objectivity with regard to the business of writing that assaults one in the prefaces, and Roth has carried this objectivity of the artist into the novel itself. He wrote, "If ever Henry [the dentist] was to turn out to be interesting, I was going to have to do it" (*COU*, 156).

When James's "Pocket Diaries" appeared in the complete edition of his *Notebooks*, that new material could only mean continued refreshment for Roth and a continued game for the reader. *The Facts*, of 1988, does more than exploit the new material, however. It and the volume that followed it, *Deception*, of 1990, constitute with *The Counterlife* Roth's tribute to James's autobiographies. They constitute a world, as well as a work on the art of fiction. For Roth the two are combined. It is interesting that he dedicated *The Counterlife* to his father and *The Facts*, also called *A Novelist's Autobiography* in its subtitle, to his brother. This serves as a clear reminder that the two books can be viewed as James's *A Small Boy and Others* and *Notes of a Son and Brother* done Roth's way.

In his counterautobiography, he is dividing what James wrote for himself and what he wrote for the public. In 1882, James wrote down the facts of his life—but impersonally—in his notebooks. Thirty-one years later, he wrote the first of his autobiographical books, *A Small Boy and Others*. There he dealt with the life of his imagination and with life with his father and family, but he had his own "truth" and his letters to his nephew show that it was James's invention. James's autobiographical creativity took place at the same time Proust and Joyce were filling their novels with autobiographical details.

In *The Facts*, Roth stepped out of the character of Zuckerman to recover the self apart from the printed facts of his life, such as those in his high-school yearbook and scattered throughout his long-sustained dialogue with his now-shed persona, Nathan Zuckerman. Roth is here trying to restore his "experience to the original, prefictionalized factuality" (*FA*, 3). He explained that to "transform myself into *myself*" after a near mental break-down, "I began rendering experience untransformed" (*FA*, 5). Perhaps, in the attempt to distinguish his truth from *the* truth, he is grappling with James's nephew's problem, the divergence from *the* truth that results from artistic intercession.

Zuckerman has the last word in a letter to Roth, who appears as himself in the novel. "You are far better off writing about me than 'accurately' re-porting your own life," he maintains, adding "You're still as much in need of me as I of you—and that I need you is indisputable" (*FA*, 161). He argues, "Your medium for the really merciless self-evisceration . . . is me" (*FA*, 185). Once the "disguises of autobiography" are abandoned and the "facts" are "handed over for imagination to work on," he holds, "there is mystery upon mystery to be uncovered" (*FA*, 184). This is precisely James's excuse for the distortions in his autobiography. Zuckerman also contends that Roth's autobiography "doesn't tell us anything of what has happened, in your life, that has brought *us* out of you" (*FA*, 194). He reiter-ates, "Your talent for self-confrontation is best served by sticking with me" (*FA*, 195). This novel is in effect Roth's notebooks, corresponding to James's *Notebooks*, but unlike James, Roth both reveals and conceals himself.

In *Deception*, Roth carried the divided self to a new level, demonstrating his power over his art. He was now the Philip of the imagination, not Zuckerman. He reviewed the fruits of the imagination in front of the lover that imagination had created for him. *Mon bon*, the muse to whom James speaks in his *Notebooks*, became for Roth a sexually realized bit of mythology, a flesh-and-blood mistress for his imagination. Roth amalgamated James's creative supports with his own, but the very idea of them depended on James.

Operation Shylock

In *Operation Shylock*, of 1993, Roth appears not only as himself but also as his double, also called Philip Roth. Zuckerman has disappeared. The double has been undermining Philip's Zionism, giving speeches commending the Diaspora and encouraging Jews to return to the country of their expulsion. There have been many doubles in literature from which Roth could have drawn his double, but there are signs his model was the alter ego in "The Jolly Corner." That would not be surprising, given Roth's long-standing obsession with James. In contrast to how James portrays his alter ego, however, Roth in his lengthy novel addresses the constant confrontation between the Philip Roth ego and the Philip Roth alter ego after a preliminary pursuit of the alter ego by the ego. This extension of his narcissism dominates the entire drama of the work. Since the conflict between Arabs and Jews seems irresoluble, it is not reasonable to expect Roth's conflict in choosing which side he will be on to be any more resoluble. *Operation Shylock* seems to have exhausted his material in its endeavor to solve the Jewish problem both politically and for him personally.

Some of James's attitudes to writing have lingered on into Roth's so-called postmodern period, and one of them is an awareness of the reader's importance to the writer. James had said that the reader must meet the author halfway, and Roth has deemed the erosion of a serious readership a major disaster. But he persists in trying to believe that such a readership, though smaller than before, still exists. The force of the double, of the alter ego who is both identical with and at odds with the original Philip Roth, in a novel that is either fiction or a true-life confession shows that at any rate Roth still reads James. In *Sabbath's Theater,* of 1995, however, James seems finally to have disappeared. With the tension between Roth and James dispelled, hope seems to have disappeared from the universe of his hero. The only thing left is sex, the one ingredient James was able to do without in most of his fiction. Roth is now able to focus only upon the importance of sex, but in this book John Milton is perhaps a substitute for James: the dialogue is, like Job's with God, religious.

The Jamesian Context in Auchincloss' and Roth's Fiction

The chief intersection between Philip Roth and Louis Auchincloss comes at the point of the importance of the family. Auchincloss' focus is on the power of the family and the impact of members of the family on the building of the country and on the creation of its values. Each author is intent on keeping up the values inculcated by families and observing how his social group's members try to retain them or to break away from them. Auchincloss' traditions ally him to James and Wharton, who were members of his social class and regional group, that is, the white Anglo-Saxon Protestant segment of New York City. He seems to be personally involved not in forming values but simply in continuing them. Thus, his fiction becomes a mirror of upper-class American, essentially New York, society rather than that of the "historian of fine consciences," as Joseph Conrad called James.

Roth, with the loss of traditional values that a Jew of the second generation undergoes in America, depended on James for values of the kind that Auchincloss had simply inherited. His absorption of James's novels and tales was so intense a literary experience that it was more than simply imposed. It colored his works from 1962 to 1991. Finally, in his novel *Patrimony*, dedicated to his dying father, he broke free of James, and James no longer entered by name. He told his own story, but with the shadow of James's autobiographical works, especially *Notes of a Son and Brother*, hovering over his writing. As James had broken away from the father figure through his portrait of the figure, Roth broke away from his father, an equally strong personality, by putting him down in his literary biographical study. Roth finally came out from "hiding behind Henry James" and came out into the open as his biological father's son. In *Operation Shylock*, the Jamesian heritage existed chiefly in the now much modified version of the alter ego from "The Jolly Corner." Yet in 1997, *American Pastoral* (see chapter 15) suggests James still exists for Roth as a stimulus.

How different is the Henry James that Auchincloss plants in his tales and novels from the James that Roth plants in his? To Roth, James is the artist, the writer who established rules of writing for his present-day colleague. To Auchincloss, James is a member of the same social class as he, a class that is now diminishing as the writing class spreads out. James, to Auchincloss, is part of his Wasp family and the Wasp family of writers. If

Auchincloss is a novelist of manners, Roth is a novelist of bad manners. His fistfight with James is an example of the anxiety of influence or the struggle of the son to overcome the father. For Auchincloss, the absorption of James seems to involve no anxiety but to furnish his quiver with its multitude of arrows.

7

IN THE VINEYARD OF THE MASTER

Never since James's time has he not figured in the craft of other writers or in their imagination of what a master of writing is. The four women I examine in this chapter—Elizabeth Bowen, Anita Brookner, Muriel Spark, and Sylvia Plath—embody four different ways of responding to James's work. These women have not been intent on re-creating the figure of James like the women who, his contemporaries, friends as well as writers, wished to present their personal impressions of the man who may also have been a severe critic of their work. The four women of this chapter are all of the post–World War I period, too young to have known James and touched by the wake of modernist writers like T. S. Eliot, Ezra Pound, and F. Scott Fitzgerald. They continued working into the postmodern period, which technically began after World War II but, with regard to altered techniques of writing, came into its own in the 1980s and 1990s under the influence of literary theory.

Elizabeth Bowen, the eldest of the four, looked to James's *What Maisie Knew*, of 1897, and *The Awkward Age* as models for updating the analysis of London's social sets, which, she decided, repeat James's patterns and can be understood through the literary devices of his two fin-de-siècle novels. Children and their corruption by adults is the content she concentrated on. Anita Brookner's interest in the isolated consciousness of her heroines follows James's attention to a different kind of consciousness, more social than hers though equally separatist. She has consequently been susceptible to the theme of *The Ambassadors* and to the support his tales have in the world of art, of which Brookner has professionally been an outstanding historian. Muriel Spark, with her original combination of skepticism and Catholicism and her easy relationship with James's work, engages in post-modern literary games. She differs from Bowen, Brookner, and Plath in that her inclusion of James seems to be that of a fellow satirist whom she appears to conspire with in her reinvention of his plots and characters.

Sylvia Plath identified with James's heroines, in particular with the two who are haunted, as she was, by a loved one's betrayal, Milly Theale and Maggie Verver. Plath wanted to surmount her personal obstacles, but she never did, and in her last poems the theme of "The Beast in the Jungle," of the beast that is unconquerable since it is death, prevails over the heroines in her doomed life story.

"On the Verge of the Henry James Country": Elizabeth Bowen

Critics of the fiction of Elizabeth Bowen (1899–1973) have often com-mented that her style was affected by James's. A biographer mentioned that in the 1930s, Virginia Woolf "warned Elizabeth of the influence of Henry James, 'she foresaw him as a danger to me'" (GL, 123). Among other things, "the habitual placing of the adverb before the verb . . . made people continually compare her style with Henry James's," and the reader of *The Heat of the Day* for a publishing house "picked out for comment [a sentence] he called 'almost more Jacobean than James'" (GL, 191). In a 1959 broadcast interview, when Bowen was questioned about this, she an-swered, "You can't say it's like catching measles, because it's a splendid style, but it's a dangerous style'" (GL, 192). Angus Wilson, in his introduc-tion in 1981 to her collected stories, wrote that the addiction to subtle meta-phors which she inherited from James, as well as her "verbal exactitudes" (GL, 78), were the basis for the connection that the critics saw.

Ten years later, A. S. Byatt, in an essay in *Passions of the Mind*, detected that *The House in Paris* is a correction of James's *What Maisie Knew*. In Bow-en's novel, Henrietta and Leopold, two children from different families, are brought to the Paris house of their chaperon, who is charged with taking the eleven-year-old girl to her grandmother and the nine-year-old boy to the mother he has never met or seen. According to Byatt, these two chil-

dren are so "equipped with the language of the secret thoughts of intelligent children" that they "make Maisie seem very much a creature of adult
artifice." The two children afford "more subtle images of the innocent or
immature perception of adult behaviour than James's Maisie."[1]

Yet, up to the present, the dependence of Bowen's novel *The Death of the
Heart*, of 1938—considered her masterpiece—on James's *The Awkward Age*
has gone unnoticed. The situation in the two novels is the same, the only
difference stemming from the change in mores during the thirty-nine years
between 1899 and 1938. A charming heroine, Anna Quayne, of the London upper classes, dominates a social set made up of her complaisant husband and men friends who are attracted and attentive to her, just as Mrs.
Brookenham dominates a similar set in *The Awkward Age*. Anna's control of
her set, which includes her lover, a much younger, irresponsible man, Eddie, referred to as her "fancy boy," is threatened by the arrival of Portia, the
fourteen-year-old stepsister of Anna's husband Thomas. According to his
father's will, Portia must live in London for a year in her stepbrother's ménage. This is an ingenious variation on the state of affairs in *The Awkward
Age*. There, Nanda Brookenham, at eighteen, is old enough to enter her
mother, Anna's, set, but others think of her as "corrupted" when she does,
because of its atmosphere of adultery. Like Nanda, who falls in love with
her mother's lover, Vanderbank, Portia falls in love with Eddie, reacting in
the intense way that an adolescent girl would to his flirtatious manner. In
The Death of the Heart, Eddie and Portia behave the only way post–World
War I young people could. Eddie's relationship with Portia, which is typical of his behavior toward women, leads her to ask him to visit her at the
seashore, where Anna has sent her to stay for the summer in the home of
Mrs. Matchett, her own old governess. Eddie flirts with one of the Matchett girls, and Portia, feeling totally alone, is finally taken in charge by
Mrs. Matchett, whose role parallels Mr. Longdon's in Nanda's rescue.
Henry James may appear in the character of the writer St. Quentin Miller,
an older man who serves as Anna's confidant and as a *ficelle* in the Jamesian
manner to further the narrative. The novel is a remarkably skillful redoing
within the framework of a later era of a young woman's "corruption," that
is, the loss of innocence incurred by merely coming downstairs into the
contagion of corrupt adults. But the difference between the Brookenham
ménage and the Quayne set is that Bowen's characters are desiccated,

1. A. S. Byatt, *Passions of the Mind* (London, 1991), 242.

whereas James's people, decadent though they may be, are capable of deep feelings.

In Bowen's *The Heat of the Day*, of 1948, which shows life after World War II in London, the plot owes more to Graham Greene than to Henry James. Yet Bowen's biographer reported that "Elizabeth knew [James's] infection showed" in the book (GL, 192). The infection manifested itself in Bowen's Jacobean predilection for metaphoric subtlety and amplification. Here are two examples: "Hesitating, he touched his moustache—as though it concealed a spring which could make his mouth fly open on something final" (*HD*, 34); "Like an ignorant looker-on at some famous game, trying to grasp the score and get the hang of the rules, he was watching to see what she would now do—expecting, evidently, to learn how far the prerogative of love went" (*HD*, 66). But Bowen's strong feelings for property, reflecting her pride in and obsession with her inherited Irish country house, have no precedent in James.

Bowen's last novel, *Eva Trout*, of 1968, twenty years later, returned to Jacobean models, but in an atmosphere that anticipated the postmodern fiction of the late 1980s and the 1990s, like Rebecca Goldstein's *The Dark Sister* and A. S. Byatt's "Precipice—Encurled." She twice in the book invoked James by name.

In the 1959 broadcast interview, Bowen stated that she could not read "James's 'more complicated' books. . . . I haven't ever read *The Ivory Tower*; he's quite beyond me there" (GL, 192). That makes it remarkable indeed how closely her Eva Trout resembles Rosanna Gaw of *The Ivory Tower*. No doubt, in order to find out that James's novel was beyond her, she had to begin to read it, and on the first couple of pages she must have met the large, blowsy heiress Rosanna Gaw, with her parasol and cigarettes. That she loved a much younger man would appear a few pages later. All the characteristics of Rosanna are in Eva, the "big heiress" (*ET*, 9) who owns a "crocodile bag" and is sometimes seen with a white bag "slung from her shoulder (à la Diana)"—a counterpart to the parasol that for Rosanna serves as a weapon à la Brünnhilde, to whom James likened her. Eva's size is constantly underlined. She is "that walking monument" (*ET*, 96), "outsize, larger-than-life in every way" (*ET*, 263). The Wagnerian overtones in *The Ivory Tower* are condensed in the name of Eva's rival, Iseult, who, with Eric, her conspirator, is trying to wrest Eva's millions from her fraudulently. Iseult corresponds to Cissy Foy in *The Ivory Tower*, who colludes with Horton Vint to gain Rosanna's fortune. It does not seem accidental that Bowen has given Iseult's mother the name of Cissie.

Eva's guardian, Constantine Ormeau, is mannered, yet "this mannered manner of his was not quite the thing; no. Yet the ambiguities had one sort of merit, or promise—one was at least on the verge of the Henry James country" (*ET,* 28). By bringing in James's name so early in the novel, Bowen gave clues to the reader, as James himself characteristically did. When Iseult, Eva's despoiler, walks on the seashore where there are scattered skeletons of fish, she thinks that Flaubert—Dickens and Browning are also mentioned in the novel—"would have been interested, James less so. What, now one came to think of it, *had* James that Dickens really had not? Or if he had, what did it amount to?" (*ET,* 118). It is as if Bowen was distancing herself from her mentor. Eva falls in love with a Cambridge undergraduate ten years her junior, whom she has known since he was a small boy, just as Rosanna's Graham Fielder is significantly her junior.

Bowen's notion in 1968 of what a postmodern novel should be lands pretty close to what such novels have become in the 1990s. In them references abound to other bits of literature, but the varied ways of the relationship require the reader's assistance in working out the complicated fantasies. There is a farcelike quality to *Eva Trout,* which takes its basic form from a book by James that she said she could not read.

"Come, Henry, We Look to You for Distraction": Bowen's Short Stories

The line "Come, Henry, we look to you for distraction" occurs in "Sunday Afternoon," a short story of 1941 that takes place during the first air raids over London. Its title suggests that Bowen looked to James's language, anyway, for more than distraction, for the most beautiful words in the English language, according to him, are "summer afternoon, summer afternoon." The general summoning of James seems to succeed in telling her how to write about a world at war, though his war had taken place a generation before. The story is set in an Irish country house, and its events take place on a beautiful Sunday afternoon in May. The guests are part of a small, very civilized group of friends who have fled wartime London and are sitting outside waiting to greet their friend Henry Russel, who has come from bombed-out London to spend the weekend with them.

The tale is peppered with allusions to James. The hostess is Mrs. Vesey; there is a Mrs. Vesey in James's "The Chaperon." The group greeting Henry Russel comprises transparently disguised members of Bowen's circle of friends, including a Sir Isaac, suggestive of Isaiah Berlin, and Lady Ottery, suggestive of Lady Ottoline Morrell. The group consequently has certain affinities with the Qu'Acre circle, which was James's set. Henry Russel's comments on wartime London, as well as those of other characters in the group, appear to have been suggested by the letters James wrote to friends during World War I, which were published in 1920 by Percy Lubbock. Russel says that the bombing, although frightening, "does not connect with the rest of life. . . . One's feelings seem to have no language for anything so preposterous" (*CSB*, 617). Another character agrees: "There is no place for it in human experience. . . . It will have no literature" (*CSB*, 618). Like James, who during his war moved to London from Rye, Russel "cannot stay long away" from London, where the action is. But James was seventy-one when World War I broke out, and Russel is only forty-three. When the young girl Maria wants to join him and the war effort in London, he, realizing that Mrs. Vesey and her friends at least have a "view of life" (*CSB*, 622) and the way it should be lived that can benefit her, refuses to expose her to the brutality and the danger of the personality's extinction that she could not keep clear of in wartime London.

The Awkward Age again shows its face, in Henry Russel's love for Mrs. Vesey when he was a young boy. This is like Mr. Longdon's young love for Lady Julia. Russel's attraction to Maria, Mrs. Vesey's niece, is a slight variation on Longdon's love for Nanda, Lady Julia's granddaughter. But there the resemblance stops, because Russel is going through a brutalizing wartime experience, and he cannot offer Maria protection at all approaching Longdon's country house. Nor does he even like her, the girl of 1941. "Maria," he says, "I can't like you. Everything you say is destructive and horrible" (*CSB*, 621). Bowen seemed to be saying that James's characters could not inhabit the world that had come about during the thirty years following his war.

A tale published in 1929, more than a decade before "Sunday Afternoon," depends very transparently on James. Its title, "Shoes: An International Episode," unites the name of an early story by James and a metaphor from his critical writing. A young English couple, Dillie and Edward Aherne, on a trip to France find the wrong pair of "female shoes" outside their hotel-room door alongside the men's shoes. High-heeled, small, and red, they are unlike Dillie's sensible brogues. Although Dillie resolves "not to be insular" (*CSB*, 243), she resents the shoes as a symbol to her husband of a sexy French woman, and his frank liking of them is to her tantamount to infidelity. When the management sends them back by mistake after she has returned them, she flings them out of the window. Her husband, by his tact, plays into her moods, including a dread of French women as mighty rivals to her sexuality and consequently as a threat to her security with her mate. This is a witty conversion of James's tale "An International Episode." Bowen's tale is a fifty-year-later update, with British-French antagonisms taking the place of the American-British.

But she seems to have been prompted to build on the way men's and women's shoes resting side by side outside hotel-room doors intimate the sexual cohabitation behind the door by a metaphor in James's essay on Gabriele D'Annunzio. Sexual passion as the Italian novelist wrote about it "has no more dignity," James maintained, "than the boots and shoes that we see, in the corridors of promiscuous hotels, standing, often in double pairs, at the doors of rooms" (*NN*, 247). James's image is very vivid, and it was to inspire one of Max Beerbohm's caricatures of him a few years later. Ingeniously, Bowen has made a charming tale out of the figure of speech.

Bowen's admiration for James is evident in her inscription, along with that by a number of other of James's devotees, of two copies of the Martin Secker edition of *The Aspern Papers*.[2] The first list of signatures is dated 1941; the signers attended the twenty-fifth anniversary observance of James's death. The second list includes fewer friends and admirers, those who were present at the centenary dinner in the Cavendish Hotel, in London, in 1943. David Garnett was among them, and this copy comes from his library (Figure 17). Elizabeth Bowen heads both lists and one feels she organized both meetings.

The Isolated Consciousness: Anita Brookner

"I suspect that if Henry James were around," the reviewer of a novel by Anita Brookner (1928–) has ventured, "the only writer he'd be reading with complete approval would be Anita Brookner."[3] The question of ap-

---

2. Both copies are in the author's collection.

3. Constance Casey, "A Judge Against Their Lives," *New York Times Book Review*, July 21, 1991, p. 14.

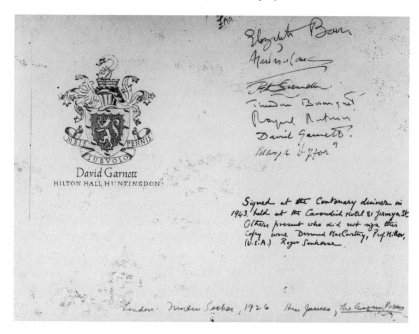

17. Inside front cover and flyleaf of David Garnett's copy of the Martin Secker edition of *The Aspern Papers,* signed by Elizabeth Bowen and several other admirers of James

From the author's collection

probation aside, he would surely recognize subtly concealed matter from his own work in Brookner's novels. Her situations re-create in contemporary life fictive states of affairs strikingly like his own.

In her first novel, *The Debut,* of 1981, titled after Balzac's novella of the same name, which was also called *A Start in Life,* it was altogether clear that Brookner's narrative strategy entails clinging to literature. Her heroine, a professor of literature, has done her doctorate on Balzac. Henry James enters the novel only when the author mentions that in "The Aspern Papers" the character of Tina also fails to gain a man's love and is equally victimized. Brookner here moved her heroine among those in Balzac's novels whom she aspires to emulate or whom she resembles. Although her next novels came out of the research library into more full-blooded life, the literary prototypes continued.

Like other women novelists of the 1980s and 1990s, Brookner inhabits a generally diffuse Jamesian atmosphere permeated by both James's emphasis on consciousness and his narrative strategy. Brookner, however, has realized how much of a disaster, socially and personally, the isolation of a consciousness can be. In her novels isolated personalities try to relate to others but have no success in doing so. In *Look at Me*, of 1983, which was Brookner's third novel, the isolation of her heroine's consciousness allows no bridge to the rest of humanity, and although the heroine yearns to escape her self-absorption and find love, she has lost the key.

Hotel du Lac, of 1984, is more specifically Jamesian. The heroine, Edith Hope, in an affair with David, who is married, goes to Switzerland for "rest" at the bidding of her friends, who are astonished that she has run away from the offer of a profitable marriage. The setting and cast seem to be vaguely out of some of James's Switzerland stories, such as "The Pension Beaurepas," of 1879, and "Fordham Castle," of 1904. Edith Hope may have got her name from Miranda Hope, James's American pensioner in Paris in "A Bundle of Letters," of 1879. The name seems more likely, however, to have come from Mrs. Warren Hope, the heroine of "The Abasement of the Northmores," for Mrs. Hope's social dislocation is, like Edith's, the result of a man's inability to fight his rival. All the characters, typically for Brookner, are rejects. All are in the Hotel du Lac to forget something. It is as if the author were punning on Dante's "Abandon all hope, ye who enter here." Edith Hope expects them to support, not abandon, her, but they do not have the capacity for that. There is something of Gilbert Osmond in Neville, who proposes to her without love, for he has a "rather well-known collection of *famille rose* dishes" (*HL*, 164). He is "attractive in a bloodless sort of way . . . a man in whom appetite might turn to some anodyne hobby, the collecting of drypoint etchings or the tracing of his own family tree" (*HL*, 163). "I am sure you love beautiful things," he tells her, and she answers, "her voice cold. 'I do not love *things* at all'" (*HL*, 164). Unlike Isabel Archer, or perhaps like her, Edith goes back to her own trap, the affair with her married lover, which she knows must end with her the loser, as Madame Vionnet would say.

Since Edith Hope is a novelist of romantic fiction, she likes to read other fiction but tends, in her "febrile agitation," to distort what she is reading. She "dreaded making nonsense of something precious to her, and, regretfully, disqualified Henry James. Nothing too big would do" (*HL*, 66). Madame de Bonneuil lives on in the hotel because she "doesn't want to see the son unhappy" (*HL*, 71). Edith feels it is time she faced reality, but "it is too late" (*HL,* 118). In this tale's hopes and disillusionments, it is like "A London Life," of 1888, and the facts to be faced, personal and sexual betrayal, are what Laura Wing in James's tale also faces.

Although Brookner has been a professor of the history of art at the Courtauld Institute, in London, her novels do not uniformly rely on pictorial icons. *Misalliance,* of 1986, is one that does. Blanche, the heroine, has failed in love. Her husband has divorced her and married a more seductive and feminine woman. Blanche, however, is intellectual and sharp and notices that the nymphs in the National Gallery succeed where the sad virgins do not. The pagans are happy, the saints are not. Blanche is an iconoclast and tells her former husband and his new wife that one can never tell when "I might make an injudicious remark or start raving on Henry James." She refers to Millie (*sic*) Theale, a "silly girl, I always thought. She should have bought that rotter outright. What else is money for?" But she finally counsels herself to "stop making stories out of these people, creating false analogies, reifying and mythologizing them. . . . I have let the National Gallery go to my head."[4] One of the pictures she comments on, Titian's *Bacchus and Ariadne,* in the National Gallery, may equally have gone to James's head in the writing of *The Princess Casamassima:* he introduces it to link Hyacinth's innocence and Christina Light's sophistication. Although Blanche's Bronzino is not the Bronzino in *The Wings of the Dove,* Brookner's analogy is modeled on James's employment of art works in novels ranging from *Roderick Hudson* through *The Outcry.*

Brookner's next novel, *Latecomers,* of 1988, further integrates her trajectories as a professor of art history and a novelist in modern-day London writing about outsiders. James's personal psychology, too, was informed by his interest in art. As a young man, he intended to become an art critic, and his fiction is filled with art. In *Latecomers,* the four characters brought up as children in London after fleeing Nazi Germany interact very much the way James's characters do in *The Golden Bowl.* Titian's *Bacchus and Ariadne,* Courbet's *Atelier,* in the Louvre, and *Madame Bovary* are all subsumed in the consciousness of Fibich, one of the men. When he revisits Germany, as he feels he must, the portrait of an Englishman by Gainsborough causes him to realize where his loyalties really lie. Fibich is taken by his friend for lunch at Durrant's Hotel, which is a small family establishment situated

4. Anita Brookner, *Misalliance* (New York, 1986), 158.

back of the Wallace Collection where distinguished art historians, as well as distinguished American writers, forgather today. It is a real, as well as a symbolic, rendezvous for Brookner, who, like James, accommodates both artistic and literary icons at the same table.

A Friend from England, of 1987, is another instance demonstrating the strong influence *The Wings of the Dove* continues to have among women writers of the 1980s and 1990s. In James's novel, the personality of Milly Theale, someone destined for death and peculiar in her personal isolation from the norm, wishes to live and relate to others in love but cannot. Rachel, the narrating heroine of Brookner's novel, has had no close family life and is thus drawn to the Livingstones, whose daughter, Heather, is even more of an enigma than Rachel, her "friend from England." But Rachel wishes to relate to others, whereas Heather, the daughter of the Livingstones, is spoiled by two adoring parents. She marries a homosexual and flees her home and family to live with a Venetian youth and his mother. Rachel and Heather are the obverse and reverse of the same coin. The full force of the title of the book emerges in the last chapter. Representing Heather's parents and as a friend of the family, Rachel goes to Venice to learn what Heather plans to do with her life. Waiting to meet her, Rachel goes to the Accademia: "I found the only picture I wanted to see. The woman suckling her child had a heavy face, immanent with meaning, but from which all explanation had been withdrawn. To her right, on the left of the picture, stood the mysterious and elegant knight, intense and remote, his face in shadow. The storm that broke on the scene bound the two together in puzzling complicity. In the background, a banal hill village. In the middle distance, two broken columns."[5] Brookner is describing *The Tempest*, by Giorgione, one of the most compelling pictures of the Italian Renaissance, in order to give a "figured objectivity," in James's phrase, to the mystery of the young woman Heather. Brookner's use of the painting is modeled on James's use of such icons as the Bronzino in *The Wings of the Dove* and the Titian in *The Ambassadors*.

Brookner, like some other women writers of the 1980s and 1990s, has been so steeped in the Jamesian canon of sensitive consciousness in the novel's point of view that the reader often feels the women consider themselves continuous with the Jamesian authority by a kind of osmosis.

5. Anita Brookner, *A Friend in England* (London, 1987), 191.

A Wink to Henry James: Muriel Spark

Although Muriel Spark (1918–) is distinguished by her originality and her ability to make each novel a truly different extension of her idiosyncratic imagination, she usually manages to shoehorn some mention of James or some trace of his originality into her fiction. In her first novel, *The Comforters,* of 1957, the main personage becomes a fictional character, anticipating the spate of postmodern novels in which an existence on two levels of reality is the norm for characters. Spark's Catholicism has taught her that fiction is not the seat of literal truth, and she develops artificial situations to the hilt. But in *The Comforters,* her plots seem to borrow from James's. The smuggling grandmother may originate in his short story "The Third Person," of 1900, about a smuggling elderly woman. From Lord Mellifont in "The Private Life," who exists only in public, disappearing when no one else is around, she may have taken Georgina Hogg's lack of any "private life whatsoever. God knows where she went in her privacy."[6]

In *Memento Mori,* of 1959, a tale of old people, someone attacks a novel by James, only to meet "James outside the Athenaeum one day and James was talking about his conscience as an artist."[7] Thereafter, James and his books interlard Spark's stories. She has acknowledged liking to toss almost irrelevant things into her tales, but somehow the references to James always seem relevant to her interest in the art of fiction. In *The Girls of Slender Means,* of 1963, one of the girls of slender means writes to him at his club, the Athenaeum. "That was foolish of you," comments a friend, "because James is dead, by the way."[8]

Vestiges of "The Aspern Papers" appear in *Territorial Rights,* of 1979, in which the locale of the Venetian palazzo conspires with two sisters who murder and bury a man in their Venetian garden. The plot re-creates in a more sinister form the atmosphere of Juliana Bordereau and her niece Tita in their palazzo, also with a garden. It is apparent that Spark knows her James of *Italian Hours* when a character repeats his reference to Cleopatra stepping ashore (*INH,* 66), again as a trope, but with the lady a different queen: "stepping ashore like the Queen of Sheba."[9] The figure of speech stems from Tiepolo's *Meeting of Anthony and Cleopatra,* in the Venetian Palazzo Labia.

6.   Muriel Spark, *The Comforters* (1957; rpr. London, 1985), 177.
7.   Muriel Spark, *Memento Mori* (Philadelphia, 1959), 96.
8.   Muriel Spark, *The Girls of Slender Means* (New York, 1963), 55.
9.   Muriel Spark, *Territorial Rights* (New York, 1979), 160.

Two years later, in *Loitering with Intent,* the writer Fleur Talbot amends her prose before sending it on to her publisher, because "I had probably been reading too much Henry James at the time." She changes *beautifully,* a word James often used, to *very well,* because "beautifully was much too much."[10] In *A Far Cry from Kensington,* of 1988, Spark's glimpse into James's "The Art of Fiction" must be the source of the passage "Of course a novelist does not have to undergo every experience, a glimpse is enough."[11] In the novel *Symposium,* of 1990, Lucian and Plato are the immediate models, but James obtrudes by the way. One character says, "One reads, sometimes, of painters who used to be available while working." Another replies, "That was in Henry James."[12] Spark was probably thinking of the sociable studio of Charles Waterlow in James's *The Reverberator,* and also that of Nick Dormer in *The Tragic Muse.* Waterlow's workshop was based on John Singer Sargent's.

Three tales in *The Stories of Muriel Spark* carry Jamesian overtones. The Daisy of "Daisy Overend" shares certain characteristics with Daisy Miller, transposed to modern London bohemia. She is as outspoken, if not more outspoken, than Daisy Miller. A girl she insults comes across "Daisy's dirty old garters" at a party and in revenge exhibits them to all, holding them with sugar tongs. Daisy is, like the earlier Daisy, disgraced in society.[13] "The Dark Glasses" seems to go back to James's "Glasses," of 1896, in addressing the subject of a girl with damaged eyesight. "The House of the Famous Poet" may have its germ in James's tale "The Birthplace," of 1903, about the house where Shakespeare was born. Her point is that a house looks different when one knows that it is the house of a famous writer. But when Muriel Spark tosses Henry James into her salad, she does so lightly and allusively with only the slightest wink in his direction.

A College Student of James: Sylvia Plath

When Sylvia Plath (1932–1963) was at Cambridge University as a Fulbright scholar, she attended lectures by Dorothea Krook, the author of *The Ordeal of Consciousness in Henry James,* of 1962 (EB, 49). After Plath came back from Cambridge and was teaching at Smith College, from which she

10. Muriel Spark, *Loitering with Intent* (London, 1981), 73.
11. Muriel Spark, *A Far Cry from Kensington* (London, 1988), 98.
12. Muriel Spark, *Symposium* (London, 1990), 25.
13. Muriel Spark, *The Stories of Muriel Spark* (London, 1985), 140.

had graduated, she frequently mentioned James in her journals. She seems to have been reading his novels, either in preparing her courses or for guidance in working out her novel, *The Bell Jar,* which was to appear in 1971. There are certain giveaway Jamesian expressions, like *Medusa-head.* This saturation in James took place when Sylvia was twenty-five years old and married to Ted Hughes, the poet, but she had begun her reading of James as an undergraduate.

Sylvia had returned to Smith to complete her studies in February, 1954, after a year away because of a breakdown, and during the spring semester she read Russian literature with great enthusiasm and began her thesis on Dostoevski. But her attention was not confined to Russian literature: "Near the end of this repeated semester . . . Newton Arvin [a professor] . . . had Sylvia reading Henry James for the first time; *The American, Portrait of a Lady,* and *The Ambassadors*" (EB, 36). A remark Plath made in her journals after coming back from Cambridge seems to derive from James's "Glasses": "I want to live each day for itself like a string of colored beads" (*JP,* 94). She "finished *What Maisie Knew*" (*JP,* 220) but ventured no comment on it. Earlier she wrote, "Finished James's book" without stating which book it was. "How much easier, how much smiling deadlier, to scrape and scrub a living off the lush trees of Joyce, of James" (*JP,* 190). When, in April, 1958, she finished *What Maisie Knew,* she commented, "Ironically Henry James's biography comforts me and I long to make known to him his posthumous reputation—he wrote in pain, gave all his life (which is more than I could think of doing—I have Ted, will have children—but few friends) and the critics insulted and mocked him, readers didn't read him. I am made crudely, for success. Does failure whet my blade?" (*JP,* 220). She also laid plans: "This summer I will study under Henry James and George Eliot for social surface, decorum" (*JP,* 220–21). At this point, she seemed to be reading James fairly intensively, and he seemed to be on her mind. On Sunday, May 11, Mother's Day, she was considering her novel, also mentioning, "I am going on with *The Wings of the Dove*" (*JP,* 223). Two days later she wrote, "Henry James teaches me hourly—he is *too* fine for me—but then I am so crude and loud that his lesson can only serve to make me less crude, not more fine—teaches me how life is circuitous, rich, sentences and acts laden with all the riches of meaning and implication. Well, I am half through *The Wings of the Dove:* Millie seems to me so damnably *good* . . . so *noble:* she sees and sees and will not flinch or be *mean,* be small." About her novel, she declared, "My novel will hardly end with love and marriage: it will be a story, like James's, of the workers and the worked, the exploiters and the exploited: of vanity and cruelty: with a *ronde*, a circle of lies and abuse in a beautiful world gone bad. The irony I record here for the novel, but also for *The Ladies' Home Journal*." And then she went on, "I am no Maggie Verver, I feel the vulgar heat of my wrong enough to gag, to spit the venom I've swallowed; but I'll take my cue from Maggie, bless the girl" (*JP*, 229). She was fascinated by Maggie's behavior in connection with the betrayal by her husband with Charlotte because she herself experienced the same kind of betrayal, or at least she thought she did. She had seen her husband come from Paradise Pond at Smith with what looked to her like a lover. Her jealousy was part of her mania, but since Maggie gets through her predicament satisfactorily, she vowed to follow her in her comportment if not in her feelings. Later, in thinking about her novel again, she resorted to James's terms: "The ghost of the unborn novel is a Medusa-head" (*JP*, 246).

Janet Malcolm, in her book *The Silent Woman*, observes that Sylvia's confrontations with Anne Stevenson, Olwyn Hughes, and A. Alvarez struck both her and Anne Stevenson as living correlates of James's fiction. Stevenson is quoted as calling herself "very Anglophile" and had "read Jane Austen and Charles Dickens and Henry James" (JM, 106). She felt herself to be very much like Sylvia, since at that time the society of poets in England was very different from what it was in the United States: "Who you went to bed with was not a matter of much importance" among English poets, and "Sylvia couldn't handle Ted acting like an English poet. She had always found it uncomfortable. There was some kind of Jamesian morality here" (JM, 107). Malcolm, after reading the letters that Stevenson gave her, felt "like the possessor of a great prize—the prize that the narrator of 'The Aspern Papers' goes to such extreme lengths to try to get" (JM, 110). Malcolm also quoted from Plath's journal the passage about her being no Maggie Verver.

Malcolm's conclusion is that a certain critical attitude to Plath "expresses the public's need to see Plath as victim, its desire to impose a Jamesian structure of American innocence versus European corruption." According to Malcolm, Plath can be seen "as Isabel Archer, let us say, and Hughes and Olwyn as Gilbert Osmond and Madam Merle on the struggle between the vivid dead girl and the ghostly English relations" (JM, 57). Malcolm also made the most of the "un-Maggie-like" response by Sylvia to Ted's presumed sexual betrayal of her. Plath did not herself extend the

Jamesian structures to the degree Malcolm was willing to in interpreting her actions. But when Plath wrote "bless the girl" about Maggie, it meant that she understood that Maggie at least solved her problems and she hoped she would too. But she never could solve the problems created by her jealousy and by the confusion between Ted and her father—at least that is one way of seeing her misfortune.

James may have had an influence on some of Plath's poems. "Pursuit" is about a woman who is hunted down by a panther, by the evil lurking in ourselves. There is a conflation of the image of the evil double from "The Jolly Corner" with the animal imagery from "The Beast in the Jungle": "The Panther's tread is on the stairs, / Coming up and up the stairs" (*CPP,* 23). In "The Colossus," which Plath composed the year after Cambridge, when she was twenty-six years old, married to Hughes, and teaching at Smith, she described the titanic but lifeless statue of her father made up of "immense skull-plates." Possibly Maggie's pagoda in the garden suggested this, with its impenetrable plates of tile representing the mysterious problem facing her in *The Golden Bowl.* Plath's colossus too can stand for her own problem: "I shall never get you put together entirely" (*CPP,* 129). In Plath's later poems of rage, certain images build up from ideas in James's fiction. In "Widow," she fears her husband's soul may "be beating . . . at her dull sense . . . against a pane of glass." Like Peter Quint's image in "The Turn of the Screw," "it looks in on, and must go on looking in on" (*CPP,* 165).

8

JAMES IN THE OTHER ARTS

James Reinvented: "The Altar of the Dead" and François Truffaut's *La Chambre verte*

A spate of films have been devoted to renderings of James's fiction.[1] *The Heiress*, produced in 1949, a version of *Washington Square; The Europeans*, in 1979; "Daisy Miller," in 1974; and *The Bostonians*, in 1984, are careful, almost reverential, productions faithful to the originals, presented with a respectful zeal to please the Master if he were around. In 1995, the revival of Ruth Goetz and Augustus Goetz's play *The Heiress*, on which the film was based, was a great box-office success. In contrast to the others, *La Chambre verte* (The green room), which François Truffaut (1932–1984) directed in 1978, is a personal and highly original film. It is based on four of James's tales, but Truffaut has adjusted the time frame, placing his film in the aftermath of the horrors of World War I, and has renamed the chief characters.

La Chambre verte centers on one of the most compelling of James's "gruesome" tales, "The Altar of the Dead," which appeared in *Terminations*, of 1895, along with three other stories, all concerned with death. Placed last in that volume, it shows how the dead are made immortal by the conscious attempt of the living to remember "them"—as James refers to the dead and

---

1. For a list of renderings of James in radio, television, and film up to 1981, see Anthony J. Mazzella, "A Selected Henry James Artsography," *Henry James Review*, III (1981), 44–58. The material in this section appeared in *Film/Literature*, VIII, no. 2 (1980), 78–83.

as Truffaut does also—through continuing ritual. Some, including F. R. Leavis, have viewed "The Altar of the Dead" as morbidly sentimental. Others, including Edel, have detected in it James's guilt after the suicide of his friend Constance Woolson. Truffaut seems to have understood, or at least projected, James's intentions better than most of his literary critics. By his creative redoing of James's fantasy he has offered the viewer the sort of appropriation James considered the ideal form of criticism.

In "The Altar of the Dead," George Stransom, who has lost his fiancée, is horrified when a seemingly inconsolable widowed friend remarries. Stransom devotes his life to trying to keep the memory of the dead alive through the ritual of lighting candles in a chapel within a Catholic church in the suburbs of London. At the same altar, a nameless woman also worships, and he is appalled to learn, when he visits her dark red drawing room, which she keeps as a shrine, that the man whose memory she is preserving is his single enemy, Acton Hague. He has refused to light a candle for Hague. In his emotional distress, he becomes seriously ill and dies, requited only by the prospect that the woman will keep his memory alive in lighting the one remaining candle.

"The Altar of the Dead" is James's only serious fictional attempt to illustrate his idea of the afterlife as essentially involving relations with the living, since it is dependent on the consciousness of those who remember. He wrote to his brother William after the death of their beloved cousin Minny Temple that he was happy to have transposed her "from this changing realm of fact to the steady realm of thought," for now she lived "as a steady unfaltering luminary in the mind rather than as a flickering wasting earth-stifled lamp" (*L*, I, 226–27).

In the story the tremendous visual effect of masses of candles is joined to Euhemerism, according to which human lives are perpetuated by being identified with stars, the symbols among the ancients of their gods and goddesses: "The word 'they' expressed enough . . . and if, in their talk, you had heard our friends use it, you might have taken them for a pair of pagans of old alluding decently to the domesticated gods" (IX, 248). James shows to what lengths Stransom's mania carries him in a wry improvisation that might have appealed to Truffaut: "There were hours at which he almost caught himself wishing that certain of his friends would now die, that he might establish with them in this manner a connection more charming than, as it happened, it was possible to enjoy with them in life" (IX, 242).

Although it is hard to view Stransom as anything but a compensated psychotic, he taps his obsession to create rather than destroy relations. He has cultivated relations not only with the dead toward whom he feels goodwill but also with a woman serving the memory of the one person he has hated. The net result is that she has brought him to stop hating his enemy and he has given her a life through his flaming memorials to the dead. Above all, he has assured himself of survival through her offices.

In the essay "Is There a Life After Death?" written in 1910, near the end of his life, James summarized his concepts, among them a law by which "consciousness gives us immensities and imaginabilities wherever we direct it. . . . Living, or feeling one's exquisite curiosity about the universe fed and fed, rewarded and rewarded—though I of course don't say definitely answered and answered—becomes thus the highest good I can conceive of. . . . The very provocation offered to the artist by the universe . . . what do I take that for but the intense desire of being to get itself personally shared?"[2]

Truffaut conveys a similar view of the immortality of the soul. But by emphasizing the woman's youth and healthy engagement with life, he makes the tensions between the necrophilic hero and the heroine more dramatic. The film maker has explained his attraction to James's tale: "In all my period films, there were actors carrying tapers or candles. . . . Without being a believer, I too—like Julien Davenne, the hero of *La Chambre verte*— love the dead. I think we forget them too fast, we don't honor them enough. Without going as far as Davenne—who is obsessed, loving the dead more than the living—I find that remembering the dead permits one to struggle against the transience of life."[3]

By altering James's time and setting for his film, Truffaut motivated the hero and rationalized his almost psychotic fixation by reference to the horrors of war. The choice of the period just after the First World War, in which France lost hundreds of thousands of men, allowed scope for inventing Davenne's enemy, the fascist demagogue, for the villain's role filled by Acton Hague in James's tale. The other alterations—in the names of the characters, the introduction of a housekeeper and her young ward, and a

---

2. Henry James, "Is There a Life After Death?" *Harper's Bazaar*, XLIV (January–February, 1910), 26, 128–29, quoted in F. O. Matthiessen, *The James Family* (New York, 1947), 610–11.

3. Annette Insdorf, *François Truffaut* (Boston, 1978), 246.

scene in an auction house—enrich the visual field and dramatize the story through episodic variety that employs recognizable icons from Truffaut's films.

The opening credits show Truffaut as Davenne wandering among the trenches, the lone survivor of his battalion. Since he also survives his wife, his burden of guilt is enormous. The film's first scene then has him consoling a friend whose young wife has also died. A nonbeliever like Stransom, he berates the priest for offering the false consolation of an afterlife. Davenne tells his friend to keep his wife's memory alive by thinking about her. Next Davenne is in an auction salesroom where he plans to bid on an amethyst ring his wife's family owns. There he meets Cécilia Mandel, played by Nathalie Baye. For the setting, Truffaut borrows from "The Beast in the Jungle," in which the luxurious Weatherend, the country house in which the hero and the heroine meet, is freighted with objects like those that would be on display at a valuable auction. The film recalls that part of James's tale where the girl identifies the place they originally met—not Rome but Pompeii, the city of the dead. Truffaut also alludes to another of James's tales, "The Way It Came," of 1896, in which a man and woman are attracted because each has had the experience of seeing a parent at the point of death while physically separated from the parent. "Théodolinde," of 1878—republished in 1885 as "Rose-Agathe"—in which a young collector of bric-a-brac falls in love with one of a pair of hairdresser's dummies, also serves Truffaut, for he has the damaged child living under the same roof with Davenne throw a stone through a hairdresser's shop window in order to take one of two such dummies as a mother substitute. Truffaut has adapted, as well, the recognition by the hero in "The Beast in the Jungle" that "he had been the man of his time, *the* man to whom nothing on earth was to have happened" (XI, 401) as one of the closing lines of the film. As Truffaut mentioned in an interview, he has also taken from James's autobiography the great loss the writer experienced at the death of Minny Temple, whom James memorialized in both *The Portrait of a Lady* and *The Wings of a Dove.*

After Davenne obtains the ring at the auction, he places it on the finger of the plaster effigy of his wife in the shrine for her in his house. At the office of *The Globe*, for which Davenne writes the obituaries, he must prepare one for his enemy, the political leader. Then he has the shock of meeting his formerly inconsolable friend with a new wife. He exclaims his censure to Cécilia, whom he also thanks for having secured the ring, but she in a spirited defense insists on the possibility of a second marriage and renewed life and happiness.

Davenne has managed to persuade the Catholic priests to let him reconstruct an abandoned chapel on the cemetery grounds for his own shrine. There, like Stransom, he fills an altar with candles dedicated to his dead friends. Cécilia helps him in setting up and maintaining the shrine. On the wall are portraits of Davenne's illustrious dead: Henry James, Oscar Wilde, and Marcel Proust. The one man Davenne refuses to memorialize happens to be Cécilia's former lover. On a visit to her "green room," the counterpart to the "red room" in James's tale, Davenne learns that his enemy has been her great passion. Severely depressed and physically exhausted, he runs to his chapel. Cécilia tries in vain to reconcile him to her love and life; as he dies his cry condenses John Marcher's thought: "I am the man to whom nothing has happened." In the final scene, Cécilia is lighting the last remaining candle for Davenne himself.

Truffaut's chapel scenes are especially effective, for the film maker has put the shrine directly in the cemetery, so that the characters move within it as if it is their total world. In spite of a close adherence to James, Truffaut has converted a story that is usually thought to be lugubrious and disagreeable to read into a film of interesting liveliness. He has done that by bringing into visual focus the largely introspective consciousness of James's main character instead of relying heavily on language and metaphor for its presentation.

The title *La Chambre verte* is taken from the color of Cécilia's room, which is itself a kind of shrine, filled with portraits of her dead lover. In "The Altar of the Dead," the woman's room has "dark red walls," which give it "the flush of life" (IX, 253). Perhaps Truffaut made the change in the spirit of the novelist in the immediately preceding film, *The Man Who Loved Women*, of 1977. The novelist changed the little girl's red dress to blue as part of transforming his experience into a work of art. Truffaut may also have considered green more consistent with Cécilia's "flush of life" and more indicative of healthy growth. But letting the film take its title from the room gives it an importance beyond those two possibilities. It conjures the green room in the Comédie Française, the salon in which the actors of the company entertain as hosts, rather than as performers, the distinguished members of the audience. Given Truffaut's immersion in James's fiction, he may have remembered the scene in *The Tragic Muse*, James's great novel of the theater, set in that green room—the "square spacious saloon, covered with pictures and relics and draped in official green velvet . . . among the portraits and scrolls, the records of a splendid history" (*TM*, 275–76). Cécilia's room, too, has its pictures and relics connected with a splendid history.

Davenne makes a ruin come to life, as preparation for making his dead friends come to life through flame. The multiplying candles in the small chapel and the mass of light they yield in the city of the dead turn night into day, an internal reference to Truffaut's film *Day for Night*, of 1973. The implicitly cinematic image dominating James's story seems to have been waiting for a film maker with Truffaut's penchant for tapers and fire. A few years after "The Altar of the Dead," James was—in "Crapy Cornelia," of 1909—to insinuate images from the early newsreels and from a moving picture he had seen of a fight.[4]

More important than the changes are the sympathies between the two creators. James and Truffaut, passionately devoted to their crafts, had the same early immersion in literary models, having both reaped the advantage of irregular schooling, which permitted intensive reading full time. Both honored their literary idols, Balzac chief among them, by including them in their art. James brought the Pension Vauquer from *Le Père Goriot* into two early tales and the Vidame de Pamiers and *Le Cousin Pons* into two later ones. *Le Cousin Pons* also made it into *The Tragic Muse*, and the hero of *The Ambassadors* is named after the hero of *Louis Lambert*. In another Truffaut film, Antoine Doinel, under the influence of *La Recherche de l'absolu*, creates an altar to Balzac. Pierre Lachenay in *The Soft Skin*, of 1964, gives a lecture on him. *Le Lys dans la vallée* is featured in *Stolen Kisses*, of 1968. Louis in *Mississippi Mermaid*, of 1969, reads *La Peau de chagrin*, and Claude Roc in *Two English Girls*, of 1971, visits Rodin's statue of Balzac. Behind James's novels lies the scheme of many of Balzac's: to mention just two, *La Fille aux yeux d'or* behind *The Bostonians*, and *Le Curé de Tours* behind *The Spoils of Poynton*. The ability of the author of *La Comédie Humaine* to fire both artists required the cooperation not only of their temperaments but of their restless observation of the variety of human types and their admiration for the creative energy Balzac, a historian of a whole society, exhibited.[5]

Truffaut's acceptance of the New Wave critic's insistence that there is a

4.   Adeline R. Tintner, *The Museum World of Henry James* (Ann Arbor, Mich., 1986), 188–96.
5.   Adeline R. Tintner, *The Book World of Henry James* (Ann Arbor, Mich., 1987), *passim*.

"personal relationship between filmmaker and film viewer" is in alignment with James's plea that the reader collaborate with the writer. James was pressing this point even as a young man of twenty-one, when he began his writing career as a literary critic—a beginning that was in step, incidentally, with Truffaut's, later, as a critic of films. Truffaut's technique of "improvisation" has affinities with James's predisposition to make metaphors that in their mounting proliferation cause his fiction, especially after 1895, to become a tissue of the pluralistic possibilities of language. Truffaut's "acts of homage" to the films, actors, and directors he admired led him to create within each film a mosaic of shots from favorite movies, in much the way James, in amplifying his intentions, incorporated bits of pillaged literary classics. Truffaut's success with James's story is not a happy accident, for it sprang from his conception of the author-director. By being personally responsible for all aspects of a film, Truffaut made his analogy between himself and James a reality: "The filmmaker/author writes with his camera as a writer writes with his pen."[6]

"Better Than Being in a Novel ... This Fairly Wallowing in a Libretto": "The Aspern Papers" as an Opera

Composers of opera have quarried James's fiction for their libretti. Douglas Moore's *The Wings of the Dove*, produced in 1961, Benjamin Britten's *The Turn of the Screw*, in 1954, and *Owen Wingrave*, in 1971, and Thea Musgrave's *The Voice of Ariadne*, in 1977, from "The Last of the Valerii," are all attempts to follow James's plots and characters faithfully, though Musgrave has taken certain liberties. *The Aspern Papers*, by Dominick Argento (1927–), first staged in Dallas in 1988, is a free, personal interpretation, like *La Chambre verte*, and, like it, involves a change of setting and the transmutation of the plot on the basis of some hints James left in the tale without acting on them. The pivot of the action is no longer the search for documentation concerning a poet's work but the pursuit of the original manuscript for an opera.

"The Aspern Papers" has inspired many film and stage adaptations. Published in 1888, it was written at what many judge to be the height of

---

6. Insdorf, *François Truffaut*, 23.
The material in this section appeared in somewhat different form as "'The Aspern Papers' and Argento's Opera," *Opera Journal*, XXVII (March, 1994), 27–37.

James's powers, with language and theme joined in harmony, long before his late style became a stumbling block. James had thought of writing the story after his great immersion in Venetian life as a guest of the Daniel Curtises in the Palazzo Barbaro. He wrote it, however, in the quiet of his equally beloved Florence, appropriately since the story line comes from a Florentine anecdote (*MY*, 218–20). James had heard about Claire Clairmont—Lord Byron's mistress and the mother of his daughter Allegra—who lived in Florence and had as a lodger a Captain Silsbee, from Boston, whose passion was Shelley. Silsbee wormed into Miss Clairmont's household, calculating to inveigle from her the surviving papers of the celebrated poet. But he refused to marry her niece, the condition she imposed, and consequently she denied him the material.

James's story concerns an overcivilized critic, journalist, and biographer who is fanatically collecting data about the object of his addiction, an "American Byron" (*AN*, 166). The nameless narrator insinuates himself into the house of Juliana Bordereau, the aged former mistress of the great poet Jeffrey Aspern. Juliana has many uninhabited rooms in the shabby Venice palazzo where she lives with Tina, her middle-aged niece. The journalist's bait is his willingness to pay an exorbitant rent for lodging and his readiness to take in hand the untended garden. His machinations fit Venice well, with its eighteenth-century history of Casanova and the statue by Verrocchio of Bartolommeo Colleoni, the great soldier of fortune. The narrator soon finds that not only has he his price but Juliana and Tina, surprisingly, have theirs. Only by marriage to Tina will he possess the long-coveted Aspern Papers. Unable to accept the unappetizing bargain, the fastidious man flees. The rejected Tina burns the papers, and the narrator never learns exactly what was in the documents.

James's story is for a quiet read, but it needs a collaboration between author and reader, if the cat-and-mouse situation in which all these Europeanized Americans pit their wits against each other is to be enjoyed fully. It needs much more to become a successful opera. That complicated art form, in which words conspire with sight and sound, demands the combined efforts of composer, stage director, designers, singers, and an orchestra who can transform the basic story into a multimedia performance from which the audience will not want to escape. In that transformation Argento has been signally successful.

Argento's first major deviation from James, apart from substituting the manuscript of an opera for a poet's papers, was in changing the Venetian scene to the area around Lake Como. *Casanova's Homecoming,* the opera Argento had written just before *The Aspern Papers,* was set in Venice, and the wish for something different in the new opera is understandable. Although readers have always felt that Venice was the very skin and bones of the tale, James himself would probably not have taken exception to Argento's move. After visiting Lake Como in 1872, he wrote in *Transatlantic Sketches,* "I made an excursion . . . which, though brief, lasted long enough to suggest to me that I too was a hero of romance with leisure for a love affair" in the "spot to which inflamed young gentlemen" of "immoral novels" invite the "wives of other gentlemen to fly with them." The beauty of the area prompted him to ask where he had seen it before: "Where, indeed, but at the opera," with the singers grouped "awaiting the conductor's signal? It was better than being in a novel — this being, this fairly wallowing, in a libretto" (*INH,* 87). Lake Como would doubtless have seemed especially appropriate for a libretto that is about composers and singers.

By making Aspern not a poet but a composer, Argento cleared the way for presenting Juliana not just as his mistress but as a great soprano. James's tale, with its dialogue, becomes the frame for a passionate story of love and betrayal, about which James had only given hints, since his focus was the fanatical scholar.

Transposing the tale to the operatic stage let it escape the bondage of the narrator's point of view. Argento could show the burning of the documents, rather than communicate the deed only through the narrator's report, as in the short story. In Argento's text, the destruction takes place after the researcher flees from marriage to Tina because she has told him about burning the score of a *Medea* that Aspern composed for Juliana over sixty-five years before. The burning of Aspern's papers coincides with the final operatic appearance of each of the characters, who one by one leave the stage as the pages, one by one, burn. James's tale has become the frame for a much earlier drama that James touched on only lightly. Argento has brilliantly created a play within a play, both dramatically beholden to Aspern's score for *Medea.* James's tale, Argento's operatic elaborations, and Aspern's opera fit together like Chinese boxes.

Argento's chief originality resides in developing a love affair that James only glancingly refers to in his tale. Another male character, the impresario Barelli, has been invented to supply Juliana with a prior lover. Argento alternated scenes of 1835 — the time of the love affair between Juliana and Aspern — with scenes of 1900, when the prying researcher comes to get the papers from Juliana. By the alternation of scenes years apart, Argento created a contrapuntal relation that is musically interesting. Longfellow's poem, "Cadenabbia, Lake of Como," sits within a barcarole at the beginning and end of the opera. The idea that the artist being researched is American is retained, but only as part of the opera's frame. Argento's changes give variety to a story that does not lend itself easily to theatrical effects. And the changes warranted making Lake Como the setting, for at the time the area was populated by singers, impresarios, directors, and composers. The famous music-publishing Ricordi family had a villa there, at which their guest Rossini created roles for Giuditta Pasta, the great soprano, and Vincenzo Bellini wrote *Norma* for her.

Yet Argento maintained James's scenario. Juliana is the same aged woman who wears a "horrible green shade which, for her, served almost as a mask," in a description lifted bodily from James's tale (VI, 291). Argento's success with the Lake Como location—the scene also of Juliana's happiness as Aspern's lover—stirs doubts about the Venetian setting for James's Juliana. The realization gradually dawns that for the former mistress of the poet Aspern, who had "treated her badly," to continue living in Venice is not particularly plausible, though James tries to justify the locale by intimating that it protects her privacy: "Venice contained so many curiosities that were greater than she" (VI, 279).

In an age when the words *adapted from* often announce a travesty, Argento's achievement is a remarkable but responsible filling-in of the gaps James left. James's narrator tells us that "there had been an impression about 1825 that [Aspern] had treated [Juliana] badly" and "had 'served' several other ladies in the same way." He asks, rhetorically, "By what passions had she been ravaged, by what sufferings had she been blanched, what store of memories had she laid away for the monotonous future?" (VI, 309). Argento answered those questions by creating a past for Juliana. James's narrator suggests that "there hovered about her name a perfume of reckless passion. . . . Was this a sign that her singer [that is, the poet Aspern] had betrayed her? . . . It was a part of my idea that the young lady had had a foreign lover (and an unedifying tragical rupture) before her meeting with Jeffrey Aspern" (VI, 309–10). Argento's liberties are not capricious but shape what James left undeveloped.

The painting of Aspern's portrait by Juliana's father now becomes an event to watch rather than hear about at second hand. While posing for it, Aspern discusses with Barelli the role he is composing for Sonia, Barelli's latest mistress. Later, declaring his own passion to the impresario's mistress, Aspern says that the women who had loved him before made him feel like "Orpheus among the maenads," close to James's "Orpheus and the Maenads" (VI, 278). Juliana overhears Aspern arranging a rendezvous across the lake with Sonia. The next scene moves ahead to 1900, after the lodger has taken Tina for a boat ride. The niece's words are from James: "She had forgotten what an attractive thing the world is" (VI, 333). When the lodger sneaks into Juliana's room for the documents, she removes her green shade to reveal her magnificent eyes, and denounces him as a "scoundrel." It is a shame that Argento did not leave this as James wrote it: his "Ah, you publishing scoundrel!" (VI, 363) has resounded through the years.[7]

The second act opens with the lodger reading from Barelli's memoirs, which retell the *Medea* story, emphasizing the heroine's vengeance on the unfaithful Jason. The opera was never seen or heard, because Barelli found only the ashes of his friend Aspern, not the unfinished manuscript, when he returned to Lake Como. In the next scene it is 1835 again, and Juliana and Aspern are celebrating the completion of *Medea*. She then gets rid of the boat Aspern was to use. His decision to swim across the lake to Sonia leads to a Shelleyan death by drowning. Argento's expansion of the affair between Juliana and Aspern intensifies the pull between the narrator's "hypocrisy and duplicity" and the equally rapacious strategies of the ancient mistress and her dependent niece in James's tale. Changing Aspern from a poet to a composer and the setting from Venice to Lake Como, with its musical reverberations and memories of a heroic period in Italian opera, complicates the pleasures of the audience and surely enriches the tale. Argento demonstrated an ingenuity that James, always interested in solving a technical problem, would have cheered.

"The Real Thing" and Tom Stoppard's *The Real Thing*

In contemporary times the words *the real thing* are usually, among literate and literary people, associated with James's tale of 1892 by that title. The Kantian *Ding an sich* is not what is at issue in James; his concern is with the difference between the real thing in life and the real thing in art. In 1982,

---

7. For a recent occurrence of the phrase, see Janet Malcolm, *The Silent Woman: Sylvia Plath and Ted Hughes* (New York, 1994), 34.

when *The Real Thing,* a play by Tom Stoppard (1937–), appeared on Broadway, its connection with James's tale became clear as the games the play's characters engage in set in relief the differences James had pointed out between the two domains' commerce with the real.

There is a certain perversity in Henry, the playwright hero. He likes jazz and pop music but seems to have a paralyzing aversion to opera, so the real thing for him, the creative artist, is not the conventional real thing. In this he is like the "I," the painter in James's "The Real Thing." Henry has put on the stage John Ford's Elizabethan drama *'Tis Pity She's a Whore* and August Strindberg's *Miss Julie,* of 1888. In both the passion is unconventional: in Ford's play it is a man's love for his sister. In both the two main characters are doomed to violence and disaster. The real thing there is useless to the people involved but good for art. The matter of the drama is worthwhile only when it becomes art. Henry's own play, *House of Cards,* is art—witty and amusing. Yet the real thing in the actor Max's life, his wife's infidelity, creates only suffering for him. Henry himself finds out, when he falls in love, that the real thing is not good for art. This confirms James's story. In that tale the real thing, Major and Mrs. Monarch, true aristocrats looking as only the real thing can look, are useless for the illustrator's art. The artist's tacky model, Miss Churm, can be a very convincing countess, even though she is a cockney, when the "alchemy of art" transforms her. Stoppard is not exulting that it is a wonderful thing for Henry to have become human and now know what it is to suffer in love. He is showing that Henry is done as an artist. There is a strong irony at the end, and one of the proofs is that the audience wants the hero to stay with his first wife, who is his proper working mate and has the same ironical attitude to life. The last line, in which Max, on the phone, tells Henry of his new wife, makes an aria da capo; the thing will go on and on, as the stage directions indicate: Annie, Henry's new wife, is described as being what Charlotte once was. James's "The Real Thing" is the warning literary presence behind Stoppard's literary play, with two other plays being acted out within Stoppard's work, both showing the most destructive forms of love, available as experiences but redeemable only when written about.

Like Strindberg, whose fanatical hatred of women was bound up with his three unsuccessful marriages, Ford presented the problem of difficult love relationships but did not solve it. Neither did Stoppard in *The Real Thing.* Strindberg suffered severe depression, about which he wrote lucidly when he recovered, and it is possible to see much the same future for Stoppard's Henry. Stoppard did pose the problem dramatically, and he under-stood that James had solved it in his terms in "The Real Thing." For both James and Stoppard, ninety years apart, the real thing in art is not the real thing in life, and it is the artist's imagination that must make a work of art out of life's raw material. James's hero, the illustrator in black and white, finds in the cockney the aristocrat that his imagination requires. For Stop-pard's Henry, the situation has become so complex that the only thing is to wish him well.

"The Author Is Indebted to Henry James": A. R. Gurney, Jr., Plays Around with James

Redoing "The Aspern Papers"

A. R. Gurney, Jr. (1930–), has written two plays that take their initial in-spiration from James's stories. The first of the two, *The Golden Age*, pro-duced in 1979, is a redoing of "The Aspern Papers." The original plot is re-tained, but the place has become New York City. Juliana has become Isabel Hastings Hoyt, the friend and perhaps lover of F. Scott Fitzgerald, and she lives in a brownstone on New York's Upper East Side. The niece Tina is now Virginia, Isabel's granddaughter, and the "publishing scoun-drel"—who, as the narrator, is nameless in James's tale—has turned into Tom, a journalist and scholar, a man of the lost generation during the golden age of American literature in the 1920s. The time between the pres-ent action and the earlier events to which it relates is sixty years, as it was between the two related sets of events in James's story.

The researcher's devotion to the Romantic poets of the early nineteenth century has been converted into a preoccupation with the romantic novel-ist and short-story writer F. Scott Fitzgerald. The lines for Isabel Hoyt were wonderfully written for the actress Irene Worth. Since Mrs. Hoyt has known the "finest writers of [her] time," Tom figures that if he can get closer to them through her, he will be able to connect. Unlike Tina, Vir-ginia is an alcoholic, a solitary drinker of brandy alexanders. Tom brings flowers for both women, miniaturizing, so to speak, the garden the narrator creates for the two women in "The Aspern Papers." Isabel, a painter, has done the portraits of the writers of the period. Virginia tells Tom that Isabel wants 50 percent of the profits when he writes about her, and an advance of ten thousand dollars. Isabel has a list of things she wants and the things she will give him in return, and she quotes Fitzgerald's remark that behind the money and "behind the Golden Age was a good long list" and behind the list were the "slaves" (*GA*, 30). She offers him the studio in which Fitzgerald stayed in her brownstone, where he can write his book. At the end of the first act she requires Tom to take Virginia to an Italian restaurant, as James's narrator had taken Tina out to see Venice.

In the second act, Isabel mentions to Virginia that she was reading *The Great Gatsby* and goes on to assert that Fitzgerald wrote a suppressed chapter about Gatsby's going to bed with Daisy Buchanan, which she has in a black notebook. When Virginia tells Tom, he is fascinated by the chance that the suppressed chapter still exists. She says, "It might be an old story, for example. By Henry James. Or it might be a play . . . she might be playing games" (*GA*, 43). Tom assures Isabel that he will take care of Virginia if she gives him the chapter. Then a scene in "The Aspern Papers" is repeated as Tom takes off his shoes and tries to steal the book while Isabel sleeps. But she catches him. A month after her death, Virginia tells him that Isabel asked her to burn the little black book to keep him from getting his hands on it. But according to her, the manuscript was not by Fitzgerald at all.

"The Beast in the Jungle" and Gurney's *Later Life*

Gurney has said that the play *Later Life*, first staged in 1984, is "very different from 'The Beast in the Jungle.' Only the obsessions of the protagonist in both works remain the same." He has written that although "I can't really call my play an *adaptation* of James, I couldn't let it be produced without some acknowledgment, hence the rather awkward credit."[8] That acknowledgment is printed on the playbill: "The author is indebted to Henry James"— just as in the published version of *The Golden Age* there is the line "Suggested by a story of Henry James" (*GA*, 4).

The action in *Later Life* takes place in a single act on an apartment terrace in a high-rise building overlooking Boston Harbor. A number of people interrupt the conversation of the two main characters, Austin and Ruth, thereby heightening the tension of their revelations to each other. The first of these outsiders at the fall party they are all attending is a man addicted to smoking, someone who, because he cannot change himself, provides a certain comic relief from the serious, conservative, controlled

8. A. R. Gurney, Jr., to Adeline R. Tintner, August 10, 1993.

appearance of Austin, the contemporary version of James's John Marcher in "The Beast in the Jungle."

The conversation between Austin and Ruth begins when she, an updated May Bartram, the heroine of James's tale, steps onto the balcony and declares that she remembers having met Austin many years ago on Capri, when Austin was in the navy. She recalls something he said to her, overlooking the bay of Naples; they mention Sorrento, the destination of the boat ride May Bartram and John Marcher take. As Austin and Ruth attempt a connection, couples keep interrupting, which is what happens in life, but finally Ruth comes out with what Austin told her at their first meeting: that he was sure that "something terrible" was "going to happen" to him in his life, that "something awful" was "going to descend on" him and "ruin" his "life forever."[9] John Marcher, too, tells May Bartram in Pompeii, before the boat ride "for the breeze" to Sorrento, that he has the "sense of being kept for something rare and strange, possibly prodigious and terrible, that [is] sooner or later to happen" to him (XI, 356).

Ruth relates that when she offered herself to Austin, he declined because he did not wish to drag her into a fate like his. Although he forgot her, she remembered him whenever something terrible happened to her: Ruth's first husband died in the war, after seven days of marriage; she lost her child of eleven years to leukemia; her fourth husband was a westerner who treated her badly.

Austin, who is still waiting for the terrible thing to happen to him, has lost his wife in a divorce after she ran off with a younger man, but her loss does not seem to bother him. With his background of Groton and Harvard, the many generations of Wasp ancestors behind him, and his talent for achieving all the goals of his social group, he seems to be protected from life itself. Judith, Ruth's friend, tells the opposite story about Ruth's current husband, a gambler, a wife beater, a rental-car agent in Las Vegas, where they live against her wishes. Bestowing on Austin a name that rhymes with Boston, Gurney, either consciously or unconsciously, followed James's naming of Miss Barrace in *The Ambassadors*, the woman who is an emissary to traveling Americans in Paris. Austin *is* Boston, the city of dead values.

Austin favors Ruth with his attentions to keep her from going off to her husband, who at least loves her. When, despite the suffering the man has caused her, she makes the choice of going to the local airport hotel, where

9. A. R. Gurney, Jr., *Later Life* (New York, 1984), 44.

he has summoned her, she opts for life. She knows that the terrible thing Austin augured has already happened: he is already dead. That is also the point of "The Beast in the Jungle": John Marcher has been dead all along, and May knows it, but her love for him enables the deathlike atmosphere surrounding him to wither her and kill her. James never says so much outright, but he lets his meaning emerge in the icons of death he has thrust into the story: the two meet in Pompeii, the city of the dead, and after May dies, Marcher frequents the cemeteries of old countries, the tombs of the pharaohs, the "Garden of Death," the "temples of gods and the sepulchres of kings" (XI, 397). Marcher realizes at the end that he should have loved May in return and "then, *then* he would have lived" (XI, 401). The knowledge of this has "something of the taste of life," but he too dies when he flings "himself . . . on [her] tomb" (XI, 402), which is where he belongs.

Gurney's living-dead Austin is a kind of zombie created by his prep school, his squash championships, his perfectionism within the standards of his class, and his failure to comprehend how living is different from not living. Ruth, acquainted with all the terrible things that living fully holds in store, has at least lived, and the wife who deserted Austin for a younger lover recognized that she was leading a death-in-life. Austin is worse than Marcher. A walking mummy of Boston and its tradition, he never achieves any insight into his own situation.

Both these plays by Gurney are eloquent and original rewritings of James's tales. Although inspired by "The Beast in the Jungle," *Later Life* carries the meaning a step further. *The Golden Age*, by contrast, is simply a restaging of "The Aspern Papers" in contemporary terms, ingenious though it is.

Two Poets and James

W. H. Auden's James

W. H. Auden (1907–1973) centered two poems on James. The first one, written in 1944, was Chapter 3 of *The Sea and the Mirror* and put James's late style, that of the prefaces to the New York Edition, into the mouth of Caliban, who speaks to the audience as if the James who wrote on the art of fiction was now speaking on the art of Shakespeare's drama. This is perhaps the only imitation of James's late style, in either writing or thinking, that does not make a caricature of his prose. It is a tribute to his style of presentation but also to the thoughts about the artistic process that he enunciated in the eighteen prefaces written between 1905 and 1909. Auden avails himself of James as a model for his own analysis of Shakespeare, the great representative of the theatrical muse. He has Caliban explain how the author of *The Tempest* was able to satisfy all the conditions the theatrical muse set. Shakespeare undertook "to explore" the theatrical muse's "vast and rambling mansion" (*CPA*, 375), as James explored his "house of fiction" (*AN*, 46). Auden is putting Shakespeare's "mirror held up to nature" before the audience in the style and in keeping with the sensibility of someone like James. The only prose section in *The Sea and the Mirror*, the passage is a prose poem by Auden, who called James the "poet of the difficult" (*CPA*, 127).

But it is in Auden's elegiac poem "At the Grave of Henry James," of 1945, that there is a full tribute to a writer who meant much to him. In his praise, he incorporated some of James's icons, such as his *bon*, or muse, and some other favorites of Auden's. He affirmed, "The flushed assault of your recognition is / The *donnée* of this doubtful hour," the time of World War II. He addresses James as "O stern proconsul of intractable provinces, / O poet of the difficult, dear addicted artist" (*CPA*, 127). He asks James to be a guide during this trying time for us who find ourselves "To be lame and blind yet burning for the Great Good Place, / To be radically corrupt yet mournfully attracted / By the Real Distinguished Thing" (CPA, 129). In 1946, in an introduction to James's *The American Scene*, Auden praised "The Great Good Place" for its spirituality.[10] In "At the Grave of Henry James," he saluted one "Who opened such passionate arms to your *Bon* when It ran / Towards you with its overwhelming reasons pleading / All beautifully in Its breast" He asked of James that "Yours be the disciplinary image that holds / Me back from agreeable wrong" (*CPA*, 129). He asked the "Master of nuance and scruple" to "Pray for me and for all writers living or dead" and to "make intercession / For the treason of all clerks" (*CPA*, 130).

Richard Howard's James

Almost thirty years later, in *Two-Part Inventions*, of 1974, Richard Howard (1929–) included "The Lesson of the Master," a dramatic dialogue between

---

10.   Henry James, *The American Scene*, intro. W. H. Auden (New York, 1946), xii, xiii.

The material in this section appeared in somewhat different form as "Richard Howard, 'The Lesson of the Master,' and Henry James," in *Edith Wharton Review*, IX (Fall, 1992), 11–14.

Edith Wharton and the male lover of a man she would have liked to love her. Nevertheless, James dominates the scene. Even the epigraph to the poem is a quotation from James—his description, in a letter, of Wharton as an "angel of devastation in her wondrous, cushioned, *general* car."[11] The epigraph establishes James's authority over the entire poem, for it is also James's lesson that is carried by the young man who accompanies Wharton to bury the ashes of Gerald Mackenzie, her friend and his lover. James has delegated the young man expressly to explain to Wharton why Mackenzie could not love her. His homoerotic tastes, comparable to those of James's entire circle of male friends, prevented him. Twenty years later, in 1994, James appears presiding again, only more directly, in two poems in Howard's collection *Like Most Revelations*. The first of the poems, "Centenary Peripeteia and Anagnoresis: Beginning with a Line by Henry James," has a title that in ordinary language means "After the passage of one hundred years, one recognizes (*anagnoresis*) that a situation has been completely reversed (*peripeteia*)." But the more mature and even more subtle Howard attached an epigraph that contains a quotation within a quotation. A. N. Wilson quotes a line from James: "The accent of Massachusetts rings up and down the Grand Canal, and the bark of Chicago disturbs the siesta." Wilson says that the last phrase of the quotation "could almost be the opening verse of a poem," and he invites someone to use it. Howard here did just that, beginning "this final phrase" of the quotation as the first line of his poem of eight three-line stanzas. As the fourth stanza, he wrote, "Now behold the reverse / situation abroad in our land: Arab glottals / astonish the ears of Fort Worth." But he saw the reversal as Jamesian: "in history's prospect the Screw always Turns / now this way now that, in the words of the Master; / and he who exults must become he who mourns" (*LM*, 21).

In the second poem, "For David Kalstone, 1932–1986," composed in 1991, a writer and critic is mourned. Howard mentions years before how, "happily trudging / to the grave of Henry James," they had made together "obeisance to that great garrulous Shade." Howard and Kalstone shared a reverence for "certain forms by fond artifice achieved: / Balanchine and Bishop and the creator of / Merton Densher. 'Denture, David? Didn't James / for once bite off less than he could chew?'" (*LM*, 80). By this pun, Howard tries to bring back the happy times he and Kalstone shared. He

11. Richard Howard, "The Lesson of the Master," in *Two-Part Inventions* (New York, 1974), 40.

ends the poem to his friend with a tribute to James, asking who would have known that "sex . . . would one day / possess the power to destroy itself? / Perhaps nobody in creation but our old / deracinated prestidigitator / whose props you so relished in the Palazzo." That was the Barbaro, where James had stayed many times before Kalstone did. James might have known, because "*his* the imagination of disaster, *his* the genius for following it out / the task has always been what The Master called / the wear and tear of discrimination" (*LM*, 81). As in "The Lesson of the Master," James in the matter of sex too could alone have foreseen the drastic penalty incurred.

States of "Hallucination": James and His Modern Illustrators

If ever a writer did not want illustrations to accompany his work, it was James. "I like so little to be illustrated (I resent it so, amiably speaking, on behalf of good prose and writing)," he wrote in a letter in 1896 apropos of the illustrations he was forced to accept for *The Other House*. At the time, magazine stories and books were regularly accoutred with black-and-white illustrations, but he felt that they were insulting to the author. In his last preface to the New York Edition, written thirteen years after the letter, he wrote that illustrations should not attempt to "relieve responsible prose of the duty of being good enough, interesting enough, and . . . pictorial enough above all *in itself*" (*AN*, 332). He was particularly annoyed because he composed, he believed, in pictures, and he wanted no other pictures to interfere with his.

Nonetheless, he admitted that fiction, including his, can legitimately affect artists in other mediums. If the plastic artist is put into a "state of hallucination" by a work of literature, he should "set up some semblance . . . in his own other medium. . . . It would quite stand off and on its own feet and thus, as a separate and independent subject of publication, [it would carry] its text in its spirit" (*AN*, 332). As an independent work of art, it—if published—should appear separately from the work of literature. He never lived to see that kind of commentary on his fiction, but it came to pass later. Two years after his death, Charles Demuth (1883–1935), put in a state of "hallucination" by "The Turn of the Screw" just at the time Edna Kenton's theory of the governess' madness was advanced, did a series of five watercolors, each meant as a separate work of art. The next year he did three watercolors based on "The Beast in the Jungle." The text does to some extent leave its traces in the handwritten quotations at the bottom of the page identifying the scene. What were, however, totally independent and clearly hallucinatory works of art were done by Peter Milton (1930–), a present-day etcher of note, fifty-five years after James's death and more than fifty years after Demuth's watercolors. No remnant of the written text attends these, and yet the spectator must have read the story, this time "The Jolly Corner," to understand many of the scenes. In the 1980s, Milton followed these with his version of "The Aspern Papers."

Two first-rate artists did illustrations for James's fiction during his lifetime. He resented one of them enough to mention his annoyance in print. After George Du Maurier's death, James recorded his displeasure with the twelve illustrations Du Maurier (1834–1896) had done for *Washington Square,* in 1880. According to James, "Every one, every thing is beautiful for Mr. Du Maurier" (*PE*, 22). Since Catherine Sloper has no beauty, no matter what way you look at her, Du Maurier solved the problem by showing her from the back and making her and everyone else's figures into stereotyped fashion mannequins like the society figures in his *Punch* illustrations. In fact, they could pass for duplicates of Major and Mrs. Monarch in "The Real Thing," the germ of which James obtained from Du Maurier. The tale gave voice to James's worry about black-and-white illustrations, and in the year he wrote it seven out of ten of his own tales were, from his point of view, badly illustrated.

John La Farge (1835–1910), the other first-rate artist who illustrated James's fiction during his lifetime, has been singularly overlooked. The one illustration he did belongs to the twentieth century, although it appeared in 1898. James never commented on the record about him or his illustration for the magazine version of "The Turn of the Screw," James's most popular tale. There is no surviving mention by a contemporary of having noticed it, and it has never been reproduced, though S. P. Rosenbaum acknowledged its existence in a short piece in the Norton Critical Edition.[12] The same illustration had headed all but one of the twelve installments in *Collier's Weekly.* It is interesting that La Farge had been the greatest single artistic influence on Henry James as a teenager, the friend

12. S. P. Rosenbaum, "A Note on John La Farge's Illustration for Henry James's *The Turn of the Screw,*" in *The Turn of the Screw,* by Henry James, ed. Robert Kimbrough (New York, 1966), 254–59.

eight years his senior who introduced him to Balzac, Merimée, and Browning. In later life he seemed to become somewhat distanced from the novelist, but it was he who said James had the "painter's eye," even if he encouraged him to become a writer rather than a painter. How the young Robert Collier, who was making innovations in the fiction of the magazine he had just inherited from his father, decided on La Farge is unknown, as are James's reactions to the choice. James knew and admired La Farge's illustrations for Browning's poems, saying so in his autobiography (*AU,* 292).

La Farge was an intellectual painter who, when photographed, posed not with his easel and palette but reading a book in front of the books in his library. He knew Continental literature and art thoroughly, since his connection to an outstanding French family of writers and artists took him to France early in life, and he passed a lot of this education on to his young American friends, the James boys. His work was a clever journey through all the European schools of painting, including those of the Italian Renaissance. He told Royal Cortissoz, his biographer, that he was familiar with all the French schools up through Symbolism. In his collaboration with Saint-Gaudens, his blending of abstract symbolic forms with realistic human forms in patterns of decorative originality is evidence of his subtle and complicated intelligence in working out pictorial problems. He had traveled to Japan and the East and was familiar with Buddhist and Asian art, including representations of many-handed gods. A long passage in *The Education of Henry Adams* that is devoted to La Farge remarks on how his meanings are often elusive because he "had no difficulty in carrying different shades of contradiction in his mind."[13] Such a man seems to have had the optimal qualities for illustrating "The Turn of the Screw."

One look at the picture convinces me that it fits contemporary interpretations of this problematic story. Here the governess is shown half-length. She has her right hand around Miles's shoulders. The two exchange loving and meaningful glances, and in typical Jamesian fashion, each is filled with the consciousness of the other.

What is surprising is that, in this presumably pre-Freudian period, La Farge has exhibited a grasp of the psychoneurotic basis for the governess' behavior and delusions. Her white right hand expresses her protective, motherly relation to Miles. Her dark right hand expresses the destructive,

---

13. Henry Adams, *The Education of Henry Adams,* intro. Leon Wieseltier (New York, 1990), 344.

mind-clutching, sexually repressed part of her nature. Her possession of the boy's soul is embedded in the usurping look to which the boy gives himself. To all appearances, La Farge anticipated the twentieth-century view that the governess is mad.

The beasts in the two identical panels flanking the main picture corroborate the message of the central panel. They are at once decorative and monstrous. Abstractions from biological grotesques, the creatures draw from the world of animals even though they stand upright like humans. They have fangs and elephantine ears, and their oxenlike feet are joined by decorative linear forms in which crustacean elements are suggested. They are symbolic of terrors, terrors that, seated in the governess' mind, are communicated in a nonspecific way to the observer. The illustration was there as a reminder to the reader installment after installment. "Make him *think* the evil, make him think it for himself," James had reasoned in his preface to the volume containing "The Turn of the Screw" (*AN*, 176). This picture leads the reader to do precisely that.

The two inhuman decorative horrors frame in sharp contrast the relationship between the governess and Miles, which is portrayed in an iconographic format that the artist had presumably discerned in sixteenth- and seventeenth-century European marriage pictures by artists like Lorenzo Lotto and Rembrandt. The loving glances and the physical contact between the governess and her charge are those of the couples in such ritual canvases. The authority for such a representation comes from the story itself. "We continued silent," relates the governess, "while the maid was with us—as silent, it whimsically occurred to me, as some young couple who, on their wedding-journey, at the inn, feel shy in the presence of the waiter" (X, 128). The story, like the picture illustrating it, seems at first sight ambiguous, but on second or third glance it lends itself not to irreconcilable alternative interpretations but to reconcilable interpretations. The unhealthy and the sound exist side by side in the governess: her delusions and their psychological ground, on the one hand, and her desire to protect the children against the dangers she perceives, on the other. The two right hands by which La Farge shows her holding on to the boy are his compressed expression of the very unambiguous fact that she is crazed.[14]

14. Adeline R. Tintner, "An Illustrator's Literary Interpretations," *A. B. Bookman's Weekly*, March 26, 1979, pp. 2275–82, reprinted in part in Tintner's *The Museum World of Henry James* (Ann Arbor, Mich., 1986), 224–26, Fig. 98.

18. *The Governess First Sees the Ghost of Peter Quint,*
from Charles Demuth's series for "The Turn of the Screw"
Philadelphia Museum of Art: Gift of Frank and Alice Osborn

Demuth's series of watercolors for "The Turn of the Screw" in 1918 and
for "The Beast in the Jungle" in 1919 were not to be published with the text
but to be shown independently.[15] Demuth put his people in contemporary
costumes and, like La Farge, he made the governess a mature woman, for
sexual repression is more likely to go with mature spinsterhood than with
the youth of the twenty-year-old governess in the story. In the first watercolor, *At a House in Harley Street,* the spinster governess is gazing at the
rather effete young bachelor who hires her. In the second (Figure 18), she
sees an invisible ghost, really the viewer, for she looks straight out of the
picture with eyes rolled, as if in a catatonic seizure. In the next two scenes
(*e.g.,* Figure 19), the children are playing; this is just before the governess
sees ghosts again (Figure 20). In the fifth watercolor (Figure 21), she embraces Miles as she inquires about his expulsion from school. Demuth has
chosen scenes in which the hysteria of the governess is about to grip her:
her first meeting with her charming boss and her fixation on him, her projection of the ghost of Peter Quint in front of the plane of the picture, her

15.   Of the five illustrations for "The Turn of the Screw," four are in the Philadelphia Museum of Art and one is in the Museum of Modern Art, in New York.

19. *The Governess, Mrs. Gross, and Children,*
from Charles Demuth's series for "The Turn of the Screw"

Philadelphia Museum of Art: Gift of Frank and Alice Osborn

20. *Flora and the Governess,*
from Charles Demuth's series for "The Turn of the Screw"

Philadelphia Museum of Art: Gift of Frank and Alice Osborn

21. *Miles and the Governess,*
from Charles Demuth's series for "The Turn of the Screw"
Philadelphia Museum of Art: Gift of Frank and Alice Osborn

seeing of Miss Jessel when no one else does. The ghosts are never part of the pictures, because they exist only in the governess' mind.

"The Beast in the Jungle" is not a ghost story but a tale of a failed human relationship, the hero of which is as obsessed as the governess. In Demuth's first scene (Figure 22), in the boat crossing the Bay of Naples to Sorrento, Marcher confesses to May Bartram having had a sense all his life that something prodigious would happen to him. In the second (Figure 23), he torments her while she is dying with his incapacity to understand their relationship. In the last scene (Figure 24), notwithstanding James's text, he flings himself on the ground next to the tomb rather than on the tomb itself.

The portfolio of twenty-one etchings that Milton did in 1977 includes seven prints for each of three segments of the story "The Jolly Corner," which had not been illustrated before. Spencer Brydon's search for his alter ego is conveyed through the "dynamics of recollection, my most essential concern," in the artist's phrase. The ambiguity of time in the sequence is consistent with Milton's approach in his other prints. He allows certain features of the story to fire his own recollection; for instance, the etching of the construction workers Brydon visits in his investigation of the house he is turning into flats (Figure 25) has a hare in the foreground, magnifying an image in the story: "If he had but stayed at home, he would have discov-

22. *Boat Ride from Sorrento,*
from Charles Demuth's series for "The Beast in the Jungle"

Philadelphia Museum of Art: Gift of Frank and Alice Osborn

23. *The Revelation Comes to May Bartram in Her Drawing Room,*
from Charles Demuth's series for "The Beast in the Jungle"

Philadelphia Museum of Art: Gift of Frank and Alice Osborn

24. *Marcher Receives His Revelation at May Bartram's Tomb,*
from Charles Demuth's series for "The Beast in the Jungle"

Philadelphia Museum of Art: Gift of Frank and Alice Osborn

25. Brydon visits construction workers during his investigation of the house.
From Peter Milton's series of etchings for "The Jolly Corner"

Courtesy Peter Milton

26. Inside the house.
From Peter Milton's series of etchings for "The Jolly Corner"
Courtesy Peter Milton

ered his genius in time really to start some new variety of awful architectural hare and run it till it burrowed in a gold-mine" (XII, 197). The viewer must know the story and remember the figure to comprehend the hare.

Three scenes realize certain metaphors from the second segment of the story, which takes place inside the house. In one (Figure 26), Milton reacts to "this stalking of a creature more subtle, yet at bay perhaps more formidable, than any beast of the forest" (XII, 210). Another is in response to the "large black-and-white squares that he remembered as the admiration of his childhood" (XII, 209). In the third (Figure 27), the "life of the town" is "under a spell." The "hard-faced houses" are "great builded voids," and Brydon makes a "choked appeal from his own open window," wanting to leave the house (XII, 220–21). Milton takes this literally and shows Brydon jumping from the window. The artist conflates memories in two categories: his memories of the story about the fictive hero's memory of the past, and his memories of his own past. The series, like the tale, is dominated by reverie.

For the third segment, first Alice Staverton, the girl who waited for Brydon, appears with Stéphane Mallarmé, who stands for Brydon, for Mallarmé is the poet of reverie (Figure 28). In the next etching, almost identical, she is in a state of undress, suggesting the sexual yearnings of Alice and

27. Brydon jumps from the window of the house.
From Peter Milton's series of etchings for "The Jolly Corner"

Courtesy Peter Milton

28. Alice Staverton and Mallarmé.
From Peter Milton's series of etchings for "The Jolly Corner"

Courtesy Peter Milton

29. Alice Staverton, James, Renoir, and Evelyn Nesbit.
From Peter Milton's series of etchings for "The Jolly Corner"
Courtesy Peter Milton

Brydon for each other. Perhaps the two dream of each other; in the story, Alice dreams of Brydon. In the next scene, James takes the place of Brydon and another image of James is there as his alter ego. The girl in the picture on the wall is based on Evelyn Nesbit, probably because of her connection with Stanford White, the architect murdered as a result of his liaison with her, for architecture concerns Brydon. Then (Figure 29), the alter ego becomes Renoir or a figure with a face much like his, testifying to the distortion of memory even when it remains connected with history. In a couple of the prints, a bull or beast, representing sexuality, appears. In the final print, there are the reconstructed house, the woman as love and sex object, and James emerging as the Brydon figure with his alter ego a reverse face. Perhaps this refers to James's suspected inversion, or homosexuality. The machinery of modern American life and twentieth-century progress recapitulates the themes in the last print.[16]

Milton integrates images of both fictive and historical persons in his temporal and spatial continuum. The originality of his statement depends

16.   A catalogue raisonné of Peter Milton's etchings, which includes the entire series devoted to "The Jolly Corner," was published by The Impressions Workshop, Boston, 1971.

on the blending or collaging of images from different time schemes and different levels of significance. An allegory can occupy the same space as a real person. The evocation of a mood of reverie that between its source and its final configuration, both in the story by James, makes its way through the private recesses of Milton's mind has the effect of providing a mode of understanding for the story through a parallel set of stimuli.

Milton has created a plastic correlative that derives its form from the story but transforms the features he selects into a private dream in which the elements originating in Spencer Brydon, in Henry James, and in Peter Milton converge and blend. The suite is truly a "hallucination" produced by the tale and, as such, by James's own estimate, is a real tribute to the writer.

Twenty-two years after completing the illustrations based on "The Jolly Corner," Milton was again moved to pictorialize a short story by James. To complement his work on the American story, he chose to delve into "The Aspern Papers," with its European background. That involved him in much greater complexity, because of the tale's multiple associations and intricate organization. No longer was the place one lonely house; it was the city of Venice, including all its reverberating echoes. The story of Byron and Shelley and Clare Clairmont is among these, as is that of James himself in Venice—his association with his brother, with his friends, with the painter Sargent, with the aristocrat Count Primoli, and with Constance Fenimore Woolson, who was closely and emotionally related to him and died there. For collaging, Milton had a much richer and more evocative horde of interrelated photographs from the Jamesian archive, and his etchings for "The Aspern Papers" drew on only a few photographs unrelated to that archive.

James seems to be affiliated with the "publishing scoundrel," for there is a small image of him in the doorway of one of the illustrations (Figure 30). The niece, Tina, stands before a collaged painting based on a portrait by John Singer Sargent: "I have appropriated and modified two of Sargent's three Miss Vickers." Milton has inserted Byron and Shelley, recognizable by their traditional Byronic shirt collars. The forward Miss Vickers is to represent, no doubt, Clare Clairmont.

Milton explained in the Afterword how his approach to "The Aspern Papers" differed from his handling of "The Jolly Corner." For the new illustrations, he decided "to skirt James's narrative and instead to take as my subject matter the same source material from which he derived his tale.

30. Tina (Tita) standing before the portrait,
with the "publishing scoundrel" at right.
From Peter Milton's series of etchings for "The Aspern Papers"

Courtesy Peter Milton

These sources, of course, gave me James himself, his family, particularly brother William; James's beloved Venice; the Palazzo Capello and its gardens, which formed the basis for the palazzo of the narrative; Shelley/Byron and Clare Clairmont; and the close friend, Constance Fenimore Woolson, who, Leon Edel believes, is almost certainly James's basis for the younger Miss Bordereau, Tina." He wanted the resonance, first, of Venice, its water and its monuments, and then of the Palazzo Capello, which he photographed for incorporation in his sequence. He subordinated the chief players of the story to their creator, focusing on the Master in the last three scenes. According to Milton, "There needed to be a point where the elaborations could begin to subside and in the end recede into silence."[17] The last scene, made from a well-known photograph of James, shows the Master writing, presumably the tale (Figure 31).

After two introductory etchings connected with Mrs. Prest's telling James about Juliana, the section "Citings of Venice" places well-known

17.   Henry James, *The Aspern Papers*, illus. Peter Milton (Boston, 1993), Afterword, unpaginated (3ʳᵈ page).

31. The Master writing.
From Peter Milton's series of etchings for "The Aspern Papers"
Courtesy Peter Milton

photographs of James and his brother in the famous Venetian tourist settings. The *sala* of the Palazzo Capello is pictured to convey the mood of
emptiness and silence in James's story (Figure 32). After the emotional climax, the currents subside in the mind of James, and he silently creates his
story at his desk.

Milton tells in detail the provenance of his archival material and its relation to the three levels on which his illustrations have content: the biographical, relating to James; the fictional, relating to the story elements
and the history of the tale's characters; and the creative, relating to Milton
himself. When Milton discovered the palazzo James chose as the home
of Juliana and Tina, it was in a state of great decay. Yet, Milton wrote,
"the grand architectural porticoes of the main towers are splendid. I spent
a haunted day photographing the majestic desolation." The architecture
seemed a comment on the "eerie aptness of James's choice to represent
his sense of a passing time in The Aspern Papers." Milton also described
his need "to shift my Byron / Shelley amalgam from Anderson/Hill to an
1855 self-portrait by the early French photographer Paul Guillard, who
brought a certain melancholy air of loss" to the "delightful eyes" and "mild
mockery" that the narrator finds in the oval Aspern portrait.

Milton also let his personal experience inform his representation of Ju-

32. Sala of the Palazzo Capello.
From Peter Milton's series of etchings for "The Aspern Papers"
Courtesy Peter Milton

liana: "For the final image of the once beautiful Juliana Bordereau I borrowed a photograph of Georgia O'Keeffe in her old age; I altered the occlusion and modified the eyes to echo James's repeated reference to the hidden, large and once beautiful eyes of the old woman" (Figure 33).

The different ways in which La Farge, Demuth, and Milton have illustrated James coordinate with twentieth-century changes in the plastic arts. La Farge, in the last years of the nineteenth century, exemplifies the Symbolist distortion of the real in his three-armed evil governess, a physiological counterpart to the Symbolist sphinxes and chimeras in the fin-de-siècle interpretation of psychological monsters. This also heralds the twentieth-century Freudian view of the human psyche, with the contradictions implicit in subconscious desires and drives. Demuth exemplifies the Post-Impressionist placement of Freudian interpretations in pictorial spaces that show the influence of Cézanne and the Cubists. Milton, however, in exploiting the potential of photography, best fulfills James's conception of acceptable illustration of a text. James would have approved of them because they form a "contribution in as different a 'medium' as possible" and do not "keep, or pretend to keep, anything like dramatic step with their suggestive matter" (*AN*, 333).

33. Juliana Bordereau and the "publishing scoundrel."
From Peter Milton's series of etchings for "The Aspern Papers"
Courtesy Peter Milton

All three of these illustrators, each in a different generation, are artists or poets—as James also saw himself: "The seer and speaker under the descent of the god is the 'poet,' whatever his form" (*AN*, 340). All three saw James's creations through the psychological lens, the premier instrument for the twentieth century's commentary on human behavior in life and art. But because Milton has achieved art that carries "its text in its spirit, just as that text correspondingly carries the plastic possibility," it is the "still more glorious tribute" that James envisioned (*AN*, 332–33).

Standing on James's Text: Rob Wynne's *Figure in the Carpet*

Rob Wynne (1950–) has designed a rug of room-size proportions decorated only with some lines from James's "The Figure in the Carpet." In that tale, the writer Hugh Vereker confesses to a young critic that he cannot understand why all those who have criticized his books have missed their whole point, the "figure in the carpet"—something he feels to be "as concrete as a bird in a cage, a bait on a hook, a piece of cheese in a mouse-trap" (IX, 283–84). For the rug's design, Wynne has chosen words describing Vereker as standing on a rug in the young critic's bedroom at a weekend country-house party they are both attending: "I can see him there still, on

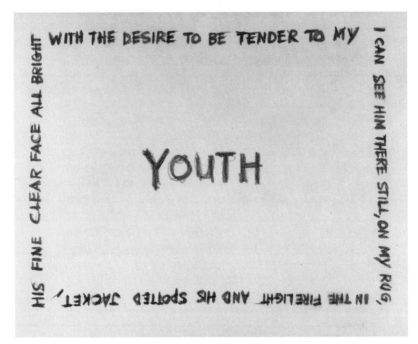

34. Rob Wynne's *Figure in the Carpet*
Courtesy Rob Wynne

my rug, in the firelight and his spotted jacket, his fine, clear face all bright
with the desire to be tender to my youth" (IX, 279–80). The words run
around the border, except for *youth,* the last word of the quotation, which is
at the center of the rug as the fulcrum of the design (Figure 34). Its five letters are larger than those at the perimeter. Wynne has thus brought the
dead metaphor "the figure in the carpet" back to life by planting it directly
in the carpet itself. The transposition of a line from the story onto a real rug
has put the essence of the tale into another medium, that of the rug weaver's art.

Wynne's work of art implicitly comments on the meaning of James's
tale. The figure in the carpet, the meaning of the writer's lifetime work, can
be learned only through a reading of the work. The critic cannot break it
down into words that improve on the words of the literary artist. Wynne's
carpet underscores that the meaning of the figure in this carpet resides in
the fact that the figure is *in* the carpet, for the message is the medium, lying
in a work that speaks for itself. His rug with its inscription concretely rep-

resents the message James intended for the reader. The spectator who stands or sits on the rug is forced not only to see it as a pictorial and literary pun, in which the design and words collaborate, but to recognize the act of reading that it entails as in union with the act of viewing. Reader and spectator are joined in cooperative action by this conceptual artist for an interplay of text and texture that is almost infinite.

Because the only design of the large rectangle is textual, there is a temptation to interpret the work as an instance of the conceptualism that has been a strong current in the visual art of the postmodern period. But conceptualism is here a kind of red herring: the text, upon being read, opens up possibilities of interpretation in a way uncharacteristic of conceptual art. The words "the figure in the carpet" come to life with the solid referent of the author standing on a rug.

The colors of the rug belie its minimalism. The center is a deep rosy red, the script is yellow, and the central motif of *youth* is turquoise. These are the colors of Giovanni Battista Tiepolo's eighteenth-century vaulted ceilings, in which the baroque blends with the Italian rococo. Wynne deliberately inverted Tiepolo's arrangement, however, by appropriating his ceiling colors for a floor covering. Together, the borrowing from the painter and the borrowing from James extend the artist's individualism and expand his reference, the limits of which depend only on the education of the mind and eye of the beholder. Wynne, in placing the rug in an environment he built for an exhibition in Monte Carlo, both limited and expanded still further the myriad proliferation of references, both visual and textual.

Wynne's rug speaks for itself as a work of art at the same time that it reinforces James's message by placing the colors of the greatest Venetian painter of the eighteenth century underfoot rather than overhead. Wynne was also turning to account certain associations of James with Tiepolo. He had slept under a Tiepolo ceiling in the Palazzo Barbaro in Venice, even if a copy had replaced the original. In "Collaboration," of 1892, James's tale of an ideal society of artists, the characters "gaze up at the distant Tiepolo in the almost palatial ceiling" (VIII, 407), a work of art that makes his studio a "temple of reconciliation" (VIII, 408). James in his travel essays often praised Tiepolo and examined Tiepolo's Venice through his own eyes.

Wynne's tapping of James goes way beyond that in the works of John La Farge, Charles Demuth, and even Peter Milton. For La Farge, a Freudian interpretation ruled. Demuth and Milton allowed themselves various visions of James's tales, but Wynne, in restricting himself to one article, the rug, and submitting to the formal limitation imposed by the size of a room and the lines he selected from "The Figure in the Carpet," has set up an infinity of interpenetrating references for the delectation of the spectator. The viewer must take on the experience of James's tale and Wynne's rug within the same compass, allowing consciousness to ricochet from the one to the other, receptive to whatever associations the adventure as reader and viewer has stirred up.

9

JAMES AND THE CRIMINOUS

A work of art ought to be constructed like a perfect crime, without a spot, without a sign of the author.

—Constantin Brancusi

The prodigious Madeleine [Smith]. . . . It represents indeed the *type*, perfect case, with nothing to be taken from it or added, and with the beauty that she precisely *didn't* squalidly suffer, but lived on to admire with the rest of us, for so many years, the rare work of art with which she had been the means of enriching humanity.

—Henry James to William Roughead

The combination of imagination and reality which is the basis of my art.

—Jeremy Brett, speaking in the role of Sherlock Holmes

With increasing frequency since just before the Second World War, detective and mystery stories have pulled James into their plots. Have the authors sensed James's interest in the criminous as a kind of obsession even before the publication of his letters to William Roughead revealed it to be that? Or have James's *Portraits of Places* and his travel pieces centered in Italy commanded their interest? Some present-day writers of mystery stories seize upon the Venetian aspect of James, with which they have become acquainted as new editions of his *Italian Hours* elicited a wider readership and "The Aspern Papers," "The Pupil," and *The Wings of the Dove* — all of which touch on criminal plots and take place in Venice — became more familiar to readers and more important to writers regardless of genre.

The trend started in England with Agatha Christie and J. I. M. Stewart, who wrote many of his suspense and detective stories under the name of Michael Innes. Stewart, as a tutor in literature at Oxford, had expertise in reading James. His specialty was the "donnish" mystery — in which the university and its professors are the bridge between scholarly interest in James and criminal detection. Carolyn Heilbrun, writing as Amanda Cross, is a proven master of this sort of mystery in the United States. Partly it was an attempt to elevate the tone of the murder story and fashion an alternative to the hard-boiled school of Raymond Chandler and Georges Simenon.

James appears very frequently in English and American murder mysteries of the 1980s and 1990s. The reading public is now thoroughly aware of James and can be depended upon to recognize icons from his best-known tales and novels. Even those who have not read him have constantly read about him and come into almost daily encounter with him in the New York *Times*. Perhaps, too, modern writers of detective fiction share James's deep interest in the relationship between the perfect crime and the perfect work of art, perpetuating a tradition going back to Oscar Wilde's praise of Thomas Wainewright as, in his forgeries, an artist of "pen, pencil, and poison."

Seeking the Ideal Reader in a *"Devotée* of Henry James": Agatha Christie and Her Jamesian Allusions

Possibly the earliest mysteries with some allusion to James or quotations from his writings are by the queen of the genre, Agatha Christie (1890–1976). In 1928, in *The Mystery of the Blue Train,* she wrote a sentence that bears a mysterious similarity to the chapter James wrote for the collaborative novel *The Whole Family.* In that chapter, the seventh, Charles, the married son of the family, says, "When you paint a picture with a brush and pigments, that is on a single plane, it can stop at your gilt frame; but when you paint one with a pen and words, that is in *all* the dimensions, how are you to stop? Of course, as Lorraine says, 'Stopping, that's art.'" In Christie's mystery, the detective, Hercule Poirot, says to Mademoiselle Zia, "You are the daughter of your father, Mademoiselle Zia. To know when to stop.

Ah! That is the art."[1] Christie may have read James's chapter in *Harper's Bazaar* or she may have read the novel itself; both were published in 1908. But perhaps James had taken it first from Arthur Conan Doyle.[2]

In her next mystery, *Thirteen at Dinner*, published in 1933, one of the murder victims presents the "pathetic figure of a young girl with all the world before her" (*TH*, 134). Comparable variants of Milton's "the World was all before them" (*Paradise Lost*, XII, 646) occur four times in *The Wings of the Dove*, once when Milly is seen "as a young person with the world before her." But Christie's phrase seems to have come from James rather than Milton, given that a young girl is the person with the world all before her. Milly Theale is virtually killed by her knowledge of her betrayal; Carlotta Adams in *Thirteen at Dinner* loses her life after an actor has her impersonate Jane Wilkinson, a well-known actress, for his own ends.

There are, in addition, echoes of James's plots, characters, motifs, and associations in Christie. Carlotta is an American monologist, reminiscent of Ruth Draper, the great American monologist for whom James wrote a monologue in 1912, although it did not appear until 1922, in the *London Mercury* and *Vanity Fair*.

James's "The Siege of London" seems also to have left its mark on *Thirteen at Dinner*. Jane Wilkinson has seduced the Duke of Merton, but his mother, the dowager Duchess of Merton, does not want her son to marry her. She appeals to Poirot to stop the marriage just as Lady Demesne appeals to Littlemore to stop the marriage of her son, Lord Demesne, to Mrs. Headway, the unrespectable American millionairess (*TH*, 142–43). The dowager duchess ends in the same defeated position as Lady Demesne, because, according to Poirot, her son "would refuse to listen to anything against the lady," nor is there "very much against her to say" (*TH*, 144). In "The Siege of London," Lady Demesne asks whether Mrs. Headway is respectable and Littlemore says she is not. But it makes no difference for the outcome: there is the same sense of the futility of trying to stop the marriage that Poirot conveys to the dowager duchess.

Christie's young duke is younger than his fiancée and as ill at ease with Jane's crowd as Sir Arthur Demesne is among Mrs. Headway's friends:

1. Agatha Christie, *The Mystery of the Blue Train* (1928; rpr. New York, 1978), 171.
2. Doyle's words are not so close to Christie's as James's: "But he had not that supreme gift of the artist, the knowledge of when to stop. He tried to improve that which was already perfect . . . and so he ruined all" (*The Return of Sherlock Holmes* [Pleasantville, N.Y., 1991], 54).

"The company in which he found himself was, so I should imagine, little to his liking. He was a strictly conservative and somewhat reactionary young man—the kind of character that seemed to have stepped out of the Middle Ages by some regrettable mistake. His infatuation for the extremely modern Jane Wilkinson was one of those anachronistic jokes that Nature so loves to play" (*TH*, 184). The same kind of attraction between opposites takes place in James's tale: "He had never seen anything like Mrs. Headway; he hardly knew by what standard to measure her. . . . Though he disapproved of it, it was precisely her foreignness that pleased him; she seemed to be as little as possible of his own race and creed" (V, 46–47).

Christie's *Murder in Three Acts*, of 1934, brings to mind James's *The Sacred Fount*, also in essence a detective novel. Mr. Satterthwaite, who recurs in several of her mysteries, is very much like the narrator of James's novel. "What is ignoble is the detective at the keyhole," James had said about the abuses and the indignities that were possible in a detective story.

Like James's nameless narrator, Satterthwaite is an "observant man. In the midst of his cogitations of the female sex in general . . . he was unable to resist saying to himself: 'Now where have I seen that particular-shaped head before?'" (*MT*, 48). Like him, he "listened to the troubles of other people and did not intrude his own" (*MT*, 118). In the manner of both James and many of his male characters, Mr. Satterthwaite was able to watch the "girl, sympathizing with her predicament. These men did not understand, but he, with his semi-feminine sensitiveness, realized her dilemma" (*MT*, 130). Observant as a detective, he remembers "fairly well where everyone had been in the room" (*MT*, 136) and, like James's narrator, keeps track of everyone. He is known to be "very clever about people. . . . It is rather his hobby, I should say" (*MT*, 169). Personifying a famous figure of speech in *The Sacred Fount*, Poirot builds a house of cards and, when he needs it no longer, "with the sweep of his hands he swept the cards from the table" (*MT*, 208).

At least fourteen of Christie's novels are concerned with a crime two people passionately involved with each other commit in collusion. The plan is for one of them to marry a rich person to get enough money so that, after they murder the victim, they will be able to have a good life together. *The Wings of the Dove* could be a model for this scenario, and *The Mysterious Affair at Styles*, of 1920, Christie's very first novel, which was also the first to introduce Poirot as her detective, follows the plot. Evelyn Howard and Alfred Inglethorp conspire to defraud Mrs. Inglethorp of her millions. Like

Kate Croy and Merton Densher, James's couple, they cultivate the impression that they are uninterested in each other. Evelyn Howard is emphatic about the aversion she feels for Alfred Inglethorp, thus diverting attention from their connection.

Gillian Gill, in her life of Agatha Christie, said that her subject put "more reliance on your knowledge of novels, particularly detective novels, than of science." She suggested that a person "highly likely to discover the murderers' identity [in *The Mysterious Affair at Styles*] is, strangely enough, a *devotée* of Henry James."[3] Gill added that Christie never mentioned reading James or *The Wings of the Dove*.

James and Christie were from the same world. Christie recorded in her autobiography that "a good many interesting people came to my house during my young days, and it seems a pity that I personally do not remember any of them!" One of these was Henry James, but she recollected only that her mother complained "that he always wanted a lump of sugar broken in two for his tea."[4] The word *always* at least testifies that he visited often. He may also have presented his books to the family.

Whether specifically indebted to James or not, Christie shared his interest in the importance of art and the value of the completely achieved artistic crime. Think of the outburst of Justice Wargrave in *And Then There Were None*, of 1939: "I have wanted—let me admit it frankly—*to commit a murder myself*. I was, or could be, an artist in crime! My imagination, sternly checked by the exigencies of my profession, waxed secretly to colossal force. I must—I must—I *must*—commit a murder! And what is more, it must be no ordinary murder! It must be a fantastical crime—something stupendous—out of the common!"[5] This is in the spirit of James's delight in Roughead's account of famous murders like those of Madeleine Smith and Mary Blandy.

"Everything's in Henry James": J. I. M. Stewart's— and Michael Innes'—Appropriation

J. I. M. Stewart (1906–1994), in his autobiography of 1987, *Myself and Michael Innes*, acknowledged that when his novel *Mark Lambert's Supper* was

3. Gillian Gill, *Agatha Christie: The Woman and Her Mysteries* (New York, 1990), 46.
4. Agatha Christie, *An Autobiography* (New York, 1977), 38.
5. Agatha Christie, *And Then There Were None* (New York, 1940), 185.

published, in 1954, some thought it a "detective story dolled up in verbal garments which absurdly evoked the shade of Henry James. This was not, I think, altogether unfair [since I had included] in the book a letter very colourably purporting to be from the pen of James himself. But I certainly didn't intend to set myself up on the stilts of another man's style."[6] Still, the novel evokes the atmosphere and general milieu of something by James. Such imitations have usually been parodies, but with Stewart there is no implication of such an intent.

Mark Lambert's Supper was the first of a series Stewart wrote after publishing many successful "donnish" mysteries as Michael Innes. In the novel, Mark Lambert, whose name conflates Lord Mark of *The Wings of the Dove* and Lambert Strether of *The Ambassadors*, is a writer and a friend of James's. It is a letter from James to Lambert that gives away the secret behind the last golden period of Lambert's books, the period corresponding to James's major phase. When Lambert's daughter, Anthea, an Oxford scientist, meets Garth Dauncey, the son of Lambert's pallid, unsuccessful painter friend, a chain of events leads to the discovery that the painter wrote Lambert's last works. In a Jamesian vein, there is at first a misunderstanding of the letter found in the newly recovered manuscript of Lambert's unpublished novel, *The End of It All*. The secret on first reading seems to be that Lambert is Garth's father, but it turns out to be that Garth's father was the author of Lambert's greatest books.

Stewart makes frequent references to *The Golden Bowl*, drawing comparisons between it and Lambert's *The Cosmopolitans*. The Settignano Memorandum Book of Lambert's is arranged like James's *Notebooks*, which had been published in 1947. In it, Lambert makes notes about *données*, as James called germinal plots, and he sets down his criticisms of a novel of James's that may be *The Awkward Age*. He records something James told him about once considering, but rejecting as a vulgar ploy, a change of plot for *The Wings of the Dove*.[7] He mentions that James is surprised by his late novels. In this, James comes across as one who cannot be fooled.

Stewart's novel *The Guardians*, published the year after the tour de force about James's friend Lambert, includes a character from American City. Thinking of Adam Verver's hometown in *The Golden Bowl*, another character inquires, "Isn't that something in Henry James?" The first answers,

6.   J. I. M. Stewart, *Myself and Michael Innes* (London, 1987), 184.
7.   J. I. M. Stewart, *Mark Lambert's Supper* (London, 1954), 92.

"Yes, sir. But then everything's in Henry James."[8] And it is tempting to think that everything that is in Henry James is also in J. I. M. Stewart's fiction. In *The Guardians*, there are glimpses of many of James's novels. Arthur Quaill is tracking down the relics and papers of an author named Fontaney, in the way the "publishing scoundrel" tracks down papers belonging to Jeffrey Aspern. Marianne Fontaney is like Tina Bordereau, except that she succeeds in marrying the man who wants her manuscripts. Even *The Portrait of a Lady* puts in an appearance through the repetition of a phrase from it. "Those signs of the highly curious he was showing her on the underside of old plates" (*PO*, 224) leaves its residue in Stewart's "obscure marks on the underside of old plates."[9]

In *A Question of Queens*, a detective story of 1956, Colin Clout, of Spenserian origin, likes *The Wings of the Dove*, as well as *Anna Karenina* and *Madame Bovary*. Stewart named the head porter Gedge, after the hero of James's "The Birthplace," of 1903, and Sir Francis Dashwood bears the last name of the man Miriam Rooth marries, Basil Dashwood, in *The Tragic Muse*. Lord Dangerfield has the same name as the lady on shipboard in James's "Pandora," of 1884.[10]

In 1957, in a mystery tale, Stewart confined his allusions to James to attributing a story called "A Second Innings" to Mark Lambert. Lambert's story approximates James's in "The Middle Years," about a second chance a writer wants but does not get. At the end of March, 1958, Stewart went up to London from Oxford for a luncheon at the Garrick Club, where Simon Nowell-Smith, Janet Adam Smith, and other Jamesians of world distinction were honoring Leon Edel, the biographer of James. Nowell-Smith "produced Stewart as a surprise," Edel remembered. "He wasn't easy to talk to: stout, stocky, loose clothes, scruffy. A nice smile, eyes wide apart. I praised *Mark Lambert's Supper*."[11] After their meeting, Stewart reviewed several volumes of Edel's biography as they were published. One of these was probably *Henry James: The Middle Years*, which appeared in 1962, for he put into his novel of 1963 many icons from *The Tragic Muse*, written in 1890, during James's middle years, and discussed in detail by Edel. In the novel, *The Last Tresilians*, Stewart quotes, for one of the four times in his books,

8.   J. I. M. Stewart, *The Guardians* (New York, 1955), 95.

9.   *Ibid.*, 220.

10.   J. I. M. Stewart, *A Question of Queens* (New York, 1956), 45–46.

11.   Leon Edel to author, March 14, 1992.

James's well-known phrase "The imagination of disaster." Many of the names in the novel are from *The Tragic Muse*, including Tresilian, although written with two *ᶴ*s there, and Nick Dallow, which combines the names of Nick Dormer and his fiancée, Julia Dallow. The fulcrum for the allusions to James is the biographer of the painter Tresilian, Thayne Delver. "I was a low fellow . . . kneeling at a keyhole" is a figure of speech he utters, and Stewart was probably influenced by the cartoon by Max Beerbohm he had often seen in the Ashmolean Museum. Delver, who seems derived from the figure of Leon Edel, is a careful and wise biographer, and is as committed to his subject as Edel was to James. "Your father's genius means a great deal to me," he tells Tresilian's son. "So I want to find out all I can about him." *The Last of the Tresilians* came so closely on the heels of the volume in which Edel analyzed *The Tragic Muse* that whether Stewart knew it or not — and in a letter he denied such an influence[12] — the pivot for the Jamesian references must be seen to lie in Delver, the biographer of Tresilian who even unconsciously was modeled on Edel.

So interested was Stewart in getting James into his narrative *Silence Observed*, published under the name of Michael Innes in 1961, that he named a young constable Henry James, allowing him to comment on that unusual fact. He had Sir John Appleby, his recurring socially well connected detective, ask Lord Mountmerton whether he ever met the author James. Mountmerton says no, for although James "went out a great deal," it was not "among the right people. . . . He moved among snobs." When Appleby asks, "Didn't he move among artists?" Mountmerton answers, "Very indifferently. . . . You no doubt know that strangest of his productions, *The Golden Bowl*. An American of enormous wealth is represented as devoted to art. . . . He simply frequents dealers, and buys the work of painters long dead. That is not, to my mind, to fulfil the duties of a patron of the arts."[13]

Edel had in 1952 discovered James's first story, published anonymously, "A Tragedy of Error." By 1965, having in his hands the story itself, Stewart wrote a takeoff on it in *A Comedy of Terrors*. Yet the substance of the tale depends on *The Sacred Fount*. The year after Edel published his discov-

12. "I did *not* have Edel in mind when inventing Delver. . . . I did have a cousin called Violet Trestrail, and I suppose Tresilian may come from that." J. I. M. Stewart to author, March 31, 1990. Stewart also wrote, however, "I recall little about that luncheon in 1958," and he asserted that he had "no visual memory of Edel." He may also have forgotten how certain vestiges of *The Tragic Muse* found their way into his novel.

13. J. I. M. Stewart [Michael Innes], *Silence Observed* (New York, 1961), 163.

ery of James's first tale, his distinguished essay on *The Sacred Fount* appeared as an introduction to Grove Press's republication of the novel. In Stewart's tale, Geoffrey notices that the narrator is concerned with "who-goes-with-whom, I suppose?" Appleby, the donnish police investigator, says, "You and Anne are not unlike the creatures in Henry James's books."[14] The novel also copies the scene in *The Sacred Fount* where the narrator notices Gilbert Long standing on the terrace.

In Stewart's *An Acre of Grass*, of 1965, there is a writer like James, and an architectural feature is described as conforming to a "similar arrangement at Henry James's house in Rye." When someone puts on an electric light at the door, it reminds the narrator of what Henry James "somewhere calls 'the white light of convenience.'"[15]

In 1967, in *Vanderlyn's Kingdom*, which has affinities with *The Golden Bowl* and *The Ambassadors*, there is a character by the name of Shefford, who has read most of the "great novels" and from them draws the lesson that "nobody must simply use anybody else." The "archetypal disaster (he would have said, pointing straight at one of the great novels) was Adam Verver's marriage to Charlotte Stant" (*VK*, 101). The relationship between Bernard Vanderlyn and his woman parallels the relationship between Verver and Stant. *The Ambassadors* insinuates itself into the novel when Shefford, whose name is close to Strether, sees two Greek boys through his binoculars—one making an obscene gesture on a fishing yacht. The scene is a counterpart to that where Strether sees Chad and Marie de Vionnet in the boat in the countryside, confirming a sexual relationship between them. As in *The Ambassadors*, there is a "big promiscuous garden party" (*VK*, 185)— a phrase late Jacobean in character. There is a marriage corresponding to Adam's marriage to Charlotte, to provide the heroine with a female companion. *Vanderlyn's Kingdom* brings *The Golden Bowl* up to date for twentieth-century readers by fitting illegitimate children and a homosexual couple into the situation of *The Golden Bowl*.

Stewart scattered fewer Jamesian comments through his Oxford quintet published under the general title of *A Staircase in Surrey* between 1975 and 1978. But in the short stories grouped together in 1969 as *Cucumber Sandwiches* there is again the phrase "the imagination of disaster." There is also a Jamesian hero with an interest in young men; this may owe some-

14. J. I. M. Stewart, *A Comedy of Terrors* (1965; rpr. New York, 1987), 52.
15. J. I. M. Stewart, *An Acre of Grass* (New York, 1965), 28.

thing to Edel's *Henry James: The Treacherous Years,* in which James's homoerotic interest in the young sculptor Hendrik Andersen is a topic. Cordenoy is based on Henry James, and the two portraits of himself he has hanging on opposite walls, one by Sargent and the other by Jacques Emile Blanche, show that Stewart was aware of the two most famous portraits of James. In "A Change of Heart," another tale in the volume, an artist stops in Switzerland at the Hotel des Trois Couronnes, the hotel at which James's Daisy Miller stays in Vevey.

In *Avery's Mission,* of 1979, *The Ambassadors* and *The Awkward Age* come together. Here the son attempts to use the material his father collected, but a woman, Mrs. Fernanda Brenton, named after Nanda in *The Awkward Age,* delivers herself, with slight modifications, of Maggie Verver's famous line in *The Golden Bowl:* "You will have to find out for yourself."[16] And in the mystery *The Open House,* of 1972, the house called Ledward resurrects a word in a list of names Henry James published in his *Notebooks:* "Ledward—Bedward—Dedward." The third occurrence of the phrase "the imagination of disaster" is there as well.

In the Oxford quintet, a character recalls that the age of forty years is, "as Henry James calls it somewhere," a "grim promontory."[17] In *The Madonna of the Astrolabe,* the fourth of the Oxford quintet volumes and concerned with a painting by Piero della Francesca, a character finds himself talking like Henry James, remarking, "It sounded like some bogus-colloquial performance out of Henry James."[18]

Honeybath's Haven, of 1977, is a rewriting of James's "The Great Good Place," but in addition the widow of Mr. Gutermann-Seuss, so prominent in *The Golden Bowl* as the art dealer, reappears in this novel, though as the widow of a different man. Her staircase "was hung with a rising tier of photographs, all the portraits of male persons, and all inscribed with greetings and signatures." Honeybath "inspected them cautiously. *Cordially, Andrew Mellon,* he read. *Yours, Samuel H. Cress*[*sic*] . . . Everybody who had ever bought anything . . . in a sufficiently big way was here."[19] Ambrose Prout

---

16.   J. I. M. Stewart, *Avery's Mission* (New York, 1979), 165.

17.   J. I. M. Stewart, *A Memorial Service* (London, 1976), 174, Vol. III of *A Staircase in Surrey,* 5 vols.

18.   J. I. M. Stewart, *The Madonna of the Astrolabe* (London, 1977), 289, Vol. IV of *A Staircase in Surrey.*

19.   J. I. M. Stewart, *Honeybath's Haven* (New York, 1978), 165.

asks, "Do you know Verver's *The Spoils of Darius?* A wonderfully revealing account of collector's mania in the great age." This refers wittily at once to "The Spoils of Poynton" and to Adam Verver, who "pitched a tent, suggesting that of Alexander furnished with the spoils of Darius" (*GB,* 40). Prout goes on, "And there's an amusing account of Verver's making a trip to Brighton to relieve Gutermann-Seuss the First of some Oriental tiles."[20]

It would be tedious to mention all the more recent books into which Stewart has introduced *The Golden Bowl.* In *Going It Alone,* a mystery of 1980, Stewart invoked *The Ambassadors* when Averell thinks, "It was all very Monet, very Renoir or Lambinet," on recalling his "favorite novel by Henry James."[21] In *My Aunt Christina and Other Stories,* of 1983, one tale contains the phrase "what dear old Henry would call a little *illustrative* action" (*MA,* 128). In the same tale someone lectures on James before a learned society of "elderly" and "eminent" gentlemen, whom James "would have described as 'belonging to the investigating classes'" (*MA,* 121). In another tale, *The Wings of the Dove* obtrudes. A son who walks off with his father's scholarly materials feels "just like the brilliant Kate Croy when she had worked it out that she and Milly Theale and Merton Densher were all going to live (or die) in the best-constructed of all possible worlds" (*MA,* 49).

In 1987, Stewart included among the "small dramatic pieces for the Third Programme" of the BBC that he was preparing one that he called "A Visit to Bly": "I was seduced by the thought that, driving to the scene of *The Turn of the Screw* in Edith Wharton's car, Henry James could be exhibited as suddenly alarmed by a roadside notice familiar to my childhood, which had read: "Motorists! Beware of the children."[22]

James Participates in the Amanda Cross Mysteries

The only true contender with Stewart for the title of master of the "donnish" mystery is Amanda Cross, who is to Carolyn Heilbrun (1926–) what Michael Innes is to Stewart. Nothing like Stewart's assumption that literary references would be understood by the cultivated consciousnesses of

20.   *Ibid.,* 171.
21.   J. I. M. Stewart, *Going It Alone* (New York, 1980), 189.
22.   Stewart, *Myself and Michael Innes,* 136–37.

educated English men and women was possible concerning Americans who had completed their university training, however. The only cultivated class in America, the academic, is but a small proportion of the population. Who else in the United States could understand all those arcane references to Shakespeare and James, Hardy and Woolf? The pedantry of the Amanda Cross mysteries is of the sort one professor displays to another. What compensates for the general awkwardness of foisting learned quotations on the American reading public is the way Cross disposes the donnish mystery so that it mirrors the liberation of women within the work force and among the university-trained members of society. Cross's twenty novels are a record of growing feminism, and the plots have gradually come to highlight issues of freedom on the campus, issues of gender, and the other issues that have pushed to the fore within the past few decades. Cross's latest books reflect her battles with Columbia University's administrative structure and her retirement from academic routines. Her mystery tales of the future may thus differ markedly from those she has already written.

Even in her early book *The James Joyce Murder,* of 1967, in which there is the quest for a lost version of "Dubliners," James's name and references to his work pop up. Two people have a relationship that "only James could have done . . . justice" (*JJ,* 62). The heroine and her husband are told to "stop behaving like characters in a Henry James novel" (*JJ,* 74). When a character says, "The abilities of the police to appreciate the complexities of a novel by Henry James . . . are considerably less than mine" (*JJ,* 78), Stewart's—and Innes'—Sir John Appleby, who has Jamesian references at his fingertips, comes to mind. Although Cross's Kate Fansler, an approximate equivalent of Appleby, cannot be subsumed under the persona of Henry James, she can be subsumed under that of Edith Wharton, which is the next best thing.

In *Poetic Justice,* of 1970, Cross evinced an original point of view concerning Lionel Trilling, a darling of the male contingent at Columbia University. Reincarnated in the book as Professor Clemance, Trilling becomes both the villain and the hero. Turning the gentle scholar who created the influential notion of the "liberal imagination" and affected at least two generations of literary critics into a man who murders by exchanging the pills of the victim captures the author's opinion, which may have been true, that Trilling did not favor women students. Trilling was accustomed to teaching the male undergraduates of Columbia College. Henry James is present as seasoning in the novel. Professor Clemance tells Kate, "I remember that you did a paper on *Portrait of a Lady*. I have never especially cared for women students. I think perhaps I was wrong in that. Perhaps there are Isabel Archers at University College." She assures him, "You taught me more—about literature, something I can only call morality, and about the honor of the profession of letters."[23] All the same, she does not shrink from manipulating him to implement the murder.

In *The Players Come Again*, of 1990, the very first page discloses that Kate has written a "study of Henry James and Thomas Hardy." The novel concerns events in the life of Emmanuel Foxx, a writer of modernist persuasion. The theme is chiefly that of the many spirited women and their interrelationships. Nellie has burned an important letter, much in the manner of "The Aspern Papers." A character deliberates, "Do I want to be the center of . . . an academic and literary debate? It will make whatever the governess in Henry James's *The Turn of the Screw* was fantasizing look like nothing."[24]

With Stewart, the appeal to James comes across as playful decoration rather than pedantry. Cross's touch is heavier: her appeal to him is more serious, underlining the moral dilemmas of the characters. There are many places where James's "morality" is sneaked into rather strained conversation, and one where Kate Fansler is accused of plagiarizing an essay on "James's use of the American heroine."[25]

It is in *Death in a Tenured Position*, of 1981, that references to James most abound. The first, however, involves an error. Cross cited a novel by James written "in the 1890's in which a young woman shows an admirer around Harvard, pointing at each of the buildings and remarking that there is no place for women in them" (*DT,* 14). She probably meant *The Bostonians*, of 1886. Kate visits the "grave of Henry James" (*DT,* 58), she feels "like a character in a James novel" (*DT,* 95), and she quotes Strether's words from *The Ambassadors:* "You're my youth" (*DT,* 97). A chapter epigraph comes from *The Portrait of a Lady* (*DT,* 125). Three years later, in *Sweet Death, Kind Death*, Kate's picture of James getting "'germs' all the time at dinner parties (ideas for stories and novels, I mean, not flu germs)" is coupled with the

---

23. Carolyn Heilbrun [Amanda Cross], *Poetic Justice* (New York, 1970), 59.

24. Carolyn Heilbrun [Amanda Cross], *The Players Come Again* (New York, 1990), 208.

25. Carolyn Heilbrun [Amanda Cross], *In the Last Analysis* (New York, 1964), 107.

comment that he "hated hearing more about the real life people than he wanted to know."[26] In *The Question of Max*, of 1976, Leon Edel's name crops up, as it does in Philip Roth's and Judith Krantz's fiction. For writers of the second half of the century to mention Edel is as good as mentioning Henry James, so closely is the Master welded to his biographer. Cross's immersion in James is not consummate like Stewart's, but so far it has always been apparent in some form.

Venice, Murder, and James, 1980s–1990s

Venice has become more and more an accustomed setting for mysteries and crime stories, and Venice now means James because of readers' growing familiarity with *The Wings of the Dove,* "The Pupil," "The Aspern Papers," and the travel essays he wrote on Venice. Out of a dozen detective stories by Julian Symons (1912–1974), the first and one of the last make specific references to James. In *Bland Beginning,* of 1949, the young champion cricketer, Anthony Shelton, finds himself bidding ten pounds for the collected works of Henry James in the Washington Square edition. He will present that to his father, since he has no interest in James himself but is after another volume at the book auction, on which he will spend a hundred guineas. The set he buys for his father is undoubtedly the New York Edition. Another character is the author of "three or four books of essays and gossip about books and authors. You know the kind of thing—how Henry James patted him on the head when he was five and said, 'I hope, my dear young friend, that you will always retain your present fine awareness of simple, and in fact incommunicable, emotion, which it is the endeavor of a lucky few, quite simply, to communicate.' "[27] In *A Criminal Comedy,* of 1985, Symons' hero is a Jamesian "poor gentleman" with a role very much like the nameless narrator's in *The Sacred Fount.* He ends up as badly as poor gentlemen do—worse, since he is murdered for his prying curiosity. In Venice, Jason Durling reminds himself constantly of James's writings, for it is how he frames his experience. Besides relating some situations that recall circumstances in James's fiction and travel writings, he is a collector of "one or two" letters by James (*CC,* 36) and his "preference" is "for a Jamesian indirectness of approach in emotional matters" (*CC,* 40).

---

26.   Carolyn Heilbrun [Amanda Cross], *Sweet Death, Kind Death* (New York, 1984), 79.
27.   Julian Symons, *Bland Beginning* (New York, 1949), 59.

Symons repeated what James wrote in *Italian Hours* after his visits to Venice: "One should arrive in Venice at the railway station, as Henry James says" (*CC*, 87). Conscious that conditions have changed since "Henry James had come to Venice by train for preference," Durling recalls as he watches the "magnificent but mouldering facades" that the "divine Henry" said that in Venice "the only sounds were human, that the sound of the gondolier is the sound of the city. . . . Then I looked at my companions and reflected that Henry James had also observed that nothing else in Venice is as disagreeable as the visitors" (*CC*, 103). Although "a century ago the divine Henry" had noticed that Venice was "a peep show and a bazaar with the barbarians in full possession," he did not know "how horrible it could now be" (*CC*, 119). When Durling looks out the window, however, he looks "almost at the Venice seen by Henry James" (*CC*, 138). The end of poor, sensitive Jason Durling is that, having discovered the lesbian relation between the two women, he must be killed, and is.

In 1992, in *A Very Venetian Murder*, Haughton Murphy, as a New York lawyer addicted to writing murder mysteries signed himself, had his hero cheerfully embark on his annual two-week visit to Venice. Murphy too boned up on James's Venetian stories and travel pieces and included in his amusing novel a reference to "The Aspern Papers"—a story so well known as James's work that the author of this mystery did not bother to mention who wrote it. Reuben Frost, the retired lawyer turned detective, visits the Marchesa Scamozzi in a converted warehouse on the Giudecca Canal. Upstairs he enters a room that is a "jumble of antiques of uncertain age and drab fabrics that bore no resemblance to the bright ones . . . produced for sale; *The Aspern Papers* came to mind."[28]

The most adept artist of the Venetian murder tale is Edward Sklepowich, a former professor of English. Now living in Venice, he has in rapid succession written two Jamesian mysteries set there. Sklepowich takes the epigraph of *Death in a Serene City*, of 1990, from one of James's essays on Venice: ". . . the refuge of endless strange secrets, broken fortunes and wounded hearts." The story is about Urbino Macintyre, a young American who has inherited a palazzo in Venice and is engaged in writing *Venetian Lives*. The problem is that his laundress has been murdered in front of the 1,100-year-old body of little Santa Teodora, itself stolen from a parish church. The Jamesian connection is by way of a writer, Clifford Voyd, a

28. Haughton Murphy, *A Very Venetian Murder* (New York, 1992), 159.

close friend of an American woman writer, Margaret Quinton, who has committed suicide after contracting the flu. This alludes to Constance Woolson's suicide, and Woolson's niece, who came down to claim her aunt's body, is evident in the young woman Adele Carstairs, the niece of the mystery's suicide. Clifford Voyd did not see that Margaret Quinton "was in love with him, that she felt encouraged, that she hoped" (*DC*, 38). In addition to embodying Woolson's relationship to James, Margaret Quinton, like Woolson, was deaf. Voyd has a young lover by the name of Christian Kobke who is, like James's friend Hendrik Andersen, Scandinavian and handsome.

Voyd is fond of saying, "To die in Venice is to be in good company," a remark from James's writings. Voyd and Krobke are staying at a hotel opposite the Salute, close to the site of Katherine De Kay Bronson's Ca' Alvisi. Voyd has a bad back because of an "old bicycle accident that flares up from time to time. It has made these indolent periods a regular part of my life" (*DC*, 171). He also adopts James's word *germ* for the source "that might become a story or—wonder of wonders!—even a novel" (*DC*, 172). Voyd is murdered when the villain of the story comes looking for information in the notebook pages of Margaret Quinton. As James removed his letters to Woolson before her niece arrived to take her effects, so Voyd burns his correspondence in a "big roaring blaze," for "it was part of an agreement he made with his correspondents. He wanted them to destroy all his letters and he would do the same with theirs. Clifford had a horror of the biographer. . . . He wanted to make things as difficult as possible" (*DC*, 209).

Even apart from the Jamesian sources of *Death in a Serene City*, Sklepowich has conjured the Jamesian atmosphere so well that there is no dissenting from the blurb on the book jacket by a fellow mystery writer: "If Henry James were alive today—and writing mysteries—*Death in a Serene City* is very much what they would look like."

Sklepowich's *Farewell to the Flesh*, of 1991, takes place during the Carnival in Venice. Urbino Macintyre is by now working on *Proust in Venice*. When Urbino and his friend Hazel Reeve pass the Ca' Rezzonico, where Browning died, he points out to her that "Browning stayed there. So did Sargent and James. In fact, James had one of his characters, an American heiress, die there after she found out that the man she loved had betrayed her" (*FF*, 287). Urbino is almost certainly wrong about James's heiress, since it is accepted that the Palazzo Leporelli in *The Wings of the Dove* is based on the Palazzo Barbaro, not the Rezzonico. Hazel says, "Women seldom die for such things except in books. . . . And when they do, they don't just 'turn' their face to the wall and expire the way she did: and neither do they will all their money to the man who deceived them" (*FF*, 288). Hazel has read the book. Urbino asks her, "But do you have any reason to believe that Val Gibbon betrayed you?" She laughs, "Betrayed! . . . You have to admit it sounds strange when you use it for someone not in a novel. The word's on your mind because of that Henry James novel, isn't it?" (*FF*, 290).

In Sklepowich's *Black Bridge*, of 1995, Woolson and her suicide are referred to directly: "She loved one of your most famous writers, Henry James. But he was afraid of physical love. You can see it in what he wrote about D'Annunzio" (*BB*, 43). Urbino picks up a "familiar volume of Henry James" (*BB*, 115), to which he returns. "It was the sad tale of the drift of a man too proud and self-absorbed to recognize and return love until it was too late" (*BB*, 116). That must be "The Beast in the Jungle," and the relevance is clear at the end. Barbara, the Contessa da Capo-Zendrini, presses Urbino about their feelings for each other: "I just wish sometimes that you would trust yourself more. . . . It isn't too late! It's never too late!" (*BB*, 222). In this novel, "The Aspern Papers" also makes an appearance. Urbino visits the palazzo in which the background is set "surrounding the private papers of a famous American poet" (*BB*, 159).

The most recent Venetian mysteries have steered away from James and the museum aspects of the city to go to the outlying districts—to the Mestre, the industrial part, to present-day political corruption, and to transvestite characters. For instance, Michael Dibdin's *Dead Lagoon*, of 1994, concentrates on the landscape of evil, including the stenches and betrayal pervasive there. But one accomplished author of several such Venetian mysteries has kept a foot in the Jamesian material. In *Death at La Fenice*, of 1992, the first of Donna Leon's crime novels set in Venice, the aristocratic Paola Brunetti, who teaches "English literature at the university" and always opts "for the most obvious choice" among the suspects her detective husband is investigating, explains that since she wrote "her dissertation on Henry James, she considered herself entitled to the release of finding the obvious in real life, since she'd never found it in his novels."[29] In *The Anonymous Venetian*, of 1995, Leon has her take on her vacation in Bolzano *The Collected Letters of Henry James*, "of formidable size," as well as "*The Sacred*

---

29. Donna Leon, *Death at La Fenice* (London, 1992), 92, 45.

Fount, having decided that this was the year she would finally have enough time to read it" (*AV,* 77). When Guido Brunetti asks his wife whether she has read the account of murder and corruption in the newspapers, she replies that she hasn't: "I've been reading the Master. *The Sacred Fount* is wonderful. *Nothing* happens, absolutely nothing" (*AV,* 163). She once took *The Golden Bowl* to Cortina, but finished it "in the first week," leaving her nothing to do except enjoy the outdoors. "She had loathed every minute of it" (*AV,* 165). But now she is "eager to finish" *The Sacred Fount,* "so that I can begin it all over again immediately" (*AV,* 165). Like any serious reader of James, she knows his work requires a second reading.

Although Leon, like James, is an American expatriate in Venice, her focus is on the city as seen by someone who lives and works there permanently. The James that Paola has read has nothing to do with Venice. But *The Sacred Fount* is a novel of detection where nothing is solved. Probably it was brought into the novel as a contrast to *The Anonymous Venetian,* where everything is solved. *The Golden Bowl* has no relation to Leon's mystery except that it is about the Italian aristocracy and thus connects to Paola Brunetti's aristocratic origins as a daughter of a Venetian count and a woman with civilized tastes in literature.

10

LINKS IN THE DAISY CHAIN

> Lo, how these fair immaculate women walk
> Behind their jocund maker . . .
> *Daisy* and *Barb* and *Chancellor* . . .
> With all their silken, all their airy kin.
> —Robert Louis Stevenson,
> "Henry James"

Instead of surveying one by one the authors who have brought James into their fiction, drama, poetry, and films in an original way, it is possible to proceed in the reverse direction, beginning with James's stories and exploring how they have attracted writers to redo them in their own way. The story most often refashioned is "Daisy Miller." From shortly after its heroine sprang from the brain of Henry James, she has continued to be alive in other pieces of literature.

Incarnations of Daisy

"Daisy Miller" was probably the most popular work of Henry James. The British loved the heroine, whose portrait horrified Americans who wanted Europeans to think well of them. It was delightful to see James pitch into Europeanized Americans in a splendid tale with a wallop. Today English speakers all over the world know Daisy. The name evokes the tale that has been published in many editions and dramatized in a brilliant film of the 1970s by Peter Bogdanovich in which Cybill Shepherd starred.

Although the story's first publication, in the *Cornhill Magazine*, was in 1878, William Dean Howells could, as late as just after World War I, write in the introduction to the Modern Library edition about the public hostility to it. In 1927, Martin W. Sampson in an introduction for an edition that the Book League of America brought out in 1929 wrote that it was ironic that James "should be best known by one of his least subtle achievements." But the American Service Edition for American troops overseas in World War II presented the story "as a concise classic, the embodiment of the spirit of her country, a girl who defies European convention."[1] And for those who no longer read, the repeated television broadcast of Bogdanovich's film since 1989 has exposed her to millions.

> The great popularity of her story was certainly due to her creator's having somehow conveyed the impression that her spirit went marching on.
> —Edmund Wilson, "The Ambiguity of Henry James"

The rewriting of "Daisy Miller" began two years after the story first appeared, and it continues in drastically postmodernized forms, as in Ruth Rendell's *Kissing the Gunner's Daughter,* of 1991. Why does Daisy's spirit go marching on, and how did the idea of Daisy come to James? In 1990, Daniel M. Fogel addressed Daisy with full scholarly panoply, in *Daisy Miller: A Dark Comedy of Manners.* He went into everything from the critical reception she received to a detailed reading of her story, and he commented on the 1909 revision and the tale's sources, which he traced to Victor Cherbuliez' *Paul Méré,* as well as to the novels of George Sand, Madame de Staël, and Ivan Turgenev. He saw the story as a "dark comedy of manners," not only because of its "pathos" but because of the "cultural determinism that finally makes it impossible for Daisy and Winterbourne to meet each other halfway."[2]

Daisy is not always understood as her maker wanted her to be—as a bit

---

1. Henry James, *Daisy Miller: An International Episode,* intro. Martin W. Sampson (New York, 1929), v; Henry James, *Daisy Miller and Other Stories,* armed forces edition (N.p., n.d.), back cover.

2. Daniel M. Fogel, *Daisy Miller: A Dark Comedy of Manners* (Boston, 1990), 97.

of "pure poetry" and a touching case of youthful misunderstanding of a loved one. But she is apparently James's most memorable character, outdistancing Isabel Archer, who also misunderstands the people around her. She has charm and seems to have bumped into James rather than been invented by him. She is the epitome of an American girl, as Isabel Archer is not unless we think of her as one who expects happiness at the hands of the world, meaning Europe, and is betrayed by it.

Frances Hodgson Burnett and Daisy

It may seem odd that Frances Hodgson Burnett (1849–1924), an author whose reputation depends on three famous classics for children—*Little Lord Fauntleroy*, of 1886, *A Little Princess*, of 1905, and probably her most famous, *The Secret Garden*, of 1911—should have had a reciprocal relation with James, who famously appealed only to adults. Not only were the two writers friends and neighbors at the turn of the century but they engaged in a certain amount of literary give-and-take. Burnett, born in Manchester, England, but transplanted to Tennessee as a result of her father's business reverses, wrote stories to help support her family, like Louisa May Alcott. Six years younger than James, she mentioned to her friend Richard Watson Gilder, the editor at Scribner's, how much she enjoyed reading her senior. Having just finished *The Europeans*, she bubbled, "All the time I am admiring Henry James and thinking how beautifully he goes all round a thing, and what excellent order he leaves it in—with no ends straggling—no gaps—no thin places. 'How clever you are,' I keep saying, 'and how neat.'"[3] Her novel *A Fair Barbarian*, of 1881, following on the heels of "Daisy Miller," has all the earmarks of a response to that famous tale, though Burnett, according to her son's biography of her, did not aspire "to 'answer' Mr. James with her 'Barbarian.'" Yet, he concedes, "She was considered, at least by some, as having done so with considerable success."[4] Plainly, she read "Daisy Miller" with great care.

The heroine of *A Fair Barbarian*, Octavia Bassett, comes to Slowbridge, a small and sleepy English village, with her father, a very rich owner of silver mines. Suddenly, in financial difficulties, he returns to the United States, leaving Octavia alone with Miss Belinda Bassett, his shy and retir-

---

3. Vivian Burnett, *The Romantick Lady* (New York, 1927), 91.
4. *Ibid.*, 106.

ing old-maid sister. Octavia, like Daisy, is dressy, showy, and laden with luxuries. She talks like Daisy: "American girls always have more things than English girls. . . . And I have more things than most American girls. Father had more money than most people" (*FB*, 22). Her exceptional prettiness attracts all the men, and her affinity with Daisy is underlined by one of her costumes, which besides being adorned with "blue ribbons" is "embroidered with field-daisies" (*FB*, 88). But chiefly what identifies her with Daisy is the problem her behavior creates. And the question arises, as with Daisy, whether to ascribe to her—in the terms of Lady Theobald, the social arbiter of the town—the "most outrageous impudence" or "innocence." Octavia has an "inscrutable and indifferent little air." A young man, Francis Barold, of proper social standing, is interested in her against his will, and in him it is possible to descry a re-creation of Winterbourne. Octavia becomes a good friend of her opposite, Lucia, the granddaughter of Lady Theobald, who is "*sure* [Octavia] is very candid and simple" (*FB*, 36)—and here, in contrast to "Daisy Miller," it is always quite obvious to the reader that the heroine is exactly that, although many of the people around her are not always sure.

When Octavia goes out on the terrace with Barold during an evening party, the sensation she causes reminds the reader of Daisy's nighttime visit to the Colosseum. Daisy becomes ill and dies; Octavia is warned that going out "in that thin dress" in the "night air" will make her sick, to say nothing of the scandal of disappearing from open view with a young man. Octavia, like Daisy, flouts social conventions, but she does not get sick. Lucia spends most of her time explaining that Octavia "is innocent of any intention to do wrong,—I am sure she is innocent" (*FB*, 167), and the reader believes her. Barold, like Winterbourne, does not wish to show any emotion: "he is so determined to hedge himself around, that one can't help suspecting that he is always guarding himself against one." Like Winterbourne, too, he spends time "analyzing his motives," and since she "made him uncomfortable often" and "her manners were not what he was accustomed to" (*FB*, 217), he is plagued by doubts. He realizes that it is hard to "marry a woman who will make mistakes" (*FB*, 219). But unlike Winterbourne, he does ask the woman about whom he is uneasy to marry him. Octavia's feelings for Barold are not those of Daisy for Winterbourne, in any case. All along she has been engaged to a young American mine owner, and they marry in an elaborate English wedding. In a fairy-tale mode, Burnett has created an

Octavia from Nevada who is a triumphant soul mate of Daisy from upstate New York.

The conjecture is that James read this novel when it appeared under the imprint of his Boston publisher, for "The Siege of London," which appeared two years after *A Fair Barbarian*, is his kind of treatment of a fair barbarian. He stressed the barbarian element in articulating his impressions of Couture's *The Romans of the Decadence* and the belief that the upper classes of England were much like the debased Romans.[5] In a letter to Charles Eliot Norton in 1886, he discussed a divorce case that he expected to "besmirch exceedingly the already very damaged prestige of the English upper class. The condition of that body seems to me to be in many ways . . . like the heavy, congested and depraved Roman world upon which the barbarians came down" (LU, I, 124).

An English Daisy

The offended American reaction to "Daisy Miller" inspired a piece of fiction "dedicated to American women" that aimed at showing Daisy's creator and the English-speaking world that not all girls misbehaving in Europe were American. In 1882, Virginia Wales Johnson (1849–1916), a young American novelist living in Europe, published the book *An English "Daisy Miller,"* a clever and readable imitation of James's tale with regard to both plot and main characters, except that the characters had become British. The locale had been changed from Vevey and Rome to Genoa, Bellagio, Venice, and the Swiss Alps. Johnson changed as well the names and positions in life of the characters. But more important, there was a shift away from James's emphasis on innocence and basic ignorance as the explanation of failure. Johnson focused on the lack of innocence and the corrupt behavior of the English newly rich. Mrs. Miller has become the snobbish, affected Lady Hooper. Ethel Hooper, her daughter—the Daisy in the story—is a self-willed, immature tomboy who joins her brother Charley in his practical jokes with a heartlessness unknown to Daisy herself (Figure 35).

The Winterbourne of the tale, Lieutenant Bowyer, awaits his rich aunt, Mrs. Everton, in Genoa. He sees Ethel "in a Boston rocking chair" pro-

---

5. Adeline R. Tintner, *Henry James and the Lust of the Eyes* (Baton Rouge, 1993), 7–22.

35. James McNeill Whistler's
Arrangement in Black and White: The Young American
Courtesy of the Freer Gallery of Art,
Smithsonian Institution, Washington, D.C.

voking shamelessly the young men who observe her through the hotel's window. Like Randolph, who hates Rome "worse and worse every day," Charley "abhors Genoa." He is a sadistic brat who prefers the "tunnel between Genoa and Alexandria, where the ladies shriek, and which will cave in some day" (*ED*, 15). As for Ethel, her unsubtle sense of fun prompts her to laugh boisterously when the rocking chair in which Lieutenant Bowyer is sitting collapses. Mrs. Everton is an accurate Mrs. Costello, only a worse snob. Ethel's behavior becomes even more shocking in Bellagio, where she enters the men's smoking room on a dare from Charley. Johnson clearly meant Ethel's rudeness to be of a different order from Daisy's when she had her unpardonably challenge the Englishman's inalienable right to his private masculine play areas. In Venice, Ethel's folly continues. Attending a performance of *Faust* unchaperoned, she and Charley escape from their servants and, like truant children, resolve to walk home, defying all the norms of seemliness.

The Chamois Hotel, in the Swiss Alps, is the scene of Ethel's final and fatal act of uncontrolled behavior. The resort, "chic because . . . inaccessible" (*ED*, 50), offers the dangers of mountain climbing to a young woman who up to now has "been lost in fog," "upset at a ball at Chillon," and "thrown from a mule" (*ED*, 51). Her destination is the Black Peak, a goal difficult of access, but she dispenses with Alpine guides. At this point, Johnson starts to highlight the good in her naughty heroine, for she is about to die. Mrs. Everton admits that Ethel has a "good heart," for she has "clothed the family" of a man lost in an avalanche. James's Giovanelli appears here as a Russian nobleman, Baron Savonieff, whose name means "soap" and whose presence is "inseparably suggestive of the blended perfumes of Atkinson's White Rose, Lubin's Ylang-Ylang, and Oriental amber" (*ED*, 52) — puns like those decorating James's tale. For Ethel's accidental fall from the mountain peak, Johnson borrows from Roderick's death in *Roderick Hudson*, though not from its ambiguity. Ethel's accident does, however, partake of the willful behavior of the original Daisy, who flouts custom and caution in daring the malarial air of the Colosseum at night. Suddenly, the tragic accident of the reckless Ethel is seen as the result of the malign doings of the courier and Balder, Mrs. Everton's maid, who have, because of their "budding attachment," arranged the itineraries of the Hooper and Everton households and tempted the rash Ethel into reckless mountain climbing. Winterbourne at the end of James's tale becomes "interested in a very clever foreign lady," and the Baron likewise soon "attaches himself to an Italian marchesa . . . ten years his senior." Johnson makes a "faded cluster of cyclamen" (*ED*, 66), not the daisy, the floral emblem of the tale. Bowyer puts the flower in his pocket, and when he is appointed to a ship, he finds a "cluster" that crumbles "to dust in his hand" (*ED*, 67).

Johnson's novella came out a year before James made "Daisy Miller" into a play with a happy ending suited to popular audiences. William Dean Howells wrote that "the American woman would [have] none of ['Daisy.'] She fancied in the poor girl a libel of her nationality, almost a libel of her sex, and failed to seize . . . her flowerlike purity." That, he believed, was because "the American woman . . . was too jealous of her own perfection to allow that innocence might be reckless."[6]

Johnson was a precocious child writer of children's stories before she advanced to adult novels. Arriving in Europe in 1875 with her mother and sister, she was, at the age of twenty-six, a kind of Daisy herself. Like the American women Howells described, she felt James's tale as an attack upon herself. But unlike Daisy, she was a proper Bostonian, descended from the famous Puritan diarist Samuel Sewall; her disaccord had to be expressed in a literary form. As far as I know, James nowhere mentioned this rewriting of his tale, but among Johnson's novels developing the international theme that James had made his own, there is one, *Tulip Place*, of 1886, that not only owes much to *Washington Square* but, oddly, anticipates *The Golden Bowl*.

Julius Chambers' *On a Margin*

Julius Chambers (1850–1920) was an early muckraker whose first book, *A Mad World*, contributed to the revision of state lunacy laws. His *On a Margin*, a now-forgotten novel published anonymously in 1884 and then under his own name in 1885, sought to expose the hidden desires and ambitions of the men who ruled Wall Street and Washington in a "rush of modern society" (*OM*, back jacket). The impact of "Daisy Miller" at the time of its writing was so strong that Chambers introduced Daisy Miller as someone his heroine meets in her travels. Cotton Mather, the main character, takes as his ward a young woman with a mind of her own who goes by the nickname Mootla, which is based on her childhood pronunciation of Martha. Not too differently from James's Annie P. Miller, nicknamed Daisy, she is "more inclined to argue than to accept the opinions of others. Humility, in her mind, meant blind subservience" (*OM*, 93).

Mootla baffles the Surgeon General: "She is absolutely controlled by impulse—a slave to the unexpected . . . erratic and odd in her habits" (*OM*, 148–49). But the doctor pronounces her to have a "case of hereditary hysteria" (*OM*, 152) that will be cured by marriage.

Cotton and Mootla go to Europe, eventually to Nice, where "Miss Daisy Miller, an alleged American girl, was met several times during the

6. William Dean Howells, *Heroines of Fiction* (2 vols; New York, 1903), II, 176.

season; but Mootla resolutely kept the presumptuous young person out of her set. The Boston girl could not tolerate the greasy Italians and impoverished Englishmen who were constantly seen in the lady's company. Her courier . . . Mootla denounced without hesitation as a blackmailer and a rascal. Mootla was slightly the elder of the two women, and was infinitely the superior of Miss Miller in intelligence, education and tact" (*OM*, 158). Why did Chambers bring in Daisy Miller from James's story? The answer may be that he conceived Mootla as a superior kind of Daisy Miller, and introducing the lesser model into the novel as a character let him exhibit the particulars of her superiority.

In "Pandora," of the same year as *On a Margin*, James himself insinuated Daisy into a new story. But he presented her only as someone the count had read about, not as someone to be met and snubbed.

A Fin-de-Siècle Daisy:
Ella D'Arcy's "The Pleasure-Pilgrim"

None of Daisy's reincarnations has been stranger than her appearance as a decadent heroine bedizened with red hair and slanty, oriental eyes, trademarks of the fin-de-siècle femme fatale (Figure 36). Along with a changed appearance, she acquired heightened sophistication in the short story Ella D'Arcy (1856/57–1937) published under the title "The Pleasure-Pilgrim" in the *Yellow Book* of April, 1895. D'Arcy is today remembered primarily as the subeditor for Henry Harland, the founder of the *Yellow Book*, but she enjoyed considerable notice at the turn of the century as a short-story writer. Harland accepted ten of her stories for his journal's thirteen issues, and they were collected in two volumes, *Monochromes*, in 1895, and *Modern Instances*, in 1898. Recently scholars have taken an interest in these books, which were reprinted in 1977 and 1984, and Benjamin Franklin Fisher IV has prepared and published a detailed bibliography of her work, as well as a secondary bibliography (BF, 191).

Clearly, D'Arcy's imagination was piqued by French writers like Marcel Prévost, whose *Les Demi-Vierges* caused a sensation when it appeared just one year before "The Pleasure-Pilgrim." James's attention too had been captured by Prévost's novel, and as I have argued elsewhere, he was to incorporate the basic problem of *Les Demi-Vierges* into *The Awkward Age*.[7]

7. Adeline R. Tintner, *The Cosmopolitan World of Henry James: An Intertextual Study* (Baton Rouge, 1991), 149–54.

36. Daisy Miller as pictured in the frontispiece
drawn by Harry McVickar for Harper's 1892 edition
of James's *Daisy Miller and An International Episode*

Prévost's book had become an international event, because its declared purpose was to sound a warning about a whole class of young French women whose mothers' lack of supervision and desire to allow their daughters some knowledge of life before marriage had permitted to ruin their chances for matrimony through "heavy petting" while preserving technical virginity.

The manner in which D'Arcy's Daisy, in the guise of a young American girl, Lulie Thayer, sexually teases a young Briton, Mr. Campbell, would have struck the readers of "Daisy Miller" as intolerable. Lulie fondles, kisses, touches, and sidles up to him, but because he has been warned that she is a confirmed flirt, he resists her even though her "younger sister" — who while not her real sister plays a part like Daisy's brother Randolph — panders to her friend's design. They all meet in a German schloss, the aristocratic owners of which have converted it into a lodging house because of their reduced circumstances. In the spirit of the fin de siècle, Lulie behaves wildly and dangerously. Campbell, unable to elude her, rejects her as brutally as a gentleman can. In spite of the rebuff, she possesses "herself of his hand, and holding it between her own, [begins] to caress it in child-like fashion, pulling the fingers apart and closing them again," but he remains "unconscious of her proceedings." She tells him, "I've always known a lot of young fellows . . . and no one ever objected to my going with them, and so I went. And I liked it . . . just kissing and making believe, and nonsense." She insists that she really loves Campbell, and to prove it she covers his hand "with kisses" (*YB,* 64). His response is to tell her to "drop that damned rot. . . . It sickens me." If she indeed loved him, he continues, her history of being "handled, fondled and God knows what besides, by this man and the other" should fill her with "such horror for yourself . . . you would up take that pistol there, and blow your brains out!" (*YB,* 65). There in the game room she does exactly that. All Campbell can do is cry, "Child, child, what have you done?" (*YB,* 66). He remains firm in his disbelief that Lulie really loved him. Nanny Dodge, Lulie's little friend, thinks she did, and because of his "cold, complacent British unresponsiveness" did not "want to live any longer." His friend Baron Mayne, on the other hand, considers the death a misadventure, convinced that Lulie "pulled the trigger from mere mischief" or that she "now demanded a sensational finale in the centre of the stage. . . . She was the most consummate little actress I ever saw." The reader has to make up his own mind. As "Daisy Miller" ends with an ambiguous reflection on what Winterbourne is doing in Geneva after Daisy's death—leaving it open whether he has learned a lesson about his character or is going on unaffected—so "The Pleasure-Pilgrim" ends with uncertainty about Lulie's final state of mind. James's delicate tale of an innocent young American who refuses to learn how to behave in a foreign society has been extended to a time in which manners have changed and has been written for the taste of that time. Daisy is now a "demi-vierge" in the French sense. She no longer flirts in the decorous way of Daisy.

James and D'Arcy met as authors in print in the first issue of the *Yellow Book* in April, 1894—he with "The Death of the Lion," she with the story "Irremediable." They clearly knew each other's work. Her title "The Pleasure-Pilgrim" harks back to James's title "A Passionate Pilgrim," and it is possible that he remembered her story "White Magic" from the *Yellow Book* of October, 1894, when he named *The Two Magics* in 1898.

D'Arcy set down her reminiscences during the 1920s but never published them. Her attitude to James was not sapless: "Gosse and Henry James, gods stepped down from a higher and older sphere, were sometimes seen at Harlands, although I think he had far more love for them than they

for him. He tried hard to form his style on James', and . . . most fortunately
. . . failed" (BF, 195).

Some of D'Arcy's contemporaries realized that she had translated a
number of Prévost's characters into her story. Richard Le Gallienne, in the
literary review *Realm* of April 26, 1895, remarked that "The Pleasure-
Pilgrim" was an "exceedingly clever story of a certain type of American
girl, recently notorious in Paris as *la demi-vierge.*" The association of "The
Pleasure-Pilgrim" with "Daisy Miller" was recognized by the reviewer of
Monochromes for the *New York Times* on June 23, 1895: "The American girl
in 'The Pleasure Pilgrim' will be called a gross caricature by people who
were annoyed by 'Daisy Miller,' but she is confessedly a unique creature—
in her tragic end and the circumstances that led to it—and probably some
of her traits, as Miss D'Arcy delineates them, are true impressions made by
certain types of American character on the European mind" (BF, 195). Lulie may have been suggested by Daisy Miller, but in answering to the fin de
siècle's idea of the femme fatale, she is a "gross caricature" of the "little figure" that was "pure poetry."

Daisy Miller on Henry James:
Robert Bridges' *Overheard in Arcady*

Another version of Daisy that appeared during James's lifetime is found in
Robert Bridges' *Overheard in Arcady*, a collection of a dozen humorous articles published in *Life* in 1894 over the signature Droch. In these Bridges
(1844–1930) presented the "households" of certain eminent writers in the
form of playlets. James's household consists of the main characters from
"The Lesson of the Master"—Henry St. George, Paul Overt, and Miss
Fancourt—and the narrator describes himself as a painter. Joining them in
their discussion of how James understood and presented their problems is
Daisy Miller, a "young American from Schenectady, N.Y." (*OV*, 15). Daisy
maintains that "if he wrote his native language we'd read him more over the
pond." Responding to St. George's perplexity over "why you Americans do
not more appreciate him," she suggests that he's "lived with you so long that
we're not onto his curves. Do you catch on? His trolley's off the American
wire" (Figure 37). She ventures that if he came to America again, he might
"learn something besides Bostonese!" (*OV*, 23). Almost twenty years after
Daisy was invented, she is in Bridges' imagination very much the slang-
loving contemporary girl, even though in James's story she never showed

37. An 1890s image of Daisy Miller,
from Robert Bridges' *Overheard in Arcady* (1894)

a proclivity toward liberties with her mother tongue; her idiosyncrasies were of behavior rather than diction. In the final article, "A Little Dinner in Arcady," Miss Daisy Miller has Mr. F. Marion Crawford, the novelist, as her escort. Although the hostess, Miss Fanny de Siècle, has the place of honor, it is Daisy who speaks her mind on how to treat young men: "We have to train all the young nobs down with sarcasm before they are endurable" (*OV,* 129).

Daisy gained mention as well in the penultimate article, in which two young recently wedded Americans are traveling through Scotland. Adrian, the young bridegroom, comments on the fashion for visiting birthplaces: "Imagine our descendants making pilgrimages to the house where our *Daisy Millers* were (according to tradition) supposed to have lived and spoken bad English" (*OV,* 123). Adrian, it seems, is less acquainted with Daisy's patterns of speech in James's story than with Bridges' aspersions against them. When the characters discuss what the American girl of the next century will be, they agree that she will display "sympathy, the result of a true insight into our 'moral predicament,' as Mr. James delights to call it. She will be a patriot and an optimist always" (*OV,* 132). Daisy in her short career always displayed exactly those qualities. But Daisy's innocence, which is her chief characteristic and the quality James wrote he meant to be her chief characteristic, is completely missed in D'Arcy's and Bridges' versions.

Edna Kenton's Two Daisies

Edna Kenton (1876–1954), a journalist, made her name in Jamesian studies by proposing in 1924 to the "ruminant reader" that the crux of the plot in "The Turn of the Screw" is the governess' hallucinations.[8] A "lifelong reader of Henry James" who heard James's lecture "The Lesson of Balzac" in 1905 in Chicago (*M,* 280), she in 1906 produced a tale, "Love Laughs at Lions," that has recently been unearthed by Robin P. Hoople.[9] In it there is a "Master of Subtleties," an expatriate author on a limited lecture tour of his native America. The copies of James's *Hawthorne* and *The Outcry* that Kenton once owned reveal that she was herself a "ruminant reader" who underlined extensively passages on every page and brought quotations from James's letters to bear on her markings.[10]

In Kenton's tale, Ellen Grattan, a serious novelist, is married to Jasper Holbrooke, who has just volunteered to her that he is the secret author of some trashy best sellers. Her books, which do not sell well, have been praised by the Master of Subtleties, a great writer who refuses "to dwell in unillusioned and disillusioning America."[11] Ellen attends one of the lectures on the Master's tour, and he asks to meet her. But when someone in the group surrounding him denigrates her husband's fiction and he demolishes it, she is hurt and refuses to go ahead with the meeting. Her husband, however, realizes that she is the novelist in the family. Surely, James is behind the Master of Subtleties. Kenton, on the basis of attending the lecture in Chicago, could describe him as "massive and clear-eyed" to Edel (*M,* 280), but she gives no rounded picture of him in her story. Only his title of

8.   Edna Kenton, "Henry James to the Ruminant Reader: *The Turn of the Screw,*" *The Arts,* VI (1924), 245–55.

9.   Robin P. Hoople, "Literary Lions and Laughing Love: Edna Kenton and Henry James, 1906," *Henry James Review,* XVII (1996), 77–84.

10.   Leon Edel purchased Edna Kenton's copies of *Hawthorne* and *The Outcry* after her death, and later I acquired them. In a shoebox, she accumulated index cards with the names of all the country houses in James's fiction.

11.   Edna Kenton, "Love Laughs at Lions," *Century Magazine,* n.s., LIV (1906), 334.

Master of Subtleties, his expatriation, and his limited visit to his native land disclose his identity.

There are indications that Kenton attempted to redo "Daisy Miller" on her own terms in her two novels. In the first, *What Manner of Man*, of 1903, she paired an ignorant, innocent girl, Clodah Rohan—the daughter of a leader of a primitive colony living on an island off the coast of Scotland—with a sophisticated painter, Kirk Thayer, who is afflicted with the "madness of art" (*MM*, 170). The painter alludes to James on the third page of the novel, when he says of his portrait of a lady friend, "Ah, isn't she a raving darling, my Portrait of a Lady!" Clodah is referred to as a "daisy" and as a "mountain daisy" (*MM*, 173), and she says of a daisy, "Dinna crush it . . . dinna no it got un'er foot" (*MM*, 269). The painter, her husband, whose "genius is just off insanity" (*MM*, 181), crushes it and, along with it, "her innocence" (*MM*, 186). Like Daisy Miller, she dies from the coldness of her lover.

In Kenton's next and only other novel, *Clem*, of 1907, her heroine comes closer to the kind of girl Daisy Miller is. Clem, the beautiful daughter of an extremely rich American speculator, is as well dressed as Daisy Miller, as candid, and as snubbed by good society. But this "Daisy" is not the victim that Clodah and Daisy Miller were. Hurt by the kind of snobbish social rejection that dogged Daisy Miller, she transcends it. In the circle of American socialites where her engagement to Reggie Wines, a young scion of wealth, has thrown her, the question is, as with Daisy Miller, whether or not she is "a wretched flirt" or a respectable girl.[12] Mrs. Wines invites her to a house party, where the men flock around her and the women shun her because of her candor and her supposedly vulgar "coon" songs. Deeply hurt by what she sees in Reggie's mother's eyes, she breaks off her engagement to Reggie and leaves the party. When Reggie accidentally inflicts a serious wound on himself—everyone thinking he has attempted suicide because he has been jilted—Clem is intercepted. She nurses him back to health, garnering the love of Mrs. Wines, who realizes the girl's goodness. She achieves happiness, however, by marrying not Reggie but another man at the party who is more appropriate for her in age and temperament.

Kenton's Clem follows James's Daisy very closely in physical, social, and personality traits. But her personality and her courage have a force that make her succeed as Daisy never could.

12. Edna Kenton, *Clem* (New York, 1907), 169.

"Daisy Miller" and F. Scott Fitzgerald's *The Great Gatsby*

If F. Scott Fitzgerald's naming his heroine in *The Great Gatsby* Daisy prompts the expectation that Daisy Miller will be apparent in her, the expectation dissipates on even casual reading, since the princess of Fitzgerald's novel is closer to the opposite of Miss Annie P. Miller, of Schenectady: she is dependent, vacillating, cowardly, and disloyal—by no means an American archetype. Yet the name Daisy is not completely a red herring, for in Jay Gatsby, the main character, a male Daisy Miller is recognizable. And there is evidence that Fitzgerald himself saw the romantic hero of his novel as a Daisy.[13]

Fitzgerald's "Absolution," a short story that appeared in the June, 1924, issue of H. L. Mencken's *American Mercury*, has a certain historical relationship to *The Great Gatsby.* Written in June, 1923, as part of an early draft, now lost, of the novel, it was not incorporated into the final manuscript. Fitzgerald wrote to his editor, Maxwell Perkins, in June, 1924, "As you know ['Absolution'] was to have been the prologue of a novel but it interfered with the neatness of the plan" (*LF,* 164). Rudolph Miller, the boy of the story, is best regarded as a preliminary view of the character who developed into James Gatz, not as the young Gatsby himself.

In the Cambridge edition of *The Great Gatsby,* Matthew J. Bruccoli has a note on "Absolution" (Appendix 1). Fitzgerald's letter to Perkins relates that "Absolution" was written before he found a "new angle"—and Bruccoli adds that by the phrase Fitzgerald "usually meant a new plot line" (*GG,* 205). One part of "Absolution" would have been a very good introduction to the character of Gatsby, but in this otherwise Jamesian novel, Fitzgerald wanted to keep everything as it was and not go back the way James was in the habit of doing. In "Absolution," when the young boy Rudolph Miller, whose name recalls Randolph Miller, Daisy Miller's younger brother, goes to a Catholic priest for confession, he discovers that the priest is the one who needs help. Drawn to the outside world, the priest appears to be obsessed by an "amusement park." He says,

---

13.   T. Jeff Evans, "F. Scott Fitzgerald and Henry James: The Raw Material of American Innocence," *Notes on Modern American Literature,* IV (1980), 206ff. The word *raw* at the end of "Daisy Miller" ("raw protuberance among the April daisies") is repeated in Fitzgerald's "how raw the sunlight was upon the scarcely created grass." This is one connection Evans sees between *The Great Gatsby* and "Daisy Miller."

It's a thing like a fair, only much more glittering. Go to one at night and stand
a little way off from it in a dark place. . . . You'll see a big wheel made of lights
turning in the air, and a long slide shooting boats down into the water. A
band playing somewhere, and a smell of peanuts—and everything will twinkle. But it won't remind you of anything, you see. It will all just hang out
there in the night like a colored balloon—like a big yellow lantern on a
pole. . . . But don't get up close . . . because if you do you'll only feel the heat
and the sweat and the life." (*SSF,* 271)

Had this been retained as the introduction, it would be evident how Daisy
Miller under the name of Rudolph Miller was reincarnated in Jay Gatsby,
a man who is in love with the glamour of life, who gives spectacular parties
so that life will be like a fair, and who is deeply innocent. If Daisy Miller is
a Byron in petticoats, Jay Gatsby is a Daisy Miller in pants.

Earlier, Fitzgerald showed an interest in imitating James in the tale
"The Lees of Happiness," but Perkins urged him to cut the first few paragraphs, because they sounded "Jamesian." Perkins wrote, "I don't think
Henry James had anything in the world to do with you at all, and so it is
not appropriate" (*CF,* 102). In the table of contents that Fitzgerald annotated for *Tales of the Jazz Age,* of 1922, he mentioned that the story "appeared in the 'Chicago Tribune,' and later obtained, I believe, the quadru-
ple gold laurel leaf or some such encomium from one of the anthologists
who at present swarm among us. The gentleman I refer to runs as a rule to
stark melodramas . . . carefully disguised by early paragraphs in Jamesian
manner which hint dark and subtle complexities to follow."[14] In 1939, Fitzgerald encouraged his daughter to read "Daisy Miller," and in another letter of the same year, to Morton Kroll, he mentioned "Daisy Miller" as one
of "the great English classics" (*LF,* 59, 593).

Paul Rosenfeld wrote to Fitzgerald that *The Great Gatsby* is "unfolded
with all the suavity of the late H. James" (*CF,* 171), and his letters pointed
out particular Jamesian elements. Jordan Baker, in the novel, has a name
that connects with Daisy Miller's by way of an utterance of Mrs. Costello's
in James's tale: "Miss Baker's, Miss Chandler's—what's her name?—Miss
Miller's intrigue with that little barber's block" (IV, 194). Interestingly,
Edmund Wilson, Fitzgerald's close friend and the reader of his manuscript,

---

14. F. Scott Fitzgerald, *Tales of the Jazz Age* (New York, 1922), x.

shared his last name with the most pathetic and tasteless character in the book, George Wilson, the garage owner, a failure who is cuckolded by a vulgar wife.

Everyone in the novel except Nick Carraway, the narrator, and Gatsby is corrupt. Jordan Baker is a liar: "She was incurably dishonest" (*GG*, 47). Perhaps Nick can be likened to Winterbourne, for he says, "But I am slow thinking and full of interior rules that act as brakes on my desires" (*GG*, 48). Gatsby seems always to be telling lies about himself, but he tells the truth so far as his short term at Oxford and his decoration from Montenegro go. As for his bootlegging, there was no other way for him to acquire the money he needed to win Daisy, who by the time he arrives with his fortune has already married. He remains true to his ideal of romantic love, whereas nobody else in the story, apart from the narrator, is true to anything.

On the dust jacket for the first edition of *The Great Gatsby* are a disembodied face, inspired by a line in *The Great Gatsby*, and a picture of a fair or amusement park that is a symbolic expression of the link with "Absolution." The fair was an image dear to Fitzgerald, and he later worked on a novel, which he never completed, called *The World's Fair*. The guests at Jay's party conduct "themselves according to the rules of behavior associated with amusement parks" (*GG*, 24), but the reference is fleeting, in contrast to "Absolution," where it is the main image.

Carraway says that Gatsby "had thrown himself into [his illusion] with a creative passion, adding to it all the time, decking it out with every bright feather that drifted his way" (*GG*, 75). Without Fitzgerald's poetic effusion, James implied the same kind of passion in Daisy. Her shy, concealing ways demonstrate a passion for Winterbourne. What is more, Gatsby changed his name from James Gatz to Jay Gatsby, as Daisy unofficially changed hers from Annie P. Miller. The young Gatz "invented just the sort of Jay Gatsby that a seventeen year old boy would be likely to invent, and to this conception he was faithful to the end" (*GG*, 77). Daisy Buchanan is the means and the source for the destruction of Fitzgerald's male Daisy. It is she who suggests to the two couples that they go to New York because of the heat. And it is the peculiar arrangement of who takes which car and how they get back from New York that is responsible for the accident in which Myrtle Wilson is killed on Long Island. When Daisy on the way home becomes a hit-and-run driver, Tom tells the police that the owner of the car is Jay, and Wilson thinks that Jay has killed his wife. Daisy retreats to Tom, who has exposed Jay to Wilson's revenge. Like Daisy Miller, Gatsby will be sacrificed; both are innocent victims, in their respective dreams, to the exigencies of reality. Nick at least has the honor of saying to Jay before he is killed, "They're a rotten crowd. . . . You're worth the whole damn bunch put together." Jay dies "concealing his incorruptible dream" (*GG*, 120), as Daisy Miller dies concealing her love for and loyalty to Winterbourne. T. S. Eliot, on reading *The Great Gatsby*, wrote to Fitzgerald, as Fitzgerald told Perkins in a letter, that he "thought it was the first step forward American fiction had taken since Henry James" (*LF*, 199). But that step would not have been what it was without James.

Vevey and the Trois Couronnes in Ernest Hemingway's "A Canary for One"

In "A Canary for One," of 1927, among the very tightly compressed stories in Ernest Hemingway's *Men Without Women*, Vevey and the Trois Couronnes hotel come up in a seemingly casual conversation in a European train compartment between a young married couple from the United States and an American woman who once lived in Switzerland. The reason the older American woman, who is deaf, left the Continent is that her daughter fell in love with a "man in Vevey," where they made their home. The man was Swiss, not American like Daisy's beloved Winterbourne, and the mother, who envies the young American wife her American husband, prevented the marriage. Although the girl did not die, she became sick, and her mother "took her away, of course." The woman is not a permissive parent like Mrs. Miller but in total control of her child's life. "I couldn't have her marrying a foreigner," she says to the couple, for though the Swiss "was from a very good family," she was once told that "no foreigner can make an American girl a good husband" (*MWW*, 105).

Vevey and the Trois Couronnes make their way into the conversation when the young wife in the compartment says, "I know Vevey. . . . We were there on our honeymoon." To the older woman's question "Where did you stop there?" she answers, "We stayed at the Trois Couronnes."

"It's such a fine old hotel," the "American lady" comments, and the younger woman agrees, "Yes, we had a very fine room and in the fall the country was lovely" (*MWW*, 107).

The "American lady" resembles Mrs. Miller in her manners, her speech, and her preference for traveling on a Cook's Tour; that is, she resembles her in her culture and in her class-distinguishing attributes, though she is not as rich as Mrs. Miller. The last line of the story renders ironic the lady's judgments about the dependability of American husbands, for the American couple is "returning to Paris to set up separate residences" (*MWW,* 108).

Vevey and the Hotel des Trois Couronnes are, of course, the Swiss resort town and the famous hotel where Daisy Miller and Winterbourne meet, but Winterbourne does not return Daisy's love as the Swiss admirer does in this tale. Hemingway's plot at first seems to have little to do with James's story, but the contrasts are significant. The American lady, who unlike Mrs. Miller takes a firm hand with "her little girl," buys a canary to take to her daughter as a consolation during her standardized tour's hourlong stopover in Palermo. The woman's care for the happiness of the bird, which is traveling in a cage in the compartment, is set off against her insensitivity to her daughter's unhappiness.

The "fine old" Trois Couronnes has been the scene of the honeymoon of this couple about to separate, just as it is the scene of Daisy's unrequited love. Given Hemingway's symbolic irony and his drastic compression in these early tales, it cannot be doubted that the invoking of Daisy's hotel has a point in the story. In this account of an American mother who is like Mrs. Miller in background but wholly unlike her in temperament, it is used to underline the irony of her stupid generalization about international marriages. Bringing severe unhappiness to her daughter because of some unreasoned cliché about foreign husbands, she has completely mistaken the nature of the marriage of her traveling companions. Mrs. Miller's inattention to her daughter's activities, which ended in Daisy's tragic midnight excursion to the Colosseum, may have given Hemingway the idea of creating another American mother, hapless in a diametrically opposite way yet equally capable of causing her daughter injury.

"A Canary for One" has interested scholars mainly because it builds around the young Hemingways' decision to separate. Their honeymoon had been spent in Switzerland, but in a town called Chamby, near Montreux, in 1922. It took place a few weeks after their marriage.[15] The reference to Vevey and the Trois Couronnes doubtless stems from "Daisy

15.   Carlos Baker, *Ernest Hemingway: A Life Story* (1968; rpr. New York, 1980), 121.

Miller," since it does not accord with the Hemingways' autobiographical details.

Since this is a tale of "men without women," it is told by a man, the young husband, but he contributes only seven spoken words within the story: "Perhaps that was because I wore braces." He then gives the tale over to the "American lady" and his wife—to the women in the tale. Since the American lady is deaf, she does not even hear those seven words: "The American lady did not hear. She was really quite deaf; she read lips, and I had not looked toward her. I had looked out of the window. She went on talking to my wife" (*MWW,* 105). Yet the young man is important to the tale, because by deciding to leave his wife he shows that he is the exception to the rule the American lady thinks applies to American husbands.

The story may not seem to fit the category of "men without women," but when the narrator arrives in Paris, he will be such a man; he will have a separate residence. What the three in the compartment view through the train windows duplicates what the Hemingways saw on their train trip in August, 1926, from Antibes to Paris. They passed a burning farm and three wrecked baggage cars. Only a few weeks after their trip, while Pauline— who was to become Hemingway's second wife—returned to the United States for a hundred-day separation from him, he wrote "A Canary for One." That was just after reading the proofs of *The Sun Also Rises* and sending them back to Perkins. He had decided to assign to Hadley all royalties from that, his most Jamesian novel and a virtual reinvention of *The Ambassadors.* James was still on Hemingway's mind as he sat in Gerald Murphy's studio in the rue Froidevaux fashioning his story.

It is part of Hemingway's narrative technique in his stripped early prose to ensure that no word is without indexical function. Having recognized Vevey and the Trois Couronnes as pointers to "Daisy Miller," we are encouraged to try to work out the relationship between "A Canary for One" and James's most popular tale. I have not yet solved the puzzle, but others too should try their hand at it.

The Two Daisies in Edmund Wilson's *I Thought of Daisy*

Edmund Wilson (1895–1972), Fitzgerald's friend and a critic of *The Great Gatsby,* published four years after that novel's appearance a novel of his own involving material and attitudes from it. He began writing *I Thought of*

Daisy in 1926 or 1927, a year or two after *The Great Gatsby* came out.[16] In a very clever, artful, and complicated way, it implants different Daisys in two women—one, Rita Cavanagh, greatly influenced by the Daisy of *The Great Gatsby*, embodiment of Jay Gatsby's dreams and illusions; the other, Daisy Coleman, the essence of the American spirit of naturalness, freshness, and tragic unfulfillment, who is drawn essentially from Daisy Miller.

Fitzgerald's Daisy Buchanan inverts the character and figure of Daisy Miller and is a paradigm for how later postmodern writers would turn certain of James's characters inside out. Daisy Buchanan is not worthy of Jay Gatsby's passionate and romantic notion of her. But Edmund Wilson has incorporated her glamour and romantic image in the figure of the talented poet Rita Cavanagh, based in part on Edna St. Vincent Millay. Rita, like Daisy Buchanan, seems to love the narrator, but she can be won away by others who flatter her and give her the financial and emotional support she needs.

Wilson's other Daisy is clearly labeled Daisy, and the hero narrator meets both of them at the same party. The two come to share lovers, and Daisy's "husband," Ray Coleman, the only character with money in the novel, corresponds to Tom Buchanan. Daisy Coleman is noted for certain qualities that some read in Daisy Miller, including "her coarseness and sharpness" (*TD*, 13). Like Daisy Miller, she dresses stylishly: she has an "ostrich-feather evening wrap that's worth three hundred dollars" (*TD*, 14). She is conspicuously "bullied by her husband" (*TD*, 15), as Daisy Miller is bullied by Winterbourne and the colony of American expatriates. "Daisy has been standing by like a bad little child reproved," with her "frank and charming grin" (*TD*, 12). The narrator resents Coleman's "failure to appreciate her" (*TD*, 13).

Daisy comes from Pittsburgh, and the character Junior Meissner, whom the narrator knew as a boy in Pittsburgh, is based on Randolph Miller from "Daisy Miller," from whom he takes his "arrogance of an over-indulged child." The narrator sees in Daisy the "real vital Pittsburgh: frank, vulgar, humorous, human!" (*TD*, 17). Wilson brings Henry James's name into the novel twice (*TD*, 49, 160). Fitzgerald liked Wilson's title (*LF*,

---

16.   Edmund Wilson, *The Twenties: From Notebooks and Diaries of the Period*, ed. Leon Edel (New York, 1975), 246. Edel wrote, "His Daisy . . . is nevertheless an extension of Henry James's Daisy Miller; so was Fitzgerald's in *The Great Gatsby*" (p. 4).

213, 216), and it may have stimulated him to try his hand at a somewhat parodic, humorous redoing of a tale that he and his Princeton friend Wilson had thus far treated so solemnly.

A Very Modern Daisy: Fitzgerald's "A Hotel Child"

In 1931, six years after *The Great Gatsby*, Fitzgerald wrote the more obvious, rather frivolous potboiler "The Hotel Child," published in the *Saturday Evening Post* of January 31, 1931. From using James's tale as the basis for the tragic elements of *The Great Gatsby*, he passed to using it as the basis for a farce, or a cartoon. This is a tale whose premise is the bafflement of Europeanized society when confronting American innocence. The Hotel des Trois Mondes, a parody of the Hotel des Trois Couronnes, is situated not in Vevey but in some nameless, fashionable resort in Europe. The Daisy is now Fifi Schwartz, an "exquisitely, radiantly beautiful Jewess whose fine, high forehead sloped gently up to where her hair, bordering it like an armorial shield, burst into lovelocks and waves and curlicues of soft dark red" (*SSF*, 599). As Daisy had been an outsider in American European circles, so Fifi is an outsider as a Jewess.

She is also like Daisy Miller in wearing wonderful dresses: "Such dresses — cerise for Chanel, mauve for Molyneux, pink for Patou; dozens of them; tight at the hips, swaying, furling . . ." The people around her, like those around Daisy Miller, say, "Such ghastly taste. . . . The stage, the shop window, the manikins' parade. What can her mother be thinking? But, then, look at her mother." Mrs. Schwartz is in the mold of Mrs. Ezra B. Miller, though she does object to the young men who try "to be engaged to" her daughter (*SSF*, 599). Among the hotel guests is the Taylor family, involved with the diplomatic service and "very Europeanized Americans," like Mrs. Costello and Mrs. Walker in James's tale, for "they had reached a position where they could hardly be said to belong to any nation at all." Their opinion was "that Fifi was as much of a gratuitous outrage as a new stripe in the flag" (*SSF*, 600).

Although there is a much larger canvas of people in this story than in "Daisy Miller," the atmosphere is the same. There is a Count Borowki, a penniless nobleman trying to marry a rich American. Fitzgerald may have considered him a variation on Giovanelli from "Daisy Miller," but Fifi allows herself to be really "engaged" to him. Fifi has a brother, as Daisy

Miller does, a brother who, too, is rather scandalous and extrovert in his behavior, with the difference that Fifi's brother, John, as a grown young man, can commit serious indiscretions, like engaging himself to the wrong people and gambling, whereas Randolph simply eats too much lump sugar and rackets around the hotel.

Mrs. Schwartz's dialogue with her daughter is couched in the same laconic terminology as Mrs. Miller's. "So I think we better go back home," she murmurs provincially after being robbed of two hundred dollars of American money (*SSF,* 605). When Fifi is reprimanded for drinking her ginger ale at the bar—since people will think she is drinking hard liquor— she reacts in Daisy Miller's way: "I never saw such a narrow-minded bunch of people in my life; always criticizing everybody and making up terrible things about them. . . . I think it would be a good thing if the hotel caught fire and burned down with all the nasty cats in it" (*SSF,* 607). Count Borowki turns out to be a well-known thief, and Lady Capps-Karr is responsible for accidentally setting the house on fire. Miss Howard, an English debutante, elopes with Count Borowki before he is apprehended and therefore cannot be compelled to appear as a witness against him. It is Fifi's visit to a local jeweler and her discovery that the Count paid for the cigarette case he gave her with a hundred-dollar American bill lifted from Fifi's mother's bureau that solves the case. So Fifi is not only a virtuous, innocent girl with brash habits and no place to wear her fancy clothing but also a sharp-eyed detective. All the nuanced implications of "Daisy Miller," subtly presented in *The Great Gatsby,* blossom forth here cartoonishly. Fifi Schwartz might pose as the Daisy Miller of the 1920s that John Held, Jr., illustrated, so playful is the spirit in which Fitzgerald created her.

Theophilus North and "Daisy Miller"

The only one of all the later versions of Daisy to be described as becoming acquainted with James's tale "Daisy Miller" is in the last novel Thornton Wilder (1897–1975) wrote, *Theophilus North,* of 1973. Wilder's hero, North, who earns a living reading to the rich in Newport, decides to read "Daisy Miller" to a young woman whose own character seems to be behind his choice. Myra Granberry is a strong-minded young woman who, because of an accident in her youth, has led a partially invalid life at odds with her spirit of independence. Her husband, who may bear some relation to Winterbourne, has convinced Theophilus that, although his young wife is difficult, she is "strong-minded and sincere" and will listen to his readings. Like Daisy, she is also "as beautiful as the morning but not as shy as the dawn" (*TN*, 192), and when she rejects readings from Jane Austen, on the grounds that Austen does not know "anything about life" (*TN*, 194), Theophilus brings her James's "Daisy Miller," the author of which he recommends as knowing about life, for he "lived in Newport when he was young" (*TN*, 195). Theophilus tells her that James got so sick of the social life in Newport that he resolved "to write it all down. . . . When he died the last book—still unfinished on his desk—was a novel laid in Newport, called *The Ivory Tower,* about the emptiness and waste of the life here." Myra takes the book and reads it herself. Although she makes no comment on the story, Wilder plainly knew what he was doing when he chose this book for this particular young woman, who "out of sheer boredom [says] the first thing that comes into [her] head" (*TN*, 196). It is almost as if Wilder thought to himself, What if Daisy did not die but continued to live, perhaps as an invalid, with Winterbourne as her husband? Would she have been happy? Mr. Granberry has a mistress on the side, just as Winterbourne, if married to Daisy, would have found it hard to detach himself from his better-educated and sophisticated woman friend in Geneva. Myra's husband seems to suffer from Winterbourne's affliction: "I can't stand being loved—loved? Worshipped." Theophilus, a deus ex machina for all the people with whom he comes into contact, admonishes Granberry, "Learn to accept love—with a smile, with a grin." If Wilder saw this inability in Winterbourne, he, being Wilder, no doubt wanted to invent a Daisy Miller who could be happy and a Winterbourne who could change his habits.[17]

Daisy and Judith Krantz's *Princess Daisy*

In 1980, the international novel, perfected by Henry James, suddenly appeared in a dazzling schlock, popular form, as the number one best-selling *Princess Daisy,* by Judith Krantz (1932–). Throughout there are evocations of "Daisy Miller," but always in the service of a twentieth-century "sensation" novel. The substantial debt to Henry James is concealed from the reader until the end, when, as James would say, Krantz gives herself away.

---

17. My attention was called to Wilder's use of "Daisy Miller" by Lyall H. Powers, in "Thornton Wilder as Literary Cubist: An Acknowledged Debt to Henry James," *Henry James Review,* VII (1985), 34–45.

One of her characters, a business tycoon, finding it impossible to sleep, reads a "few more pages of Leon Edel's five-volume biography of Henry James. This great scholarly work, detailed, leisurely and undoubtedly good for him, had the virtue of not being a page-turner." It occupies him "until about five in the morning," as Hilly Bijur tries hard "not to think only about James churning out books in London [he] had never read."[18] Krantz, on the other hand, has read and thought about James's books, as her previous novels establish. Writers from the 1950s who have been steeped in James do not use the name Daisy without expecting some resonance from his most popular tale.

Not that there is much similarity between the lives and experiences of the two Daisys apart from their innocence. James's Daisy, the victim of her innocence, dies as a result of events flowing from her hurt feelings when Winterbourne does not respond to her. Krantz's Daisy Valensky is innocent to a certain degree, as well, and is a victim of her half brother's brutality, but she goes on to success. To have a best seller, Krantz had to satisfy the dreams of female readers, after all. In a strange and postmodern transformation of the ending of "Daisy Miller," where, at a piteous funeral, the young girl's grave in the Protestant cemetery of Rome is covered with daisies, Daisy Valensky is dressed and wreathed in daisies, thousands of which have been gathered for an extravagant advertising campaign. Daisy Valensky rides in triumph with her dog "on a leash of silver sequined ribbons into which a bunch of daisies had been threaded."[19]

Both Daisys take a lively interest in exceptionally showy and expensive clothing. In the name of Daisy Valensky's lover — North — and in the frosty role he plays in their affair in Venice, there is a vestige of the chilly Winterbourne. Both Daisys want love from their cold lovers, and both Daisys are courageous and generous. But in the trajectory of their lives there is no similarity. To argue that the pestiferous younger brother, Randolph, in James's tale becomes in Krantz's novel the older half brother Ram, the evil influence in Daisy Valensky's life, would surely be to torture the evidence.

The only responsible conclusion is that a contemporary novelist well versed in James could easily have modeled on James's Daisy the character of a young girl also named Daisy living in both the United States and Eu-

18. Judith Krantz, *Princess Daisy* (New York, 1980), 450.
19. *Ibid.,* 493.

rope, gifted with great beauty and innocence, and taken advantage of by those without sensitivity to the poetry of her being. But the possibility of such a daisy chain of association depends on the reader's response and not only on the intentions of the writer.

A Postmodern Daisy: Daisy Turned Inside Out in Ruth Rendell's *Kissing the Gunner's Daughter*

Since 1925, when Fitzgerald took the tack of reversing Daisy Miller's character in Daisy Buchanan, writers have shown that James's Daisy is still an inspiration even if it is also a challenge to vary her personality enough to achieve a different slant. In the 1990s, literary effort has yielded a criminal Daisy who is the villainess of a suspense novel.

The first novel in which Ruth Rendell (1930–), writing as Barbara Vine, transmogrified a character of Henry James's was *The House of Stairs*, of 1988. She there converted Milly Theale from a virtuous, victimized rich young American into a distorted, murderous criminal—a beautiful creature that many of the characters in the book adore, as characters in *The Wings of the Dove* adore Milly Theale, but who turns out to be evil personified. In *Kissing the Gunner's Daughter*, of 1992, Rendell submitted Daisy Miller to the same process. Both on the dust jacket and within the book, Bernini's statue *Apollo and Daphne* is an icon for the metamorphosis. In the leading character, Daisy Flory, James's Daisy has gone from being an innocent girl living in the garden of life to being revealed as a greedy thief and murderess.

Until the last pages of the novel, Daisy is depicted in a way suggesting James's Daisy. At the very onset it transpires that she is named after Davina Flory, her grandmother, but that everyone calls her Daisy (*KG*, 39). Daisy Miller too goes by her pet name. As Daisy Miller is throughout James's tale treated as a flower in a floral setting, so Daisy Flory, her family name also floral, lives in an artificially structured environment that her grandmother, a distinguished anthropologist and arborealist, has created for the home she shares with her daughter, Naomi, and her granddaughter. Nicholas Virson, a friend of Daisy's family, brings her a "dozen red roses in bud. . . . Her right hand, the good hand, rested on their stems and on the pink and gold patterned paper in which they were wrapped" (*KG*, 89). When Daisy Miller arrives at Mrs. Walker's house, she is carrying a bouquet. When Virson leaves

the hospital, he walks off carrying the roses he carried in (*KG*, 91), like Giovanelli. Daisy Flory, through most of the novel, acts like Daisy Miller, as if
her heart has been broken. The floral motif recurs in the name of Joanne
Garland, the partner of Daisy's mother in their antique shop (*KG*, 94). The
novel is deliberately overfloriated, presumably to summon up the atmosphere of Daisy Miller, whose suitor always bears a "stack of flowers" and
who is always seen in a garden. Daisy Flory wears an American western
outfit of jeans because "these people were to be shown the real Daisy, what
she wanted to be, a free spirit, even an outrageous spirit, dressing as she
pleased and doing as she liked" (*KG*, 310). Like Daisy Miller, she grieves,
and her reason is very much like Daisy Miller's: "Because the man she loved
and who she believed loved her had shot her" (*KG*, 366).

The book ends with Daisy and Thanny Hogarth, who turns out to have
been her secret lover, sitting together in the conservatory, handling the jewels presumed to have been stolen by some outsider (*KG*, 378). The surprise
is that it is Daisy who, with her lover, has murdered the whole family.

Alice James Thinking of Daisy via Susan Sontag

In 1993, a year after Rendell's *Kissing the Gunner's Daughter*, Daisy reverted
to her old self of 1878 when she appeared as part of a monologue of a postmodern Alice James in Susan Sontag's play *Alice in Bed*. Alice, on a trip,
though only in her imagination, to Rome, remembers that her brother
"Harry told me about a girl who went to the Colosseum at night and caught
pneumonia and died." Unlike Alice, though, that girl was not alone: "She
went there with a man—but I like to think of being alone . . . in Rome, even
though it's a city where women are harassed when walking about alone"
(*AL*, 82).

Daisy Miller continues to inhabit the imagination of those who write
about James even when they touch on her as tangentially as Sontag did in
this play about Alice as a victim of her family. Daisy is pertinent exactly as
a victim of her society, the American colony in Rome. According to Sontag,
Alice in Rome "will imagine not only her freedom but the weight of the
past" (*AL*, 116), and she in her fancy allies herself with the past. Like her
brother Henry and Margaret Fuller, "with their idyllic memories of a separate, papal Rome," she too is someone for whom "the mind is the past, and
the mind is Rome" (*AL*, 83). Sontag wrote, "All is fiction, of course, in my
play" (*AL*, 116).

Daisy and David Leavitt's "The Term Paper Artist"

"The Term Paper Artist" is a novella of 1997 by David Leavitt (1961–), a writer easy in his gay life who writes with a humor that reaches every kind of reader, gay or straight—unlike, for instance, James McCourt, whose *Time Remaining* (see below, p. 361) purveys a more specifically gay humor. In this tale, Leavitt uses a narrative device that partially explains his "plagiarism" of an episode in Stephen Spender's life in his novel *While England Sleeps* (1993). In "The Term Paper Artist," the narrating character, named David Leavitt, says, "Writers often disguise their lives as fiction. The thing they almost never do is disguise fiction as their lives" (*AR*, 72). Leavitt in this story has dressed his fiction as autobiography, but the reader should not be taken in. The novella is another postmodern twist on storytelling.

David has been approached by Eric, the son of friends of his parents with whom he is staying in California, to write a term paper that the undergraduate needs if he is to make it into the Stanford University School of Business. David becomes amenable to writing the essay, since the twenty-year-old appeals to him and is offering blandishments. David, who never received less than an A on a paper at Yale, knows he can handle the topic assigned by the professor, a Henry James expert, which is to "compare and contrast Lucy's and Daisy's responses to Italy in Forster's *A Room with a View* and James's *Daisy Miller*" (*AR*, 21). When Eric broached the matter to David by asking if he had read "Daisy Miller," David answered with a certain amount of contempt, "Of course" (*AR*, 20). He was at first shocked by the proposal of sex as payment, remonstrating to Eric, "I'm a famous writer. I have a novel under contract with Viking Penguin. You know, Viking Penguin, that gigantic publisher, the same one that published *Daisy Miller*." But Eric answered, "I've got something you want. You've got something I need. We make a deal" (*AR*, 22). When David accepts and looks at Eric's notes, he finds much to criticize:

> "First of all, you're wrong about Daisy. She's not nearly so knowing as you make out."
> "How so?"
> "It's the whole point. She's actually very innocent, maybe the most innocent character in the story."

David goes on, "Innocence can . . . mean unawareness that what other people think matters" (*AR*, 22). This definition of Daisy's innocence is one

rarely met with in criticism, and it goes far toward explaining Daisy's reck-
lessness about her reputation within the American colony in Rome.

David's and Eric's comments about E. M. Forster's *A Room with a View* do
not display the same critical acumen, but they clarify the greater enthusiasm both young men have for Forster. As David says, "I'll always admire
James. But I'll never love him. He's too—I don't know. Fussy. Also, he
never gets under Italy's skin, which is odd, because Forster does, and he
spends so much less time there" (*AR,* 23). David does a little work on the
two writers, which includes reading P. N. Furbank's life of Forster. He
seems to have doctored or misread Edel's words about the tea both writers
shared, for instead of quoting "head rather fat but fine," he leaves out the
word *head* (*M,* 389). David feels that Forster, who wrote a poem to a youth
he saw on the way back from tea with James, "wouldn't have warmed much
to James, that conscientious objector in the wars of sexuality, preempted
from battle by virtue of his 'obscure hurt' (how coy, how typically Jamesian, that phrase!). Whereas Forster, dear Forster, was in his own way the
frankest of men" (*AR,* 26). Forster gets better marks as a gay man from David because Forster supported Radclyffe Hall, but "James distanced himself from Oscar Wilde during his trial, fearful lest the association should
taint. And this seems natural: fear, in the Jamesian university, seems natural." David is expressing the current view of James as homoerotic but too
fearful to act on his feelings, whereas Forster "would have betrayed his
country before he betrayed his friend" (*AR,* 27). So often forgotten is that
Forster was of a younger generation than James.

Rereading the two works as preparation for writing the paper, David
smiles at some of the things he reads in Forster, and specifically at two
things he reads in "Daisy Miller." He is amused "when Randolph Miller
said, 'You bet,'" and when Winterbourne "reflected on that depth of Italian
subtlety, so strangely opposed to Anglo-Saxon simplicity, which enables
people to show a smoother surface in proportion as they're more acutely
displeased.' That was good. That was James at his best" (*AR,* 28). The two
classics make David happy, and he writes in a fever of joy.

His paper of course earns an A from the female professor, who views
"Daisy Miller" as a novel, not a short story: "In my view *Daisy Miller* must
be looked upon as a novel" (*AR,* 34). Eric gets not only an A but exemption
from the final, and his paper is to be nominated for a prize. The professor
never once doubts that Eric wrote it, for David, as he puts it, has written it
"like something a smart college junior might write. I mean as opposed to

something Elizabeth Hardwick or Susan Sontag might write" (*AR*, 35). At the same time the deal with Eric is finally consummated, David's own agent has a "done deal" for the "paperback of *While England Sleeps*, as well as my new novel" (*AR*, 37). The narrator David Leavitt acquires a local reputation for writing papers in exchange for sexual pleasure, and turns out seven term papers in all. The last one he does is for a Mormon student, who is full of the sense of sinning but all the same awakens to his own homosexuality.

"The Term Paper Artist," at the end of the twentieth century, recalls in its sexuality the emphasis on sex at the end of the nineteenth century in Ella D'Arcy's "The Pleasure-Pilgrim." Although Leavitt is the first gay writer to give Daisy her due, it is not surprising that as a comfortably gay writer, he is partial to Forster over James. James was a fearful, perhaps latently gay personality. Forster came out of the closet toward the end of his life, when the times allowed him to do so. James could only be apprehensive, given his Puritan New England background and Wilde's trials. But that David Leavitt the narrator, who responds to the gifts of both writers, emphasizing their sexual nature, has more to say about James's work than about Forster's—apart from Forster's being more lovable than James—establishes his respect for "Daisy Miller." Daisy enters the world of gay literary creativity through David Leavitt's insight into what is seriously innocent in her behavior. She greets the new century with her quality intact.

11

THE PORTRAIT OF A LADY

The Allure of the Title: Pound, Eliot, and Hemingway

The modernists Ezra Pound (1885–1972), T. S. Eliot (1888–1965), and Ernest Hemingway (1898–1961) were fascinated by *The Portrait of a Lady*, particularly by its title. When James used the title for his novel of 1881, he was adopting a phrase from the world of art. By the time the modernists began to use it, the phrase had lost its primary connection with painting. Because of the admiration Pound, Eliot, and Hemingway had for James, the phrase, for them, brought his novel to mind first of all. The development of feminism surely accelerated the presence in others' writings of Isabel Archer, a heroine trapped by her own choice in pursuing the good marriage. Pound translated the title of the novel into French and in 1912 called a poem "Portrait d'une femme." This poem recollects Walter Pater's essay on *La Gioconda* besides relating to James's *The Portrait of a Lady*, or rather, Isabel Archer. Moreover, it was to enter into Eliot's naming of a poem "Portrait of a Lady" in 1917. In Eliot's lines the lady expressing herself to the narrator entertains the same illusions about life that Isabel Archer does, especially illusions paralleling those Isabel Archer has about Gilbert Osmond. The lady expects, because of what her friends have told her, to find a kinship with the narrator. She expects a fulfilling relation with him — and presumably he is one among many. But the narrator has no intention of forming a close tie with her, and he manages to slip from her tentacles. Eliot's lady has been nurtured on the same kinds of romantic hopes as Isabel Archer, hopes comparable to Emma Bovary's. All three women suffer the same kind of disillusionment. Eliot's poem, written just two years after James's death, omitted the definite article from the title, as did the one by Pound, who was even more saturated in James than Eliot was.[1]

Pound's other references to *The Portrait of a Lady* are sometimes elusive, however, as in his poem "Hugh Selwyn Mauberley," which he described as a "study in form, an attempt to condense the James novel. Meliora speramus."[2] In any case, Eliot seems to have attempted a similar condensation, for his "Portrait of a Lady" compresses almost a year into its lines. It begins in December, when the lady first meets the narrator and tells him how much her friends mean to her and that she hopes he will be one of them (*CPE*, 19). In April, the lady bores the narrator by attempting to entangle him in her web of feelings. During October, the lady receives the news that the narrator is going abroad, and the poem ends with the narrator's realization that, given her greater age, she may die at any time and that his attitude to her, of boredom and smiling contempt, is not really justified. This is a condensed novel, perhaps not exactly that of *The Portrait of a Lady*, but one about a distinguished older lady of certain pretensions who expects too much from the young men who pay her dutiful calls. To that extent it is a variation on the theme of James's novel.

Eliot's lady shares Isabel Archer's romantic illusions about the good life and suffers a loss of illusions comparable to what Isabel Archer experiences after marrying Gilbert Osmond. The lady of Eliot's poem has illusions about the perfect friendship she expects to enjoy with a younger man who visits her. He, however, does not wish to be bound in the relationship she envisions. When he evades her desires, the lady "can hardly understand" why he leaves. He tells us he reads "the comics and the sporting page" (*CPE*, 21), one side of many the lady does not realize exist in him.

In the last lines of "Portrait of a Lady," the narrator understands that the lady has given more than he has given her credit for. She could be, like

1. Christopher Ricks has shown how many words and phrases from James's work appear in Eliot's early poetry. See T. S. Eliot, *Inventions of the March Hare: Poems, 1909–1917*, ed. Christopher Ricks (New York, 1997).

2. Ezra Pound to Felix E. Schelling, July 8, 1922, in *The Letters of Ezra Pound*, ed. D. D. Paige (New York, 1950), 180.

Pound's lady in "Portrait d'une femme," *his* "Sargasso Sea," for "Great minds have sought you—lacking someone else." Although Eliot's portrait is of a repetitive bore, what the narrator does not convey is the qualities in her that have made him go so often to see her. As Pound stated clearly and Eliot may imply, there is "Nothing that's quite your own. / Yet this is you." The lady has her own worth.[3]

Nine years after Eliot's poem, Ernest Hemingway, of the next generation, wrote a poem he entitled "Portrait of a Lady." This was part of an unpublished essay on Gertrude Stein that he composed in Paris around 1926, after his friendship with Stein had ended. The first seventeen lines are in a prose format: "Now we will say it with a small poem. A poem that will not be good. . . . A mean poem. A poem written by a man with a grudge," and so on. After that, two short lines are indented: "Gertrude Stein was never crazy / Gertrude Stein was very lazy."[4] And under these is written, "Now that it is all over perhaps it made a great difference if it was something that you cared about." The poem's development in its final lines achieves the tone of the concluding lines of Eliot's poem. And in a poem that follows it called "Sequel," Hemingway definitely invoked Eliot's poem, beginning it with a variation on the first line of Eliot's last stanza:

> Well! and what if she should die some afternoon,
>
> . . . .
>
> Should die and leave me sitting pen in hand
>
> . . . .
>
> Doubtful, for a while
> Not knowing what to feel or if I understand
>
> . . . .
>
> Would she not have the advantage, after all?
>
> . . . .
>
> And should I have the right to smile? (*CPE,* 23.)

Hemingway's poem reads,

---

3. Ezra Pound, *Personae* (New York, 1909), 61. Eliot later considered using another of James's titles, *In the Cage,* but decided against it. See T. S. Eliot, *The Waste Land: A Facsimile and Transcript of the Original Drafts, Including the Annotations of Ezra Pound,* ed. Valerie Eliot (London, 1971), 10, 11.

4. Nicholas Gerogiannis, ed., *Ernest Hemingway: 88 Poems* (New York, 1979), 90 (Editor's note: "Paris, *ca.* 1926.").

> So if she dies
> And if you write of it
> Being a writer and a shit
> Dulling it so you sleep again at night,
>
> Alone   or telling it to whores . . . [5]

In those lines Hemingway has reached the same conclusion as the narrator of Eliot's poem.

Hemingway's "Portrait of a Lady" is a kind of ultimate parody of Isabel Archer, now incarnated in Gertrude Stein, whom he rejects as an influence through the lens of Eliot's poem, granting in his sequel that Miss Stein had the advantage of him, the writer and self-confessed "shit." In filtering through the imaginations of Pound, Eliot, and Hemingway, the legacy of James's influential novel about a heroine who "affronts her destiny" has been colored more by their talents than by his. But the light beam originated in James's fiction.

In the Wake of Pound, Eliot, and Hemingway: Martha Gellhorn's "Portrait of a Lady"

In 1941, Martha Gellhorn (1908–1998) included in her collection of short stories, *The Heart of Another,* a tale she called "Portrait of a Lady." She probably had read the poem of the same title that her husband, Ernest Hemingway, wrote about Gertrude Stein fifteen years earlier. Gellhorn placed her story in Finland during the war between Russia and the Finns. A rich young American woman, Ann Maynard, is on an escorted tour of the front. She is a journalist who looks on war as a romantic adventure, and she makes herself especially attractive to the group of officers and pilots in the Officer's Club without considering the consequences. Mrs. Maynard's effect on the men seems to draw from the impression Isabel Archer makes on Edward Rosier four years after her marriage to Gilbert Osmond: Rosier "took his course to the adjoining room and met Mrs. Osmond coming out of the deep doorway. She was dressed in black velvet; she looked high and splendid. . . . Now, at all events, framed in the gilded doorway, she struck our young man as the picture of a gracious lady" (NYE, IV, 105). Not dressed in black velvet, Mrs. Maynard is wearing the closest modern

5. *Ibid.,* 90.

equivalent, a "black ski-suit that was perfectly cut and very warm and black ski boots. Her white sweater came up high around her neck and she had on a beaver great coat with the hood now thrown back. . . . Ben knew how expensive she was and he admired expensiveness" (*HA*, 58). The men all look at her with great interest, and she is immediately attracted to one of them, Lieutenant Lahti, who has shot down four Russian planes in a day. She says to him, "This is my first war" (*HA*, 64). But someone else thinks that "she is just a spoiled, beautiful crazy who travels around wanting anything she sees" (*HA*, 66). She approaches the war and her seduction of Lieutenant Lahti the way Isabel Archer approaches Osmond—in a spirit of adventure. The risks for her are equally great, and she loses out on her vision of the perfect marriage. She is fully conscious of the risks of the affair, but she pushes it anyway. After she has kept Lahti up all night, he dies in an engagement with an enemy plane. What she learns is that the war "could happen to anyone, it could happen to you" (*HA*, 121). She no longer cares about creating a portrait of a lady by standing in a doorway and exciting the women-deprived men. She is totally disillusioned and reacts to the death of the lieutenant very much as Isabel does when Ralph dies at Gardencourt and she returns to Rome and reality.

Philip Roth's *Letting Go*

In 1988, in *The Facts*, which bridged the genres of fiction and autobiography, Philip Roth told the reader that in his first novel, *Letting Go*, twenty-six years earlier, he had freed himself from the "awesome graduate school authority of Henry James, whose *Portrait of a Lady* had been a virtual handbook during the early drafts of *Letting Go*" (*FA*, 157). The reader of that first novel can see clearly that Roth succeeded, on the contrary, in imprisoning not only himself but his novel and his heroine within a grotesque construal of *The Portrait of a Lady*. Roth recalled in *The Facts* that he and his fellow graduate students at the University of Chicago spoke of Isabel Archer as a shiksa—that is, a Gentile (*FA*, 114)—and that they enjoyed long discussions on whether Osmond "wasn't really a Jew" (*FA*, 115). In *Letting Go*, Isabel becomes another shiksa in the character of Libby Herz. Roth has availed himself of the very Jamesian strategy—especially evident in *The Awkward Age*—of having his characters misplace, carry, and refer to a well-known book in order to underline its symbolic function relative to his plot and characterization. *Letting Go* begins with the deathbed letter in which the mother of Gabe, the hero, confesses to "pushing and pulling at people with a clear conscience" because she has wanted to influence them, though now she realizes that the influence she exerted has made her entire family unhappy. Gabe, the consciousness of the book, is in the army, and his one connection with the "world of feeling" is "not the world itself but Henry James, whom I had lately begun to read" (*LET,* 3). When he receives his mother's letter, he is "reading *Portrait of a Lady* and it was into its pages that I slid the envelope." He lends the book to a fellow graduate student, Paul Herz, whose wife, Libby, reads it and talks about it. Like Minny Temple and Alice James, Libby is an invalid, and like Isabel Archer, she has had a miscarriage. Frustrated in her marriage, she is impressed with the first scene in the novel, especially by the "rug on the lawn." According to Libby, Isabel "likes rugs on lawns. . . . That's the least of it. She wants to put rugs on other people's lawns," and on Osmond, "and more than Osmond . . . she wants to alter what can't be altered. . . . Isabel's trouble is she wants to change others, but a man comes along who can alter her . . . Caspar Good-wood—and what happens? She gets the shakes, she gets scared" (*LET,* 9). Libby sees Isabel as "one of those pushers-around of men," but Gabe says he has always found Isabel "virtuous and charming" (*LET,* 10). Gabe real-izes that Libby has found his mother's letter and that "she could no more appreciate my mother's dilemma than she could Isabel Archer's." He ar-gues that Isabel "shows herself to have a lot of guts in the end" (*LET,* 11). It is clear that Libby is an annoying nag to her husband and is acting out her desire to influence and alter someone besides herself. "She wouldn't let the poor guy alone" (*LET,* 15).

Some time later when Gabe meets Libby in the supermarket, she has finished James's novel. She has to admit that Isabel *has* a lot of courage in the end, but she speculates that it is more likely stubbornness than true courage. From then on, the novel revolves among characters whose rela-tionships imprison them in the way Libby judges James's heroine to be imprisoned.

What is especially hard for the reader of James to accept is the arbitrary reading Roth, through Libby, takes of Isabel Archer. He forces the behav-ior of his characters to conform to a trait that Libby finds in Isabel but that is farfetched in the extreme: that Isabel is someone who manipulates people. The point of James's novel is that in the name of freedom poor Isa-bel finds herself manipulated into a marriage in which she must remain. Roth apparently wants us to think that Libby is also trapped in a marriage she has trouble accepting. But is she? Her husband, Paul, seems to be the one trapped, yet the author has scanted Paul's character. In his first attempt to come to terms with James's work—which seems to have provided him with an entire world removed from his own parochial Jewish community—he failed to make a plausible use of it, however ingenious his idea of bringing *The Portrait of a Lady* into his characters' lives in body and soul.

The Portrait of a Lady in Fiction of the 1980s and 1990s

In nine contemporary novels and three movies, reflections, at times dim and attenuated, are discernible from *The Portrait of a Lady.* Apparent in them are the difficulties of modern writers in accepting Isabel's destiny.

Ursula Perrin's *Old Devotions*

Old Devotions, of 1983, by Ursula Perrin (1935–), appears to be a kind of "free arrangement" of *The Portrait of a Lady,* even to the point of stressing the attitudes to marriage of her heroine, Isabel. The heroine has had one husband, Walter, and a lover, David, who has divorced his wife and wants, after things cool off, to marry her. She loves Douglas—who corresponds to James's Gilbert Osmond. She looks to herself "shiny-faced and slightly comic, a prim, tart-tongued lady—Henrietta Stackpole?—out of some Henry James novel" (*OD,* 30). When discussing Margaret's dinner party, Morgan says it was good "talking about Henry James. How intelligent can you get?" Morgan says, "It's your *idea* of marriage that worries me. . . . You are seeing life through a haze of Henry James. All that drawing room stuff, all those elegant, deep conversations" (*OD,* 68). She answers, "You can't even read, for Christ's sake. Henry James was a realist. If you look at his characters closely . . ." (*OD,* 69). Her mother told her "Seize the day" (*OD,* 82)—which is "Live all you can" from *The Ambassadors.* Isabel recounts, "I was leading a stable, pleasing existence but often felt sad in the evening: I knew it couldn't last. Like the hero of a famous Henry James story (was his name Marcher? yes, Marcher), I sensed catastrophe coming" (*OD,* 91). "I was thirty-four and rediscovering Henry James, Debussy, Vuillard" (*OD,* 140). Sarah, the drug kid, is "reading Henry James"—*The Wings of the Dove*—because her mother is dying of leukemia.

In spite of the jumble of references, Perrin defines her main Jamesian source as *The Portrait of a Lady*, and her heroine Isabel, facing the same problems that Isabel Archer faces, winds up with the same kind of solutions.

Judith Krantz's *I'll Take Manhattan* and *Scruples Two*

Halfway through Judith Krantz's *I'll Take Manhattan*, a best-selling popular novel published in 1986, Maxi, the heroine, has "become, she flattered herself, an updated Henry James heroine, a woman with a past that was only dimly known; whose present was tantalizingly private yet illuminated by the blaze of her independence, her family, her fortune, and—why not be blunt—her face; a woman whose future held infinite promise."[6] The character she is thinking of has to be Isabel Archer. Her present "blaze of independence"—the particular that has been the keynote of Isabel's life—makes her successful, because Maxi is not trapped. This is a schlock novel, in which Maxi has to succeed, in contrast to Isabel. Maxi's fortune parallels the fortune Ralph gets his father to leave Isabel. Rocco corresponds to one of the suitors for Isabel's hand. The second husband, the sick Dan Brady, corresponds to the sick Ralph, who gets a fortune to leave to Isabel with a slight change of direction. Black Dan Brady, from Australia, is an "oddly elegant sacred cow," like Ralph. The equivalent in Krantz's book of Isabel's third suitor, Lord Warburton, is Oswald, Earl of Kirkgordon. Maxi's mother, Lily, is another Jamesian character: perhaps Madame Merle is her model. Lily is involved sexually with Cutter Amberville, a man who has lived in hatred and envy of his successful brother, Zachary, and who has a bastard by Lily named Justin.

Justin corresponds to the bastard of Madame Merle and Gilbert Osmond, Pansy. There is a pun involved here. Whereas Madame Merle and Osmond's little bastard daughter is called Pansy, Lily and Cutter produce a bastard son who is a pansy, a homosexual boy whose tastes involve him with a crook who plants drugs on him. Justin, who has known about his bastardy since prep school, throws his father down the stairs when Cutter tells him about it. Developing James's Pansy into a gay illegitimate boy-child is surely a postmodern update written to achieve a best-seller clientele and redeemed in the author's eyes by the association with James.

In Judith Krantz's first novel, *Scruples*, of 1978, there is a wealthy widow

6. Judith Krantz, *I'll Take Manhattan* (New York, 1986), 183.

who establishes in Beverly Hills the most elegant boutique in the world, which she calls Scruples. This woman, Billie Ikehorn Orsini, a descendant of the Winthrops, was the unattractive daughter of a Boston doctor and a girl with no matrimonial or other kind of future before she married an elderly multimillionaire. Her mother died early, like Catherine Sloper's in *Washington Square*. Krantz employed the figure of a balloon for romanticism tied to reality, as James did in his preface to *Roderick Hudson*. Billie is "trying to keep her world tied down and under her control as if it were a runaway balloon. It was time to let the balloon loose and allow it to take her with it . . . with a light hand at the controls."[7]

Fifteen years later, in 1993, *Scruples Two* was published and continued the saga. Cora Middleton de Lioncourt in her nineteenth year marries a man of forty-nine. The count she marries is very much like Osmond in *The Portrait of a Lady*. He believes that life should be "easy, idle and spent in the pursuit of beautiful objects. His collection of antiques is the one passion to which he dedicated all his time and much of his inheritance."[8] Cora, though, is an improvement on Isabel Archer, for she has "not neglected her own development in the course of twenty-three years of marriage to a man who had nothing to recommend him but exquisite taste" and for whom "his wife, like his apartment, was a reflection of his taste."[9]

What Maisie Knew, The Portrait of a Lady, perhaps *The Spoils of Poynton,* "The Private Life," and some parts of *The Ambassadors* are also in this book. Clearly Judith Krantz has absorbed Henry James. But the most fundamental source is *The Portrait of a Lady*, the favorite of many women today because James's novel acts as a cautionary tale for them.

Anita Brookner's *A Closed Eye*

The casual reader does not immediately see the subtext of Anita Brookner's *A Closed Eye*, of 1991. The novel is written so well and persuasively that a robust appreciation of it is possible even when the subtext is not noticed. The first clue the fully open eye taking in *A Closed Eye* will hit upon is in the epigraph, which is identified as from James's early novella "Madame de Mauves." It is necessary to keep this passage in mind in order to under-

---

7. Judith Krantz, *Scruples* (New York, 1978), 468.
8. Judith Krantz, *Scruples Two* (New York, 1993), 179.
9. *Ibid.,* 182.

stand the novel whose title is taken from it: "She strikes me as a person who is begging off from full knowledge—who has struck a truce with painful truth, and is trying awhile the experiment of living with closed eyes" (*CLO*, 3). The context of this is young Longmore's letter, which explains the unhappy Madame de Mauves to her friend. Just before the lines of the epigraph, Longmore writes, "She believed her husband was a hero of rose-colored romance, and he turns out to be not even a hero of very sad-colored reality. For some time now she has been sounding her mistake, but I don't believe she has touched the bottom of it yet." Then, after the lines of the epigraph, he goes on, "In the dark she tries to see again the gilding on her idol" (III, 162). But if the plot of Brookner's novel is, as I maintain, based on *The Portrait of a Lady*, the question arises why Brookner begins with a quotation from "Madame de Mauves." There is the obvious answer that the short story is a forerunner of *The Portrait of a Lady*, with many things taking place in it that will be completely developed seven years later in the novel. But there is also the secondary consideration that the style in which Brookner is writing comes very close to that of "Madame de Mauves," insofar as both involve a reliance on exposition over dialogue. In each the chief character has a dream embodying the frustrations of waking life. In James's novella, Euphemia de Mauves eludes Longmore in his dream, just as Freddie eludes Harriet in *A Closed Eye*.

The best clue to the linkage between *A Closed Eye* and *The Portrait of a Lady* lies in the first name, Merle, of Mrs. Blakemore, the mother of Harriet, Brookner's heroine. Harriet mentions early in the story that Merle means "blackbird" and that her mother is "adept at keeping secrets" (*CLO*, 202). Mr. Latif, their landlord and benefactor, is the true father of Harriet, supposedly the daughter of Merle and Hugh, and Merle and Mr. Latif, along with Hugh, have married her off to Freddie Lytton, Hugh's rich army chum. Now, Merle is an unusual name, but it occurs in *The Portrait of a Lady*, where Madame Serena Merle, with Osmond, tries unsuccessfully to marry off Pansy, their bastard daughter, an innocent convent-bred girl, to Lord Warburton through the offices of Isabel Archer. Brookner appears to have set herself the task of writing a novel in which a latter-day Pansy gets married to the modern equivalent of Warburton. Like James's Pansy, Harriet, although not convent-bred, has been told nothing about life. She has spent her years in the back room of her mother's dress shop. Like Pansy, too, she has a physical disadvantage—a facial birthmark, as against Pansy's below-average height.

In order to see how this plot is rewritten, it is necessary to read between the lines. It seems that Mr. Latif, upon Harriet's marriage, gives Merle and her husband a sum of money vast enough to procure them an elegant flat in Brighton. This comes out, however, only by piecing together such seemingly irrelevant details as that Mr. Latif comes to the shop often because he is sorry that Harriet must do "her lessons at the back of the shop, with only the *impotent* father for company, for so he thought of him. It was perhaps pity for Harriet (or was it for Merle, who accepted his embraces?) that kept him from raising the rent" (*CLO*, 19; italics mine). There are occasional innocent-sounding references to Mr. Latif's putting his hand on Merle's arm or on her breast. Only at a second reading, which Brookner, in another sign of imitating James's fictional strategy, seems to force the reader into, do these clues fit together.

Near the beginning of the novel, Hugh presents his nominal daughter with a "doughnut on a cracked plate" (*CLO*, 17) — damaged in the way Madame Merle believes herself to be: "I've been shockingly chipped and cracked. I do very well for service yet, because I've been cleverly mended" (*PO*, 166).

The chief axis of the plot of this modern version of *The Portrait of a Lady* is Merle, who does get her daughter married off to somebody rich, though to a man who resembles Sidney Traffle of James's late story "Mora Montravers" more than Osmond, for like Sidney, Freddie Lytton spends his time in art galleries — liking "Dutch pictures . . . best" (*CLO*, 209) — rather than producing, as Osmond, who is a draftsman as well as a collector, does. The real counterpart to Osmond, once the screen is penetrated, turns out to be Mr. Latif.

Harriet eventually bears a daughter, Imogen. Brookner's imagination confects for her a child who is exactly her opposite — beautiful, successful, and cruel. Imogen has the "life force," like both Madame Merle and Merle Blakemore. She is Harriet's greatest illusion, for the child turns out to repudiate her parents, to think only of money, and to be corrupt. Her baseness is communicated in a few lines at the end of the book in which Lizzie, the child of Harriet's glamorous friends but temperamentally close to Harriet's recessive personality, recalls helping Imogen when she arrived at her apartment with "chattering teeth, the odour of blood. . . . So much blood, which she had cleaned" (*CLO*, 261). Something criminal had occurred: an illegal abortion or possibly a murder.

Brookner seems to have learned certain narrative techniques from her lifelong assimilation of James, among them the placing of clues capable of revealing the subtext of a novel on a rereading. In disclosing a Jamesian subtext, Brooker is pointing her book at the reader versed in the Master, but she does not lose sight of the general reader, who can discern a consistent and satisfying pattern apart from understanding the subtext. Her heroine in *A Closed Eye* begs off from a full knowledge of life, but Brookner herself never shirks unpleasant aspects. Her eyes are always open to reality, never refusing to respond to the multiform world.

Woody Allen's *Husbands and Wives*

Countless young women can think of their goals and situations by reference to Isabel Archer. Accordingly, the effect of *The Portrait of a Lady* seems only to mount as the century moves on, particularly in novels by women. Yet one man, the imaginative parodist and filmmaker Woody Allen (1935–), spotted in James's novel an irresistible opportunity for a cinematic moment of great wit. In the film *Husbands and Wives*, which he produced and directed in 1992 and in which he performed, Professor Gabe Roth, enamored of a young student, kisses her at her twenty-first birthday party in a kitchen on East End Avenue, on New York's Upper East Side. Coinciding with the kiss is a storm's shaft of bright lightning over the East River. In the New York Edition of *The Portrait of a Lady*, Caspar's kiss is "like white lightning, a flash that spread, and spread again, and stayed. . . . So had she heard of those wrecked and under water following a train of images before they sink. But when darkness returned she was free" (NYE, IV, 436). As Isabel rejects Caspar despite his ability to stir her sexually, so Gabe returns from the enchantment and overwhelming erotic act of that kiss free of it and its dangers. Allen has transferred the consciousness of James's heroine to a twentieth-century male professor with strong neurotic tendencies. It is a mark of comedic genius to set a strictly Manhattan type upon the cultural deposits of the work of literature his contemporaries most value, or at least find most serviceable for their creative ends. Is there a hint in the name Gabe Roth? Gabe is the hero of Philip Roth's *Letting Go* who lends his copy of *The Portrait of a Lady* to his friend Paul Herz.

Allen conducted ten years of intense literary self-education during the 1960s. According to Adam Gopnik, the "outward sign" of this "was all the jokes he made about it. One after another of the classics of modernism came up for inspection, got passed through the prism of his special gift, and came out transformed." Hemingway, Kafka, Camus, Kierkegaard, and Bellow were among the writers he parodied, seemingly "always at ease in the comic limbo between high art and Manhattan reality."[10] If Allen never did a literary parody of Henry James, he made up for the omission in his brilliant cinematic one-liner. Gopnik wrote, "The concrete realities in Woody's writing are so concrete that they are not just funny; they evoke a world."[11] Allen goes beyond this in the simultaneous kiss and lightning bolt, where a concrete cinematic act of barely a minute's duration lays open the whole world of *The Portrait of a Lady*. In all the erotic acts narrated since *The Aeneid*, a kiss like lightning occurs only in James's metaphor and Woody Allen's concretization of it in film.

Carol De Chellis Hill's *Henry James' Midnight Song*

Carol Hill's *Henry James' Midnight Song*, of 1993, brings only one work of James's fiction into the partylike ambience of her cosmopolitan crew of geniuses—James, Wharton, Freud, Jung, and company—and that is *The Portrait of a Lady*. In Hill's novel, one of the banker's children, Cecily Main, wants to be a character of literature, like Isabel. She is convinced that only by being "written" will she feel she is really alive: "The only way to be alive [is] to be a character." The literary character most alive to her is Isabel. Cecily chides James for sending "Isabel back to Rome and Mr. Osmond."[12] She desires, by becoming Isabel Archer, not only to turn her own fate around but also to change the course of events in *The Portrait of a Lady*. Somehow we are grateful that Hill did not allow her to do this—that there is at least this limitation on the refashioning of the events the assembled characters engage in. But Cecily's preoccupation with Isabel Archer underscores the continuing hold this character's personality and perplexities have on women. In *The Portrait of a Lady*, James took up the cudgels for the spirited women of the 1880s whose misconceptions concerning deceptive males exposed them to disappointment and put them into destructive hands—gifted women who realized their mistake after it was too late. It is a cautionary tale in the wake of *The Feminine Mystique*, but by making the

---

10. Adam Gopnik, "The Outsider," *New Yorker*, October 25, 1993, pp. 86, 89.
11. *Ibid.*, 89.
12. Carol De Chellis Hill, *Henry James' Midnight Song* (New York, 1993), 86.

novel the focus of young girls of the fin de siècle, a generation after Isabel Archer, Hill exhibits how its relevance has remained steady over the decades.

Bernardo Bertolucci's *Stealing Beauty*

The movie *Stealing Beauty*, on which Bernardo Bertolucci was at work in Tuscany as I wrote this section, is, according to a reviewer, a "Jamesian tale of a younger American girl who comes to Europe seeking answers." Although the idea was Bertolucci's, Susan Minot wrote the script. The story concerns nineteen-year-old Lucy, who visits for a week with an English expatriate family, friends of her dead mother's, in Tuscany. Despite many threads, the story is reputed to remain simple, a "kind of 1990's film version of a Henry James novel. 'Stealing Beauty' centers around what man Lucy will choose. Mr. Bertolucci calls her 'an Isabel Archer in Tuscany, a young American woman who is both very strong and very vulnerable.'"[13] The legacy of James's novel casts its shadow over what will undoubtedly be a very postmodern and very Italian film even though Minot, a descendant of New England Brahmins, is the author of *Folly*, a Jamesian novel in which *The Bostonians* and other works by James appear.

Jane Campion's Feminist *The Portrait of a Lady*

An article in a fashion journal in 1988, "Jamesian Dressing," quoted a young designer of such clothing, Severine Perraudin, as saying, "Isabel, in *The Portrait of a Lady*, could be a woman of our time. What I want to capture is the spirit of contradiction found in all of James's women, to bring it into my clothes—the modesty mingled with seduction."[14]

This view of Isabel as being sexually aware was fully developed in 1996 in Joan Campion's film *The Portrait of a Lady*. On the whole, Campion's film shows a return to James's text from postmodern transformation, though the Australian director has expressed the text in feminist, as well as Freudian, terms. What the development of Isabel's character in the film implies is her overcoming a fear of overt sexuality. Campion (1935?–) conspicuously

---

13.   Celestine Bohlen, "Wine and Women in Tuscany," *New York Times*, August 27, 1995, Arts and Leisure Sec., p. 10.
14.   See Jean Bond Rafferty, "Jamesian Dressing," *Elle* (September, 1988).

did not accede to James's limit of a single kiss. His revision of the text in 1908 for the New York Edition brought Isabel into the twentieth century and made her part of James himself at that late stage of his life. Campion remade Isabel into a heroine typical of the end of the century. Her Isabel is at first tethered to her nineteenth-century history but in the end overcomes her inhibitions. Wherever the original novel gives Campion an inch, she takes an ell.

Early on, Isabel is ready to be physically embraced and, in one of her fantasies, she imagines that her three suitors—Lord Warburton, Ralph Touchett, her consumptive cousin, and Caspar Goodwood, her American friend—are fondling and caressing her simultaneously, which she likes. She responds to Gilbert Osmond not chiefly because of his exquisite taste but because of his mesmeric physical power, which he wields over her as he does over his former mistress, Serina Merle, and in the film, over his very sexually developed and surprisingly tall daughter, Pansy. In the novel, Pansy is so short as to reduce her chances for a decent marriage, in her father's eyes. But Campion turns her into a nubile, full-sized charmer in order to emphasize the erotic relation Osmond has with his three women— Serina, Isabel, even his daughter.

John Malkovich, who plays Osmond, had success as Valmont in *Les Liaisons dangereuses*, and his sexual proclivities here continue to be carefully based on the Marquis de Sade. Campion's Osmond abuses Isabel cruelly and sadistically. James depicted Osmond's egotistic nature by more subtle character traits, but an audience in 1996 would have felt cheated without physical violence. The imprisonment—personal, physical, and moral— that Osmond's manipulative behavior constitutes is iconified by the spatial constriction of the film, in which there is only a rare use of vistas or views of spatial depth, with the spectator hemmed in by the front planes of the space.

Isabel's repressed desires are at the core of most of the events that Campion depicts. At the beginning of Isabel's sojourn in Europe, she is beset by her unconscious desires for sensual and sexual fulfillment, and her response to the advances of her suitors is both attraction and puritanical repulsion. But after a few years of marriage, her desire for Osmond's caresses is redirected by his sadism, for it becomes clear that his passions seek to punish her physically rather than satisfy her awakened sexuality. It is kissing with others that she now wants, and she gets what she wants with remarkable frequency, culminating in the kisses on Ralph's deathbed, which she initiates. The climax of James's novel lies in the reaction of Isabel to the single passionate kiss of Goodwood. In Campion's film, that kiss is not Goodwood's but is Isabel's voluntary and passionate act. Fully released from her inhibitions, she takes the sexual initiative. The end of the novel has Isabel remembering her duty and returning to Osmond, presumably to watch over Pansy's future; the film's ending is more open. In retreating to the Garden Court House after kissing Goodwood, she turns around to face us and him. The intimation is that it will not be too long before Henrietta Stackpole's prediction "just you wait" comes true.

Campion is faithful to James in her own fashion. In casting Nicole Kidman as Isabel, Campion takes Minny Temple, James's blue-eyed, sprightly cousin, as the model for the heroine, and the viewer seems to see her in her very life. If James could in 1908 make *The Portrait of a Lady* of 1881 into a novel about a heroine who is quite different in her responses to sex and life than the earlier Isabel Archer, Campion is only following in his footsteps with her Isabel on the brink of the twenty-first century.

Isabel as Lambert Strether: Diane Johnson's *Le Divorce*

"I suppose because I went to film school, I think of my story as a sort of film," Isabel Walker says in the first line of *Le Divorce,* of 1997, by Diane Johnson (1934–). This is a West Coast Isabel, from southern California, who has come to Paris on a mission very much like Lambert Strether's in *The Ambassadors:* to rescue her stepsister, Roxeanne, from a bad marriage.

The book's epigraph, a quotation from a letter James sent William Dean Howells, primes the reader to expect some relationship between the novel and James. In the letter, James compares Howells to Zola but states, "You have a wholly different consciousness. You see a totally different side of a different race. Man isn't at all one, after all—it takes so much of him to be American, to be French, etc." The import of this would be more evident if Johnson had continued her quotation: "The only thing is to take them and what they do and to allow them absolutely and utterly their conditions. This alone, for the taster, secures freedom of enjoyment" (*L,* III, 282; the date of the letter should be May 27, 1890). This thought more or less sums up *Le Divorce.*

Isabel Walker is, at both the beginning and the end of the book, reminiscent of Isabel Archer. One of her American friends in Paris, Janet Hutchinson, fills Madame Merle's role by discussing how French women dress, and the word *merles* appears on the last page of the volume: "Little teeny birds plunged into pots of foie gras . . . are they called greves? Grebes? Merles?" (*LD*, 309). Crockery looms big in *The Portrait of a Lady*, with Mr. Touchett opening the action with his own peculiar cup and saucer, Madame Merle viewing herself as a badly cracked cup, and Rosier collecting china figurines. In *Le Divorce*, Mrs. Pace, the expatriate writer, talks about crockery, a tureen of value gets stolen, and Isabel wants to buy one for her elderly lover.

Johnson's employment of a supposed painting by Georges de La Tour of Saint Ursula—ironically, here, the saint of virgins—borrows from the Jamesian technique of textual clarification by way of pictures, as in the comparison of Ralph Touchett to a Watteau (or a Lancret for the New York Edition) and of Chad Newsome to Titian's *Portrait of a Young Man with a Glove*.

Johnson's Isabel is called Isabel Walker purposefully, for nobody pays much attention to her as a young woman and everyone uses her to walk dogs and children. The villain uses her to try to keep the police from his tracks, for this is a murder story and Charles-Henri, Roxy's unfaithful young husband, has been murdered by the husband of his mistress.

There is a vigil in Johnson's novel (*LD*, 169)—by Isabel when her sister is hospitalized after an attempted suicide—but it is not the center of the book the way the vigil in *The Portrait of a Lady* is. Although it takes place at noon—an odd time for a hospital vigil—it has an effect on Isabel Walker that is pretty much the same as that of Isabel Archer on herself: she feels about people that she cannot "know them, nor they me, and we were all alone" (*LD*, 184).

Not only is Isabel's objective in going to Paris similar to Strether's but the milieu of expatriate Americans and a French family in which she finds herself is similar to what is in *The Ambassadors*, as well. Strether is enamored of Marie de Vionnet, and Isabel Walker takes on some of the qualities of Marie, especially in her awareness that she is "without protection. I would be discarded. I knew that" (*LD*, 211). She is in that regard less innocent than Isabel Archer. She knows the score, and unlike James's virginal heroine, she comes to Europe with carnal knowledge but no acquaintance with love. That she has to attain through Edgar, her elderly lover, a distinguished Frenchman with a career as a statesman and a television personality—although, like Strether, she will gain nothing for herself at the end. Every indication is that she will continue to be used through the rest of her life. When Edgar's wife says that the American girl is a "famous type, of fearless ingenuity," she sees something in Isabel that probably is not there.

In *Le Divorce*, there are at least three references to the novels of James. One of Isabel's friends, Janet, is a "reminder of former days when American girls with money or style came over here and hunted for European husbands, counts or Rothschilds, as in the novels of Henry James" (*LD*, 13). Later, Roxy thinks how her parents, Chester and Margreeve, have "been intimating that [she has] fallen into the hands of impoverished European fortune hunters, like a victim out of Henry James" (*LD*, 228).

Before the book ends, Isabel records that she has "drawn a moral the opposite of the one intended" and is "on the wrong side, as in the novels of Henry James, which Mrs. Pace has suggested I read" (*LD*, 305).

Johnson's novel concludes with Isabel either about to follow Edgar, which would flout social strictures, or about to become the mistress of another cabinet minister, which is more likely. Like Strether, she comes away from Paris with "nothing for myself" except the knowledge that love can be a disturbing experience. *Le Divorce*, in the manner of *The Portrait of a Lady*, is, in James's phrase, "of its very nature an 'ado,' an ado about something" (*AN*, 48). Although James wrote that his Isabel "should be herself complex" (*AN*, 52), Isabel Walker is only an intelligent but rather simple-minded, very sexually adventurous, perhaps "presumptuous," girl.

James's Isabel "affronts her destiny," but Isabel Walker speaks of "controlling my destiny." The person who is aware of affronting destiny is Edgar, who says on television, "At one time I thought my destiny would be as a statesman" (*LD*, 251). He decides to go to Zagreb, which means that the affair with Isabel is ended. Isabel recognizes, "I was immediately doomed" (*LD*, 252). Isabel Archer learns the same thing, and Marie de Vionnet always knows it. Edgar's consanguinity with Gilbert Osmond and Chad Newsome is apparent.

Roxy, who, pregnant with her second child and abandoned by her young husband, attempts suicide but fails, emerges the more triumphant of the two sisters. Roxeanne and Chad are the two characters who have successful careers not only in the novels but presumably after the novels close.

Isabel Walker and Strether alike attempt to rescue family members who need no rescuing. Instead they are themselves caught off guard by what France says to them. But at bottom Isabel Walker is another Isabel Archer, who is disillusioned by her romance with an older civilization.

James and Juvenilia: Barbara Ware Holmes's *Letters to Julia*

It is not often that a distinguished author of literature directed to adults reaches a status where it is thought essential that children be aware of him. This has happened to Shakespeare, and in Charles Lamb and Mary Lamb's *Tales from Shakespeare* children of preteen years can get to know the great Elizabethan dramatist. It has now happened to James as well, in Barbara Ware Holmes's *Letters to Julia,* for readers upward of twelve years old. *The Portrait of a Lady* is so in the foreground of literary prefigurations of the modern woman that even a novel directed to a young readership—which once had to content itself with Nancy Drew mysteries—revolves around a heroine who consciously models herself on Isabel Archer and attempts to define her individuality against an environment that can ultimately doom her. As Holmes (1945–) has put it, her book is "concerned with what happens to the passionate and intellectually curious young mind when it is enforced to awaken in an environment where there is little to nourish or reflect it back—in particular, an imaginative and artistically gifted young woman who longs for someone to affirm that her insights and talents will have value in the world at large, when they so clearly do not at home."[15]

In *Letters to Julia,* Liz Beech, an aspiring young writer fifteen years old, conducts a correspondence with Julia, an editor at Springtime Press, which publishes Books for Young Readers. The novel adroitly orchestrates not just the correspondence between the editor and the high-school student but also the student's journal and her first novel as it is written chapter by chapter. Isabel Archer is appealed to both as a spur to writing and as an example of moral principles. Holmes has explained the part that *The Portrait of a Lady* has in her novel's structure: "When I set my character to reading, I handed her Isabel Archer, a heroine whose fine and hungry intellect struggled to blossom in an age when the greatest use of the female mind was judged to be the appending of it to a man's. The coming of age in a per-

---

15.   Barbara Ware Holmes to Adeline R. Tintner, February 7, 1997.

son endowed with the isolated perceptions of an artist is a story which holds at its core the making of true triumph or tragedy."[16]

Julia writes to Liz of the "spunky Miss Archer" and marvels that Liz, at her age, can master a book as difficult as *The Portrait of a Lady* (*LJ*, 54). The word *destiny*, which James uses in connection with Isabel in his preface, crops up more than once, and Liz writes, particularly in her journal entries, about meeting *her* destiny. The problems facing Liz appear to relate to those of Isabel Archer, and when one of her friends tells her that trying to be a writer is "better than drifting" (*LJ*, 104), there is the echo of Henrietta Stackpole's figure of speech for describing Isabel's life (*PO*, 153). As Liz reads *The Portrait of a Lady* for an English class, she becomes angry with James for allowing Isabel to marry Osmond. But she eventually realizes that he is deliberately trying to "shock and make us think" (*LJ*, 105). She decides to write her class paper on the flower imagery in James's novel. She is also impressed by the way the book begins (*LJ*, 219) and notices that "everywhere you look there are stories without endings" (*LJ*, 220). *The Portrait of a Lady* is mentioned some seventeen times in *Letters to Julia*. Liz goes on to collect "sentences about Isabel Archer that sound like me. The last one was the best one. The best one is 'her imagination was by habit ridiculously active; when the door was not open it jumped out of the window'" (*LJ*, 58). Thinking this "a wonderful image" (*LJ*, 59), Liz likes to repeat it as describing her own imagination.

Although Liz's family is dysfunctional, to say the least, she gradually begins to understand and accept it through her relationship with Julia. The artful introduction of a crisis in the editor's life, changing her from just a mentor to, besides, a fellow sufferer, shows Holmes to be an experienced writer, capable of eliciting the complexity of all her characters. Ultimately, that includes Liz's father and mother. Both student and mentor surmount their difficulties by becoming serious writers—even if one is still in her apprenticeship. Julia's loss of her parents and her job and the threat of the loss of her family home in Virginia bring on a nervous breakdown, but her recourse is to write about her experiences. Liz learns to be a writer not only by gaining a perspective on her troubled family but also by observing the more tragic events in Julia's life. Isabel Archer is portrayed as having the potential for an artist's career without being able to achieve that career. Liz,

16. *Ibid.*

from her intelligent reading of James and from her intimacy with a mature mind, is able to avoid Isabel's defeat. What she learns from Isabel's accommodation to her predicament and to her mistaken choice in marriage is that finding oneself in a fix requires the courage to adjust to it with resourcefulness rather than resignation. She learns to adapt to her parents' peculiarities while convincing them that higher education will be her salvation, preparing her for a writer's career.

Two Gay Novels Invoke Isabel Archer:
Lev Raphael's *Let's Get Criminal* and Edmund White's
The Farewell Symphony

Isabel Archer is borrowed as a model in two recent gay novels. The first, by Lev Raphael, is *Let's Get Criminal* (1996). It is an academic mystery that shows us a narrator whose lover, Stefan, had a secret affair years earlier with a murdered assistant professor of Canadian literature at the university where they all taught. When the narrator learns about this affair, he begins "to feel like Isabel Archer in *The Portrait of a Lady,* where she finally realizes what her husband is like" (*LGC,* 41). This analogy does not surprise the reader, since the narrator's specialty is Henry James and Edith Wharton (*LGC,* 2). He repeats this comparison to his cousin Sharon when he tells her that he "had been feeling like Isabel Archer in *The Portrait of a Lady*" (*LGC,* 45), reminding the reader of the similarity between Stefan and Gilbert Osmond. Sharon suggests that a better model for himself than Isabel would be "Alexis on *Dynasty*" (*LGC,* 45).

On the heels of this mystery comes Edmund White's *The Farewell Symphony* (1997), in which the narrator, a writer, reports to the reader in specific detail his sexual exploits, as well as his friendships, with certain barely disguised, well-known poets, critics, and translators. Isabel Archer appears here not as an analogic figure for the narrator directly but for a character in one of his novels with whom he identifies himself. Alyx, the character, is "compounded" of two girls he actually knew "and Henry James's Isabel Archer" (*FS,* 155). Because of an emotional crisis she experiences with a gay man and woman "who exalt independence," Alyx "decides she must marry but chooses unwisely—the handsome, cruel, gold-digging Osmond" (*FS,* 155). The next reminder of James's novel occurs when the narrator, on his first trip to Venice, mentions that he sees "the house where

James finished *Portrait of a Lady*" (*FS*, 336), information he probably obtained from Leon Edel's *Henry James: The Conquest of London* (*CL*, 438).

The attraction of these two gay novelists to James's novel might be explained by their sensitivity to the tragedy of Isabel's choice of a life partner as well as their own identification with Isabel herself. They also might be acknowledging a connection between their own homosexuality and James's homoeroticism, for he, in his revised 1907 *The Portrait of a Lady*, seems also to have identified himself with Isabel.[17]

17.   See my "In the Dusky, Crowded, Heterogeneous Book-Shop of the Mind: The Iconography of *The Portrait of a Lady*," *Henry James Review*, VII (1986), 156.

12

THE AMBASSADORS

Whether writers agree or not with James that *The Ambassadors* is the "best 'all round' of my productions" (*FW,* 1304), at least seven have paid him the tribute of borrowing extensively from the work, which represents the mid-age crisis of a civilized man. The seven, running from James Thurber to James McCourt, do not include such writers as Hemingway in *The Sun Also Rises* and Fitzgerald in "Babylon Revisited" (see above, pp. 183–84, 175–76), who also make references to it.

Louis Auchincloss' Two *Ambassadors*

The first of Louis Auchincloss' borrowings from *The Ambassadors* is in a short story in the 1950 collection *The Injustice Collectors.* There he adapts the main plot of James's novel in a tale called "The Ambassadress." James's Sarah Pocock becomes in Auchincloss' story the hero's sister, Edith McLean, and Jim Pocock becomes her husband George. They have come over from the United Sates to Paris to rescue the hero, Tony, Auchincloss' Chad Newsome, from the arms of a twice-married and twice-divorced beautiful woman with whom he has been dallying on the Lido in Venice. Edith's strategy for turning Tony off Mrs. Gwladys Kane, the divorcée, and having him marry her husband's niece is much cleverer than Sarah Po-cock's approach. Edith chooses to become an enthusiastic friend of Mrs.

Kane, which infuriates Tony more than anything else. In his anger, he gets drunk with Diana, the niece and a counterpart to Mamie Pocock, Jim Pocock's niece. Only at the end is it patent that this has all been Edith's design to get him to play into her hands. In the retelling of the story of Chad Newsome and the Pococks, the ambassadors from Woollett, Massachusetts, who take over from Lambert Strether when he is unable to hate Madame de Vionnet, Tony is the exponent of "live all you can," Strether's advice to Little Bilham in Gloriani's garden. Tony says, "I affirm life!"[1] When Tony says to Gwladys, "You sound like a character in a Henry James novel,"[2] Auchincloss makes sure we do not miss the point.

The second of Auchincloss' borrowings from *The Ambassadors* is *The Rector of Justin*, of 1964, a novel recording the life of Mr. Prescott, the headmaster of Justin Martyr, a boys' preparatory school in New England. Mrs. Prescott is consigned to a wheelchair, and a character recounts in his journal, "When I mentioned Henry James she stopped me. 'You know he dictated the later novels . . . but of course it's not odd at all. He always wanted to be read aloud, and how could he know how it would sound unless he thought aloud?'" The journal keeper, Brian, reads to her then from *The Ambassadors*, "one other soul in this dark male world that cares about beautiful things" (*REJ*, 15–16).

Mr. Prescott says about *The Ambassadors*, "It has all that is gorgeous in the master, all that is sublime. And all that is ridiculous." Mrs. Prescott asks, "What do you mean, ridiculous?" and her husband replies, "Simply that it has nothing whatever to do with life on this poor planet of ours." To her rejoinder, "It has a great deal to do with *my* life," he queries, "Do you see yourself, my dear, as a Lambert Strether?" She is insistent. "Certainly I do! . . . Strether didn't know until he saw Paris that he'd wasted his life. Well, it took more than Paris to teach me that. It took this abominable wheelchair!" (*REJ*, 19).

Mr. Prescott explains to Brian, "My wife . . . takes James too seriously. . . . For every three parts genius he is one part ass." He continues, "Strether imbibes Paris through every pore. He is revived and rejuvenated. Yet what spoils it all for him? The simple fact that Chad Newsome . . . turns out to have a French mistress." Mrs. Prescott says, "His vision will sustain him. His vision of Paris. Of life!" (*REJ*, 20).

1. Louis Auchincloss, *The Injustice Collectors* (Boston, 1950), 167.
2. *Ibid.*, 173.

Another character, Horace Havistock, knew James, and he tells Brian that there are several letters "to me in it" (*REJ*, 51), meaning the correspondence edited by Lubbock. The references to *The Ambassadors* are picked up again when Mr. Prescott lies dying. That ties the end of the novel to its beginning: "November 1. Mrs. Prescott surprised me today by asking me to skip to the great chapter in Gloriani's studio where Strether warns Little Bilham not to waste his life as he has done" (*REJ*, 17).

In the most recent years, Auchincloss has written fewer novels and has concentrated on groups of short stories collected under a unifying theme and on literary essays. In *The Style's the Man*: *Reflections on Proust, Fitzgerald, Wharton, Vidal, and Others*, a volume published in 1994, one essay, "Portrait of the Artist as Strether," centers on James. Auchincloss picks up Strether's life after the novel ends. Pointing out that in the *Notebooks*, James addresses his muse with passion, as he never does any real person in his correspondence (*SM*, 84), and that he had only one nonmelodramatic plot, *The Ambassadors*, "where the drama is largely confined to the mind of the reflector of the action: Strether," Auchincloss ventures that "Strether, in short, might be the one comment that [James] felt should be made about his own life as a writer." For "Strether is like James in many ways." He is a passive man who accepts the mission given him by a strong woman, but in Paris he discovers "all that he has missed in the first fifty-five years of his existence. . . . He is redeemed; he lives at last, but as an artist lives, in his own enlightenment." It is not that the affairs of other human beings "are not important, but . . . they do not really want him to be concerned with their affairs" (*SM*, 85). Chad will do what he wants in any case, and "in the meantime Strether has discovered what life — or at least his own life — is all about" (*SM*, 86). From this point Auchincloss continues and completes *The Ambassadors* with a focus on Strether's future. In a page and a quarter he writes a virtual prospectus for a sequel to *The Ambassadors*:

Strether in the end will return to Woollett, Massachusetts, but he will have no more influence on the lives of his friends there than he has had on those of his friends in Paris. Chad will probably marry Mamie Pocock; in any event, he will marry someone very like her. Mrs. Newsome, Chad's mother, will not become Mrs. Strether, but her life will be the same as it was before she considered that alternative. . . . And in Paris Madame de Vionnet will be *triste* for a while over the loss of Chad, but she will be French and realistic and adaptable. Poor Maria Gostrey will be the only person to have been permanently affected by Strether, for she has loved him, but she, as James himself once said, is only a *ficelle*—a piece of string to hold the plot together—and how sorely can a *ficelle* suffer? I seem almost to make something out of the fact that only a *ficelle*, i.e., not a real person, could fall in love with James-Strether.

So the only person whose life *will* be changed is Strether himself. He will be a different man, a man with a vision, for his experience has turned him into an artist—after all, he has expressed to himself the whole novel that we have read—and as an artist he will stand apart from the others in a loneliness that presumably has its own compensating ecstasy.

Strether's vision came when he was fifty-five; James's own must have happened much earlier. . . . But in composing his plan for *The Ambassadors* he could still have identified himself with the nonwriting Strether, musing on what might have been his fate in Woollett, possessed of an artist's imagination but of no art. (*SM*, 86–87)

Auchincloss saw the envisioned sequel as double edged—as working out the future Auchincloss prophesied for Strether but also as spelling out James's biography of himself, in Strether's character.

The Ambassadors with "a Difference of Design": W. M. Spackman's Version

W. M. Spackman (1905–1990), a professor of the classics who had dosed himself heavily on James through the years, wrote a new version of *The Ambassadors* in 1983 entitled *A Difference of Design*. The names of the characters are the same as those in James's novel with only slight alterations. Maria Gostrey becomes Maria Godfrey, Chad Newsome becomes Chad Newman, and Strether becomes Sather. Spackman has above all taken the line "live all you can" to mean that every one of his characters must get into bed as often as possible and stay there as long as possible with as many consenting mates as possible.

The story line is pretty much the same as in *The Ambassadors* except that most of the conversations that take place among characters seated in chairs in James's novel take place lying in bed in Spackman's. Spackman writes as if Strether has decided to follow all the advice he has given to Little Bilham and is now living life to the hilt as late-twentieth-century society understands that. James's Strether resists the love of Maria Gostrey, as well as the overtures by Marie de Vionnet. Sather—the name combines *Strether* and *father*—has affairs with both. Strether, who finds it hard to accept the fact that people have affairs at all, has in Sather adjusted to the "difference in design" entailed by the last part of the twentieth century. Maria Godfrey has become much younger than her thirty-year-old original in James's novel and the Countess Fabienne—Marie de Vionnet updated—is no older. Moving Sather right into bed with Maria and, in the last scene, having him enchant a very willing Fabienne, who has had enough of Chad, Spackman parodies cleverly the style, conversations, and set scenes familiar from *The Ambassadors*. The home of the Newman family is in Iowa—Woollett, Massachusetts, today sounding too worldly-wise for Spackman's purpose. The family manufactures "couplings" (*DD*, 11), parts connecting two electrical circuits, important and lucrative necessities in modern industry. Couplings is also a pun on the chief activity of the novel, in which the personal "circuits" of Fabienne and Chad, Maria Godfrey and Sather, Maria Godfrey and Bingham (James's Little Bilham), and prospectively, Sather and Fabienne are joined.

Sather is an investor and financial adviser for Mrs. Newman, the strong-minded woman from Iowa who has sent him to investigate why her son Chad is remaining in Paris and to bring him home. Sather is not an editor of a literary journal like Strether, since that job is without prestige today, and a millionaire widow would probably not be inclined to rely on its holder to be her emissary. Spackman in effect did to Strether what James in "The Jolly Corner," published six years after *The Ambassadors* and after a return from his trip of 1904–1905 to the United States, did to his hero, Spencer Brydon, when he had him forgo a life of dilettantish musing in Europe to become a real estate tycoon. Sather is not nearly as out of things as Strether is. He is just temperamentally the same—a laconic, fifty-year-old widower of long standing who talks in a way that parodies Strether and who is having a midlife crisis. Beyond this, Spackman implements other authorial decisions of James's, but with a difference. His entire first chapter, like James's, is put into the consciousness of a single person, but because Spackman seems to feel that today's ideal consciousness is a woman's, the Countess Fabienne is the person. Even Sarah Pocock must conform to late-century mores. She is coupled with Waymarsh, who keeps his name from *The Ambassadors* but now travels with Mrs. Pocock as her live-in lover. The "improvement" Strether detects in Chad is transformed into Sather's "improvement" by his endless affairs with young girls: "Obviously, they improved *him*, what on earth else! It was women men learned manners from, wasn't it? And always has been; bedroom and drawing room both. So why *not* the more the better?"(*DD*, 92).

It is as if Spackman said, Okay, James thought *The Ambassadors* was the best 'all round' of his novels, but how do we rewrite it today, by what 'difference in design' can we make it an interesting novel for contemporary readers? He followed James's example of invoking a classic by which to measure the story he is writing. To Sather, who over an elegant meal talks about his mission to save Chad, Maria Godfrey says, "Oh dear, it sounds practically like a novel we had to wade through in American Lit, Henry James or somebody. Are you quite sure she's bad for him?" (*DD*, 51). Spackman seems not to have trusted the reader to see the parallel without help. His is a correction as well as a parody of its model, and through his idiosyncratic language, with its hyperbolic syntax, he needles James's late style with his own mannered prose.

A Japanese Version: Yasunari Kawabata's *The Sound of the Mountain*

The Sound of the Mountain, of 1970, by Yasunari Kawabata (1899–1972), does not involve a point-by-point transposition of *The Ambassadors* in the way of Spackman's novel but concentrates on the role of a middle-aged man, like Strether sent as an ambassador—in this case, to solve a family problem that often figures in Japanese fiction.[3] When Shingo, a sixty-two-year-old man with a wife, son, daughter, and two grandchildren, discovers that his son, Shuichi, has a mistress, Kinu, his secretary persuades him to intercede to get rid of her for the family's sake. Shingo's consciousness dominates the book, and his Strether-like innocence of life is stressed: "I am an aged man and I have not yet climbed Mount Fiji" (*SO*, 82). He feels that his closely circumscribed married life has deprived him of many experiences. When he arrives at Kinu's house, he thinks "the woman beautiful" (*SO*, 234). Shingo is affected, as Strether is, by the comeliness and distress of the woman his mission requires him to oppose. "As he got into a cab, Shingo wondered whether it might not be better to effect a reconciliation between Shuichi and the woman," and no more than Strether does he "like to think of the ineptness" with which he has faced the mistress of the young

---

3. Donald D. Stone is my authority for saying that the situation is recurrent in Japanese fiction.

man he is charged with rescuing (*SO*, 235). Shingo has dreams about embracing young girls, and he enjoys having a teenage geisha fall asleep in his arms. But like Strether, at the end he feels it is too late, and he says to his son, "There was something in the paper about old lotuses. Remember? Some ancient seeds that sent out shoots that finally bloomed" (*SO*, 252). The novel concludes with Kinu showing her great affection for Shingo and developing an interest in starting a shop with Shingo's divorced daughter, Fusako.

"Live All You Can" in Anita Brookner's *Fraud*

At first glance, Anita Brookner's *Fraud*, of 1992, seems to escape Henry James's influence. Anna Durrant, a "woman in middle years, living alone in apparently comfortable circumstances," has been "missing for some four months" (*FR*, 5). But, in a novel that begins and ends as a detective story, it is with the complicity of Henry James that Anna can put herself into a position to detect what is wrong with herself. Living in the shadow of her mother, a well-off widow, Anna is a victim of a "fraud . . . perpetrated on me by the expectations of others" (*FR*, 221). Only at the end of her saga, when she reveals that she has been living in Paris, does it become apparent that there is a relevance to her dreary life and her unfruitful relations with her egotistical associates in a thought Mrs. Marsh, an octogenarian, has in reflecting about her divorced daughter, that "being young enough was a different matter. Live all you can, she thought. Dear Henry James" (*FR*, 31). For it is Paris that leads Anna to realize what her position in life has been. How the atmosphere of Paris discloses truth is broached at Gloriani's garden party in *The Ambassadors*, just before Strether admonishes Little Bilham to "live all you can." There, Little Bilham, Miss Barrace, and Strether are conversing, and Miss Barrace says, "We're all looking at each other — and in the light of Paris one sees what things resemble. That's what the light of Paris seems always to show. It's the fault of the light of Paris — dear old light! . . . Everything, every one shows." Strether counters, "But for what they really are?" He presses, "Does Madame de Vionnet do that? I mean really show for what she is?" (*AM*, 133–34). Anna's discovery of what she really is accords with this conception of how Paris dissipates a fraudulent view of life and reveals real identities.

There are also two references to art in *Fraud* that recall James's citing of museum masterpieces. In Paris, Anna visits the Louvre and looks at the many portraits by Ingres. Anna gives us the impression of finding that painter to express well the feeling of frustration and limitations that dogs her life. In the Borghese Gallery, in Rome, Dr. Halliday thinks of Titian's *Sacred and Profane Love*. Dr. Halliday is a masculine correlate of Anna in his frustrations, and the inference is that he will have a relationship with her after the novel is over. As if reshuffling the cards taken from James's deck, Brookner has devised a happy ending for the seemingly doomed personalities who coexist in her novel. Like other novelists of the 1980s and 1990s, she reassembles things learned from James's fiction to illuminate behavior associated with the problems of a woman alone today.

In both *Fraud* and the novel before it, *A Closed Eye*, of 1991, Brookner has a hidden strategy in handling Jamesian icons. She thus emulates James's way with hidden strategies, especially when he appropriated the writings of others. Her continued reference in some form to Jamesian precedents has become infinitely sophisticated; it is her subtlety in this that makes her novels, dealing so strictly with one kind of feminine personality and temperament, bearable and even absorbing to readers familiar with James. She follows the Master in arranging her own highly cultivated audience, which she can presume to be familiar with the works of literature and art that she injects into her narrative.

James Thurber's "A Call on Mrs. Forrester (After Rereading, in My Middle Years, Willa Cather's 'A Lost Lady' and Henry James' 'The Ambassadors')"

In technique, James Thurber's "A Call on Mrs. Forrester (After Rereading, in My Middle Years, Willa Cather's 'A Lost Lady' and Henry James' 'The Ambassadors')" differs from other borrowings from *The Ambassadors*. Although written in 1948, just after the Second World War, it possesses certain characteristics of the postmodern novel. Thurber (1894–1961) chose for his setting the small town in Nebraska where Willa Cather placed *A Lost Lady*. The first-person narrator adopts the voice of Cather's Neil Herbert, grown middle-aged. He was once in love with Marian Forrester but is disillusioned by her infidelities toward her husband. Caught in the rain outside her house as he comes to make another visit, he fantasizes what will happen when he confesses to her that he now loves Madame de Vionnet.

"I beg you to remember it was once said of Mme. de Vionnet that when she touched a thing, the ugliness, God knows how, went out of it," he would defend his beloved, but he could hear Marian sneering that "she lost her lover, for all her charm" (*AD*, 271).[4] At that point he would be impelled to stalk out of the house in anger but would by mistake end in the hall closet rather than outside the front door. Marian would look witheringly on this, a "calamity Mme. de Vionnet would ignore" (*AD*, 272). He concludes that he will "carry lilacs, one of these summers, to the house on the Boulevard Malesherbes, and take Mme. de Vionnet to a matinée of 'Louise,' have a white port with her at one of the little terraces at the quietest corner of the Parc Monceau. . . . Since, in the best Henry James tradition, I will get nothing out of this for myself, it ought to make up for something. I could do worse than spend my last summers serenely, sipping wine, clop-clopping around town, listening to good music, kissing a lady's hand at her door, going to bed early and getting a good night's sleep" (*AD*, 272–73).

In this charming literary invention drawing from novels written twenty years apart, the narrator's consciousness chooses James's gentle and aristocratic Parisian over Willa Cather's deteriorated midwesterner. As he waits outside Mrs. Forrester's house, he imagines the humiliating encounter ahead and realizes that he prefers the manners of Madame de Vionnet in 1903. Thurber's placement of himself within the sphere of two novels distinguishes his original short concoction as one of the first postmodern manipulations of literary characters in which the author deconstructs received sequences. Thurber's invention anticipated the flood of such manipulations thirty years later.

A Criminal Strether: Patricia Highsmith's *The Talented Mr. Ripley*

Patricia Highsmith (1921–1995), like Thurber, is a forerunner of the postmodern novelists of the 1980s and 1990s. Highsmith has widened the path for novelists to subvert James's original intentions by constructing their own fantasies on his foundation.

Highsmith wrote five novels based on the adventures of Tom Ripley, a charming and likable con man with whom the reader sympathizes yet who is enabled to live in his delightful style only by the money he has amassed from his remorseless murder of many men. He occupies a villa near Paris

---

4. This piece appeared first in the *New Yorker* of June 19, 1948.

and is married to a young, beautiful, and well-to-do woman who never asks too many questions. The first of the five novels, *The Talented Mr. Ripley,* of 1955, begins, like *The Ambassadors,* with the appointment by the parent of a son loitering in Europe of someone who knows the son to persuade him to return to the United States and enter the family business. In the first chapter, Mr. Herbert Greenleaf follows Tom into a New York bar and tries to engage him to go to Mongibello, a town south of Naples, with all expenses paid, in order to get Dickie, his son, to stop his amateur painting, leave his girl friend, and return to take his place in the business. Mr. Greenleaf has settled on Tom to undertake the mission because the young man has a slight prior acquaintance with Dickie. As Tom leaves Mr. Greenleaf's house, where over dinner they have clinched their arrangement, Mr. Greenleaf, "chuckling again," asks Tom if he has "read a certain book by Henry James." He answers, "I'm sorry to say I haven't, sir, not that one."[5] If the reader has not guessed which book that is, the answer is plain when Tom goes to the first-class library on the ship to inquire, "Have you Henry James' *The Ambassador?*" The novel is not there, but because he feels "he ought to read it," he tracks it down in the cabin-class library. A first-class passenger tells him, though, that he is "not allowed to take books from the cabin-class library,"[6] and that is the end of the signal to the reader to think of James's novel, even if Tom gets the title slightly wrong.

Beginning service as Mr. Greenleaf's ambassador, Tom gets into Dickie's good graces and wins him away from his girl friend. But then Tom decides to do away with him and take on his identity. He drowns him, makes a false will in his own favor that will ensure him a permanent income, and as he jumps from being Tom to impersonating Dickie and back again, he is forced to kill Freddie, Dickie's friend. Cleverly and deviously Tom avoids being suspected of killing the two men, and the reader is always on his side. In Tom there is a violent transmutation of a parental ambassador from someone who can feel satisfaction in "not, out of the whole affair, to have got anything for myself" (*AM,* 457) into someone who gets everything for himself. That includes a lovely villa in the country near Paris, priceless masterpieces of art, and a collection of music. Tom surely does "live all you can," and he is true to Strether's pronouncement that "it doesn't so much matter what you do in particular, so long as you have your life" (*AM,* 161).

5. Patricia Highsmith, *The Talented Mr. Ripley* (New York, 1955), 21.
6. *Ibid.,* 31.

According to Highsmith, Tom indeed has his life, a wonderful, beautiful life out of it. In rhythm with Tom, readers let their morality be co-opted by that of the hero. In the four remaining novels about Ripley, Tom goes on murdering his victims and charming the reader. Ripley as a morally perverted Strether anticipated what postmodern novelists of the 1980s and 1990s would do to James's characters, as well as to James as a figure. Romanesque sculptors used the remains of classical sculpture lying about them to create new art forms; among postmodern writers, the intact work of art is smashed and some of the pieces are assembled in a format decided on by the creator.

Hattie Jaques: James McCourt's Gay Novel *Time Remaining*

Surprising as it may seem, *The Ambassadors* occupies some ten pages of *Time Remaining,* the novel of 1993 by James McCourt (1941–) about gay life in New York City and the Hamptons. James's novel is the book Odette O'Doyle, the transvestite performance artist and onetime NYU literature student who is the hero of the book, reads, analyzes, and satirically puts into the context of his gay sensibility. McCourt's filtering of James's masterpiece through the gay imagination and culture is at once hilarious and supremely clever. Odette, "like every other ostentatiously educated American on a train in Europe," discusses James's novel with a European lady professor:

> I was actually reading—rereading—Henry James. *The Ambassadors* . . . I hadn't looked at it since N.Y.U., when and where—need I tell you—you weren't allowed to *open your mouth and say 'boo'* if you hadn't read it. It and at least a half dozen others, and unless you'd also taken—or, at any rate—audited Leon Edel's course. And had formed—or let's say *forged*—as a *direct consequence* of your reading an explication of the texts, a *point of view on adult life.* . . . And at N.Y.U. you couldn't get anybody to even show you his snapshots of the Amalfi coast or play you his Piaf records until you said something about poor old Hattie Jaques. (*TR,* 229)

He tells how he had *The Ambassadors* "in my lap . . . remembering the summer I took the Edel course: one novel per lecture for a month—hilarious. I wanted to do my paper on the so-called *little thing* that makes the fortune the sexpot we used to call Chapstick Nuisance lives on in sin on the

Rive Gauche—the commodity he's supposed to go back to Asshole, Mass., to oversee the manufacture of. . . . I decided it was toilet paper. Edel was not amused, so I did one on 'the Polish Joke as Paradigm of Reaction in *The Ambassadors*.'" He insists that "Lamebrain Stretcher, looking up . . . at his quarry's windows on the Boulevard Malesherbes was but a silhouette compared to Swann looking up in desperation at Odette's" (*TR*, 230). He feels Proust superior to James, "who for me is nothing much more than a desperado appealing mainly to adolescents and refugees who have only ever listened at doorways or peeked through keyholes . . . to go down-and-out with the gorgeous prematurely gray-streaked Chapstick into the Parisian night." He concedes, however, that "Hattie did concoct good stories, implemented in some very gay diction" (*TR*, 231).

Pitted against Odette's gay perception of *The Ambassadors* is the reaction of the professor on the train. Through her words, McCourt's respect for James shines clearly. Odette's opinions do not represent the author's. The woman professor insists that Hattie "knew—really *knew* about women, but Marcel Proust knew only, really, about duchesses." She says that James "understood women as *types*—which was all they were . . . permitted to be. . . . Exemplary types, cautionary types, types, to be sure, with many *facets*. . . . Marcel Proust . . . on the other hand understood them—women—as *personnages*" (*TR*, 232). The importance of James to McCourt, and to Odette, is evident in the amount of space devoted to the one literary work that this brilliantly satirical novel awash in the icons and parlance of the gay culture of the 1970s and 1980s canvasses.

Many authors today, from writers of serious literature to writers of detective stories, introduce homosexual characters, but few have given us the locutions of the gay culture that after existing for four decades has almost been destroyed by AIDS. Because of the death of so many of the characters in *Time Remaining*, the novel is as elegiac as it is satirical. The juxtaposition of the gay reading of James's novel with the traditional reading in Edel's courses and alongside Edel's biographical volumes augurs all kinds of future dialogues in which James's masterpiece can participate.

13

THE GOLDEN BOWL

or years, *The Golden Bowl* has been considered James's masterpiece, the realization of everything he learned in Europe and in his own life, and it has continued to appeal to the wilder imaginations of the 1980s and 1990s. Although it had its heyday in the 1960s and 1970s, when its place as a philosophical novel began to be assessed—preparing the way for Martha Nussbaum to make it the focus of an elaborate and convincing philosophical argument—it still has a hold on postmodern novelists. The "golden bowl" has, at any rate, become part of our inheritance, and its flaw—the crack in the crystal—has entered our everyday language. When a writer for the *New York Times Book Review* makes a comparison to "extruded golden bowls with nearly undetectable flaws," she is safe in assuming that her readers do not have to be told that she has in mind the golden crystal bowl in James's novel.[1]

Elizabeth Taylor's "A Troubled State of Mind"

Elizabeth Taylor (1912–1975) traveled the way of other twentieth-century writers in selecting part of a novel or tale by James and then developing it

---

1. Martha Nussbaum, "Flawed Crystals: James's *The Golden Bowl* and Literature as Moral Philosophy," *New Literary History,* XV (1983), 25–50; Maureen Howard, "In the Heart of the Heart of the Text," *New York Times Book Review,* March 19, 1997, p. 6.

the way she felt it should be developed. Read after her short story, "A Troubled State of Mind," of 1951, James's *The Golden Bowl* seems artificial and unreal, as it does not before reading Taylor's story. What she has done is attend to the relationship between two schoolmates, one of whom becomes the stepmother of the other. Since *The Golden Bowl* is the one important locus in modern literature where that situation occurs, her story immediately predisposes the reader to expect a connection with James. In James's novel, when Maggie Verver, married to Prince Amerigo, feels she is depriving her father, Adam, of her company, she plants in him the idea of marrying Charlotte, her boarding-school friend. Since, abnormally, that marriage does not change the close rapport between Maggie and her father, Charlotte and Amerigo are more or less driven to become intimate.

In Taylor's story, Sophy, the daughter of Colonel Vellacott, has been away at school in Switzerland all year. Suddenly she hears that her schoolmate Lalage, who has often visited as a houseguest of the Vellacotts over the years and who, like Sophy, is only eighteen years old, has married Sophy's father, in his fifties. As, in *The Golden Bowl*, Adam and Charlotte write to Maggie and Amerigo to let her know of their marriage, so Lalage and the colonel write to Sophy at school with their news. The colonel, a widower like Adam, is a distinguished jurist, and the difference between his age and Lalage's is even greater than that between Adam and Charlotte. Sophy is considerably upset to return to an altered household where she is no longer at the center and her chum, now "Madam," has taken the place of her mother. Like Charlotte, Lalage at first holds the reins of power, but at the end of "A Troubled State of Mind," Sophy takes them from her just as, at the end of *The Golden Bowl*, Maggie saves her marriage and dooms Charlotte to exile with Adam. But at first, depressed by the new situation, Sophy decides to take a job and leave the household. Before she can do that, however, the two girls fall back into their adolescent relationship and the colonel becomes upset that his wife has turned into an adopted daughter. Since Lalage is an orphan and wanted to escape the hell of a secretarial job, she was glad to marry the colonel. Like Charlotte, she is saved by her husband from a poverty-stricken spinsterhood.

Although no Prince Amerigo exists in this tale, an equivalent young male, Graham Dennis, celebrating his twenty-first birthday, falls in love with Sophy, and she with him. Lalage becomes bitterly conscious of having lost her position as wife as well as the freedom to love a man her own age. The tale ends with Lalage's feeling even more excluded than Sophy felt at the beginning. In this it follows the general curve of *The Golden Bowl*, in which Charlotte, having married the rich Adam Verver, is deprived of the love of someone her own age.

Yet the dynamics of "A Troubled State of Mind" are very different from those of *The Golden Bowl*. James ignored the oddity of a parental relationship between young women of the same age. He concentrated on how the two couples go about satisfying certain specific needs. In James's novel, the daughter and father go on in their abnormally close relationship so that the Prince and Charlotte must console themselves until Maggie becomes aware of how she has been eliminated from her husband's life. The peculiarity of two schoolmates being related as stepmother and stepdaughter does not seem to enter the picture at all. In Taylor's short story, it is the entire situation. In addition, Taylor tells the reader what the colonel thinks and feels about the changes occurring between his wife and daughter, whereas Adam's point of view has to be inferred from the way he acts, especially from his final determination to take Charlotte away from Maggie and the Prince, which solidifies only when his daughter gives him the high sign. Taylor's story amounts to an original recombination of the facts in the basic situation of Maggie and Charlotte.

Iris Murdoch's *An Unofficial Rose*

In the hands of Iris Murdoch (1919–), the psychology of the couple Mildred and Humphrey in *An Unofficial Rose*, of 1962, easily assumes the habiliments of the Assinghams of *The Golden Bowl*. As A. S. Byatt has written, "These are the people of James's and Forster's fiction, and this perhaps makes them feel artificial and unreal even when they are not" (*PM*, 171). Mildred and Humphrey are an amusing and perfectly reasonable transposition of the Assinghams into contemporary English life. Mildred recounts to her husband what takes place in the novel, as Mrs. Assingham does to Bob, her husband, only Humphrey is homosexual and has a fling with Penn, the young cousin from Australia. Emma Sands, the aging mystery writer, lives with Lindsay, a young woman companion. The valuable object that functions like the crystal bowl in *The Golden Bowl* is the small golden Tintoretto *Susanna at Her Bath*. Byatt found the novel filled with the "obtrusive presence of Henry James, and with him, of John Bayley's reading of *The Golden Bowl*." She decided that "Iris Murdoch in writing *An Unofficial Rose* was not essentially different from George Eliot's greedy reworking of

Goethe" (*PM*, 171). Can we assume that Murdoch is in this very complicated work commenting on how differently the behavior of the protagonists of *The Golden Bowl* would have been had they been English rather than American?

Muriel Spark's Maggie in *The Takeover*

Muriel Spark's *The Takeover*, of 1976, effects the kind of inversion of James's novel that especially appeals to postmodern writers. Her very rich American heroine is named Maggie, like James's; she is also married to an Italian aristocrat. He, the Marchese Berto, owns a beautiful Palladian villa that is being vandalized. But here everyone is corrupt: Maggie sleeps with an Italian servant, who is also sleeping with her daughter-in-law, as well as with another servant. Maggie, her son the Principino, and her husband the Marchese recall the trio in *The Golden Bowl*. As in Spackman's version of *The Ambassadors*, the action takes place in bed instead of in armchairs and sofas. But Spark's corrupt Maggie manages to regain her fortune and to outwit the native Italians. She is equal to rescuing her life, as Maggie Verver is to rescuing hers.

A Take-Off in a Novel of Adultery:
W. M. Spackman's *A Little Decorum, for Once*

In 1985, two years after rewriting *The Ambassadors*, W. M. Spackman did a turn on *The Golden Bowl*, calling it *A Little Decorum, for Once*. Spackman extends the situation in James's novel by creating two younger couples—the novelist hero Scrope Townshend's daughter, Sibylla, and her classmate, Amy, who take each other's husbands as lovers. The younger people discuss how their parents' generation went out of its way in its adulterous relations "to protect each other's spouse's feelings . . . the way in daddy's novels it's not just unkind not to, it's inexcusable! They loved whoever they were married to *too*" (*LI*, 18). That is also the norm in *The Golden Bowl*, where the Prince and Charlotte are careful not to hurt Adam and Maggie. According to Sibylla, Scrope finds the seduction scene between Anna and Vronsky in *Anna Karenina* so decorous that he contends, "The scene could have been written by Henry James!" (*LI*, 19). Spackman pleads for a little decorum from the younger generation.

There is a parallel between Adam Verver's marriage to the much younger woman Charlotte and the older writer Scrope's sexual dalliance with a Scandinavian in her early twenties (*LI*, 23). The second and pointedly explicit mention of James occurs when Mrs. Tench-Fenton, in discussion with Charles about his article on Ovid, tells him that at least he is not like those "characters in Henry James who have to have minor characters explain things to them all the time" (*LI*, 55). This seems to be a jab at Mrs. Assingham, who explains to both her unimaginative husband and the reader what has happened and will happen. Later, Spackman lampoons the breaking of the golden bowl by telling how a girl avenges herself on a faithless lover by breaking not only a "beautiful little Sheraton chair she'd given him" but "every plate dish cup saucer bowl mug and glass into pieces on the floor!" (*LI*, 80). This novel seems to cross *The Golden Bowl* with Ovid's *Ars Amatoria,* and the fantasy is in an idiosyncratic style. Scrope too, like Spackman and James, "invents his own dialect, stylizing" (*LI*, 107).

A Revision in Dance: The Pilobolus Version

James is not off limits to any artist. Witness the dance characterization of his work mounted by Pilobolus in 1988. In the dance called "The Golden Bowl," the unnamed Charlotte Stant is an on-stage narrator relating "successive revelations of moral deceit," or so Anna Kisselgoff, the dance critic for the New York *Times,* discerned from the composition of four dancing characters, including Charlotte. Charlotte has become a flapper from the 1920s who recalls her adulterous affair with the Prince. The other dancing characters are also unnamed, but the narration renders the dance close in plot to James's novel, showing how the "supposedly innocent daughter [Maggie] in fact manipulates the supposedly sophisticated lovers." There is a burlesque quality to the action when Adam Verver is seen "groveling at the feet of . . . his beloved daughter." Incest is now implied. Amerigo is a "hapless prince" whom Maggie treats as a pet. Charlotte is "deceived by those she deceived." The ending is changed, and instead of Maggie resolving the situation, a final waltz metaphorically conveys that the four people will "live unhappily ever after."[2] The Pilobolus version corresponds to the line of criticism that interprets Maggie as an arch manipulator of the adulterous couple. The motif of incest is a postmodern touch.

2.   Anna Kisselgoff, "James's 'Golden Bowl' According to Pilobolus," *New York Times,* December 26, 1988, Sec. C.

A. S. Byatt Possesses *The Golden Bowl:*
The Art of *Déja-Dit* in *Possession*

A. S. Byatt (1936–) works *The Golden Bowl* into her novel *Possession*, of 1990, in an interesting, ingenious, and poetic fashion. *Possession* concerns the search for the biographical facts about Randolph Henry Ash, an invented Victorian poet probably based on Robert Browning. A young research fellow of the present day finds two letters from Ash to the equally celebrated woman poet Christabel LaMotte, also invented, who is reminiscent of Christina Rossetti. With the help of a young professor, he unearths evidence of a romance between the two poets and assists in the discovery that a child was born of their love affair. Ash is presented in an authorized biography called *The Great Ventriloquist* as having had the ability to place his voice into the poetry of others.

One of the many poems in the novel, "The Great Collector," is composed of words and phrases from a passage in Henry James's *The Golden Bowl* and is about the collector in Byatt's novel, Mortimer P. Cropper. In this poem by Ash, I have italicized the words taken from James:

> His taste, that was his passion, brought him then
> To *bourgeois parlours, grey and grim back* rooms,
> *All redolent of Patriarchal teas,*
> Pacing behind a lustrous, smiling Jew,
> All decorous, 'twixt brute *mahogany,*
> *Meuble* or chest, and solid *table,* clothed
> *Smug* in its Sabbath calm, *in indigo,*
> *Faded maroon* and bistre *cotton* stripes —
> He'd see, perhaps, *extracted one by one,*
> *From three times locked,* but plumply *vulgar drawers*
> From *satchels soft of oriental silk,*
> To spread *in ordered and in matched array,*
> *So tenderly unmuffled and revealed*
> *The immemorial amethystine blue*
> Of twenty *ancient Damascene glazed tiles*
> As bright as heaven's courts, as subtle-hued
> As living sheen upon the peacock's neck.
> And then his soul was satisfied, and then

The material in this section appeared in somewhat different form in the Correspondence department of the *Henry James Review,* XII (1991), 181–83.

He tasted honey, then in those dead lights
Alive again, he knew his life, and gave
His gold, to gaze and gaze.[3]

In the relevant passage of *The Golden Bowl*, I have italicized the words appearing also in Ash's poem. Adam Verver, the great collector who is the model for Cropper, is at Brighton with Charlotte, and together they visit the house of Mr. Gutermann-Seuss to look at some Damascene tiles:

> Such places were not strange to him when they took the form of *bourgeois* back-*parlours*, a trifle ominously *grey and grim* from their north light, at watering-places prevailingly homes of humbug, or even when they wore some aspect still less, if not perhaps still more, insidious. He had been everywhere, pried and prowled everywhere, going, on occasion, so far as to risk, he believed, life, health and the very bloom of honour; but where, while precious things, *extracted one by one from thrice-locked* yet often *vulgar drawers* and *soft satchels* of old *oriental silk*, were impressively ranged before him, had he, till now, let himself, in consciousness, wander like one of the vague? . . . [Mr. Gutermann-Seuss made a] repeated act of passage between a featureless *mahogany meuble* and a *table* so virtuously disinterested as to look fairly *smug* under a *cotton cloth of faded maroon and indigo, all redolent of patriarchal teas.* The *Damascene tiles,* successively, and *oh so tenderly, unmuffled and revealed,* lay there at last in their full harmony and their venerable splendour. . . . The infinitely ancient, the immemorial *amethystine blue of the glaze,* scarcely more meant to be breathed upon, it would seem, than the cheek of royalty—this property of *the ordered and matched* array had inevitably all its determination for him. (*GB*, 171–72)

An interviewer has posed a question to Byatt: "It is interesting that you use in *Possession* the form of what one might call the literary detective story in which the hunt for documents becomes a way of dramatizing and exploring all kinds of dubious human motives—*The Aspern Papers* is a classic example—and that you link this with the modern university world, the global campus. What drew you to that kind of story?"[4]

Byatt answered,

3. A. S. Byatt, *Possession* (New York, 1990), 103.
4. *Conversations with Critics* (Manchester, Eng., 1994), 58.

It was partly—and one must tread carefully—watching the greed of real scholars. It was partly, as you say, Henry James. There is a big joke in *Posses-sion* about Adam Verver in *The Golden Bowl*, who bought Charlotte Stant and took her back to an American city; James sees this as the acquiring of people by profit, but also, I think, sees the American millionaire as a possible savi-our as well as a possible destroyer. Mortimer Cropper's collection in my novel is called the Stant Collection, in memory of Adam Verver, and the whole poem about the Great Collector is actually a description of Adam Verver from *The Golden Bowl*. It goes into blank verse in my novel. I didn't have to change almost any of James's words or add any, except a little bit of Balzac and Swedenborg at the end."[5]

Byatt is, in this novel as well as in other pieces of her fiction, playing a "kind of game with modern theories of intertextuality (a modern text, 'reading' an ancient one by quoting a 'rearrangement,' to use a Jamesian word)." As part of a general contemporary concern with truth telling and lying in fiction, Byatt is unapologetic about the "use, conscious and uncon-scious, of the *déja-dit* in current fiction." The placement of James's descrip-tion of the oriental tiles from *The Golden Bowl* within a poetic response pre-sented as Ash's even though Ash died fifteen years before *The Golden Bowl* appeared has resulted in a more inventive context. The end product is "*my* fiction," in much the way that James thought of the facts he manipulated in *Notes of a Son and Brother* as "*my* truth." The game in *Possession* is played with scholarly "theories." Byatt says that her novel is "about greedy reading and so is my writing—a kind of writerly raid on scholarly dogmatics and theories."[6]

In "People in Paper Houses" in her book of essays *Passions of the Mind*, she gives examples of other novelists of the postmodern period who have wrestled with the "problem of veracity and the fictive." Julian Mitchell in *The Undiscovered Country*, of 1968, has created a model for later novels such as Rebecca Goldstein's *The Dark Sister*. In Mitchell's novel there are two parts, the first about the author, a real person with "a cast of real people and a plot of real events" (*PM*, 179). The second part is about his fictional friend. According to the friend, Charles, the earlier part of the novel, though purportedly "real," is not. The first part is changed when seen

5. *Ibid.*, 64.
6. A. S. Byatt to author, August 6, 1991.

through the second, ostensibly "unreal" part, which is done as a parody. Narrative manipulation of this sort is one of the aims of postmodern fiction.

In Norman Mailer's *Harlot's Ghost*, of 1991, the same games of reality and fiction occur not in experimental verbal intricacies like those of contemporary Continental and English novelists but in the book's content. The division is between reality in the spy's world and reality as someone knows it who is not privy to the spy's commitments and activities. One of the special agents taps the binding of *The Golden Bowl*, which he asserts was "much studied by Lenin and Dzerzhinsky." He goes on, "*Golden Bowl*. Perfect symbol for capitalism, of course Dzerzhinsky would read such work.... We spent weeks analyzing what Dzerzhinsky got from *The Golden Bowl*."[7] Doubtless mouthing Mailer's criticism of James, another character says, "Henry James is a quince pie as large as the Mojave Desert. It's a pity. Put Hemingway's heart in him and James would have been a writer to equal Stendhal or Tolstoy."[8]

7. Norman Mailer, *Harlot's Ghost* (New York, 1991), 580–81.
8. *Ibid.*, 144.

14

SOME TWICE-TOLD TALES

"The Turn of the Screw"
Frances Hodgson Burnett's *The Secret Garden*

It is not surprising that "The Turn of the Screw," James's best-known short story, captured the imagination of several modern writers at the turn of the twentieth century, although it is curious that one of these should be the author of *Little Lord Fauntleroy*, Frances Hodgson Burnett. In Burnett's *The Secret Garden*, of 1911, the very plot, involving two children who are not precious to the relative in charge of their care, has an affinity to James's tale, as do their responses to good and evil influences.

And though there are traces of Charlotte Brontë in the orphanage of Mary Lennox, Burnett's heroine, they too may have passed through the filter of James's "The Turn of the Screw." In India, Mary's parents both die from cholera in the course of a day, leaving the child the only survivor of her family. Like the children in "The Turn of the Screw," she is sent to the great house of an uncle. He, Mr. Archibald Craven, has no interest in her, does not want to see her, and like the master in "The Turn of the Screw," refuses to "be troubled by anythin' when he's here."[1] Mary and her unloved and sickly cousin, Colin, whom she discovers hidden in the house, are bad

---

1. Frances Hodgson Burnett, *The Secret Garden* (1911; rpr. New York, 1987), 28.

children in the way Flora and Miles are bad—and for the same reason, namely, that they are unloved, as Burnett clearly stated. James had by implication offered the same cause for the behavior of Flora and Miles when he wrote that he wished to picture the "helpless plasticity of childhood that isn't dear or sacred to *some*body" (*L,* IV, 84).

James's influence appears as well in the invocation of magic in *The Secret Garden:* "There is Magic in there—good magic. . . . Even if it isn't real Magic . . . we can pretend it is." To this, Mary says, "It's Magic . . . but not black. It's as white as snow."[2] That recalls *The Two Magics,* of 1898, which included James's two stories "The Turn of the Screw" and "Covering End," examples of black magic and white magic. Craven behaves like Dr. Sloper in *Washington Square,* who hates his daughter because his beautiful and beloved wife died giving birth to a clumsy and dull girl. Craven hates his son because his beautiful and beloved wife has died giving birth to a hysterical and ill boy. Unlike "The Turn of the Screw," however, Burnett's children's classic ends happily. The children become joyful and healthy, and the responsible adults learn their lesson.

The Secret Garden was dear to Burnett's heart and is a memorial to her own rose garden at Maytham, her rented house only six miles from James's Lamb House, in Rye. Beginning in 1895, at the time of *Guy Domville,* the two writers corresponded and maintained considerable intimacy. What Burnett probably did not know was that James had on October 24, 1883, anonymously reviewed her play *Young Folks' Ways,* adapted from her short story "Esmeralda," though an article in *The Athenaeum* "definitely stated that the criticism was from the pen of Henry James."[3] He made a careful summary of a complicated story but said that it is "mawkish and unreal, and after the first act there is scarcely any attempt to tell it."[4] Since James burned his correspondence, no letters from Burnett to him survive. But in one of his to her, he thanked her for a magnificent gift of fruit in the typical burlesque of thank-you notes by which he acknowledged gifts. He signed that letter "Machiavelli H. James." In at least two letters, he referred to her as a "genius," and he voiced the expectation of having tea in the magnificent house she rented at 63 Portland Place, in London. Probably thinking

---

2. *Ibid.,* 246.
3. Henry James, *The Scenic Art,* ed. Allan Wade (New Brunswick, N.J., 1948), 197.
4. *Ibid.,* 195.

of *A Little Princess,* he called Burnett the "princess of Maytham." Although forced to read some of her manuscripts, he never publicly criticized them apart from the review of her play. And even then he seemed to divine where her genius lay, for he wrote of seeing in the play "elements of a touching simplicity, put together with an ingenuousness which would be commendable in a moral tale for the young."[5] Burnett must have been interested in reading *What Maisie Knew,* James's book about children; at any rate she owned a copy, for in 1914, Phyllis DeKay wrote that Burnett had lent it to her. Burnett's basic realism is in alignment with James's approach in his fiction about youngsters. Moreover, Burnett shared James's urge to depict the "helpless plasticity of childhood" when a child is not loved.

Rumer Godden's *The Peacock Spring*

Rumer Godden (1907–1996), who lived at Lamb House for a number of years, absorbed Henry James to the extent that the underlying pattern of *The Peacock Spring,* of 1975, which is laid in India, clearly derives from "The Turn of the Screw." Sir Edward Gwithian, a British official representing the United Nations in New Delhi some time after World War II, summons his two daughters from Cerne, their English school, where they have been perfectly happy. The children of two different marriages, they are fifteen and twelve years old. The younger, Halcyon, is temperamentally like her mother, Sir Edward's divorced second wife, and she is precociously susceptible to falling in love. Una, the older daughter, has been very close to her father, but she is extremely suspicious about her father's decision to call them to India. Although in their father's custody, the girls were allowed to lead their own life at the English school, but now it appears that they will have to live with their father and a governess he has procured for them. Una and Halcyon feel they are being "posted around like parcels."[6] Una's mistrust turns out to be warranted. As the girls learn when they arrive, Sir Edward is in a liaison with the beautiful Eurasian Alix Lamont, and public attitudes will allow her to live in the house only on the pretext that the two girls are in her charge.

In "The Turn of the Screw," the arrangements made for two children in

5. *Ibid.,* 193.
6. Rumer Godden, *The Peacock Spring* (New York, 1975), 15.

whom their uncle is not interested are shaped to satisfy his selfish desires. The arrangements for Una and Halcyon similarly have greater benefit for adults than for them. When the girls get to India, they are exposed to corrupting forces a vigilant parent would have protected them against. Young Halcyon falls in love with Vikram Singh, a former raja and the polo-playing captain of the president's bodyguard who is now deprived of his once large fortune. Because Halcyon's mother has heard through the grapevine of the young girl's wild passion for this man, Sir Edward has to send her to a convent school. Meantime, Una, who wished to prepare at Cerne for entrance to a university, finds that Alix is not up to teaching her mathematics at the level she requires. Deviously she gets to know Ravi, the young assistant gardener on her father's estate, who is an unpublished but gifted poet. Since her father attends only to his mistress, Una finds the love she needs in the young gardener, but she also finds herself pregnant. She and Ravi leave the estate at the time Sir Edward marries his mistress. Ravi, who resists taking responsibility for his unborn child and is too young and too egocentric to accept the notion of being a father, ends up with Una at his grandmother's house. When Sir Edward finds out where Una has fled, he travels to bring her home. He wants her to have an abortion and is horrified by the idea of a half-caste child in the family, which, ironically, also upsets his Eurasian mistress. The evil governess, who has whipped Una because of disobedience, demonstrates, surprisingly, genuine concern for the unborn child and the future of the young girl. Una's miscarriage allows the scandal to be concealed, and the girl is sent back to the boarding school in England. Halcyon is put in the custody of her mother and sent to a school in Connecticut. But Sir Edward, after the disclosure of the corrupt aspects of Alix' character, still loves her, and they leave Delhi for his new posting in Bangkok.

The theme of Godden's novel, too, is James's: the "helpless plasticity of childhood that isn't dear or sacred to *some*body" (*L*, IV, 84). Besides transferring the story to India, where she spent many years, Godden has made the character of the governess more flexible and has changed the little boy and girl to two adolescent girls. The story is told from the point of view of the older daughter, whose intelligence and insight into the situation cannot avert her yearnings for the accustomed paternal attentions. In addition, Una and Halcyon, unlike Miles and Flora, are in the end returned to more healthful surroundings.

Taking "The Turn of the Screw" As Far As It Can Go: Peter Straub's *Ghost Story*

Peter Straub (1943–) has said that his novel *Ghost Story,* of 1979, "refers back to the classic American novels and stories of the genre by Henry James and Nathaniel Hawthorne. . . . I was moved by a desire to look into, examine and play with the genre—to take these 'classic' elements as far as they could go" (*GS,* jacket flap). That story by James he has taken as far as he can is "The Turn of the Screw." Five men meet as what they called the Chowder Society, and each one tells a ghost story. Sears James, whose name is indicative, goes first with a tale about two of the Bate children, Fenny and Constance, who take orders from their elder brother, Gregory. An evil influence, he forbids them to attend school. Fenny and Constance are clearly based on Flora and Miles of "The Turn of the Screw," and Gregory on the evil Peter Quint. If, to Sears James, Fenny's behavior seems "corrupt; it frightened me" (*GS,* 68), his impression agrees with the conclusion of the local minister, who has told him that Fenny is not bad, "but he is corrupt" (*GS,* 69), and that Gregory is the corrupter. The depth of the corruption, exceeding anything in "The Turn of the Screw," is clearly spelled out: Gregory has had sexual relations with both the young children. He has forced them into heterosexual and homosexual incest. After the two kill Gregory, he becomes a revenant, like Peter Quint.

The governess sees Peter Quint on the fortifications of the house at Bly, and Sears James sees Gregory "up on the hill staring down at me" (*GS,* 73) and again in town "just intensely staring at me" (*GS,* 74). Sears James reacts comparably to the governess and struggles to wrest Gregory's power over the two younger children from him. He sees Gregory's face "in the window" of the schoolroom, much as the governess observes Peter Quint's face at the window at Bly. The scene after Sears James grabs Fenny follows almost exactly the final scene in "The Turn of the Screw." As Sears James relates the events to the Chowder Society, he assured Fenny, "He won't get you—*I* have you! He knows he's lost you forever!"

> "Where is he?" Fenny shrieked again, pushing at me. "Where is Gregory?"
> "*There,*" I said, and turned him around to face the window. He was already *jerking* himself around, and we both stared then at an empty window—there was nothing out there but an empty dark sky. I felt triumphant—I had won. I gripped Fenny's arm with all the strength of my victory, and he gave a shout

of pure despair. He toppled forward, and I caught him as if he were jumping into the pit of hell itself. Only a few seconds later did I realize what *I* had caught: his heart had stopped, and I was holding a *dispossessed* body. He had gone over for good. (*GS*, 77; italics mine)

Here is the related sequence of actions in "The Turn of the Screw": Having seen Peter Quint at the window, the governess hears Miles say, "It's *he?*" To the governess' question "Whom do you mean by 'he'?" Miles responds, "Peter Quint—you devil." She counters, "Where?" and adds, "What does he matter now, my own—what will he *ever* matter? *I* have you . . . but he has lost you for ever!"

But he had already *jerked* straight round, stared, glared again, and seen but the quiet day. With the stroke of the loss I was so proud of he uttered the cry of a creature hurled over an abyss, and the grasp with which I recovered him might have been that of catching him in his fall. I caught him, yes, I held him—it may be imagined with what a passion; but at the end of a minute I began to feel what it truly was that I held. We were alone with the quiet day, and his little heart, *dispossessed*, had stopped. (X, 138; italics mine)

Elizabeth Taylor's "Poor Girl"

It has always been assumed that the governess loves the master in "The Turn of the Screw." The interchange between the outside narrator and Douglas in the framing prologue seems to indicate that, and Edmund Wilson assumed it in his essay "The Ambiguity of Henry James," in 1934. But the governess never sees the master after her two interviews. What does come out in the story and what Douglas may be referring to when he declares the governess "was in love" and that "she couldn't tell her story without its coming out" (X, 17) are the patently erotic passages between her and little Miles. Miles is a tangible substitute for his uncle, and there are many passages in which James brings that out. But the passion manifest in the tale is between Miles and the governess, not between the governess and the master. This part of "The Turn of the Screw" carries so much freight that interpretations will go on indefinitely.

Elizabeth Taylor took off from this juncture in "Poor Girl," of 1951. She bestowed the name Florence Chasty on the governess and in the very first paragraph of the tale thrust the reader into James's story: "Miss Chasty's first pupil was a flirtatious little boy" (*BL*, 169). Florence's charge, Hilary, who is her Miles, is only seven years old. He is precocious: "Sometimes she thought that he despised his childhood, regarding it as a waiting time which he used only as a rehearsal for adult life" (*BL*, 165). The aggressive partner in this flowering of love is the boy of seven. In contrast, the governess in "The Turn of the Screw" is twenty years old and Miles is ten, duplicating the ten-year difference between the governess and Douglas, who is in love with her, and the strange passion between the governess and Miles—who refers to it as "this queer business of ours," and "the way you bring me up. And all the rest" (X, 102)—is sustained by the two in more equal measure. Hilary, who is "already more sophisticated than his young governess," disturbs her "with his air of dalliance" (*BL*, 169). Hilary's familiarity in addressing Miss Chasty as "my dear girl" reprises Miles's in addressing his governess as "my dear." When the governess and Miles are in church, he seems to take her arm and position himself so as to be in contact with her as they sit in the pew; Hilary leans against Florence "heavily." But she feels "as if he were not leaning against her at all, but against someone in the future." When this happens, "she would blush, as if he were a grown man, and her heart could be heard beating quickly. . . . Once he proposed to her and she had the feeling that it was a proposal-rehearsal" (*BL*, 170). He tells her, "You could wait for me to grow up, I can do that quickly enough." The physical relation between Miles and the governess develops progressively, ending in the passionate embrace just before he dies. The governess has an "absolute conviction of his secret precocity . . . the poison of an influence that I dared but half to phrase" that makes him "appear as accessible as an older person" (X, 103). The "dandified" Hilary is sniffing around Miss Chasty like an animal in rut from the beginning.

Taylor brings into her story the two parents of the boy, who are deeply implicated in the romance between child and governess. Florence unconsciously responds to Hilary's addresses by giving off a heavy odor of physical desire. The father, Mr. Wilson, is a philanderer ready to take advantage of the situation. Mrs. Wilson, extremely jealous, watches him carefully and notices a red stain on a teacup. The swishing of silk underwear beneath the governess' inexpensive cotton skirt and her musky odor of sexuality adumbrate the appearance of the "ghost" in the story.

This is how it happens. Mr. Wilson tries to make love to her, and she, in spite of overt resistance, responds. Her repressed feelings seem to have been summoned by his sexual advances, leading to the supposition of a "suppressed wantonness" that has "hovered beneath her primness" (*BL*,

181). Although the governess unconsciously seemed to want Mr. Wilson's advances, "she felt an enormous sense of disappointment, almost as if he were the wrong person embracing her in the dark" (*BL,* 189). There is no doubt that she would have preferred Hilary's advances. She is discharged, and as she makes her way out she sees a young woman on the stairs wearing a "tunic which scarcely covered the knees, a hat like a helmet, ... matching a long necklace of glass beads which swung on her flat bosom. ... Silk rustled against her silken legs and all of the staircase ... was full of fragrance." Since the clothes, "unlike anything that Florence had ever seen" (*BL,* 214), are of the 1920s, a generation after Florence's story with the Wilsons, the surmise is that this is the ghost of a future governess who will care for the little girlchild who accompanies her. The man with whom this ghost exchanges secret messages must be Hilary grown up. It is Hilary that Florence has wanted, as the governess in James's story wants little Miles, both his soul and his personal beauty, and not his uncle, the master.

Reinventions of James's fiction can enable us to see plainly things that eluded us before. Until Taylor wrote this version of "The Turn of the Screw," I too had assumed that the person the governess is in love with is the master, whom she wants to please. But "Poor Girl" causes us to notice that the relationship between her and Miles is indeed that of a love affair. Miles flirts with her, and it is Miles to whom she responds.

Rewritings from Different Points of View: Michael Winner's *The Nightcomers* and Joyce Carol Oates's "Accursed Inhabitants of the House of Bly"

Of two approaches to "The Turn of the Screw" from a point of view different from that of the governess—the point of view dominating James's tale—the first is the film *The Nightcomers,* of 1972, directed by Michael Winner; the second, Joyce Carol Oates's short story "Accursed Inhabitants of the House of Bly," of 1994, is based on the cast of characters and the plot as James conceived them. *The Nightcomers* is an excursion away from the original story insofar as it takes the point of view of the children and occupies itself with what happened before the governess came to Bly. As a prequel to "The Turn of the Screw," it gives an entirely different account of the deaths of Miss Jessel and Peter Quint. It, like Oates's story, is a reaction, explicit and specific, to the so-called ambiguity of James. *The Nightcomers* has the children themselves arrange and accomplish the deaths of the two lovers. They manage to sink the boat the governess is in so that she drowns, and they orchestrate the circumstances of the death of the drunken Quint so as not to be held responsible. The two children are evil, and at the film's end, when the governess who is to replace Miss Jessel arrives, we are in a position to look at James's tale with the prior knowledge that the children are murderers.

The originality with which Oates (1938–) imbues "Accursed Inhabitants of the House of Bly" depends on adopting the point of view of the ghosts of Miss Jessel and Peter Quint, the two dead lovers. They have "crossed over," that is, they are dead and have become ghouls, yet they still experience desire and can influence human beings. Eventually they will reach the point where they disappear completely, but that has not happened yet when the replacement governess comes to Bly. Unlike *The Nightcomers*, Oates's tale is coeval with James's. The view of the governess, as well as of the other characters—Flora and Miles, the master and Mrs. Grose—through the eyes of the ghosts is as chilling and spellbinding as anything observed in "The Turn of the Screw."

The scenes where Peter Quint appears to the governess from the tower of the mansion and where the governess sees Miss Jessel at the lake do not lose their spookiness but are, if anything, intensified. The master is more cruel than in "The Turn of the Screw," yet also extremely concerned about the homosexuality of his nephew Miles, which Oates has made explicit in Miles's grasping for love and his attachment to Quint, as well as in his expulsion from school, here Eton. But the ghosts do not get their way as they do in James's tale. Miles is not killed, either by the governess or by Quint, who in this tale wants him dead so that he can enter the world of the ghoul and they can continue their love. Oates's story ends with the governess sending both spirits to their final resting place: "*We must have imagined that, if Evil could be made to exist, Good might exist as rightfully.*"[7] The governess, who is good and a Christian, is thus the heroine. By her strong will and virtue she destroys the evil influence of the ghosts, and Miles survives. Oddly enough, notwithstanding the cheerful ending, the hauntings that make up the main part of the tale are as scary as the ones in "The Turn of the Screw." For Oates the ghosts are evil but they act out of love. She is testimony that the interpretation of the ghosts as projections resulting from the governess' mental illness is no longer universally accepted. Some readers may prefer

---

7.   Joyce Carol Oates, *Haunted: Tales of the Grotesque* (New York, 1994), 282.

James's ambiguity, but the straightforward account by the leading contemporary writer of grotesques is refreshing, at least to those who have read the original. Appreciating the brilliance of Oates's invention requires the reader to compare the two versions of the events. It is the tension between them that maximizes the grotesquerie and shock value in Oates's story. Winner's *The Nightcomers* and Oates's "Accursed Inhabitants of the House of Bly" both get their power from the reader's acquaintance with James's tale.

Hilary Bailey's *Miles and Flora: A Sequel to Henry James' The Turn of the Screw*

Three years after Oates's "Accursed Inhabitants of the House of Bly," Hilary Bailey in *Miles and Flora: A Sequel to Henry James' The Turn of the Screw*, of 1997, attempted to harness the theories that the ghosts are real and that they are hallucinations. The two theories are like two horses running a race that ends in a contested final. The narrative mechanics of Bailey by which the two attitudes to the existence of the ghosts are presented deserve admiration for their ingenuity and well-maintained suspense. Her sequel is indeed a thriller.

Bailey has retained a number of characters with their original names from "The Turn of the Screw." Flora, the dead Miles, and Mrs. Grose appear under their original names; the governess, whom James did not name, becomes Elaine Selsden. Douglas, who appears in the prologue of James's tale, is brought into Bailey's story as Tom Brett, still enamored of the governess. The master returns under the name of Geoffrey Bennett, with his wife, Beth. Bly is still Bly, and Jessel and Quint are still Jessel and Quint.

Two *ficelles* are needed to advance the plot. One is Marguerite, Elaine's younger sister, who is also a governess but a healthy-minded one. The other is Henry Reeve, an echo of James himself, who unites the plot of the governesses—all three now live in Strand, a small village in Sussex—with that of the master and the doings at Bly, which is possible because Henry is a friend of Geoffrey Bennett's. Once Bailey has sketched the cast of characters and their roles in connection with the tragic occurrences at Bly, she draws the reader cleverly into a rapidly developing plot of horrors that resorts to no gothic elements in the manner of Oates but adheres more closely to the genteel tradition of nineteenth-century ghost stories, such as Wilkie Collins' and Sheridan LeFanu's.

It is 1914, and Flora is now a girl in her early twenties engaged to a young aristocrat. All goes well until she sees the ghost of her brother, Miles, as a young soldier — *miles* in Latin means just that. She comes apart, abstracted by "Miles as he would have been, had he grown up,"[8] and her relations with her fiancé and his family become uncertain as the signs of her hysteria or madness become more pronounced. She faints at the altar, and life becomes difficult for both families. In the parallel plot, Elaine, the nervous governess, thinks that Henry Reeve is smitten with her, and she sexually harasses him. He, though, has become attached to her younger sister, Marguerite, who has been conducting a correspondence with Mrs. Grose, who in this novel can read and write. The housekeeper's letters remind Marguerite and the reader of the horrors that have taken place at Bly under the spell of Miss Jessel and Peter Quint. Elaine is more and more out of control. She writes to Tom Brett and summons him from his job in order to take up residence with him against his will in London. When he escapes her by going back to his family in Scotland, where she had been a governess to his sisters after leaving Bly, she joins Mrs. Grose, who comes to Strand to see her, in table-tapping and inducing séances to invoke the ghosts of Miss Jessel and Peter Quint. Flora only gets worse. After Elaine and Mrs. Grose are rescued from their lodgings because of a fire, the two women are put into an asylum. All three are finally abandoned to the ghosts of Jessel, Quint, and Miles. But Marguerite and Henry Reeve are joined in marriage, showing that at least one governess is sane and capable of a normal relationship with a man. The reader lands between believing that the ghosts are the hallucinations of unbalanced women and believing that they are actual presences.

The additions to the original story are arresting. Flora breaks down, although in James's story she seems to have been taken out of the evil atmosphere before it could harm her. James had placed his story in the 1860s or 1870s, but Bailey took the time of the story to have been the time of its writing, 1898, which permits Flora to be in her early twenties in 1914, at the beginning of World War I. In James's tale, Mrs. Grose does not see the ghost; only the governess sees it. Here, Elaine, Mrs. Grose, and Flora all see ghosts. Something that makes it especially difficult for the reader to decide whether the ghosts are real is that an outsider also apparently sees a ghost:

8. Hilary Bailey, *Miles and Flora: A Sequel to Henry James' The Turn of the Screw* (London, 1997), 171.

a policeman, after the fire, notices an unknown man coming out of the building. The preoccupation of the era with psychical research tempers the tale as Mrs. Grose and Elaine try to summon up those who have died.

Bailey seems to combine both theories. Her novel is in the traditions of both the gothic novel and the modern psychological thriller. Her answer to the ambiguity of James is a bipartisan attitude to the ghosts. The development of the plot, which gradually builds to an ending in which none of the horrors of James's tale have been reduced, may not require a prior reading of "The Turn of the Screw" for its enjoyment. It is unlikely, however, that an innocent reader of this genre exists today, someone who does not know James's most famous story.

"Brooksmith"

"Brooksmith," James's story of 1891 involving a Platonized manservant, had until the second half of the twentieth century received little serious attention. Joseph Conrad, however, was reported to have liked it best of the stories in the collection James published in 1892 as *The Lesson of the Master* (see above, p. 145). And now four writers with strikingly different cultural backgrounds have transposed and reconstructed it.

Elizabeth Taylor's "A Dedicated Man"

Elizabeth Taylor began her "A Dedicated Man," of 1965, by introducing a waiter very much like the valet Brooksmith. As Brooksmith is ruined, in a sense, by being the servant of Mr. Offord, a superior man who conducts a salon of superior minds in a London house, so the waiter Silcox is undone by his dedication to working in a superior hotel suited to his superior service. He persuades a middle-aged waitress, Edith, to pose as his wife so that they can qualify as a couple for jobs he considers worthy of their talents. For they both, "being snobbish," were "galled at having to wait on noisy, sunburnt people who wore freakish and indecent holiday clothes and could not pronounce *crêpes de volaille*, let alone understand what it meant" (*DED*, 112). Silcox prides himself on his impeccable comportment as a waiter, and "his deference would have that touch of condescension which would make customers angle for his good will. . . . 'Maurice always looks after me,' they would say" (*DED*, 113). The Royal George Hotel meets his standards. As part of the trappings of the sham marriage, he shows off a picture of a son.

The tale is told from Edith's point of view, and she leaves no doubt that for her Silcox is "simply . . . the Establishment." He is "always a waiter," and she always thinks "of him dressed as a waiter" (*DED*, 117). Silcox' professionalism is consummate, like Brooksmith's, and "to turn something over in flaming brandy in a chafing-dish crowned Silcox's evening." As Brooksmith models his behavior on his employer's, Silcox models his "on that of his own most difficult customers" and seems "to be retaliating by doing so." Not only is he "very lordly and full of knowledge and criticism" (*DED*, 118) but he is willing to exploit Edith for his own success. Since he on principle does not talk about his private affairs, Edith can defy him by speaking of the boy to others and inventing a story about him. When, accidentally, she finds out that the boy is Silcox' son by an early marriage, she embroiders her chitchat by saying that the youth has been disgraced "for theft" (*DED*, 131). After Silcox beats her, she decides to leave, but before she does, she plants some silver-plated spoons from the dining room in the drawer of their chest, to give the impression that the boy gets his thievery from his father. She hopes that "the whole world will know, and may decide where they can lay the blame" (*DED*, 131).

This variation on "Brooksmith" illustrates by implication how the valet in James's story, likewise dedicated to achieving the highest level of his calling, would relate to a wife. He would be rigid and inflexible and would distort human values as necessary in pursuing his calling. Taylor's version of "Brooksmith" has a certain resemblance to *The Remains of the Day*, by Kazuo Ishiguro (see below, pp. 384–86), which portrays the inflexibility of a butler who models his values on those of the man he serves.

Daniel Stern's "Brooksmith by Henry James: A Story"

A transformation of "Brooksmith" in *Twice-Told Tales*, of 1989, by Daniel Stern (1928–), is sometimes used as a text for interracial relations in writing courses. It is one of six literary transformations in the volume, the others being of works by Sigmund Freud, Ernest Hemingway, Lionel Trilling, and E. M. Forster. Dedicated to Muriel Shine, a well-known James scholar and professor, Stern's "Brooksmith by Henry James: A Story" creates from her the character of Celia Morris, a teacher of literature, whose lawyer husband has recently died, so that she is forced back into teaching college English. The memory of her husband as someone who nurtured artists and musicians and made his home into an "oasis of song, poetry and general conversation" links Stern's "Brooksmith" to James's "Brooksmith," in which Mr. Offord keeps a distinguished salon.

Celia assigns two stories for reading in her class at City University: one, "Sonny's Blues," by James Baldwin, for the blacks, and another, "Brooksmith," by James, for the whites. By mistake, however, she assigns James's tale to Zoë, a spirited black woman. Stern relates that "Brooksmith" is the "tale of a butler at one of those Jamesian salons of the imagination, so spoiled by the quality of the discourse at his master's evenings that he cannot survive the man's death and all that vanishes with it" (*TT,* 101). He adds that James's Brooksmith resembles Celia's husband, who was also an "artist without an art, attending those who owned and exercised the gifts." But the semiliterate Zoë gets the true point of the story: "Brooksmith be spoiled by being only part way into the beautiful world of his master Mister Offard. It can be a curse on you, they let you in part way so you can't go back and they hate for you to go forward" (*TT,* 103). The girl declares, "*I am Brooksmith*" (*TT,* 104). Her aim is to be a nurse, but her family, mostly made up of prostitutes, is against her completing her education. Celia gets her a science tutor and awards her a good grade in English. Zoë makes it.

The story's narrator, a young actor who has been helped by Celia's husband, visits Celia when she is hospitalized with a serious illness a few years later and finds Zoë, now a qualified nurse, taking care of her. When, out of theatrical work, the actor falls back on teaching drama, he decides to have his class read "Brooksmith," with an eye to discerning the "central dramatic conflict" (*TT,* 107). He makes the "interesting discovery" from James's *Notebooks* that the model for Brooksmith had been Mrs. Duncan Stewart's lady's maid, who remarked to her employer's daughter after the woman died, "*What is your loss to mine? You continue to live with clever, cultivated people; but I fall again into my own class. I shall never see such company—hear such talk—again.*" He was "wonderfully struck by the possibilities of transformation" (*TT,* 108). If Brooksmith could be a "lady's maid . . . then why not a Brooklyn black trying to escape the prostitute's fate? And who could know what he'd be the next time?" (*TT,* 108–109).

Kazuo Ishiguro's *The Remains of the Day*

The Remains of the Day, also of 1989, by Kazuo Ishiguro (1954–), since made into a successful movie, strikes the reader as reconstructing the character of Brooksmith. The butler Stevens is like Brooksmith in having spent his years as a devoted servant. He has been head butler of a great house belonging to the famous Lord Darlington, who helped frame much of the foreign policy preceding the Second World War and, favoring accommodation with the Nazis, almost succeeded in involving England's new king in German intrigue. Like Brooksmith, Stevens found it ennobling "to serve the great gentleman of our time in whose hands civilization had been entrusted," and he lapped up the atmosphere of the house. After inferior posts, he had been "rewarded at last with the opportunity to serve Lord Darlington" (*RD*, 116). Yet, unlike Brooksmith, he had a trust in his master that was purely professional, not personal. His attitude was that of a general leading an army, because his staff, in contrast to Brooksmith's sole footman, consisted of a regiment of servants over whom he ruled like a despot, subjecting everything to his rigorous professional standards. While his father, a butler before him, was dying in Darlington Hall, Stevens persevered with his duties, which involved a secret conference in the house among the diplomatic heads of Europe. He followed his master's edict that the Jewish girls employed at the Hall must be fired, and later, when his master repented his action and asked him to find the girls, he simply did not do so.

The great books in the house, with great ideas, did not rub off on him, for Miss Kenton, the housekeeper, found him reading a "sentimental love story" of the kind left in ladies' bedrooms. He deemed such reading an "extremely efficient way to maintain and develop one's command of the English language" (*RD*, 167), for "elegant dialogue" was "of much practical value" to him, especially with the ladies (*RD*, 168). He is convinced that "a butler of any quality must be seen to *inhabit* his role, utterly and fully" (*RD*, 169). The delight Brooksmith takes in the company of his civilized master and in the atmosphere of his master's salon stems from being not only his butler but also "his most intimate friend" (VIII, 16). Mr. Offord has said that what Brooksmith likes is the "talk—mingling in the conversation," although Brooksmith never "permit[ted] himself this freedom . . . what Mr. Offord alluded to was a participation more intense than any speech could have represented" (VIII, 17). The crux of James's story lies in the question the narrator asks: "To what was this sensitive young man of thirty-five, of the servile class, being educated?" (VIII, 17). Stevens, like Brooksmith, never entered the educated conversation, except when he was delegated to tell a young man the "facts of life," something he could not do at all, because he was personally removed from natural life. When the "great men" summoned for the conference regarding the fate of Europe ask him for his opinion of the complicated political machinations he has witnessed, he cannot offer any. That was exactly what they expected in asking the question.

P. G. Wodehouse's Jeeves, J. M. Barrie's Crichton, and James's Brooksmith are the ancestors of Ishiguro's Stevens, though he, like each of them, is distinctly himself. Jeeves solves the problems of the idiot aristocrat who is his master. Crichton, although lord of the island, relinquishes his elevated role when he returns to British society. Brooksmith, who has been bred to a superior kind of life through intimacy with his employer, is out of his element with any other master and dies of despair. Stevens is an autocrat who exercises power because he is fanatical in devotion to the "dignity" of his profession. His attitude is dangerously close to the fanaticism of Hitler and his regime, but his outlook lets him adapt to another master when Lord Darlington dies. At the end of Stevens' weeklong motor trip, during which he recapitulates his professional life, he questions his superloyal submission to the duties of his job. "Lord Darlington wasn't a bad man," he decides, though "he made his own mistakes." That train of thought leads him, a prizer of "dignity above all," to admit, "I can't even say I made my own mistakes. Really—one has to ask oneself—what dignity is there in that?" (*RD*, 243). But his professionalism prevails, and he begins to practice the bantering that his new American boss, who has bought Darlington Hall, expects of him. Stevens' professionalism dictates that he mold himself to the preferences of his new employer. Brooksmith, on the other hand, is not a professional; he is a sensitive man who recognizes the Arcadia Mr. Offord has constructed with his help and recoils from anything less.

Ishiguro has not deconstructed Brooksmith; he has reconstructed him. The rhetorical question of the narrator of "Brooksmith"—"But to what was this sensitive young man of thirty-five, of the servile class, being educated?"—is one that Stevens cannot ask himself. Not all-knowing like Jeeves, not prepared to take extraordinary steps under desperate conditions like Crichton, not oversensitive like Brooksmith, Stevens is purely and simply the creature of his training, a dehumanized fossil of an outmoded tradition, a robot of the class system. The type is on its way to disappearing. Yet, at bottom, Ishiguro's intent is the same as James's. Both servants illustrate the sacrifice of human beings to a class system that can never reward them. Zoë, in Stern's "twice-told tale," understands the trap and with the help of her English teacher avoids it.

A Feminist Version: Angela Huth's "Mistral"

Angela Huth (1938–) would doubtless never have written "Mistral," of 1994, without the example of "Brooksmith." In Huth's feminist short story, Annie Hawker has worked as a housekeeper for eleven years in the French provincial country home of a couple of gentlemen when an incident takes place that marks her independence from them, as well as her dependence on them. She has always had a desire to write, and the story is her attempt to record her relationship with the two now-elderly gentlemen of means. She originally accepted her position as a way to enliven and improve her rather humdrum existence after her husband died. The cluster of houses Mr. Gerald and Mr. Arthur own in the south of France is the answer to her wishes. "Oh, it's paradise, as I tell my sister. I know how lucky I am." Mr. Gerald, like Mr. Offord of "Brooksmith," cultivates a garden, although this one is real, not a drawing room, and he has "planted the whole place" with flowers and fruits.[9] The men planned to make a colony for artists, in the vein of Mr. Offord's salon in "Brooksmith," but it never worked out. Although Mrs. Hawker does not know what the two gentlemen do, they seem to have aesthetic tastes and one may be a collector of antique pottery.

Annie Hawker was not the first Brooksmith to be a woman, for Stern's black student saw herself as Brooksmith. But Huth's is the first retelling from the point of view of a woman servant introduced to a higher level of life. Casting Brooksmith as a woman goes back to the germ of James's story in Mrs. Duncan Stewart's lady's maid (see above, p. 384). Mr. Gerald's garden suits Mrs. Hawker in the way Mr. Offord's intellectually superior salon suits Brooksmith, aptly since "Mr. Offord's drawing-room was indeed Brooksmith's garden" (VIII, 14). But there are great differences between the tales just because this servant is a woman and this is the age of feminism. She more or less accommodates herself to being called Mrs. Hawker and not Annie as a "little barrier, to denote my position as employee rather than as friend," whereas Mr. Offord's home had the atmosphere of a men's club in which Brooksmith was a member. By contrast, Mrs. Hawker encounters all kinds of barriers: "What exactly was my place?"[10]

During an especially hot mistral, one of the men in irritation addresses Annie Hawker as "woman" when he lashes out at her for the number of hot

---

9. Angela Huth, "Mistral," *New Yorker,* May 16, 1994, p. 88.
10. *Ibid.,* 89.

casseroles she has prepared during the hot spell: "Did you hear what I said, Mrs. Hawker, woman?" That word "cut me to the quick. *Woman!* Indicating chattel, inferior, nuisance."[11] When teatime comes and she is late, they are again critical. At that point she lets them have it, calling them useless and parasites. She hurls fruit, china, glasses, and a bag of flour. Released from her anger, she retires to her room to write the account that constitutes the tale. She combats her dependence on her bosses by becoming a writer. Brooksmith does not have a comparable resourcefulness, and he dies a frustrated man. In addition, Mrs. Hawker's tirade causes the men to realize that they are dependent on her for their sybaritic life. They make amends by serving dinner to her: she has become their friend. It is the woman servant's demand for equality and the circumstances by which she acquires it that are Huth's original turn on the basic story line of "Brooksmith." Mr. Offord's servant has been the "occult artist" (VIII, 15) behind Mr. Offord's life. Annie Hawker has similarly sustained the paradise of her two bosses, but her outburst has made them realize that her art, in this day and age, must not be occult: it must be open, and it must be recognized.

What Maisie Knew and *The Awkward Age* as Joint Sources

The redoings of James extend to the most popular of contemporary fiction—even to Danielle Steel, who has twice taken a Jamesian approach to showing life from the point of view of a small child. In *The Finer Things*, of 1990, the child Janey reenacts Maisie's life. With her father a dope dealer, she is the center of unsavory experiences. In *Kaleidoscope*, of 1987, Steel redid "The Turn of the Screw" by writing of three orphaned sisters who are separated because an uncle rejects his responsibilities to them.

Ruth Rendell's *The Crocodile Bird*

Since Barbara Vine and Ruth Rendell are the same person and since *The House of Stairs* (see below, pp. 400–402) and *Kissing the Gunner's Daughter* (see above, pp. 323–24) give evidence of reinventing *The Wings of the Dove* and "Daisy Miller" respectively, it is not surprising that certain impulses in

11. *Ibid.*, 91.

The Crocodile Bird, of 1993, seem to come from James—in this instance from *What Maisie Knew* and *The Awkward Age*. The story of the murder of three men by Eve Beck is told by her daughter, Liza, in segments that begin when she is four, then eleven, and finally sixteen. The murder that the child of four witnesses is as incomprehensible as the various marital arrangements that Maisie, the eight-year-old heroine in James's novel, observes between her parents. Only when Liza is eleven is the second murder revealed to her. When she is sixteen and her mother is arrested, she finds herself about to repeat her mother's fatal pattern. A rape victim of three truck drivers while she was an Oxford undergraduate, Eve has been driven to murder her later lovers, but the education she has given her child keeps Liza from acting out similar murderous impulses and leads her to seek a formal education. With a cache of her mother's money, she strikes out to create her own identity. This is almost unrecognizably a twist on what happens at the end of *The Awkward Age* to Nanda, another teenager but one who lives in a much more protected milieu. Nanda detaches herself from her mother's corrupt circle and becomes the adopted daughter of a man of high moral principles who once loved her grandmother.

Rendell's title refers to a bird that lives in a crocodile's mouth and can warn the animal when harm is near. Liza, for both her mother and herself, plays the role that this bird symbolizes. Her growing up with only the company of the great classics has saved her life. Rendell's enumeration of the titles of these classics seems prompted by the role that Nanda's shelf of great classics plays in *The Awkward Age*. Both young girls are protected from the corruption of their surroundings by the influence of the great books. But Liza has no father figure beyond the characters in the books. Unlike Mrs. Brookenham, Eve loves her daughter, and her eccentric ways of bringing her up are the consequence of her own cruel history. Liza's circumstances are so acutely desperate that it is only the discipline gained from her reading that allows her to break from her mother's trajectory.

It is hard to read a work of fiction that involves the point of view of a small female child on the events in her life without thinking of *What Maisie Knew*. In the case of *The Crocodile Bird*, Rendell, a sophisticated reader of James's work, counterpoints the small child's view with that of the adolescent girl capable of loving the grown man in *The Awkward Age*. The counterpoint imparts a startling rhythm to a story very removed from the atmosphere of James's novels.

Joyce Johnson's *What Lisa Knew*

Joyce Johnson's *What Lisa Knew*, of 1990, is about a case in which life copied art with ultimate cruelty. In 1989, six-year-old Lisa Steinberg was found beaten to death in her adoptive parents' bathroom. Hedda Nussbaum, her mother, lived in a sadomasochistic relationship with Joel Steinberg. Both were on drugs as well, and Steinberg had beaten their adopted daughter frequently during her short life. James's title *What Maisie Knew* is obviously behind Johnson's title for her piece of "faction." About Lisa we know very little except that she seems to have accepted her beatings calmly, probably mimicking her mother, who accepted her disfiguration at the hands of the man she lived with and idolized. Lisa appears to have adored her adoptive father too and accepted what he did to her as part of the way life was. The child was outgoing, bright, and gregarious and to her teachers showed no signs of abnormality or abuse. Like Maisie, she accepted the life she led as being the only life she knew. When she displeased her father and he asked, "What am I supposed to do with you?" she answered, "You're supposed to hit me" (*WL*, 228). Johnson wrote that "what Lisa knew will never be known" (*WL*, 242).

Johnson employs as an additional metaphor "The Turn of the Screw," the general theme of which corresponds to the Steinberg scandal. "Even after the twelve-week Steinberg trial," wrote Johnson, "the story of what really happened to Lisa remains as mysterious and inconclusive as Henry James's *The Turn of the Screw*, which is also about children at the mercy of evil surrogate parents who use them in their games with each other. The Steinberg case, too, remains open to endless interpretation, another classic in the making" (*WL*, 239). Hedda Nussbaum comes across as another Miss Jessel under the domination of a sadistic Peter Quint. The two James fictions, one of a child's accommodation to a lack of loving attention from her parents, and the other about the murder of a young boy by a selfish narcissist, create a literary backdrop for one of the most horrifying cases in contemporary times.

"The Great Good Place"

The "Ultimate Dream": James Hilton's *Lost Horizon*

Twenty-five years after James's "The Great Good Place" first appeared in print, it entered modern literature in Hemingway's "Big Two-Hearted

River" (see above, pp. 181–83) and Fitzgerald's "The Diamond As Big As the Ritz" (see above, p. 176). But a more fully realized parallel to James's tale exists in James Hilton's extended novel of adventure, *Lost Horizon*, which was published in 1933. Shangri-La, the great good place conceived by Hilton (1900–1954), is better known than James's "place" as the ideal earthly paradise, partly because of the successful movie made from Hilton's novel. Yet James's fantasy retreat is also part of the literate reader's experience and vocabulary. Both places are idealizations that serve as outlets for the frustrations in life and the longing for happiness in twentieth-century man.

James's "great good place" occupies the dreams of a work-stressed famous writer whose memory has shut down on him because of the pressures he endures. But he is able to drift off in sleep to a monastery-like world where his time is his own and the refreshment thorough enough to enable him to return to his normal daily routine.

In *Lost Horizon*, Conway, a famous soldier and adventurer, has been kidnapped, with three others, and transported by plane to the earthly paradise of the Tibetan monastery of Shangri-La, where he is to succeed the Grand Lama. Shangri-La, or the Valley of the Blue Moon, has everything someone tired of the stresses of modern life could wish for: luxury enjoyed in an ideal climate reached by pressing beyond the formidable barrier of an icy and snow-laden mountain range. It is possible to leave its precincts, but the penalty is a loss of the youth that Shangri-La's atmosphere perpetuates and supports. Yet Conway chooses to leave in order to help a dissatisfied younger colleague in the kidnapped group travel home. He then, after a period of amnesia, tries to find his way back. The story is presented as an adventure, but there is evidence within the narrative that the reader is to see it as another "ultimate dream" like that of "The Great Good Place." For no facts authenticate the narrative of his experiences. My surmise is that Hilton had James's tale in front of him when he thought up his novel, published in the aftermath of World War I and on the eve of World War II. Like James's story, Hilton's novel has a framing scene of a group of four friends, including both a first-person narrator and the person who recounts certain events to the others. This person, in Hilton's novel, is Sanders, a young pilot who talks to his friends about the background of the book's inner story as he sits with them at a restaurant table. His word is the only assurance anyone can have that the adventure really took place.

A few years before the dinner in the restaurant, a plane had been kidnapped in Baskul, India, with Conway on it, but the event had been hushed up. At the dinner—besides Sanders and the narrator, who is a neurologist—are the novelist Rutherford and Wyland, a secretary of the embassy, who is giving the dinner. As in "The Turn of the Screw," someone tells the first-person narrator that he is about to give him a manuscript. Here it is Rutherford giving it to the neurologist because of his knowledge about amnesia. Conway did not write the manuscript, but Rutherford has reconstructed the sequence of events in the third person on the basis of conversations he had with Conway. They met in a Chinese hospital, where Conway was being treated for amnesia, then spent a number of days together on a boat going from China northward, during which Conway gradually recovered his memories and shared them with the pilot.

In the first chapter, the very first sight outside the plane that has deposited the four kidnapped people shows a close kinship with the "great good place" of James's tale. In James's story, the opening words are, "George Dane had waked up to a bright new day, the face of nature well washed by last night's downpour and shining as with high spirits . . . the great glare of recommencement, in short, fixed in his patch of sky" (XI, 13). In *Lost Horizon,* Conway sees that "the surrounding sky had cleared completely . . . range upon range of snow-peaks . . . merging towards the west in a horizon that was fierce, almost garish in coloring . . . a sheer white wall that seemed part of the sky itself." The sun shines on the snow, flaming "it into a superb and dazzling incandescence" (*LH,* 35). There is a correspondence here with what James calls the "trumpet-blare of the sky" (XI, 15). Loss of memory is adumbrated by James when George Dane in the prologue to his dream vision forgets about those who are coming to luncheon and the young man who is coming to breakfast. His man, Brown, calls his attention to his forgetfulness.

In *Lost Horizon* and "The Great Good Place" alike, the experiences of the protagonist are described in the third person, although the protagonist's consciousness seems to direct the narrative. In metaphoric language of a greater density than in any other tale by James, "The Great Good Place" resorts to the word *avalanche* (XI, 17) to communicate the pressures of George Dane's world, and the Conway party walks toward the Valley of the Blue Moon, where "thunder and avalanches resounded from the snow-fields above" (*LH,* 59). Dane appreciates the silence of the "great good place," as Conway is gratified by the quiet in Shangri-La.

The "charm" of their surroundings acts on both men: the "puzzle of Shangri-La . . . was beginning to exercise" over Conway a "rather charming fascination" (*LH*, 76), and for Dane the general charm is an "absence of everything" (XI, 19). For both heroes, charm and oddity are associated (XI, 19; *LH*, 76). The earthly paradises are in both cases monasterial. The one Conway enters is a Tibetan monastery, and in the "great good place," visitors are "brothers . . . for the time, as in a great monastery" (XI, 22). In each case the origin of the utopia seems to have sprung from a single creative mind. The "great good place" began "in a splendid thought, in a real stroke of genius. . . . On the day it came home to the right mind this dear place was constituted" (XI, 23). "What . . . overhung . . . all . . . was some original inspiration, but confirmed, unquenched, some happy thought of an individual breast. . . . Yet the wise mind was everywhere—the whole thing, infallibly, centred . . . in . . . a consciousness . . . how like his own!" (XI, 31). In *Lost Horizon*, the mind behind the monastery and the kind of life lived there is Father Perrault, 250 years old, who has had Conway abducted to be his successor. In talking with the High Lama, Conway senses a "calm intelligence brooding gently over every diversion." He thinks how satisfied he is in the "serene world that Shangri-La offered him, pacified rather than dominated by its single tremendous idea" (*LH*, 173). The Lama tells his chosen replacement to "add to it the touch of your own mind" (*LH*, 181). The "wise mind" created a dream in "The Great Good Place" and what was tantamount to a dream in *Lost Horizon*. After Conway's interview with the Lama, he wonders "if all that he called to mind were part of a waking or a sleeping vision" (*LH*, 147). The conviction that assails the reader all along, that the place has been experienced not in reality but through a dream vision, is ratified in the last line of the novel, which refers to the "strange ultimate dream of Blue Moon." The question asked in the last sentence, before the novel's abrupt end, is, "Do you think you will ever find it?" That the "great good place" is a dream is declared from the beginning, and this aspect is reiterated by imputing to it a "mere dream-sweetness" (XI, 30).

The bath is very important in both paradises. Hilton's emphasis on the modern plumbing in Shangri-La may well have been suggested by the opening metaphors in "The Great Good Place," for Dane sees the "great good place" as a kind of bath in itself. He wants "just to *be* there, to stay in the bath . . . the broad, deep bath of stillness" (XI, 20). Hilton's baths are bathtubs brought from Akron, Ohio, across the barrier of forbidding mountains. They are part of the miracle of the place, and they are emblematic of how the conveniences of modern life are inseparable from this dream of wish fulfillment.

The friendly Brother in "The Great Good Place" tells Dane that any other than "our horrible time . . . is only a dream. We really know none but our own" (XI, 26). Conway does not realize this, although the reader does, for all through *Lost Horizon* the knowledge that Shangri-La is but a dream in spite of all the specificity is clearly if subtly indicated. Witness the amnesia of Conway, the absence of data on the geographical location (which is not marked on any map), the loss of all the passengers except Conway. The entire narrative has for its authority only a novelist with a fine imagination who has assembled Conway's recollections from notes. The neurologist narrator conveniently limits himself to the last question and the last line of the novel: "Do you think he will ever find it?" It is a utopian dream that the hero concocts out of desire and imagination and that an ingenious novelist organizes for him. James's tale is an overt dream made possible by a sympathetic young man who takes over Dane's authorial duties while Dane lives for a time in his nonsectarian dream monastery.

The "deep anesthetizing tranquillity" (*LH*, 63) of Shangri-La and a "pleasant mingling of physical ease and mental alertness which seems to him of all sensations the most truly civilized" (*LH*, 65) are characteristics of James's "The Great Good Place," where a want of ease is impossible. The seclusion of Shangri-La is symbolized by the physical dangers of the approach, and of the "great good place" by the small number who can know that it exists: "Think . . . of all the people who haven't and who never will!" (XI, 21).

Although Conway has been allotted the epochal responsibility of continuing to live in this, his ideal, place and of saving civilization from the oncoming disastrous war, he leaves it for the sake of a younger colleague who cannot journey out without his help. Dane also leaves his "great good place," but he can go back any time he needs to. His place is not approached through a barrier of ice and snow and insupportable temperatures. All he has to do is close his eyes and feel the need. Despite the difference in ease of access, Conway does leave, attesting that he as much as Dane can feel the urge to return to action.

In "The Great Good Place," the "very essence of the bliss" is that there is "nothing now to time" (XI, 21). In *Lost Horizon*, Conway is told, "You will have Time—that rare and lovely gift that your Western countries have lost the more they have pursued it" (*LH*, 141).

It may be that the conviction of the brothers in James's tale that they can always escape to this place ("When we want it again we shall find it"; XI, 38) leads Conway to try to regain his lost place, against the seemingly insuperable odds. In any case, on the eve of another World War that may destroy civilization, Hilton is aware how impossible it will be to find the dream place once more.

In a powerful opening metaphor, Dane wants to get away from the "newspapers too many . . . each with its hand on the neck of the other, so that the row of their bodiless heads was like a series of decapitations" (XI, 13). This may have caught Hilton's imagination, for when Mr. Barnard, an American capitalist and one of the four kidnapped men, asks for newspapers, he is told that there are none.

Conway's attitude toward his "dream" may have been suggested by lines from "The Great Good Place": "They saw the increasing rage of life and the recurrent need, and they wondered proportionately whether to return to the front when their hour should sharply strike would be the end of the dream" (XI, 39). An almost inexplicable need to return "to the front" and "to make an end of the dream" impels Conway, but it is on the note of his desire to return to Shangri-La that the novel ends.

What makes Conway leave with Mallinson is that "it came to him that a dream had dissolved . . . at the first touch of reality." He knew too "that his mind dwelt in a world of its own, Shangri-La in microcosm, and that this world also was in peril" (*LH*, 197). This conforms with Dane's knowledge that "they must return to the front sooner or later" (XI, 39). James's use of the word *front* ties up with Hilton and Conway's premonition of World War II that is inherent in their feeling that the world is in peril. The necessity of rejoining the struggle, which Hilton seems to have imported from James's tale, gives the reader a moment of disbelief by requiring Conway to leave a place that so satisfies him. Conway himself muses, "How strange . . . that this secret sanctuary should be forsaken by one who had found in it such happiness!" (*LH*, 197). Frank Capra's movie a few years later turned everything right for Conway too, but only by letting him find Shangri-La again and stay there. As James had in his library contemporary Victorian renderings of utopias—Samuel Butler's *Erewhon*, of 1872; Edward Bellamy's *Looking Backward*, of 1887; William Morris' *News from Nowhere*, of 1890—but found little use for them as literary models, so Hilton found

most earlier and contemporaneous versions of utopias of little use, including J. M. Barrie's boy's neverland in *Peter Pan*, of 1904; H. G. Wells's
ideal in *A Modern Utopia*, of 1905; and Aldous Huxley's in *Brave New World*,
of 1932. As a result, he may have reached back to James's version.

Graham Greene's *The Comedians*

Graham Greene's three essays on James show the extraordinary identification he felt with his predecessor and the belief he held that a religious
sense pervades James's oeuvre. In the earliest of the essays, "Henry James:
The Private Universe," of 1933, he described *The Ivory Tower* as giving out
a "sense of evil religious in its intensity" (*LC*, 21). He concluded that
James's "pity" and its "final justice" make him "rank with the greatest of
creative writers" (*LC*, 30). In "Henry James: The Religious Aspect," also of
1933, he recognized that "neither a philosophy nor a creed ever emerged"
from James's deep religious sense (*LC*, 38). Greene went through all of
James's fiction and discovered in such stories as "The Altar of the Dead"
and in such episodes as Strether's finding comfort in visiting the Cathedral
of Notre Dame the evidence he sought of James's religious parti pris. Yet it
is puzzling that he missed "The Great Good Place" in his amassing of evidence, for there the yearning for the part of Catholicism that James could
accept—namely, the retreat—is expressed explicitly and the role of the
monk or hermit, which always appealed to him, is scrutinized. Later
Greene became conscious of his oversight and embedded the story in *The
Comedians*, a novel of violence and murder published in 1965, thirty-two
years after the essay. In *The Comedians*, which demonstrates the "confused
comedy of our lives" (*COM*, 64), Brown, the hero and narrator, who incidentally has the same last name as George Dane's manservant in "The
Great Good Place," has inherited the Hotel Trianon, in Port-au-Prince,
from his mother. His life there with his lover, Martha, the wife of an ambassador to Haiti, seems to re-create for him the "great good place," he tells
the reader. But unlike Dane, who can retreat to his place whenever he
needs to refresh himself, Brown will lose the Hotel Trianon forever. Brown
has at least a nodding acquaintance with James's story: "I tried to read in a
paper-back volume of his short stories Henry James's *Great Good Place*,
which someone long ago had left behind; I wanted to forget that tomorrow
was Monday, but I failed. 'The wild waters of our horrible times,' James
had written, and I wondered what temporary break in the long enviable

Victorian peace had so disturbed him. Had his butler given notice?" (*COM*, 309).

By implication, he draws a comparison between Dane's place and his hotel, his great good place: "It was in a sense a family tomb. I put *The Great Good Place* down and went upstairs with a lamp. I thought it possible—if things went wrong—that this might be the last night I would spend in the Hotel Trianon" (*COM*, 309). It is natural that Brown's "great good place" would be lost, for things always go wrong in Greene's novels.

Greene needed no special insight to descry James's receptivity to the Catholic idea of a retreat, since James stated it in so many words: "The place, the time, the way were, for those of the old persuasion, always there. . . . They can always get off—the blessed houses receive. So it was high time that we—we of the great Protestant peoples, still more . . . should learn how to get off, should find somewhere *our* retreat and remedy" (XI, 24). In the retreat, the "agnostic Catholic" could meet the Protestant, and consequently "The Great Good Place" is the one tale in which Greene could observe James inspired to appropriate a part of Catholicism.

J. I. M. Stewart's *Honeybath's Haven*

A novel of suspense, *Honeybath's Haven*, written by J. I. M. Stewart under the name of Michael Innes, makes extended reference to James's "The Great Good Place." Published in 1977, the novel concerns two painters, one of whom, Honeybath, a portraitist, puts down a deposit, sight unseen, on a sumptuous dwelling called Hanwell Court: "Would it prove to be what Henry James had thought of as the Great Good Place, or would it turn out to be a well-upholstered funk-hole of a depressing sort?" (*HH*, 28). When he sees it, he decides that it is an "institution standing up for oddity [that has] much to commend it" (*HH*, 51). But actually Hanwell Court turns out not to be the "great good place": "It had turned out—utterly mysteriously—to be the Great Bad Place instead" (*HH*, 98).

The Wings of the Dove

Gertrude Stein's *Things As They Are*

Gertrude Stein's early novella *Things As They Are*, written in 1903, just a year after the publication of *The Wings of the Dove*, converts the trio of Kate Croy, Milly Theale, and Merton Densher into a triangle of women. The short novel by Stein (1874–1946) went unpublished until 1950, and it is still hard to come by. The triadic relationship, so dear to James, and present also in *The Bostonians* in Olive Chancellor, Verena Tarrant, and Basil Ransom, correlates in *Things As They Are* with a love triangle in Stein's own life. Her conscious linkage of her novella with *The Wings of the Dove* is apparent first in Kate Croy's being mentioned in the text. The character who is the counterpart of Kate, Helen Thomas, says, "Like Kate Croy she would tell me 'I shall sacrifice nothing and nobody' and that's just her situation, she wants and will try for everything, and hang it all, I am so fond of her and do somehow so much believe in her that I am willing to help as far as within me lies" (*TAT,* 75).[12]

Sophie Neathe is the novella's Milly Theale, insofar as she has a hold on Helen because of her money. The third woman, Adele, through whose consciousness the short novel is told, has been seduced by Helen, who cheats on her relationship with Sophie. Stein described Helen as the "handsome English girl" (*TAT,* 4), a phrase James used of Kate (IX, 171). Like Kate, Helen is a "woman of passions but not emotions" (*TAT,* 4).[13]

About the line "I shall sacrifice nothing and nobody," Alice B. Toklas recorded in a letter that when Stein wrote that, "in 1903 in a novelette . . . she quotes Kate Croy."[14] But the line does not occur in James's book, and a careful reading of Stein leaves it clear that she is not quoting James but is putting into the mouth of Helen the kinds of words that Kate might have said.

Stein's novella does not follow the plot of *The Wings of the Dove;* the connection is strictly in the characters, with Helen seemingly the recipient of most of the legacy from James's novel. Like Kate Croy, she has an impossible family and must get away from them. She therefore accepts the financial patronage of her friend Sophie and conceals her new love for Adele from her. Helen prevails with Adele by making physical advances Adele is not ready for. Kate and Helen exhibit the same desperate need for love. Adele achieves Densher's eventual clarity of vision when she realizes that "in order to accomplish her ends Helen would not hesitate to cause her any

---

12. The original title was *Q. E. D., Quod Erat Demonstrandum,* but for publication it was changed to a phrase used by Stein in the novella.

13. See Charles Caramello, "Reading Gertrude Stein Reading Henry James; or, Eros Is Eros Is Eros," *Henry James Review,* VI (1985), 182–203.

14. Edward Burns, ed., *Staying on Alone: The Letters of Alice B. Toklas* (New York, 1973), 84.

amount of pain [which] gave her a sense of sick despondency" (*TAT,* 68). Helen might say, equally with Kate, "I don't like it, but I'm a person, thank goodness, who can do what I don't like" (NYE, XX, 226).

Toklas' letters disclose that *The Wings of the Dove* was favorite reading of Stein's and that *Things As They Are* was the point of departure for her "Melanctha" in *Three Lives,* with a change of skin color. Adele calls Helen a "blooming Anglo-Saxon. You know what you want and you go and get it." She is "passionate but not emotional, capable of great sacrifice but not tender-hearted" (*TAT,* 31).

Sophie demonstrates her taste and money through her elegant apartment, which permits the same assumptions as Milly's Palazzo Leporelli. Sophie's "kinship with decadent Italy" is "purely spiritual," like Milly's (*TAT,* 21). Adele has a "number of friends of whom [Adele's family members] do not approve" (*TAT,* 34). That puts her in Densher's situation vis-à-vis Mrs. Lowder's circle, for Kate's aunt wants her to marry into the British aristocracy. Like Densher, who is passive toward Kate, Adele has "always doubted her own courage and distrusted her capacity to meet a difficulty if she had not inured herself to it beforehand" (*TAT,* 40).

Charles Caramello has pursued further the relationship between James and Stein, and he has ascertained that Stein had been in a "difficult lovers' triangle in which she lost May Bookstaver to Mabel Haynes."[15] By developing certain complications in Stein's life, the book transmits the legacy of *The Wings of the Dove* in the free and, for its time, unusual form of a lesbian novel. There had been another lesbian novel, Rhoda Broughton's *Dear Faustina,* in 1897, but it approaches the lesbian relationship from the point of view of a man, the fiancé of the young woman seduced by Faustina. Stein, by telling her story from the point of view of a woman, inaugurates the twentieth-century stream of novels about lesbians.

A Deconstruction: Barbara Vine's *The House of Stairs*

The Wings of the Dove seems to be the novel by James that modern English writers see as paradigmatic of his work, by virtue of rendering the sin of betrayal concrete in the pact between Kate Croy and Merton Densher. Writers return to this theme, and to *The Wings of the Dove,* again and again. Probably the most spectacular postmodern exploitation of the theme is in

15. Charles Caramello to *Henry James Review,* X (1989), 216.

The House of Stairs, of 1988, which reverses Milly Theale's role. In this novel, by Ruth Rendell writing as Barbara Vine, the character in Milly's role is not an object of pity and sympathy. She is a murderer. Vine has made her as evil as she made Daisy Miller.

On the dust jacket of the novel there is a picture of a house of stairs, and at the top of it, through a large window that reaches the floor, can be seen the face of Lucrezia Panciatichi, from the portrait by Bronzino but in reverse. In the reversal is a clue to the author's intention: the novel is a redoing of *The Wings of the Dove,* but in reverse. Elizabeth Vetch, the narrator, who fears that Huntington's chorea, the inherited disease that killed her mother, will also kill her, finds a substitute mother in Cosette. Cosette gives Elizabeth some books, including a complete set of the novels of Henry James, "with *The Wings of the Dove* present, showing no sign of special wear, bearing no marks of time or pressure or pain. But why should it? It was not this copy in tooled blue leather, stamped with gold print, which Bell picked up and looked at, idly turning the pages, inquiring of me indifferently what it was about" (*HS,* 31). Bell, a beautiful young woman with "hair the colour of tarnished brass, plaited and tied up on top of her head" (*HS,* 63), is the character associated with Milly Theale and, like her, with the woman in Bronzino's portrait. Sometimes Bell is "all in black—like James's Milly Theale" (*HS,* 100). She has "never read anything more demanding than the *Evening News* or a fortune-teller's manual" (*HS,* 31). Elizabeth once planned "to be a teacher. I was going to write a thesis on Henry James" (*HS,* 94).

Critics believe Bronzino's portrait of Lucrezia Panciatichi, which hangs at the Uffizi, in Florence, to have been the inspiration behind the painting James described in *The Wings of the Dove* as hanging in the "great gilded historic chamber" at Matcham. Bell, actuated by her resemblance to the painting at the Uffizi, buys a print of it in Florence and hangs it in her bedroom (*HS,* 105). But then it becomes related in her mind to bad things and she puts it in her drawer: "I look at the space where I tried hanging the Bronzino but couldn't, couldn't face the sight of it" (*HS,* 32). Elizabeth, looking at the picture, is "reminded . . . of Bell's interest in *The Wings of the Dove,* of her surprising request to hear the plot of it, of the conspiracy" (*HS,* 106). Her immediate need for money to pay for treatment causes her to reflect, "With the example of Henry James before me, knowing James as thoroughly as I did, I might have at least tried to write something that was an examination of the human heart, but I didn't. I wanted money . . . I had to have it all now" (*HS,* 112). So she writes lurid best sellers. Cosette dresses

Bell in a costume resembling Lucrezia's dress, and "Lucrezia Panciatichi comes in — or Milly Theale" (*HS*, 146–47). The reproduction of Lucrezia looks "down at the living Lucrezia," and in that setting "two women, one of them surely herself, enter . . . each other's arms and [make] love" (*HS*, 148). Here is evident a postmodernist attempt to coalesce the Bronzino in its actuality as a reproduction with Bell in the picture's costume, who as Lucrezia but also as Milly Theale becomes a partner in a lesbian embrace with Elizabeth, the writer and narrator of the novel. There are many levels to James, and many levels to Barbara Vine.

Bell picks up *The Awkward Age*, which Elizabeth is reading, and asks whether this is the one "about the girl that looks like me." Elizabeth answers, "No, that's *The Wings of the Dove*." When Bell asks what that is about, Elizabeth tells her the plot: "That was all I ever did. . . . The plot was enough, the melodramatic central spring of the novel which James makes somehow sensational but subtle, tenuous, like life." She adds, "I suppose it was the painting that anchored her to it" (*HS*, 159). At the arrival of Mark, Bell's brother, Bell is again wearing "nothing but black" (*HS*, 160). Later she wears a white cheesecloth costume resembling the white dress Milly has on when she gives her party in Venice (*HS*, 171). According to the author, James said, "There is a limit to the impunity with which one can juggle with truth" (*HS*, 176). But there is no limit to Barbara Vine's juggling. She brings in many references to other heroines in James's novels. Bell is likened to a Christine (*HS*, 191) — the heroine, spelled differently, of *The Princess Casamassima* — and she picks up the novel *What Maisie Knew* (*HS*, 193). But the main icon, and the heroine with whom Bell is steadily identified, is Milly Theale–Lucrezia Panciatichi: "It is a noble face Bell has, Lucrezia Panciatichi's, aristocratic, serene" (*HS*, 217).

Mark gets the idea of marrying Cosette, who is dying from cancer, in order to obtain her money: "Bell and Mark had tried to re-live the plot of a novel and it had failed — as indeed the conspiracy in *The Wings of the Dove* fails" (*HS*, 257). The perversity of the identification of Bell with Milly Theale emerges with the knowledge that she is a murderer who has also murdered in the past. When she was twelve years old, she murdered her three-year-old sister out of sibling rivalry, and now she murders Mark by pushing him out of the window. She goes to prison, but Elizabeth in her will leaves everything to her. Will Elizabeth die of her hereditary disease, or will Bell kill again? The conclusion is inevitable that Elizabeth is courting death by the woman she loves. Vine has rewritten Milly Theale as a vil-

lain and not a heroine, injecting enough of Kate Croy into her for that purpose but preserving her charismatic effect on all the other characters in the
book, especially on Elizabeth, the girl novelist who is drenched in the work
of James.

The American

Apart from Willa Cather's interpretation of James's *The American* in *Alexander's Bridge*, of 1912, there are few instances of that novel's leaving its
mark on later fiction. But one play seems distinctly to recall James's second
novel, published in 1877.

Lillian Hellman's *The Little Foxes*

According to David Higdon, a scene in *The Little Foxes*, of 1939, by Lillian
Hellman (1905–1984), "bears striking similarities to a scene in James's *The
American.*" In Hellman's play, Regina Giddens refuses to give her husband,
Horace Giddens, the medicine necessary to keep an attack from killing
him. In *The American*, the Marquise de Bellegarde's husband dies because
of her denying him medicine. The Marquis, aware of what his wife has
dealt him, entrusts to their servant, Mrs. Bread, a piece of paper disclosing
his wife's deeds. That paper is what affords Newman an opportunity—
which he passes up—to blackmail the Bellegardes. As Higdon wrote, "Like
the Marquis, Horace dies because his wife withholds medicine at a crucial
moment; and in both scenes, characters suggest that the illness comes because the man is 'paying for his dissipations.'"[16]

Hellman acknowledged in *Pentimento* that her diaries from the end of
1938 "could convince me now that *Watch on the Rhine* came out of Henry
James. . . . I was driving back to the farm . . . when I began to think of
James's *The American* and *The Europeans.*" It is Higdon's conclusion that
James's macabre plot, in which there is "the corruptly powerful Marquise
de Bellegarde, her murder of her husband, her dominance over her children, and her ruthless desire to secure her own way assisted Hellman" in
The Little Foxes as well.[17] Her borrowing may have been either conscious
or unconscious.

---

16. David Leon Higdon, "Henry James and Lillian Hellman: An Unnoted Source,"
Henry James Review, VI (1985), 134.

17. *Ibid.*, 135.

15

ADDITIONAL JAMES FICTION

Works Seldom Treated

Some of the novels and tales of James that are seldom appropriated by other fiction are in marked contrast to the most popular and best known of his works.

"Nona Vincent" and Elizabeth Robins'
The Florentine Frame

Leon Edel has reconstructed the triadic relationship between Elizabeth Robins, the young Ibsen interpreter; Mrs. Florence Bell, the wealthy patroness of the theater and a minor playwright; and Henry James, who in the 1890s was aspiring to be a serious playwright himself (*TY*, 30–39). In connection with that aspiration he met both the patroness and the actress. Edel detects in James's charming tale "Nona Vincent," of 1892, a dramatization of the relationship of the three. James placed himself in the character of Allan Wayworth, a young playwright who makes his reputation because of Mrs. Alsager (based on Mrs. Bell) and who marries the young, untutored actress Violet Grey (partly based on Elizabeth Robins). On the surface, this is one of the few Jamesian tales with a happy ending. But that is just on the surface, because an integral part of the story is that Mrs. Alsager, who would never dare tell of her love—unlike Nona Vincent, the heroine of the young man's play—quietly retreats to Torquay so as discreetly to remove herself from the triangle after she learns that the actress is in love with the playwright, who can get produced only because of the older woman's connections.

Seventeen years later, in 1909, Robins (1862–1952), with her acting career behind her, wrote a novel, *The Florentine Frame*, that takes off from "Nona Vincent." Robins' heroine, Mrs. Isabella Roscoe, is a rich widow of a prosperous patron of the university, and once introduced to Chester Keith, a young playwright, she serves as his muse much as Mrs. Alsager served as Allan's. Robins has amplified James's short tale, concentrating on the tremendous love the playwright has for Mrs. Roscoe. But in Robins' novel the third person is not a young actress but Mrs. Roscoe's adolescent daughter, who falls in love with the playwright and, in her ingenuousness—her name is Genie—proposes. He tries writing a letter begging off, but Professor Fanshawe, the mouthpiece for many of the novel's comments about playwriting, forgets to deliver it. When Mrs. Roscoe learns about the betrothal, she backs away from Keith's declaration of how much he loves her, because she puts her child's happiness before her own. Mrs. Alsager simply moves away from the scene, but Mrs. Roscoe dies. Her unrequited love for the young man divests her of any wish to survive a serious attack of the flu. The object denominated by the title *The Florentine Frame* functions for Robins in the way the object referred to by *The Golden Bowl* does for James. The picture frame is the iconic center of Robins' novel, epitomizing Mrs. Roscoe's feelings for the young man. Professor Fanshawe and Keith see another such frame at an art gallery. It has "ivory wings with silver feathers framing an oval," and Keith is interested enough in looking at the "rival example" that Mrs. Roscoe owns to pay a visit to her. Her frame was made as an altar to feature a madonna and child, but she considers it not a shrine but "only a very personal sort of picture-frame."[1] Nevertheless, she has never found a picture she considers worthy of it. Before she dies, she places a picture of Keith within it.

Robins has broadened James's "Nona Vincent" by spelling out the suppressed love that Mrs. Roscoe feels for Keith and has made it the central part of the novel. The one hint James gave of the strength of the feelings suppressed by Mrs. Alsager when she withdraws after infusing Vivian with the right take on her role is in the succinct statement she offers Allan

1.　Elizabeth Robins, *The Florentine Frame* (London, 1909), 44, 45.

of the gulf between herself and Nona. Mrs. Alsager ejaculates, "She simply tells her love — I should never do that" (VIII, 161). James made it clear that Allan reveres Mrs. Alsager but is not the least bit in love with her, and Mrs. Alsager knows that herself. In contrast, Keith and Mrs. Roscoe love each other passionately; although Keith brings himself to declare it, Mrs. Roscoe, like Mrs. Alsager, never does.

It is interesting that the single redoing of "Nona Vincent" that I have been able to find came from the pen of one of the participants of the friendship behind James's tale. Who better than Robins would have something different to say about the situation? But she did not give an autobiographical tone to her novel; she rewrote the piece of fiction into which James converted his experience. Possibly she was making a comment on how Mrs. Bell felt about James, although at the time he was a stout middle-aged man well-known for his platonic relations with women. Robins was a close friend of Mrs. Bell's,[2] and James's tale supports the suspicion that he too may have had an inkling of an emotional tie by which the patroness was bound to him.

Is *The Princess Casamassima* in Lionel Trilling's *The Middle of the Journey?*

The Princess Casamassima is one of the few ambitious novels by James that not only met with an unwelcoming reception when it was published but also never entered the fabric of other novelists' production. Perhaps Lionel Trilling's *The Middle of the Journey,* of 1947, with its Dantesque title, owes something to the novel. Those who argue that there is a one-to-one relationship between elements in the two novels are usually able to give few specifics, and their argument goes little beyond the fact that Trilling (1905–1975) published his novel in the same year he was working on his famous introduction to *The Princess Casamassima* for the Macmillan edition of 1948. Those who have attempted to make a firmer case for a relationship have had a hand in reviving interest in Trilling's works in general. Daniel O'Hara has referred to Trilling's theory of reading as "magnanimous" self-creation.[3] Trilling's brilliant introductory essay to *The Princess Casamas-*

---

2. Elizabeth Robins, *Theatre and Friendship: Some Henry James Letters* (New York, 1932), *passim.*

3. Daniel T. O'Hara, *Lionel Trilling: The Work of Liberation* (Madison, Wis., 1988).

sima fitted in with the mind-set of the immediate post–World War II generation, for whom there was a poignant conflict between revolutionary impulses and the life of culture, as expressed in Hyacinth's suicide. Engendering this was the experience of American sympathizers of the Soviet revolution. *The Middle of the Journey* provided Trilling with a conceptual structure for placing *The Princess Casamassima* in a context of acceptability to the "liberal imagination" that was also a context of revolutionary disillusionment.

In an unpublished paper, John Kimmey attempts to show how *The Middle of the Journey* was influenced by *The Princess Casamassima* by analyzing the relationships between the characters in the two novels. At the core of Trilling's novel is a concern with the nature of guilt—a consequence of Freud's influence on him—and of personal responsibility. Susan is a twelve-year-old child whose recitation of a song by William Blake has come in for criticism by the hero, John Laskell, a family friend. Laskell's reprimand confuses her when she plays her part in a school dramatization, with the result that she stumbles on her lines. When her father, disappointed and mortified, slaps her, the blow, in connection with her heart condition, causes her death. The responsibility for this touches all the characters, none of whom corresponds closely to a main character in *The Princess Casamassima, pace* upholders of the idea that there is a one-to-one relationship. For Laskell is not really a political person, even if "the picture of the world that presented itself to his mind was a great sea of misery, actual or to come." That, after all, is a Keatsian, rather than Jamesian, note. Since almost one-third of the book is concerned with Laskell's convalescence from a serious attack of scarlet fever, the stories by James that come to mind are "Longstaff's Marriage," of 1878, and "A Most Extraordinary Case," of 1868, in both of which the consciousness of invalids takes over. The rich liberal Kermit Simpson is perhaps based on Corliss Lamont or Dwight Macdonald, American "revolutionaries" who also edited journals, but the overriding issue of *The Middle of the Journey* has no linkage with the way politics functions in *The Princess Casamassima* when it figures in Hyacinth's choice between political activity and acceptance of the values of the society his political activity aims to destroy. For Trilling, the question is, who is guilty for the death of the child—Laskell, who demoralizes young Susan, or the father, who has not been a good parent to her or a good husband to Emily, the child's mother, and who lands the smack that kills? When the four men, four radicals, who are visiting the small rural town decide to pay for the funeral of the child, they simply stir up the antagonism of the community, which wishes to take care of the matter themselves. Their gesture is an attempt at easing their guilt over the untimely death, which seems not to be involved with their politics but to be occasioned by the difference in manner of living between them and people who are not of their class. The critical efforts to identify Nancy Croom, the well-to-do fellow traveler, with the Princess, Laskell with Hyacinth Robinson, Emily Dodd with Millicent Henning, and Gifford Maxim with Paul Muniment seem forced and unsatisfactory.

John Kimmey emphasizes the guilt experienced by Laskell, whose consciousness presides over *The Middle of the Journey* as Hyacinth's does over *The Princess Casamassima*. He sees this guilt as deeply influenced by the guilt in *The Princess Casamassima*, although the pre-Freudian James thought of it not as guilt but as treachery and shame. According to Kimmey, in *The Princess Casamassima* the "dualism, reflecting the world of [Hyacinth's] French 'plebeian mother' and his English 'super-civilized sire,' is at the heart of his awareness and guilt." His argument is that Trilling was influenced "not so much by James's cast of characters, but by the guilt psychology that underlies Laskell's relationship with his friends," which has its pattern in the guilt psychology of Hyacinth in his relationships. Laskell's most acute feelings of guilt stem from his mistake in overtraining Susan for her poetry recitation. Kimmey spells out a host of specific differences between Trilling's characters and James's. All the same, he is conscious how "subtly Trilling has caught James's 'imagination of disaster' and how earnestly he strives to approach his 'imagination of love.'"[4] This, the last line of Kimmey's paper, alludes to the last line of Trilling's essay on *The Princess Casamassima*: "James had the imagination of disaster, and that is why he is immediately relevant to us; but together with the imagination of disaster he had what the imagination of disaster often destroys and in our time is daily destroying, the imagination of love" (*LIB*, 92). One might also say that Trilling's allegiance to the "liberal imagination" is a commitment to the "imagination of liberalism."

Although there are no direct correlations between characters in the two novels, and although such a fanatic as Gifford Maxim—first a revolutionary and then a religious convert—is not even conceivable in the gallery of

---

4. John Kimmey, "*The Princess Casamassima* and *The Middle of the Journey*" (Photocopy of typescript in author's possession), 2, 7, 18.

revolutionaries in *The Princess Casamassima*, there is some commonality between Hyacinth and Laskell. Hyacinth's search for love among his friends, a love that might have turned him away from conflict with the revolutionaries, is unrewarded, and he kills himself as a result. Laskell's search for "moral realism" leads him to realize that Susan's death was precipitated not only by her father's failure to love her but also by his own failure to treat her with love when she was rehearsing and by his failure really to love Emily, who has provided him with the reality of love. Shortcomings in Laskell's personal rapport with Emily and Susan, rather than his tepid, disillusioned political past, are at the heart of the tragedy.

But surely the political aspect of Trilling's novel must have some relationship with the political aspect of James's novel, contemporary critics are apt to suppose. I think it is, rather, that the writing of *The Middle of the Journey*, in which the problem is one of responsibility to a moral stand, affected Trilling's interpretation of *The Princess Casamassima* in his essay. The political stance of American liberals in the 1940s was as multiform as that of political revolutionary action in James's novel, going from aloof sympathy to political anarchism. Trilling, by clarifying his own political and moral position—that of the liberal imagination—in his novel, defined his critical response to *The Princess Casamassima*. That came about precisely because it was his intention in *The Middle of the Journey* to write a political novel in the mold of James but fitted to the politics of New York intellectuals in the 1940s, some of whom still adhered to Stalinism—though his hero did not. Trilling insisted in his essay that one of the "themes which make the pattern of *The Princess Casamassima*" is the "sense of guilt and unreality which may come to members of the upper classes and the strange complex efforts they make to find innocence and reality" (*LIB*, 61). That is also the theme of *The Middle of the Journey*, where Laskell finds love with Emily but withholds the love he really feels from Susan. These two women embody innocence and reality. *The Middle of the Journey* prepared the way for reading *The Princess Casamassima* in a different way.

Trilling's attachment to James is stressed in the portrait of him that Carolyn Heilbrun, writing as Amanda Cross, embeds in the character of Professor Clemance of *Poetic Justice* (see above, p. 290). After Clemance accidentally kills a man through Kate's connivance, she says to him, since he is not being prosecuted, "If you want in the old moral way to pay a price, remember that the University College is now almost certainly assured of con-

tinued existence and development."[5] The thought that the moral human being must pay a price derives from Trilling's essay: "Civilization has a price
and a high one. . . . All civilizations are alike in that they renounce something for something else. We do right to protest this in any given case . . .
and we do right to get as much as possible for as little as possible; but we
can never get everything for nothing" (*LIB*, 84). *Poetic Justice* ends with
Clemance saying, "As to the price I pay, you need never concern yourselves
about the appropriate enormity of that."[6]

Even before executing this clearly drawn portrait of Trilling, Amanda
Cross put into the mouth of Dr. Barrister, one of her characters in another
Kate Fansler novel, an observation that relates to the introductory essay to
The Princess Casamassima: "One of those highbrow critics has discovered, I
understand, a new sort of novel about the young man from the provinces. I
was a young man from the provinces."[7] Dr. Barrister is referring to Trilling's characterization of Hyacinth Robinson as a provincial youth, comparable to Balzac's heroes. That notion has dominated all the subsequent criticism on James's novel. Dr. Barrister, however, is incriminating himself by
his remark, since his oblique reference to Trilling is circumstantial evidence that he knew the murdered girl, who talked to him about Kate's lecture on Trilling, and the acquaintanceship proves his guilt.

"The Romance of Certain Old Clothes" and Elizabeth Bowen's "Hand in Glove"

One of Elizabeth Bowen's stories, "Hand in Glove," of 1952, is heavily indebted to James's "The Romance of Certain Old Clothes," of 1868, reprinted in 1885 in *Stories Revived.* James's tale is set in an earlier time, the
eighteenth century, and so is Bowen's, in the twentieth century at its turn.
In James's tale, two young sisters in America, Viola and Perdita, love the
same young British aristocrat, Arthur Lloyd. They are also equally enamored of fashion and clothing. The suitor marries the younger Perdita, who
dies giving birth to a little girl. On her deathbed, she makes her husband
promise to keep her trunkload of trousseau finery intact under lock and

5. Carolyn Heilbrun [Amanda Cross], *Poetic Justice* (New York, 1970), 162.
6. *Ibid.*
7. Carolyn Heilbrun [Amanda Cross], *In the Last Analysis* (New York, 1964), 56.

key for their daughter, since she knows that Viola craves beautiful clothes. Arthur eventually marries the jealous, earlier rejected Viola, who is the more statuesque of the sisters and therefore the better clotheshorse, in order that his daughter may receive good care. But Arthur loses money, and since he is unable to buy her the finery her sister enjoyed, she covets all the more her sister's wardrobe. She knows that it lies "languishing in thankless gloom in the dusty attic" (I, 315) and that Arthur keeps the key "wrapped in a little packet" (I, 317). Her husband finds her near the open chest: "Viola had fallen backward from a kneeling posture. . . . On her limbs was the stiffness of death, and on her face . . . the terror of something more than death. . . . And on her bloodless brow and cheeks there glowed the marks of ten hideous wounds from two vengeful ghostly hands" (I, 319).

In Bowen's adaptation, there remain, besides the displacement of events to an earlier time, two sisters out for the same marital catch, the unauthorized access to clothes in a trunk in the attic, and the murder by strangulation of a plundering young woman. But Bowen modified the plot ingeniously. The avenger in "Hand in Glove" is not one of the sisters but their aunt, who lives with them, occupying a back bedroom under the attic where the trunks full of finery she accumulated in her great social life in India are stored. The sisters in "The Romance of Certain Old Clothes" have a "certain native-grown gentle *brusquerie* and wildness" (I, 298), and the sisters Ethel and Elysia Trevor, in "Hand in Glove," have "ingenuity and agility." Since they take "leading parts in theatricals" (*CSB*, 768) and sing duets, they clandestinely select from their aunt's trunks and restitch the clothing. They discover that "all that they were short of was evening gloves," which were in the trunk they could not open, for "all other locks had yielded to pulls or picking," but not that one (*CSB*, 768). The aunt keeps the keys for this trunk on her person in a silk sack. The sisters' own gloves, having to be constantly cleaned, smell of benzene, but Lord Fred, the English aristocrat on whom Ethel is setting her cap, has "since childhood recoiled from the breath of benzine" (*CSB*, 773). Ethel notices that his interest in her flags when they dance closely. Going to her aunt's room to get the key, she ends in an altercation that is fatal for her aunt. Ethel takes the bag with the keys from the corpse, heads for the attic, opens the trunk, and flings "herself forward on to that sea of kid, scrabbling and searching" (*CSB*, 775). One of the gloves seems to be occupied by a hand that clutches "Ethel's front hair . . . and drags her head down. She begins to choke among the sachets and tissue — then the glove lets go . . . and makes its leap at her throat" with such force that "during the strangling of Ethel, the seams of the glove split." The glove, ironically, "would have been too small" for Ethel to wear (*CSB*, 775).

Only one hand strangles Ethel, in contrast to the "two vengeful ghostly hands" in James's tale. Bowen has put her modernist stamp on a tale James liked well enough to include in his first book of stories, *A Passionate Pilgrim*, of 1875. It was the only ghost tale in the volume. Although he did not select it for his New York Edition, it was reprinted after his death in his first collected edition, of 1921–1923. In 1948, it appeared in *The Ghostly Tales of Henry James*, edited by Leon Edel, and Elizabeth Bowen may have read it there, no more than four years before her rewriting. James's neogothic tale has never been hidden from readers.

"The Beldonald Holbein" and Louis Auchincloss' *The House of Five Talents*

Although the heaviest debt in Louis Auchincloss' *The House of Five Talents*, of 1960, is to Edith Wharton's unfinished novel, *The Buccaneers*, Auchincloss is still in this novel looking over James's shoulder, particularly in the chapter about Mrs. Millinder's becoming an art collector. Gussie Millinder begins her acquisitions with a "Holbein of an unknown English lady (aetatis suae 37)."[8] James's tale "The Beldonald Holbein," of 1901, was based on a portrait of Lady Butts by Holbein that in real life Isabella Stewart Gardner came to own. At the top of this painting is the inscription "Anno Aetatis Suae LVII." The subject of the portrait in *The House of Five Talents* looks just like Mrs. Millinder, as Lady Butts was supposed to resemble Mrs. Gardner, who at the time James wrote his story was also in her fifty-seventh year: "The subject even looks a bit like Mama: white, square-jawed, intelligent."[9] Perhaps the effect of Henry James is most apparent in the way the reader is expected to look over the shoulder of Mrs. Millinder, the narrator, who in each chapter interferes in the life of a different one of five relatives. Although she is sure her effect is positive, the reader sees the damage she has done to the happiness of all her victims. From behind her shoulder it is possible to apprehend that she is an interfering busybody who does harm to everyone around her, but first of all to herself.

8. Louis Auchincloss, *The House of Five Talents* (Boston, 1960), 188.
9. *Ibid.*, 188.

The *Tragic Muse* and Louis Auchincloss' *The Dark Lady*

Auchincloss' spin-off of *The Tragic Muse* in *The Dark Lady*, of 1977, is a more subtle piece of craftsmanship than his earlier redoing of *The Ambassadors*. There are many references to plays: to *Romeo and Juliet*, *Twelfth Night*, *Troilus and Cressida*, and to Racine's *Phèdre*. The main character of the novel is Elesina, a young actress who, encouraged by an elderly spinster who is her friend to break up a millionaire's marriage and get the man for herself, is a variation on Miriam Rooth of *The Tragic Muse*. When, after her marriage, she is taxed with being still on the stage at Broadlawns, the estate of which she is mistress, she responds, "But I'm on it! Do you know Henry James's *The Tragic Muse?* It's the best novel ever written about an actress." But she takes issue with James's heroine's determination not to give up the stage to marry a young diplomat and accept a future as an ambassadress: "Ah, how James saw it, the idiocy of any man's thinking that a real actress could even consider balancing love against the stage! But now I begin to see something that James didn't see. She *might* have wanted to add the part of ambassadress—in diamonds—to her roles."[10] Elesina runs for Congress after the death of her husband. She thereby achieves a rather dramatic political equivalent of becoming an ambassadress. Rounding out the parallels to *The Tragic Muse,* she also, like Miriam Rooth, marries her manager.

Roderick Hudson and John O'Hara's *Ourselves to Know*

John O'Hara (1905–1970) went to *Roderick Hudson* to set the stage and situate two of the principal characters in *Ourselves to Know*, of 1960, in which a man of Jamesian sensibilities and a peaceful way of life murders his wife. Unlike James, the hero of O'Hara's novel fails to realize in time that marriage does not suit him. The relationship between Roderick Hudson and Rowland Mallet is clearly the model for the friendship between the two young men in O'Hara's novel, with some reversals in characterization. The painter Chester Calthorpe is based on the sculptor Roderick, although his friend, Robert Millhauser, who corresponds to Rowland, does not support him financially, for each pays his own way when they travel to Europe together in the 1870s. But Chester has chosen Robert "to be the steadying influence," and he relies on his "stolid German nature" (*OK*, 44). He remarks on Robert's sounding "so Dutchy," a reminder of Rowland's true "Dutch

---

10.   Louis Auchincloss, *The Dark Lady* (Boston, 1977), 134.

ancestry" (NYE, I, 13). Robert admires Chester "for his independence, and fearlessness. . . . He didn't rebel quietly, on the sly. He did it openly and took the consequences, even if the consequences cost him things he wanted very much" (*OK*, 47). This is much in the manner of Roderick.

Gerald Higgins, the narrator, to whom Robert has entrusted his auto-biographical memoirs, ties Robert's experience of Europe to his admiration for Henry James: "Consciously or not, he was an admirer, I suspected, of the late Henry James. His prose style was similar to, if not imitative of, James's travel essays." Gerald notices that Robert has quoted a phrase, "the swarming democracy of your fellow tourists," which "he did not put in quotation marks and which I remembered from my limited reading of James" (*OK*, 79). What Robert has written manages "to transport" Gerald "back to the 1870's, to make that time and all of his time come alive to me, and he had done it through his own personality and not by his imitations of Henry James" (*OK*, 85).

On the trip to Europe, with Robert as chaperon and Chester as a fla-grantly unconstrained and sensual artist, the two men fall out. After Ches-ter reveals himself to be a rampant homosexual, Robert breaks away, characterizing his position relative to Chester with a phrase that James employed as a title when he says, "I'm not your guest on this trip. I'm your traveling companion" (*OK*, 92). The two men do not see each other again until the end of the book. Some years after the journey to Europe, the un-emotional Robert falls violently in love with a woman half his age. They marry, but she deceives him openly. When he murders her, the provocation of her behavior and the fine reputation he enjoys among the townspeople mean that he is released after serving a very short time in prison. On the day he is about to go home, Chester reappears. Ironically, in *Ourselves to Know*, it is the figure patterned on Rowland who goes amok, murdering a wife who is a more contemporary and vivid remake of Christina Light, the wife Roderick did not kill but who drove him to suicide. Chester, the reck-less homosexual painter, has been saved by his Catholicism, and he be-comes a lay priest. Both men have an acquaintance with monasteries. Rob-ert sees his jail as a comfortable monastery; Chester does the hard work of priests in his. The reader is bound to conclude that Robert Millhauser should have learned from Henry James's decision to remain celibate.

Gerald's interest in the life of a murderer who does not pay the penalty usually exacted seems to reproduce James's in the existence criminals led after avoiding the death penalty or lifetime incarceration. Writing to William Roughead, the historian of crime, in 1914, James extolled the "prodigious Madeleine" Smith, who had emerged from a trial years before with the verdict of "guilt not proven." For James, her trial represented the "perfect case . . . or the beauty that she precisely *didn't* squalidly suffer, but lived on to admire with the rest of us . . . the rare work of art with which she had been the means of enriching humanity." James showed a fascination with the life Smith led "during the time . . . when I used to hear of her, as married and considered, after a long period in Australia, the near neighbour, in Onslow Gardens, of my old friends the Lyon Playfairs" (LU, II, 386–87). A large part of O'Hara's book is concerned with Robert's completely uneventful life after his crime, as a model citizen in his hometown.

The American Scene and Philip Roth's *American Pastoral*

In 1997, two years after Philip Roth unburdened himself of the bitter and rage-filled puppeteer's story, *Sabbath's Theatre,* he returned to Jamesian material in *American Pastoral.* His manner of decanting from James has changed, however. There are no references to James, nor are there any quotations, and the work that appears to have spurred Roth is not among James's fiction. Rather, it is *The American Scene,* the last book of James's travel essays, written in the wake of his trip to America in 1904 and 1905 after twenty years of absence. Roth's move here is unanticipated, and the evidence for ascribing it to him lies only in the first few pages of James's impressions of America, which include a short summary of his reaction to the New Jersey shore, where his publisher, Colonel Harvey, took him shortly after his arrival. This is the only text in which James paid any attention to the state of New Jersey, and in it he seemed to be challenging a writer to follow through on his observation of the way rich Jews were living in palatial houses, like those in Deal Beach. Roth's New Jersey youth and his obsession with James and with Jews as a people would undoubtedly have led him to read James's account.

James and Harvey arrived by steamboat, surrounded by a "rare collection of young men of business returning, as the phrase is, and in the pride of their youth and their might, to their 'homes,'" and "if treasures of 'type' were not here to be disengaged, the fault would be all [the spectator's] own." A few lines later, James began his page-long description of impressions that would ripen "like golden apples, on the tree." His experiences "sharpened . . . that consciousness of strolling in the orchard that was all one's own to pluck, and counting, overhead, the apples of gold," as he called "those thick-growing items of the characteristic that were surely going to drop into one's hand, for vivid illustration, as soon as one could begin to hold it out" (*AS*, 6). For him it was an "adventure, unmistakably, to have a revelation made so convenient—to be learning at last, in the maturity of one's powers, what New Jersey might 'connote.' This was nearer than I had ever come to any such experience." He described the grandiose dwellings as a "close stringing of more or less monstrous pearls" (*AS*, 7). They struck him as "florid creations waiting . . . for their justification, waiting for the next clause in the sequence, waiting in short for life, for time, for interest, for character, for identity itself to come to them" (*AS*, 8). He saw in them the "expensive as a power by itself . . . really exerting itself in a void that could make it no response" (*AS*, 9). These houses seemed to him to say, "We are only instalments, symbols, stop-gaps. . . . Expensive as we are, we have nothing to do with continuity, responsibility, transmission." They held the "sharp interest of the match everywhere and everlastingly played between the short-cut and the long road" (*AS*, 11).

He explained: "Money, in fact, *is* the short-cut" (*AS*, 11). His question was, "What turn, on the larger, the general stage, was the game going to take?" (*AS*, 12). It was clear to him that it would constitute "drama, and *that* drama; than which nothing could be more to the occult purpose of the confirmed, the systematic story-seeker":

> The very *donnée* of the piece could be given, the subject formulated: the great adventure of a society reaching out into the apparent void for the amenities, the consummations, after having earnestly gathered in so many of the preparations and necessities. . . . What would lurk beneath this . . . to thicken the plot from stage to stage and to intensify the action? The story-seeker would be present, quite intimately present, as the general effort [proceeded] to gouge an interest *out* of the vacancy. . . . Never would be such a chance to see how the short-cut works, and if there be really any substitute for roundabout experience, for troublesome history, for the long, the immitigable process of time. It was a promise, clearly, of the highest entertainment. (*AS*, 13)

This challenge seems to be met, three generations later, by the story seeker Roth, interested in his Jewish heritage and his New Jersey background. His hero in *American Pastoral* is the successful Jewish businessman Seymour Levov. Blond like a Wasp, a star athlete, and the picture of normality, Levov looks as if he belongs to one of the ruling families that date back to the revolutionary history of the state. First the reader sees Levov as he appeared to Nathan Zuckerman when they were in high school together. In the account by Nathan that follows, Roth has answered James's invitation. It turns out that there is no shortcut to giving oneself and one's family a background in New Jersey's history. Levov's daughter, Merry, becomes a terrorist of the sixties, killing a number of people. She is in hiding, and Levov and his wife, a former New Jersey beauty queen, are contending with shattered lives. The success of three generations of Levovs as glove manufacturers, or of Dawn Levov in breeding cattle in a carefully appointed pastoral milieu, is to no avail. Merry's terrorism has shattered the arcadia. The dream of reason produces monsters, as Goya showed, and Merry is the tragic result of Levov's good intentions underwritten by money and the desire for assimilation into the American mainstream.

Whether Roth consciously took up James's challenge or fulfilled his task unconsciously is probably irrelevant. As a Jew, a New Jerseyite, and a writer old enough to have seen three generations of rich assimilated Jews aspire to the American arcadia, he is equipped by birth, by life, and by a commitment to his Jewish origins to show that there is no shortcut. The fourth generation of assimilated Jews produces a terrorist daughter who shatters the pastoral fantasy. Levov, who fancied himself Johnny Appleseed scattering his apple trees all over America, not plucking the golden fruit there for hungerers after impressions who are just passing through, cannot sustain a pastoral achieved by the shortcut wealth has given him.

Postmodern Treatments

"The Diary of a Man of Fifty" and Jean Pavans' *Retour à Florence*

Ernest Dowson was much impressed by James's "The Diary of a Man of Fifty," and its influence appears in a number of Dowson's short stories (see above, pp. 148–51). About a hundred years later, Jean Pavans, a French playwright, novelist, and translator of James's work, produced a French adaptation of the tale.[11] The French mind had found "The Altar of the

---

11. Translations by Jean Pavans of works by Henry James include *La Scène américaine* (Paris, 1993), *Heures italiennes* (Paris, n.d.), and Volumes I and II of *Oeuvres complètes de Henry James: Nouvelles, 1864–1875* and *Nouvelles, 1876–1888*.

Dead" appealing to the imagination (see above, pp. 241–47) but rarely read James's earlier tales. But Pavans has deemed "The Diary of a Man of Fifty" effective enough to make into a play. Performed in 1986 at the Théâtre du Rond-point, in Paris, and directed by Jean Louis Barrault, *Retour à Florence* has dialogue almost completely in James's words. Pavans has also made changes, however, that are true to his critical evaluation of James. First, he has given the nameless narrator a name, as a way of fleshing out his reality. For the performance he becomes Stanley Ferguson. In the preface to the one-act play, Pavans disagrees with James's decision not to include the story in the New York Edition on the ground that the plot was too "trivial." Pavans believes that the narrator of "The Diary of a Man of Fifty"—along with the narrator of *The Sacred Fount*, which James also rejected for republication—has an illusory certitude that love is a murderer or vampire (*RF,* 8). Pavans elects to develop the "affrontisements psychologiques" between four persons, and his play makes vivid the encounters between a mature man and a young man, and between them and the two Biancas of Florence, mother and daughter. Pavans has noticed that encounters of a similar nature take place in other of James's works—between Dencombe and Dr. Hugh in "The Middle Years," and between Lambert Strether and Little Bilham in *The Ambassadors.* They also occurred in James's later life between him and the young men he favored—among them Hendrik Andersen, Jocelyn Persse, and Hugh Walpole.

The introduction by Pavans, in three scenes, of the ghost of the dead Countess Salvi, the elder Bianca, was inspired by "The Altar of the Dead" to let the countess shed light on the obsessive delusions of Stanley Ferguson. That enabled Pavans—who substituted Venice for the side trip, eliminating the original story's Bologna—to create a brief but charming digression in which Stanley tells Bianca Scarabelli, the daughter, "In your wonderful country there is a city for each state of mind, and if your city [Florence], Countess, inflamed my young heart, at present it is Venice that exalts the maturity of this old organ" (*RF,* 75).[12] Venice is the "miraculous city whose consciousness tells us that age and isolation are the basis of happiness" (*RF,* 76). The suggestion that Stanley has an idée fixe in believing that the Countess Salvi was a liar and a temptress and that her daughter is betraying in an identical manner her suitor, young Stamner, comes from James. In "The Diary of a Man of Fifty," Stamner tells the narrator, "You

12. Throughout this section, the translations from the French are mine.

have at any rate what we call a fixed idea" (IV, 421). Pavans makes it contemporary when the Countess Scarabelli tells him, "You have in every sense what's called *une idée fixe*" (*RF,* 76). The basic scenario is in James's tale, but Pavans has admirably orchestrated the interactions between the four characters to create the opposition between a man whose idée fixe distorts reality and the other characters. The dramatic transactions between the four reveal that the mother's feelings for Ferguson were nothing like what he thought them to be and that the bond between the daughter and her young suitor cannot, on any reasonable examination, be considered analogous to Ferguson's relationship to the mother, whether that was real or illusory.

It is Pavans' accomplishment to extract from James's curious tale a drama of Racinian distinction about a man obsessed by his own ego. The ghost of the mother points out to him how his ego rules: "It is always yourself that you see in me" (*RF,* 64). It is also the mother, the woman he thought he loved, whom he sees in her daughter. The appearance of the ghost of the Countess Salvi allows Ferguson and Stamner to expose their thoughts and feelings to each other in a way they could not while the countess was alive.

Pavans does not take up the meaning of the painting by Andrea del Sarto that hangs on the walls of the Florentine palace, although he mentions that it is there. In James's story, the narrator perceives an analogy not only between his case and Stamner's but also between the painting and the countess, for Andrea's wife, the subject, was unfaithful before and after their marriage. Pavans lets a painting by Raphael in the Pitti Palace, *The Madonna of the Chair,* look out over one of the meetings of the ghost and Ferguson. The ghost never appears in the countess' home but only in public places. Pavans is representative of his generation of French writers in being attracted to the deeper psychology in James, evident even in his earlier tales.

Playing with Theories of Intertextuality: "The Private Life" and A. S. Byatt's "Precipice-Encurled"

A. S. Byatt's confessed aim in her intellectually keen manipulations of existing prose and poetry is to play a "kind of game with modern theories of intertextuality (a modern text reading an ancient one by quoting and 'rearrangement,' to use a Jamesian word)."[13] When she has encountered this

---

13. A. S. Byatt to author, August 6, 1991.

in others, she has defined it as "not parody, not pastiche, not plagiarism —
but a good and greedy reading, by a great writer" (*PM*, 167). In modern
times, the narrative technique was apparent in the novels of Angus Wilson,
especially in his *No Laughing Matter*, of 1967. There a "game" is played by a
family, and the family itself is a constituent of the game: "A reverberation is
set up between their literary factitiousness and their own sense of this."
The complex situation "produces a new, a novel kind of acute disorder and
discomfort in the reading experience" (*PM*, 169).

"The Private Life" has impelled at least two writers to reinvention of the
Jamesian in their own work. Noël Coward, in *Private Lives*, took the notion
of doubles, applying it to two couples who separate and then rejoin and will
continue to do so (see above, pp. 166–67). Almost fifty years later, Byatt
has preferred to take bodily from James's tale the passages that refer to
Robert Browning — the nineteenth-century writer behind Clare Vawdrey
and his double in "The Private Life." Coward's appropriation was popular
and directed to a theatergoing audience; Byatt's is for a sophisticated literary readership. His shared the theater's nontheoretical bias, whereas hers
is an answer to the vogue in academic circles for theories of fiction writing:
"I was playing games with scholarly theories and Browning's mixing of
fact-fiction in *The Ring in the Book*, a postmodernist text if there ever was
one," she wrote of her tale "Precipice-Encurled," of 1987.[14] Three years
prior to the publication of *Possession* (see above, pp. 368–71), and more ex-
perimentally, Byatt attempted in "Precipice-Encurled" to show how the
novelist and the poet possess each other. The tale, one in her collection of
short stories *Sugar and Other Stories*, has a title that comes from some lines
by Browning:

> What I love best in all the world
> is a castle, precipice-encurled
> In a gash of the wind-grieved Apennines.[15]

As in *Possession*, Browning is the hero, this time under his own name. In the
tale we may find a key to the principle behind Byatt's system of literary appropriation, that of *déja-dit*.

The story is Byatt's re-rendering in her own terms of the relationship be-

14. *Ibid.*
15. Quoted *ibid.*

tween the English poet and Mrs. Bronson, an American friend of his living in Venice in the Ca'Alvisi, a house in which Browning often stayed and worked. She was also a close friend of Henry James's, and he wrote about her in a prefatory note to her article "Browning in Venice," reprinted in *Italian Hours*. The scholar in Byatt's tale sees, in the relation between Mrs. Bronson and Browning, that the lady was the "inapprehensive object" of a "dormant passion needing but a look / To burst into immense life!"[16]—another quotation from Browning's poetry. The scholar "combs the facts this way" (*SU*, 188). In the remainder of the tale, the scholar appears to reconstitute the relationship between the two people by virtue of his possession of relevant facts, many of them depending on a slight repositioning of lines and words taken from James's prefatory note to "Browning in Venice," as well as from "The Private Life." The epigraph to the tale, also by Browning, underlines the point Byatt wished to make in her story: "Is fiction, which makes fact alive, fact too?" Byatt's excerpting of whole sentences more or less intact as the material from which she makes her own fiction is a narrative technique that seems geared to a contemporary attitude to the *déja-dit*. The already written text is removed from its moorings and is therefore free to be appropriated by anyone. There is hence no such thing as plagiarism involved; the lines and words belong to whoever can put them to use. The principle is not a long step from the appropriation of the literary heritage begun by James himself, then extended by Ezra Pound and T. S. Eliot. Peter Ackroyd, in his fiction, has reconstituted the life of Thomas Chatterton and Oscar Wilde, but Byatt has absorbed the whole Victorian period, including James's fiction.

Even in *The Virgin in the Garden*, of 1979, Byatt had quoted Eliot's "Tradition and the Individual Talent" and brought in the name of Alexander Wedderburn—with Edward T. Cook one of the authors of the classic *Life of John Ruskin*—as well as "A Local Habitation," by Wordsworth.

In "Precipice-Encurled," Byatt wrote, "It has been said of her that she would exchange a Tintoretto for a cabinet of tiny gilded glasses" (*SU*, 185). Compare James in *Italian Hours:* "She would have given a Tintoretto or two, I think, without difficulty, for a cabinet of tiny gilded glasses" (*INH*, 78). More strikingly, she had Browning sitting in a hotel with a balcony "face to face with a great, bristling primeval glacier" (*SU*, 188). James's very first line of "The Private Life" begins, "We talked of London, face to

16. *The Complete Poetic and Dramatic Works of Robert Browning* (Boston, 1895), 991.

face with a great bristling, primeval glacier" (VIII, 189). Browning's sister says to him as he works, "You can't write in the dark, Robert" (*SU*, 194). That depends on a memorable scene from "The Private Life" where the narrator penetrates the darkened room in which Vawdrey, Browning's private self, is writing. "It was equally natural that in the absence of its occupant the room should be dark" (VIII, 204), but in the dark he sees a "figure seated at a table" (VIII, 205). The sister sees a "rug thrown over a chair" (*SU*, 194). This is a collaging of James's prose: "a figure I had at first taken for a travelling-rug thrown over a chair." The narrator adds, "If you're busy, I won't disturb you" (VIII, 205). Byatt wrote, "If you're busy, I won't disturb you" (*SU*, 194). James went on, "Why was he writing in the dark?" (VIII, 205). Byatt wrote, "You can't write in the dark, Robert, it is bad for your eyes" (*SU*, 194).

Byatt quoted from "The Private Life," but without quotation marks. She at times took a series of words from James's tale and lined them up recognizably but with the elimination of certain of his words. Consider her lines:

He addressed himself to women exactly as he addressed himself to men, this affronted narrator complained; he gossiped to all men alike, talking no better to clever folk than to dull. He was loud and cheerful and copious, his opinions were sound and second-rate, and of his perceptions, it was too mystifying to think. (*SU*, 195)

And then James's:

He might have been always in the same company, so far as he recognized any influence from age or condition or sex: he addressed himself to women exactly as he addressed himself to men, and gossiped with all men alike, talking no better to clever folk than to dull. I used to feel a despair at his way of liking one subject—so far as I could tell—precisely as much as another: there were some I hated so myself. I never found him anything but loud and cheerful and copious, and I never heard him utter a paradox or express a shade or play with an idea. . . . His opinions were sound and second-rate, and of his perceptions it was too mystifying to think. (VIII, 191–92)

Byatt's Browning worries about signing a birthday book just as James's narrator does, who "always . . . took some time to recall" his birth date. He "hesitated between two days" (VIII, 203). In "Precipice-Encurled," Browning professes "not to remember on which of two days he had been born . . . he never could be certain" (*SU*, 195).

From the fiction by James about Browning, Byatt has seized what she would treat as facts about Browning in producing her own fiction. Her method gets its strength from the energy of the passages she has selected, and it is a bold and noticeable departure from the methods of the other postmodern writers who have sought sustenance in James.

"The Aspern Papers" and James Michener's *The Novel*

I'm present all right, says the narrator of The Aspern Papers.
    You, sir, are an unmitigated scoundrel, says Strether, and you don't even know it. Out and out flawed as a consciousness.
                                        —Christine Brooke-Rose, *Textermination*

In 1991 — the year of Christine Brooke-Rose's academic roundup *Textermination,* which among the many literary characters it brought to life included the narrator of "The Aspern Papers" — James A. Michener (1907–1997) took the same tale as both the prime example of integrity in writing and the supreme text by which to measure human morality. It provided the substantive literary content, as well as the moral, of Michener's *The Novel*. In the way Michener has organized his material, there is also a suggestion of a Jamesian technical device, that of viewing events from separate points of view. The four parts of his novel are divided among the Writer, the Editor, the Critic, and the Reader, all of whom, like the two couples in *The Golden Bowl*, are closely connected. The critic, Streibert, is pursuing an advanced degree from Columbia University, where he meets Professor Devlan, of Oxford University, a man "laudatory of Henry James and his severely controlled type of narration" (*NV*, 203). Streibert makes a trip with Devlan into Venice, knowing that James "set the rules" for references to the city and for knowing how to make fiction out of its architectural embellishments. Devlan tells Streibert that John Cumnor, the "rather unpleasant English authority" in "The Aspern Papers," who "also wanted the papers, could have been me, and the young American could easily have been you." By pointing out James's procedure in "The Aspern Papers," Devlan teaches Streibert that a certain "chain of words . . . will bring to life real human beings in a real human setting" (*NV*, 217) and that "serious art is a communication between equals on exalted levels. Nothing else is worth trying" (*NV*, 218). Later in the summer, the two men meet again in Athens, and Devlan reads to the critic from "The Aspern Papers" in a carefully chosen rendezvous in an olive grove. Devlan, in a fit of emotion, chooses the section in which Miss Tina proposes marriage to the "publishing scoundrel" as a price for the documents he wants, and then he continues to the end of the story. When the critic asks why Devlan has read the end of the story — "What does it signify?" (*NV*, 262) — Devlan replies that it illustrates "what we seek when we write. To fill a throbbing moment with revelation, with meaning, human passion." Devlan has made of James's tale a kind of biblical text out of which he can draw the great lesson for writers who wish to reach the highest levels of creativity, and also a text for the revelation of his own passionate human feelings for a friend he knows he is seeing for the last time.

"The Aspern Papers" and A. N. Wilson's Quartet of Novels

A. N. Wilson (1950–) wrote a quartet of novels between 1988 and 1996 that, many clues attest, takes its plot from "The Aspern Papers." The first of the novels, *Incline Our Hearts*, of 1988, exactly one hundred years after the publication of James's tale, introduces Raphael Hunter, who has written a biography of the famous English writer James Petworth Lampitt and who is now at work in bringing out a volume of Lampitt's letters. A member of Lampitt's family is "wary" of this biographer and of "publishing scoundrels" in general.[17] Wilson places quotation marks around the phrase of opprobrium, for the words are well known from "The Aspern Papers." When Juliana catches the narrator going through her desk, she exclaims, "Ah! You publishing scoundrel!" (VI, 361). Hunter has insinuated in his life of Lampitt that the writer's friendship with Henry James and Hugh Walpole marks him as homoerotic, if not actively homosexual. Lampitt's book *Lagoon Longings*, about Venice, is permeated by the Venetian aspects of James's tale.

In the second novel, *A Bottle in the Smoke*, of 1990, Hunter has become a celebrity and television personality. He is the utter fulfillment of James's "publishing scoundrel," a media success. He learns that Lampitt as a young man visited James at Rye, from which Hunter infers that there were homosexual experiences between James and him. In the third volume, *The Daughters of Albion*, of 1992, it comes out that Hunter murdered Lampitt,

17. A. N. Wilson, *Incline Our Hearts* (New York, 1988), 148.

and later he is suspected of murdering Virgil D. Everett, a great collector of material relating to Lampitt, in an effort to obtain items he wants. Hunter goes through Lampitt's desk, as James's nameless narrator goes through Miss Bordereau's. He in addition seduces all the women who have been involved with Lampitt for the biographical lore he can unearth. This volume concentrates on the correspondence between Lampitt and James, and it transpires that as a young man Lampitt had served as an amanuensis of James in "Lamb's House" (*sic*) and had taken James's dictation for the chapter in *The Ambassadors* in which Strether advises Little Bilham, "Live all you can!" A letter James wrote to Lampitt is found, and Wilson imitates with some verisimilitude James's style when, in the fourth volume, *Hearing Voices*, of 1996, he presents it in its entirety.

Many facets of James's biography and fiction undergird the extension of the plot from "The Aspern Papers," but the controlling objective of their introduction seems to be to frame a postmodern flowering of James's manipulative narrator. Hunter, in his obsession to become the "greatest English biographer since Boswell,"[18] has become a scoundrel for the late twentieth century who does not shrink from seduction and murder as means to his end.

It is no accident that both Michener's *Novel* and Wilson's quartet are concerned with homosexuality. The unstated assumption seems to be that, in James's tale, the narrator's avoidance of marriage with Tina Bordereau is a manifestation of his homosexuality. In Michener's novel, the two men's feelings are deeply and erotically intertwined. In Wilson's quartet, Raphael Hunter's homosexual drive colors his attitude to his biographical subject. Hunter can perform bisexually as long as his sexual partners offer something that might prove his biographical allegations.

One thing that is sure is that Julian Ramsay, the novel's narrator, is heterosexual. In *Hearing Voices*, Hunter's seduction of Ramsay's fiancée unhinges the narrator, and he rehearses his offender's malefactions, truly devilish in quality and quantity.

The Europeans and Maureen Howard's *Natural History*

Maureen Howard's *Natural History* is, true to its name, a detailed account of actual events during the nineteenth century in Bridgeport, Connecticut.

18. *Ibid.*

It is also a novel about a present-day resident, in whose life the history of the town reverberates. Incorporating James Joyce's way with Dublin in a remodeled stream of consciousness and availing herself of techniques of montage and notebook insertion, Howard (1930–) brings in everything she can from the history of a town that for her typifies the American dream and the rude awakening from it.

Toward the end of World War II, a society woman kills a soldier, and the investigator of the murder is Billy Bray, a swaggering detective connected with the Bridgeport courthouse and the father of the hero, James Bray. The Bridgeport home of the Brays is riddled with sex, crime, and moral confusion and out of this swirl James Bray rises to success. But what is particularly interesting in the present connection is that, with all the references to Chekhov, Mark Twain, and other literary giants, the literary character James Bray looks to for a disguise is Felix Young in James's *The Europeans*. Introducing James Bray in disguise by invoking the passage in *The Europeans* in which the character appears, Howard conveys how Bray is like his model: "He has taken a room near the university under the name of Felix Young, a sinister professor in one of his mild disasters, talky script devoid of action. . . . Yeah, he is Felix" (*NH*, 223). The reference to James's novel affords Howard the opportunity to show what her hero does with his disguise as Felix Young. He assumes the painter's eye of James's good-natured Felix. James wrote, "Felix was immensely entertained. He had called it a comical country, and he went about laughing at everything he saw. You would have said that American civilization expressed itself to his sense in a tissue of capital jokes. . . . Felix might have passed for an undispirited young exile revisiting the haunts of his childhood" (*EU*, 14). Later, he added, "Felix himself continued to be in high good-humour. Brought up among ancient customs and in picturesque cities, he yet found plenty of local colour in the little Puritan metropolis" (*EU*, 16). As Felix prepares to visit the Wentworths, the cousins he and his sister, Eugenia, have come to see near Boston, she instructs him, "You will go and examine, and report. You will come back and tell me who they are and what they are; their number, gender, their respective ages—all about them. Be sure you observe everything; be ready to describe to me the locality, the accessories—how shall I say it?—the *mise en scène*" (*EU*, 17). The very term *mise en scène* is repeated by Howard. After she describes the students of Professor Felix Young as these "new immigrants" with their "new dreams," she continues, "Felix Young sees this more clearly than James Bray who levitates in his opening shots, all *mise en scène* stuff ending in an indulgent frame" (*NH*, 225). The final words of instruction by Eugenia to Felix indicate where Howard got her book's title. When Felix asks how he should tell the innocent American Wentworths about Eugenia's European marriage into the German aristocracy, Eugenia answers, "Tell my story in the way that seems to you most—natural" (*EU*, 18). In other words, he is to make it part of their natural history. Not much later in *The Europeans*, there is a glancing allusion to natural history in the zoological sense. Mr. Wentworth says to his transatlantic relatives, "It seems natural that we should know each other," and Eugenia replies, "Ah, there comes a moment in life when one reverts, irresistibly, to one's natural ties—to one's natural affections" (*EU*, 38). It is as if she is protesting against being seen as an exotic specimen in a museum of natural history.

Henry James appears again in *Natural History* when Glenda, the Radcliffe graduate who is James Bray's publicity agent, reads the "late Henry James" (*NH*, 342). This seems almost a deliberate counterbalance to the preoccupation with the early James that is inherent in a focus on *The Europeans*, a nod to the preference of the literati for works of the "major phase." When today's novelists look to James's fiction, it is either to the early fiction—*Washington Square*, *The Portrait of a Lady*, and *The Europeans*—or else to the major phase. The middle novels and stories of the realistic phase are with a few exceptions not often invoked. The assumption must be that when Howard chose Felix Young as the alias of her hero, it was to recall the past of a more innocent America: "He's after, with Felix's help . . . call it an aura of trust and purpose, a giddy, gung-ho innocence—a moment in the grand American city, of dramatic reversal" (*NH*, 227).

"The Beast in the Jungle" and Brad Leithauser's *Seaward*

> In Henry James's story "The Beast in the Jungle," the beast is the fear that is always threatening us. The final act, when it comes, will be to show us where the failure of our expectation lay. The fall of man is only too real when it comes to ourselves.
>
> —Alfred Kazin, in his journal

Alfred Kazin, a leading literary critic from the 1960s to the 1990s, has mused about "The Beast in the Jungle," "But that is a marvelous fable, isn't it, coming from a writer-virgin, who acted in life only by writing? . . . Yet Henry James manages now to make his reader feel like an accomplice. He proved that, whatever his withdrawals as a man, his valor as a writer was enough—and overreaching."

Brad Leithauser's *Seaward*, of 1993, can be taken as illustrative of how the myth of whatever the beast stands for in the minds of those who have read James's story affects postmodern writers. Kazin sees the tale's theme as the "fear that is always threatening us"; others see it as not only the fear of death but death itself. In its vague definition the beast stands for the essential tragedy of mortality, as well as the tragedy that springs from not facing up to what mortality really is and not taking advantage of its antidote, the love between human beings. Leithauser (1953–) portrays Tony Seward, his novel's hero, as an ordinary man who has had an extraordinary experience of a mystical cast. A Princeton graduate, a Washington lawyer, and a pole-vaulting champion, Tony can soar upward without straining and thereby reaches heights others do not. Betsy, his wife, who has been accidentally drowned, seems to appear to him as a ghostly apparition. He tries to interpret the experience by talking to two of his friends. At the beginning of the novel, he also tells the story of his life to a young woman on a plane and adds, "I'd like to have the experience just once before I die of seeing somebody who is somehow *larger than life*" (*SE*, 14). The connection with "The Beast in the Jungle" is apparent in his continuing "odd inarticulate disgruntled sensation—one burrowing all the way back into his childhood—that there was something, some not yet divulged *something* . . . to serve which he had been placed upon this planet" (*SE*, 44). In "The Beast in the Jungle," the hero too waits for a great role, discovering only after the woman who loves him dies that he was so concerned with his own place in life that he did not respond to her love and fulfill the great role open to him as her lover.

There is another affinity to "The Beast in the Jungle" in his, "one raw day in Charlottesville, hurling himself headlong, eyes hotly blind with weeping, onto Betsy's grave." He is one of the "living damned who at some point in their lives had seen, as he had seen, something so unthinkable it was never once more even in dreams to be fully approached: your wife unreally bleached and unreally bloated" (*SE*, 51). Even though he is "on the very edge of forty," he has always felt that "he was born for some as yet undefined purpose" (*SE*, 52). The illumination in his cabin frightens him, for it seems to be an appearance of his wife (*SE*, 140). His friend explains him as being someone who has waited "all his life for what he used to call his *one extraordinary thing*" (*SE*, 112). In spite of this normal, contemporary man's

ordinary life, people have to understand that he is "somebody who entertains visions . . . and this is his fate and these are something he alone can negotiate." He gives away his niece, Diana, in marriage so that it should
"never be said of him that he failed to bring the girl safely to shore" (*SE*,
384). That fulfillment of an obligation frees him from his feeling of guilt.

Incidentally, also in 1993, there appeared in a movie a character who
suggests the hero of "The Beast in the Jungle." Whether the author saw
him so is debatable, but the critic did, for those who do the reviews for the
daily papers and magazines are steeped in James. Anthony Lane, of the
New Yorker, found the coldhearted hero of *Un Coeur en hiver* to be a "descendant of John Marcher in 'The Beast in the Jungle,' the man 'to whom nothing on earth was to have happened.'" The beautiful heroine, who is a talented musician, makes an "exasperated appeal as the hero decides what to
do about her."

James's Ghost Stories and Alison Lurie's *Women and Ghosts*

Any Jamesian reading Alison Lurie's collection of tales, *Women and Ghosts,*
from 1994, will notice that among the nine stories, three seem to illustrate
what Harold Bloom would call "poetic misprision," new misreadings on
themes originally explored by a predecessor—in Lurie's case, Henry
James in his fiction in the ghostly genre. The differences between the three
stories by Lurie (1926–) and the three by James pivot on her originality
and personal idiosyncrasies. In each, the intertextual reader is prompted to
recognize the original but also clearly conditioned to see how new Lurie's
treatment of the theme is.

"The Highboy" relates to James's "Sir Dominick Ferrand," of 1892, in
which a davenport desk bought by Peter Baron, a poor young writer, contains a hidden drawer filled with incriminating love letters between an
aristocrat and a young governess. The illegitimate daughter of their union,
Mrs. Ryves, a young widow with a small boy living in the same boarding-
house as Baron, receives an uncanny message of danger when the young
author tries to use the material he has discovered: "Some secret sympathy
had made her vibrate—had touched her with the knowledge that he had
brought something to light" (VIII, 360). The hidden cache comes to Peter's
notice only when the small boy begins "to bang on the surface" of the desk.
Peter hears the hollow sound and investigates. The concealment was possi-

ble owing to the peculiar shape of the davenport, with six small drawers "of different sizes, inserted sideways." The papers "haunt" Mrs. Ryves, although she does not know their content (VIII, 357, 379). Baron is about to negotiate a deal with the editor of the journal the *Promiscuous Review*, which will publish his find. But as he reads the letters, his concern for the young woman deepens, and he ends up burning them, so that she never learns what they were about. The "inscrutable davenport" (VIII, 385), which shows no emotion and evinces no anthropomorphic tendencies, is different from Lurie's Chippendale highboy. Her story begins with the sentence: "Even before I knew more about that piece of furniture, I wouldn't have wanted it in my house." The narrator is discussing a piece of furniture that will show malice toward everyone. Its large ugliness, the "color of canned prunes" (*WG*, 40), upends the loveliness of Peter Baron's davenport. Lurie's tale is a take on James's idea, but she has turned it around, as she did also in the other two derived ghost stories. Buffy, the narrator's sister-in-law—rich, comfortable, and modern, in contrast to Peter and Mrs. Ryves—seriously loves the ugly piece of furniture she owns. Her personality and her love for the highboy—which parallels Peter's liking for the davenport—are also reminiscent of Mrs. Gereth's love for her collection of valuable furniture in *The Spoils of Poynton*. In "Sir Dominick Ferrand," when the letters are burned, the link to the past is destroyed and the ghost that plagues Mrs. Ryves's mind disappears. James's statement in his preface to *The Spoils of Poynton* that "the 'things' are . . . exerting their ravage without remorse" metaphorically suggests the animate nature of Buffy's brutal highboy. But James called the furniture pieces "magnificently passive," whereas Lurie makes her highboy malevolently aggressive. It bruises Buffy's grandchildren (returning the damaging of the davenport by Mrs. Ryves's little boy), but Buffy's concern for her highboy is more intense than any feeling for her grandchildren. Buffy shares Mrs. Ryves's almost extrasensory perception, yet, like Mrs. Gereth, she cares "too much for her furniture" (*WG*, 49). She is able to sense that her highboy is "getting upset" (*WG*, 51) by the talk about being put into a museum. Left to be inferred is that this is the motive the highboy has in killing her "accidentally," since upon the accidental death, Buffy's unaltered will leaves the piece to a family and not an institution.

Lurie's "In the Shadow" recalls James's "Sir Edmund Orme," of 1891, the story of a benevolent ghost that appears to a woman who, having jilted a man years ago, caused his suicide. Now, whenever her young daughter is about to jilt a suitor, his ghost reappears, but only to the mother. She is a very different person from Lurie's Celia Zimmern, a twenty-nine-year-old career diplomat working in the American embassy in London, who is engaged to Dwayne Mudd. After Dwayne is killed in an auto accident, his ghost appears to Celia whenever she is about to become intimate with another man. Then, in a "semi-transparent" form, he heckles her about her choice and badgers her to stop her lovemaking. In order to flee the jealous ghost, she gives up her job in London and takes one at the embassy in Goto, Africa, but he persists. This ghost is different from that of Sir Edmund Orme in being aggressive and voluble. Sir Edmund's ghost mixes with people fully materialized and never says a word. Celia feels that the accident in which Dwayne lost his life is her fault because she did not go to the party where Dwayne drank himself into the state that resulted in his death. Dwayne gave Celia a Cartier watch that had belonged to his mother. When her lady guru in Goto makes her give the watch to her, the ghost, divested of his maternal link to Celia, finally disappears.

The last of the tales, "The Double Poet," shares with James's "The Private Life" the conceit of a double. Coward and Byatt have also played with this (see above, pp. 166–68, 419–20). In Lurie's tale, the narrator, Karo McKay, is, like James's Vawdrey, a poet of distinction. Since it is the late twentieth century, she is a poet in residence at a university. And Karo finds James's idea of a double appealing: "To have a stand-in who would take my place for all the tedious chores that go with giving a reading but aren't mentioned in the contract: someone who would be polite and charming to the nervous students who meet the flight, make conversation at long receptions, sign books, give interviews to local newspapers and radio stations — Yes, that's what I'd wish for, if wishes were horses — Pegasus?" (*WG,* 154–55). But the double Karo gets is a monster who forces her to face herself. She discovers that someone posing as her has been making appearances, but as an interfering interloper. Her double, known to the reader as the Non-Karo, misrepresents her and delivers herself of literary judgments the real Karo would never venture. But the double does make Karo realize that she is an impostor herself, since the person she projects in her public profile and the person who pursues monetary advantage have nothing to do with her real, creating self. After the shenanigans of the Non-Karo bring on a breakdown, she realizes that her self-presentation as a modern publicized poet has been a fake front. Lurie is making a caustic comment on the ruinous public-relations expectations that today's creative artist must meet. Beyond instigating a lie, they are a health hazard and a burden on the artist's sensibilities.

"The Beast in the Jungle" and Saul Bellow's *The Actual*

One well-informed critic sees in Saul Bellow's novella *The Actual*, of 1997, a contemporary version of "The Beast in the Jungle," and finds that Harry Trellman, Bellow's hero, has "more than a passing resemblance to the hero of James's famous tale," John Marcher. She concludes that the novella can only be described as a "Bellovian variation on James."[19] The "Bellovian variation," if that is what it is, in any case strays from James in its kind of hero and in its matter and material. Bellow (1915–) has written about contemporary Chicago, the world of successful finance, and a heroine who is a somewhat vulgar go-getter even if her name, Amy, is an anagram of May Bartram's. Both fictions are fantasies of their writers' old age, and both heroes are out of touch with reality. John Marcher withholds love from May, but for an entirely different reason than Harry withholds love from Amy, for Harry knows but cannot express that he loves Amy, whereas Marcher is oblivious of the love between him and May. May's love for him is as unspoken as Harry's for Amy. Marcher's obtuse obsession with his fate makes him aware of nothing outside himself. There is a way in which Harry is Marcher's opposite: he is "observant," and his love, existing only in fantasy, keeps him from declarations until the very end of the novella. What is more, the milieu and the two heroines' personalities are so different that, without this critic's perception, the resemblance between the two works might go unnoticed.

She does not detail further similarities between the two novellas, except for commenting that Harry too "has spent his entire life waiting and withholding." She might have mentioned that Bellow seems to make use of two main settings from James's tale. One is the country house Weatherend, and the other is the cemetery where May has been buried. Weatherend sets the tone for the expertise about paintings and interior decoration that Bellow has allotted to Amy. Amy selects furniture and paintings for the Adletskys and the Heisingers, both collectors of valuable works of art, as May

19. Michiko Kakutani, "Eluding Entanglements, and So Eluded by Love," *New York Times*, April 25, 1997, Sec. C, p. 28.

Bartram attends to the contents of Weatherend. Both May and Amy can command reality, whereas Marcher and Harry live in their own world, Harry finding excuses in his accidental similarity to an Asian ("I have a Chinese look").[20] But Harry, unlike Marcher, is an observer at dinner parties, and that quality leads the trillionaire Adletsky to take him on as part of his "brain trust." Perhaps Bellow's dining-out hero is named Harry because there is something of the social Henry James in him. The benign character of Harry's fantasies differs from the evil in those of someone like Madge Heisinger, who thinks up schemes, such as a divorce registry, that she wants Amy to run with her. But Amy's good sense makes her reject such unrealistic scams. Both Amy and May, however, are dependent at certain stages of their lives on their aunts' charity, and Bellow may have arranged this similarity.

At the end of *The Actual,* James's cemetery scene comes in, though for a reversal of James's ending. Bellow reverses Marcher's realization of the failure of his life by permitting Harry the revelation that allows him to make up for his former mistakes. He is able to declare his love as Amy re-buries her husband, and he proposes marriage. Thus he unites his fantasy with his "actual." Bellow has made a happy fable out of James's tragic adventure into the dark places within personal relationships.

20.   Saul Bellow, *The Actual* (New York, 1997), 2.

16

THE "JAMESIAN" NOVEL AND SHORT STORY

The "Jamesian" Novel

During the period of socialist thinking in the 1930s, especially among New York intellectuals, there arose the concept of the "Jamesian novel." It emerged at a time when there was an ambivalence among socialists about the novels of Henry James. Certain leaders of socialist thinking, like Philip Rahv, were scholars and teachers who esteemed James as a very great novelist but reacted against his fascination with the upper classes. They took an interest in the form of his fiction, if not particularly in its content. Mary McCarthy, another of the leaders of the group, framed a notion of what a "Jamesian novel" was: "The Jamesian model remains a standard, an archetype, against which contemporary impurities and laxities are measured," she wrote in *Ideas and the Novel.* Struggling to make her account less vague, she continued that James "invented a peculiar new kind of fiction, more refined, more stately, than anything known before, purged, to the limit of possibility, of the gross traditional elements of suspense, physical action, inventory, description of places and persons, apostrophe, moral teaching." He "etherealized the novel." From today's point of view, she seems completely wrong about James, though not about the "Jamesian" novel that flourished just before and just after the Second World War. She complained that James's characters never discuss politics and "never dis-

pute what they have looked at." Her assertion ignores a profusion of coun-
terexamples, from the Reverend Mr. Babcock's discussions of Luini's
paintings in *The American* to the articulation of impressions in front of the
Bronzino portrait in *The Wings of the Dove*. She also wrote that James's
people "are virtually never seen reading . . . even a guidebook." Isabel Archer often appears with a book, and in "Travelling Companions" a guidebook is never out the hands of the two main characters.[1] The category
of the "Jamesian novel" betrays a careless reading of James that is perpetuated by those who follow in the footsteps of the genre's definers even
today.

In the posthumously published book *Intellectual Memoirs*, of 1992, Mc-
Carthy referred to James's grip on her friends in the literary world of the
1930s: "Philip [Rahv's] long love-affair with James had begun; at Vassar I
hadn't cared for him. . . . Fred Dupee was a natural Jamesian." As to the
short story "Cruel and Barbarous Treatment," which became the first chapter of the novel *The Company She Keeps*, the book that made her famous, she
recalled, "I know for a fact that when I wrote that piece I was feeling the effects of reading a lot of Henry James; yet today I cannot find James here
either."[2] The presence of James is not as invisible as McCarthy thought. In
the volume's first chapter, she included the phrase "The Real Thing" twice,
and in "Portrait of the Intellectual as a Yale Man," she wrote, "She had
showed him the cage of his own nature. He had accommodated himself to
it, but he could never forgive her. Through her he had lost his primeval innocence."[3] That echoes the need of "The Beast in the Jungle" (XI, 402).
McCarthy's stories are Jamesian to the degree that they are thematic tales
playing with variations, in which metaphors predominate as they do in
James's later style. McCarthy was good at metaphors.

Diana Trilling in her intellectual memoirs continued to employ McCarthy's concept of a "Jamesian novel." Isabel Bolton's two novels manifest the
genre's defining characteristics, according to her.[4] In Bolton's *Do I Wake or
Sleep*, of 1946, as well as in *Many Mansions*, of 1952, there is the Jamesian
device of a first-person narrator who reviews her life in thoughtful recollection. But at least Bolton applied her technique so as to enable gradual reve-

1. Mary McCarthy, *Ideas and the Novel* (New York, 1980), 5.
2. Mary McCarthy, *Intellectual Memoirs: New York, 1936–1938* (New York, 1992), 36.
3. Mary McCarthy, *The Company She Keeps* (New York, 1942), 246.
4. Diana Trilling, *The Beginning of the Journey* (New York, 1993).

lations in a plot that has a number of surprises in it. Her novels fall outside McCarthy's definition of a "Jamesian novel" insofar as things do happen. In both novels, the heroine is educated and gifted with the skills of writing, and within her contemplation there exist paragraphs of keen critical judgment. In *Many Mansions*, Miss Sylvester, an eighty-four-year-old woman living by herself in a small hotel in New York City, writes a novel about her life, which turns out to be much more dramatic than the opening chapter portends. Having been made pregnant as a young girl by the husband of a cousin, she gives birth to a boy in Florence. The child is immediately adopted, and for a while no trace of him remains for her. But by chance he reappears in her life as a ne'er-do-well who rents a room in her home. She never lets him find out that she is his mother. The novel is "Jamesian" only in the most diffuse way, and it is probably but one of a countless number of such novels written after the 1930s.

The genre McCarthy demarcated has become completely watered down in the 1990s. In Damien Wilkins' *The Miserables*, of 1993, a latter-day version of the "Jamesian novel," there seems no perceptible intrusion of plot, character, or quotation from James, but there is a first-person narrator of sensibility and aesthetic predisposition.

The "Jamesian" Short Story: Jonathan Keates's *Soon to Be a Major Motion Picture*

Along with the "Jamesian novel," there is also a place for the "Jamesian" short story. In 1997, a good example of that appeared in Jonathan Keates's collection of stories *Soon to Be a Major Motion Picture*. We have seen how the Venetian crime tale of the 1970s and 1980s insisted on its relation to Henry James, mentioning within them usually either his Venetian tale, "The Aspern Papers," or his personal connection with the city. At the close of the 1990s, there seemed to be a number of Henry Jameses in the fiction of gay writers, following James McCourt's *Time Remaining* of 1993.

An example of such a "Jamesian" character appears in Keates's collection. In the story "La Dolce Prospettiva" he clearly attempts an imitation of James's middle-late style and civilized approach to the American experience of Venice. Keates's ability to invent metaphors seems to imply a saturation in James's short stories. A reviewer for the *Times Literary Supplement* sees the hero of the tale, "a secretive New England professor," as experiencing a "Henry Jamesian predicament in modern Venice."[5] She must see behind his avoidance of the emotional entanglement that a rich American woman wishes to engage him in a repetition of Constance Fenimore Woolson's similar attempt to engage James's affections, which were homoerotically related to his young men acolytes. The reviewer sees the professor specifically as a "Jamesian art historian."

The story concerns an American woman so rich that "from her money . . . nuns might have built themselves a cathedral" (DP, 86–87). She has hired a distinguished professor of art history to guide her through her experiences with the art of Europe. His "face bore the lines and marks of old America, of the patrician enlightenment which had planted New England with libraries and institutes . . . in an unshakable confidence . . . as to the ultimate rightness of its considered discriminations" (DP, 87). This suggests something of Henry James, as well as Bernard Berenson. The woman's interest is one of desire for the professor, and she awaits an opportunity to disclose this kind of interest in him. But the opportunity never comes, even in the Venetian church in which an altarpiece shows, among the three saints' pictures, a figure of St. Sebastian that stirs the professor emotionally. For the professor, there is "the peculiar kind of truth accorded to his sensibilities by a picture or a statue" (DP, 93). In his apartment, his collection of small works of art "mattered more than the people he invited to fit among them" (DP, 94). The depiction of St. Sebastian reminds him of his love for a young man forty years ago. The professor is "'introduced' at Palazzo Barbaro" (DP, 98), a place that had been frequented by James, and his trained young art historians, whom he loved, remind the reader steeped in James of the Master's young acolytes. In the picture of St. Sebastian the saint's "right arm was raised to grasp the arrow shaft jutting from his lower neck" (DP, 102), reminding the professor of the pose of his young lover years ago, a pose beckoning him to make love to him.

The language used by Keates in this story, the Venetian art, the reference to homosexual arousal all contribute to suggest the presence of the now universally conceded homoerotic James, as well as does the complex texture of the prose. All these elements are situated in the city that, from James's recently republished *Italian Hours* containing his five remarkable essays on Venice, have made all educated English and American readers learn to associate that city with James himself.

5.   Julia O'Faolain, "Con Brio," *Times Literary Supplement*, April 18, 1997, p. 23.

17

THE AFTERLIFE OF THE LIFE: LEON EDEL'S BAEDEKER TO JAMES

> Boswell has been waiting in line for three years. I'd promised to get to him as soon as I finished Henry James and I still have 'The Ambassadors,' 'The Golden Bowl,' 'The Awkward Age' and four volumes of Edel's biography to go.
>
> —Russell Baker, in the *New York Times*

The five-volume biography of Henry James by Leon Edel (1907–1997) has been a Baedeker not only to those wishing to visit the James continent but also to those wanting to annex parts of it. Annexing the Master is aided by annexing the masterpiece about the Master.

For some people, the biography has come to take the place of James and is all of James they ever read. As the Samuel Johnson who dominates the imagination of the English-speaking world is Boswell's, so the Henry James who occupies present-day attention is Edel's. When, in 1980, the international novel—if not invented, at least perfected by James—appeared in the number one best-selling novel, *Princess Daisy*, by Judith Krantz, she concealed her substantial debt to him until the end, only then being will-

The material in this chapter appeared in somewhat different form as "Biography and the Scholar: *The Life of Henry James*," in Gloria G. Fromm, ed., *Essaying Biography: A Celebration for Leon Edel* (Honolulu: University of Hawaii Press, 1986), 21–36.

ing, as James would say, to give herself away. There, a business tycoon, finding it impossible to sleep in spite of pills, reads a "few more pages of Leon Edel's five-volume biography of Henry James" (see above, p. 322).

Not only the cosmetic king but also his creator has gone to James by way of Edel, the path by which the audience the great novelist courted to little avail all his life has finally made its way to him. Much the same is true in France, where in 1990 Edel's one-volume abridgment of the five-volume biography was translated into French and published as *Une Vie* to the excitement of the literary community. The only complaint was that the work did not tell enough about James's eccentric personality and erotic life. The French have apparently been spoiled by the eccentricities of Edgar Allan Poe, William Faulkner, and Dashiell Hammett; they prefer the American authors they read about to be dysfunctional and psychologically intriguing. The French *littérateurs* wanted answers that the biographer felt the facts did not yield. James is now the object of a cult in France, for he is thought of as an American Proust.

Edel's life of James has taken the place of James's own works for a large proportion of the reading public because he has made the "figure" of James assimilable. The quintet of volumes turns into a five-act play in which the hero is James and the other characters are his novels and tales. Each volume has its own climax, its shock of discovery, and its problems and solutions. The work has gained from Edel's maturity, for the twenty years over which the biography was published were for him a period of growth not only as a scholar and writer but as an artist. The five-volume set was followed, in 1977, by a two-volume edition in England that Edel at the time called his definitive version. The greatly reduced price of the five-volume American paperback edition, of 1978, captured another large audience, and in 1985 the one-volume edition reached a still more sizable community of readers who had neither the patience nor the preparation to persevere through the five volumes.

Often, enthusiastic devourers of Edel's life of James vow to complement that reading with a reading of James's total oeuvre. They begin nobly but never get beyond one or two titles. James's fiction turns out to consist for them, as for Krantz's cosmetic tycoon, of "books [they] had never read" and would never read. These readers are content to take the word of a compelling and gifted writer about the excellence of James's books. They want James's story.

The five-volume edition, in the richness of its details and judgments, was gradually absorbed by novelists and short story writers interested in James. After the publication, in 1953, of the first volume, *The Untried Years*, in which Edel applied his Freudian technique and analytical skills to James's childhood and youth, those details and judgments started filtering into new fiction. Although Fred Kaplan in a biography of 1991 included interesting letters not previously published, he uncovered substantially little to modify Edel's basic factual account of James's life. Cynthia Ozick has written charmingly of her unthinking response to James, which she corrected only after reading Edel's biography. At the age of seventeen, she plunged into "The Beast in the Jungle" and immediately became the older Henry James, who wrote the tale when he was sixty. As she recounted, it was only after reading a

> certain vast and subtle book that I understood what had happened to me. The book was not by Henry James, but about him. Nowadays we give this sort of work a special name: we call it a non-fiction novel. I am referring of course to Leon Edel's ingenious and beautiful biography of Henry James, which is as much the possession of Edel's imagination as it is of the exhilaratingly reported facts of James's life. In Edel's rendering, I learned what I had never before taken in—but the knowledge came in the Jamesian way, too late. What I learned was that Henry James himself had not always been the elderly bald-headed Henry James!—that he too had once been twenty-two years old.[1]

If James is present in others' novels and short stories, so is Leon Edel. In Philip Roth's *Deception*, there is no mention of James but only of Edel. When the writer, lying in bed with his mistress, asks her what she would do if, after his death, she were approached to give her version of the author, she answers, "This is a very handy device to get me to reveal myself, isn't it? But I ain't talking. It has to be Leon Edel or I'm not saying a thing" (*DE*, 71). In *Zuckerman Unbound*, Roth quoted from a letter of James's to Paul Bourget, which, at that time, the Bourget heirs had allowed to be published only in part, and only in Edel's *Henry James: The Middle Years*. There was no other source from which Roth could have obtained it.

Discussing biography in relation to Zuckerman's life, Roth wrote in *Deception*, "What interests [the biographer] is the terrible ambiguity of the 'I,'

1. Lyall Powers, ed., *Leon Edel and Literary Art* (Ann Arbor, Mich., 1987), 114.

the way a writer makes a myth of himself and, particularly, *why*" (*DE*, 98). Roth had evidently read Edel's collection of essays *Writing Lives: Principia Biographica*, of 1984, or *Literary Biography*, of 1957, and paid attention to what Edel said about "myth." In *Writing Lives*, Edel discussed the two myths that matter to biographers: "the myth we perceive with our eyes and sense of observation; and the covert myth, which is a part of the hidden dreams of our biographical subjects, and which even they would have difficulty to describe because these are lodged in the unconscious, in the psyche."[2] Also echoing this passage from Edel, Roth wrote in *Deception*, "It's the dream biography—the author died young. . . . It's really the biography every biographer wants to write because the *issue* is biography" (*DE*, 100). It is fitting that as Roth wound down the Jamesian presence in his fiction, he should have adverted to Edel's approach to biography and shown how it has affected the biographical elements in his own fiction. Edel replaced James for Roth when the situation required replacement.

It should be obvious that fiction that enfolds material about James has been not only more abundant but also more soundly grounded in fact since the volumes of Edel's biography started to have their effect. Some writers who have fallen under the spell of James have done so because they have also been under the spell of Edel. At least three writers besides Roth who have markedly relied on James for material have mentioned Edel in their writings: Carolyn Heilbrun (under the pen name of Amanda Cross), James McCourt, and Sylvia Plath. Amanda Cross, in *The Question of Max*, of 1977, refers to how the James family gave permission to Edel to write the novelist's biography: "Look at the James family. They gave Edel complete domain until he finished the biography, and never regretted it."[3] In James McCourt's *Time Remaining*, Odette O'Doyle, the transvestite narrator who joins the gay stories together, goes on about Edel's course on James at NYU. Edel's course was the open sesame to James's work, and Edel the supreme authority on it. In the journals of Sylvia Plath for 1958, after Edel's *The Untried Years* appeared, there is the comment "Henry James's biography consoled me and I longed to make known to him his public acclamation."[4]

Since *Henry James: The Master*, the fifth and final volume, came out in

2. Leon Edel, *Writing Lives* (New York, 1984), 161.
3. Carolyn Heilbrun [Amanda Cross], *The Question of Max* (New York, 1977), 63.
4. *The Journals of Sylvia Plath* (New York, 1982), 219.

1972, writers interested in bringing James into their work have had an almost limitless supply of facts at hand. One on which they seem to fixate is
the burning of James's personal correspondence, which they find almost as
suggestive as James's "obscure hurt," described in an earlier volume.
James Lord mentions the destruction of the letters in *Picasso and Dora: A
Personal Memoir,* of 1993.[5] James Mellow, who reviewed Lord's book for the
New York Times Book Review, remarked that although Lord had "destroyed
all raw materials" that went into his volume, he "had not hesitated to tell
all" about the triangular relationship between himself and Picasso and
Dora Maar. "Strangely," Mellow continued, "after having told so much, if
not everything, about himself and significant others, he concludes with this
abrupt confession: 'To me one of the most moving literary events of modern
time is Henry James's great bonfire of personal papers in 1909.'"[6]

Katherine Anne Porter is another writer of distinction who has looked
into at least one volume of Edel's life, *Henry James: The Treacherous Years,* for
the wisdom and critical judgments of James's biographer. I have before me
a copy of that volume signed by Porter and dated February 17, 1972.[7] In
ink, she has heavily underlined parts of the introduction, including where
Edel states that James's novels and tales "constitute a remarkable series of
technical experiments devoted to modes of indirect narration and a refin-
ing of the novelist's omniscience" (*TY,* 14). Porter's notes show how greatly
Edel's judgments can engage the creative writer. She has marked the sentence in which Edel calls attention to James's kinship with Proust and
Freud, and then with incisive strokes the sentence "Thus in three different
cities of the Old World three different men were embarked at this singular
moment of the history of mind and psyche on journeys into a personal 'dark
backward and abysm.'" Of the three—that is, Proust, Freud, and James—
Edel continued, "James wrote with a profound intuition but with the least
self-awareness" (*TY,* 15). Porter was also interested in the justification
Edel offered for his "biographical method" (*TY,* 16). "The works of a
writer," he has always contended, "are in every way the primary source of
a literary biography." She responded to Edel's insistence that "an artist's
work is less accidental than it has seemed" and that "there exists an equally

---

5. James Lord, *Picasso and Dora: A Personal Memoir* (New York, 1993).

6. James R. Mellow, "Jousting with the Minotaur," *New York Times Book Review,* July 18,
1993, p. 1.

7. Katherine Anne Porter's copy is in the author's possession.

consistent unconscious effort—an inescapable use of the buried materials of life and experience—to which the artist constantly returns" (*TY*, 17). The assumption must be that Porter was reading Edel's biography as a work of art itself rather than just as a pipeline to James's works of art.

Perhaps the first of modern writers to acknowledge the artist in Edel was Edith Wharton, who wrote in a letter recommending Edel for a Guggenheim award that the young man who had met with her to learn about James had the "sympathy and understanding to lift a work of erudition to the level of literature."[8] Wharton foresaw what Edel's *Life* would be even before he started writing it; she had sampled his work in his published doctoral dissertation, *Les Années dramatiques*.

In A. S. Byatt's *Possession* (see above, pp. 367–69), Mortimer P. Cropper, the biographer of Byatt's poet, Randolph Ash, exerts himself "to know as far as possible everything he did—everyone who mattered to him, every little preoccupation he had." Besides being patterned on Adam Verver, this painstaking and brilliant biographer is probably a fictive portrait of Leon Edel, for in Byatt's theory of possession, in order to possess James, it would be necessary to possess Edel.

James wrote to Whistler, "With the artist the artist communicates" (*L*, IV, 43), and the Edel who communicates with James also communicates what he knows about James to the artists at work after him, from writers like Philip Roth to etchers like Peter Milton. But Edel has also been appropriated by readers who have never read and may never read James.

Each generation constructs its own view of a great writer, and other biographies of James have come after his. Edel himself, in *Henry James: A Life*, the one-volume compression published in 1985 of his five-volume edition, updated the earlier volumes written as much as thirty-two years before. In it Edel tried to bridge the generation gap, pointing to the new direction that James studies would take. In his preface he wrote that sexuality was now more openly discussed and investigated than it had been when he prepared the five volumes. He also admitted that he had had to take into consideration the feelings of the James family members from whom he had gained permission to publish material. "I am not trying to suggest that I have, in my revisions, gone in quest of a 'sex life' or even a 'love life' for Henry

---

8.   Leon Edel to author, April, 1994. Wharton's recommendation was reported to Edel by Gordon Ray.

James; my data remains the same."[9] Two more recent biographies, Fred Kaplan's *Henry James: The Imagination of Genius*, of 1992, and Sheldon Novick's *Henry James: The Young Master*, of 1996, try to show, the latter rather more than the former, that James had a love life. Both biographers report on the feelings James had for Vasili Zhukovski in similar words. Kaplan says, "James briefly fell in love." Novick's words are, "He was in love."[10] The love was homoerotic according to Kaplan, homosexual according to Novick. Novick admits, however, that James's approaches were not reciprocated. Still, without any substantial foundation in fact, he is convinced that James had the human reactions to emotional experience, that he knew what love was about. Both writers rely on parts of the vast correspondence of James that Edel did not comment on or quote from, but they come up with nothing radically new in the data of James's life. Kaplan shares the tendency of the 1990s to read more into James's tales than had been customary—to discover in them James's attitudes to his family, to love, and to his own problems. Treating "The Pupil" as capturing a homoerotic experience between the young boy and his tutor shows how readings of some of James's tales have extended beyond those of Edel's generation. Kaplan identifies James with both Isabel Archer and Pansy in *The Portrait of a Lady* and sees in the plot of Isabel's imprisonment in an unhappy marriage James's perception of his family life as dominated by his father. Novick has come up with the discovery of a review by James of an actress' performance, anonymously printed. Some of the other supporting evidence in his first volume is fairly exiguous. In support of his ascription of homosexuality, he interprets James's notebook entry about his "initiation" as referring to his sexual initiation. It may not be possible to prove exactly what James meant, but it is at least as plausible to think he was referring to his acceptance as a contributor to several American periodicals—to his initiation into the literary life.

No one knows how much of the mostly speculative material about James's emotional life future scholars will absorb, but it is in conformity with certain fiction incorporating his figure. In fiction, though, a degree of speculation and exaggeration is permissible that is not acceptable in biography.

9.   Leon Edel, *Henry James: A Life* (New York, 1985), xi.

10.   Fred Kaplan, *Henry James: The Imagination of Genius* (New York, 1992), 171; Sheldon Novick, *Henry James: The Young Master* (New York, 1996), 342.

In Novick's book, James is seen as a normal man, except for the objects of his sexual feelings. In a letter to the *Wall Street Journal*, Novick stressed that he saw James as using his own experiences in his fiction, the "ordinary experiences of life." Novick maintained, "I am not primarily concerned in my book with James's sexual orientation, which no scholar now doubts was primarily homosexual, but with the manner in which he used his memories to create a new kind of realistic fiction. The point is not that James was a closeted gay man, but that he had vivid memories of the ordinary experiences of life; his books were spun from these and not neurotic fantasies, as past biographers have claimed."[11]

By contrast, the picture of James in a collection of essays published in 1995 and edited by David McWhirter is of a "vulnerable, sexually anxious, and lonely writer." Edel's "awesome" Master and Novick's "young" Master join in these essays a set of Jameses who are "anxious, conflicted, marginal."[12] In the majority of the essays in the book biographical attitudes to James are in evidence, and these are often diametrical opposites. What unifies the essays is that biography seems to be the dominant focus, as it is in current Jamesian studies. "Creative" literary biographers and not only storytellers and novelists have come into the legacy of Henry James.

11.   Sheldon Novick, "James's 'Initiation'" (Letter to the editor), *Wall Street Journal*, November 13, 1996, Sec. A, p. 23.

12.   David McWhirter, ed., *Henry James's New York Edition: The Construction of Authorship* (Stanford, Calif., 1995), xxiv, xxv.

INDEX